Imperialism

A Study

by

J. A. HOBSON

New Introduction by
PHILIP SIEGELMAN

Ann Arbor Paperbacks
The University of Michigan Press

First edition as an Ann Arbor Paperback 1965
Copyright by George Allen & Unwin Ltd., 1938
Reprinted by special arrangement
Introduction copyright © by The University of Michigan 1965
All rights reserved
ISBN 0-472-06103-8
Published in the United States of America by
The University of Michigan Press and
in Rexdale, Canada, by John Wiley & Sons Canada, Limited
Manufactured in the United States of America

1983   1982   1981   1980   9   8   7   6

INTRODUCTION

By Philip Siegelman

Hobson's *Imperialism* was a powerful—and in some cases definitive—influence on Lenin, Hilferding, Kautsky, Rosa Luxemburg, Bakunin, and on virtually all later significant treatments of the subject. Since the substantive content of Hobson's analysis has been subjected to damaging and skeptical criticism, it is rather his influence on later thinkers that constitutes his greatest importance. But *Imperialism: A Study* is also of great interest, as we shall see, to intellectual historians, to students of the British Empire, to political and economic theorists, as well as to other social scientists.

The totality of John Atkinson Hobson's career (1858-1940) has yet to be definitively studied. But the writings of his many prominent friends and associates, together with his own prolific testimony, provide abundant data about his life and his work. His own output runs to more than thirty volumes, including *Confessions of an Economic Heretic* (1938), a kind of intellectual autobiography written a few years before his death. He was also a prodigious journalist and essayist for numerous English liberal newspapers and periodicals, including the *Manchester Guardian, Progressive Review, Westminister Review,* and the *Nation.* And if we could somehow measure his verbal output as a teacher, university lecturer, and participant in socialist, liberal, egalitarian, and ethical causes, we would be confronted with a staggering production. But it is only to an examination of a few of the recurrent motifs evidenced throughout his career and relevant to *Imperialism* that we shall direct our attention.

Hobson's childhood and adolescence "were cast in the calmest and most self-confident years of the mid-Victorian era, when peace, prosperity, and progress appeared to be the permanent possession of most civilized nations."[1] His father was the editor and part proprietor of a liberal newspaper in Derby, a position that assured young John of the advantages customary to one "born and bred in the middle stratum of the middle class of a middle-sized industrial town of the Midlands." Economics, politics, and religion all appeared to him to be governed by an unseen invisible hand which avoided stagnation and assured a "gradual orderly improvement in the standard of living, the working conditions, and the behavior of most classes." But Hobson was soon to be disabused of the efficacy of laissez-faire in the market place or as part of his theodicy. From the corner of his vision, Hobson observed the ragged poor lurking in Derby's "Back Lane"; and in the Established Church his sense of reason was affronted by the "doctrines of the atonement and of everlasting punishment for unrepentant sinners." Such difficulties led him by early manhood to abandon his commitment to orthodox Christianity and begin articulating the creed he was later to call "economic humanism." By the time he reached Oxford his heterodoxy was distinct enough for him to become a self-designated "religious heretic." When in his later career as an "economic heretic" Hobson "for long travelled almost alone" (this is R. H. Tawney's characterization), we can sense some

---

[1] All quotations are from the writings of J. A. Hobson unless otherwise noted.

of the fruits of these early preparatory intellectual struggles. It is all of a piece too, when we learn that his first published essays dealt with that intellectual cause célèbre, *Essays and Reviews* (1861), and with "Mr. Gladstone and Genesis."

The outlines of Hobson's "economic heresy" did not take self-conscious shape until the middle 1880's; his actual systematic study of economics dates, roughly, from about this time as well. Before that, he lists as pre-university influences in the mid-1870's Mill's *On Liberty* and *Utilitarianism* and acknowledges a "profound influence" in Herbert Spencer's *The Study of Sociology,* a work that persuaded Hobson, and so many others, that the scientific study of social institutions was possible. In general, while at Oxford he "heard nothing to disturb [his] complacent acceptance of the beneficent and equitable operation of laws of supply and demand in their laissez-faire environment." But in later years, when he came to review this part of his career, he readily acknowledged the presence of "seeds of doubt" about whether or not the "justice, necessity, and finality of the existing economic system" did, in fact, conform to the "order of Nature." Some of the accepted principles of capitalist economics appear, even at that early time, to have "stuck in [his] gizzard."

No part of this early career may seem at first glance to be vitally or directly correlated with a work like *Imperialism.* But we may, perhaps, assess its relevance indirectly by noting that much of the tone of Hobson's early intellectual struggles reveals a familiar leitmotif evidenced in the thought of numerous contemporaries. To be sure, their skepticism about the established order was to take radically different directions. Yet, such diverse thinkers and writers as Ibsen, Havelock Ellis, Tolstoi, Freud, Nietzsche, Shaw, and Frank Harris were unnerved, each in his own way, by a sharp sense of disparity between the real and the ideal; between the formal, official, surface view of things and the disorderly, irrational, selfish reality of events. Freud, for example, felt that the official bourgeois sexual morality was at odds with man's instinctual nature: unacknowledged and obscured tensions and conflicts between unconscious, illicit wishes and the prohibitions of civilization created repression and neurosis. Hobson's criticism was less obviously dramatic, less driven to the substrata of man's nature, more externalized and institutional in its focus. But he too sensed a disjunction between the official and the real, between the formal principles of laissez faire and the realities of rapacious economic competition and aggrandizement, between the professions of government motives in the Boer War and the realities of the operations of entrepreneurs and financial adventurers. It was, in part, out of this sense of dislocation that *Imperialism* emerged.

In addition to this motif of the institutionalized façade, at least two other relevant themes recur in Hobson's life and thought. The first is his lifelong attachment to social movements, idealist and liberal societies, movements that were "rationalistic, ethical, political, aesthetic," protesting "against the sort of civilization that was emerging under mechanized capitalism." In this formative stage of his career, he "was not a Socialist, Marxian, Fabian"; he rejected Christian Socialism, and indeed was not a Christian or a sectarian of any recognizable kind, though his "opinions and feelings were beginning to move in the direction of Socialism." He was a member of the London Ethical Society during the time he was employed as a teacher in the Oxford University Extension Movement, a position that gave him the opportunity to lecture in the provinces on "practical issues relating to working-class life." This meliorative aspect of Hobson's thought is, perhaps, the soil out of which his technical economic studies grew. Here in varied guises, we see the activist side of Hobson as political economist, both broadly and technically conceived. He was to have a lifelong concern for the study of the authoritative allocation of values and power, and for the examination of that border area where politics and economics meet and mesh. This concern is visible directly in works such as *Democracy After the War, Towards International Government, Democracy,* as well as in his admiration for new works in political psychology, such as Harold Laski's *Grammar of Politics.* At other times it was evidenced in ideas and inspirations derived from friendships and discussions with men like Prince Kropotkin, the Indian nationalist leader G. K. Gokhale, L. T. Hobhouse, and others. Part of this strain, especially that connected with Hobson's strong attachment to Hobhouse, is probably more readily recognizable to Americans as the expression of a John Deweyite kind of political philosophy. He was deeply sympathetic with the attempts to establish sociology as a scientific discipline. He saw the study of sociology as an indispensable partner to his own attempts to develop an ethically oriented "welfare economics."

Many of his activities and intellectual debts reveal themselves from this perspective: his friendship and admiration for Thorstein Veblen and Graham Wallas, his sympathy with Bernard Bosanquet's attempts "to furnish thought and leadership to movements for the amelioration of the condition of the working class," perhaps especially his affinity for Ruskin (*John Ruskin; Social Reformer,* 1898). From Ruskin he "drew the basic thought for [his] subsequent economic writings, viz., the necessity of going behind the current monetary estimates of wealth, cost, and utility, to reach the body of human benefits and satisfactions which gave them a real meaning." Hobson was himself acutely—and accurately —aware of possible methodological and epistemological reproaches that such exhortations might be judged too naive or "value-oriented" by a rigorous, quantified, or "positivist" social science. (He later addressed himself to some of these difficulties in *Free Thought in the Social Sciences*, 1926.) During the 1880's and 1890's, including the period of the composition of *Imperialism*, he readily concedes that he was often fumbling for the fuller conception of economics implied by such contemporary usages as political economy, political sociology, and the like. This part of Hobson would undoubtedly have applauded Hannah Arendt's explorations in the etiology of late nineteenth- and twentieth-century imperialism (*The Origins of Totalitarianism*, 1951) which stressed the interdependence of politics (totalitarianism) and of economics and racism (imperialism) in the rise of modern European dictatorships.

Hobson's other main intellectual preoccupation throughout his career was his theory of underconsumption and oversavings, probably the unwobbling pivot central to all his thought. His earliest articulation of these ideas came to him through a chance association with a businessman named A. F. Mummery (also an outdoorsman and a famous mountaineer) whose special economic idée fixe was a theory of oversavings. Hobson tried at first "to counter his arguments by the use of the orthodox economic weapons," but eventually Mummery persuaded him that excessive savings was a crucial dysfunctional element in British capitalism "responsible for the underemployment of capital and labor in periods of bad trade." The result of this association was a book under joint authorship, *The Physiology of Industry* (1889), characterized by Hobson "as the first open step in my heretical career."[2]

[2] Hobson was later to discover that his sin was not quite so original as he had believed: similar notions had, in fact, been set forth by eighteenth- and nineteenth-century thinkers such as Shaftesbury, Berkeley, and Malthus.

He was convinced that the orthodox economists of his day recoiled from the originality of his thesis and from its implications; seemingly he was opposing personal thrift and questioning what had been the long-established doctrine that savings ought never to be limited because they increased "the capital structure and the fund for paying wages." For Hobson, oversavings on the part of capitalists resulted in underconsumption by the workers, a wretched distribution of industrial gains, recurrent depressions, and crippling underemployment. Thus far, it is clear, we are dealing with a critical analysis of capitalism, a task that Hobson set himself more explicitly in his "first solid piece of economic writing," *The Evolution of Modern Capitalism, A Study of Machine Production.* Hobson was dealing here with the social consequences of capital formation—an area which he regarded throughout his life as central to the larger problem of establishing a just and humane social order. This concern was to be a lifelong preoccupation of Hobson's. At this early date, however, he had not yet been impelled to apply these criticisms of capitalism to the nexus of economics and international politics, the connection between the internal dynamics of British laissez faire and those foreign political-economic adventures which in the last sixty years have commonly come to be called "imperialist."

A recent scholarly synthesis restates effectively the notion that the theme of imperialism may be said to have arisen during and out of the Boer War:

> The Boer War was, indeed, more than a local clash of two nations and opposing political and economic interests. It was more than a chapter in the history of the industrialization of Africa. In the career of imperialism it was an essential turning point. It made the

word an international slogan in Europe, just as the Spanish War had made it a slogan in America. It also gave rise to the world-wide misinterpretation of the Boer War as a capitalist plot. That misinterpretation became the basis of all subsequent theories of imperialism. Imperialism as a political and economic theory first emerged during and immediately after the Boer War. It originated in England.[3]

It originated, in fact, from Hobson's pen. Hobson himself also regarded the war as crucial to his articulation of the concept of imperialism: "The Boer War was both a turning-point in my career and an illumination to my understanding of the real relations between economics and politics . . ." Hobson drew on current news accounts of the troubles in the Transvaal for an essay on "Imperialism" which appeared in the *Contemporary Review* in March 1899. The essay caught the eye of L. T. Hobhouse, then the chief political writer of the *Manchester Guardian*. At his initiative Hobson was hired by the *Guardian* to go to South Africa as a correspondent. On Hobson's return, he published *The War in South Africa* (1900), a book made up of the articles written for the *Manchester Guardian,* together with other material. From 1900-1902 Hobson was arguing that the diamond monopoly and the rapacious economic adventurers who were exploiting the Rand had created the war and had used their influence to discredit the government of the Transvaal. In these and other articles he began to cast his revulsion with the Boer War into terms consistent with his broodings of the previous decade on the shortcomings of capitalism. For example, in

[3] Richard Koebner and Helmut Dan Schmidt, *Imperialism, The Story and Significance of a Political Word,* 1840-1960 (New York: Cambridge University Press, 1964). The history of the term "imperialism" prior to Hobson is authoritatively explored in this work.

"The Economic Taproot of Imperialism"[4] Hobson sketched out part of the larger argument of *Imperialism: A Study*— that the great industrialists and banking houses fashioned imperialist adventures as a way of providing profitable high-interest-bearing investments for their surplus capital. The idea was taking shape in Hobson's publications that imperialism was not only a tool of particular capitalists but rather that imperialism in the form of military aggrandizement was the mode, par excellence, of capitalist expansion.[5] Another study, *The Psychology of Jingoism* (1901), dealt with these same themes; all may be regarded as preliminary to *Imperialism: A Study* (1902), which became the synthetic composite of these earlier efforts.

What Hobson had done was to define imperialism so that henceforth most users of the term would, willy-nilly, be talking about economic imperialism. Hobson's analysis of the war in South Africa became his paradigm for explaining the international consequences of capitalist underconsumption and oversavings:

> As one nation after another enters the machine economy and adopts advanced industrial methods, it becomes more difficult for its manufacturers, merchants and financiers to dispose profitably of their economic resources, and they are tempted more and more to use their Governments in order to secure for their particular use some distant undeveloped country by annexation and protection . . . Everywhere appear excessive powers of production, excessive capital in search of investment. It is admitted by all businessmen that the growth of

[4] This was both the title of an article (*Contemporary Review*, Vol. LXXXII, August 1902) and the title of Chapter IV of *Imperialism: A Study*.

[5] I owe this observation to Koebner and Schmidt, *op. cit.*, p. 252.

> the powers of production in their country exceeds the growth in consumption, that more goods can be produced than can be sold at a profit, and that more capital exists than can find remunerative investment. It is this economic condition of affairs that forms the taproot of Imperialism.[6]

Imperialism could now be seen, according to Hobson, as a spreading excrescence, the outward sign of domestic disorder. But we must underscore one fundamental point about Hobson's assault on capitalist imperialism: despite the overwhelming attractiveness of his basic point of view to Lenin and to a host of communist, Marxist, and socialist theorists, Hobson himself never advocated abolition of capitalism. True, his "most destructive heresy" involved a criticism of the market economy as being an unfair mode of distribution "whether under monopoly or so-called competitive conditions." He continued to advocate "rapid and important structural changes . . . in the material and social environment," public planning, utilization of the taxing power to correct inequities and maldistribution, and similar reforms. Hobson felt that it was by no means inevitable that imperialist expansion should be the concomitant of any attempt to establish a democratic, dynamic, industrial capitalist society. Finally, we might note that his studies of Marxism led him to reject the efficacy of the dialectic, the theory of class conflict, and the labor theory of value as instruments of social analysis. Hobson's form of socialism seems to have lacked any doctrinaire component.

Before concluding these remarks, we should at least point to that massive area of indispensable inquiry dealing with Hobson's influence on subsequent thinkers—Lenin, Kautsky, Luxemburg, to cite the most obvious, each of whom explicitly

[6] *Imperialism: A Study*, pp. 80-81.

acknowledged his debt to Hobson. Lenin's thesis (in *Imperialism: The Highest Stage of Capitalism*, 1916) became dogma for virtually all of the subsequent Marxist and communist considerations of the subject. For Lenin, the cataclysm of World War I hopefully signified the death knell of capitalism. Predictably, he went beyond Hobson in describing imperialism as the inevitable and final aggressive phase of a dying capitalist social order which had turned to overseas expansion in its last desperate effort to sustain its pernicious system of human exploitation. The transmutations of Hobson's theories by radicals of the left continue to this day and are deserving of systematic study by students of international affairs.

Finally, we should mention the large body of literature that is critical of Hobson's *Imperialism*. For one outstanding example, the reader is referred to Professor D. K. Fieldhouse's cogent and skillful assessment.[7] Pursuing a number of carefully documented criticisms, Fieldhouse charges that Hobson's argument is reductivist, that it relies on an excessively discontinuous view of nineteenth-century British history, that its data are often inadequate, that it gives a false reality to nonexistent correlations between unrelated sets of data, and that the notion of an embarrassment of excess capital (which could not be invested at home because of the underconsumption factor) is not consistent with new studies by C. Paish, A. K. Cairncross, R. Nurske, and others. This series of revisions is an interesting chapter in the history of ideas. The task of unraveling the tangled web of past usages, of sorting out influences, of reassembling our data with renewed skepticism—all these are necessary steps toward the formation of more rigorous theories about the nature of imperialism

[7] D. K. Fieldhouse, " 'Imperialism': An Historiographical Revision," *The Economic History Review*, Second Series, Vol. XIV, No. 2 (1961).

and of the empirical world. The study of mistaken or partly valid theories is important to the task of contemporary theory formation. It is an activity as fundamental to political science and the political economist's search for truth as is the reconstruction of the past to the conduct of psychoanalysis, history, cultural anthropology, or any of the other time-bound disciplines.

PREFACE TO THE FIRST EDITION

THIS study of modern Imperialism is designed to give more precision to a term which is on everybody's lips and which is used to denote the most powerful movement in the current politics of the Western world. Though Imperialism has been adopted as a more or less conscious policy by several European States and threatens to break down the political isolation of the United States, Great Britain has travelled so much faster and farther along this road as to furnish in her recent career the most profitable guidance or warning.

While an attempt is made to discover and discuss the general principles which underlie imperialist policy, the illustration of that policy is mainly derived from the progress of British Imperialism during the last generation, and proceeds rather by diagnosis than by historical description.

In Part I the economic origins of Imperialism are traced, with such statistical measurements of its methods and results as are available.

Part II investigates the theory and the practice of Imperialism regarded as a "mission of civilization," in its effects upon "lower" or alien peoples, and its political and moral reactions upon the conduct and character of the Western nations engaging in it.

The book is addressed to the intelligence of the minority who are content neither to float along the tide of political opportunism nor to submit to the shove of some blind "destiny," but who desire to understand political forces in order that they may direct them.

Those readers who hold that a well-balanced judgment consists in always finding as much in favour of any political course as against it will be discontented with the treatment given here. For the study is distinctively one of social pathology, and no endeavour is made to disguise the nature of the disease.

The statistics given in Part I are derived, when the source is not stated, from the " Statistical Abstracts " published by the Government, reinforced in some instances, by figures derived from the *Statesman's Year Book*.

I am indebted to the editor of the *Financial Reform Almanac* for permission to reproduce the valuable diagram illustrative of British expenditure from 1870, and to the editors of the *Speaker*, the *Contemporary Review*, the *Political Science Quarterly*, and the *British Friend* for permission to embody in chapters of this volume articles printed in these magazines.

I desire also to express my gratitude to my friends Mr. Gilbert Murray and Mr. Herbert Rix for their assistance in reading most of the proof-sheets and for many valuable suggestions and corrections.

JOHN A. HOBSON.

August, 1902.

In this revised edition, facts and figures have been, as far as possible, brought up to date, a number of additions and deletions have been made, and in some instances the line of argument has been recast.

J. A. H.

September, 1905.

CONTENTS

CONTENTS

IMPERIALISM

IMPERIALISM: A STUDY

NATIONALISM AND IMPERIALISM

AMID the welter of vague political abstractions to lay one's finger accurately upon any "ism" so as to pin it down and mark it out by definition seems impossible. Where meanings shift so quickly and so subtly, not only following changes of thought, but often manipulated artificially by political practitioners so as to obscure, expand, or distort, it is idle to demand the same rigour as is expected in the exact sciences. A certain broad consistency in its relations to other kindred terms is the nearest approach to definition which such a term as Imperialism admits. Nationalism, internationalism, colonialism, its three closest congeners, are equally elusive, equally shifty, and the changeful overlapping of all four demands the closest vigilance of students of modern politics.

During the nineteenth century the struggle towards nationalism, or establishment of political union on a basis of nationality, was a dominant factor alike in dynastic movements and as an inner motive in the life of masses of population. That struggle, in external politics, sometimes took a disruptive form, as in the case of Greece, Servia, Roumania, and Bulgaria breaking from Ottoman rule, and the detachment of North Italy from her unnatural alliance with the Austrian Empire. In other cases it was a unifying or a centralising force, enlarging the area of nationality, as in the case of Italy and the Pan-Slavist movement in

3

Russia. Sometimes nationality was taken as a basis of federation of States, as in United Germany and in North America.

It is true that the forces making for political union sometimes went further, making for federal union of diverse nationalities, as in the cases of Austria-Hungary, Norway and Sweden, and the Swiss Federation. But the general tendency was towards welding into large strong national unities the loosely related States and provinces with shifting attachments and alliances which covered large areas of Europe since the break-up of the Empire. This was the most definite achievement of the nineteenth century. The force of nationality, operating in this work, is quite as visible in the failures to achieve political freedom as in the successes ; and the struggles of Irish, Poles, Finns, Hungarians, and Czechs to resist the forcible subjection to or alliance with stronger neighbours brought out in its full vigour the powerful sentiment of nationality.

The middle of the century was especially distinguished by a series of definitely " nationalist " revivals, some of which found important interpretation in dynastic changes, while others were crushed or collapsed. Holland, Poland, Belgium, Norway, the Balkans, formed a vast arena for these struggles of national forces.

The close of the third quarter of the century saw Europe fairly settled into large national States or federations of States, though in the nature of the case there can be no finality, and Italy continued to look to Trieste, as Germany still looks to Austria, for the fulfilment of her manifest destiny.

This passion and the dynastic forms it helped to mould and animate are largely attributable to the fierce prolonged resistance which peoples, both great and small, were called on to maintain against the imperial designs of Napoleon.

4

The national spirit of England was roused by the tenseness of the struggle to a self-consciousness it had never experienced since " the spacious days of great Elizabeth." Jena made Prussia into a great nation ; the Moscow campaign brought Russia into the field of European nationalities as a factor in politics, opening her for the first time to the full tide of Western ideas and influences.

Turning from this territorial and dynastic nationalism to the spirit of racial, linguistic, and economic solidarity which has been the underlying motive, we find a still more remarkable movement. Local particularism on the one hand, vague cosmopolitanism upon the other, yielded to a ferment of nationalist sentiment, manifesting itself among the weaker peoples not merely in a sturdy and heroic resistance against political absorption or territorial nationalism, but in a passionate revival of decaying customs, language, literature and art ; while it bred in more dominant peoples strange ambitions of national " destiny " and an attendant spirit of Chauvinism.

The true nature and limits of nationality have never been better stated than by J. S. Mill.

" A portion of mankind may be said to constitute a nation if they are united among themselves by common sympathies which do not exist between them and others. This feeling of nationality may have been generated by various causes. Sometimes it is the effect of identity of race and descent. Community of language and community of religion greatly contribute to it. Geographical limits are one of the causes. But the strongest of all is identity of political antecedents, the possession of a national history and consequent community of recollections, collective pride and humiliation, pleasure and regret, connected with the same incidents in the past."[1]

---

[1] *Representative Government*, chap. xvi.

It is a debasement of this genuine nationalism, by attempts to overflow its natural banks and absorb the near or distant territory of reluctant and unassimilable peoples, that marks the passage from nationalism to a spurious colonialism on the one hand, Imperialism on the other.

Colonialism, where it consists in the migration of part of a nation to vacant or sparsely peopled foreign lands, the emigrants carrying with them full rights of citizenship in the mother country, or else establishing local self-government in close conformity with her institutions and under her final control, may be considered a genuine expansion of nationality, a territorial enlargement of the stock, language and institutions of the nation. Few colonies in history have, however, long remained in this condition when they have been remote from the mother country. Either they have severed the connexion and set up for themselves as separate nationalities, or they have been kept in complete political bondage so far as all major processes of government are concerned, a condition to which the term Imperialism is at least as appropriate as colonialism. The only form of distant colony which can be regarded as a clear expansion of nationalism is the self-governing British colony in Australasia and Canada, and even in these cases local conditions may generate a separate nationalism based on a strong consolidation of colonial interests and sentiments alien from and conflicting with those of the mother nation. In other " self-governing " colonies, as in Cape Colony and Natal, where the majority of whites are not descended from British settlers, and where the presence of subject or " inferior " races in vastly preponderating numbers, and alien climatic and other natural conditions, mark out a civilization distinct from that of the " mother country," the conflict between the colonial and the imperial ideas has long been present in the forefront of the consciousness of politicians. When Lord Rosmead spoke of the permanent presence of the imperial factor as " simply an absurdity," and Mr. Rhodes spoke of its " elimination," they were championing a " colonialism " which is more certain in the course of time to develop by inner growth into a separate " nationalism " than in the case of the Australasian and Canadian colonies, because of the wider divergence, alike of interests and radical conditions of life, from the mother nation. Our other colonies are plainly representative of the spirit of Imperialism rather than of colonialism. No considerable proportion of the population consists of British settlers living with their families in conformity with the social and political customs and laws of their native land : in most instances they form a small minority wielding political or economic sway over a majority of alien and subject people, themselves under the despotic political control of the Imperial Government or its local nominees. This, the normal condition of a British colony, was well-nigh universal in the colonies of other European countries. The " colonies " which France and Germany established in Africa and Asia were in no real sense plantations of French and German national life beyond the seas ; nowhere, not even in Algeria, did they represent true European civiliza-tion ; their political and economic structure of society is wholly alien from that of the mother country.

Colonialism, in its best sense, is a natural overflow of nationality ; its test is the power of colonists to transplant the civilization they represent to the new natural and social environment in which they find themselves. We must not be misled by names ; the " colonial " party in Germany and France is identical in general aim and method with the " imperialist " party in England, and the latter is the truer title. Professor Seeley well marked the nature of

7

Imperialism. "When a State advances beyond the limits of nationality its power becomes precarious and artificial. This is the condition of most empires, and it is the condition of our own. When a nation extends itself into other territories the chances are that it cannot destroy or completely drive out, even if it succeeds in conquering, them. When this happens it has a great and permanent difficulty to contend with, for the subject or rival nationalities cannot be properly assimilated, and remain as a permanent cause of weakness and danger."[1]

The novelty of recent Imperialism regarded as a policy consists chiefly in its adoption by several nations. The notion of a number of competing empires is essentially modern. The root idea of empire in the ancient and mediæval world was that of a federation of States, under a hegemony, covering in general terms the entire known recognized world, such as was held by Rome under the so-called *pax Romana*. When Roman citizens, with full civic rights, were found all over the explored world, in Africa and Asia, as well as in Gaul and Britain, Imperialism contained a genuine element of internationalism. With the fall of Rome this conception of a single empire wielding political authority over the civilized world did not disappear. On the contrary, it survived all the fluctuations of the Holy Roman Empire. Even after the definite split between the Eastern and Western sections had taken place at the close of the fourth century, the theory of a single State, divided for administrative purposes, survived. Beneath every cleavage or antagonism, and notwithstanding the severance of many independent kingdoms and provinces, this ideal unity of the empire lived. It formed the conscious avowed ideal of Charlemagne, though as a practical ambition confined to Western Europe. Rudolph of Habsburg not

---

[1] " Expansion of England," lect. iii.

merely revived the idea, but laboured to realize it through Central Europe, while his descendant Charles V gave a very real meaning to the term by gathering under the unity of his imperial rule the territories of Austria, Germany, Spain, the Netherlands, Sicily, and Naples. In later ages this dream of a European Empire animated the policy of Peter the Great, Catherine, and Napoleon. Nor is it impossible that Kaiser Wilhelm III held a vision of such a world-power.

Political philosophers in many ages, Vico, Machiavelli, Dante, Kant, have speculated on an empire as the only feasible security for peace, a hierarchy of States conforming on the larger scale to the feudal order within the single State.

Thus empire was identified with internationalism, though not always based on a conception of equality of nations. The break-up of the Central European Empire, with the weakening of nationalities that followed, evoked a new modern sentiment of internationalism which, through the eighteenth century, was a flickering inspiration in the intellectual circles of European States. " The eve of the French Revolution found every wise man in Europe— Lessing, Kant, Goethe, Rousseau, Lavater, Condorcet, Priestley, Gibbon, Franklin—more of a citizen of the world than of any particular country. Goethe confessed that he did not know what patriotism was, and was glad to be without it. Cultured men of all countries were at home in polite society everywhere. Kant was immensely more interested in the events of Paris than in the life of Prussia. Italy and Germany were geographical expressions ; those countries were filled with small States in which there was no political life, but in which there was much interest in the general progress of culture. The Revolution itself was at bottom also human and cosmopolitan. It is, as Lamartine said, ' a date in the human mind,' and it is because of that fact that all the carping of critics like Taine cannot prevent us from seeing that the character of the men who led the great movements of the Revolution can never obliterate the momentous nature of the Titanic strife. The soldiers of the Revolution who, barefooted and ragged, drove the insolent reactionaries from the soil of France were fighting not merely for some national cause, but for a cause dimly perceived to be the cause of general mankind. With all its crudities and imperfections, the idea of the Revolution was that of a conceived body of Right in which all men should share."[1]

This early flower of humane cosmopolitanism was destined to wither before the powerful revival of nationalism which marked the next century. Even in the narrow circles of the cultured classes it easily passed from a noble and a passionate ideal to become a vapid sentimentalism, and after the brief flare of 1848 among the continental populace had been extinguished, little remained but a dim smouldering of the embers. Even the Socialism which upon the continent retains a measure of the spirit of internationalism is so tightly confined within the national limits, in its struggle with bureaucracy and capitalism, that " the international " expresses little more than a holy aspiration, and has little opportunity of putting into practice the genuine sentiments of brotherhood which its prophets have always preached.

Thus the triumph of nationalism seems to have crushed the rising hope of internationalism. Yet it would appear that there is no essential antagonism between them. A true strong internationalism in form or spirit would rather imply the existence of powerful self-respecting nationalities which seek union on the basis of common national needs and interests. Such a historical development would be far

[1] W. Clarke, *Progressive Review*, February, 1897.

more conformable to laws of social growth than the rise of anarchic cosmopolitanism from individual units amid the decadence of national life.

Nationalism is a plain highway to internationalism, and if it manifests divergence we may well suspect a perversion of its nature and its purpose. Such a perversion is Imperialism, in which nations trespassing beyond the limits of facile assimilation transform the wholesome stimulative rivalry of varied national types into the cutthroat struggle of competing empires.

Not only does aggressive Imperialism defeat the movement towards internationalism by fos.ering animosities among competing empires : its attack upon the liberties and the existence of weaker or lower races stimulates in them a corresponding excess of national self-consciousness. A nationalism that bristles with resentment and is all astrain with the passion of self-defence is only less perverted from its natural genius than the nationalism which glows with the animus of greed and self-aggrandisement at the expense of others. From this aspect aggressive Imperialism is an artificial stimulation of nationalism in peoples too foreign to be absorbed and too compact to be permanently crushed. We welded Africanderdom into just such a strong dangerous nationalism, and we joined with other nations in creating a resentful nationalism until then unknown in China. The injury to nationalism in both cases consists in converting a cohesive, pacific internal force into an exclusive, hostile force, a perversion of the true power and use of nationality. The worst and most certain result is the retardation of internationalism. The older nationalism was primarily an inclusive sentiment ; its natural relation to the same sentiment in another people was lack of sympathy, not open hostility ; there was no inherent antagonism to prevent nationalities from growing and thriving side by side. Such in the main was the nationalism of the earlier nineteenth century, and the politicians of Free Trade had some foundation for their dream of a quick growth of effective, informal internationalism by peaceful, profitable intercommunication of goods and ideas among nations recognizing a just harmony of interests in free peoples.

The overflow of nationalism into imperial channels quenched all such hopes. While co-existent nationalities are capable of mutual aid involving no direct antagonism of interests, co-existent empires following each its own imperial career of territorial and industrial aggrandisement are natural necessary enemies. The full nature of this antagonism on its economic side is not intelligible without a close analysis of those conditions of modern capitalist production which compel an ever keener " fight for markets," but the political antagonism is obvious.

The scramble for Africa and Asia virtually recast the policy of all European nations, evoked alliances which cross all natural lines of sympathy and historical association, drove every continental nation to consume an ever-growing share of its material and human resources upon military and naval equipment, drew the great new power of the United States from its isolation into the full tide of competition ; and, by the multitude, the magnitude, and the suddenness of the issues it had thrown on to the stage of politics, became a constant agent of menace and of perturbation to the peace and progress of mankind. The new policy exercised the most notable and formidable influence upon the conscious statecraft of the nations which indulge in it. While producing for popular consumption doctrines of national destiny and imperial missions of civilization, contradictory in their true import, but subsidiary to one another as supports of popular Imperialism, it evoked a calculating, greedy type of Machiavellianism, entitled " real-politik " in Germany, where it was made, which remodelled the whole art of diplomacy and erected national aggrandisement without pity or scruple as the conscious motive force of foreign policy. Earth hunger and the scramble for markets were responsible for the openly avowed repudiation of treaty obligations which Germany, Russia, and England had not scrupled to defend. The sliding scale of diplomatic language, hinterland, sphere of interest, sphere of influence, paramountcy, suzerainty, protectorate, veiled or open, leading up to acts of forcible seizure or annexation which sometimes continue to be hidden under " lease," " rectification of frontier," " concession," and the like, was the invention and expression of this cynical spirit of Imperialism. While Germany and Russia were perhaps more open in their professed adoption of the material gain of their country as the sole criterion of public conduct, other nations were not slow to accept the standard. Though the conduct of nations in dealing with one another has commonly been determined at all times by selfish and shortsighted considerations, the conscious, deliberate adoption of this standard at an age when the intercourse of nations and their interdependence for all essentials of human life grow ever closer, is a retrograde step fraught with grave perils to the cause of civilization.

PART I

THE ECONOMICS OF IMPERIALISM

CHAPTER I

THE MEASURE OF IMPERIALISM

QUIBBLES about the modern meaning of the term
Imperialism are best resolved by reference to concrete
facts in the history of the last sixty years. During that
period a number of European nations, Great Britain being
first and foremost, annexed or otherwise asserted political
sway over vast portions of Africa and Asia, and over numerous
islands in the Pacific and elsewhere. The extent to which
this policy of expansion was carried on, and in particular
the enormous size and the peculiar character of the British
acquisitions, were not adequately realized even by those
who pay some attention to Imperial politics.

The following lists, giving the area and, where possible,
the population of the new acquisitions, are designed to
give definiteness to the term Imperialism. Though derived
from official sources, they do not, however, profess strict
accuracy. The sliding scale of political terminology along
which no-man's land, or hinterland, passes into some kind
of definite protectorate is often applied so as to conceal
the process ; " rectification " of a fluid frontier is continually
taking place ; paper " partitions " of spheres of influence
or protection in Africa and Asia are often obscure, and in
some cases the area and the population are highly speculative.

In a few instances it is possible that portions of territory
put down as acquired after 1870 may have been ear-marked
by a European Power at some earlier date. But care is
taken to include only such territories as have come within
this period under the definite political control of the Power

15

to which they are assigned. The figures in the case of Great Britain are so startling as to call for a little further interpretation. I have thought it right to add to the recognized list of colonies and protectorates[1] the " veiled Protectorate " of Egypt, with its vast Soudanese claim, the entire territories assigned to Chartered Companies, and the native or feudatory States in India which acknowledged our paramountcy by the admission of a British Agent or other official endowed with real political control.

All these lands are rightly accredited to the British Empire, and if our past policy is still pursued, the intensive as distinct from the extensive Imperialism will draw them under an ever-tightening grasp.[2]

In a few other instances, as, for example, in West Africa, countries are included in this list where some small dominion had obtained before 1870, but where the vast majority of the present area of the colony is of more recent requisition. Any older colonial possession thus included in Lagos or Gambia is, however, far more than counter-balanced by the increased area of the Gold Coast Colony, which is not included in this list, and which grew from 29,000 square miles in 1873 to 39,000 square miles in 1893.

The list is by no means complete. It takes no account of several large regions which passed under the control of our Indian Government as native or feudatory States, but of which no statistics of area or population, even approximate were available. Such are the Shan States, the Burma Frontier, and the Upper Burma Frontier, the districts of Chitral, Bajam, Swat, Waziristan, which came under our

---

[1] The Statistical Abstract for British Empire in 1903 (Cd. 2395, pub. 1905), gives an area of 9,631,100 sq. miles and a population of 360,646,000.

[2] The situation is that of 1905. The transfer of large regions from the control of our Foreign Office to that of our Colonial Office is a register of the tightening process. Northern and Southern Nigeria underwent this change in 1900, the E. African Protectorate, Uganda, and Somaliland in 1904.

	Date of Acquisition.	Area Square Miles.	Population.
EUROPE—			
Cyprus	1878	3,584	237,022
AFRICA—			
Zanzibar and Pemba . .	1888 }	} 1,000,000	{ 200,000
East Africa Protectorate .	1895 }		{ 2,500,000
Uganda Protectorate .	1894–1896	140,000	3,800,000
Somali Coast Protectorate .	1884–1885	68,000	(?)
British Central Africa Protectorate . . .	1889	42,217	688,049
Lagos	to 1899	21,000	3,000,000
Gambia	to 1888	3,550	215,000
Ashantee	1896–1901	70,000	2,000,000
Niger Coast Protectorate .	1885–1898	{ 400,000 to 500,000	{ 25,000,000 to 40,000,000
Egypt	1882	400,000	9,734,405
Egyptian Soudan . .	1882	950,000	10,000,000
Griqualand West . .	1871–1880	15,197	83,373
Zululand	1879–1897	10,521	240,000
British Bechuanaland .	1885	51,424	72,736
Bechuanaland Protectorate	1891	275,000	89,216
Transkei	1879–1885	2,535	153,582
Tembuland . . .	1885	4,155	180,130
Pondoland . . .	1894	4,040	188,000
Griqualand East . .	1879–1885	7,511	152,609
British South Africa Charter	1889	750,000	321,000
Transvaal . . .	1900	117,732	1,354,200
Orange River Colony .	1900	50,000	385,045
ASIA—			
Hong Kong (littoral) .	1898	376	102,284
Wei-hai-wei . . .	—	270	118,000
Socotra	1886	1,382	10,000
Upper Burma . . .	1887	83,473	2,046,933
Baluchistan . . .	1876–1889	130,000	500,000
Sikkim	1890	2,818	30,000
Rajputana (States) . }		{ 128,022	{ 12,186,352
Burma (States) . . }	since 1881	{ 62,661	{ 785,800
Jammu and Kashmir . }		{ 80,000	{ 2,543,952
Malay Protected States .	1883–1895	24,849	620,000
North Borneo Co. . .	1881	31,106	175,000
North Borneo Protectorate.	1888	—	—
Sarawak	1888	50,000	500,000
British New Guinea . .	1888	90,540	350,000
Fiji Islands . . .	1874	7,740	120,124

"sphere of influence" in 1893, and have been since taken under a closer protectorate. The increase of British India itself between 1871 and 1891 amounted to an area of 104,993 square miles, with a population of 25,330,000, while no reliable measurement of the formation of new native States within that period and since is available. Many of the measurements here given are in round numbers, indicative of their uncertainty, but they are taken, wherever available, from official publications of the Colonial Office, corroborated or supplemented from the *Statesman's Year Book*. They will by no means comprise the full tale of our expansion during the thirty years, for many enlargements made by the several colonies themselves are omitted. But taken as they stand they make a formidable addition to the growth of an Empire whose nucleus is only 120,000 square miles, with 40,000,000 population.

For so small a nation to add to its domains in the course of a single generation an area of 4,754,000 square miles[1] with an estimated population of 88,000,000, is a historical fact of great significance.

Accepting Sir Robert Giffen's estimate[2] of the size of our Empire (including Egypt and the Soudan) at about 13,000,000 square miles, with a population of some 400 to 420 millions (of whom about 50,000,000 are of British race and speech), we find that one-third of this Empire, containing quite one-fourth of the total population of the Empire, was acquired within the last thirty years of the nineteenth century. This is in tolerably close agreement with other independent estimates.[3]

---

[1] Sir R. Giffen gives the figures as 4,204,690 square miles for the period 1870–1898.
[2] "The Relative Growth of the Component Parts of the Empire," a paper read before the Colonial Institute, January, 1898.
[3] See table, "British Colonies and Dependencies," on page 20.

The character of this Imperial expansion is clearly exhibited in the list of new territories.

Though, for convenience, the year 1870 has been taken as indicative of the beginning of a conscious policy of Imperialism, it will be evident that the movement did not attain its full impetus until the middle of the eighties. The vast increase of territory, and the method of whole-sale partition which assigned to us great tracts of African land, may be dated from about 1884. Within fifteen years some three and three-quarter millions of square miles were added to the British Empire.[1]

Nor did Great Britain stand alone in this enterprise. The leading characteristic of that modern Imperialism, the competition of rival Empires, was the product of this same period. The close of the Franco-German war marked the beginning of a new colonial policy in France and Germany, destined to take effect in the next decade. It was not unnatural that the newly-founded German Empire, surrounded by powerful enemies and doubtful allies, and perceiving its more adventurous youth drawn into the United States and other foreign lands, should form the idea of a colonial empire. During the seventies a vigorous literature sprang up in advocacy of the policy[2] which took shape a little later in the powerful hands of Bismarck. The earliest instance of official aid for the promotion of German commerce abroad occurred in 1880 in the Government aid granted to the " German Commercial and Plantation Association of the Southern Seas." German connexion with Samoa dates from the same year, but the definite advance of Germany upon its Imperialist career began in 1884, with a policy of African protectorates and annexations

[1] *Liberalism and the Empire*, p. 341.
[2] Fabri's *Bedarf Deutschland der Colonien* was the most vigorous and popular treatise.

BRITISH COLONIES AND DEPENDENCIES, 1900.[1]

	Area Square Miles.	Estimated Population.
EUROPEAN DEPENDENCIES . . .	119	204,421
ASIATIC DEPENDENCIES—		
India (1,800,258 square miles, 287,223,431 inhabitants)	1,827,579	291,586,688
Others (27,321 square miles, 4,363,257 inhabitants)		
AFRICAN COLONIES	535,398	6,773,360
AMERICAN COLONIES	3,952,572	7,260,169
AUSTRALASIAN COLONIES . . .	3,175,840	5,009,281
Total	9,491,508	310,833,919
PROTECTORATES—		
Asia	120,400	1,200,000
Africa (including Egypt, Egyptian Soudan)	3,530,000	54,730,000
Oceania	800	30,000
Total Protectorates . . .	3,651,200	55,960,000
Grand total	13,142,708	366,793,919

of Oceanic islands. During the next fifteen years she brought under her colonial sway about 1,000,000 square miles, with an estimated population of 14,000,000. Almost the whole of this territory was tropical, and the white population formed a total of a few thousands.

Similarly in France a great revival of the old colonial spirit took place in the early eighties, the most influential of the revivalists being the eminent economist, M. Paul Leroy-Beaulieu. The extension of empire in Senegal and Sahara in 1880 was followed next year by the annexation of Tunis, and France was soon actively engaged in the scramble for Africa in 1884, while at the same time she was fastening her rule on Tonking and Laos in Asia. Her

[1] Compiled from Morris' *History of Colonization*, vol. ii, p. 87, and *Statesman's Year Book*, 1900. Figures for 1933-4 are given in the Appendix, p. 369.

acquisitions between 1880 and 1900 (exclusive of the extension of New Caledonia and its dependencies) amounted to an area of over three and a half million square miles, with a native population of some 37,000,000, almost the whole tropical or sub-tropical, inhabited by lower races and incapable of genuine French colonization.

Italian aspirations took similar shape from 1880 onwards, though the disastrous experience of the Abyssinian expeditions gave a check to Italian Imperialism. Her possessions in East Africa are confined to the northern colony of Eritrea and the protectorate of Somaliland.[1]

Of the other European States, two only, Portugal[2] and Belgium, enter directly into the competition of this new Imperialism. The African arrangements of 1884–6 assigned to Portugal the large district of Angola on the Congo Coast, while a large strip of East Africa passed definitely under her political control in 1891. The anomalous position of the great Congo Free State, ceded to the King of Belgium in 1883, and growing since then by vast accretions, must be regarded as involving Belgium in the competition for African empire.

Spain may be said to have definitely retired from imperial competition. The large and important possessions of Holland in the East and West Indies, though involving her in imperial politics to some degree, belong to older colonialism : she takes no part in the new imperial expansion.

Russia, the only active expansionist country of the North, stood alone in the character of her imperial growth, which differed from other Imperialism in that it was principally Asiatic in its achievements and proceeded by direct extension of imperial boundaries, partaking to a

[1] In the year 1905.

[2] Portugal's true era of Imperialism in Africa, however, dates back two centuries. See Theal's fascinating story of the foundation of a Portuguese Empire in *Beginnings of South African History* (Fisher Unwin).

larger extent than in the other cases of a regular colonial policy of settlement for purposes of agriculture and industry. It is, however, evident that Russian expansion, though of a more normal and natural order than that which characterises the new Imperialism, came definitely into contact and into competition with the claims and aspirations of the latter in Asia, and was advancing rapidly during the period which is the object of our study.

The entrance of the powerful and progressive nation of the United States of America upon Imperialism by the annexation of Hawaii and the taking over of the relics of ancient Spanish empire not only added a new formidable competitor for trade and territory, but changed and complicated the issues. As the focus of political attention and activity shifted more to the Pacific States, and the commercial aspirations of America were more and more set upon trade with the Pacific islands and the Asiatic coast, the same forces which were driving European States along the path of territorial expansion seemed likely to act upon the United States, leading her to a virtual abandonment of the principle of American isolation which hitherto dominated her policy.

The comparative table of colonisation (page 369), compiled from the *Statesman's Year Book* for 1900 by Mr. H. C. Morris,[1] marked the expansion of the political control of Western nations in 1905.[2]

The political nature of British Imperialism may be authoritatively ascertained by considering the governmental relations which the newly annexed territories have held with the Crown.

Officially,[3] British " colonial possessions " fall into three

[1] *Cf.* his *History of Colonization*, vol. ii, p. 318 (Macmillan & Co.).
[2] Figures for the years 1934–5 are given in the Appendix, p. 369.
[3] See the " Colonial Office List."

	Number of Colonies.	Area. Square Miles.		Population.	
		Mother Country.	Colonies, &c.	Mother Country.	Colonies, &c.
United Kingdom	50	120,979	11,605,238	40,559,954	345,222,239
France . .	33	204,092	3,740,756	38,517,975	56,401,860
Germany . .	13	208,830	1,027,120	52,279,901	14,687,000
Netherlands .	3	12,648	782,862	5,074,632	35,115,711
Portugal . .	9	36,038	801,100	5,049,729	9,148,707
Spain . .	3	197,670	243,877	17,565,632	136,000
Italy . .	2	110,646	188,500	31,856,675	850,000
Austria-Hungary	2	241,032	23,570	41,244,811	1,568,092
Denmark . .	3	15,289	86,634	2,185,335	114,229
Russia . .	3	8,660,395	255,550	128,932,173	15,684,000
Turkey . .	4	1,111,741	465,000	23,834,500	14,956,236
China . .	5	1,336,841	2,881,560	386,000,000	16,680,000
U.S.A. . .	6	3,557,000	172,091	77,000,000	10,544,617
Total . .	136	15,813,201	22,273,858	850,103,317	521,108,791

classes—(1) " Crown colonies, in which the Crown has the entire control of legislation, while the administration is carried on by public officers under the control of the Home Government ; (2) colonies possessing representative institutions, but not responsible government, in which the Crown has no more than a veto on legislation, but the Home Government retains the control of public affairs ; (3) colonies possessing representative institutions and responsible government, in which the Crown has only a veto on legislation, and the Home Government has no control over any officer except the Governor."

Now, of the thirty-nine separate areas which were annexed by Great Britain after 1870 as colonies or protectorates, not a single one ranks in class 3 and the Transvaal alone in class 2.

The new Imperialism established no single British colony endowed with responsible self-government. Nor, with the

exception of the three new States in South Africa, where white settlers lived in some numbers, is it seriously pretended that any of these annexed territories was being prepared and educated for representative, responsible self-government; and even in these South African States there is no serious intention, either on the part of the Home Government or of the colonists, that the majority of the inhabitants shall control the government.

It is true that some of these areas enjoy a measure of self-government, as protectorates or as feudatory States, under their own native princes. But all these in major matters of policy are subject to the absolute rule of the British Government, or of some British official, while the general tendency is towards drawing the reins of arbitrary control more tightly over protectorates, converting them into States which are in substance, though not always in name, Crown colonies. With the exception of a couple of experiments in India, the tendency everywhere has been towards a closer and more drastic imperial control over the territories that have been annexed, transforming protectorates, company rule, and spheres of influence into definite British States of the Crown colony order.

This is attributable, not to any greed of tyranny on the part of the Imperial Government, but to the conditions imposed upon our rule by considerations of climate and native population. Almost the whole of this new territory is tropical, or so near to the tropics as to preclude genuine colonisation of British settlers, while in those few districts where Europeans can work and breed, as in parts of South Africa and Egypt, the preoccupation of the country by large native populations of " lower races " precludes any considerable settlement of British workers and the safe bestowal of the full self-government which prevails in Australasia and Canada.

The same is true to an even more complete extent of the Imperialism of other continental countries. The new Imperialism nowhere extended the political and civil liberties of the mother country to any part of the vast territories which, after 1870, fell under the government of Western civilized Powers. Politically, the new Imperialism was an expansion of autocracy.

Taking the growth of Imperialism as illustrated in the expansion of Great Britain and of the chief continental Powers, we find the distinction between Imperialism and colonisation closely borne out by facts and figures, and warranting the following general judgments :—

First—Almost the whole of this imperial expansion was occupied with the political absorption of tropical or sub-tropical lands in which white men will not settle with their families.

Second—Nearly all the lands were thickly peopled by " lower races."

Thus this recent imperial expansion stands entirely distinct from the colonization of sparsely peopled lands in temperate zones, where white colonists carry with them the modes of government, the industrial and other arts of the civilization of the mother country. The " occupation " of these new territories was comprised in the presence of a small minority of white men, officials, traders, and industrial organisers, exercising political and economic sway over great hordes of population regarded as inferior and as incapable of exercising any considerable rights of self-government, in politics or industry.

CHAPTER II

THE COMMERCIAL VALUE OF IMPERIALISM

THE absorption of so large a proportion of public interest, energy, blood and money in seeking to procure colonial possessions and foreign markets would seem to indicate that Great Britain obtained her chief livelihood by external trade. Now this was not the case. Large as was our foreign and colonial trade in volume and in value, essential as was much of it to our national well-being, nevertheless it furnished a small proportion of the total industry of the nation.

According to the conjectural estimate of the Board of Trade " the proportion of the total labour of the British working classes which was concerned with the production of commodities for export (including the making of the instruments of this production and their transport to the ports) was between one-fifth and one-sixth of the whole."[1]

If we suppose the profits, salaries, etc., in connexion with export trade to be at the same level with those derived from home trade, we may conclude that between one-fifth and one-sixth of the income of the nation comes from the production and carriage of goods for export trade.

Taking the higher estimate of the magnitude of foreign trade, we should conclude that it furnished employment to one-fifth of our industrial factors, the other four-fifths being employed in supplying home markets.

But this must not be taken as a measure of the net value

[1] Cd. 1761, p. 361.

of foreign trade to our nation, or of the amount of loss that would have been sustained by a diminution of our foreign markets. We are not entitled to assume that a tariff-policy or some other restrictive policy on the part of foreign nations which gradually reduced our export trade would imply an *equivalent* loss of national income, and of employment of capital and labour in Great Britain. The assumption, sometimes made, that home demand is a fixed amount, and that any commodities made in excess of this amount must find a foreign market, or remain unsold, is quite unwarranted. There is no necessary limit to the quantity of capital and labour that can be employed in supplying the home markets, provided the effective demand for the goods that are produced is so distributed that every increase of production stimulates a corresponding increase of consumption.

Under such conditions a gradual loss of foreign markets would drive more capital and labour into industries supplying home markets ; the goods this capital and labour produced would be sold and consumed at home. Under such circumstances some loss would normally be sustained, because it could be reasonably assumed that the foreign market that was lost was a more profitable one than the new home market which took its place ; but that loss would certainly be much smaller than the aggregate of the value of trade thus transferred ; it would, in fact, be measured by the reduction in profit, and perhaps in wages, attending the substitution of a less remunerative home market for a more remunerative foreign market.

This argument, of course, does not imply that Great Britain could dispense with her external markets, and be no great sufferer in trade and income. Some considerable foreign markets, as we know, are an economic necessity to her, in order that by her exports she may purchase foods and materials which she cannot produce, or can only produce at a great disadvantage.

This fact makes a considerable external market a matter of vital importance to us. But outside the limit of this practical necessity the value of our foreign markets must rightly be considered to be measured, not by the aggregate value of the goods we sell abroad, but by the superior gain from selling them abroad as compared with selling them (or corresponding quantities of other goods) at home. To assume that if these goods are not sold abroad, neither they nor their substitutes could be sold, even at lower prices, in the home market, is quite unwarranted. There is no natural and necessary limit to the proportion of the national product which can be sold and consumed at home. It is, of course, preferable to sell goods abroad where higher profit can be got by doing so, but the net gain to national industry and income must be measured not by the value of the trade done, but by its more profitable nature.

These reflections are required to make us realize (1) that the importance of external trade is not rightly measured by the proportion its volume and value bear at any given time to those of home trade; and (2) that it is by no means essential to the industrial progress of a nation that her external trade should under all conditions keep pace with her home trade.

When a modern nation has attained a high level of development in those industrial arts which are engaged in supplying the first physical necessaries and conveniences of the population, an increasing proportion of her productive energies will begin to pass into higher kinds of industry, into the transport services, into distribution, and into professional, official and personal services, which produce goods and services less adapted on the whole for international trade than those simpler goods which go to build the lower

Year.	Trade (in Millions).	Value per Head of Population.	Year.	Trade (in Millions).	Value per Head of Population.
		£ s. d.			£ s. d.
1870	547		1885	642	
1871	615		1886	619	
1872	669		1887	643	
1873	682		1888	686	
1874	668		1889	743	
Average	636	**19 19 3**	Average	666	18 4 5
1875	655		1890	749	
1876	632		1891	744	
1877	647		1892	715	
1878	616		1893	682	
1879	612		1894	682	
Average	632	18 16 6	Average	715	18 14 10
1880	697		1895	703	
1881	694		1896	738	
1882	720		1897	745	
1883	732		1898	764	
1884	686		1899	805	
Average	706	20 1 3	Average	753	**18 15 6**

Figures for the years 1910-1934 are given in the Appendix, p. 370.

stages of a civilization.[1]   If this is true, it would appear that, whereas up to a certain point in the development of national life foreign trade will grow rapidly, after that point a decline, not in absolute size or growth but in relative size and growth, will take place.

There is some reason to hold that Great Britain had, in 1905, reached an industrial level where external trade, though still important, will be relatively less important in her national economy.

Between 1870 and 1900, as the above table shows, the

[1] See *Contemporary Review*, August, 1905, in which the author illustrates this tendency by the statistics of occupations in various nations.

value of our foreign trade had not grown so fast as our population. Whereas upon the generally accepted estimate the growth of the income of the nation during these three decades was from about £1,200,000,000 to £1,750,000,000, yielding an increase of about 10 per cent. in the income per head of the population, the value of foreign trade per head had positively shrunk.

Although the real increase in volume of external trade was considerable when the general fall of prices after 1870 is taken into account, it remains quite evident that neither volume nor value of external trade had kept pace during this period with volume and value of internal trade.[1]

Next, let us inquire whether the vast outlay of energy and money upon imperial expansion was attended by a growing trade within the Empire as compared with foreign trade. In other words, does the policy tend to make us more and more an economically self-sufficing Empire ? Does trade follow the flag ?

The figures in the table facing represent the proportion which our trade with our colonies and possessions bears to our foreign trade during the last half of the nineteenth century.

A longer period is here taken as a basis of comparison in order to bring out clearly the central truth, viz., that Imperialism had no appreciable influence whatever on the determination of our external trade until the protective and preferential measures taken during and after the Great War. Setting aside the abnormal increase of exports to our colonies in 1900–1903 due to the Boer War, we perceive that the proportions of our external trade had changed

---

[1] The four years subsequent to 1899 show a considerable increase in value of foreign trade, the average value per head for 1900-1903 working out at £21 2s. 5d. But this is abnormal, due partly to special colonial and foreign expenditure in connexion with the Boer War, partly to the general rise of prices as compared with the earlier level.

PERCENTAGES OF TOTAL VALUES.

Annual Averages.	Imports into Great Britain from		Exports from Great Britain to	
	Foreign Countries.	British Possessions.	Foreign Countries.	British Possessions.
1855–1859	76·5	23·5	68·5	31·5
1860–1864	71·2	28·8	66·6	33·4
1865–1869	76·0	24·0	72·4	27·6
1870–1874	78·0	22·0	74·4	25·6
1875–1879	77·9	22·1	67·0	33·0
1880–1884	76·5	23·5	65·5	34·5
1885–1889	77·1	22·9	65·0	35·0
1890–1894	77·1	22·9	66·5	33·5
1895–1899	78·4	21·6	66·0	34·0
1900–1903	77·3	20·7	63·0	37·0

This table (Cd. 1761 p. 407) refers to merchandise only, excluding bullion. From the export trade, ships and boats (not recorded prior to 1897) are excluded. In exports British produce alone is included. Figures for the years up to 1934 are given in the Appendix, p. 371.

very little during the half century; colonial imports slightly fell, colonial exports slightly rose, during the last decade, as compared with the beginning of the period. Although since 1870 such vast additions have been made to British possessions, involving a corresponding reduction of the area of " Foreign Countries," this imperial expansion was attended by no increase in the proportions of intra-imperial trade as represented in the imports and exports of Great Britain during the nineteenth century.

From the standpoint of the recent history of British trade there is no support for the dogma that " Trade follows the Flag." So far we have examined the question from the point of view of Great Britain. But if we examine the commercial connexion between Great Britain and the colonies from the colonial standpoint, asking whether the external trade of our colonies tends to a closer union with the mother country what result do we reach ?

The elaborate statistical investigation of Professor Alleyne Ireland into the trade of our colonial possessions strikes a still heavier blow at the notion that trade follows the flag. Taking the same period, he establishes the following two facts :—

" The total import trade of all the British colonies and possessions has increased at a much greater rate than the imports from the United Kingdom." " The total exports of all the British colonies and possessions have increased at a much greater rate than the exports to the United Kingdom."[1]

The following table[2] shows the gradual decline in the importance to the colonies of the commercial connexion with Great Britain since 1872–75, as illustrated in the proportion borne in the value of their exports from and their imports to Great Britain as compared with the value of the total imports and exports of the British colonies and possessions :—[1]

Four-Yearly Averages.	Percentages of Imports into Colonies, &c., from Great Britain.	Percentages of Exports from Colonies, &c., into Great Britain.
1856–1859	**46.5**	**57.1**
1860–1863	41·0	65·4
1864–1867	38·9	57·6
1868–1871	**39.8**	**53.5**
1872–1875	43·6	54·0
1876–1879	41·7	50·3
1880–1883	42·8	48·1
1884–1887	38·5	43·0
1888–1891	36·3	39·7
1892–1895	32·4	36·6
1896–1899	**32.5**	**34.9**

[1] *Tropical Colonization*, Page 125.

[2] Founded on the tables of Professor Ireland (*Tropical Colonization*, pp. 98–101), and revised up to date from figures in the Statistical Abstract of Colonial Possessions, Cd. 307.

[1] Figures for the years 1913–4, 1924–9, 1933–4 are given in the Appendix, pp. 372–3.

In other words, while Great Britain's dependence on her Empire for trade was stationary, the dependence of her Empire upon her for trade was rapidly diminishing.

The actual condition of British trade with foreign countries and with the chief groups of the colonies respectively may be indicated by the following statement[1] for the year ending December, 1901 :—

	Imports from.		Exports to.	
	Value.	Percentage.	Value.	Percentage.
	£		£	
Foreign Countries . . .	417,615,000	80	178,450,000	63½
British India	38,001,000	7	39,753,000	14
Australasia . . .	34,682,000	7	26,932,000	9½
Canada	19,775,000	4	7,797,000	3
British South Africa .	5,155,000	1	17,006,000	6
Other British Possessions .	7,082,000	1	10,561,000	4
Total	522,310,000	100	280,499,000	100

It is thus clearly seen that while imperial expansion was attended by no increase in the value of our trade with our colonies and dependencies, a considerable increase in the value of our trade with foreign nations had taken place. Did space permit, it could be shown that the greatest increase of our foreign trade was with that group of industrial nations whom we regard as our industrial enemies, and whose political enmity we were in danger of arousing by our policy of expansion—France, Germany, Russia, and the United States.

One more point of supreme significance in its bearing on the new Imperialism remains. We have already drawn

[1] " Cobden Club Leaflet," 123, by Harold Cox. Figures for the year 1934-5 are given in the Appendix, p. 371.

attention to the radical distinction between genuine colonialism and Imperialism. This distinction is strongly marked in the statistics of the progress of our commerce with our foreign possessions.

The results of an elaborate investigation by Professor Flux[1] into the size of our trade respectively with India, the self-governing colonies and the other colonies may be presented in the following simple table :—[2]

	Percentages of imports from Great Britain.		Percentage of Exports to Great Britain.	
	1867–71.	1892–96.	1867–71.	1892–96.
India	69·2	71·9	52·6	33·2
Self-governing Colonies . .	57·5	59·2	55·4	70·3
Other Colonies . . .	34·3	26·4	46·4	29·3

Professor Flux thus summarises the chief results of his comparisons : " The great source of growth of Britain's colonial trade is very clearly shown to be the growth of trade with the colonies to which self-government has been granted. Their foreign trade has nearly doubled, and the proportion of it which is carried on with the mother country has increased from about 56½ per cent. to 65 per cent.

Later statistics[3] distinguishing British trade with India, the self-governing colonies and other colonies and possessions impress the same lesson from the standpoint of Great Britain in an even more striking manner.

[1] " The Flag and Trade," *Journal of Statistical Society*, September, 1899. Vol. lxii, pp. 496–98.
[2] Figures for the years 1913-4, 1924-9 and 1933-4 are given in the Appendix, p. 371.
[3] Statistical Abstract for the British Empire from 1889 to 1903. (Cd. 2395 pp. 25–28). Full tables of the Export and Import trade of Great Britain with the several parts of the Empire for the years 1904 to 1934, are given in the Appendix, pp. 372–3.

VALUE OF IMPORTS INTO GREAT BRITAIN FROM THE SEVERAL PARTS OF THE EMPIRE (000,000 OMITTED).

	1889	1890	1891	1892	1893	1894	1895	1896	1897	1898	1899	1900[1]	1901	1902	1903
Self-governing Colonies	51	52	57	58	58	62	67	64	77	80	80	69	68	71	84
India . . .	37	33	33	34	28	31	29	27	26	29	29	31	34	32	37
Other possessions .	15	15	16	15	15	17	16	16	16	16	18	19	17	19	16

VALUE OF EXPORTS FROM GREAT BRITAIN INTO THE SEVERAL PARTS OF THE EMPIRE

	1889	1890	1891	1892	1893	1894	1895	1896	1897	1898	1899	1900	1901	1902	1903
Self-governing Colonies . .	48	44	45	39	37	35	43	47	45	44	48	55	59	68	66
India . . .	40	45	39	37	38	36	31	38	37	38	40	41	46	42	45
Other possessions . .	15	17	15	14	14	15	14	13	13	15	17	18	18	17	18

These tables show that whereas the import and the export trade with our self-governing colonies exhibited a large advance, our import trade alike with India and the "other possessions" was virtually stagnant, while our export trade with these two parts shows a very slight and very irregular tendency to increase.

Now the significance of these results for the study of modern Imperialism consists in the fact that the whole trend of this movement was directed to the acquisition of lands and populations belonging not to the self-governing order but to the "other possessions." Our expansion was almost wholly concerned with the acquisition of tropical and sub-tropical countries peopled by races to whom we have no serious intention of giving self-government. With the exception of the Transvaal and the Orange River

[1] Fall-off in imports from self-governing colonies 1900-2 is due entirely to stoppage in gold imports from South Africa.

Colony, none of our acquisitions since 1870 belonged, even prospectively, to the self-governing group, and even in the case of the two South African states, the prospective self-government was confined to a white minority of the population. The distinctive feature of modern Imperialism, from the commercial standpoint, is that it adds to our empire tropical and sub-tropical regions with which our trade is small, precarious and unprogressive.

The only considerable increase of our import trade since 1884 is from our genuine colonies in Australasia, North America, and Cape Colony ; the trade with India has been stagnant, while that with our tropical colonies in Africa and the West Indies has been in most cases irregular and dwindling. Our export trade exhibits the same general character, save that Australia and Canada show a growing resolution to release themselves from dependence upon British manufactures ; the trade with the tropical colonies, though exhibiting some increase, is very small and very fluctuating.

As for the territories acquired under the new Imperialism, except in one instance, no serious attempt to regard them as satisfactory business assets is possible.

The following table (page 39) gives the official figures of the value of our import and export trade with our tropical and sub-tropical possessions for the beginning of the present century. Bullion and specie are included in both accounts.

The entire volume of our export trade with our new protectorates in Africa, Asia and the Pacific amounted to not more than some nine millions sterling, of which more than six millions took place with the Malay Protected States, and was largely through traffic with the Far East. The entire volume of the import trade consisted of about eight millions sterling, half of which is with the same Malay States. At whatever figure we estimate the profits in this

38

British Trade with New Possessions.[1]	Imports from	Exports to
	£	£
Cyprus	83,842	132,445
Zanzibar Protectorate . . .	114,088	88,777
British East Africa Protectorate (including Uganda) . . .	123,006	17,274
Somaliland	389,424[2]	333,842[2]
Southern Nigeria Protectorate .	1,228,959	922,657
Northern Nigeria Protectorate . .	240,110	68,442
Lagos	641,203	366,171
Gambia	142,560	15,158
British North Borneo . .	275,000	368,000
Malay Protected States . .	4,100,000	6,211,000
Fiji	30,567	10,161
British Solomon Islands Protectorate	—	32,203
Gilbert and Ellice Islands Protectorate	20,359	21,502
British New Guinea . . .	—	62,891
Leeward Islands . . .	168,700	67,178
Windward Islands	739,095	305,224

trade, it forms an utterly insignificant part of our national income, while the expenses connected directly and indirectly with the acquisition, administration and defence of these possessions must swallow an immeasurably larger sum.

Apart from its quantity, the quality of the new tropical export trade was of the lowest, consisting for the most part, as the analysis of the Colonial Office shows, of the cheapest textile goods of Lancashire, the cheapest metal goods of Birmingham and Sheffield, and large quantities of gunpowder, spirits, and tobacco.

Such evidence leads to the following conclusions bearing upon the economics of the new Imperialism. First, the external trade of Great Britain bore a small and diminishing proportion to its internal industry and trade. Secondly, of the external trade, that with British possessions bore a diminishing proportion to that with foreign countries.

[1] Cd. 2395 and Cd. 2337.
[2] Trade with British possessions as well as with Great Britain is here included.

Thirdly, of the trade with British possessions the tropical trade, and in particular the trade with the new tropical possessions, was the smallest, least progressive, and most fluctuating in quantity, while it is lowest in the character of the goods which it embraces.

CHAPTER III

IMPERIALISM AS AN OUTLET
FOR POPULATION

THERE is a widely prevalent belief that imperial expansion is desirable, or even necessary, in order to absorb and utilize the surplus of our ever-growing population. "The reproductive powers of nature," runs the argument, "brook no restraint : the most dominant force in history is the tendency of population to overflow its ancient banks, seeking fuller and easier subsistence. Great Britain is one of the most congested areas in the world ; her growing population cannot find enough remunerative occupation within these islands ; professional and working-classes alike find it more and more difficult to earn a decent and secure living, every labour market is overstocked, emigration is a prime economic necessity. Now, those who under such pressure leave our shores consist largely of the strongest and most energetic stuff the nation contains. Many of these people, whose permanent alienation would be a heavy loss, have been saved to the Empire by the policy of imperial expansion : they have settled either in vacant places of the earth which they have seized and kept under British rule, or in places where they have set up a definitely British supremacy over lower races of existing inhabitants. It is our most urgent national interest that this surplus emigrant population shall settle in lands which are under the British flag, and we must therefore maintain a constant policy of extending the political control of Great Britain so as to cover the new homes to which these people betake themselves in pursuit of employment." This motive is closely linked with other economic motives relating to trade and investments. The establishment of British trade, and especially of British capital, in foreign lands naturally attracts a certain British population ; traders, engineers, overseers, and mechanics are needed as entrepreneurs and managers. So wherever a new area was opened up to our trade and capital the nucleus of an outlander population was formed. Hence, of necessity, sprang up a crop of political issues, an outlander problem : the British outlanders, not satisfied with the foreign rule, demanded the intervention of their home Government. Thus the duty of protecting British subjects in a foreign country has been identified with the duty of protecting British property, not merely the personal property of the outlanders, often a trivial matter, but the far larger stakes of the home investors. But apart from these cases of special interest, wherever any considerable number of British subjects settles in a savage or semi-civilized country they have a " right " to British protection, and since that protection can seldom be made effective without the exercise of direct British authority, the imperial ægis of Great Britain must be spread over all such areas, when a convenient occasion for such expansion should present itself.

Such has been the accepted theory and practice. What validity did it possess as an argument for imperial expansion ? Let me first ask : Was England over-populated, and was the prospect of further increase such as to compel us to " peg out claims for posterity " in other parts of the world ? The facts are these. Great Britain is not and was not so thickly populated as certain prosperous industrial areas in Germany, the Netherlands, and China : along with every recent growth of population has come a far greater growth of wealth and of the power to purchase food and other subsistence. The modern specialization of industry has caused a congestion of population upon certain spots which may be injurious in some ways to the well-being of the nation, but it cannot be regarded as over-population in the sense of a people outgrowing the means of subsistence. Nor have we reason to fear such over-population in the future. It is true that our manufactures and commerce may not continue to grow as rapidly as in the past, though we have no clear warrant from industrial statistics for this judgment : but if this be so, neither is our population likely to increase so fast. Of this we have clear statistical evidence : the diminution of the rate of growth of our population, as disclosed by the recent censuses, is such as to justify the conclusion that, if the same forces continue to operate, the population of Great Britain will be stationary by the middle of the century.

There exists, then, no general necessity for a policy of expansion in order to provide for over-population, present or prospective. But supposing it had been necessary for an increasing surplus of our population to emigrate, was it necessary for us to spend so large a part of our national resources, and to incur such heavy risks, in seizing new territory for them to settle upon ?

The total emigration of Britons represents no large proportion of the population ; that proportion during the years of imperial expansion perceptibly diminished : of the emigrants less than one-half settled in British possessions, and an infinitesimally small fraction settled in the countries acquired under the new Imperialism. These most instructive facts are established by the following official table, giving the statistics of emigration from 1884 to 1903, the year from which the full tide of imperial expansion is to be dated :—

NUMBER OF OUTWARD BOUND PASSENGERS OF BRITISH AND IRISH ORIGIN, FROM THE UNITED KINGDOM TO COUNTRIES OUT OF EUROPE.[1]

Year.	Passengers to					Total.
	United States.	British North America.	Australia and New Zealand.	Cape of Good Hope and Natal.	Other Places.	
1884	155,280	31,134	44,255	—	11,510	242,179
1885	137,687	19,828	39,395	—	10,724	207,644
1886	152,710	24,745	43,076	3,897	8,472	232,900
1887	201,526	32,025	34,183	4,909	8,844	281,487
1888	195,986	34,853	31,127	6,466	11,496	279,928
1889	168,771	28,269	28,294	13,884	14,577	253,795
1890	152,413	22,520	21,179	10,321	11,683	218,116
1891	156,395	21,578	19,547	9,090	11,897	218,507
1892	150,039	23,254	15,950	9,891	10,908	210,042
1893	148,949	24,732	11,203	13,097	10,833	208,814
1894	104,001	17,459	10,917	13,177	10,476	156,030
1895	126,502	16,622	10,567	20,234	11,256	185,181
1896	98,921	15,267	10,354	24,594	12,789	161,925
1897	85,324	15,571	12,061	21,109	12,395	146,460
1898	80,494	17,640	10,693	19,756	12,061	140,644
1899	92,482	16,410	11,467	14,432	11,571	146,362
1900	102,797	18,443	14,922	20,815	11,848	168,825
1901	104,195	15,757	15,350	23,143	13,270	171,715
1902	108,498	26,293	14,345	43,206	13,370	205,662
1903	123,663	59,652	12,375	50,206	14,054	259,950

Regarded as a measure of the outflow of "surplus" population, even these figures are excessive in two ways. In the first place, they include considerable numbers of travellers and casual visitors who were not real emigrants, Secondly, to measure aright the net emigration, we must set against these figures the immigration figures. The net reduction of our population by emigration is thus reduced to an average, during the years 1895–1900 to 31,474 per annum.

The "boom" in North-West Canada and in the colonies

[1] Number of passengers for the years 1912–1934 are given in the Appendix, p. 374.

of South Africa perceptibly increased the flow at the turn of the century. But the rest of our Empire has absorbed a very small proportion of our emigrants. The number sailing for " other parts " of the Empire in 1903 was 8,719, and of these the number of actual settlers in the new tropical dominions would be a mere handful.

A certain quantity of military and official employment is afforded by the new Imperialism to the influential upper classes, a few engineers, missionaries, prospectors, and overseers of trading and industrial undertakings get temporary posts, but as a contribution towards the general field of employment the new Imperialism is an utterly insignificant factor.

No substantial settlement of Britons was taking place in 1905 upon any of the areas of the Empire acquired since 1870, excepting the Transvaal and the Orange River Colony, nor was it likely that any such settlement would take place. The tropical character of most lands acquired under the new Imperialism renders genuine colonisation impossible : there was no true British settlement in these places ; a small number of men spent a short broken period in precarious occupations. The new Empire was even more barren for settlement than for profitable trade.

CHAPTER IV

ECONOMIC PARASITES OF IMPERIALISM

I

SEEING that the Imperialism of the last six decades is clearly condemned as a business policy, in that at enormous expense it has procured a small, bad, unsafe increase of markets, and has jeopardised the entire wealth of the nation in rousing the strong resentment of other nations, we may ask, " How is the British nation induced to embark upon such unsound business ? " The only possible answer is that the business interests of the nation as a whole are subordinated to those of certain sectional interests that usurp control of the national resources and use them for their private gain. This is no strange or monstrous charge to bring ; it is the commonest disease of all forms of government. The famous words of Sir Thomas More are as true now as when he wrote them : " Everywhere do I perceive a certain conspiracy of rich men seeking their own advantage under the name and pretext of the commonwealth."

Although the new Imperialism has been bad business for the nation, it has been good business for certain classes and certain trades within the nation. The vast expenditure on armaments, the costly wars, the grave risks and embarrassments of foreign policy, the checks upon political and social reforms within Great Britain, though fraught with great injury to the nation, have served well the present business interests of certain industries and professions.

It is idle to meddle with politics unless we clearly recognise this central fact and understand what these sectional interests are which are the enemies of national safety and the commonwealth. We must put aside the merely sentimental diagnosis which explains wars or other national blunders by outbursts of patriotic animosity or errors of statecraft. Doubtless at every outbreak of war not only the man in the street but the man at the helm is often duped by the cunning with which aggressive motives and greedy purposes dress themselves in defensive clothing. There is, it may be safely asserted, no war within memory, however nakedly aggressive it may seem to the dispassionate historian, which has not been presented to the people who were called upon to fight as a necessary defensive policy, in which the honour, perhaps the very existence, of the State was involved.

The disastrous folly of these wars, the material and moral damage inflicted even on the victor, appear so plain to the disinterested spectator that he is apt to despair of any State attaining years of discretion, and inclines to regard these natural cataclysms as implying some ultimate irrationalism in politics. But careful analysis of the existing relations between business and politics shows that the aggressive Imperialism which we seek to understand is not in the main the product of blind passions of races or of the mixed folly and ambition of politicians. It is far more rational than at first sight appears. Irrational from the standpoint of the whole nation, it is rational enough from the standpoint of certain classes in the nation. A completely socialist State which kept good books and presented regular balance-sheets of expenditure and assets would soon discard Imperialism ; an intelligent *laissez-faire* democracy which gave duly proportionate weight in its policy to all economic interests alike would do the same. But a State in which certain well-organised business interests are able to outweigh the weak, diffused interest of the community is bound to pursue a policy which accords with the pressure of the former interests.

In order to explain Imperialism on this hypothesis we have to answer two questions. Do we find in Great Britain any well-organised group of special commercial and social interests which stand to gain by aggressive Imperialism and the militarism it involves ? If such a combination of interests exists, has it the power to work its will in the arena of politics ?

What is the direct economic outcome of Imperialism ? A great expenditure of public money upon ships, guns, military and naval equipment and stores, growing and productive of enormous profits when a war, or an alarm of war, occurs ; new public loans and important fluctuations in the home and foreign Bourses ; more posts for soldiers and sailors and in the diplomatic and consular services ; improvement of foreign investments by the substitution of the British flag for a foreign flag ; acquisition of markets for certain classes of exports, and some protection and assistance for British trades in these manufactures ; employment for engineers, missionaries, speculative miners, ranchers and other emigrants.

Certain definite business and professional interests feeding upon imperialistic expenditure, or upon the results of that expenditure, are thus set up in opposition to the common good, and, instinctively feeling their way to one another, are found united in strong sympathy to support every new imperialist exploit.

If the £60,000,000[1] which may now be taken as a minimum expenditure on armaments in time of peace were subjected to a close analysis, most of it would be traced directly to

[1] In 1905 ; now, in 1938, £200,000,000.

the tills of certain big firms engaged in building warships and transports, equipping and coaling them, manufacturing guns, rifles, ammunition, 'planes and motor vehicles of every kind, supplying horses, waggons, saddlery, food, clothing for the services, contracting for barracks, and for other large irregular needs. Through these main channels the millions flow to feed many subsidiary trades, most of which are quite aware that they are engaged in executing contracts for the services. Here we have an important nucleus of commercial Imperialism. Some of these trades, especially the shipbuilding, boilermaking, and gun and ammunition making trades, are conducted by large firms with immense capital, whose heads are well aware of the uses of political influence for trade purposes.

These men are Imperialists by conviction ; a pushful policy is good for them.

With them stand the great manufacturers for export trade, who gain a living by supplying the real or artificial wants of the new countries we annex or open up. Manchester, Sheffield, Birmingham, to name three representative cases, are full of firms which compete in pushing textiles and hardware, engines, tools, machinery, spirits, guns, upon new markets. The public debts which ripen in our colonies, and in foreign countries that come under our protectorate or influence, are largely loaned in the shape of rails, engines, guns, and other materials of civilization made and sent out by British firms. The making of railways, canals, and other public works, the establishment of factories, the development of mines, the improvement of agriculture in new countries, stimulate a definite interest in important manufacturing industries which feeds a very firm imperialist faith in their owners.

The proportion which such trade bears to the total industry of Great Britain is not great, but some of it is extremely influential and able to make a definite impression upon politics, through chambers of commerce, Parliamentary representatives, and semi-political, semi-commercial bodies like the Imperial South African Association or the China Society.

The shipping trade has a very definite interest which makes for Imperialism. This is well illustrated by the policy of State subsidies now claimed by shipping firms as a retainer, and in order to encourage British shipping for purposes of imperial safety and defence.

The services are, of course, imperialist by conviction and by professional interest, and every increase of the army, navy and air force enhances the political power they exert. The abolition of purchase in the army, by opening the profession to the upper middle classes, greatly enlarged this most direct feeder of imperial sentiment. The potency of this factor is, of course, largely due to the itch for glory and adventure among military officers upon disturbed or uncertain frontiers of the Empire. This has been a most prolific source of expansion in India. The direct professional influence of the services carries with it a less organised but powerful sympathetic support on the part of the aristocracy and the wealthy classes, who seek in the services careers for their sons.

To the military services we may add the Indian Civil Service and the numerous official and semi-official posts in our colonies and protectorates. Every expansion of the Empire is also regarded by these same classes as affording new openings for their sons as ranchers, planters, engineers, or missionaries. This point of view is aptly summarised by a high Indian official, Sir Charles Crossthwaite, in discussing British relations with Siam. "The real question was who was to get the trade with them, and how we could make the most of them, so as to find fresh markets for our goods and also employment for those superfluous articles of the present day, our boys."

From this standpoint our colonies still remain what James Mill cynically described them as being, " a vast system of outdoor relief for the upper classes."

In all the professions, military and civil, the army, diplomacy, the church, the bar, teaching and engineering, Greater Britain serves for an overflow, relieving the congestion of the home market and offering chances to more reckless or adventurous members, while it furnishes a convenient limbo for damaged characters and careers. The actual amount of profitable employment thus furnished by our recent acquisitions is inconsiderable, but it arouses that disproportionate interest which always attaches to the margin of employment. To extend this margin is a powerful motive in Imperialism.

These influences, primarily economic, though not un-mixed with other sentimental motives, are particularly operative in military, clerical, academic, and Civil Service circles, and furnish an interested bias towards Imperialism throughout the educated circles.

II

By far the most important economic factor in Imperialism is the influence relating to investments. The growing cosmopolitanism of capital has been the greatest economic change of recent generations. Every advanced industrial nation has been tending to place a larger share of its capital outside the limits of its own political area, in foreign countries, or in colonies, and to draw a growing income from this source.

No exact or even approximate estimate of the total amount of the income of the British nation derived from foreign

investments is possible. We possess, however, in the income
tax assessments an indirect measurement of certain large
sections of investments, from which we can form some
judgment as to the total size of the income from foreign and
colonial sources, and the rate of its growth.

These returns give us a measure of the amount and
growth of the investments effected by British citizens
in foreign and colonial stocks of a public or semi-public
character, including foreign and colonial public securities,
railways, etc. The income from these sources is computed
as follows :—[1]

	£
1884	33,829,124
1888	46,978,371
1892	54,728,770
1896	54,901,079
1900	60,266,886
1903	63,828,715

From this table it appears that the period of energetic
Imperialism coincided with a remarkable growth in the
income for foreign investments.

These figures, however, only give the foreign income
which can be identified as such. The closer estimates
made by Sir R. Giffen and others warrant the belief that
the actual income derived from foreign and colonial investments amounted to not less than £100,000,000, the capital
value of the same reaching a sum of about £2,000,000,000.[2]

Income tax returns and other statistics descriptive of
the growth of these investments indicate that the total
amount of British investments abroad at the end of the
nineteenth century cannot be set down at a lower figure

[1] Figures for the years 1929–1933 are given in the Appendix, p. 375.
[2] See Appendix, p. 375.

than this. Considering that Sir R. Giffen regarded as " moderate " the estimate of £1,700,000,000 in 1892, the figure here named is probably below the truth.

Now, without placing any undue reliance upon these estimates, we cannot fail to recognise that in dealing with these foreign investments we are facing the most important factor in the economics of Imperialism. Whatever figures we take, two facts are evident. First, that the income derived as interest upon foreign investments enormously exceeded that derived as profits upon ordinary export and import trade. Secondly, that while our foreign and colonial trade, and presumably the income from it, were growing but slowly, the share of our import values representing income from foreign investments was growing very rapidly.

In a former chapter I pointed out how small a proportion of our national income appeared to be derived as profits from external trade. It seemed unintelligible that the enormous costs and risks of the new Imperialism should be undertaken for such small results in the shape of increase to external trade, especially when the size and character of the new markets acquired were taken into consideration. The statistics of foreign investments, however, shed clear light upon the economic forces which dominate our policy. While the manufacturing and trading classes make little out of their new markets, paying, if they knew it, much more in taxation than they get out of them in trade, it is quite otherwise with the investor.

It is not too much to say that the modern foreign policy of Great Britain has been primarily a struggle for profitable markets of investment. To a larger extent every year Great Britain has been becoming a nation living upon tribute from abroad, and the classes who enjoy this tribute have had an ever-increasing incentive to employ the public

53

policy, the public purse, and the public force to extend the field of their private investments, and to safeguard and improve their existing investments. This is, perhaps, the most important fact in modern politics, and the obscurity in which it is wrapped has constituted the gravest danger to our State.

What was true of Great Britain was true likewise of France, Germany, the United States, and of all countries in which modern capitalism had placed large surplus savings in the hands of a plutocracy or of a thrifty middle class. A well-recognised distinction is drawn between creditor and debtor countries. Great Britain had been for some time by far the largest creditor country, and the policy by which the investing classes used the instrument of the State for private business purposes is most richly illustrated in the history of her wars and annexations. But France, Germany, and the United States were advancing fast along the same path. The nature of these imperialist operations is thus set forth by the Italian economist Loria :

" When a country which has contracted a debt is unable, on account of the slenderness of its income, to offer sufficient guarantee for the punctual payment of interest, what happens ? Sometimes an out-and-out conquest of the debtor country follows. Thus France's attempted conquest of Mexico during the second empire was undertaken solely with the view of guaranteeing the interest of French citizens holding Mexican securities. But more frequently the insufficient guarantee of an international loan gives rise to the appointment of a financial commission by the creditor countries in order to protect their rights and guard the fate of their invested capital. The appointment of such a commission literally amounts in the end, however, to a veritable conquest. We have examples of this in Egypt, which has to all practical purposes become a British province, and in Tunis, which has in like manner become a dependency of France, who supplied the greater part of the loan. The Egyptian revolt against the foreign domination issuing from the debt came to nothing, as it met with invariable opposition from capitalistic combinations, and Tel-el-Kebir's success bought with money, was the most brilliant victory wealth has ever obtained on the field of battle."[1]

But, though useful to explain certain economic facts, the terms " creditor " and " debtor," as applied to countries, obscure the most significant feature of this Imperialism. For though, as appears frcm the analysis given above, much, if not most, of the debts were " public," the credit was nearly always private, though sometimes, as in the case of Egypt, its owners succeeded in getting their Government to enter a most unprofitable partnership, guaranteeing the payment of the interest, but not sharing in it.

Aggressive Imperialism, which costs the taxpayer so dear, which is of so little value to the manufacturer and trader, which is fraught with such grave incalculable peril to the citizen, is a source of great gain to the investor who cannot find at home the profitable use he seeks for his capital, and insists that his Government should help him to profitable and secure investments abroad.

If, contemplating the enormous expenditure on armaments, the ruinous wars, the diplomatic audacity or knavery by which modern Governments seek to extend their territorial power, we put the plain, practical question, *Cui bono ?* the first and most obvious answer is, the investor.

The annual income Great Britain derives from commissions on her whole foreign and colonial trade, import and export, was estimated by Sir R. Giffen[2] at £18,000,000 for 1899, taken at 2¼ per cent., upon a turnover of £800,000,000.

[1] Loria, *The Economic Foundations of Politics*, p. 273 (George Allen & Unwin).
[2] *Journal of the Statistical Society*, vol. xlii, p. 9.

This is the whole that we are entitled to regard as profits on external trade. Considerable as this sum is, it cannot serve to yield an economic motive-power adequate to explain the dominance which business considerations exercise over our imperial policy. Only when we set beside it some £90,000,000 or £100,000,000, representing pure profit upon investments, do we understand whence the economic impulse to Imperialism is derived.

Investors who have put their money in foreign lands, upon terms which take full account of risks connected with the political conditions of the country, desire to use the resources of their Government to minimise these risks, and so to enhance the capital value and the interest of their private investments. The investing and speculative classes in general have also desired that Great Britain should take other foreign areas under her flag in order to secure new areas for profitable investments and speculation.

III

If the special interest of the investor is liable to clash with the public interest and to induce a wrecking policy, still more dangerous is the special interest of the financier, the general dealer in investments. In large measure the rank and file of the investors are, both for business and for politics, the cat'spaws of the great financial houses, who use stocks and shares not so much as investments to yield them interest, but as material for speculation in the money market. In handling large masses of stocks and shares, in floating companies, in manipulating fluctuations of values, the magnates of the Bourse find their gain. These great businesses—banking, broking, bill discounting, loan floating, company promoting—form the central ganglion of international capitalism. United by the strongest bonds of organisation, always in closest and quickest touch with one another, situated in the very heart of the business capital of every State, controlled, so far as Europe is concerned, chiefly by men of a single and peculiar race, who have behind them many centuries of financial experience, they are in a unique position to manipulate the policy of nations. No great quick direction of capital is possible save by their consent and through their agency. Does any one seriously suppose that a great war could be undertaken by any European State, or a great State loan subscribed, if the house of Rothschild and its connexions set their face against it ?

Every great political act involving a new flow of capital, or a large fluctuation in the values of existing investments, must receive the sanction and the practical aid of this little group of financial kings. These men, holding their realised wealth and their business capital, as they must, chiefly in stocks and bonds, have a double stake, first as investors, but secondly and chiefly as financial dealers. As investors, their political influence does not differ essentially from that of the smaller investors, except that they usually possess a practical control of the businesses in which they invest. As speculators or financial dealers they constitute, however, the gravest single factor in the economics of Imperialism.

To create new public debts, to float new companies, and to cause constant considerable fluctuations of values are three conditions of their profitable business. Each condition carries them into politics, and throws them on the side of Imperialism.

The public financial arrangements for the Philippine war put several millions of dollars into the pockets of Mr. Pierpont Morgan and his friends ; the China-Japan war, which saddled the Celestial Empire for the first time with a public debt, and the indemnity which she will pay to her European invaders in connexion with the recent conflict, bring grist to the financial mills in Europe ; every railway or mining concession wrung from some reluctant foreign potentate means profitable business in raising capital and floating companies. A policy which rouses fears of aggression in Asiatic states, and which fans the rivalry of commercial nations in Europe, evokes vast expenditure on armaments, and ever-accumulating public debts, while the doubts and risks accruing from this policy promote that constant oscillation of values of securities which is so profitable to the skilled financier. There is not a war, a revolution, an anarchist assassination, or any other public shock, which is not gainful to these men ; they are harpies who suck their gains from every new forced expenditure and every sudden disturbance of public credit. To the financiers " in the know " the Jameson raid was a most advantageous coup, as may be ascertained by a comparison of the " holdings " of these men before and after that event ; the terrible sufferings of England and South Africa in the war, which was a sequel of the raid, has been a source of immense profit to the big financiers who have best held out against the uncalculated waste, and have recouped themselves by profitable war contracts and by " freezing out " the smaller interests in the Transvaal. These men are the only certain gainers from the war, and most of their gains are made out of the public losses of their adopted country or the private losses of their fellow-countrymen.

The policy of these men, it is true, does not necessarily make for war ; where war would bring about too great and too permanent a damage to the substantial fabric of industry, which is the ultimate and essential basis of speculation, their influence is cast for peace, as in the dangerous quarrel between Great Britain and the United States regarding

Venezuela. But every increase of public expenditure, every oscillation of public credit short of this collapse, every risky enterprise in which public resources can be made the pledge of private speculations, is profitable to the big money-lender and speculator.

The wealth of these houses, the scale of their operations, and their cosmopolitan organisation make them the prime determinants of imperial policy. They have the largest definite stake in the business of Imperialism, and the amplest means of forcing their will upon the policy of nations.

In view of the part which the non-economic factors of patriotism, adventure, military enterprise, political ambition, and philanthropy play in imperial expansion, it may appear that to impute to financiers so much power is to take a too narrowly economic view of history. And it is true that the motor-power of Imperialism is not chiefly financial : finance is rather the governor of the imperial engine, directing the energy and determining its work : it does not constitute the fuel of the engine, nor does it directly generate the power. Finance manipulates the patriotic forces which politicians, soldiers, philan-thropists, and traders generate ; the enthusiasm for expansion which issues from these sources, though strong and genuine, is irregular and blind ; the financial interest has those qualities of concentration and clear-sighted calculation which are needed to set Imperialism to work. An ambitious statesman, a frontier soldier, an overzealous missionary, a pushing trader, may suggest or even initiate a step of imperial expansion, may assist in educating patriotic public opinion to the urgent need of some fresh advance, but the final determination rests with the financial power. The direct influence exercised by great financial houses in " high politics " is supported by the control which they exercise over the body of public opinion through the Press, which, in every " civilised " country, is becoming more and more their obedient instrument. While the specifically financial newspaper imposes " facts " and " opinions " on the business classes, the general body of the Press comes more and more under the conscious or unconscious domination of financiers. The case of the South African Press, whose agents and correspondents fanned the martial flames in this country, was one of open ownership on the part of South African financiers, and this policy of owning newspapers for the sake of manufacturing public opinion is common in the great European cities. In Berlin, Vienna, and Paris many of the influential newspapers have been held by financial houses, which used them, not primarily to make direct profits out of them, but in order to put into the public mind beliefs and sentiments which would influence public policy and thus affect the money market. In Great Britain this policy has not gone so far, but the alliance with finance grows closer every year, either by financiers purchasing a controlling share of newspapers, or by newspaper proprietors being tempted into finance. Apart from the financial Press, and financial ownership of the general Press, the City has notoriously exercised a subtle and abiding influence upon leading London newspapers, and through them upon the body of the provincial Press, while the entire dependence of the Press for its business profits upon its advertising columns has involved a peculiar reluctance to oppose the organised financial classes with whom rests the control of so much advertising business. Add to this the natural sympathy with a sensational policy which a cheap Press always manifests, and it becomes evident that the Press has been strongly biased towards Imperialism, and has lent itself with great facility to the suggestion of financial or political Imperialists who have desired to work up patriotism for some new piece of expansion.

Such is the array of distinctively economic forces making for Imperialism, a large loose group of trades and professions seeking profitable business and lucrative employment from the expansion of military and civil services, and from the expenditure on military operations, the opening up of new tracts of territory and trade with the same, and the provision of new capital which these operations require, all these finding their central guiding and directing force in the power of the general financier.

The play of these forces does not openly appear. They are essentially parasites upon patriotism, and they adapt themselves to its protecting colours. In the mouth of their representatives are noble phrases, expressive of their desire to extend the area of civilisation, to establish good government, promote Christianity, extirpate slavery, and elevate the lower races. Some of the business men who hold such language may entertain a genuine, though usually a vague, desire to accomplish these ends, but they are primarily engaged in business, and they are not unaware of the utility of the more unselfish forces in furthering their ends. Their true attitude of mind was expressed by Mr. Rhodes in his famous description of "Her Majesty's Flag" as "the greatest commercial asset in the world."[1]

APPENDIX

Sir R. Giffen estimated the income derived from foreign sources as profit, interest and pensions in 1882 at £70,000,000, and in a paper read before the Statistical Society in March, 1899 he estimated the income from the same sources for the

[1] It will be observed that this, like not a few other words of revelation, has been doctored in the volume, *Cecil Rhodes : his Political Life and Speeches*, by " Vindex " (p. 823).

current year at £90,000,000. It is probable that this last figure is an underestimate, for if the items of foreign income not included as such under the income-tax returns bear the same proportion to those included as in 1882, the total of income from foreign and colonial investments should be £120,000,000 rather than £90,000,000. Sir R. Giffen hazarded the calculation that the new public investments abroad in the sixteen years 1882–1898 amounted to over £800,000,000, " and though part of the sum may have been nominal only, the real investment must have been enormous."

Mr. Mulhall gave the following estimate of the size and growth of our foreign and colonial investments after 1862 :

Year.					Amount.	Annual Increase.
					£	Per cent.
1862	.	.	.	.	144,000,000	—
1872	.	.	.	.	600,000,000	45·6
1882	.	.	.	.	875,000,000	27·5
1893	.	.	.	.	1,698,000,000	74·8

This last amount is of especial interest, because it represents the most thorough investigation made by a most competent economist for the *Dictionary of Political Economy.* The investments included under this figure may be classified under the following general heads :—

Loans.		Million £.	Railways.		Million £.	Sundries.		Million £.
Foreign	.	525	U.S.A.	.	120	Banks	.	50
Colonial	.	225	Colonial	.	140	Lands	.	100
Municipal	.	20	Various	.	128	Mines, &c.	.	390
		770			388			540

In other words, in 1893 the British capital invested abroad represented about 15 per cent. of the total wealth of the United Kingdom ; nearly one-half of this capital was in the form of loans to foreign and colonial Governments ; of the rest a large proportion was invested in railways, banks, telegraphs, and other public services, owned, controlled, or vitally affected by Governments, while most of the remainder was placed in lands and mines, or in industries directly dependent on land values.[1]

[1] Total (Nominal) British investments overseas for the years 1929–1933 are given in the Appendix, p. 375.

CHAPTER V

IMPERIALISM BASED ON PROTECTION

A BUSINESS man estimating the value of an extension of his business will set the increased costs against the increased takings. Is it unreasonable that a business nation should adopt the same course ? From this stand-point our increased military and naval expenditure during recent years may be regarded primarily as insurance premiums for protection of existing colonial markets and current outlay on new markets.

In order to test the finance of the new Imperialism, let us compare the growth of expenditure on armaments and wars since 1884 with the increased value of colonial trade[1] (page 65).

Now, though there are no means of ear-marking the expenditure which might rank as insurance upon old markets or that which is spent upon acquiring new markets, it is not unreasonable to saddle the new Imperialism with the whole of the increase and to set against it the value of the trade of the new acquisitions. For though it might be claimed that the aggressive commercialism of rival European States raised the insurance rate upon the old markets, it cannot be contended that Great Britain's expenditure on arma-ments need have increased had she adopted firmly and consistently the full practice of Cobdenism, a purely defen-sive attitude regarding her existing Empire and a total abstinence from acquisition of new territory. The increased hostility of foreign nations towards us in the last thirty

[1] Figures for the years 1904–1931 are given in the Appendix, p. 376.

64

Year.	Armaments and War.	Colonial Trade. Import and Export Trade with Possessions.
	£	£
1884	27,864,000	184,000,000
1885	30,577,000	170,000,000
1886	39,538,000	164,000,000
1887	31,768,000	166,000,000
1888	30,609,000	179,000,000
1889	30,536,000	188,000,000
1890	32,772,000	191,000,000
1891	33,488,000	193,00,0000
1892	33,312,000	179,000,000
1893	33,423,000	170,000,000
1894	33,566,000	172,000,000
1895	35,593,000	172,000,000
1896	38,334,000	184,000,000
1897	41,453,000	183,000,000
1898	40,395,000	190,000,000
1899	64,283,000	201,000,000
1900	69,815,000	212,000,000
1901	121,445,000	219,000,000
1902	123,787,000	223,000,000
1903	100,825,000	232,000,000

years of the nineteenth century may be regarded as entirely due to the aggressive Imperialism of those years, and the increased expenditure on armaments may, therefore, reasonably rank in a business balance-sheet as a cost of that policy.

So, taken, this new expenditure was nothing else than a huge business blunder. An individual doing business in this fashion could not avoid bankruptcy, and a nation, however rich, pursuing such a policy is loaded with a millstone which must eventually drag her down.

In total contravention of our theory that trade rests upon a basis of mutual gain to the nations that engage in it, we undertook enormous expenses with the object of " forcing " new markets, and the markets we forced were small, precarious, and unprofitable. The only certain and palpable result of the expenditure was to keep us continually embroiled with the very nations that were our best customers, and with whom, in spite of everything, our trade made the most satisfactory advance.

Not only were these markets not worth what they cost us, but the assumption that our trade would have been proportionately less had they fallen into the hands of rival and Protectionist nations is quite groundless. If, instead of squandering money upon these territorial acquisitions, we had let any or all of them pass into the possession of France, Germany, or Russia, in order that these countries might spend their money, instead of us spending our money, in acquiring and developing them, is it certain that our foreign trade would not have grown by at least as much as our colonial trade might have shrunk? The assumption that there is only a given quantity of trade, and that if one nation gets any portion of it another nation loses just so much, shows a blind ignorance of the elements of international trade. It arises from a curiously perverse form of separatism which insists upon a nation keeping a separate account with every other nation, and ignoring altogether the roundabout trade which is by far the most important business of an advanced industrial nation.

France seizing Madagascar practically extirpated direct British trade with the Malagasy; Germany, by her occupation of Shan-tung, deprived us of all possibility of trade with this Chinese province. But it by no means followed that France and Germany could or would keep to themselves the whole advantage of these new markets. To make any such supposition implies a complete abandonment of the principles of Free Trade. Even were the whole of China portioned out among the other industrial nations, each imposing tariffs which virtually prohibited direct trade between Great Britain and China—the most extreme assumption of a hostile attitude—it by no means follows that England would not reap enormous benefits from the expansion of her foreign trade, attributable in the last resort to the opening up of China. Even the feeblest recognition of the intricacies of foreign trade should make us aware that an increased trade with France, Germany, or Russia, either directly or through other nations trading with them might have given us our full share of the wealth of Chinese trade, and proved as beneficial as any direct share of trade with China which at great expense and peril we might have secured. The assignment of spheres of influence in China or in Africa to France, Germany, or Russia, which they might have sought to monopolise for purposes of trade, does not imply, as seems to be believed, a corresponding loss of markets to England. The intricate and ever-growing industrial co-operation of the civilized nations through trade does not permit any nation to keep to herself the gain of any market she may hold. It is not difficult to conceive cases where another nation might enjoy a larger share of the results of a trade than the nation which owned the private markets of this trade.

These were the commonplaces of the economics of Free Trade, the plainest lessons of enlightened common sense. Why were they forgotten?

The answer is that Imperialism repudiates Free Trade, and rests upon an economic basis of Protection. Just in so far as an Imperialist is logical does he become an open and avowed Protectionist.

If the fact of France or Germany seizing for its exclusive use a market which we might have seized necessarily reduces our aggregate external trade by the amount of this market, it is only reasonable that when we seize a territory we should take the same means to keep its market for ourselves.

Imperialism, when it shakes off the " old gang " of politicians who had swallowed Free Trade doctrine when they were young, openly adopts the Protectionism required to round off this policy.

Imperialism naturally strives to fasten to the mother country the markets of each new territorial acquisition, convinced that only by such separate increments can the aggregate of our trade grow ; and by the success of this policy it must justify the enormous national outlay which Imperialism involves. Free Trade trusts for the increase of our foreign trade to the operation of the self-interest of other trading nations. Her doctrine is that, though it were better for us and for them that they should give us free admission to their colonial and home markets, their protec-tive tariff, even though it prohibits us from trading directly with their colonies, does not shut us out from all the benefits of their colonial development. Through the ordinary operation of competition in European markets the rubber trade which France does in East Africa helps to increase the supply and to keep down the price of rubber for English consumers, just as the bounties which continental countries pay to sugar producers enable British boys and girls to enjoy cheap sweets.

There is, then, nothing vaguely hypothetical about these indirect gains. Every business man can trace certain concrete advantages of goods and prices which come to us from the development of colonies by Protectionist countries. The " open door " is an advantage to our trade, but not a necessity. If we have to spend vast sums and incur vast risks in keeping " doors open " against the wishes of our best customers, it is more profitable to let them close these doors and take our gain by the more indirect but equally certain processes of roundabout trade. At present Great Britain is in a stronger position than any other nation to practise this policy of abstinence, because she possesses in her carrying trade by sea a most effective guarantee that she will obtain an adequate share of the net gains from new markets opened up by foreign nations. Though no complete statistics are available, it is known that a very large proportion of the trade, not only between England and foreign countries, but between foreign countries trading among themselves and with their possessions, is carried by British ships. So long as this continues, England, apart from her share obtained in roundabout trade, must participate directly and in a most important manner in the trade advantages of foreign markets belonging to our European trade competitors.

These considerations ought to make us willing that other nations should do their share of expansion and development, well contented to await the profit which must accrue to us from every increase of world-wealth through ordinary processes of exchange. We have done our share, and more, of the costly, laborious, and dangerous work of opening up new countries to the general trade of Western industrial nations ; our later ventures were more expensive and less profitable to us than the earlier ones, and further labours of expansion seemed to conform to a law of diminishing returns, yielding smaller and more precarious increments of trade to a larger outlay of material and intellectual capital. Had we not reached, or even passed, the limit of the most profitable outlay of our national energy and resources ? Will not enlightened self-interest impel us to leave to other active and ambitious nations—France, Russia, Germany, Japan—the work of developing new tropical or sub-tropical countries ? If it is necessary that Western industrial civilization shall undertake the political and commercial management of the whole world, let these nations take their share. Why should we do all the work and get so little from it ? On the assumption that backward countries must be developed by foreign countries for the general good, a reasonable economy of power will apportion the work which remains to the " Imperialism " of other nations. Even if these other nations were disposed to shirk their share, it would pay us better to persuade them to undertake it rather than further to load our overladen shoulders. Since these other nations are not only eager to do their share, but by their jealousy at our undertaking their work continually threaten to wreck the peace of Europe, it seems sheer madness for Great Britain to weaken herself politically and financially by any further process of expansion.

CHAPTER VI

THE ECONOMIC TAPROOT OF
IMPERIALISM

NO mere array of facts and figures adduced to illustrate the economic nature of the new Imperialism will suffice to dispel the popular delusion that the use of national force to secure new markets by annexing fresh tracts of territory is a sound and a necessary policy for an advanced industrial country like Great Britain.[1] It has indeed been proved that recent annexations of tropical countries, procured at great expense, have furnished poor and precarious markets, that our aggregate trade with our colonial possessions is virtually stationary, and that our most profitable and progressive trade is with rival industrial nations, whose territories we have no desire to annex, whose markets we cannot force, and whose active antagonism we are provoking by our expansive policy.

But these arguments are not conclusive. It is open to Imperialists to argue thus : " We must have markets for our growing manufactures, we must have new outlets for the investment of our surplus capital and for the energies of the adventurous surplus of our population : such expansion is a necessity of life to a nation with our great and growing powers of production. An ever larger share of our population is devoted to the manufactures and commerce of towns, and is thus dependent for life and work upon food and raw

[1] Written in 1905.

71

materials from foreign lands. In order to buy and pay for these things we must sell our goods abroad. During the first three-quarters of the nineteenth century we could do so without difficulty by a natural expansion of commerce with continental nations and our colonies, all of which were far behind us in the main arts of manufacture and the carrying trades. So long as England held a virtual monopoly of the world markets for certain important classes of manufactured goods, Imperialism was unnecessary. After 1870 this manufacturing and trading supremacy was greatly impaired: other nations, especially Germany, the United States, and Belgium, advanced with great rapidity, and while they have not crushed or even stayed the increase of our external trade, their competition made it more and more difficult to dispose of the full surplus of our manufactures at a profit. The encroachments made by these nations upon our old markets, even in our own possessions, made it most urgent that we should take energetic means to secure new markets. These new markets had to lie in hitherto undeveloped countries, chiefly in the tropics, where vast populations lived capable of growing economic needs which our manufacturers and merchants could supply. Our rivals were seizing and annexing territories for similar purposes, and when they had annexed them closed them to our trade. The diplomacy and the arms of Great Britain had to be used in order to compel the owners of the new markets to deal with us: and experience showed that the safest means of securing and developing such markets is by establishing ' protectorates ' or by annexation. The value in 1905 of these markets must not be taken as a final test of the economy of such a policy; the process of educating civilized needs which we can supply is of necessity a gradual one, and the cost of such Imperialism must be regarded as a capital outlay, the fruits of which posterity would reap. The new markets might not be large, but they formed serviceable outlets for the overflow of our great textile and metal industries, and, when the vast Asiatic and African populations of the interior were reached, a rapid expansion of trade was expected to result.

" Far larger and more important is the pressure of capital for external fields of investment. Moreover, while the manufacturer and trader are well content to trade with foreign nations, the tendency for investors to work towards the political annexation of countries which contain their more speculative investments is very powerful. Of the fact of this pressure of capital there can be no question. Large savings are made which cannot find any profitable investment in this country ; they must find employment elsewhere, and it is to the advantage of the nation that they should be employed as largely as possible in lands where they can be utilized in opening up markets for British trade and employment for British enterprise.

" However costly, however perilous, this process of imperial expansion may be, it is necessary to the continued existence and progress of our nation ;[1] if we abandoned it we must be content to leave the development of the world to other nations, who will everywhere cut into our trade, and even impair our means of securing the food and raw materials we require to support our population. Imperialism is thus seen to be, not a choice, but a necessity."

The practical force of this economic argument in politics is strikingly illustrated by the later history of the United States. Here is a country which suddenly broke through a conservative policy, strongly held by both political parties,

---

[1] " And why, indeed, are wars undertaken, if not to conquer colonies which permit the employment of fresh capital, to acquire commercial monopolies, or to obtain the exclusive use of certain highways of commerce ? " (Loria, *Economic Foundations of Society*, p. 267).

bound up with every popular instinct and tradition, and flung itself into a rapid imperial career for which it possessed neither the material nor the moral equipment, risking the principles and practices of liberty and equality by the establishment of militarism and the forcible subjugation of peoples which it could not safely admit to the condition of American citizenship.

Was this a mere wild freak of spread-eaglism, a burst of political ambition on the part of a nation coming to a sudden realization of its destiny? Not at all. The spirit of adventure, the American " mission of civilization," were as forces making for Imperialism, clearly subordinate to the driving force of the economic factor. The dramatic character of the change is due to the unprecedented rapidity of the industrial revolution in the United States from the eighties onwards. During that period the United States, with her unrivalled natural resources, her immense resources of skilled and unskilled labour, and her genius for invention and organization, developed the best equipped and most productive manufacturing economy the world has yet seen. Fostered by rigid protective tariffs, her metal, textile, tool, clothing, furniture, and other manufactures shot up in a single generation from infancy to full maturity, and, having passed through a period of intense competition, attained, under the able control of great trust-makers, a power of production greater than has been attained in the most advanced industrial countries of Europe.

An era of cut-throat competition, followed by a rapid process of amalgamation, threw an enormous quantity of wealth into the hands of a small number of captains of industry. No luxury of living to which this class could attain kept pace with its rise of income, and a process of automatic saving set in upon an unprecedented scale. The investment of these savings in other industries helped to

74

bring these under the same concentrative forces. Thus a great increase of savings seeking profitable investment is synchronous with a stricter economy of the use of existing capital. No doubt the rapid growth of a population, accustomed to a high and an always ascending standard of comfort, absorbs in the satisfaction of its wants a large quantity of new capital. But the actual rate of saving, conjoined with a more economical application of forms of existing capital, exceeded considerably the rise of the national consumption of manufactures. The power of production far outstripped the actual rate of consumption, and, contrary to the older economic theory, was unable to force a corresponding increase of consumption by lowering prices.

This is no mere theory. The history of any of the numerous trusts or combinations in the United States sets out the facts with complete distinctness. In the free competition of manufactures preceding combination the chronic condition is one of " over-production," in the sense that all the mills or factories can only be kept at work by cutting prices down towards a point where the weaker competitors are forced to close down, because they cannot sell their goods at a price which covers the true cost of production. The first result of the successful formation of a trust or combine is to close down the worse equipped or worse placed mills, and supply the entire market from the better equipped and better placed ones. This course may or may not be attended by a rise of price and some restriction of consumption : in some cases trusts take most of their profits by raising prices, in other cases by reducing the costs of production through employing only the best mills and stopping the waste of competition.

For the present argument it matters not which course is taken ; the point is that this concentration of industry in " trusts," " combines," etc., at once limits the quantity of capital which can be effectively employed and increases the share of profits out of which fresh savings and fresh capital will spring. It is quite evident that a trust which is motived by cut-throat competition, due to an excess of capital, cannot normally find inside the " trusted " industry employment for that portion of the profits which the trust-makers desire to save and to invest. New inventions and other economies of production or distribution within the trade may absorb some of the new capital, but there are rigid limits to this absorption. The trust-maker in oil or sugar must find other investments for his savings : if he is early in the application of the combination principles to his trade, he will naturally apply his surplus capital to establish similar combinations in other industries, econo-mising capital still further, and rendering it ever harder for ordinary saving men to find investments for their savings.

Indeed, the conditions alike of cut-throat competition and of combination attest the congestion of capital in the manufacturing industries which have entered the machine economy. We are not here concerned with any theoretic question as to the possibility of producing by modern machine methods more goods than can find a market. It is sufficient to point out that the manufacturing power of a country like the United States would grow so fast as to exceed the demands of the home market. No one acquainted with trade will deny a fact which all American economists assert, that this is the condition which the United States reached at the end of the century, so far, as the more developed industries are concerned. Her manufactures were saturated with capital and could absorb no more. One after another they sought refuge from the waste of competition in " combines " which secure a measure of profitable peace by restricting the quantity of operative capital. Industrial and financial princes in oil, steel, sugar, railroads, banking, etc., were faced with the dilemma of either spending more than they knew how to spend, or forcing markets outside the home area. Two economic courses were open to them, both leading towards an abandonment of the political isolation of the past and the adoption of imperialist methods in the future. Instead of shutting down inferior mills and rigidly restricting output to correspond with profitable sales in the home markets, they might employ their full productive power, applying their savings to increase their business capital, and, while still regulating output and prices for the home market, may " hustle " for foreign markets, dumping down their surplus goods at prices which would not be possible save for the profitable nature of their home market. So likewise they might employ their savings in seeking investments outside their country, first repaying the capital borrowed from Great Britain and other countries for the early development of their railroads, mines and manufactures, and afterwards becoming themselves a creditor class to foreign countries.

It was this sudden demand for foreign markets for manufactures and for investments which was avowedly responsible for the adoption of Imperialism as a political policy and practice by the Republican party to which the great industrial and financial chiefs belonged, and which belonged to them. The adventurous enthusiasm of President Theodore Roosevelt and his " manifest destiny " and " mission of civilization " party must not deceive us. It was Messrs. Rockefeller, Pierpont Morgan, and their associates who needed Imperialism and who fastened it upon the shoulders of the great Republic of the West. They needed Imperialism because they desired to use the public resources of their country to find profitable employment for their capital which otherwise would be superfluous.

It is not indeed necessary to own a country in order to do trade with it or to invest capital in it, and doubtless the United States could find some vent for their surplus goods, and capital in European countries. But these countries were for the most part able to make provision for themselves : most of them erected tariffs against manufacturing imports, and even Great Britain was urged to defend herself by reverting to Protection. The big American manufacturers and financiers were compelled to look to China and the Pacific and to South America for their most profitable chances ; Protectionists by principle and practice, they would insist upon getting as close a monopoly of these markets as they can secure, and the competition of Germany, England, and other trading nations would drive them to the establishment of special political relations with the markets they most prize. Cuba, the Philippines, and Hawaii were but the *hors d'œuvre* to whet an appetite for an ampler banquet. Moreover, the powerful hold upon politics which these industrial and financial magnates possessed formed a separate stimulus, which, as we have shown, was operative in Great Britain and elsewhere ; the public expenditure in pursuit of an imperial career would be a separate immense source of profit to these men, as financiers negotiating loans, shipbuilders and owners handling subsidies, contractors and manufacturers of armaments and other imperialist appliances.

The suddenness of this political revolution is due to the rapid manifestation of the need. In the last years of the nineteenth century the United States nearly trebled the value of its manufacturing export trade, and it was to be expected that, if the rate of progress of those years continued, within a decade it would overtake our more slowly advancing export trade, and stand first in the list of manufacture-exporting nations.[1]

This was the avowed ambition, and no idle one, of the keenest business men of America ; and with the natural resources, the labour and the administrative talents at their disposal, it was quite likely they would achieve their object.[2] The stronger and more direct control over politics exercised in America by business men enabled them to drive more quickly and more straightly along the line of their economic interests than in Great Britain. American Imperialism was the natural product of the economic pressure of a sudden advance of capitalism which could not find occupation at home and needed foreign markets for goods and for investments.

The same needs existed in European countries, and, as is

[1] EXPORT TRADE OF UNITED STATES, 1890-1900.

Year.				Agriculture.	Manufactures.	Miscellaneous.
				£	£	£
1890	.	.	.	125,756,000	31,435,000	13,019,000
1891	.	.	.	146,617,000	33,720,000	11,731,000
1892	.	.	.	142,508,000	30,479,000	11,660,000
1893	.	.	.	123,810,000	35,484,000	11,653,000
1894	.	.	.	114,737,000	35,557,000	11,168,000
1895	.	.	.	104,143,000	40,230,000	12,174,000
1896	.	.	.	132,992,000	50,738,000	13,639,000
1897	.	.	.	146,059,000	55,923,000	13,984,000
1898	.	.	.	170,383,000	61,585,000	14,743,000
1899	.	.	.	156,427,000	76,157,000	18,002,000
1900	.	.	.	180,931,000	88,281,000	21,389,000

[1] Post-war conditions, with the immense opportunities afforded for exports of American goods and capital brought a pause and a temporary withdrawal from imperialist policy.

[2] " We hold now three of the winning cards in the game for commercial greatness, to wit—iron, steel and coal. We have long been the granary of the world, we now aspire to be its workshop, then we want to be its clearing-house." (The President of the American Bankers' Association at Denver, 1898.)

admitted, drove Governments along the same path. Over-production in the sense of an excessive manufacturing plant, and surplus capital which could not find sound investments within the country, forced Great Britain, Germany, Holland, France to place larger and larger portions of their economic resources outside the area of their present political domain, and then stimulate a policy of political expansion so as to take in the new areas. The economic sources of this movement are laid bare by periodic trade-depressions due to an inability of producers to find adequate and profitable markets for what they can produce. The Majority Report of the Commission upon the Depression of Trade in 1885 put the matter in a nutshell. " That, owing to the nature of the times, the demand for our commodities does not increase at the same rate as formerly ; that our capacity for production is consequently in excess of our requirements, and could be considerably increased at short notice ; that this is due partly to the competition of the capital which is being steadily accumulated in the country." The Minority Report straightly imputed the condition of affairs to " over-production." Germany was in the early 1900's suffering severely from what is called a glut of capital and of manufacturing power : she had to have new markets ; her Consuls all over the world were " hustling " for trade ; trading settlements were forced upon Asia Minor ; in East and West Africa, in China and elsewhere the German Empire was impelled to a policy of colonization and protectorates as outlets for German commercial energy.

Every improvement of methods of production, every concentration of ownership and control, seems to accentuate the tendency. As one nation after another enters the machine economy and adopts advanced industrial methods, it becomes more difficult for its manufacturers, merchants, and financiers to dispose profitably of their economic resources, and they are tempted more and more to use their Governments in order to secure for their particular use some distant undeveloped country by annexation and protection.

The process, we may be told, is inevitable, and so it seems upon a superficial inspection. Everywhere appear excessive powers of production, excessive capital in search of investment. It is admitted by all business men that the growth of the powers of production in their country exceeds the growth in consumption, that more goods can be produced than can be sold at a profit, and that more capital exists than can find remunerative investment.

It is this economic condition of affairs that forms the taproot of Imperialism. If the consuming public in this country raised its standard of consumption to keep pace with every rise of productive powers, there could be no excess of goods or capital clamorous to use Imperialism in order to find markets : foreign trade would indeed exist, but there would be no difficulty in exchanging a small surplus of our manufactures for the food and raw material we annually absorbed, and all the savings that we made could find employment, if we chose, in home industries.

There is nothing inherently irrational in such a supposition. Whatever is, or can be, produced, can be consumed, for a claim upon it, as rent, profit, or wages, forms part of the real income of some member of the community, and he can consume it, or else exchange it for some other consumable with some one else who will consume it. With everything that is produced a consuming power is born. If then there are goods which cannot get consumed, or which cannot even get produced because it is evident they cannot get consumed, and if there is a quantity of capital and labour which cannot get full employment because its products cannot get consumed, the only possible explanation of this paradox is the refusal of owners of consuming power to apply that power in effective demand for commodities.

It is, of course, possible that an excess of producing power might exist in particular industries by misdirection, being engaged in certain manufactures, whereas it ought to have been engaged in agriculture or some other use. But no one can seriously contend that such misdirection explains the recurrent gluts and consequent depressions of modern industry, or that, when over-production is manifest in the leading manufactures, ample avenues are open for the surplus capital and labour in other industries. The general character of the excess of producing power is proved by the existence at such times of large bank stocks of idle money seeking any sort of profitable investment and finding none.

The root questions underlying the phenomena are clearly these : " Why is it that consumption fails to keep pace automatically in a community with power of production ? " " Why does under-consumption or over-saving occur ? " For it is evident that the consuming power, which, if exercised, would keep tense the reins of production, is in part withheld, or in other words is " saved " and stored up for investment. All saving for investment does not imply slackness of production ; quite the contrary. Saving is economically justified, from the social standpoint, when the capital in which it takes material shape finds full employment in helping to produce commodities which, when produced, will be consumed. It is saving in excess of this amount that causes mischief, taking shape in surplus capital which is not needed to assist current consumption, and which either lies idle, or tries to oust existing capital from its employment, or else seeks speculative use abroad under the protection of the Government.

But it may be asked, " Why should there be any tendency

to over-saving ? Why should the owners of consuming power withhold a larger quantity for savings than can be serviceably employed ? " Another way of putting the same question is this, " Why should not the pressure of present wants keep pace with every possibility of satisfying them ? " The answer to these pertinent questions carries us to the broadest issue of the distribution of wealth. If a tendency to distribute income or consuming power according to needs were operative, it is evident that consumption would rise with every rise of producing power, for human needs are illimitable, and there could be no excess of saving. But it is quite otherwise in a state of economic society where distribution has no fixed relation to needs, but is determined by other conditions which assign to some people a consuming power vastly in excess of needs or possible uses, while others are destitute of consuming power enough to satisfy even the full demands of physical efficiency. The following illustration may serve to make the issue clear. " The volume of production has been constantly rising owing to the development of modern machinery. There are two main channels to carry off these products—one channel carrying off the product destined to be consumed by the workers, and the other channel carrying off the remainder to the rich. The workers' channel is in rock-bound banks that cannot enlarge, owing to the competitive wage system preventing wages rising *pro rata* with increased efficiency. Wages are based upon cost of living, and not upon efficiency of labour. The miner in the poor mine gets the same wages per day as the miner in the adjoining rich mine. The owner of the rich mine gets the advantage —not his labourer. The channel which conveys the goods destined to supply the rich is itself divided into two streams. One stream carries off what the rich ' spend ' on themselves for the necessities and luxuries of life. The other

is simply an ' overflow' stream carrying off their ' savings.'
The channel for spending, i.e. the amount wasted by the
rich in luxuries, may broaden somewhat, but owing to the
small number of those rich enough to indulge in whims
it can never be greatly enlarged, and at any rate it bears
such a small proportion to the other channel that in no
event can much hope of avoiding a flood of capital be hoped
for from this division. The rich will never be so ingenious
as to spend enough to prevent over-production. The
great safety overflow channel which has been continuously
more and more widened and deepened to carry off the
ever-increasing flood of new capital is that division of the
stream which carried the savings of the rich, and this is not
only suddenly found to be incapable of further enlargement, but actually seems to be in the process of being
dammed up."[1]

Though this presentation over-accentuates the cleavage
between rich and poor and over-states the weakness of the
workers, it gives forcible and sound expression to a most
important and ill-recognised economic truth. The " overflow " stream of savings is of course fed not exclusively
from the surplus income of " the rich "; the professional
and industrial middle classes, and to some slight extent the
workers, contribute. But the " flooding " is distinctly
due to the automatic saving of the surplus income of rich
men. This is of course particularly true of America, where
multi-millionaires rise quickly and find themselves in
possession of incomes far exceeding the demands of any
craving that is known to them. To make the metaphor
complete, the overflow stream must be represented as re-
entering the stream of production and seeking to empty
there all the " savings " that it carries. Where competition
remains free, the result is a chronic congestion of productive

[1] *The Significance of the Trust*, by H. G. Wilshire.

power and of production, forcing down home prices, wasting large sums in advertising and in pushing for orders, and periodically causing a crisis followed by a collapse, during which quantities of capital and labour lie unemployed and unremunerated. The prime object of the trust or other combine is to remedy this waste and loss by substituting regulation of output for reckless over-production. In achieving this it actually narrows or even dams up the old channels of investment, limiting the overflow stream to the exact amount required to maintain the normal current of output. But this rigid limitation of trade, though required for the separate economy of each trust, does not suit the trust-maker, who is driven to compensate for strictly regulated industry at home by cutting new foreign channels as outlets for his productive power and his excessive savings. Thus we reach the conclusion that Imperialism is the endeavour of the great controllers of industry to broaden the channel for the flow of their surplus wealth by seeking foreign markets and foreign investments to take off the goods and capital they cannot sell or use at home.

The fallacy of the supposed inevitability of imperial expansion as a necessary outlet for progressive industry is now manifest. It is not industrial progress that demands the opening up of new markets and areas of investment, but mal-distribution of consuming power which prevents the absorption of commodities and capital within the country. The over-saving which is the economic root of Imperialism is found by analysis to consist of rents, monopoly profits, and other unearned or excessive elements of income, which, not being earned by labour of head or hand, have no legitimate *raison d'être*. Having no natural relation to effort of production, they impel their recipients to no corresponding satisfaction of consumption : they form a surplus wealth, which, having no proper place in the normal economy of production and consumption, tends to accumulate as excessive savings. Let any turn in the tide of politico-economic forces divert from these owners their excess of income and make it flow, either to the workers in higher wages, or to the community in taxes, so that it will be spent instead of being saved, serving in either of these ways to swell the tide of consumption— there will be no need to fight for foreign markets or foreign areas of investment.

Many have carried their analysis so far as to realise the absurdity of spending half our financial resources in fighting to secure foreign markets at times when hungry mouths, ill-clad backs, ill-furnished houses indicate countless unsatisfied material wants among our own population. If we may take the careful statistics of Mr. Rowntree[1] for our guide, we shall be aware that more than one-fourth of the population of our towns is living at a standard which is below bare physical efficiency. If, by some economic readjustment, the products which flow from the surplus saving of the rich to swell the overflow streams could be diverted so as to raise the incomes and the standard of consumption of this inefficient fourth, there would be no need for pushful Imperialism, and the cause of social reform would have won its greatest victory.

It is not inherent in the nature of things that we should spend our natural resources on militarism, war, and risky, unscrupulous diplomacy, in order to find markets for our goods and surplus capital. An intelligent progressive community, based upon substantial equality of economic and educational opportunities, will raise its standard of consumption to correspond with every increased power of production, and can find full employment for an un-

[1] *Poverty : A Study of Town Life.*

limited quantity of capital and labour within the limits of the country which it occupies. Where the distribution of incomes is such as to enable all classes of the nation to convert their felt wants into an effective demand for commodities, there can be no over-production, no under-employment of capital and labour, and no necessity to fight for foreign markets.

The most convincing condemnation of the current economy is conveyed in the difficulty which producers everywhere experience in finding consumers for their products : a fact attested by the prodigious growth of classes of agents and middlemen, the multiplication of every sort of advertising, and the general increase of the distributive classes. Under a sound economy the pressure would be reversed : the growing wants of progressive societies would be a constant stimulus to the inventive and operative energies of producers, and would form a constant strain upon the powers of production. The simultaneous excess of all the factors of production, attested by frequently recurring periods of trade depression, is a most dramatic exhibition of the false economy of distribution. It does not imply a mere miscalculation in the application of productive power, or a brief temporary excess of that power ; it manifests in an acute form an economic waste which is chronic and general throughout the advanced industrial nations, a waste contained in the divorcement of the desire to consume and the power to consume.

If the apportionment of income were such as to evoke no excessive saving, full constant employment for capital and labour would be furnished at home. This, of course, does not imply that there would be no foreign trade. Goods that could not be produced at home, or produced as well or as cheaply, would still be purchased by ordinary process of international exchange, but here again the pressure would be the wholesome pressure of the consumer anxious to buy abroad what he could not buy at home, not the blind eagerness of the producer to use every force or trick of trade or politics to find markets for his " surplus " goods.

The struggle for markets, the greater eagerness of producers to sell than of consumers to buy, is the crowning proof of a false economy of distribution. Imperialism is the fruit of this false economy ; " social reform " is its remedy. The primary purpose of " social reform," using the term in its economic signification, is to raise the wholesome standard of private and public consumption for a nation, so as to enable the nation to live up to its highest standard of production. Even those social reformers who aim directly at abolishing or reducing some bad form of consumption, as in the Temperance movement, generally recognise the necessity of substituting some better form of current consumption which is more educative and stimulative of other tastes, and will assist to raise the general standard of consumption.

There is no necessity to open up new foreign markets ; the home markets are capable of indefinite expansion. Whatever is produced in England can be consumed in England, provided that the " income " or power to demand commodities, is properly distributed. This only appears untrue because of the unnatural and unwholesome specialisation to which this country has been subjected, based upon a bad distribution of economic resources, which has induced an overgrowth of certain manufacturing trades for the express purpose of effecting foreign sales. If the industrial revolution had taken place in an England founded upon equal access by all classes to land, education and legislation, specialisation in manufactures would not have gone so far (though more intelligent progress would have been made, by reason of a widening of the area of selection of inventive and organising talents) ; foreign trade would have been less important, though more steady ; the standard of life for all portions of the population would have been high, and the present rate of national consumption would probably have given full, constant, remunerative employment to a far larger quantity of private and public capital than is now employed.[1] For the over-saving or wider consumption that is traced to excessive incomes of the rich is a suicidal economy, even from the exclusive standpoint of capital ; for consumption alone vitalises capital and makes it capable of yielding profits. An economy that assigns to the " possessing " classes an excess of consuming power which they cannot use, and cannot convert into really serviceable capital, is a dog-in-the-manger policy. The social reforms which deprive the possessing classes of their surplus will not, therefore, inflict upon them the real injury they dread ; they can only use this surplus by forcing on their country a wrecking policy of Imperialism. The only safety of nations lies in removing the unearned increments of income from the possessing classes, and adding them to the wage-income of the working classes or to the public income, in order that they may be spent in raising the standard of consumption.

Social reform bifurcates, according as reformers seek to achieve this end by raising wages or by increasing public taxation and expenditure. These courses are not essentially

[1] The classical economists of England, forbidden by their theories of parsimony and of the growth of capital to entertain the notion of an indefinite expansion of home markets by reason of a constantly rising standard of national comfort, were early driven to countenance a doctrine of the necessity of finding external markets for the investment of capital. So J. S. Mill : " The expansion of capital would soon reach its ultimate boundary if the boundary itself did not continually open and leave more space " (*Political Economy*). And before him Ricardo (in a letter to Malthus) : " If with every accumulation of capital we could take a piece of fresh fertile land to our island, profits would never fall."

contradictory, but are rather complementary. Working-class movements aim, either by private co-operation or by political pressure on legislative and administrative government, at increasing the proportion of the national income which accrues to labour in the form of wages, pensions, compensation for injuries, etc. State Socialism aims at getting for the direct use of the whole society an increased share of the " social values " which arise from the closely and essentially co-operative work of an industrial society, taxing property and incomes so as to draw into the public exchequer for public expenditure the " unearned elements " of income, leaving to individual producers those incomes which are necessary to induce them to apply in the best way their economic energies, and to private enterprises those businesses which do not breed monopoly, and which the public need not or cannot undertake. These are not, indeed, the sole or perhaps the best avowed objects of social reform movements. But for the purposes of this analysis they form the kernel.

Trade Unionism and Socialism are thus the natural enemies of Imperialism, for they take away from the " imperialist " classes the surplus incomes which form the economic stimulus of Imperialism.

This does not pretend to be a final statement of the full relations of these forces. When we come to political analysis we shall perceive that the tendency of Imperialism is to crush Trade Unionism and to " nibble " at or parasitically exploit State Socialism. But, confining ourselves for the present to the narrowly economic setting, Trade Unionism and State Socialism may be regarded as complementary forces arrayed against Imperialism, in as far as, by diverting to working-class or public expenditure elements of income which would otherwise be surplus savings, they raise the general standard of home consumption and abate the pressure for foreign markets. Of course, if the increase of working-class income were wholly or chiefly " saved," not spent, or if the taxation of unearned incomes were utilised for the relief of other taxes borne by the possessing classes, no such result as we have described would follow. There is, however, no reason to anticipate this result from trade-union or socialistic measures. Though no sufficient natural stimulus exists to force the well-to-do classes to spend in further luxuries the surplus incomes which they save, every working-class family is subject to powerful stimuli of economic needs, and a reasonably governed State would regard as its prime duty the relief of the present poverty of public life by new forms of socially useful expenditure.

But we are not here concerned with what belongs to the practical issues of political and economic policy. It is the economic theory for which we claim acceptance—a theory which, if accurate, dispels the delusion that expansion of foreign trade, and therefore of empire, is a necessity of national life.

Regarded from the standpoint of economy of energy, the same " choice of life " confronts the nation as the individual. An individual may expend all his energy in acquiring external possessions, adding field to field, barn to barn, factory to factory—may " spread himself " over the widest area of property, amassing material wealth which is in some sense " himself " as containing the impress of his power and interest. He does this by specialising upon the lower acquisitive plane of interest at the cost of neglecting the cultivation of the higher qualities and interests of his nature. The antagonism is not indeed absolute. Aristotle has said, " We must first secure a livelihood and then practise virtue." Hence the pursuit of material property as a reasonable basis of physical comfort would be held true economy by the wisest men ; but the absorption of time, energy, and interest upon such quantitative expansion at the necessary cost of starving the higher tastes and faculties is condemned as false economy. The same issue comes up in the business life of the individual : it is the question of intensive *versus* extensive cultivation. A rude or ignorant farmer, where land is plentiful, is apt to spread his capital and labour over a large area, taking in new tracts and cultivating them poorly. A skilled, scientific farmer will study a smaller patch of land, cultivate it thoroughly, and utilise its diverse properties, adapting it to the special needs of his most remunerative markets. The same is true of other businesses ; even where the economy of large-scale production is greatest there exists some limit beyond which the wise business man will not go, aware that in doing so he will risk by enfeebled management what he seems to gain by mechanical economies of production and market.

Everywhere the issue of quantitative *versus* qualitative growth comes up. This is the entire issue of empire. A people limited in number and energy and in the land they occupy have the choice of improving to the utmost the political and economic management of their own land, confining themselves to such accessions of territory as are justified by the most economical disposition of a growing population ; or they may proceed, like the slovenly farmer, to spread their power and energy over the whole earth, tempted by the speculative value or the quick profits of some new market, or else by mere greed of territorial acquisition, and ignoring the political and economic wastes and risks involved by this imperial career. It must be clearly understood that this is essentially a choice of alternatives ; a full simultaneous application of intensive and extensive cultivation is impossible. A nation may either, following the example of Denmark or Switzerland, put brains into agriculture, develop a finely varied system of public education, general and technical, apply the ripest science to its special manufacturing industries, and so support in progressive comfort and character a considerable population upon a strictly limited area ; or it may, like Great Britain, neglect its agriculture, allowing its lands to go out of cultivation and its population to grow up in towns, fall behind other nations in its methods of education and in the capacity of adapting to its uses the latest scientific knowledge, in order that it may squander its pecuniary and military resources in forcing bad markets and finding speculative fields of investment in distant corners of the earth, adding millions of square miles and of unassimilable population to the area of the Empire.

The driving forces of class interest which stimulate and support this false economy we have explained. No remedy will serve which permits the future operation of these forces. It is idle to attack Imperialism or Militarism as political expedients or policies unless the axe is laid at the economic root of the tree, and the classes for whose interest Imperialism works are shorn of the surplus revenues which seek this outlet.

CHAPTER VII

IMPERIALIST FINANCE

THE analysis of economic forces in the foregoing chapter explains the character which public finance assumes in States committed to an imperialist policy. Imperialism, as we see, implies the use of the machinery of government by private interests, mainly capitalists, to secure for them economic gains outside their country. The dominance of this factor in public policy imposes a special character alike upon expenditure and taxation.

The accompanying diagram[1] brings into clear light the main features of the national expenditure of Great Britain during the last three decades of the nineteenth century.

The first feature is the rate of growth of national expenditure taken as a whole. This growth has been far faster than the growth of foreign trade. For whereas the average yearly value of our foreign trade for 1870–75, amounting to £636,000,000, increased in the period 1895–1903 to £868,000,000, the average public expenditure advanced over the same period from £63,160,000 to £155,660,000. It is far faster than the growth of the aggregate national income, which, according to the rough estimates of statisticians, advanced during the same period from about £1,200,000,000, to £1,750,000,000. The rate of growth has greatly quickened during the latter half of the period in question, for, leaving out of consideration war expenditure, the rise of ordinary imperial expenditure has been from £87,423,000 in 1888 to £128,600,000 in 1900.

[1] Appendix, p. 379.

The most salient feature of the diagram is the small and diminishing proportion of the national revenue expended for what may be regarded as directly productive purposes of government. Roughly speaking, over two-thirds of the money goes for naval and military expenditure, and for the payment of military debts, about six shillings in the pound being available for education, civil government, and the dubious policy of grants in aid of local taxation.[1]

The only satisfactory incident disclosed by the table was the growing amount and proportion of public money spent on education. A substantial part of the sum expended as aid to local taxation has simply gone as a dole to landowners.

The direct military and naval expenditure during the period has increased faster than the total expenditure, the growth of trade, of national income, or any other general indication of national resources. In 1875 the army and navy cost less than 24½ millions out of a total expenditure of 65 millions ; in 1903 they cost nearly 79 millions out of a total of 140 millions.

The enormous expenditure upon the South African war was followed by a large permanent increase in these branches of expenditure, amounting to an addition of not less than £32,000,000 per annum.

This growth of naval and military expenditure from about 25 to 79 millions in a little over a quarter of a century is the most significant fact of imperialist finance. The financial, industrial, and professional classes, who, we have shown, form the economic core of Imperialism, have used their political power to extract these sums from the nation in order to improve their investments and open up new fields for capital, and to find profitable markets for their

[1] A portion of the money expended under the head National Debt should, however, be regarded as productively expended, since it has gone towards reduction of the debt. Between 1875 and 1900 a reduction of £140,000,000, equal to about £5,800,000 per annum, has been effected.

surplus goods, while out of the public sums expended on these objects they reap other great private gains in the shape of profitable contracts, and lucrative or honourable employment.

The financial and industrial capitalists who have mainly engineered this policy, employing their own genuine convictions to conceal their ill-recognised business ends, have also made important bribes or concessions to other less directly benefited interests in order to keep their sympathy and ensure their support.

This explains the large and growing grants in aid of local taxation, almost the whole of which, interpreted by a scientific regard to incidence of taxation, must be considered as a subsidy to landowners. The support of the Church and of the liquor trade has been more cheaply purchased; the former by relief of rates on tithes and increased grants for Church schools, the latter by a policy of masterly inaction in the matter of temperance reforms and special consideration in regard to taxation.

In making the capitalist-imperialist forces the pivot of financial policy, I do not mean that other forces, industrial, political, and moral, have no independent aims and influences, but simply that the former group must be regarded as the true determinant in the interpretation of actual policy.

We have identified almost all the organised interests, commonly summed under the head of Capitalism, including land-capital, with Imperialism. Most of them participate directly in one or other of the two sorts of gain which attend this policy: the interest, trade profits, or employment furnished by the imperialist policy, or the interest, profit, or employment connected with military and civil expenditure itself.

It cannot be too clearly recognised that increasing public

expenditure, apart from all political justification, is a direct source of gain to certain well-organised and influential interests, and to all such Imperialism is the chief instrument of such increasing expenditure.

While the directors of this definitely parasitic policy are capitalists, the same motives appeal to special classes of the workers. In many towns most important trades are dependent upon Government employment or contracts ; the Imperialism of the metal and shipbuilding centres is attributable in no small degree to this fact. Members of Parliament freely employ their influence to secure contracts and direct trade to their constituents, and every growth of public expenditure enhances this dangerous bias.

The clearest significance of imperialist finance, however, appears on the side, not of expenditure, but of taxation. The object of those economic interests which use the public purse for purposes of private gain is in large measure defeated if they have first to find the money to fill that purse. To avert the direct incidence of taxation from their own shoulders on to those of other classes or of posterity is a natural policy of self-defence.

A sane policy of taxation would derive the whole or the main part of the national revenue from unearned increments of land values and from profits in trades which, by virtue of some legal or economic protection screening them from close competition, are able to earn high rates of interest or profit. Such taxation would be borne most easily, falling upon unearned elements of incomes, and would cause no disturbance of industry. This, however, would imply the taxation of precisely those elements which constitute the economic taproot of Imperialism. For it is precisely the unearned elements of income which tend towards an automatic process of accumulation, and which, by swelling the stream of surplus capital seeking markets of investment or markets for the surplus goods it helps to make, direct political forces into Imperialism. A sound system of taxation would, therefore, strike at the very root of the malady.

On the other hand, were the capitalist-imperialist forces openly to shift the burden of taxation on to the shoulders of the people, it would be difficult under popular forms of government to operate such an expensive policy. The people must pay, but they must not know they are paying, or how much they are paying, and the payment must be spread over as long a period as possible.

To take a concrete example. The medley of financial and political interests which inveigled Great Britain into spending some two hundred millions of public money, in order to obtain for them control of the land and mineral resources of the South African Republics, could not possibly have achieved their object if they had been compelled to raise the money by sending round a tax-gatherer to take from every citizen in hard cash the several pounds which constituted his share of the taxes—the share which by more crooked ways was to be got out of him.

To support Imperialism by direct taxation of incomes or property would be impossible. Where any real forms of popular control existed, militarism and wars would be impossible if every citizen was made to realise their cost by payments of hard cash. Imperialism, therefore, makes everywhere for indirect taxation ; not chiefly on grounds of convenience, but for purposes of concealment. Or perhaps it would be more just to say that Imperialism takes advantage of the cowardly and foolish preference which the average man everywhere exhibits for being tricked out of his contribution to the public funds, using this common folly for its own purposes. It is seldom possible for any Government, even in the stress of some grave emergency, to impose an income-tax ; even a property-tax is commonly evaded in cases of personal property, and is always unpopular. The case of England is an exception which really proves the rule.

The repeal of import duties and the establishment of Free Trade marked the political triumph of the new manufacturing and commercial plutocracy over the land-owning aristocracy. Free Trade was so profitable to the former classes in securing cheap importation of raw materials, and in cheapening the subsistence of labour at a time when England's priority in new industrial methods offered an indefinitely rapid expansion of trade, that they were willing to support the reimposition of the income-tax which Peel proposed in 1842 in order to enable him to repeal or reduce the import duties. When the sudden financial stress of the Crimean war came on the country the Free Trade policy was in the prime of its popularity and success, and a Liberal ministry, in preference to a reversion to Protection which would otherwise have been inevitable, gave permanency to the tax, extending the area of its application and making its removal more difficult by further repeals of import duties. No Government could now remove it, for the new unpopularity caused by finding adequate substitutes would have outweighed the credit gained by its removal, while its productivity and calculability are advantages shared in an equal degree by no other mode of taxation.

Some allowance may also be made for the principles and personal convictions of political financiers trained in the English science of political economy, and still more for the temptation of competing parties to seek the favour of the newly enfranchised populace by a well-paraded policy of class taxation. The seething revolutionism of the mid-century throughout Europe, the rapid growth of huge industrial centres throughout England, with their masses of ill-explored poverty and their known aptitude for ignorant agitation, made the establishment of formal democracy seem a most hazardous experiment, and both parties were in a mood to conciliate the new monster by doles or bribery. When the break-up of the old Liberal party in 1885–86 had for the first time thrown the vast preponderance of personal property on to the same side as real property, a genuinely democratic budget with a progressive income-tax and a substantial death duty became possible and seemed expedient. It is not necessary to deny that Sir William Harcourt and his colleagues were sincerely convinced of the justice as well as the expediency of this policy; but it must be remembered that no alternative was open, in face of the need of increased funds for Imperialism and education, except a *volte face* upon the Free Trade principles they had most stoutly championed, and a dangerous attack upon trade interests which might recoil upon the working classes, whose cause they were anxious to espouse. The financial attack on " property," embodied in the progressive income tax and death duties, must be regarded, then, as an exceptional policy, due mainly to a combination of two causes— the difficulty of reverting suddenly to the abandoned practice of Protection, and the desire to conciliate the favour of the new unknown democracy.

Hence the anomaly of Imperialism attended by direct taxation. In no other country have the political conditions operated so. Upon the Continent Militarism and Imperialism have thriven upon indirect taxation, and have enabled the agricultural and manufacturing interests to defeat easily any movement towards Free Trade by urging the needs of revenue through tariffs. In Great Britain it seems unlikely that the policy of direct taxation upon property and income for imperial purposes will be carried any further. The Government of the propertied classes has shaken itself free from the traditions of Free Trade;

the leaders and the overwhelming majority of the rank and file are avowed Protectionists so far as agriculture and certain staple industries are concerned. They are no longer seriously frightened by the power of the people as implied by a popular franchise, nor are they prepared to conciliate it by further taxes upon property; they have experimented with the temper of " the monster," and they think that by the assistance of " the trade " and the Church he is quite manageable, and can be cajoled into paying for Imperialism through protective duties. " Panem et circenses " interpreted into English means cheap booze and Mafficking. Popular education, instead of serving as a defence, is an incitement towards Imperialism; it has opened up a panorama of vulgar pride and crude sensationalism to a great inert mass who see current history and the tangled maze of world movements with dim, bewildered eyes, and are the inevitable dupes of the able organised interests who can lure, or scare, or drive them into any convenient course.

Had the Liberal party stood by the principles of peace, retrenchment, and reform, refusing to go beyond the true " colonialism " of such men as Molesworth, and rejecting the temptations to a " spirited foreign policy " dictated by bond-holders, they might have been able to resist the attack upon Free Trade. But a Liberal party committed to a militant Imperialism whose rapidly growing expense is determined chiefly by the conduct of foreign Powers and the new arts of scientific warfare was in a hopeless dilemma. Its position as a buffer party between the propertied classes organised as Conservatism and the unorganised pressure of a loose set of forces striving to become a Socialist labour party dictated moderation, and the personnel of its leaders, still drawn from the propertied classes, prevented it from making any bold attempt to work Imperialism upon a basis of direct taxation upon property, raising the income and proper taxes to cover every increasing need of imperialist finance. It had neither the pluck nor the principle to renounce Imperialism or to insist that the classes who seek to benefit by it shall pay for it.

There is then no reason to impute to Liberalism either the desire or the power to defray the expenses of militant Imperialism by a further pursuance of progressive taxation of incomes and property. While the conveniences of finance may have prevented the repeal of taxation which was so productive, it would not be carried further ; when expenditure is placed again upon a normal footing the income-tax would be reduced and all increase of normal expenditure (estimated by a statistical authority at £20,000 000 for military services alone) will be defrayed by indirect taxation.

Now any considerable calculable increase of revenue by indirect taxation means the abandonment of Free Trade. A large steady income of such a kind can only be raised by duties upon imports of necessaries and prime conveniences of life and trade. It is of course quite immaterial to urge that taxation for revenue is not Protection. If import duties are raised on sugar and tea, if they are imposed upon wheat and flour, foreign meat and raw materials of our staple manufactures, or upon finished manufactured goods competing in our market, it matters not that the object be revenue, the economic effect is Protection.

It is probable that imperialist finance is not yet prepared to admit the name or the full economic policy of Protection.[1] The preparatory steps can find other names. A countervailing duty upon beet-sugar poses as an instrument of Free Trade : once admitted, it introduces a whole train of countervailing duties by parity of reasoning. A tax on

[1] The ensuing discussion of Protection relates to the probabilities of the year of this study, 1905.

prison-made goods, on the ground that they are subsidised and so produced under " cost " price, is logically followed by similar protection against all products of " sweated " foreign industry. An export duty upon coal may well be followed by similar duties on the export of engines and machinery, which similarly aid the growth of our manu-facturing rivals. But the most formidable mask of Protection will take the shape of military necessity. A military nation surrounded by hostile empires must have within her boundaries adequate supplies of the sinews of war, efficient recruits, and a large food supply. We cannot safely rely upon the fighting capacities of a town-bred population, or upon food supplies from foreign lands. Both needs demand that checks be set upon the excessive concentration of our population in towns, and that a serious attempt be made to revive agriculture and restore the people to the soil.

There are two methods which seem possible. The one is a large radical scheme of land reform interfering with the rights of landowners by compulsory purchase or leasing on the part of public bodies, with powers to establish large numbers of small farmers on the soil with loans of capital sufficient to enable them to live and work upon the soil. The other method is Protection, the re-imposition of taxes on imported grain, cattle, fruit, and dairy produce, with the object of stimulating agriculture and keeping the population on the soil.

Given the political sway of the possessing classes, it is certain that the latter course will be preferred. The land-owning and the industrial interests are now sufficiently blended to render it impossible for the town industrialist to refuse assistance to the rural landowner. The dole in relief of rates is a convincing testimony to this truth. Political economists may prove that the chief result of " Protection," in as far as it protects, is to raise the rent of land, that a corn tax will raise the price of bread, and by raising real wages injure profits, and that if the tax really succeeded in stimulating intensive cultivation and self sufficiency for food supply it would not assist the revenue. The Protectionist will not be dismayed by the contradictory positions he is required to hold, for he will be aware that the people whose votes he craves cannot hold two arguments in their heads at the same time for purposes of comparison.

The demand for agricultural protection in order to keep upon the soil a peasantry with sound physique and military aptitudes is likely to outweigh all economic objections in the near future, and it is quite possible that Protection may here be tempered by such carefully devised land reforms as shall place a new " yeoman " class upon British soil, and a substantial sum as purchase money plus compensation for disturbance in the pockets of British landlords.

One other secret avenue to Protection is through the shipbuilding trade. Here is a case not for taxation but for bounties. If England is to be strong for contest in war and trade she must keep open for herself the highways of commerce, and must own ships and men adaptable for purposes of defence. England's great foreign trade was undoubtedly built up in the first instance by the aid of the navigation laws, and the same combination of political exigencies and commercial interests will make towards a revival of this policy. Such are the main streams of tendency towards Protection. But there is no reason to suppose that the policy will be confined to agriculture, sugar and other subsidised imports, export duties upon coal, and bounties on shipbuilding. The leading branches of the textile, metal, and other staple manufactures whose monopoly even in the home market is threatened by the progressive industries of Germany, Holland, and the United States had long lost that confident reliance on Free Trade which they entertained when England's paramountcy in the manufacturing arts was unquestioned. The local specialization of industries places a most formidable weapon in the hands of the protectionist politician. In spite of the financial and intellectual aid given to the Free Trade movement by certain manufacturing interests, Protection stands as the producer's policy, Free Trade as the consumer's. The specialization of localities enables a politician to appeal to the separate trade interests of a single town or neighbourhood, and to convince not only its capitalists but its workers of the gain that would accrue to them if their trade was protected against what is termed unfair competition of foreigners : nothing is said about what they will lose as consumers in the diminished purchasing power of their profits and wages, the result of Protection to the trades of other localities. This appeal made to the separate interests of producers is almost certain to be successful in a people of low education and intelligence. Any attempt to put the other side by representing the result of Protection to be a general rise of prices is commonly met by a confident denial that this result will follow, though it is commonly admitted that wages and profits will rise in the particular local trade to whose self-interest the protectionist appeal is addressed.

It is, however, probable that an attempt will be made to conceal the whole character of the protectionist policy by a misty atmosphere of Imperialism. Protection will not be Protection, but Free Trade within the Empire ; a protectionist tariff will hide its exclusive side and masquerade as an Imperial Zollverein. Great economic changes, requiring the use of political machinery, invent that machinery. The Imperialism of England, essentially though not exclusively an economic thing, will strive to cover the protective system of finance it favours, by a great political achievement, entitled Federation of the Empire. This avenue to Protection would in any case have been essayed by Imperialism, as indeed the curious attempt of Mr. Chamberlain in 1897 testifies. The abnormally rapid swelling of financial needs due to the disastrous policy in South Africa merely precipitates this policy and gives it political occasion. It will be sought to exploit the enthusiastic loyalty of the colonists exhibited in their rally round the mother country in the South African war for purposes of formal federation on a basis which shall bind them to contribute money and men to the protection and expansion of the Empire. The probability of success in this attempt to secure imperial federation is a matter for separate consideration. It is here named as one of the avenues to Protection.

In many ways it thus appears that Protection is the natural ally of Imperialism.

The economic root of Imperialism is the desire of strong organized industrial and financial interests to secure and develop at the public expense and by the public force private markets for their surplus goods and their surplus capital. War, militarism, and a " spirited foreign policy " are the necessary means to this end. This policy involves large increase of public expenditure. If they had to pay the cost of this policy out of their own pockets in taxation upon incomes and property, the game would not be worth the candle, at any rate as far as markets for commodities are concerned. They must find means of putting the expense upon the general public. But in countries where a popular franchise and representative government exist this cannot be successfully done in an open manner. Taxation must be indirect and must fall upon such articles of consumption or general use as are part of the general standard of consumption and will not shrink in demand or give way to substitutes under the process of taxation. This protection not only serves the purposes of imperial finance, taxing the impotent and ignorant consumer for the imperial gains of the influential economic interests, but it seems to furnish them a second gain by securing to them as producers their home market which is threatened by outside competition, and enabling them to raise their prices to the home consumers and so reap a rise of profits. To those who regard foreign trade in its normal condition as a fair interchange of goods, and services, it may seem difficult to understand how these economic interests expect to exclude foreign goods from their market, while at the same time pushing their goods in foreign markets. But we must remind such economists that the prime motive force here is not trade but investment : a surplus of exports over imports is sought as the most profitable mode of investment, and when a nation, or more strictly its investing classes, is bent on becoming a creditor or parasitic nation to an indefinite extent, there is no reason why its imports and exports should balance even over a long term of years. The whole struggle of so-called Imperialism upon its economic side is towards a growing parasitism, and the classes engaged in this struggle require Protection as their most serviceable instrument.

The nature and object of Protection as a branch of imperialist finance is best illustrated in the case of Great Britain, because the necessity of subverting an accepted Free Trade policy lays bare the different methods of Protection and the forces upon which it relies. In other nations committed to or entering upon an imperialist career with the same ganglia of economic interests masquerading as patriotism, civilization, and the like, Protection has been the traditional finance, and it has only been necessary to extend it and direct it into the necessary channels.

Protection, however, is not the only appropriate financial method of Imperialism. There is at any given time some limit to the quantity of current expenditure which can be met by taxing consumers. The policy of Imperialism to be effective requires at times the outlay of large unforeseen sums on war and military equipment. These cannot be met by current taxation. They must be treated as capital expenditure, the payment of which may be indefinitely deferred or provided by a slow and suspensible sinking fund.

The creation of public debts is a normal and a most imposing feature of Imperialism. Like Protection, it also serves a double purpose, not only furnishing a second means of escaping taxation upon income and property otherwise inevitable, but providing a most useful form of investment for idle savings waiting for more profitable employment. The creation of large growing public debts is thus not only a necessary consequence of an imperialist expenditure too great for its current revenue, or of some sudden forced extortion of a war indemnity or other public penalty. It is a direct object of imperialist finance to create further debts, just as it is an object of the private money-lender to goad his clients into pecuniary difficulties in order that they may have recourse to him. Analysis of foreign investments shows that public or State-guaranteed debts are largely held by investors and financiers of other nations; and history shows, in the cases of Egypt, Turkey, China, the hand of the bond-holder, and of the potential bond-holder, in politics. This method of finance is not only profitable in the case of foreign nations, where it is a chief instrument or pretext for encroachment. It is of service to the financial classes to have a large national debt of their own. The floating of and the dealing in such public loans are a profitable business, and are means of exercising important political influences at critical junctures. Where floating capital constantly tends to excess, further debts are serviceable as a financial drainage scheme.

Imperialism with its wars and its armaments is undeniably responsible for the growing debts of the continental nations, and while the unparalleled industrial prosperity of Great Britain and the isolation of the United States have enabled these great nations to escape this ruinous competition during recent decades, the period of their immunity is over ; both, committed as they seem to an Imperialism without limit, will succumb more and more to the moneylending classes dressed as Imperialists and patriots.[1]

[1] The later passages of this chapter describing the probable plunge towards Protection are left as written in 1901, two years before Mr. Chamberlain's dramatic espousal of a full Protection.

PART II

THE POLITICS OF IMPERIALISM

CHAPTER I

THE POLITICAL SIGNIFICANCE
OF IMPERIALISM

I

THE curious ignorance which prevails regarding the
political character and tendencies of Imperialism
cannot be better illustrated than by the following passage
from a learned work upon " The History of Colonization "[1] :
" The extent of British dominion may perhaps be better
imagined than described, when the fact is appreciated that,
of the entire land surface of the globe, approximately one-
fifth is actually or theoretically under that flag, while more
than one-sixth of all the human beings living in this planet
reside under one or the other type of English colonization.
The names by which authority is exerted are numerous,
and processes are distinct, but the goals to which this mani-
fold mechanism is working are very similar. According
to the climate, the natural conditions and the inhabitants
of the regions affected, procedure and practice differ. The
means are adapted to the situation ; there is not any irrevo-
cable, immutable line of policy ; from time to time, from
decade to decade, English statesmen have applied different
treatments to the same territory. Only one fixed rule of
action seems to exist ; it is to promote the interests of the
colony to the utmost, to develop its scheme of government
as rapidly as possible, and eventually to elevate it from the
position of inferiority to that of association. Under the
charm of this beneficent spirit the chief colonial establish-

[1] Morris, vol. ii, p. 80.

113

ments of Great Britain have already achieved substantial freedom, without dissolving nominal ties; the other subordinate possessions are aspiring to it, while, on the other hand, this privilege of local independence has enabled England to assimilate with ease many feudatory States into the body politic of her system." Here then is the theory that Britons are a race endowed, like the Romans, with a genius for government, that our colonial and imperial policy is animated by a resolve to spread throughout the world the arts of free self-government which we enjoy at home,[1] and that in truth we are accomplishing this work.

Now, without discussing here the excellencies or the defects of the British theory and practice of representative self-government, to assert that our "fixed rule of action" has been to educate our dependencies in this theory and practice is quite the largest misstatement of the facts of our colonial and imperial policy that is possible. Upon the vast majority of the populations throughout our Empire we have bestowed no real powers of self-government, nor have we any serious intention of doing so, or any serious belief that it is possible for us to do so.

Of the three hundred and sixty-seven millions of British subjects outside these isles, not more than eleven millions, or one in thirty-four, have any real self-government for purposes of legislation and administration.[2]

Political freedom, and civil freedom, so far as it rests upon the other, are simply non-existent for the overwhelming majority of British subjects. In the self-governing colonies of Australasia and North America alone is responsible representative government a reality, and even there considerable populations of outlanders, as in West Australia,

[1] " The British Empire is a galaxy of free States," said Sir W. Laurier in a speech, July 8, 1902.
[2] Figures for the period of this study, ca. 1903.

or servile labour, as in Queensland, have tempered the genuineness of democracy. In Cape Colony and Natal events testify how feebly the forms and even the spirit of the free British institutions have taken root in States where the great majority of the population were always excluded from political rights. The franchise and the rights it carries remain virtually a white monopoly in so-called self-governing colonies, where the coloured population was, in 1903, to the white as four to one and ten to one respectively.

In certain of our older Crown colonies there exists a representative element in the government. While the administration is entirely vested in a governor appointed by the Crown, assisted by a council nominated by him, the colonists elect a portion of the legislative assembly. The following colonies belong to this order : Jamaica, Barbados, Trinidad, Bahamas, British Guiana, Windward Islands, Bermudas, Malta, Mauritius, Ceylon.

The representative element differs considerably in size and influence in these colonies, but nowhere does it out-number the non-elected element. It thus becomes an advisory rather than a really legislative factor. Not merely is the elected always dominated in numbers by the non-elected element, but in all cases the veto of the Colonial Office is freely exercised upon measures passed by the assemblies. To this it should be added that in nearly all cases a fairly high property qualification is attached to the franchise, precluding the coloured people from exercising an elective power proportionate to their numbers and their stake in the country.

The entire population of these modified Crown colonies amounted to 5,700,000 in 1898.[1]

The overwhelming majority of the subjects of the British

[1] In all essential features India and Egypt are (1903) to be classed as Crown colonies.

Empire are under Crown colony government, or under protectorates.[1] In neither case do they enjoy any of the important political rights of British citizens ; in neither case are they being trained in the arts of free British institu-tions. In the Crown colony the population exercises no political privileges. The governor, appointed by the Colonial Office, is absolute, alike for legislation and adminis-tration ; he is aided by a council of local residents usually chosen by himself or by home authority, but its function is merely advisory, and its advice can be and frequently is ignored. In the vast protectorates we have assumed in Africa and Asia there is no tincture of British representative government ; the British factor consists in arbitrary acts of irregular interference with native government. Exceptions to this exist in the case of districts assigned to Chartered Companies, where business men, animated avowedly by business ends, are permitted to exercise arbitrary powers of government over native populations under the imperfect check of some British Imperial Commissioner.

Again, in certain native and feudatory States of India our Empire is virtually confined to government of foreign relations, military protection, and a veto upon grave internal disorder, the real administration of the countries being left in the hands of native princes or headmen. However excellent this arrangement may be, it lends little support to the general theory of the British Empire as an educator of free political institutions.

Where British government is real, it does not carry freedom or self-government ; where it does carry a certain amount of freedom and self-government, it is not real. Not five per cent. of the population of our Empire are possessed of any appreciable portion of the political and civil liberties which are the basis of British civilization.

[1] Situation in 1903.

Outside the eleven millions of British subjects in Canada, Australia, and New Zealand, no considerable body is endowed with full self-government in the more vital matters, or being "elevated from the position of inferiority to that of association."[1]

This is the most important of all facts for students of the present and probable future of the British Empire. We have taken upon ourselves in these little islands the responsibility of governing huge aggregations of lower races in all parts of the world by methods which are antithetic to the methods of government which we most value for ourselves.

The question just here is not whether we are governing these colonies and subject races well and wisely, better than they could govern themselves if left alone, or better than another imperial European nation could govern them, but whether we are giving them those arts of government which we regard as our most valuable possessions.

The statement in the passage which we quoted, that underneath the fluctuations of our colonial policy throughout the nineteenth century lay the " fixed rule " of educating the dependencies for self-government, is so totally and manifestly opposed to historical records and to the testimony of loyal colonial politicians in all our colonies as to deserve no further formal refutation. The very structure of our party government, the ignorance or open indifference of colonial ministers of the elder generations, the biassed play of colonial cliques and interests, reduced the whole of our colonial government for many decades to something between a see-saw and a game of chance : the nearest approach to any " fixed rule " was the steady prolonged pressure of some commercial interest whose political aid was worth purchase. That any such " beneficent spirit " as is recorded

[1] All the facts and figures given here and elsewhere relate to the period of this study, 1903.

consciously presided over the policy applied to any class of colonies during the larger half of the nineteenth century is notoriously false. To those statesmen to whom the colonies were not a tiresome burden, they were a useful dumping-ground for surplus population, including criminals, paupers and ne'er-do-weels, or possible markets for British trade. A few more liberal-minded politicians, such as Sir W. Molesworth and Mr. Wakefield, regarded with sympathetic interest the rising democracies of Australasia and Canada. But the idea of planning a colonial policy inspired by the motive of teaching the arts of free representative self-government not merely was not the " fixed rule," but was not present as a rule at all for any responsible Colonial Secretary in Great Britain.

When the first dawn of the new Imperialism in the seventies gave fuller political consciousness to " empire," it did indeed become a commonplace of Liberal thought that England's imperial mission was to spread the arts of free government, and the examples of Australia and Canada looming big before all eyes suggested that we were doing this. The principles and practices of representative government were " boomed " ; Liberal pro-consuls set on foot imposing experiments in India and in the West Indies ; the progress of the South African colonies suggested that by fairly rapid degrees the various populations of the Empire might attain substantial measures of self-government ; and the larger vision of a British Empire, consisting in the main or altogether of a union of self-governing States, began to dazzle politicians.

Some persons—though a diminishing number—still entertain these notions and believe that we are gradually moulding the British Empire into a set of substantially self-governing States. Our position in India is justified, they think, by the training we are giving the natives in good government, and when they hear of " representative " elements in the government of Ceylon or of Jamaica they flatter themselves that the whole trend of imperial government is directed to this end. Admitting the facts regarding the small proportion of present political liberty throughout the Empire, they urge that this arises from the necessary regard we have to the mode of educating lower races : the vast majority of our subjects are " children " and must be trained slowly and carefully in the arts of responsible self-government.

Now such persons are suffering from a great and demonstrable delusion if they suppose that any appreciable number of the able energetic officials who practically administer our Empire from Downing Street, or on the spot, either believe that the populations which they rule are capable of being trained for effective free self-government, or are appreciably affected in their policy by any regard to such a contingency in the near or remote future. Very few British officials any longer retain the notion that we can instruct or are successfully instructing the great populations of India in the Western arts of government. The general admission or conviction is that experiments in municipal and other government conducted under British control on British lines are failures. The real success of our Indian Government admittedly consists in good order and justice administered autocratically by able British officials. There is some training of native officials for subordinate, and in rare instances for high offices, but there is no pretence that this is the chief or an important aim or end, nor is there the least intention that these native officials shall in the future become the servants of the free Indian nation rather than of the bureaucratic Imperial Government.

In other instances, as in Egypt, we have used natives for certain administrative work, and this training in lower offices is doubtless not without its value. Our practical success in preserving order, securing justice and developing the material resources of many of our colonies has been largely due to the fact that we have learnt to employ native agents wherever possible for detailed work of administration, and to adapt our government, where it can be safely done, to native conditions. The retention of native laws and customs or of the foreign system of jurisprudence imposed by earlier colonists of another race,[1] while it has complicated government in the final court of the Privy Council, has greatly facilitated the detailed work of administration upon the spot.

Indeed the variety, not only of laws but of other modes of government in our Empire, arouses the enthusiastic admiration of many students of its history. " The British Empire," we are told, " exhibits forms and methods of government in almost exuberant variety. The several colonies at different times of their history have passed through various stages of government, and in 1891 there are some thirty or forty different forms operating simultaneously within our Empire alone. At this moment there are regions where government of a purely despotic kind is in full exercise, and the Empire includes also colonies where the subordination of the colonial government has become so slight as to be almost impalpable."[2]

[1] " Every country conquered or ceded to the Crown of England retains such laws and such rules of law (not inconsistent with the general law of England affecting dependencies) as were in force at the time of the conquest or cession, until they are repealed by competent authority. Now, inasmuch as many independent States and many dependent colonies of other States have become English dependencies, many of the English dependencies have retained wholly or in part foreign systems of jurisprudence. Thus Trinidad retains much of the Spanish law ; Demarara, Cape of Good Hope, and Ceylon retain much of the Dutch law ; Lower Canada retains the French civil law according to the " coutume de Paris " ; St. Lucia retains the old French law as it existed when the island belonged to France " (Lewis, *Government of Dependencies*, p. 198).

[2] Caldecott, *English Colonization and Empire*, p. 121.

Whether this is a striking testimony to the genius for "elasticity" of our colonial policy, or an instance of haphazard opportunism, one need not here discuss.[1]

The point is that an examination of this immense variety of government disposes entirely of the suggestion that by the extension of our Empire we have been spreading the type of free government which is distinctively British.

The present condition of the government under which the vast majority of our fellow-subjects in the Empire live is eminently un-British in that it is based, not on the consent

---

[1] What "elasticity" actually signifies in Colonial Office government may be illustrated by the following testimony of Miss Kingsley in regard to West Africa. "Before taking any important steps the West African governor is supposed to consult the officials at the Colonial Office, but as the Colonial Office is not so well informed as the governor himself is, this can be no help to him if he is a really able man, and no check on him if he is not an able man. For, be he what he may, he is the representative of the Colonial Office; he cannot, it is true, persuade the Colonial Office to go and involve itself in rows with European continental Powers, because the Office knows about them; but if he is a strong-minded man with a fad, he can persuade the Colonial Office to let him try that fad on the natives or the traders, because the Colonial Office does not know the natives nor the West African trade. You see, therefore, you have in the governor of a West African possession a man in a bad position. He is aided by no council worth having, no regular set of experts; he is held in by another council equally non-expert, except in the direction of continental politics. . . . In addition to the governor there are the other officials, medical, legal, secretarial, constabulary, and customs. The majority of them are engaged in looking after each other and clerking. Clerking is the breath of the Crown colony system, and customs what it feeds on. Owing to the climate it is practically necessary to have a double staff in all these departments—that is what the system would have if it were perfect; as it is, some official's work is always being done by a subordinate; it may be equally well done, but it is not equally well paid for, and there is no continuity in policy in any department, except those which are entirely clerk, and the expense of this is necessarily great. The main evil of this want of continuity is, of course, in the governors—a governor goes out, starts a new line of policy, goes home on furlough leaving in charge the colonial secretary, who does not by any means always feel enthusiastic towards that policy, so it languishes. The governor comes back, goes at it again like a giant refreshed, but by no means better acquainted with local affairs for having been away; then he goes home again or dies, or gets a new appointment; a brand-new governor comes out, he starts a new line of policy, perhaps has a new colonial secretary into the bargain : anyhow the thing goes on wavering, not advancing. The only description I have heard of our policy in West African colonies that seems to me to do it justice is that given by a medical friend of mine, who said it was a coma accompanied by fits."—(*West African Studies*, pp. 328–330).

of the governed, but upon the will of imperial officials ; it does indeed betray a great variety of forms, but they agree in the essential of un-freedom. Nor is it true that any of the more enlightened methods of administration we employ are directed towards undoing this character. Not only in India, but in the West Indies, and wherever there exists a large preponderance of coloured population, the trend, not merely of ignorant, but of enlightened public opinion, is against a genuinely representative government on British lines. It is perceived to be incompatible with the economic and social authority of a superior race.

When British authority has been forcibly fastened upon large populations of alien race and colour, with habits of life and thought which do not blend with ours, it is found impossible to graft the tender plants of free representative government, and at the same time to preserve good order in external affairs. We are obliged in practice to make a choice between good order and justice administered autocratically in accordance with British standards, on the one hand, and delicate, costly, doubtful, and disorderly experiments in self-government on British lines upon the other, and we have practically everywhere decided to adopt the former alternative. A third and sounder method of permitting large liberty of self-government under a really loose pro-tectorate, adopted in a few instances, as in Basutoland, part of Bechuanaland, and a few Indian States, meets with no great favour and in most instances seems no longer feasible. It cannot be too clearly recognised that the old Liberal notion of our educating lower races in the arts of popular government is discredited, and only survives for platform purposes when some new step of annexation is urged upon the country.

The case of Egypt is a *locus classicus*. Here we entered the country under the best auspices, as deliverers rather than as conquerors; we undoubtedly conferred great economic benefits upon large sections of the people, who are not savages, but inheritors of ancient civilised traditions. The whole existing machinery of government is virtually at our disposal, to modify it according to our will. We have reformed taxation, improved justice, and cleansed the public services of many corruptions, and claim in many ways to have improved the condition of the fellaheen. But are we introducing British political institutions in such wise as to graft them on a nation destined for progress in self-government ?

The following statement of Lord Milner may be regarded as typical, not of the fossilised, old-world official, but of the modern, more enlightened, practical Imperialist :—

" I attach much more importance, in the immediate future of Egypt, to the improvement of the character and intelligence of the official class than I do to the development of the representative institutions with which we endowed the country in 1883. As a true born Briton (*sic!*), I, of course take off my hat to everything that calls itself Franchise, Parliament, Representation of the People, the Voice of the Majority, and all the rest of it. But, as an observer of the actual condition of Egyptian society, I cannot shut my eyes to the fact that popular government, as we understand it, is for a longer time than any one can foresee at present out of the question. The people neither comprehend it nor desire it. They would come to singular grief if they had it. And nobody, except a few silly theorists, thinks of giving it to them."[1]

Yet here we went into this country upon the express understanding that we should do precisely what Lord Milner says we have no intention of doing, viz. teach the

[1] *England in Egypt*, pp. 378, 379.

people to govern themselves within the space of a few years and then leave them to work their government.

I am not here, however, concerned to discuss either the value of the governmental work which we are doing or our right to impose our authority upon weaker populations. But the fact is plain that the British Empire is not to any appreciable extent a training ground in the British arts of free government.

In the light of this inquiry, directed to the Empire as a whole, how do we regard the new Imperialism? Almost the whole of it, as we have seen, consists of tropical or sub-tropical territory, with large populations of savages or "lower races"; little of it is likely, even in the distant future, to increase the area of sound colonial life. In the few places where English colonists can settle, as in parts of the South African States, they will be so largely outnumbered by dark populations as to render the adoption of free representative government impracticable.

In a single word, the New Imperialism has increased the area of British despotism, far outbalancing the progress in population and in practical freedom attained by our few democratic colonies.

It has not made for the spread of British liberty and for the propagation of our arts of government. The lands and populations which we have annexed we govern, in so far as we govern them at all, by distinctively autocratic methods, administered chiefly from Downing Street, but partly from centres of colonial government, in cases where self-governing colonies have been permitted to annex.

II

Now this large expansion of British political despotism is fraught with reactions upon home politics which are deserving of most serious consideration. A curious blindness seems to beset the mind of the average educated Briton when he is asked to picture to himself our colonial Empire. Almost instinctively he visualises Canada, Australasia, and South Africa—the rest he virtually ignores. Yet the Imperialism which is our chief concern, the expansion of the last quarter of the nineteenth century, has nothing in common with Canada and Australasia, and very little with " white man's Africa."

When Lord Rosebery uttered his famous words about " a free, tolerant and unaggressive Empire," he can scarcely have had in mind our vast encroachments in West and Central Africa, in the Soudan, on the Burmese frontier, or in Matabeleland. But the distinction between genuine Colonialism and Imperialism, important in itself, is vital when we consider their respective relations to domestic policy.

Modern British colonialism has been no drain upon our material and moral resources, because it has made for the creation of free white democracies, a policy of informal federation, of decentralisation, involving no appreciable strain upon the governmental faculties of Great Britain. Such federation, whether it remains informal with the slight attachment of imperial sovereignty which now exists, or voluntarily takes some more formal shape, political or financial, may well be regarded as a source of strength, political and military.

Imperialism is the very antithesis of this free, wholesome colonial connection, making, as it ever does, for greater complications of foreign policy, greater centralisation of power, and a congestion of business which ever threatens to absorb and overtax the capacity of parliamentary government.

The true political nature of Imperialism is best seen

by confronting it with the watchwords of progress accepted in the middle of the nineteenth century by moderate men of both great parties in the State, though with interpretations, varying in degree—peace, economy, reform, and popular self-government. Even now we find no formal abandonment of the principles of government these terms express, and a large section of professed Liberals believe or assert that Imperialism is consistent with the maintenance of all these virtues.

This contention, however, is belied by facts. The decades of Imperialism have been prolific in wars ; most of these wars have been directly motived by aggression of white races upon " lower races," and have issued in the forcible seizure of territory. Every one of the steps of expansion in Africa, Asia, and the Pacific has been accompanied by bloodshed ; each imperialist Power keeps an increasing army available for foreign service ; rectification of frontiers, punitive expeditions, and other euphemisms for war have been in incessant progress. The *Pax Britannica*, always an impudent falsehood, has become a grotesque monster of hypocrisy ; along our Indian frontiers, in West Africa, in the Soudan, in Uganda, in Rhodesia fighting has been[1] well-nigh incessant. Although the great imperialist Powers kept their hands off one another, save where the rising empire of the United States found its opportunity in the falling empire of Spain, the self-restraint has been costly and precarious. Peace as a national policy is antagonized not merely by war, but by militarism, an even graver injury. Apart from the enmity of France and Germany, the main cause of the vast armaments which have drained the resources of most European countries is their conflicting interests in territorial and commercial expansion. Where thirty years ago there existed one sensitive spot in our

[1] The situation in 1903.

relations with France, or Germany, or Russia, there are a dozen now; diplomatic strains are of almost monthly occurrence between Powers with African or Chinese interests, and the chiefly business nature of the national antagonisms renders them more dangerous, inasmuch as the policy of Governments passes under the influence of distinctively financial juntos.

The contention of the *si pacem vis para bellum* school, that armaments alone constitute the best security for peace, is based upon the assumption that a genuine lasting antagonism of real interests exists between the various peoples who are called upon to undergo this monstrous sacrifice.

Our economic analysis has disclosed the fact that it is only the interests of competing cliques of business men—investors, contractors, export manufacturers, and certain professional classes—that are antagonistic; that these cliques, usurping the authority and voice of the people, use the public resources to push their private interests, and spend the blood and money of the people in this vast and disastrous military game, feigning national antagonisms which have no basis in reality. It is not to the interest of the British people, either as producers of wealth or as tax-payers, to risk a war with Russia and France in order to join Japan in preventing Russia from seizing Corea; but it may serve the interests of a group of commercial politicians to promote this dangerous policy. The South African war, openly fomented by gold speculators for their private purposes, will rank in history as a leading case of this usurpation of nationalism.

War, however, represents not the success, but the failure of this policy; its normal and most perilous fruit is not war, but militarism. So long as this competitive expansion for territory and foreign markets is permitted to misrepresent itself as " national policy " the antagonism of interests seems real, and the peoples must sweat and bleed and toil to keep up an ever more expensive machinery of war.

Were logic applicable in such cases, the notion that the greater the preparation for war the smaller the probability of its occurrence might well appear a *reductio ad absurdum* of militarism, implying, as it does, that the only way to secure an eternal world peace is to concentrate the entire energy of all nations upon the art of war, which is thus rendered incapable of practice.

With such paradoxes, however, we need not concern ourselves. The patent admitted fact that, as a result of imperial competition, an ever larger proportion of the time, energy, and money of " imperialist " nations is absorbed by naval and military armaments, and that no check upon further absorption is regarded as practicable by Imperialists, brings " militarism " into the forefront of practical politics. Great Britain and the United States, which have hitherto congratulated themselves on escaping the militarism of continental Europe, are now rapidly succumbing. Why ? Does any one suggest that either nation needs a larger army for the protection of its own lands or of any of its genuine white settlements in other lands ? Not at all. It is not pretended that the militarization of England is required for such protective work. Australia and New Zealand are not threatened by any power, nor could a British army render them adequate assistance if they were ; equally impotent would British land forces be against the only Power which could conceivably attack our Canadian Dominion ; even South Africa, which lies on the borderland between colony and tropical dependency, cannot ultimately be secured by the military power of England. It is our mistaken annexation of tropical and sub-tropical territories, and the attempt to govern "lower races," that is driving us down the steep road to militarism.

If we are to hold all that we have taken since 1870 and to compete with the new industrial nations in the further partition of empires or spheres of influence in Africa and Asia, we must be prepared to fight. The enmity of rival empires, openly displayed throughout the South African war, is admittedly due to the policy by which we have forestalled, and are still seeking to forestall, these rivals in the annexation of territory and of markets throughout the world. The theory that we may be compelled to fight for the very existence of our Empire against some combination of European powers, which is now used to scare the nation into a definite and irretrievable reversal of our military and commercial policy, signifies nothing else than the intention of the imperialist interests to continue their reckless career of annexation. In 1896 Lord Rosebery gave a vivid description of the policy of the last two decades of the century, and put forth a powerful plea for peace.

"The British Empire . . . needs peace. For the last twenty years, still more during the last twelve, you have been laying your hands, with almost frantic eagerness, on every tract of territory adjacent to your own or desirable from any other point of view which you thought it desirable to take. That has had two results. I daresay it has been quite right, but it has had two results. The first result is this, that you have excited to an almost intolerable degree the envy of other colonizing (*sic !*) nations, and that, in the case of many countries, or several countries rather, which were formerly friendly to you, you can reckon—in consequence of your colonial policy, whether right or wrong—not on their active benevolence, but on their active malevolence. And, secondly, you have acquired so enormous a mass of territory that it will be years before you can settle it or control it, or make it capable of defence or make it amenable to the acts of your administration. . . . In twelve years you have added to the Empire, whether in the shape of actual annexation or of dominion, or of what is called a sphere of influence, 2,600,000 square miles of territory . . . to the 120,000 square miles of the United Kingdom, which is part of your Empire, you have added during the last twelve years twenty-two areas as large as that United Kingdom itself. I say that that marks out for many years a policy from which you cannot depart if you would. You may be compelled to draw the sword—I hope you may not be ; but the foreign policy of Great Britain, until its territory is consolidated, filled up, settled, civilized, must inevitably be a policy of peace."[1]

After these words were uttered, vast new tracts of un-digested empire were added in the Soudan, in East Africa, in South Africa, while Great Britain was busily entangling herself in obligations of incalculable magnitude and peril in the China seas, and the prophet who spoke this warning was himself an active instrument in the furtherance of the very folly he denounced.

Imperialism—whether it consists in a further policy of expansion or in the rigorous maintenance of all those vast tropical lands which have been ear-marked as British spheres of influence—implies militarism now and ruinous wars in the future. This truth is now for the first time brought sharply and nakedly before the mind of the nation. The kingdoms of the earth are to be ours on condition that we fall down and worship Moloch.

Militarism approaches Great Britain with the following dilemma. If the army needed for defence of the Empire is to remain upon a voluntary basis, consisting of selected material obtained by application of economic inducements,

[1] Edinburgh, October 9, 1896.

a considerable increase either of the regular forces or the militia can only be obtained by a rise of pay so large as to tempt men, not from the unskilled labour market or the agricultural districts as heretofore, but from the skilled artisan classes of the towns. It requires but slight consideration to perceive that every fresh increment of the army will involve an appeal to a class accustomed to a higher standard of wage, and that the pay for the entire army must be regulated by the rate of pay needed to secure this last increment. Recruiting in time of war is always brisker than in time of peace, other motives blending with the distinctly economic motive. Every increase of our forces on a peace footing will involve a far more than proportionate increase in the rate of pay—how large an increase experiment alone can teach. It seems quite likely that in a period of normally good trade our voluntary army could only be increased 50 per cent. by doubling the former rate of pay, or by other improved conditions of employment involving an equivalent rise of cost, and that, if we required to double the size of our standing army, we should have to treble the rate of pay. If, on the other hand, the prospect of some such enormous increase of military expenditure should lead us to abandon the purely voluntary basis, and have recourse to conscription or some other form of compulsory service, we could not fail to suffer in average fighting calibre. Such selection of physique and morale as prevailed under the voluntary system would now disappear, and the radical unfitness of a nation of town-dwellers for arduous military service would be disclosed. The fatuous attempt to convert ineffective slum-workers and weedy city clerks into tough military material, fit for prolonged foreign service, or even for efficient home defence, would be detected, it may be hoped, before the trial by combat with a military Power drawing its soldiers from the soil. A nation, 70 per cent. of whose inhabitants are denizens of towns, cannot afford to challenge its neighbours to trials of physical force, for in the last resort war is determined neither by generalship nor superiority of weapons, but by those elements of brute endurance which are incompatible with the life of industrial towns.

The full danger of the dilemma of militarism is only perceived when the indirect is added to the direct expenditure. An army, volunteer or conscript, formed out of town material would take longer training or more frequent exercise than a peasant army ; the waste of labour power, by withdrawing the youth of the nation from their early training in the productive arts in order to prepare them for the destructive art, would be greater, and would impair more grievously the skilled industries than in nations less advanced in the specialized trades and professions. The least of these economic injuries would be the actual loss of labour time involved in the withdrawal ; far graver would be the damage to industrial skill and character by withdrawing youths at the period of best docility and aptitude for skilled work and subjecting them to a distinctively mechanical discipline, for though the slum-dweller and the clodhopper may gain in smartness and alertness by military training, the skilled labouring classes will lose more by the crushing of individual initiative which professional militarism always involves.

At a time when the call for free, bold initiative and individual enterprise and ingenuity in the assimilation of the latest scientific and technical knowledge for the arts of industry, for improved organization and methods of business, becomes most urgent to enable us to hold our own in the new competition of the world—at such a time to subject the youth of our nation to the barrack system, or to any form of effective military training, would be veritable suicide. It is to no purpose to reply that some of our keen commercial competitors, notoriously Germany, are already saddled with this burden ; the answer is that, if we can hardly hold our own with Germany while she bears this burden, we shall hand over to her an easy victory if we assume a still heavier one.[1] Whatever virtues are attributed to military discipline by its apologists, it is admitted that this training does not conduce to industrial efficiency. The economic cost of militarism is therefore twofold ; the greatly increased expense of the army must be defrayed by an impoverished people.

So far, I have regarded the issue on its narrowly economic side. Far more important are the political implications of militarism. These strike at the very root of popular liberty and the ordinary civic virtues. A few plain reflections serve to dispel the sophistical vapours which are used to form a halo round the life of the soldier. *Respice finem.* There exists an absolute antagonism between the activity of the good citizen and that of the soldier. The end of the soldier is not, as is sometimes falsely said, to die for his country ; it is to kill for his country. In as far as he dies he is a failure ; his work is to kill, and he attains perfection as a soldier when he becomes a perfect killer. This end, the slaughter of one's fellow-men, forms a professional character, alien from, and antagonistic to, the character of our ordinary citizen, whose work conduces to the preservation of his fellow-men. If it be contended that this final purpose, though informing and moulding the structure and functions of an army, operates but seldom and slightly upon the consciousness of the individual soldier, save upon the battlefield, the answer is that, in the absence from consciousness of this end, the entire routine of the soldier's life, his drill, parades, and whole

[1] Refers, of course, to the situation in 1903.

military exercise, is a useless, purposeless activity, and that these qualities exercise a hardly less degrading influence on character than the conscious intention of killing his fellow-men.

The psychical reactions of military life are indeed notorious ; even those who defend the utility of an army do not deny that it unfits a man for civil life. Nor can it be maintained that a shorter general service, such as suffices for a citizen army, escapes these reactions. If the service is long and rigorous enough to be effective, it involves these psychical reactions, which are, indeed, part and parcel of military efficiency. How clearly this is set forth by Mr. March-Phillips in his admirable appreciation of the common soldier's life !

" Soldiers as a class (I take the town-bred, slum-bred majority, mind) are men who have discarded the civil standard of morality altogether. They simply ignore it. This is, no doubt, why civilians fight shy of them. In the game of life they don't play the same rules, and the consequence is a good deal of misunderstanding, until finally the civilian says he won't play with the Tommy any more. In soldiers' eyes lying, theft, drunkenness, bad language, etc., are not evils at all. They steal like jackdaws. As to language, I used to think the language of a merchant ship's fo'c'sle pretty bad, but the language of Tommies, in point of profanity, quite equals, and, in point of obscenity, beats it hollow. This department is a speciality of his. Lying he treats with the same large charity. To lie like a trooper is quite a sound metaphor. He invents all sorts of elaborate lies for the mere pleasure of inventing them. Looting, again, is one of his perpetual joys. Not merely looting for profit, but looting for the sheer fun of the destruction, etc."[1] The fidelity of this description is attested by the

[1] *With Remington*, by L. March-Phillips, pp. 131, 132.

sympathy which the writer displays with the soldierly attributes that accompany, and, in his opinion, atone for, these breaches of the civilian rules.

" Are thieving and lying and looting and bestial talk very bad things ? If they are, Tommy is a bad man. But, for some reason or other, since I got to know him, I have thought rather less of the iniquity of these things than I did before."

This judgment is itself a striking comment on militarism. The fact that it should be given by a man of sterling character and culture is the most convincing testimony to the corrupting influence of war.

To this informal witness may be added the significant evidence of Lord Wolseley's *Soldier's Pocket-book*.

" As a nation, we are brought up to feel it a disgrace to succeed by falsehood ; the word ' spy ' conveys in it something as repulsive as slave. We will keep hammering away with the conviction that honesty is the best policy, and that truth always wins in the long run. These pretty little sentences do well enough for a child's copy-book, but the man who acts upon them in war had better sheathe his sword for ever."

The order and progress of Great Britain during the nine-teenth century was secured by the cultivation and practise of the ordinary civic and industrial virtues, assisted by certain advantages of natural resources and historical contingencies. Are we prepared to substitute the military code of ethics or to distract the national mind and conduct by a perpetual conflict of two warring principles, the one making for the evolution of the good citizen, the other for the evolution of the good soldier ?

Ignoring, for the present, distinctively moral degradation of this reversion from industrial to military ethics, we cannot but perceive that the damage done to commercial morality must react disastrously upon the wealth-producing power of the nation, and sap the roots of imperial expenditure.

But one loophole of escape from this dilemma presents itself, an escape fraught with still graver peril. The new Imperialism has been, we have seen, chiefly concerned with tropical and sub-tropical countries where large " lower races " are brought under white control. Why should Englishmen fight the defensive or offensive wars of this Empire, when cheaper, more numerous, and better-assimilated fighting material can be raised upon the spot, or transferred from one tropical dominion to another ? As the labour of industrial development of tropical resources is put upon the " lower races " who reside there, under white superintendence, why should not militarism be organized upon the same basis, black or brown or yellow men, to whom military discipline will be " a wholesome education," fighting for the British Empire under British officers ? Thus can we best economize our own limited military material, keeping most of it for home defence. This simple solution—the employment of cheap foreign mercenary armies—is no new device. The organization of vast native forces, armed with " civilized " weapons, drilled on " civilized " methods, and commanded by " civilized " officers, formed one of the most conspicuous features of the latest stages of the great Eastern Empires, and afterwards of the Roman Empire. It has proved one of the most perilous devices of parasitism, by which a metropolitan population entrusts the defence of its lives and possessions to the precarious fidelity of " conquered races," commanded by ambitious pro-consuls.

One of the strangest symptoms of the blindness of Imperialism is the reckless indifference with which Great Britain, France, and other imperial nations embarked on this perilous dependence. Great Britain has gone

farthest. Most of the fighting by which we have won our
Indian Empire was done by natives; in India, as later
in Egypt, great standing armies were placed under British
commanders; almost all the fighting associated with our
African·dominions, except in the southern part, was done
for us by natives. How strong the pressure was to reduce
the proportion of British soldiers employed in these countries
to a bare minimum of safety is amply illustrated in the case
of India, when the South African emergency drove us to
reduce the accepted minimum by more than fifteen thousand
men, while in South Africa itself we established a dangerous
precedent by employing large numbers of armed natives
to fight against another white race.

Those best acquainted with the temper of the British
people and of the politicians who have the direct determination of affairs will understand how readily we may be
drawn along this perilous path. Nothing short of the
fear of an early invasion of these islands will induce the
British people to undergo the onerous experience of a
really effective system of compulsory military service; no
statesman except under the shadow of a serious menace
of invasion will dare to press such a plan. A regular
provision for compulsory foreign service will never be
adopted when the alternative of mercenary native armies
remains. Let these " niggers " fight for the empire in
return for the services we render them by annexing and
governing them and teaching them " the dignity of labour,"
will be the prevailing sentiment, and " imperialist " statesmen will be compelled to bow before it, diluting with British
troops ever more thinly the native armies in Africa and
Asia.

This mode of militarism, while cheaper and easier in
the first instance, implies less and less control from Great
Britain. Though reducing the strain of militarism upon

the population at home, it enhances the risks of wars, which become more frequent and more barbarous in proportion as they involve to a less degree the lives of Englishmen. The expansion of our Empire under the new Imperialism has been compassed by setting the " lower races " at one another's throats, fostering tribal animosities and utilising for our supposed benefit the savage propensities of the peoples to whom we have a mission to carry Christianity and civilization.

That we do not stand alone in this ignominious policy does not make it better, rather worse, offering terrible prophetic glimpses into a not distant future, when the horrors of our eighteenth century struggle with France in North America and India may be revived upon a gigantic scale, and Africa and Asia may furnish huge cock-pits for the struggles of black and yellow armies representing the imperialist rivalries of Christendom. The present tendencies of Imperialism plainly make in this direction, involving in their recoil a degradation of Western States and a possible *débâcle* of Western civilization.

In any event Imperialism makes for war and for militarism, and has brought a great and limitless increase of expenditure of national resources upon armaments. It has impaired the independence of every nation which has yielded to its false glamour. Great Britain no longer possesses a million pounds which it can call its own ; its entire financial resources are mortgaged to a policy to be dictated by Germany, France, or Russia. A move from any of these Powers can force us to expend upon more battleships and military preparations the money we had designed to use for domestic purposes. The priority and reckless magnitude of our imperial expansion has made the danger of an armed coalition of great Powers against us no idle chimera. The development of their resources along the lines of the new industrialism, on the one hand, by driving them to seek foreign markets, brings them in all parts of the world against the vexatious barriers of British possessions ; on the other, has furnished them with ample means of public expenditure. The spread of modern industrialism tends to place our " rivals " on a level with ourselves in their public resources. Hence, at the very time when we have more reason to fear armed coalition than formerly, we are losing that superiority in finance which made it feasible for us to maintain a naval armament superior to any European combination.

All these perils in the present and the future are the fruits of the new Imperialism, which is thus exposed as the implacable and mortal enemy of Peace and Economy. How far the military aspect of Imperialism has already eaten into the resources of modern European States may be judged by the following table showing the growth of expenditure of the various great European States on military equipment in the last generation :—

MILITARY EXPENDITURE OF GREAT EUROPEAN POWERS.[1]

	1869–1870.	1897–1898.
	£	£
Great Britain	22,440,000	40,094,000
France	23,554,000	37,000,000
Russia	15,400,000	35,600,000
Germany	11,217,000	32,800,000
Austria	9,103,000	16,041,000
Italy	7,070,000	13,510,000
Totals	88,784,000	175,045,000

For the whole body of European States the increase has been from £105,719,000 in 1869–1870 to £208,877,000 in 1897–1898.

[1] See Appendix, p. 378, for expenditure of the Powers on Defence in 1934.

139

III

There are those who deny the antagonism of Imperialism and social reform. "The energy of a nation like ours, they urge, is not to be regarded as a fixed quantity, so that every expenditure upon imperial expansion implies a corresponding restriction for purposes of internal progress ; there are various sorts of energy demanding different outlets, so that the true economy of British genius requires many domestic and external fields of activity ; we are capable at one and the same time of imperial expansion in various directions, and of a complex energy of growth in our internal economy. The inspiration of great achievements throughout the world reacts upon the vitality of the British nation, rendering it capable of efforts of internal progress which would have been precluded by the ordinary course of smug insular self-development."

Now it is needless to argue the incompatibility of social reform with imperialism on any abstract principle regarding the quantity of national energy. Though limits of quantity exist underneath the finest economy of division of labour, as indeed is illustrated on the military plane by the limits which population imposes upon the combination of aggressive expansion and home defence, these limits are not always easy to discover and are sometimes capable of great elasticity. It cannot, therefore, be contended that the sound intellectual stuff which goes into our Indian Civil Service involves a corresponding loss to our home professions and official services, or that the adventurous energy of great explorers, missionaries, engineers, prospectors and other pioneers of empire could and would have found as ample a field and as sharp a stimulus for their energies within these islands. The issue we are considering—that of Imperialism—does not in its main political and social effects turn upon any such exact considerations of quantitative economy of energy, nor does the repudiation of Imperialism imply a confinement within rigid territorial limits of any individual or co-operative energy which may find better scope abroad. We are concerned with economy of governmental power, with Imperialism as a public policy. Even here the issue is not primarily one of quantitative economy, though, as we shall see, that is clearly involved. The antagonism of Imperialism and social reform is an inherent opposition of policy involving contradictory methods and processes of government. Some of the more obvious illustrations of this antagonism are presented by considerations of finance. Most important measures of social reform, the improvement of the machinery of public education, any large handling of the land and housing questions in town and country, the public control of the drink traffic, old-age pensions, legislation for improving the condition of the workers, involve considerable outlay of public money raised in taxation by the central or local authorities. Now Imperialism, through the ever-growing military expenditure it involves, visibly drains the public purse of the money which might be put to such purposes. Not only has the Exchequer not sufficient money to expend on public education, old-age pensions, or other State reforms ; the smaller units of local government are similarly crippled, for the taxpayers and the ratepayers are in the main the same persons, and when they are heavily mulcted by taxes for unproductive State purposes they cannot easily bear increased rates.

Every important social reform, even if it does not directly involve large public expenditure, causes financial disturbances and risks which are less tolerable at times when public expenditure is heavy and public credit fluctuating and embarrassed. Most social reforms involve some attack on vested interests, and these can best defend themselves when active Imperialism absorbs public attention. When legislation is involved, economy of time and of governmental interest is of paramount importance. Imperialism, with its " high politics," involving the honour and safety of the Empire, claims the first place, and, as the Empire grows, the number and complexity of its issues, involving close, immediate, continuous attention, grow, absorbing the time of the Government and of Parliament. It becomes more and more impossible to set aside parliamentary time for the full unbroken discussion of matters of most vital domestic importance, or to carry through any large serious measure of reform.

It is needless to labour the theory of this antagonism when the practice is apparent to every student of politics. Indeed, it has become a commonplace of history how Governments use national animosities, foreign wars and the glamour of empire-making, in order to bemuse the popular mind and divert rising resentment against domestic abuses. The vested interests, which, on our analysis, are shown to be chief prompters of an imperialist policy, play for a double stake, seeking their private commercial and financial gains at the expense and peril of the commonwealth. They at the same time protect their economic and political supremacy at home against movements of popular reform. The city ground landlord, the country squire, the banker, the usurer, and the financier, the brewer, the mine-owner, the ironmaster, the shipbuilder, and the shipping trade, the great export manufacturers and merchants, the clergy of the State Church, the universities, and great public schools, the legal trade unions and the services have, both in Great Britain and on the Continent, drawn together for common political resistance against attacks upon the power, the property, and the privileges which in various forms and degrees they represent. Having conceded under pressure the form of political power in the shape of elective institutions and a wide franchise to the masses, they are struggling to prevent the masses from gaining the substance of this power and using it for the establishment of equality of economic opportunities. The collapse of the Liberal party upon the Continent, and now in Great Britain, is only made intelligible in this way. Friends of liberty and of popular government so long as the new industrial and commercial forces were hampered by the economic barriers and the political supremacy of the *noblesse* and the landed aristocracy, they have come to temper their " trust " of the people by an ever-growing quantity of caution, until within the last two decades[1] they have either sought political fusion with the Conservatives or have dragged on a precarious existence on the strength of a few belated leaders with obsolescent principles. Where Liberalism preserves any real strength, it is because the older struggle for the franchise and the primary liberties has been delayed, as in Belgium and in Denmark, and a *modus vivendi* has been possible with the rising working-class party. In Germany, France, and Italy the Liberal party as a factor in practical politics has either disappeared or is reduced to impotence ; in England it now stands convicted of a gross palpable betrayal of the first conditions of liberty, feebly fumbling after programmes as a substitute for principles. Its leaders, having sold their party to a confederacy of stock gamblers and jingo sentimentalists, find themselves impotent to defend Free Trade, Free Press, Free Schools, Free Speech, or any of the rudiments of ancient Liberalism. They have alienated the confidence of the people. For many years they have been permitted to conduct a sham fight and to call it politics ; the people thought it real until the South African war furnished a

[1] Referring to the last twenty years of the nineteenth century.

decisive dramatic test, and the unreality of Liberalism became apparent. It is not that Liberals have openly abandoned the old principles and traditions, but that they have rendered them of no account by dallying with an Imperialism which they have foolishly and futilely striven to distinguish from the firmer brand of their political opponents. This surrender to Imperialism signifies that they have preferred the economic interests of the possessing and speculative classes, to which most of their leaders belong, to the cause of Liberalism. That they are not conscious traitors or hypocrites may be readily conceded, but the fact remains that they have sold the cause of popular reform, which was their rightful heritage, for an Imperialism which appealed to their business interests and their social pre-possessions. The mess of pottage has been seasoned by various sweeter herbs, but its " stock " is class selfishness. The majority of the influential Liberals fled from the fight which was the truest test of Liberalism in their generation because they were " hirelings," destitute of firm political principle, gladly abandoning themselves to whatever shallow and ignoble defences a blear-eyed, raucous " patriotism " was ready to devise for their excuse.

It is possible to explain and qualify, but this remains the naked truth, which it is well to recognise. A Liberal party can only survive as a discredited or feeble remnant in England, unless it consents definitely to dissever itself from that Imperialism which its past leaders as well as their opponents, have permitted to block the progress of domestic reforms.

There are individuals and sections among those who have comprised the Liberal party whose deception has been in large measure blind and involuntary, because they have been absorbed by their interest in some single important issue of social reform, whether it be temperance,

144

land tenure, education, or the like. Let these men now recognize, as in honesty they can scarcely fail to do, that Imperialism is the deadly enemy of each of these reforms, that none of them can make serious advance so long as the expansion of the Empire and its satellite (militarism) absorb the time, the energy, the money of the State. Thus alone is it still possible that a strong rally of Liberals might, by fusion or co-operation with the political organisations of the working classes, fight Imperialism with the only effectual weapon, social reconstruction on the basis of democracy.

IV

The antagonism with democracy drives to the very roots of Imperialism as a political principle. Not only is Imperialism used to frustrate those measures of economic reform now recognized as essential to the effectual working of all machinery of popular government, but it operates to paralyse the working of that machinery itself. Representative institutions are ill adapted for empire, either as regards men or methods. The government of a great heterogeneous medley of lower races by departmental officials in London and their nominated emissaries lies outside the scope of popular knowledge and popular control. The Foreign, Colonial, and Indian Secretaries in Parliament, the permanent officials of the departments, the governors and staff who represent the Imperial Government in our dependencies, are not, and cannot be, controlled directly or effectively by the will of the people. This subordination of the legislative to the executive, and the concentration of executive power in an autocracy, are necessary consequences of the predominance of foreign over domestic politics. The process is attended by a decay of party spirit and party action, and an insistence on the part of the autocracy, whether it be a Kaiser or a Cabinet, that all effective party criticism is unpatriotic and verges on treason. An able writer, discussing the new foreign policy of Germany, summarises the point of view of the expansionists : " It is claimed by them that in foreign affairs the nation should stand as one man, that policies once entered upon by the Government should not be repudiated, and that criticism should be avoided as weakening the influence of the nation abroad. . . . It is evident that when the most important concerns of a nation are thus withdrawn from the field of party difference, party government itself must grow weak, as dealing no longer with vital affairs. . . . Thus, as the importance of the executive is enhanced, that of the legislative is lowered, and parliamentary action is looked down upon as the futile and irritating activity of unpractical critics. If the governmental measures are to be adopted inevitably, why not dispense with the irritating delay of parliamentary discussion ? "[1]

The Kaiser's speech at Hamburg, October 19, 1899, condenses the doctrine thus : " The face of the world has changed greatly during the last few years. What formerly required centuries is now accomplished in a few months. The task of Kaiser and Government has consequently grown beyond measure, and a solution will only be possible when the German people renounce party divisions. Standing in serried ranks behind the Kaiser, proud of their great fatherland, and conscious of their real worth, the Germans must watch the development of foreign States. They must make sacrifices for their position as a world-power, and, abandoning party spirit, they must stand united behind their prince and emperor."

Autocratic government in imperial politics naturally

[1] *World Politics*, by P. S. Reinsch, pp. 300, 301 (Macmillan & Co.).

reacts upon domestic government. The intricacy of the departmental work of the Home Office, the Board of Trade, of Education and other important offices has favoured this reaction, which has taken shape in government by administrative orders in accordance with large powers slipped into important statutes and not properly challenged or safeguarded amid the chaotic hurry in which most governments are driven in legislation. It is noticeable that in America a still more dangerous practice has sprung up, entitled "government by injunction," in which the judiciary is virtually empowered to issue decrees having the effect of laws with attendant penalties for specific acts.

In Great Britain the weakening of "party" is visibly attended by a decline of the reality of popular control. Just in proportion as foreign and colonial policy bulks more largely in the deliberative and administrative work of the State is government necessarily removed from the real control of the people. It is no mere question of economy of the time and energy of Parliament, though the dwindling proportion of the sessions devoted to consideration of domestic questions represents a corresponding decline of practical democracy. The wound to popular government penetrates far deeper. Imperialism, and the military, diplomatic, and financial resources which feed it, have become so far the paramount considerations of recent Governments that they mould and direct the entire policy, give point, colour and character to the conduct of public affairs, and overawe by continual suggestions of unknown and incalculable gains and perils the nearer and more sober processes of domestic policy. The effect on parliamentary government has been great, quick, and of palpable import, making for the diminution of the power of representative institutions. At elections the electorate is no longer invited to exercise a free, conscious, rational choice between the representatives of different intelligible policies; it is invited to endorse, or to refuse endorsement, to a difficult, intricate, and hazardous imperial and foreign policy, commonly couched in a few well-sounding general phrases, and supported by an appeal to the necessity of solidarity and continuity of national conduct—virtually a blind vote of confidence. In the deliberations of the House of Commons the power of the Opposition to oppose has been seriously and progressively impaired : partly by alteration in the rules of the House, which have diminished the right of full discussion of legislative measures in their several stages, and impaired the privileges of the Commons, viz., the right of discussing grievances upon votes of Supply, and of questioning ministers regarding the conduct of their offices ; partly by a forcible encroachment of the Government upon the rights and privileges formerly enjoyed by private members in moving resolutions and in introducing bills. This diminution of the power of opposition is only the first of a series of processes of concentration of power. The Government now claims for its measures the complete disposal of the time of the House whenever it judges such monopoly to be desirable.

Within the Government itself the same centripetal forces have been operative. "There can," writes Mr. Bryce, "be no doubt that the power of the Cabinet as against the House of Commons has grown steadily and rapidly, and it appears (1901) to be still growing."[1]

So the Cabinet absorbs the powers of the House, while the Cabinet itself has been deliberately and consciously expanded in size so as to promote the concentration of real power in an informal but very real "inner Cabinet," retaining some slight selective elasticity, but virtually consisting of the Prime Minister and the Foreign and

[1] *Studies in History and Jurisprudence,* Vol. i, p. 177.

Colonial Secretaries and the Chancellor of the Exchequer. This process of centralisation of power, which tends to destroy representative government, reducing the House of Commons to be little more than a machine for the automatic registration of the decrees of an unelected inner Cabinet, is chiefly attributable to Imperialism.[1] The consideration of delicate, uncertain intelligence affecting our relations with foreign Powers, the accepted necessity of secrecy in diplomacy, and of expeditious, unobtrusive action, seem to favour and even to necessitate a highly centralised autocratic and bureaucratic method of government.

Amid this general decline of parliamentary government the "party system" is visibly collapsing, based as it was on plain cleavages in domestic policy which have little significance when confronted with the claims and powers of Imperialism. If the party system is destined to survive in British politics, it can only do so by the consolidation of all sections opposed to the "imperialist" practices to which Liberal as well as Conservative ministries have adhered during recent years. So long as Imperialism is allowed to hold the field, the only real political conflict is between groups representing the divergent branches of Imperialism, the men upon the spot and the Home Government, the Asiatic interests of India and China and the forward policy in Africa, the advocates of a German alliance or a Franco-Russian alliance.

[1] An experienced observer thus records the effect of these changes upon the character and conduct of members of Parliament : " For the most part, as in the country, so in the House, the *political* element has waned as a factor. The lack of interest in constitutional matters has been conspicuous. . . . The 'Parliament man' has been disappearing ; the number of those desirous of furthering social and industrial reforms has been waning. On the other hand, those who have been anxious to grasp such opportunities of various kinds outside its work and duties as are afforded by membership of the House of Commons, and who are willing to support the Government in the division lobby without being called upon to do much more, came up in large numbers in 1895 and 1900, and now form a very large proportion, if not the majority, of the House of Commons " (Mr. John E. Ellis, M.P., *The Speaker*, June 7, 1902).

V

Imperialism and popular government have nothing in common : they differ in spirit, in policy, in method. Of policy and method I have already spoken ; it remains to point out how the spirit of Imperialism poisons the springs of democracy in the mind and character of the people. As our free self-governing colonies have furnished hope, encouragement, and leading to the popular aspirations in Great Britain, not merely by practical successes in the arts of popular government, but by the wafting of a spirit of freedom and equality, so our despotically ruled dependencies have ever served to damage the character of our people by feeding the habits of snobbish subservience, the admiration of wealth and rank, the corrupt survivals of the inequalities of feudalism. This process began with the advent of the East Indian nabob and the West Indian planter into English society and politics, bringing back with his plunders of the slave trade and the gains of corrupt and extortionate officialism the acts of vulgar ostentation, domineering demeanour and corrupting largesse to dazzle and degrade the life of our people. Cobden, writing in 1860 of our Indian Empire, put this pithy question : " Is it not just possible that we may become corrupted at home by the reaction of arbitrary political maxims in the East upon our domestic politics, just as Greece and Rome were demoralised by their contact with Asia ? "[1]

Not merely is the reaction possible, it is inevitable. As the despotic portion of our Empire has grown in area, a larger and larger number of men, trained in the temper and methods of autocracy as soldiers and civil officials in our Crown colonies, protectorates, and Indian Empire, reinforced by numbers of merchants, planters, engineers, and overseers, whose lives have been those of a superior caste living an

[1] Morley, *Life of Cobden*, Vol. ii, p. 361.

artificial life removed from all the healthy restraints of ordinary European society, have returned to this country, bringing back the characters, sentiments, and ideas imposed by this foreign environment. The South and South-West of England is richly sprinkled with these men, many of them wealthy, most of them endowed with leisure, men openly contemptuous of democracy, devoted to material luxury, social display, and the shallower arts of intellectual life. The wealthier among them discover political ambitions, introducing into our Houses of Parliament the coarsest and most selfish spirit of " Imperialism," using their imperial experience and connexions to push profitable companies and concessions for their private benefits, and posing as authorities so as to keep the yoke of Imperialism firmly fixed upon the shoulders of the " nigger." The South African millionaire is the brand most in evidence : his methods are the most barefaced, and his success, social and political, the most redoubtable. But the practices which are writ large in Rhodes, Beit, and their parliamentary confederates are widespread on a smaller scale ; the South of England is full of men of local influence in politics and society whose character has been formed in our despotic Empire, and whose incomes are chiefly derived from the maintenance and furtherance of this despotic rule. Not a few enter our local councils, or take posts in our constabulary or our prisons : everywhere they stand for coercion and for resistance to reform. Could the incomes expended in the Home Counties and other large districts of Southern Britain be traced to their sources, it would be found that they were in large measure wrung from the enforced toil of vast multitudes of black, brown, or yellow natives, by arts not differing essentially from those which supported in idleness and luxury imperial Rome.

It is, indeed, a nemesis of Imperialism that the arts

and crafts of tyranny, acquired and exercised in our unfree Empire, should be turned against our liberties at home. Those who have felt surprise at the total disregard or the open contempt displayed by the aristocracy and the plutocracy of this land for infringements of the liberties of the subject and for the abrogation of constitutional rights and usages have not taken sufficiently into account the steady reflux of this poison of irresponsible autocracy from our " unfree, intolerant, aggressive " Empire.

The political effects, actual and necessary, of the new Imperialism, as illustrated in the case of the greatest of imperialist Powers, may be thus summarised. It is a constant menace to peace, by furnishing continual temptations to further aggression upon lands occupied by lower races and by embroiling our nation with other nations of rival imperial ambitions ; to the sharp peril of war it adds the chronic danger and degradation of militarism, which not merely wastes the current physical and moral resources of the nations, but checks the very course of civilization. It consumes to an illimitable and incalculable extent the financial resources of a nation by military preparation, stopping the expenditure of the current income of the State upon productive public projects and burdening posterity with heavy loads of debt. Absorbing the public money, time, interest and energy on costly and unprofitable work of territorial aggrandisement, it thus wastes those energies of public life in the governing classes and the nations which are needed for internal reforms and for the cultivation of the arts of material and intellectual progress at home. Finally, the spirit, the policy, and the methods of Imperialism are hostile to the institutions of popular self-government, favouring forms of political tyranny and social authority which are the deadly enemies of effective liberty and equality.

CHAPTER II

THE SCIENTIFIC DEFENCE OF IMPERIALISM

I

THOUGH it can hardly be denied that the ambitions of individuals or nations have been the chief conscious motives in Imperialism, it is possible to maintain that here, as in other departments of human history, certain larger hidden forces operate towards the progress of humanity. The powerful hold which biological conceptions have obtained over the pioneers in the science of sociology is easily intelligible. It is only natural that the laws of individual and specific progress so clearly discerned in other parts of the animal kingdom should be rigorously applied to man ; it is not unnatural that the deflections or reversals of the laws of lower life by certain other laws, which only attain importance in the higher psychical reaches of the *genus homo*, should be underrated, misinterpreted, or ignored. The biologist who enters human history often finds himself confronted by intellectual antagonists who regard him as an interloper, and seek to raise the barrier between human and animal development. Indeed, from the ranks of the biological profession itself, scientists of such eminence as Huxley and A. R. Wallace have lent themselves to this separatism, distinguishing the ethical or spiritual progress of the human race from the general cosmic process, and endowing men with qualities and with laws of action different in kind from those which obtain in the rest of the animal kingdom. A reaction against the abrupt dogmatism of this position has led many others to an equally abrupt and equally dogmatic assertion of the laws of the lower forms of physical struggle and selection which explain or describe progress in lower animals as sufficient for all purposes of sociology.

Sociologists have shown themselves in some cases eager to accept this view, and apply it to defend the necessity, the utility, and even the righteousness of maintaining to the point of complete subjugation or extermination the physical struggle between races and types of civilization.

Admitting that the efficiency of a nation or a race requires a suspension of intestine warfare, at any rate à l'outrance, the crude struggle on the larger plane must, they urge, be maintained. It serves, indeed, two related purposes. A constant struggle with other races or nations is demanded for the maintenance and progress of a race or nation ; abate the necessity of the struggle and the vigour of the race flags and perishes. Thus it is to the real interest of a vigorous race to be " kept up to a high pitch of external efficiency by contest, chiefly by way of war with inferior races, and with equal races by the struggle for trade routes and for the sources of raw material and of food supply." " This," adds Professor Karl Pearson, " is the natural history view of mankind, and I do not think you can in its main features subvert it."[1]

Others, taking the wider cosmic standpoint, insist that the progress of humanity itself requires the maintenance of a selective and destructive struggle between races which embody different powers and capacities, different types of civilization. It is desirable that the earth should be peopled, governed, and developed, as far as possible, by the races which can do this work best, i.e. by the races of highest " social efficiency " ; these races must assert their right by

[1] *National Life from the Standpoint of Science*, p. 44 (Black, 1901).

conquering, ousting, subjugating, or extinguishing races of lower social efficiency. The good of the world, the true cause of humanity, demands that this struggle, physical, industrial, political, continue, until an ideal settlement is reached whereby the most socially efficient nations rule the earth in accordance with their several kinds and degrees of social efficiency. This principle is clearly enunciated by M. Edmond Demolins, who describes it as being " as indisputable as the law of gravitation.

" When one race shows itself superior to another in the various externals of domestic life, it *inevitably* in the long run gets the upper hand in public life and establishes its predominance. Whether this predominance is asserted by peaceable means or feats of arms, it is none the less, when the proper time comes, officially established, and afterwards unreservedly acknowledged. I have said that this law is the only thing which accounts for the history of the human race, and the revolutions of empires, and that, moreover, it explains and justifies the appropriation by Europeans of territories in Asia, Africa, and Oceania, and the whole of our colonial development."[1]

The western European nations with their colonies represent the socially efficient nations, in various degrees. Some writers, American and English, such as Professor Giddings and Mr. Kidd, believe that the Teutonic races, and in particular the Anglo-Saxon branches, represent the highest order of efficiency, in which notion they are supported by a little group of Anglophil Frenchmen.

This genuine and confident conviction about " social efficiency " must be taken as the chief moral support of Imperialism. " Human progress requires the maintenance of the race struggle, in which the weakest races shall go under while the ' socially efficient ' races survive and flourish :

[1] *Boers or British ?* p. 24.

we are the ' socially efficient ' race." So runs the imperialist argument.

Now, thus closely stated, the meaning of the term " socially efficient " becomes evident. It is simply the antithesis of " weak," and is equivalent to " strong in the struggle of life." Taken at the first blush it suggests admitted moral and intellectual virtues of some broad general kind, and is afterwards taken to imply such qualities. But applied in the present " natural history " sense it signifies nothing more or less than capacity to beat other races, who, from their failure, are spoken of as " lower." It is merely a repetition of the phrase " survival of the fittest," the meaning of which is clear when the question is put, " Fittest to do what ? " and the answer follows, " Fittest to survive."

It is true that " social efficiency " seems to imply much more than mere fighting capacity in war and trade, and, if we were to take into account all qualities which go to make a good society, we should include much more ; but from our present " natural history " standpoint it is evident that these must be excluded and only those included which aid directly in the struggle.

Giving, then, the proper value to the terms, it simply comes to this. " In the history of man, as throughout nature, stronger races have continually trampled down, enslaved, and exterminated other races." The biologist says : " This is so rooted in nature, including human nature, that it must go on." He adds : " It has been the prime condition and mode of progress in the past, therefore it is desirable it should go on. It must go on, it ought to go on."

So easily we glide from natural history to ethics, and find in utility a moral sanction for the race struggle. Now, Imperialism is nothing but this natural history doctrine regarded from the standpoint of one's own nation. We represent the socially efficient nation, we have conquered and acquired dominion and territory in the past : we must go on, it is our destiny, one which is serviceable to ourselves and to the world, our duty.

Thus, emerging from natural history, the doctrine soon takes on a large complexity of ethical and religious finery, and we are wafted into an elevated atmosphere of " imperial Christianity," a " mission of civilization," in which we are to teach " the arts of good government " and " the dignity of labour."

II

That the power to do anything constitutes a right and even a duty to do it, is perhaps the commonest, the most " natural " of temperamental fallacies. Even Professor Pearson does not avoid it, when, after an able vindication of the necessity of intra-race selection and of race struggle, he speaks of " our right to work the unutilised resources of earth, be they in Africa or in Asia."[1]

This belief in a " divine right " of force, which teachers like Carlyle, Kingsley, Ruskin did so much to foster, is primarily responsible for the transmutation of a natural history law into a moral enthusiasm.

Elsewhere I have dwelt with so much insistence on the more sordid and calculating motives which direct Imperialism that I am anxious here to do justice to the nobler aspects of the sentiment of Imperialism, interpreted through a naïve rendering of science into a gospel of arduous chivalry. Such a revelation is conveyed in the charming nature and buoyant career of Hubert Hervey, of the British South African Chartered Company, as rendered by his fellow-adventurer, Earl Grey. In his career we have Imperialism at its best in action, and what is better for our purpose, a

[1] *National Life*, p. 46.

most ingenuous and instructive attempt to set forth the gist of the imperialist philosophy.

"Probably every one would agree that an Englishman would be right in considering his way of looking at the world and at life better than that of the Maori or Hottentot, and no one will object in the abstract to England doing her best to impose her better and higher view on those savages. But the same idea will carry you much farther. In so far as an Englishman differs in essentials from a Swede or Belgian, he believes that he represents a more perfectly developed standard of general excellence. Yes, and even those nations nearest to us in mind and sentiment—German and Scandinavian—we regard on the whole as not so excellent as ourselves, comparing their typical characteristics with ours. Were this not so, our energies would be directed to becoming what they are. Without doing this, however, we may well endeavour to pick out their best qualities and add them to ours, believing that our compound will be superior to the foreign stock.

"It is the mark of an independent nation that it should feel thus. How far such a feeling is, in any particular case, justified, history alone decides. But it is essential that each claimant for the first place should put forward his whole energy to prove his right. This is the moral justification for international strife and for war, and a great change must come over the world and over men's minds before there can be any question of everlasting universal peace, or the settlement of all international differences by arbitration. More especially must the difficulty caused by the absence of a generally recognised standard of justice be felt in the case of contact between civilized and uncivilized races. Is there any likelihood of the gulf between the white and the black man being bridged within any period of time that we can foresee? Can there be any doubt that the white man must, and will, impose his superior civilization on the coloured races ? The rivalry of the principal European countries in extending their influence over other continents should lead naturally to the evolution of the highest attainable type of government of subject races by the superior qualities of their rulers."[1]

Here is the undiluted gospel of Imperialism, the fact of physical stuggle between white races, the fact of white subjugation of lower races, the necessity based upon these facts, the utility based upon the necessity, and the right or duty upon the utility. As a revelation of the purer spirit of Imperialism it is not to be bettered. The Englishman believes he is a more excellent type than any other man ; he believes that he is better able to assimilate any special virtues others may have ; he believes that this character gives him a right to rule which no other can possess. Mr. Hervey admits that the patriotic Frenchman, the German, the Russian feels in the same way his sense of superiority and the rights it confers on him ; so much the better (and here he is in line with Professor Pearson), for this cross-conviction and these cross-interests intensify the struggle of white races, and ensure the survival and progressive fitness of the fittest.

So long as we regard this Imperialism exclusively from the standpoint of the English, or any other single nation, its full *rationale* escapes us. It is essential to the maintenance of the struggle of nations, which is to quicken vigour and select the fittest or most efficient, that each competitor shall be stimulated to put forth his fullest effort by the same feelings regarding the superiority, the destiny, the rights and imperial duties of his country as the English imperialist entertains regarding England. And this is just what we seem to find.

[1] *Memoir of Hubert Hervey*, by Earl Grey (Arnold, 1899).

The Englishman is genuinely confident in the superior fitness of England for any work she may essay in the civilization of the world. This is the supreme principle of the imperialist statesman, so well expressed in Lord Rosebery's description of the British Empire as "the greatest secular agency for good the world has ever seen," and in Mr. Chamberlain's conviction[1] that "the Anglo-Saxon race is infallibly destined to be the predominant force in the history and civilization of the world." Of the superior competence of Englishmen for all purposes of government, quite irrespective of climatic, racial, or any other conditions, there is no touch of doubt in the average man. "Why, I suppose you imagine we could undertake to govern France better than Frenchmen can govern her ?" I heard put as an ironical poser in a discussion on British capacity. The triumphant retort, "Why, of course I do," was no rhetorical paradox, but a perfectly genuine expression of the real conviction of most Englishmen.

Now, the French Chauvinist, the German colonialist, the Russian Pan-Slavist, the American expansionist, entertain the same general conviction, with the same intensity, regarding the capacity, the destiny, the rights of their own nation. These feelings have, perhaps, come more clearly into the forefront of our national consciousness than in the case of any other nation, but events are rapidly educating the same imperial aspirations in all our chief industrial and political competitors.

"In our own day Victor Hugo declares France 'the saviour of nations,' and bursts out, 'Non, France, l'univers a besoin que tu vives ! Je le redis, la France est un besoin des hommes.' Villari, echoing the illustrious Gioberti, claims for Italy the primacy among nations. The Kaiser tells his people, 'Der alte gute Gott has always been on

[1] *Foreign and Colonial Speeches*, p. 6.

our side.' M. Pobyedonostseff points to the freedom of Russia from the shibboleths of a decadent civilization, and looks to the young and vigorous Slavonic stock as the residuary legatee of the treasures and conquests of the past. The Americans are not less confident than in the days of Martin Chuzzlewit that it is their mission to ' run this globe'."[1]

Nor are these barren sentiments ; in various parts of the world they have inspired young soldiers, politicians, and missionaries to a practical direction of the resources of France, Germany, Italy, Russia, the United States towards territorial expansion.

We are now in a position to restate and test the scientific basis of Imperialism regarded as a world-policy. The maintenance of a military and industrial struggle for life and wealth among nations is desirable in order to quicken the vigour and social efficiency of the several competitors, and so to furnish a natural process of selection, which shall give an ever larger and intenser control over the government and the economic exploitation of the world into the hands of the nation or nations representing the highest standard of civilization or social efficiency, and by the elimination or subjugation of the inefficient shall raise the standard of the government of humanity.

This statement withdraws the issue from the purely national—political, and from the distinctively ethical stand-points, referring it back to its scientific basis in the laws or analogies of biology.

Here we can profitably start from a statement of Professor K. Pearson. " History shows me one way, and one way only, in which a high state of civilization has been produced, namely, the struggle of race with race, and the survival of the physically and mentally fitter race. If men want to

[1] G. P. Gooch in *The Heart of the Empire*, p. 333

know whether the lower races of man can evolve a higher type, I fear the only course is to leave them to fight it out among themselves, and even then the struggle for existence between individual and individual, between tribe and tribe, may not be supported by that physical selection due to a particular element, on which, probably, so much of the Aryans' success depended."

Now, assuming that this is a true account of the evolution of civilization during the past, is it essential that the same methods of selection must dominate the future? or are there any forces which have been coming into play during the later periods of human history that deeply modify, suspend, and even reverse the operations of selective forces that dominate the rest of nature?

In the very work from which I quote, Professor Pearson furnishes a complete answer to his own contention for the necessity of this physical struggle between races.

In the last sentence of the passage given above, he seems to recognize the utility in lower races of the physical struggle for life between "individuals" in the same tribe. But his general position as a "socialist" is very different. In order that a tribe, a nation, or other society may be able to compete successfully with another society, the individual struggle for life within the society itself must be suspended. The conpetitive vigour, the social efficiency, of the nation requires a saving of the friction of individual competition for life or for the means of life. Now this is in itself a reversal of the generally recognized law of progress throughout the animal world, in which the struggle for food and other livelihood is held to be essential to the progress of the species, and this though every species is engaged in more or less direct competition for food, etc., with other species. Co-operation, social solidarity, is indeed recognized as an adjunct of progress in many of the higher species, but the struggle between individuals for a restricted supply of food or other necessaries is maintained as a leading instrument of progress by rejection of the physically unfit.

Now Professor Pearson justly recognizes and boldly admits the danger which attends the humanitarianism that has in large measure suspended the " struggle for life " among individuals, and has incited modern civilized nations to secure for all individuals born in their midst the food, shelter, and other necessaries enabling them to grow to maturity and to propagate their kind.

He sees quite clearly that this mere suspension of the individual struggle for life not only is not essential to the solidarity and efficiency of the nation, but that it impairs those virtues by burdening society with a horde of physical and moral weaklings, who would have been eliminated under earlier forms of the struggle for life. He rightly enforces the doctrine that a nation which is reproduced from its bad stock more than from its better stock is doomed to deterioration of physique and morale. It is as essential to the progress of man as to that of any other animal, as essential in the future as in the past, that reproduction shall be from the better stock and that the worst stock shall be eliminated. Humanitarianism and the sense of social solidarity by no means recognize, or even admit, that this condition should be sacrificed ; they merely impose new methods on the process of selection.

Irrational nature selects wastefully and with the maximum of pain and misery, requiring innumerable individuals to be born in order that they may struggle and perish. Rational humanity would economize and humanize the struggle by substituting a rational, social test of parenthood for the destruction of children by starvation, disease, or weakness.

To prevent reproduction from bad stock, however difficult and dangerous it may be, is obviously the first duty of an organized society, acting alike in its own self-defence and for the interests of its individual members. It is not necessary for the safety and progress of society that "unfit" children ˜hould die, it is necessary that they should not be born, and ultimately the society which prospers most in the character of its members will be the one which best fulfils this preventive duty.

Yet, when Professor Pearson passes from a society of individuals to the society of nations, which we call humanity, he insists upon retaining the older, cruder, irrational method of securing progress, the primitive struggle for physical existence. Why? If it is profitable and consistent with progress to put down the primitive struggle for life among individuals with one another, the family and tribal feuds which survive even in fairly developed societies, and to enlarge the area of social internal peace until it covers a whole nation, may we not go farther and seek, with hope, to substitute international peace and co-operation, first among the more civilized and more nearly related nations, and finally throughout the complete society of the human race? If progress is helped by substituting rational selection for the struggle for life within small groups, and afterwards within the larger national groups, why may we not extend the same mode of progress to a federation of European States, and finally to a world-federation? I am not now concerned with the grave practical difficulties besetting such an achievement, but with the scientific theory.

Although a certain sort of individual efficiency is sacrificed by repressing private war within a tribe or nation, it is rightly judged that the gain in tribal or national unity and efficiency outweighs that loss. May not a similar biological and rational economy be subserved by substituting government for anarchy among nations? We admit that a nation is strengthened by putting down internecine tribal warfare;

what finality attaches to the arbitrary social group we term a " nation " which obliges us to reverse the economy applicable to tribes when we come to deal with nations ?

Two objections are raised against this idea of internationalism. One is historical in its nature ; it consists in a denial that a society of nations does or can exist at the present time or in any future which concerns us. The physical and psychical relations which exist between nations, it is urged, have no real analogy with those existing between individuals or tribes within a nation. Society is dependent on a certain homogeneity of character, interests, and sympathies of those who form it. In the ancient world this was seldom found of sufficient strength save among close neighbours, and the city-state was the true social type ; the actual and positive relations of these city-states with one another were commonly those of war, modified by transitory compacts, which rarely led them into any truly national unity. In such a condition close-welded co-operation of citizens was essential as a condition of civic survival and progress, and a struggle for life between the several city-states was a means of progress in accordance with the biological law. The nation-state stands now where the city-state stood in ancient Greece or mediæval Italy ; there remains the same historical and even ethical necessity to retain the struggle between nations now as to retain the inter-civic struggle in earlier times.

Social psychologists attempt to fortify this position by laying emphasis upon the prime psychical condition of a national life. The possible area of a genuine society, a nation, is determined by the extension of a " consciousness of kind," an " ethical like-mindedness."[1] This may be applied as a limiting condition by a " little Englander " or as an expansive principle to justify imperial expansion,

[1] Professor Giddings, *Empire and Democracy*, pp. 10, 51.

according to the quantity and quality of like-mindedness taken as the basis of social unity in a " nation " or an " empire." The most precise statement of this doctrine in its application as a barrier to ethical and political internationalism is that of Dr. Bosanquet. " The nation-state is the widest organization which has the common experience necessary to found a common life."[2] He carries the finality of the national type of society so far as virtually to repudiate the ethical fact and the utility of the conception of humanity. " According to the current ideas of our civilization, a great part of the lives which are being lived and have been lived by mankind are not lives worth living, in the sense of embodying qualities for which life seems valuable to us. This being so, it seems to follow that *the object of our ethical idea of humanity is not really mankind as a single community*. Putting aside the impossibilities arising from succession in time, we see that no such identical experience can be pre-supposed in all mankind as is necessary to effective membership of a common society and exercise of a general will."[1] Though a subtle qualification follows, based on the duty of States to recognize humanity, not as a fact but as a type of life, " and in accordance with it to recognize and deal with the rights of alien individuals and communities," the real upshot of this line of thought is to emphasise the ethical self-sufficiency of a nation and to deny the validity of any practical standard of the conduct of nations towards one another, at any rate so far as the relations between higher and lower, or eastern and western, nations are concerned.

This view is stoutly supported by some sociologists and statesmen from the juridical standpoint. There can, we are told, be no real " rights " of nations because there exists no " sanction," no recognized tribunal to define and

[1] *The Philosophical Theory of the State*, p. 320.   [2] *Op. cit.* p. 329.

enforce rights.[1] The legal rigour of this position I am not greatly concerned to question. It may here suffice to say that the maintenance under ordinary conditions of treaty relations, international credit and exchange, a common postal, and within narrower limits, a common railway system, not to mention the actual machinery of conventions and conferences for concerted international action, and the whole unwritten law of war and international courtesies, embassies, consulates, and the like—all these things rest upon a basis of recognition of certain reciprocal duties, the neglect or violation of which would be punished by forfeiture of most favoured nations' treatment in the future, and by the reprobation and the possibly combined intervention of other States.

III

We have here at least a real beginning of effective international federation, with the rudiments of legal sanction for the establishment and enforcement of rights.

The studied ignoring of those vital facts in the more recent statecraft, and the reversion, alike of legal theorists and high politicians of the Bismarck school, to a nationalism which emphasises the exclusive rather than the inclusive aspect of patriotism and assumes the antagonism of nations as an all-important and a final fact, form the most dangerous and discreditable factor of modern politics. This conduct in politics we have already in part explained in our analysis of the economic driving forces that exhibit certain sectional interests and orders within the nation usurping the national will and enforcing their private advantages, which rest upon international antagonism, to the detriment of the national advantage, which is identical with that of other nations.

[1] On this point see the admirable chapter " International Rights " in L. T. Hobhouse's *Democracy and Reaction* (Unwin, 1904).

This obstinate halt in the evolution of such relations at the limit of political nationality now reached will be recognized as the most difficult of all present political phenomena for the future historian to explain. The community of interests between nations is so great, so multifarious, and so obvious, the waste, pain, and damage of conflicts so gross and palpable, that to those who do not understand the strong sectional control in every modern State it may well appear that some natural barriers, race, boundaries, or colour make any real extension of " society " outside the area of nationality impossible.

But to ascribe finality to nationalism upon the ground that members of different nations lack " the common experience necessary to found a common life " is a very arbitrary reading of modern history. Taking the most inward meaning of experience, which gives most importance to the racial and traditional characters that mark the divergences of nationality, we are obliged to admit that the fund of experience common to peoples of different nationality is growing with great rapidity under the numerous, swift, and accurate modes of intercommunication which mark the latest phases of civilization. It is surely true that the dwellers of large towns in all the most advanced European States, an ever-growing proportion of the total population, have, not merely in the externals of their lives, but in the chief formative influences of their reading, their art, science, recreation, a larger community of experience than existed a century ago among the more distant members of any single European nation, whether dwelling in country or in town. Direct intercommunication of persons, goods, and information is so widely extended and so rapidly advancing that this growth of " the common experience necessary to found a common life " beyond the area of nationality is surely the most mark-worthy feature of the age. Making, then, every due allowance for the subjective factors of national character which temper or transmute the same external phenomena, there surely exists, at any rate among the more conscious and more educated sections of the chief European nations, a degree of true " like-mindedness," which forms the psychical basis of some rudimentary internationalism in the field of politics. Indeed it is curious and instructive to observe that while some of those most insistent upon " like-mindedness " and " common experience," as the tests of a true social area, apply them in defence of existing nationalities and in repudiation of attempts to absorb alien nationalities, others, like Professor Giddings, apply them in the advocacy of expansion and Imperialism.

Surely there is a third alternative to the policy of national independence on the one hand, and of the right of conquest by which the more efficient nation absorbs the less efficient nation on the other, the alternative of experimental and progressive federation, which, proceeding on the line of greatest common experience, shall weave formal bonds of political attachment between the most " like-minded " nations, extending them to others as common experience grows wider, until an effective political federation is established, comprising the whole of " the civilized world," i.e. all those nations which have attained a considerable fund of that " common experience " comprised under the head of civilization.

This idea does not conflict with the preservation of what is really essential and valuable in nationalism, nor does it imply a suspension or abolition of any form of struggle by which the true character of a nation may express itself, in industry, in politics, in art or literature.

If it be objected that the requisite amount of " like-mindedness " or " common experience " does not exist

even among the nations most subjected to modern assimil-
ative influences, that the forces of racial and national
antagonism even there preclude any truly effective union,
I can only repeat that this is a matter for experiment, and
that the experiment has never been tried. Racial and
national antagonisms have been so fed, fostered, and
inflamed, for the class and personal ends and interests
which have controlled politics, that the deeper underlying
sympathies and community of different peoples have
never been permitted free expression, much less political
assertion. The most potent and pervasive forces in the
industrial, intellectual, and moral life of most European
races, so far as the masses of the peoples are concerned, have
so rapidly and closely assimilated during the last century
as of necessity to furnish a large common body of thought
and feeling, interests and aspirations which furnish a
" soul " for internationalism.

The main economic conditions affecting the working life
of the masses of the peoples, both in town and country,
on the one hand, the matter and methods of education
through the school, the church, the press upon the other,
show features of similarity so much stronger and more
numerous than those of difference as to make it a safe
assertion that the " peoples " of Europe are far closer akin
in actual interests than their governments, and that this
common bond is already so strong as to furnish a solid and
stable foundation for political federal institutions, if only
the obstruction of class governments could be broken down
and the real will of the peoples set in the seat of authority.
To take the commonest of concrete instances, it is at least
probable that the body of the workers in different countries
who fight and pay for wars would refuse to fight and pay in
the future if they were allowed to understand the real
nature of the issues used to inflame them.

If this view is correct, the mere facts that wars still occur and that national animosities are continually flaring up must not be taken as proof that sufficient common sympathy and experience does not exist between the different nations to render impossible a suspension of physical conflict and the establishment of a political machinery required to maintain peace.

To hold this position it is not necessary to exaggerate the extent of this international community of interests. If any considerable amount of real community exists, it furnishes the spirit which should and might inform a body of political institutions. Here is the significance of the recent[1] Hague Conference, alike in its successes and its failure. Its success, the mere fact that it was held and the permanent nucleus of internationalism it created, attests a real and felt identity of interests among different nations in the maintenance of peace ; its failure and the open derision expressed by many politicians merely indicate the presence in high places of cliques and classes opposed in their interests and feelings to those of the peoples, and the necessity of dethroning these enemies of the people if the new cause of internationalism is to advance. Secure popular government, in substance and in form, and you secure internationalism : retain class government, and you retain military Imperialism and international conflicts.

IV

In following out the psychical argument against regarding nations as final social areas, I seem to have wandered very far from the biological basis, the alleged necessity of maintaining conflicts between nations for purposes of " natural selection." In reality I have come round precisely

[1] 1901.

to the point of divergence. Assuming it were possible to enthrone the will of the peoples and so to secure institutions of internationalism with a suspension of war, would the individuality of a nation suffer, would it lose vigour, become less efficient and perish ? Is the maintenance of physical conflict essential to the " natural selection " of nations ?

Turn to the suspension of the cruder physical struggle which takes place in the evolution of tribal or national solidarity. As such national organization becomes stronger and more skilful the ravages of intestine strife, starvation, and certain diseases cease to be selective instruments, and the kind of individual fitness which was tested by them is superseded ; the vast expenditure of individual energy formerly engaged in protecting life and in securing necessaries of life is reduced to insignificant dimensions ; but the struggle for individual life is not abated, it is simply shifted on to higher planes than that of bare animal existence, nourishment and propagation. Instead of struggling for these simpler vital ends, individuals now struggle with all the extra energy spared from the earlier struggles for other ends of an enlarged and more complex life, for comfort and wealth, for place and personal honour, for skill, knowledge, character, and even higher forms of self-expression, and for services to their fellow-men, with whom they have identified themselves in that expanded individuality we term altruism or public spirit.

Individuality does not suffer but greatly gains by the suppression of the lower struggle ; there is more energy, greater scope for its expression, a wider field of close competitors ; and higher and more varied forms of fitness are tested and evoked. It is not even true that the struggle ceases to be physical ; the strain and the support of the higher forms of struggle, even in the topmost intellectual and moral planes, are largely physical ; the health and nervous energy which take part in the struggles of the law or literature or on any intellectual arena are chief requisites if not the supreme determinant of success. In all the higher forms of struggle an elimination of the physically unfit is still maintained, though the criteria of physical unfitness are not quite the same as in the primitive human struggles. How arbitrary are the convenient distinctions between physical, intellectual, and moral qualities and defects is nowise better illustrated than in the elaborate methods which modern complex civilization evolves for the detection, degradation, and final extinction of bad stock whose " degeneracy " is attested not less by physical than by mental and moral stigmata. The struggle for physical fitness never flags, but the physical forms part of a higher and more complex test of character determined by a higher standard of social utility. The point is this : national government, or State socialism, using the term in its broad sense, as a coercive and educative force, does not, in so far as it is wisely exercised, diminish the individual struggle, repress individual vigour, reduce the arena for its display. It does just the opposite ; it quickens and varies the struggle ; by equalising certain opportunities it keeps a fairer ring, from which chance or other factors alien to personal fitness are excluded ; it admits on more equal terms a larger number of competitors, and so furnishes a better test of fitness and a more reliable selection of the fittest.

Professor Pearson rightly urges that truly enlightened national government will insist on mending the slow, painful, and irregular elimination of bad stock which goes on through progressive degeneracy by substituting some rational control of parentage, at least to the extent of preventing through public education, or if necessary by law, the propagation of certain surely recognized unfitnesses.

Does a nation thus firmly planted in rational self-government, with individual competition within its ranks conducted most keenly upon a wide variety of different fields, furnishing the keenest incentive to the education and display of every kind of personal originality, really require a maintenance of the crude form of physical struggle with other nations in order to maintain its character and progress ? If individuality does not disappear with the removal of the cruder struggle for life within the nation, why should the valid force of nationality disappear if a corresponding change takes place in the nature of international conflict ?

Biology furnishes no reason for believing that the competition among nations must always remain a crude physical struggle, and that the substitution of " rational " for " natural " selection among individual members of a nation cannot be extended to the selection of nations and of races.

V

The history of past nations indeed gives an appearance of natural necessity to imperial expansion and to the military policy which is its instrument, and many who deplore this necessity accept it. An American writer in a brilliant monograph[1] argues the perpetual necessity of wars of conquest and of the Imperialism which such wars express, as following from " the law of decreasing returns." A population on a limited area of land not only tends to grow but actually grows faster than the food supply that is available ; improvement in the arts of cultivation does not enable a people to obtain full subsistence for its growing population, hence a natural and necessary pressure for access to new rich land, and conflicts with and victories over neighbours who seek to hold their own, or are even

[1] " War and Economics," by Professor E. van Dyke Robinson, *Political Science Quarterly*, Dec. 1900.

actuated by the same needs of territorial expansion. Hunger is a necessary spur to migration, and where emigrants, planting themselves successfully upon new fertile lands, formerly unoccupied or occupied by people whom they have subjugated, desire to retain the political union with the mother country, an unlimited expansion of national areas ensues. Whether such expansion takes shape in genuine colonization or in what is here properly distinguished as Imperialism, involving centralized government and forcible control of " inferior races," matters little to this wide argument. The essence of this policy is the acquisition of an expanding area for food supply. A nation with growing population must either send a constant flow of population into other lands to grow food for themselves, or, failing this, it must produce at home an ever-growing surplus of manufactures which evade the law of decreasing returns and find markets for them, so as to obtain payment in food from foreign lands, which, in their turn, are thus forced more quickly to experience the pinch of the same natural law. As more nations pursue this course they either realize directly the pressure of the law driving them to find new lands for their surplus population, or they find themselves embroiled in an ever fiercer competition with rival manufacturing nations seeking a share in an over-stocked or too slowly expanding market for manufactures. Imperialism lies in both directions, and cannot be avoided. " The cause of war is as permanent as hunger itself, since both spring from the same source, the law of diminishing returns. So long as that persists, war must remain, in the last analysis, a national business undertaking, designed to procure or preserve foreign markets, that is, the means of continued growth and prosperity. ' Chacun doit grandir ou mourir'. "[1]

[1] Robinson, *Political Science Quarterly*, p. 622.

Now the finality of this alleged necessity has often been subjected to incidental criticism, so far as Great Britain is concerned. Imperialism, it has been shown, is not in fact necessitated in order to obtain by trade an increased food supply which should keep pace with the growth of British population, nor has it chiefly been engaged in forwarding such trade; still less is it engaged in finding land upon which our surplus population may subsist and multiply.

But the validity of the whole argument from natural history is contestable. As man grows in civilization, i.e. in the art of applying reason to the adjustment of his relations with his physical and social environment, he obtains a corresponding power to extricate himself from the necessity which dominates the lower animal world. He can avoid the necessity of war and expansion in two ways, by a progressive mitigation of the law of diminishing returns in agriculture and the extractive arts, and by limiting the rate of growth of population. The tendency of rational civilization is to employ both methods. It may fairly be maintained that reason is educated in individual men, and is applied to further a co-operative policy, chiefly by acts of choice which are directed to avoid the hardships and perils of war and the expansive practices. In animal life, and in man just so far as he resembles other animals, war and extension of territory form the only means of providing for a growth of population which is determined by a mere interaction of sexual instincts and physical conditions of environment. But from very early times this dominion of irrational forces, which finds direct expression in " the law of diminishing returns," is qualified by two sets of checks. On the one hand, improvements in agriculture and the beginnings of trade increase the quantity of human life which a given piece of land is able to support; on the other, customs relating to marriage and maintenance of children, often of a degraded character, such as exposure or infanticide, are added to the " natural " checks upon increase of population. Both forces represent the crude beginnings of " reason " or conscious human policy in its struggle to overcome the play of the non-rational forces of nature. Throughout history, so far as it is known, these rational forces have been so slow and feeble in their application as only to moderate or postpone the operation of " the law of decreasing returns." But this need not always continue to be the case. There is some ground to believe that both sets of rational checks may in the future be amply adequate to suspend or overcome the limitations of matter so far as the food supply of a nation on a given area is concerned. Progress in agriculture even of the most progressive nations of the past was very slow : modern science, which has achieved such marvels in revolutionizing the manufacturing and transport industries, is beginning more and more to concentrate its power on agriculture in such wise that the pace of progress in this art may be vastly accelerated. When the sciences of agricultural chemistry and botany are adequately reinforced by mechanics, scientific method being duly guided and enriched by garnering the empirical wisdom of great agricultural races whose whole practical genius has been centred for countless ages on minute cultivation, like the Chinese, and when to such improved knowledge of agricultural arts is added a perfection of co-operative labour for those processes where this yields a true economy, the possibilities of intensive cultivation are virtually unlimited. These new conditions of a national policy of agriculture are themselves so important as to make it easily conceivable that a nation keenly set upon utilizing them might for a long time to come reverse the operation of " the law of diminishing returns " extracting from its own proper lands an increasing stock of food to meet its "natural" growth of population without a more than proportionate increase of labour engaged in agriculture. In face of recent experiments in intensive and scientific agriculture and the practical substitution of skilled gardening for unskilled farming, it is impossible to deny that such a triumph of the laws of mind over the laws of matter is probable in the most highly intelligent peoples. There are already manifested throughout Gteat Britain certain signs of such a set towards agriculture as took place in England during the middle of the eighteenth century and led them to relatively great improvements in crop growing and stock breeding. If a brief fashion and sportive interest on the part of a small well-to-do class could then produce what is not wrongly described as an "agricultural revolution," what might not be achieved now by vastly greater numbers, capital, and intelligence directed in a public policy and wielding the accumulated knowledge of modern science? Many causes consciously contribute towards such a brilliant revival of British agriculture. The growing sense of the hygienic and military perils which attend a nation of town dwellers, whose powers of forcible resistance are impaired in just proportion as their dependence upon precarious foreign supplies of food increases, is driving the issue of restoring a people to the land into the forefront of politics. Modern scientific transport, hitherto centripetal in its main economy, now seems to tend more to become centrifugal, while the wider spread of culture does something, and may do much, to cause a moral and æsthetic revolt against the life and work of towns. A careful and drastic system of land reform which should aim at the net economy of individual enterprise and co-operative aid for agriculture is of course in Great Britain a prior condition to all rapid and effective progress. All these conditions are within the power of man, and belong to rational policy; once secured, it is at least probable that private incentives to gain, bringing brain and capital to bear upon the land, might in this or any other industrial country produce so vast an increase of the productiveness of the soil as to destroy completely all speciousness which history attaches to the necessity of expansion for purposes of food supply.

It is not necessary here to discuss the part played respectively by public policy and private initiative in the development of this economy of intensive cultivation. It is sufficient to insist that it furnishes the larger half of a complete answer to the alleged natural necessity of expansion. The other half has reference to a rational control of the growth of population, which must in any sound national economy tend more and more to replace the wasteful and cruel prodigality which nature unchecked by reason here as elsewhere displays. However difficult it may be, rational control of the quantity and quality of population is quite essential to the physical and moral progress of a species which has striven successfully to suspend or stay the cruel and wasteful checks which disease, famine, pestilence, internecine warfare, and early savage usages employed in the struggle for existence. To stay the "natural" checks, and to refuse to substitute "rational" checks, is to promote not merely the unrestricted growth of population, but the survival and multiplication of the physically and morally unfit, the least effective portion of the population, which is able to be born, reared, and to propagate its kind. How far the operation of the great public policy of preventing the propagation of certain definite forms of unfitness can best be left to the free play of individual interest and discretion, illuminated by the growing knowledge of biological science, or how far such private determination must be reinforced by public pressure, is a matter with which we need not here concern ourselves.

But there is every reason to believe that both quantitative and qualitative checks upon the " natural " growth of population are already operative in modern civilized communities, that they are already appreciably affecting the general growth of population, and that their operation is likely to continue in the future. With the spread of biological and moral education the methods of moderating the growth of population may be expected to come more truly " rational," and in particular the increasing economic liberty and enlightenment of women will contribute to the efficacy of this reasonable self-restraint. This second check upon the false necessity assigned to the law of decreasing returns is not unrelated to the first. It is, in fact, its true complement. Taken by itself the improvement in methods of obtaining food might not suffice to do more than to postpone or hold in check for a period the law of limitation of the food supply obtainable from a national area. But if the same forces of human reason which substitute intensive for extensive cultivation of the soil are at work imposing the same substitution in the cultivation of the species, checking the merely quantitative increase in order to secure a higher quality of individuation, this mutual reinforcement may secure the triumph of rational policy over the untamed forces of natural history.

I have laboured this issue at some length because it is required in order to bring home the distinctively rational character of that choice of national life against which Imperialism sins so fatally. There is no natural necessity for a civilized nation to expand the area of its territory, in order either to increase its production of food and other forms of material wealth, or to find markets for its increased products. Progress, alike for the nation and for the individual, consists in substituting everywhere an intensive or qualitative for an extensive or quantitative economy. The low-skilled farmer is given to spread his capital and labour over a large area of poorly cultivated land, wherever a large quantity of free or cheap land is available; the skilled, competent farmer obtains a larger net return by concentrating his productive power upon a smaller area scientifically cultivated, recognizing that the best use of his productive resources imposes a limit on the size of his farm. So with the economy of national resources—the craving and the necessity of expansion are signs of barbarism; as civilization advances and industrial methods become more highly skilled and better differentiated, the need for expansion of territory is weakened, the progress of the nation concerns itself more and more with the intensive or qualitative development of its national resources. Size of territory can never be eliminated as a condition of progress, but it becomes relatively less important with each step from barbarism to civilization, and the idea of indefinite expansion as necessary or good is opposed to reason and sane policy. This was recognized by the most profound of ancient thinkers. " There is," wrote Aristotle, " a certain degree of greatness fit for States as for all other things, living creatures, plants, instruments, for each has its proper virtue and faculty, when neither very little nor yet excessively great."[1] That the tendency has ever been to excess is the commonplace of history. The true greatness of nations has been educated by the concentrated skill in the detailed development of limited national resources which the contracted area of the State has developed in them. " It is to the burning vitality of compact, independent nations, the strong heart in the small body, to Judæa and to Athens, to Rome the republic, to the free cities of Italy, Germany,

[1] *Politics*, vii. 4.

and Flanders, to France, to Holland, and to England the island, that we owe the highest achievements in the things that make life most worth living."[1]

If imperial expansion were really nothing other than a phase of the natural history of a nation it would be as idle to protest against it as to argue with an earthquake. But the policy of civilized States differs from that of uncivilized States in resting more largely upon deliberate conscious choice, partaking more definitely of the character of conduct. The same growth of collective reason which makes it technically possible for a nation to subsist and prosper by substituting an intensive for an extensive economy of national resources enables it by deliberate exercise of will to resist the will of the older " destiny " by which nations attaining a certain degree of development were led by a debilitating course of Imperialism to final collapse.

VI

Thus met, the biological argument is sometimes turned on to another track.

" If these nations," it is argued, " are no longer called upon to struggle for food, and check their growth of population while they increase their control over their material supplies, they will become effete for purposes of physical struggle ; giving way to an easy and luxurious life, they will be attacked by lower races multiplying freely and maintaining their military vigour, and will succumb in the conflict." This is the danger indicated by Mr. C. H. Pearson in his interesting book *National Life and Character*. The whole argument, however, rests on a series of illusions regarding actual facts and tendencies.

It is not true that the sole object and result of the

[1] *Imperium et Libertas*, by Bernard Holland, p. 12.

stoppage of individual warfare has been to increase the efficiency of the nation for the physical struggle with other nations. As man has grown from barbarism towards civilization, the struggle to adapt his material and social environment to purposes of better livelihood and life has continuously tended to replace the physical struggle for the land and food supply of other nations. This is precisely the triumph of intensive over extensive cultivation : it implies a growing disposition to put that energy which formerly went to war into the arts of industry, and a growing success in the achievement. It is the need of peaceful, steady, orderly co-operation for this work, as the alternative to war, and not the needs of war itself, that furnishes the prime motive towards a suspension of internecine struggles, at any rate in most societies. This is a matter of pivotal importance in understanding social evolution. If the sole or main purpose of suspending individual conflict was to strengthen the purely military power of a tribe or nation, and the further evolution of society aimed at this sort of social efficiency, it might well be attended by the decay of individual freedom and initiative, by the sacrifice of individuality to a national life. The fact that this result has not occurred, that in modern civilized nations there exist far more individual freedom, energy, and initiative than in more primitive societies, attests the truth that military efficiency was not the first and sole object of social organization. In other words, the tendency of growing civilization on the national scale has been more and more to divert the struggle for life from a struggle with other nations to a struggle with environment, and so to utilize the fruits of reason as to divert a larger and larger proportion of energy to struggles for intellectual, moral, and æsthetic goods rather than for goods which tax the powers of the earth, and which, conforming to the law of diminishing returns are apt to bring them into conflict with other nations.

As nations advance towards civilization it becomes less needful for them to contend with one another for land and food to support their increasing numbers, because their increased control of the industrial arts enables them to gain what they want by conquering nature instead of conquering their fellow-men.

This truth does not indeed disclose itself readily with its full brilliancy to the eyes of modern civilized peoples, whose greed for foreign wealth and foreign lands seems as fruitful a source of war as in more primitive times. The illusion that it is necessary and advantageous to fight for new territory and distant markets, while leaving most imperfectly developed the land and markets of their own nation, is slow to be dispelled. Its sources have been already explored ; it has been traced to the dominance of class interests in national politics. Democracy alone, if it be attainable, will serve to fasten on the national mind the full economy of substituting the inner struggle with the natural environment for the outer struggle with other nations.

If, as seems possible, the civilized white nations, gradually throwing off the yoke of class governments whose interests make for war and territorial expansion, restrict their increase of population by preventing reproduction from bad stock, while they devote their energies to utilizing their natural resources, the motives of international conflict will wane, and the sympathetic motives of commerce and friendly intercourse will maintain permanent peace on a basis of international union.

Such a national economy would not only destroy the chief motives of war, it would profoundly modify the industrial struggle in which governments engage. Democracies chiefly concerned with developing their own markets would not need to spend men and money in fighting for the chance of inferior and less stable foreign markets. Such rivalry as was retained would be the rivalry not of nations but of individual manufacturers and merchants within the nation ; the national aspect of industrial warfare, by tariffs and bounties and commercial treaties, would disappear. For the dangers and hostilities of national commercial policies are due, as we have seen, almost entirely to the usurpation of the authority and political resources of the nations by certain commercial and financial interests. Depose these interests, and the deep, true, underlying harmonies of interest between peoples, which the prophets of Free Trade dimly perceived, will manifest themselves, and the necessity of permanent industrial warfare between nations will be recognized as an illusion analogous in nature and origin to the illusion of the biological necessity of war.

The struggle for life is indeed a permanent factor in social progress, selection of the physically fit is a necessity, but as men become more rational they rationalize the struggle, substituting preventive for destructive methods of selection, and raising the standard of fitness from a crudely physical robustness to one which maintains physical endurance as the raw material of higher psychical activities. Thus, while men no longer fight for food, their personal fitness is maintained, the struggle and the fitness are both raised to a higher plane. If this can take place in the struggle of individuals, it can take place in the struggle of nations. The economy of internationalism is the same as that of nationalism. As individuality does not disappear, but is raised and quickened by good national government, so nationality does not disappear but is raised and quickened by internationalism.

War and commercial tariffs are the crudest and most

wasteful forms of national struggles, testing the lowest forms of national fitness. Let international government put down wars and establish Free Trade, the truly vital struggles of national expression will begin. As in the case of individuals, so now of nations, the competition will be keener upon the higher levels ; nations having ceased to compete with guns and tariffs will compete with feelings and ideas.

Whatever there is of true original power and interest in the Celtic, the Teutonic, the various blends of Latin and Slavonic races can only bear its fruit in times of peace.

So far as nationality or race has any distinct character or value for itself and for the world, that value and character are expressed through work. Hitherto the absorption of so much national energy upon military, and in later times rude industrial occupations, has checked the higher forms of national self-expression ; while the permanent hostility of international relations has chilled the higher intercourse and prevented what is really great and characteristic in the national achievements of art, literature, and thought from penetrating other nations, and so by subtle educative processes laying the foundation of true feelings of humanity, based, as such feelings must be, not on vague imaginative sympathy, but upon common experience of life and a common understanding. Peaceful intercourse between nations is thus not merely the condition, but the powerful stimulus of national energy and achievement in the higher arts of life ; for the self-appreciation of national pride can never furnish so wholesome an incentive or so sound a criterion of human excellence as the impartial judgment of civilized humanity, no longer warped by baser patriotic prejudices, but testing what is submitted to it by the impartial universal standard of humanity. A few rare individual men of genius in art and literature, a few more in science and in religion, have broken the barriers of nationality and have become fertilizing, humanizing forces in other nations—such men as Jesus, Buddha, Mahomet, Homer, Shakespeare, Plato, Aristotle, Kant, Copernicus, Newton, Darwin. A larger number of great men have exercised some real and abiding influence upon the little world of science and letters which in the middle ages had attained an internationalism lost in the rise of militant nationalism and being slowly rediscovered in our own age.

But outside these conquests of personal genius the broad streams of national influence and achievement which might have fertilized the wide plains of the intellectual world have been confined within their narrow national channels. Nationalism as a restrictive and exclusive force, fostering political and industrial enmities and keeping down the competition of nationalities and races to the low level of military strife, has everywhere checked the free intercourse requisite for the higher kinds of competition, the struggle of languages, literatures, scientific theories, religious, political, and social institutions, and all the arts and crafts which are the highest and most important expressions of national as of individual life.

VII

This thought unearths the lowest root fallacy of the crude biological sociology, the assumption that there is one sort of national efficiency and that it is tested by a contest of military or commercial power. The only meaning that can be given to the " social efficiency " of a nation identifies it with the power it displays of adapting itself to its physical environment and of altering that environment to help the adaptation ; the attainments in religion, law, politics, intellectual life, industry, etc., are the expressions of this social efficiency. Bearing this in mind, it is evident that for concrete purposes of comparison there are many kinds of social efficiency, and that the notion that civilization is a single beaten track, upon which every nation must march, and that social efficiency, or extent of civilization, can be measured by the respective distances the nations have gone, is a mischievous delusion.

The true social efficiency, or civilization, of a nation only shows itself in its more complex achievements and activities. The biologist who understood his science would recognize that a true test of the efficiency of nations demanded that the conflict of nations should take place not by the more primitive forms of fight and the ruder weapons in which nations are less differentiated, but by the higher forms of fight and the more complex intellectual and moral weapons which express the highest degree of national differentiation. This higher struggle, conducted through reason, is none the less a national struggle for existence, because in it ideas and institutions which are worsted die, and not human organisms. The civilization of the world can only proceed upon the higher planes on condition that this struggle of national ideals and institutions is waged by a free field of competitors, and this struggle cannot be effectively maintained unless the lower military and industrial struggles cease.

Biology always demands as a condition of progress the competition of individuals, but as reason grows in the nation it closes the ring and imposes laws, not to stop the struggle, but to make it a fairer test of a fuller form of individual fitness. Biology demands as a condition of world-progress that the struggle of nations or races continue ; but as the world grows more rational it will in similar fashion rationalize the rules of that ring, imposing a fairer test of forms of national fitness.

The notion of the world as a cock-pit of nations in which round after round shall eliminate feebler fighters and leave in the end one nation, the most efficient, to lord it on the dung-hill, has no scientific validity. Invoked to support the claims of militant nationalism, it begins by ignoring the very nature and purposes of national life, assuming that uniformity of character and environment which are the negation of nationalism.

The belief that with the stoppage of war, could it be achieved, national vigour must decay, is based on a complete failure to recognize that the lower form of struggle is stopped for the express purpose and with the necessary result that the higher struggle shall become possible. With the cessation of war, whatever is really vital and valuable in nationality does not perish ; on the contrary, it grows and thrives as it could not do before, when the national spirit out of which it grows was absorbed in baser sorts of struggle.

Internationalism is no more opposed to the true purposes of nationalism than socialism within the nation, rightly guided, is hostile to individualism. The problem and its solution are the same. We socialize in order that we may individuate ; we cease fighting with bullets in order to fight with ideas.

All the essentials of the biological struggle for life are retained, the incentive to individual vigour, the intensity of the struggle, the elimination of the unfit and the survival of the fittest.

The struggle has become more rational in mode and purpose and result, and reason is only a higher form of nature.

VIII

The shortsightedness of this school of biological sociologists is nowhere more strikingly displayed than by the exclusive attention they pay to the simpler form of struggle, the direct conflict of individuals and species, to the exclusion of the important part played by " crossing " as a means of progress throughout organic life.

The law of the fertility of " crosses " as applied to civilization or " social efficiency " alike on the physical and psychical plane requires, as a condition of effective operation, internationalism. It is of course true that throughout history the " crossing " of national types has been largely achieved by means of war, conquest, and subjugation. But this, though subserving progress in the long run, has been a most wasteful, indirect, and unsafe method, the selection being determined by no clear view of the future or of any higher purpose of social efficiency. Just in proportion as internationalism promotes free intercourse between nations for higher purposes of peaceful interest, will blending of races by intermarriage be determined on grounds of affinity more fruitful of improved racial efficiency, and new modifications of species more numerous and more novel will compete with one another as factors in the civilization of the world, raising the character and intensity of the competition and enhancing the pace of human progress.

Nay, we may carry the biological analogy still farther, following the insistence of Professor Pearson regarding the necessity of bringing direct social pressure, of public opinion or of law, to prevent the fatal process of breeding from " bad stock." If the ordinary processes of physical degeneracy within the nation do not suffice for the elimination of bad stock, but must be supplemented by some direct prohibition of bad parentage, it might be necessary in the interests of humanity that similar measures should be enforced upon the larger scale by the mandates of organized humanity. As lower individuals within a society perish by contact with a civilization to which they cannot properly assimilate themselves, so " lower races " in some instances disappear by similar contact with higher races whose diseases and physical vices prove too strong for them. A rational stirpiculture in the wide social interest might, however, require a repression of the spread of degenerate or unprogressive races, corresponding to the check which a nation might place upon the propagation from bad individual stock. With the other moral and practical issues involved in such a proposal we need not here concern ourselves ; regarded exclusively from a biological standpoint, that course would seem to follow from the application of direct rational rejection of bad stock upon the smaller scale of national life. The importance of this consideration rests upon the fact that this rejection of unsound racial stock implies the existence of an international political organization which has put down war and has substituted this rational for the cruder national selection and rejection of races.

Whether a nation or a society of nations will ever proceed as far as this, or, going farther, will attempt the fuller art of stirpiculture, encouraging useful " crosses " of families or races, may be matter of grave doubt ; but if the maintenance and improvement of the national stock ever warranted such experiments, we are entitled to insist that logic would justify the application of the same rule in the society of nations.

Again, while it is questionable how far the law of the utility of cross-fertilization is transferable from the world of physical organisms to the psychical realm in its literal bearing, the more general applicability cannot be disputed. That scientific theories, religious, social, and political arts and institutions gain by free, friendly, vital intercourse with other theories, arts and institutions, undergoing serviceable accretions, excretions, and modifications, is a commonplace of intellectual life. Whether, therefore, we regard the contact of ideas and feelings and the arts they animate as a direct struggle for existence, in which the worse or falser perish and the better and truer survive, or as a friendly intercourse in which each selects and assimilates something from the others, internationalism is as essential to the efficiency of these processes as nationalism itself.

It is only when we realize the true nature of this spread and fertilization of ideas, arts, and institutions, the riper fruits of the spirit of a nation, that we realize the legitimate as distinguished from the illegitimate expansion, the valid significance of empire. When nations compete to take one another's lives or land or trade, the dominion which the conqueror establishes has no element of permanence ; another turn of the military or commercial tide wipes out the victory and leaves scarce a ripple in the sands. But the influence exerted through acts of peace is more lasting, more penetrating, and more glorious. Shakespeare, Byron, Darwin, and Stevenson have done incomparably more for the influence of England in the history of the world than all the statesmen and soldiers who have won victories or annexed new provinces. Macaulay has well said it, " There is an empire exempt from all natural sources of decay—that empire is the imperishable empire of our art and our morals, our literature and our law." This antagonism between the extensive empire and the intensive empire is not rhetorical, it is grounded upon biological necessities.

The essential conditions of the lower struggle for the life and land and trade of others preclude the higher and more profitable competition of ideas by which the empire of the national mind is extended : it is not merely the economy of energy which determines that the national vigour cannot at the same time engage effectively in both struggles ; but, far more important, the very nature of the lower struggle drives each nationality to feed upon itself in insolent, exclusive pride, inhibiting the receptivity of other nations.

Effective internationalism is the only sound basis of competition and rational selection among nations. In the cruder form of the human struggle, accident, or numbers, or some primitive force or cunning, may secure the success of a people whose " social efficiency " is of a low order, impermanent and unproductive, while it stamps out or checks the growth of a people whose latent powers of achievement and capacities of progress are far superior. Only in proportion as racial or national selection is rationally guided and determined does the world gain security against such wastes and such calamities. An international government alone can furnish adequate protection to weak but valuable nationalities, and can check the insolent brutality of powerful aggressors, preserving that equality of oppotunities for national self-expression which is as essential to the commonwealth of nations as to the welfare of the several nations.

Only by raising the crude, fragmentary, informal, often insincere beginning of international government into a stronger, more coherent, and more complex authority can the struggle for life proceed upon the highest arena of competition, selecting the finest forms of social efficiency.

One further objection to the final efficacy of a federation of civilized nations demands consideration. Suppose a federal government of Western nations and their colonial offspring to be possible in such wise that internal conflicts were precluded, this peace of Christendom would be constantly imperilled by the " lower races," black and yellow, who, adopting the arms and military tactics now discarded by the " civilized races," would overwhelm them in barbarian incursions, even as the ruder European and Asiatic races overwhelmed the Roman Empire. We cannot get the whole world to the level of civilization which will admit it into the alliance ; the Powers outside will be a constant menace, and if the main purpose of federation is to eliminate militarism from the economy of national life, the attainment of this purpose will render effective resistance to such invaders no longer possible. This has been the universal fate of Empires in the past ; what talisman could this latest federal Empire possess enabling it to escape ? To this objection we may make this preliminary answer. Two factors in the older Empires have primarily contributed to weaken their powers of resistance against outside " barbarians," and to strengthen and stimulate the zeal of the invaders. There is first the habit of economic parasitism, by which the ruling State has used its provinces, colonies, and dependencies in order to enrich its ruling class and to bribe its lower classes into acquiescence. This bleeding of dependencies, while it enfeebles and atrophies the energy of the imperial people, irritates and eventually rouses to rebellion the more vigorous and less tractable of the subject races ; each repression of rebellion rankles in the blood, and gradually a force of gathering discontent is roused which turns against the governing Power.

The second factor, related to the first, consists in that form of " parasitism " known as employment of mercenary forces. This is the most fatal symptom of imperial infatuation, whereby the oppressor at once deprives himself of the habit and instruments of effective self-protection and hands them over to the most capable and energetic of his enemies.

This fatal conjunction of folly and vice has always contributed to bring about the downfall of Empires in the past. Will it prove fatal to a federation of Western States ?

Obviously it will, if the strength of their combination is used for the same parasitic purposes, and the white races, discarding labour in its more arduous forms, live as a sort of world-aristocracy by the exploitation of "lower races," while they hand over the policing of the world more and more to members of these same races. These dangers would certainly arise if a federation of European States were simply a variant of the older Empires, using a *pax Europæa* for similar purposes and seeking to maintain it by the same methods as those employed under the so-called *pax Romana*. The issue is a great one, furnishing, in fact, the supreme test of modern civilization.

Is it possible for a federation of civilized States to maintain the force required to keep order in the world without abusing her power by political and economic parasitism ?

CHAPTER III

MORAL AND SENTIMENTAL FACTORS

I

ANALYSIS of the actual course of modern Imperialism has laid bare the combination of economic and political forces which fashions it. These forces are traced to their sources in the selfish interests of certain industrial, financial, and professional classes, seeking private advantages out of a policy of imperial expansion, and using this same policy to protect them in their economic, political, and social privileges against the pressure of democracy. It remains to answer the question, " Why does Imperialism escape general recognition for the narrow, sordid thing it is ? " Each nation, as it watches from outside the Imperialism of its neighbours, is not deceived ; the selfish interests of political and commercial classes are seen plainly paramount in the direction of the policy. So every other European nation recognizes the true outlines of British Imperialism and charges us with hypocrisy in feigning blindness. This charge is false ; no nation sees its own shortcomings ; the charge of hypocrisy is seldom justly brought against an individual, against a nation never. Frenchmen and Germans believe that our zeal in promoting foreign missions, putting down slavery, and in spreading the arts of civilization is a false disguise conveniently assumed to cover naked national self-assertion. The actual case is somewhat different.

There exists in a considerable though not a large proportion of the British nation a genuine desire to spread Christianity among the heathen, to diminish the cruelty and other sufferings which they believe exist in countries less fortunate than their own, and to do good work about the world in the cause of humanity. Most of the churches contain a small body of men and women deeply, even passionately, interested in such work, and a much larger number whose sympathy, though weaker, is quite genuine. Ill-trained for the most part in psychology and history, these people believe that religion and other arts of civiliza-tion are portable commodities which it is our duty to convey to the backward nations, and that a certain amount of compulsion is justified in pressing their benefits upon people too ignorant at once to recognize them.

Is it surprising that the selfish forces which direct Imperialism should utilize the protective colours of these disinterested movements ? Imperialist politicians, soldiers, or company directors, who push a forward policy by portraying the cruelties of the African slave raids or the infamous tyranny of a Prempeh or a Theebaw, or who open out a new field for missionary enterprise in China or the Soudan, do not deliberately and consciously work up these motives in order to incite British public. They simply and instinctively attach to themselves any strong, genuine elevated feeling which is of service, fan it and feed it until it assumes fervour, and utilize it for their ends. The politician always, the business man not seldom, believes that high motives qualify the political or financial benefits he gets : it is certain that Lord Salisbury really believed that the South African war, for which his Govern-ment was responsible, had been undertaken for the benefit of the people of South Africa, and would result in increased liberty and happiness ; it is quite likely that Earl Grey thought that the Chartered Company which he directed was animated by a desire to improve the material and moral condition of the natives of Rhodesia, and that it was attaining this object.

So Leopold, King of the Belgians, claimed for his government of the Congo—" Our only programme is that of the moral and material regeneration of the country." It is difficult to set any limit upon the capacity of men to deceive themselves as to the relative strength and worth of the motives which affect them : politicians, in particular, acquire so strong a habit of setting their projects in the most favourable light that they soon convince themselves that the finest result which they think may conceivably accrue from any policy is the actual motive of that policy. As for the public, it is only natural that it should be deceived. All the purer and more elevated adjuncts of Imperialism are kept to the fore by religious and philanthropic agencies : patriotism appeals to the general lust of power within a people by suggestions of nobler uses, adopting the forms of self-sacrifice to cover domination and the love of adventure. So Christianity becomes " imperialist " to the Archbishop of Canterbury, a " going out to all the world to preach the gospel " ; trade becomes " imperialist " in the eyes of merchants seeking a world market.

It is precisely in this falsification of the real import of motives that the gravest vice and the most signal peril of Imperialism reside. When, out of a medley of mixed motives, the least potent is selected for public prominence because it is the most presentable, when issues of a policy which was not present at all to the minds of those who formed this policy are treated as chief causes, the moral currency of the nation is debased. The whole policy of Imperialism is riddled with this deception. Although no candid student of history will maintain for a moment that

the entrance of British power into India, and the chief steps
leading to the present British Empire there, were motived
by considerations other than our own political and commercial aggrandisement, nothing is more common than to
hear the gains which it is alleged the natives of the country
have received from British rule assigned as the moral
justification of our Indian Empire. The case of Egypt
is a still more striking one. Though the reasons openly
assigned for the British occupation of Egypt were military
and financial ones affecting our own interests, it is now
commonly maintained that we went there in order to
bestow the benefits which Egyptians have received from
our sway, and that it would be positively wicked of us
to keep the pledge we gave to withdraw within a short
term of years from the country. When the ordinary
Englishman reads how " at no previous period of his
history has the fellah lived under a Government so careful
to promote his interests or to preserve his rights,"[1] he
instinctively exclaims, " Yes, that is what we went to
Egypt for," though, in point of fact, the play of " Imperialism " which carried us there was determined by quite other
considerations. Even if one supposes that the visible
misgovernment of Egypt, in its bearing on the life of the
inhabitants, did impart some unselfish element to our
conduct, no one would suggest that as an operative force
in the direction of our imperial policy such motive has ever
determined our actions.[2] Not even the most flamboyant

[1] *England in Egypt*, p. 97.

[2] How far the mystification of motives can carry a trained thinker upon politics
may be illustrated by the astonishing argument of Professor Giddings, who, in
discussing " the consent of the governed " as a condition of government, argues
that " if a barbarous people is compelled to accept the authority of a state more
advanced in civilization, the test of the rightfulness or wrongfulness of this
imposition of authority is to be found, not at all in any assent or resistance at the
moment when the government begins, but only *in the degree of probability* that,
after full experience of what the government can do to raise the subject population
to a higher plane of life, *a free and rational consent will be given* by those who have

Imperialist contends that England is a knight-errant, everywhere in search of a quest to deliver oppressed peoples from oppressive governments, regardless of her own interests and perils. Though perhaps not so inefficient, the Russian tyranny was quite as oppressive and more injurious to the cause of civilization than the government of the Khedive, but no one proposed that we should coerce Russia, or rescue Finland from her clutches. The case of Armenia, again, attests the utter feebleness of the higher motives. Both the Government and the people of Great Britain were thoroughly convinced of the atrocious cruelties of Turkey, public opinion was well informed and thoroughly incensed, Great Britain was expressly pledged by the Cyprus Convention to protect Armenia; but the " cause of humanity " and the " mission of civilization " were powerless either for interference or for effective protest.

Aggressive Imperialism, as our investigation has shown, is virtually confined to the coercion by stronger or better-armed nations of nations which are, or seem to be, weaker and incapable of effective resistance; everywhere some definite economic or political gain is sought by the imperial aggressor. The chivalrous spirit of Imperialism leads neither Great Britain nor any other Western nation to assail a powerful State, however tyrannous, or to assist a weak State reputed to be poor.

The blending of strong interested with weak disinterested forces is indeed characteristic of the age. It is the homage which Imperialism pays to humanity. But just as the

come to understand all that has been done " (*Empire and Democracy*, p. 265). Professor Giddings does not seem to recognize that the entire weight of the ethical validity of this curious doctrine of retrospective consent is thrown upon the act of judging *the degree of probability that a free and rational consent will be given*, that his doctrine furnishes no sort of security for a competent, unbiassed judgment, and that, in point of fact, it endows any nation with the right to seize and administer the territory of any other nation on the ground of a self-ascribed superiority and self-imputed qualifications for the work of civilization.

mixture known as "philanthropy and 5 per cent." is distrusted in the ordinary business world, so in the larger policy of nations the same combination is by right suspect. When business is harnessed with benevolence the former is commonly allowed to determine the direction and to set the pace. Doubtless it says something for the moral sensibility of a nation that a gainful course is rendered more attractive by a tincture of disinterestedness. But the theory and the practice in modern history often border so closely on hypocrisy that we cannot feel surprise that unfriendly foreigners apply the term to them. What, for example, can we say of the following frank description of Imperialism by Sir George now Lord Baden-Powell ? " The ultimate unit, the taxpayer—whether home or colonial —looks for two groups of results as his reward. On the one hand, he hopes to see Christianity and civilization *pro tanto* extended ; and, on the other, to see some compensating development of industry and trade. Unless he, or ' his servants the Government,' secure either or both these results, the question must be plainly asked, Has he the right, and is he right, to wage such wars ? "[1]

What is the mode of equating the two groups of results ? how much Christianity and civilization balance how much industry and trade ? are curious questions which seem to need an answer. Is not the ultimate unit in his capacity of taxpayer liable to lay more stress upon the asset which admits of monetary measurement, and to undervalue the one that evades arithmetic ?

" To combine the commercial with the imaginative " was the aim which Mr. Rhodes ascribed to himself as the key of his policy. The conjunction is commonly described by the word " speculation," a word whose meaning becomes more sinister when politics and private business are so

[1] Addendum to *The Downfall of Prempeh*.

inextricably interwoven as they were in the career of Mr. Rhodes, who used the legislature of Cape Colony to support and strengthen the diamond monopoly of De Beers, while from De Beers he financed the Raid, debauched the constituencies of Cape Colony, and bought the public press, in order to engineer the war, which was to win him full possession of his great " thought " the North.[1]

II

It may safely be asserted that, wherever " the commercial " is combined with " the imaginative " in any shape or sort, the latter is exploited by the former. There is a brand of " Christian Imperialist " much commended in certain quarters, the " industrial missionary," who is designed to float Christianity upon an ocean of profitable business, inculcating theological dogmas in the intervals of teaching the material arts and crafts. " To the sceptical Chinese the interest manifested by a missionary in business affairs would go far towards dispelling the suspicions which now attach to the presence in their midst of men whose motives they are unable to appreciate, and therefore condemn as unholy." " Immense services might be rendered to our commercial interests if only the members of the various missions in China would co-operate with our Consuls in the exploitation of the country, and the introduction of commercial as well as of purely theological ideas to the Chinese intelligence."[2] This revelation of the mercantile uses of Christianity by a British Consul leaves little to be desired in point of frankness. Its full significance is, however, only perceived when it is reinformed by the naïve confession of Lord Hugh Cecil. " A great many people

[1] " The North is my thought " (*Cecil Rhodes : His Political Life and Speeches*, p. 613.).
[2] Passages from a recent report of the British Consul at Canton.

were most anxious to go with their whole hearts into what might be called the imperial movement of the day, but had, as it were, a certain uneasiness of conscience whether, after all, this movement was quite as unpolluted by earthly considerations as they would desire it to be. He thought that by making prominent to our own minds the importance of missionary work we should to some extent sanctify the spirit of Imperialism."[1]

We are well aware that most British missionaries are quite untainted by admixture of political and commercial motives, and that they set about their work in a single spirit of self-sacrifice, eager to save the souls of the heathen, and not a whit concerned to push British trade or " sanctify the spirit of Imperialism." Indeed, it is quite evident that, just in proportion as the suspicions of worldly motives appear in missionary work, so the genuinely spiritual influence evaporates. The whole history of missionary work in China is one long commentary on this text. The early Catholic missionaries, relying on the authority of their holy lives and teaching, won not only security, but wide influence, both among the masses and in the governing circles, introducing not only Christianity, but the elements of Western science. Though they made no large numbers of converts, they constituted a powerful factor in the civilization of the great Eastern Empire. But the introduction in the nineteenth century of national and sectarian competition in missionary enterprise, each mission using freely the diplomatic and even the military resources of some European State for its defence or propagation, has inhibited the play of spiritual forces, generating suspicions which, only too well grounded, have changed the early receptiveness into a temper of fanatical hostility.

[1] An address at the annual meeting of the Society for the Propagation of the Gospel, May 4, 1900.

" It must be very difficult," writes an educated Chinaman, " for the mandarins to dissociate the missionaries
from the secular power, whose gunboats seem ever ready
to appear on behalf of their respective Governments. . . .
The Chinese have watched with much concern the sequence
of events—first the missionary, then the Consul, and at
last the invading army. They had scarcely forgotten the
loss of Annam in this way when the German action in
Shan-tung created a profound sensation amongst all classes
of the literati." " We cannot wonder that the Chinese
officials should hate the missionaries. Their Church is
an *imperium in imperio*, propagating a strange faith and
alienating the people from that of their ancestors. The
missionaries are not amenable to Chinese laws, and in
some cases have acted in a high-handed manner in the
protection of their converts. In this lies one of the secrets
of the mysterious hatred entertained against ' the friends
of China ' as the missionaries call themselves."[1]

How injurious to the cause " whose kingdom is not
of this earth " is this alliance with politics and armaments
might appear too obvious for discussion. Yet it is quite
evident that sincere men are prepared to support the use
of political and military force in order to open fields for
missionary enterprise, and that the missionary, who is by
turns trader, soldier, and politician, seems a most desirable
instrument of civilization.

How close in motive and in conduct this combination really
is may be thus illustrated from the history of the Soudan.

" Detachments of officers and men from every regiment,
British and Egyptian, were conveyed across the Nile in
the gunboats to take part in the Gordon memorial service,
and to witness the hoisting of the British flag on the ruins

[1] *The Chinese Crisis from Within*, by Wen Ching, pp. 10, 12, 14 (Grant
Richards).

of Khartoum. . . . Surrounded by the soldiers he had directed with terrible and glorious effect, the successful general ordered the flags to be hoisted. . . . The officers saluted, the men presented arms, and the band played the Egyptian National Anthem and our own. Then the Sirdar called for three cheers for Her Majesty. . . . The memorial service followed, and the solemn words of the English Prayer Book were read in that distant garden. . . . The bands played their dirge and Gordon's favourite hymn, ' Abide with Me ' ; a gunboat on the river crashed out the salute. . . . The Highlanders played a long lament, and thus the ceremony was duly fulfilled. Nine thousand of those who would have prevented it lay dead on the plain of Omdurman. Other thousands were scattered in the wilderness, or crawled wounded to the river for water."[1] While the writer of this passage omits the final touch, the deliberate shooting of wounded crawlers by troops under British commanders, the picture is profoundly suggestive, with its strange amalgam of the British flag, " Abide with Me," and the avenging of Gordon.

Yet it is evident that those who ascend to the misty heights of Imperialism are able to unite these diverse jarring factors in " a higher synthesis," and while deploring, often in earnest, the necessity of the maxim and the gun-boat, find a glorious justification in the higher ends of a civilization promoted by such means. The Western nations are, according to this gospel, rapidly realizing a beneficent control of the earth which will, in the near future, secure general peace and the industrial, scientific, and moral supremacy of Western arts.

> Fly, happy, happy sails, and bear the Press,
> Fly, happy with the mission of the Cross,
> Knit land to land, and blowing heavenward,
> Enrich the markets of the golden year.

[1] *The River War*, by Winston Churchill, vol. ii, pp. 204-206.

This is the benevolent theory. Let Sir Charles Dilke's estimate of our acquisitions in tropical Africa serve for commentary.

" If we cannot make the most fertile of the West India Islands pay, how can we expect to make countries which are far less healthy and less fertile in the very heart of Africa, return a profit ? Our people have been interested in Africa through their traditional desire to suppress the evils of the slave trade, and to pay conscience money in these days for the sins, in connexion with slavery, of their predecessors ; but it is probable that we have done more harm by promoting the partition of Africa and the creation, in the name of liberty, of such governments as that of the Congo Free State than the harm which our grandfathers did to Africa by their participation in African slavery and the slave trade."[1]

III

The psychical problem which confronts us in the advocates of the mission of Imperialism is certainly no case of hypocrisy, or of deliberate conscious simulation of false motives. It is partly the dupery of imperfectly realized ideas, partly a case of psychical departmentalism. Imperialism has been floated on a sea of vague, shifty, well-sounding phrases which are seldom tested by close contact with fact. " It is not in size and variety alone that English dominion is unique. Its crowning glory is its freedom,"[2] writes Mr. Henley, doubtless believing what he says. The suggestion of these words is that the " freedom " we enjoy in these isles is common to our fellow-subjects throughout the British Empire. This suggestion is false, as we have seen, but phrase-mongering Imperialism does not recognize its falsehood. The largest and most essential

[1] *The British Empire*, p. 114.   [2] *Imperialism*, p. 7.

facts of Imperialism, political, economic, moral, are commonly unknown to the average " educated " Briton. To him our Empire is composed of a number of free, self-governing States, which are in close and growing industrial relations with us ; individual and racial freedom and equal justice prevail everywhere ; Christianity and British moral ideals are rapidly winning their way over the vast populations of the lower races, which gladly recognize the superiority of our ideas and characters and the benefits which they receive from British rule. These vague, hasty notions are corrected by no close study of facts and figures : the only substance which they commonly possess is the assertion of some friends or relatives who are " on the spot " in some British possessions and whose individual testimony is made to sustain a pile of imperialist notions. How many persons, during the South African war, based their convictions regarding the " outlander grievances " and the character and motives of the Boer Government upon the impassioned statement of some single dweller in Johannesburg, who had virtually no contact with Boers and knew nothing of grievances, excepting through the Rhodesian press, which fashioned them !

To what extent Imperialism lives upon " masked words "[1] it is difficult to realize unless we turn to the language of diplomacy, the verbal armoury of Imperialism. Paramount power, effective autonomy, emissary of civilization, rectification of frontier, and a whole sliding scale of

---

[1] " There are masked words droning and skulking about us in Europe just now which nobody understands, but which everybody uses and most people will also fight for, live for, or even die for, fancying they mean this or that or the other of things dear to them. There never were creatures of prey so mischievous, never diplomatists so cunning, never poisons so deadly, as these masked words ; they are the unjust stewards of all men's ideas ; whatever fancy or favourite instinct a man most cherishes he gives to his favourite masked word to take care of for him ; the word at last comes to have an infinte power over him, and you cannot get at him but by its ministry " (Ruskin, *Sesame and Lilies*, p. 29).

terms from " hinterland " and " sphere of interest " to
" effective occupation " and " annexation " will serve as
ready illustrations of a phraseology devised for purposes
of concealment and encroachment. The Imperialist who
sees modern history through these masks never grasps the
" brute " facts, but always sees them at several removes,
refracted, interpreted, and glozed by convenient renderings.
Some measure of responsibility for his ignorance he retains,
for he must often be aware that the truth is not told him
and that he is refusing to penetrate the disguises. This
persistent evasion of naked truth endows him sometimes with
an almost preternatural power of self-deceit. Mr. Lecky
writes : " Of all forms of prestige, moral prestige is the
most valuable, and no statesman should forget that one of
the chief elements of British power is the moral weight that
is behind it."[1] The vast majority of " educated " Englishmen genuinely believe that England's greatest gain from
the Boer war is an enhancement of her " moral prestige " !

An error so monstrous is only made intelligible by reference
to another curious psychical factor. Nowhere is the
distrust of what is termed " logic " as a guide for public
conduct, so firmly rooted as in England : a course of
conduct which stands out sharply " logical " is in itself
suspect. The practice of " party " government has so
commonly made " compromises " a necessity that we
have come to believe that our national progress is due to
this necessity, and that if the sharper and more rapid
application of " ideas " had been feasible, we should, by
following them, have been led into false paths involving
much trouble of retracing steps, or over the brink of some
revolutionary peril. Though sound " compromise " is
no wise illogical, but is simply logic applied within certain
limits of time and environment, it easily degenerates into

[1] *The Map of Life.*

the opportunism of an idle policy **of** short-range utility. The complexity of modern politics in such a country as Great Britain, reacting on the exigencies and temptations of a party system, has driven the habit of " compromise " to such foolish extremes as to corrupt the political intelligence of the nation. Elsewhere the same tendency has been operative, but has been checked or modified by a narrow and more consciously definite policy on the part of a ruling monarch or a ruling class, by the limits of a written constitution, and, in some of the Latin nations, by an inherent and widespread belief in the value of ideas as operative forces in politics. In England, and indeed throughout Anglo-Saxondom, a sort of cheery optimism has commonly usurped the seat of intelligent direction, a general belief in " national destiny," which enables us " somehow to muddle through," and advises us " to do the best we can and not look too far ahead." Now, with the disdain of history and the neglect of sociological laws which this implies I am not here so much concerned as with the injurious reaction wrought upon the mind of the citizen confronted with some new event which challenges his judgment. Our rough-and-ready, hand-to-mouth, " take-what-you-can-get " politics have paralysed judgment by laming the logical faculty of comparison. Not being required to furnish to ourselves or others clear, consistent reasons for our short-range expediencies of public conduct, we have lost all habit of mental consistency, or, putting it conversely, we have developed a curious and highly dangerous aptitude for entertaining incompatible and often self-contradictory ideas and motives.

One or two extreme concrete instances will serve as illustrations of the damage done to the public intelligence by the absence of all sense of clear logical order in the conduct of affairs. At the beginning of the South African war the numerical insignificance of the Boers was regarded as an aggravation of their insolence in entering upon strife with the greatest Empire of the world. But the numerical smallness did not in the least interfere with the equally genuine belief and feeling that we were contending with a Power as large, numerically, as ourselves, which were required to support the sense of triumph when we won a victory, or to turn the edge of shame when our tiny adversary inflicted a defeat upon us. The shifts of detailed mendacity and curious invention to which we were driven in the course of the war by the necessity of keeping up this double and contradictory belief will doubtless attract the attention of the psychological historian, how the numbers alternately and automatically expanded and contracted according as it was sought to impress upon the nation the necessity of voting large supplies of troops and money, or else to represent the war as " nearly over " and as having lapsed into a trifling guerilla struggle. Or take another instance. It was possible for informed politicians to maintain at one and the same time that our conduct in providing food and shelter to the families whose property we had destroyed in South Africa was an act of unprecedented generosity, and to defend the right to sell by public auction their farms in order to defray the very cost of keep which was the ground for our self-commendation. These two contentions could be uttered in the House of Commons by the same minister and accepted by the nation without any recognition of their inconsistency. Why ? Simply from a practical inhibition of the faculty of comparison. A line of action is pursued from the felt pressure of some close expediency : afterwards some " reasons " must be found for it, some justification given : no attempt is made before or after the action to see it as a whole with its causes and its consequences, and so there is no clear comparison of actual motives and results. This genius of inconsistency, of holding conflicting ideas or feelings in the mind simultaneously, in watertight compartments, is perhaps peculiarly British. It is, I repeat, not hypocrisy; a consciousness of inconsistency would spoil the play: it is a condition of the success of this conduct that it should be unconscious. For such inconsistency has its uses. Much of the brutality and injustice involved in " Imperialism " would be impossible without this capacity. If, for example, the British mind had been sufficiently consistent to have kept clearly before it the fact that 400 millions of people were contending with a body less than a quarter of a million, whatever view was held as to the necessity and justice of the war, much of its detailed barbarism and all the triumphant exultation on success would have been impossible.

There is of course much more than this in the psychology of Imperialism, but there are two main factors, the habit and capacity of substituting vague and decorative notions, derived through " masked words," for hard naked facts, and the native or acquired genius of inconsistency. Great Britain would be incapable of this policy if she realized in clear consciousness the actual play of motives and their results. Most of the men who have misled her have first been obliged to mislead themselves. There is no enthusiasm in hypocrisy, and even bare-faced greed furnishes no adequate stimulus to a long policy. Imperialism is based upon a persistent misrepresentation of facts and forces, chiefly through a most refined process of selection, exaggeration, and attenuation, directed by interested cliques and persons so as to distort the face of history.

The gravest peril of Imperialism lies in the state of mind of a nation which has become habituated to this deception and which has rendered itself incapable of self-criticism.

For this is the condition which Plato terms " the lie in the soul "—a lie which does not know itself to be a lie.

One of the marks of this diseased condition is a fatal self-complacency. When a nation has succumbed to it, it easily and instinctively rejects all criticism of other nations as due to envy and malice, and all domestic criticism is attributed to the bias of anti-patriotism. In more primitive nations the lusts of domination and material acquisition which underlie Imperialism express themselves freely and unconsciously: there is little self-complacency because there is little self-consciousness. But nations which have grown in self-consciousness as far as the Western European nations seek to stimulate and feed their instinctive lusts by conscious reflection. Hence the elaborate weaving of intellectual and moral defences, the ethics and sociology of empire which we have examined.

The controlling and directing agent of the whole process, as we have seen, is the pressure of financial and industrial motives, operated for the direct, short-range, material interests of small, able, and well-organized groups in a nation. These groups secure the active co-operation of statesmen and of political cliques who wield the power of "parties," partly by associating them directly in their business schemes, partly by appealing to the conservative instincts of members of the possessing classes, whose vested interest and class dominance are best preserved by diverting the currents of political energy from domestic on to foreign politics. The acquiescence, even the active and enthusiastic support, of the body of a nation in a course of policy fatal to its own true interests is secured partly by appeals to the mission of civilization, but chiefly by playing upon the primitive instincts of the race.

The psychology of these instincts is not easy to explore, but certain prime factors easily appear. The passion which a French writer describes as kilometritis,[1] or milo-mania,

[1] M. Novicov, *La Federation de l'Europe*, p. 158.

the instinct for control of land, drives back to the earliest times when a wide range of land was necessary for a food supply for men or cattle, and is linked on to the " trek " habit, which survives more powerfully than is commonly supposed in civilized peoples. The " nomadic " habit bred of necessity survives as a chief ingredient in the love of travel, and merges into " the spirit of adventure " when it meets other equally primitive passions. This " spirit of adventure," especially in the Anglo-Saxon, has taken the shape of " sport," which in its stronger or " more adventurous " forms involves a direct appeal to the lust of slaughter and the crude struggle for life involved in pursuit. The animal lust of struggle, once a necessity, survives in the blood, and just in proportion as a nation or a class has a margin of energy and leisure from the activities of peaceful industry, it craves satisfaction through " sport," in which hunting and the physical satisfaction of striking a blow are vital ingredients. The leisured classes in great Britain, having most of their energy liberated from the necessity of work, naturally specialize on " sport," the hygienic necessity of a substitute for work helping to support or coalescing with the survival of a savage instinct. As the milder expressions of this passion are alone permissible in the sham or artificial encounters of domestic sports, where wild game disappears and human conflicts more mortal than football are prohibited, there is an ever stronger pressure to the frontiers of civilization in order that the thwarted " spirit of adventure " may have strong, free play. These feelings are fed by a flood of the literature of travel and of imaginative writing, the security and monotony of the ordinary civilized routine imparting an ever-growing fascination to the wilder portions of the earth. The milder satisfactions afforded by sport to the upper classes in their ample leisure at home are imitated by the industrial masses, whose time and energy for recreation have been growing, and who, in their passage from rural to town conditions, have never abandoned the humbler sports of feudal country life to which from time immemorial they had been addicted. " Football is a good game, but better than it, better than any other game, is that of man-hunting."[1]

The sporting and military aspects of Imperialism form, therefore, a very powerful basis of popular appeal. The desire to pursue and kill either big game or other men can only be satisfied by expansion and militarism. It may indeed be safely said that the reason why our army is so inefficient in its officers, as compared with its rank and file, is that at a time when serious scientific preparation and selection are required for an intellectual profession, most British officers choose the army and undertake its work in the spirit of " sport." While the average " Tommy " is perhaps actuated in the main by similar motives, " science " matters less in his case, and any lack of serious professional purpose is more largely compensated by the discipline imposed on him.

But still more important than these supports of militarism in the army is the part played by " war " as a support of Imperialism in the non-combatant body of the nation. Though the active appeal of " sport " is still strong, even among townsmen, clear signs are visible of a degradation of this active interest of the participant into the idle excitement of the spectator. How far sport has thus degenerated may be measured by the substitution every-where of a specialized professionalism for a free amateur exercise, and by the growth of the attendant vice of betting, which everywhere expresses the worst form of sporting excitement, drawing all disinterested sympathy away

[1] Baden-Powell, *Aids to Scouting*, p. 124.

from the merits of the competition, and concentrating it upon the irrational element of chance in combination with covetousness and low cunning. The equivalent of this degradation of interest in sport is Jingoism in relation to the practice of war. Jingoism is merely the lust of the spectator, unpurged by any personal effort, risk, or sacrifice, gloating over the perils, pains, and slaughter of fellow-men whom he does not know, but whose destruction he desires in a blind and artificially stimulated passion of hatred and revenge. In the Jingo all is concentrated on the hazard and blind fury of the fray. The arduous and weary monotony of the march, the long periods of waiting, the hard privations, the terrible tedium of a prolonged campaign, play no part in his imagination ; the redeeming factors of war, the fine sense of comradeship which common personal peril educates, the fruits of discipline and self-restraint, the respect for the personality of enemies whose courage he must admit and whom he comes to realize as fellow-beings—all these moderating elements in actual war are eliminated from the passion of the Jingo. It is precisely for these reasons that some friends of peace maintain that the two most potent checks of militarism and of war are the obligation of the entire body of citizens to undergo military service and the experience of an invasion.

Whether such expensive remedies are really effectual or necessary we are not called on to decide, but it is quite evident that the spectatorial lust of Jingoism is a most serious factor in Imperialism. The dramatic falsification both of war and of the whole policy of imperial expansion required to feed this popular passion forms no small portion of the art of the real organizers of imperialist exploits, the small groups of business men and politicians who know what they want and how to get it.

Tricked out with the real or sham glories of military

heroism and the magnificent claims of empire-making, Jingoism becomes a nucleus of a sort of patriotism which can be moved to any folly or to any crime.

IV

Where this spirit of naked dominance needs more dressing for the educated classes of a nation, the requisite moral ans intellectual decorations are woven for its use; the church, the press, the schools and colleges, the political machine, the four chief instruments of popular education, are accommodated to its service. From the muscular Christianity of the last generation to the imperial Christianity of the present day is but a single step; the temper of growing sacerdotalism and the doctrine of authority in the established churches well accord with militarism and political autocracy. Mr. Goldwin Smith has rightly observed how "force is the natural ally of superstition, and superstition knows it well."[1] As for the most potent engine of the press, the newspaper, so far as it is not directly owned and operated by financiers for financial purposes (as is the case to a great extent in every great industrial and financial centre), it is always influenced and often dominated by the interests of the classes which control the advertisements upon which its living depends; the independence of a paper with a circulation so large and firm as to "command" and to retain advertisements in the teeth of a policy disliked by the advertising classes is becoming rarer and more precarious every year, as the cluster of interests which form the business nucleus of Imperialism becomes more consolidated and more conscious in its politics. The political machine is "an hireling,"

[1] Letter in *The Manchester Guardian*, October 14, 1900.

because it is a machine, and needs constant repair and lubrication from the wealthy members of the party ; the machinist knows from whom he takes his pay, and cannot run against the will of those who are in fact the patrons of the party, the tightening of whose purse-strings will automatically stop the machine. The recent Imperialism both of Great Britain and America has been materially assisted by the lavish contributions of men like Rockefeller, Hanna, Rhodes, Beit to party funds for the election of " imperialist " representatives and for the political instruction of the people.

Most serious of all is the persistent attempt to seize the school system for Imperialism masquerading as patriotism. To capture the childhood of the country, to mechanize its free play into the routine of military drill, to cultivate the savage survivals of combativeness, to poison its early understanding of history by false ideals and pseudo-heroes, and by a consequent disparagement and neglect of the really vital and elevating lessons of the past, to establish a " geocentric " view of the moral universe in which the interests of humanity are subordinated to that of the " country " (and so, by easy, early, natural inference, that of the " country " to that of the " self "), to feed the always overweening pride of race at an age when self-confidence most commonly prevails, and by necessary implication to disparage other nations, so starting children in the world with false measures of value and an unwillingness to learn from foreign sources—to fasten this base insularity of mind and morals upon the little children of a nation and to call it patriotism is as foul an abuse of education as it is possible to conceive. Yet the power of Church and State over primary education is being bent consistently to this purpose, while the blend of clericalism and autocratic academicism which dominates the secondary education of this country pours its enthusiasm into the same evil channel.[1] Finally, our centres of highest culture, the universities, are in peril of a new perversion from the path of free inquiry and expression, which is the true path of intellectual life. A new sort of "pious founder" threatens intellectual liberty. Our colleges are, indeed, no longer to be the subservient defenders of religious orthodoxy, repressing science, distorting history, and moulding philosophy to conserve the interests of Church and King. The academic studies and their teachers are to employ the same methods but directed to a different end : philosophy, the natural sciences, history, economics, sociology, are to be employed in setting up new earthworks against the attack of the disinherited masses upon the vested interests of the pluto-cracy. I do not of course represent this perversion as destructive of the educational work of the colleges : the services rendered in defence of "conservatism" may even be regarded in most cases as incidental : only perhaps in philosophy and economics is the bias a powerful and pervasive one, and even there the individuality of strong independent natures may correct it. Moreover, it is need-less to charge dishonesty against the teachers, who commonly think and teach according to the highest that is in them. But the actual teaching is none the less selected and controlled, wherever it is found useful to employ the arts of selection and control, by the business interests playing on the vested academic interests. No one can follow the history of political and economic theory during the last century without recognizing that the selection and rejection of ideas, hypothesis, and formulæ, the moulding of them into schools or tendencies of thought, and the propagation of them in the intellectual world, have been plainly directed by the pressure of class interests. In political

[1] For striking illustrations *cf.* Spencer's *Facts and Comments*, pp. 126–7.

218

economy, as we might well suspect, from its close bearing upon business and politics, we find the most incontestable example. The " classical " economics in England were the barely disguised formulation of the mercantile and manufacturing interests as distinguished from, and opposed to, the landowning interest on the one hand, the labouring interest on the other, evoking in later years other class economics of " protection " and of " socialism " similarly woven out of sectional interests.

The real determinants in education are given in these three questions : " Who shall teach ? What shall they teach ? How shall they teach ? " Where universities are dependent for endowments and incomes upon the favour of the rich, upon the charity of millionaires, the following answers will of necessity be given : " Safe teachers. Safe studies. Sound (i.e. orthodox) methods." The coarse proverb which tells us that " he who pays the piper calls the tune " is quite as applicable here as elsewhere, and no bluff regarding academic dignity and intellectual honesty must blind us to the fact.

The interference with intellectual liberty is seldom direct, seldom personal, though both in the United States and Canada some instances of the crudest heresy-hunting have occurred. The real danger consists in the appointment rather than in the dismissal of teachers, in the determination of what subjects shall be taught, what relative attention shall be given to each subject, and what text-books and other apparatus of instruction shall be used. The subservience to rank and money, even in our older English universities, has been evinced so nakedly, and the demands for monetary aid in developing new faculties necessarily looms so large in academic eyes, that the danger here indicated is an ever-growing one. It is not so much the weight of the " dead hand " that is to be feared as that of the living : a college so unfortunate as to harbour teachers who, in handling vital issues of politics or economics, teach truths deeply and obviously antagonistic to the interests of the classes from whom financial aid was sought, would be committing suicide. Higher education has never been economically self-supporting ; it has hardly ever been fully organized from public funds ; everywhere it has remained parasitic on the private munificence of wealthy persons. The peril is too obvious to need further enforcement : it is the hand of the prospective, the potential donor that fetters intellectual freedom in our colleges, and will do so more and more so long as the duty of organizing public higher education for a nation out of public funds fails of recognition.

The area of danger is, of course, far wider than Imperialism, covering the whole field of vested interests. But, if the analysis of previous chapters is correct, Imperialism stands as a first defence of these interests : for the financial and speculative classes it means a pushing of their private businesses at the public expense, for the export manufacturers and merchants a forcible enlargement of foreign markets and a related policy of Protection, for the official and professional classes large openings of honourable and lucrative employment, for the Church it represents the temper and practice of authority and the assertion of spiritual control over vast multitudes of lower people, for the political oligarchy it means the only effective diversion of the forces of democracy and the opening of great public careers in the showy work of empire-making.

This being so, it is inevitable that Imperialism should seek intellectual support in our seats of learning, and should use the sinews of education for the purpose. The millionaire who endows Oxford does not buy its men of learning outright, need not even stipulate what should be taught. But the practical pressure of Imperialism is such that when a professional appointment is made in history it is becoming more difficult for a scholar with the intellectual outlook of a John Morley, a Frederick Harrison, or a Goldwin Smith to secure election, or for a political economist with strong views on the necessity of controlling capital to be elected to a chair in economics. No formal tests are necessary; the instinct of financial self-preservation will suffice. The price which universities pay for preferring money and social position to intellectual distinction in the choice of chancellors and for touting among the million-aires for the equipment of new scientific schools is this subservience to the political and business interests of their patrons : their philosophy, their history, their economics, even their biology must reflect in doctrine and method the consideration that is due to patronage, and the fact that this deference is unconscious enhances the damage done to the cause of intellectual freedom.

Thus do the industrial and financial forces of Imperialism, operating through the party, the press, the church, the school, mould public opinion and public policy by the false idealization of those primitive lusts of struggle, domination and acquisitiveness, which have survived throughout the eras of peaceful industrial order, and whose stimulation is needed once again for the work of imperial aggression, expansion, and the forceful exploitation of lower races. For these business politicians biology and sociology weave thin convenient theories of a race struggle for the subjugation of the inferior peoples, in order that we, the Anglo-Saxon, may take their lands and live upon their labours ; while economics buttresses the argument by representing our work in conquering and ruling them as our share in the division of labour among nations, and history devises reasons why the lessons of past empire do not apply to ours while social ethics paints the motive of " Imperialism " as the desire to bear the " burden " of educating and elevating races of " children." Thus are the " cultured " or semi-cultured classes indoctrinated with the intellectual and moral grandeur of Imperialism. For the masses there is a cruder appeal to hero-worship and sensational glory, adventure and the sporting spirit : current history falsified in coarse flaring colours, for the direct stimulation of the combative instincts. But while various methods are employed, some delicate and indirect, others coarse and flamboyant, the operation everywhere resolves itself into an incitation and direction of the brute lusts of human domination which are everywhere latent in civilized humanity, for the pursuance of a policy fraught with material gain to a minority of co-operative vested interests which usurp the title of the commonwealth.

CHAPTER IV

IMPERIALISM AND THE LOWER RACES

I

THE statement, often made, that the work of imperial expansion is virtually complete is not correct. It is true that most of the " backward " races have been placed in some sort of dependence upon one or other of the " civilized " Powers as colony, protectorate, hinterland, or sphere of influence. But this in most instances marks rather the beginning of a process of imperialization than a definite attainment of empire. The intensive growth of empire by which interference is increased and governmental control tightened over spheres of influence and protectorates is as important and as perilous an aspect of Imperialism as the extensive growth which takes shape in assertion of rule over new areas of territory and new populations.

The famous saying, attributed to Napoleon, that " great empires die of indigestion " serves to remind us of the importance of the imperialist processes which still remain after formal " expansion " has been completed. During the last twenty years of the last century Great Britain, Germany, France, and Russia had bitten off huge mouthfuls of Africa and Asia which are not yet chewed, digested, or assimilated. Moreover, great areas still remain whose independence, though threatened, is yet unimpaired.[1]

Vast countries in Asia, such as Persia, Thibet, Siam,

[1] The reader is reminded that this and ensuing remarks relate to the situation at the beginning of the century.

Afghanistan, are rapidly forging to the front of politics as likely subjects of armed controversy between European Powers with a view to subjugation ; the Turkish dominions in Asia Minor, and perhaps in Europe, await a slow, precarious process of absorption ; the paper partition of Central Africa teems with possibilities of conflict. The entrance of the United States into the imperial struggle throws virtually the whole of South America into the arena ; for it is not reasonable to expect that European nations, with settlements and vast economic interests in the southern peninsula, will readily leave all this territory to the special protection or ultimate absorption of the United States, when the latter, abandoning her old consistent isolation, has plunged into the struggle for empire in the Pacific.

Beyond and above all this looms China. It is not easy to suppose that the lull and hesitancy of the Powers will last, or that the magnitude and manifest risks of disturbing this vast repository of incalculable forces will long deter adventurous groups of profit-seekers from driving their Governments along the slippery path of commercial treaties, leases, railway and mining concessions, which must entail a growing process of political interference.

It is not my purpose to examine here the entanglement of political and economic issues which each of these cases presents, but simply to illustrate the assertion that the policy of modern Imperialism is not ended but only just begun, and that it is concerned almost wholly with the rival claims of Empires to dominate " lower races " in tropical and sub-tropical countries, or in other countries occupied by manifestly unassimilable races.

In asking ourselves what are the sound principles of world policy and of national policy in this matter, we may at first ignore the important differences which should affect our conduct towards countries inhabited by what appear to be definitely low-typed unprogressive races, countries whose people manifest capacity of rapid progress from a present low condition, and countries like India and China, where an old civilization of a high type, widely differing from that of European nations, exists.

Before seeking for differences of policy which correspond to these conditions, let us try to find whether there are any general principles of guidance in dealing with countries occupied by " lower " or unprogressive peoples.

It is idle to consider as a general principle the attitude of mere *laissez faire*. It is not only impracticable in view of the actual forces which move politics, but it is ethically indefensible in the last resort.

To lay down as an absolute law that " the autonomy of every nation is inviolable " does not carry us very far. There can no more be absolute nationalism in the society of nations than absolute individualism in the single nation. Some measure of practical internationality, implying a " comity of nations," and some relations of " right " and " duty " between nations, are almost universally admitted. The rights of self-government, implied by the doctrine of autonomy, if binding in any sense legal or ethical on other nations, can only possess this character in virtue of some real international organization, however rudimentary.

It is difficult for the strongest advocate of national rights to assert that the people in actual occupation or political control over a given area of the earth are entitled to do what they will with " their own," entirely disregarding the direct and indirect consequences of their actions upon the rest of the world.

It is not necessary to take extreme cases of a national policy which directly affects the welfare of a neighbouring State, as where a people on the upper reaches of a river like the Nile or the Niger might so damage or direct the flow as to cause plague or famine to the lower lands belonging to another nation. Few, if any, would question some right of interference from without in such a case. Or take another case which falls outside the range of directly other-regarding actions. Suppose a famine or flood or other catastrophe deprives a population of the means of living on their land, while unutilized land lies in plenty beyond their borders in another country, are the rulers of the latter entitled to refuse an entrance or a necessary settlement ? As in the case of individuals, so of nations, it will be generally allowed that necessity knows no laws, which, rightly interpreted, means that the right of self-preservation transcends all other rights as the prime condition of their emergence and exercise.

This carries us on an inclined plane of logic to the real issue as ably presented by Mr. Kidd, Professor Giddings, and the " Fabian " Imperialists. It is an expansion of this plea of material necessity that constitutes the first claim to a control of the tropics by " civilized " nations. The European races have grown up with a standard of material civilization based largely upon the consumption and use of foods, raw materials of manufacture, and other goods which are natural products of tropical countries. The industries and the trade which furnish these commodities are of vital importance to the maintenance and progress of Western civilization. The large part played in our import trade by such typically tropical products as sugar, tea, coffee, indiarubber, rice, tobacco, indicates the dependence of such countries as Great Britain upon the tropics. Partly from sheer growth of population in temperate zones, partly from the rising standard of material life, this dependence of the temperate on the tropical countries must grow. In order to satisfy these growing needs larger and larger tracts of tropical country must be cultivated, the cultivation must be better and more regular, and peaceful and effective trade relations with these countries must be maintained. Now the ease with which human life can be maintained in the tropics breeds indolence and torpor of character. The inhabitants of these countries are not " progressive people "; they neither develop the arts of industry at any satisfactory pace, nor do they evolve new wants or desires, the satisfaction of which might force them to labour. We cannot therefore rely upon the ordinary economic motives and methods of free exchange to supply the growing demand for tropical goods. The resources of the tropics will not be developed voluntarily by the natives themselves.

" If we look to the native social systems of the tropical East, the primitive savagery of Central Africa, to the West Indian Islands in the past in process of being assisted into the position of modern States by Great Britain, or the black republic of Hayti in the present, or to modern Liberia in the future, the lesson seems everywhere the same ; it is that there will be no development of the resources of the tropics under native government."[1]

We cannot, it is held, leave these lands barren ; it is our duty to see that they are developed for the good of the world. White men cannot " colonize " these lands and, thus settling, develop the natural resources by the labour of their own hands ; they can only organize and superintend the labour of the natives. By doing this they can educate the natives in the arts of industry and stimulate in them a desire for material and moral progress, implanting new " wants " which form in every society the roots of civilization. It is quite evident that there is much force in this presentation of the case, not only on material but on moral grounds ; nor can it be brushed aside because it is liable

[1] Kidd, *The Control of the Tropics*, p. 53 (Macmillan & Co.).

to certain obvious and gross abuses. It implies, however, two kinds of interference which require justification. To step in and utilize natural resources which are left undeveloped is one thing, to compel the inhabitants to develop them is another. The former is easily justified, involving the application on a wider scale of a principle whose equity, as well as expediency, is recognized and enforced in most civilized nations. The other interference whereby men who prefer to live on a low standard of life with little labour shall be forced to harder or more continuous labour, is far more difficult of justification.

I have set the economic compulsion in the foreground, because in point of history it is the *causa causans* of the Imperialism that accompanies or follows.

In considering the ethics and politics of this interference, we must not be bluffed or blinded by critics who fasten on the palpable dishonesty of many practices of the gospel of " the dignity of labour " and " the mission of civilization." The real issue is whether, and under what circumstances, it is justifiable for Western nations to use compulsory government for the control and education in the arts of industrial and political civilization of the inhabitants of tropical countries and other so-called lower races. Because Rhodesian mine-owners or Cuban sugar-growers stimulate the British or American Government to Imperialism by parading motives and results which do not really concern them, it does not follow that these motives under proper guidance are unsound, or that the results are undesirable.

There is nothing unworthy, quite the contrary, in the notion that nations which, through a more stimulative environment, have advanced further in certain arts of industry, politics, or morals, should communicate these to nations which from their circumstances were more backward, so as to aid them in developing alike the material resources of their land and the human resources of their people. Nor is it clear that in this work some " inducement, stimulus, or pressure " (to quote a well-known phrase) or in a single word, " compulsion," is wholly illegitimate. Force is itself no remedy, coercion is not education, but it may be a prior condition to the operation of educative forces. Those, at any rate, who assign any place to force in the education or the political government of individuals in a nation can hardly deny that the same instrument may find a place in the civilization of backward by progressive nations.

Assuming that the arts of " progress," or some of them, are communicable, a fact which is hardly disputable, there can be no inherent natural right in a people to refuse that measure of compulsory education which shall raise it from childhood to manhood in the order of nationalities. The analogy furnished by the education of a child is prima facie a sound one, and is not invalidated by the dangerous abuses to which it is exposed in practice.

The real issue is one of safeguards, of motives, and of methods. What are the conditions under which a nation may help to develop the resources of another, and even apply some element of compulsion in doing so ? The question, abstract as it may sound, is quite the most important of all practical questions for this generation. For that such development will take place, and such compulsion, legitimate or illegitimate, be exercised, more and more throughout this new century in many quarters of this globe, is beyond the shadow of a doubt. It is the great practical business of the country to explore and develop, by every method which science can devise, the hidden natural and human resources of the globe.

That the white Western nations will abandon a quest on which they have already gone so far is a view which does not deserve consideration. That this process of development may be so conducted as to yield a gain to world-civilization, instead of some terrible *débâcle* in which revolted slave races may trample down their parasitic and degenerate white masters, should be the supreme aim of far-sighted scientific statecraft.

II

To those who utter the single cry of warning, " *laissez faire*, hands off, let these people develop their resources themselves with such assistance as they ask or hire, undisturbed by the importunate and arrogant control of foreign nations," it is a sufficient answer to point out the impossibility of maintaining such an attitude.

If organized Governments of civilized Powers refused the task, they would let loose a horde of private adventurers, slavers, piratical traders, treasure hunters, concession mongers, who, animated by mere greed of gold or power, would set about the work of exploitation under no public control and with no regard to the future ; playing havoc with the political, economic, and moral institutions of the peoples, instilling civilized vices and civilized diseases, importing spirits and firearms as the trade of readiest acceptance, fostering internecine strife for their own political and industrial purposes, and even setting up private despotisms sustained by organized armed forces. It is unnecessary to revert to the buccaneering times of the sixteenth century, when a " new world " was thrown open to the plunder of the old, and private gentlemen of Spain or England competed with their Governments in the most gigantic business of spoliation that history records. The story of Samoa, of Hawaii, and a score of South Sea Islands in quite recent years, proves that, at a time when every sea is a highway, it is impossible for the most remote land to escape the intrusion of " civilized " nations, represented by precisely their most reckless and debased specimens, who gravitate thither in order to reap the rapid fruits of licence. The contact with white races cannot be avoided, and it is more perilous and more injurious in proportion as it lacks governmental sanction and control. The most gigantic modern experiment in private adventure slowly yielded its full tale of horrors in the Congo Free State, while the handing over of large regions in Africa to the virtually unchecked government of Chartered Companies has exposed everywhere the dangers of a contact based on private commercialism.[1]

To abandon the backward races to these perils of private exploitation, it is argued forcibly, is a barbarous dereliction of a public duty on behalf of humanity and the civilization of the world. Not merely does it leave the tropics to be the helpless prey of the offscourings of civilized nations ; it opens grave dangers in the future, from the political or military ambitions of native or imported rulers, who, playing upon the religious fanaticism or the combative instincts of great hordes of semi-savages, may impose upon them so effective a military discipline as to give terrible significance to some black or yellow " peril." Complete isolation is no longer possible even for the remotest island ; absolute self-sufficiency is no more possible for a nation than for an individual : in each case society has the right and the need to safeguard its interests against an injurious assertion of individuality.

[1] Chartered Company government is not necessarily bad in its direct results. It is, in fact, little else than private despotism rendered more than usually precarious in that it has been established for the sake of dividends. A " managing director " may be scrupulous and far-sighted, as Sir G. T. Goldie in the Niger Company, or unscrupulous and short-sighted, as Mr. Rhodes in the South African Chartered Company. The unchecked tyranny of the managing director may be illustrated by the evidence of the Duke of Abercorn, tendered to the South African Committee. " Mr. Rhodes had received a power of attorney to do precisely what he liked without consultation with the Board, he simply notifying what was done."

Again, though there is some force in the contention that the backward natives could and would protect themselves against the encroachments of private adventurers, if they had the assurance that the latter could not call upon their Government for assistance or for vengeance, history does not lead us to believe that these powers of self-protection however adequate against forcible invasions, would suffice to meet the more insidious wiles by which traders, prospectors, and political adventurers insinuate their poisons into primitive societies like that of Samoa or Ashanti.

So far, we have established two tentative principles. First, that all interference on the part of civilized white nations with " lower races " is not prima facie illegitimate. Second, that such interference cannot safely be left to private enterprise of individual whites. If these principles be admitted, it follows that civilized Governments *may* undertake the political and economic control of lower races—in a word, that the characteristic form of modern Imperialism is not under all conditions illegitimate.

What, then, are the conditions which render it legitimate ? They may be provisionally stated thus : Such interference with the government of a lower race must be directed primarily to secure the safety and progress of the civilization of the world, and not the special interest of the interfering nation. Such interference must be attended by an improvement and elevation of the character of the people who are brought under this control. Lastly, the determination of the two preceding conditions must not be left to the arbitrary will or judgment of the interfering nation, but must proceed from some organized representation of civilized humanity.

The first condition is deduced directly from the principle of social utility expanded to its widest range, so as to be synonymous with " the good of humanity." Regarding the conduct of one nation towards another we can find no other standard. Whatever uncertainty or other imperfection appertains to such a standard, regarded as a rule for international policy, any narrower standard is, of necessity, more uncertain and more imperfect. No purely legal contentions touching the misapplication of the term " right " to international relations, in the absence of any form of " sanction," affects our issue. Unless we are prepared to re-affirm in the case of nations, as the all-sufficient guide of conduct, that doctrine of " enlightened selfishness " which has been almost universally abandoned in the case of individuals, and to insist that the unchecked self-assertion of each nation, following the line of its own private present interest, is the best guarantee of the general progress of humanity, we must set up, as a supreme standard of moral appeal, some conception of the welfare of humanity regarded as an organic unity. It is, however, needless to insist upon the analogy between the relation of an individual to the other individuals of his society, and that of one society towards another in the commonwealth of nations. For, though cynical statesmen of the modern Macchiavelli school may assert the visible interest of their country as the supreme guide of conduct, they do not seriously suggest that the good of humanity is thus attained, but only that this wider end has no meaning or appeal for them. In the light of this attitude all discussion of general principles " justifying " conduct is out of place, for " just " and " justice " are ruled out *ab initio*. The standard here proposed would not, however, in point of fact, be formally rejected by any school of political thinkers who were invited to find a general law for the treatment of lower races. No one would assert in so many words that we had a right to sacrifice the good of any other nation, or of the world at large, to our own private national gain.

In England, certainly, Lord Rosebery's declaration that the British Empire is " the greatest secular agency for good known to the world " would everywhere be adopted as the fundamental justification of empire.

Lord Salisbury expressly endorsed the principle, asserting that " the course of events, which I should prefer to call the acts of Providence, have called this country to exercise an influence over the character and progress of the world such as has never been exercised in any Empire before " ; while the Archbishop of Canterbury propounded a doctrine of " imperial Christianity " based upon the same assumptions. It may, then, fairly be understood that every act of " Imperialism " consisting of forcible interference with another people can only be justified by showing that it contributes to " the civilization of the world."

Equally, it is admitted that some special advantage must be conferred upon the people who are the subject of this interference. On highest ground of theory, the repression, even the extinction, of some unprogressive or retrogressive nation, yielding place to another more socially efficient and more capable of utilizing for the general good the natural resources of the land, might seem permissible, if we accepted unimpaired and unimproved the biological struggle for existence as the sole or chief instrument of progress. But, if we admit that in the highest walks of human progress the constant tendency is to substitute more and more the struggle with natural and moral environment for the internecine struggle of living individuals and species, and that the efficient conduct of this struggle requires the suspension of the lower struggle and a growing solidarity of sentiment and sympathy throughout entire humanity, we shall perceive two important truths. First, " expansion," in order to absorb for the more " progressive " races an ever larger portion of the globe, is not the "necessity" it once appeared, because progress will take place more and more upon the qualitative plane, with more intensive cultivation alike of natural resources and of human life. The supposed natural necessity for crowding out the lower races is based on a narrow, low, and purely quantitative analysis of human progress.

Secondly, in the progress of humanity, the services of nationality, as a means of education and of self-development, will be recognized as of such supreme importance that nothing short of direct physical necessity in self-defence can justify the extinction of a nation. In a word, it will be recognized that "le grand crime internationnel est de détruire une nationalité."[1] But even those who would not go so far in their valuation of the factor of nationality will agree that it is a sound practical test of conduct to insist that interference with the freedom of another nation shall justify itself by showing some separate advantage conferred upon the nation thus placed in an inferior position : partly, because it seems obvious that the gain to the general cause of civilization will chiefly be contained in or compassed by an improvement in the character or condition of the nation which is the subject of interference ; partly, because the maxim which recognizes the individual person as an end, and requires State government to justify itself by showing that the coercion it exercises does in reality enlarge the liberty of those whom it restrains, is applicable also to the larger society of nations. Without unduly pressing the analogy of individual and nation as organisms, it may safely be asserted that imperial interference with a "lower race" must justify itself by showing that it is acting for the real good of the subject race. Mr. Chamberlain is no sentimentalist, and his declaration may

[1] M. Brunetière, quoted *Edinburgh Review*, April, 1900.

rank as a *locus classicus* upon this matter. "Our rule over the territories [native] can only be justified if we can show that it adds to the happiness and prosperity of the people."

The moral defence of Imperialism is generally based upon the assertion that in point of fact these two conditions are fulfilled, viz. that the political and economic control forcibly assumed by " higher " over " lower races " does promote at once the civilization of the world and the special good of the subject races. The real answer, upon which British Imperialists rely in defending expansion, is to point to actual services rendered to India, Eygpt, Uganda, etc., and to aver that other dependencies where British government is less successful would have fared worse if left either to themselves or to another European Power.

Before considering the practical validity of this position, and the special facts that determine and qualify the work of " civilizing " other races, it is right to point out the fundamental flaw in this theory of " Imperialism," viz. the non-fulfilment of the third condition laid down above. Can we safely trust to the honour, the public spirit, and the insight of any of the competing imperial races the subordination of its private interests and ends to the wider interests of humanity or the particular good of each subject race brought within its sway ?

No one, as we point out, contends that so perfect a natural harmony exists that every nation, consciously following its own chief interest, is " led " as " by an invisible hand " to a course of conduct which necessarily subserves the common interest, and in particular the interest of the subject race. What security, then, can possibly exist for the practices of a sound Imperialism fulfilling the conditions laid down ? Does any one contend that the special self-interest of the expanding and annexing nation is not a chief, or indeed the chief conscious determinant in each step of practical Imperialism ? Prima facie it would seem reasonable to suppose that many cases would occur in which the special temporary interests of the expanding nation would collide with those of the world-civilization, and that the former would be preferred. It is surely unreasonable to take as proof of the fulfilment of the conditions of sane Imperialism the untested and unverified *ipse dixit* of an interested party.

III

While it is generally agreed that the progress of world-civilization is the only valid moral ground for political interference with " lower races," and that the only valid evidence of such progress is found in the political, industrial, and moral education of the race that is subjected to this interference, the true conditions for the exercise of such a " trust " are entirely lacking.

The actual situation is, indeed, replete with absurdity. Each imperialist nation claims to determine for itself what are the lower races it will take under its separate protection, or agrees with two or three neighbours to partition some huge African tract into separate spheres of influence ; the kind of civilization that is imposed is never based on any sober endeavour to understand the active or latent progressive forces of the subject race, and to develop and direct them, but is imported from Europe in the shape of sets arts of industry, definite political institutions, fixed religious dogmas, which are engrafted on alien institutions. In political government progress is everywhere avowedly sacrificed to order, and both alike are subservient to the quick development of certain profitable trading industries, or to the mere lust of territorial aggrandisement. The recurrent quarrels of the armed white nations, each insisting on his claim to take up the white man's burden in some fresh quarter of the globe ; the trading companies seeking to oust each other from a new market, the very missionaries competing by sects and nationalities for " mission fields," and using political intrigue and armed force to back their special claims, present a curious commentary upon the " trust for civilization " theory.[1]

It is quite evident that this self-assertive sway lacks the first essentials of a trust, viz. security that the " trustee " represents fairly all the interested parties, and is responsible to some judicial body for the faithful fulfilment of the terms of the trust. Otherwise what safeguard exists against the abuse of the powers of the trustee ? The notorious fact that half the friction between European nations arises from conflicting claims to undertake the office of " trustee for civilization " over lower races and their possessions augurs ill alike for the sincerity of the profession and the moral capacity to fulfil it. It is surely no mark of cynicism to question closely this extreme anxiety to bear one another's burdens among the nations.

This claim to justify aggression, annexation, and forcible government by talk of duty, trust, or mission can only be made good by proving that the claimant is accredited by a body genuinely representative of civilization, to which it acknowledges a real responsibility, and that it is in fact capable of executing such a trust.

[1] From *The Times*, February 24, 1902—

" Hong-Kong, February 22.

" The German missionaries who escaped after the mission house at Frayuen was destroyed by Chinese have returned. It is reported from Canton that the French bishop intends to protect the natives who destroyed the Berlin mission station. The first information showed that hostility existed on the part of the Catholics towards the native Protestants, but it is believed that the aggressors assumed Catholicism as a subterfuge. If the bishop defends them, the situation of the missions in Kwang-tung will become complicated."

In a word, until some genuine international council exists, which shall accredit a civilized nation with the duty of educating a lower race, the claim of a " trust " is nothing else than an impudent act of self-assertion. One may well be sceptical about the early feasibility of any such representative council ; but until it exists it would be far more honest for " expanding " nations to avow commercial necessity or political ambition as the real determinant of their protection of lower races than to feign a " trust " which has no reality. Even were international relations more advanced, and the movement begun at the Hague Conference solidified in a permanent authoritative body, representative of all the Powers, to which might be referred not only the quarrels between nations, but the entire partition of this " civilizing " work, the issue would still remain precarious. There would still be grave danger lest the " Powers," arrogating to themselves an exclusive possession of " civilization," might condemn to unwholesome and unjust subjection some people causing temporary trouble to the world by slow growth, turbulence or obnoxious institutions, for which liberty might be the most essential condition of progress. Apart from such genuine misapprehensions, there would exist the peril of the establishment of a self-chosen oligarchy among the nations which, under the cloak of the civilizing process, might learn to live parasitically upon the lower races, imposing upon them " for their own good " all the harder or more servile work of industry, and arrogating to themselves the honours and emoluments of government and supervision.

Clear analysis of present[1] tendencies points indeed to some such collusion of the dominant nations as the largest and gravest peril of the early future. The series of treaties and conventions between the chief European Powers,

[1] Relates to the period in which this book was written, 1903.

beginning with the Berlin African Conference of 1885, which fixed a standard for the "amicable division" of West African territory, and the similar treaty in 1890, fixing boundaries for English, German and Italian encroachments in East Africa, doubtless mark a genuine advance in the relations of the European Powers, but the objects and methods they embody throw a strange light upon the trust theory. If to the care of Africa we add that of China, where the European Powers took common action in "the interests of civilization," the future becomes still more menacing. While the protection of Europeans was the object in the foreground, and imposed a brief genuine community of policy upon the diverse nations, no sooner was the immediate object won than the deeper and divergent motives of the nations became manifest. The entire history of European relations with China in modern times is little else than one long cynical commentary upon the theory that we are engaged in the civilization of the Far East. Piratical expeditions to force trade upon a nation whose one principle of foreign policy was to keep clear of foreigners, culminating in a war to compel the reception of Indian opium ; abuse of the generous hospitality given for centuries to peaceful missionaries by wanton insults offered to the religious and political institutions of the country, the forcible exaction of commercial and political "concessions" as punishment for spasmodic acts of reprisal, the cold-blooded barter of murdered missionaries for the opening of new treaty ports, territory at Kiao Chow, or a new reach of the Yang-Tse for British trading vessels ; the mixture of menace, cajolery, and bribery by which England, Russia, Germany, France, and Japan laboured to gain some special and separate railway or mining concessions, upon terms excluding or damaging the interest of the others ; the definite assumption by Christian bishops and missionaries of political authority, and the arrogant and extensive use of the so-called right of "extra-territoriality," whereby they claim, not only for themselves but for their alleged converts and protégés, immunity from the laws of the land— all these things sufficiently expose the hollowness in actual history of the claims that considerations of a trust for civilization animate and regulate the foreign policy of Christendom, or of its component nations. What actually confronts us everywhere in modern history is selfish, materialistic, short-sighted, national competition, varied by occasional collusion. When any common international policy is adopted for dealing with lower races it has partaken of the nature, not of a moral trust, but of a business "deal."

It seems quite likely that this policy of "deals" may become as frequent and as systematic in the world of politics as in the world of commerce, and that treaties and alliances having regard to the political government and industrial exploitation of countries occupied by lower races may constitute a rude sort of effective internationalism in the early future.

Now, such political arrangements fall short in two important respects of that genuine trust for civilization which alone could give moral validity to a "civilized" control of lower peoples. In the first place, its assignment of a sphere of interest or a protectorate to England, to Germany, or Russia, is chiefly determined by some particular separate interest of that country by reason of contiguity or other private convenience, and not by any impartial consideration of its special competence for the work of civilization. If, for example, European Powers were really animated by the desire to extend Western civilization to China for her own good and that of the world, they might more favourably essay this task by promoting the influence of Japan than by inserting their own alien occidentalism.

But no one proposes to delegate to Japan this " trust "; every nation thinks of its own present commercial interests and political prestige.

Secondly, the civilization of the lower races, even according to accepted Western lights, is nowhere adopted as the real aim of government. Even where good political order is established and maintained, as in Egypt or India, its primary avowed end, and its universally accepted standard of success, are the immediate economic benefits attributed thereto. The political government of the country is primarily directed everywhere to the rapid, secure, effective development of the national resources, and their profitable exploitation by native labour under white management. It is maintained and believed that this course is beneficial to the natives, as well as to the commerce of the controlling power and of the world at large. That Indians or Egyptians are better off to-day than they were before our autocratic sway, not merely in economic resources but in substantial justice, may be quite true ; it may even be accredited to us that many of our governors and officials have displayed some disinterested concern for the immediate well-being of the races committed (by ourselves) to our trust. But it can nowhere be sincerely contended that either we or any other Christian nation are governing these lower races upon the same enlightened principles which we profess and some-times practise in governing ourselves. I allude here not to methods of government, but to ends. In the more en-lightened European States and their genuine colonies, though present economic considerations bulk largely enough, they do not absorb the present and the future of public policy ; provision is made for some play of non-economic forces, for the genuine culture of human life and character, for progress alike in individual growth and in the social growth which comes by free processes of self-government. These are regarded as essential conditions of the healthy growth of a nation. They are not less essential in the case of lower nations, and their exercise demands more thought and more experiment. The chief indictment of Imperialism in relation to the lower races consists in this, that it does not even pretend to apply to them the principles of education and of progress it applies at home.

IV

If we or any other nation really undertook the care and education of a " lower race " as a trust, how should we set about the execution of the trust ? By studying the religions, political and other social institutions and habits of the people, and by endeavouring to penetrate into their present mind and capacities of adaptation, by learning their language and their history, we should seek to place them in the natural history of man ; by similar close attention to the country in which they live, and not to its agricultural and mining resources alone, we should get a real grip upon their environment. Then, carefully approaching them so as to gain what confidence we could for friendly motives, and openly discouraging any premature private attempts of exploiting companies to work mines, or secure concessions, or otherwise to impair our disinterested conduct, we should endeavour to assume the position of advisers. Even if it were necessary to enforce some degree of authority, we should keep such force in the background as a last resort, and make it our first aim to understand and to promote the healthy free operations of all internal forces for progress which we might discover.

Natural growth in self-government and industry along tropical lines would be the end to which the enlightened policy of civilized assistance would address itself.

Now, what are the facts ? Nowhere has any serious organized attempt been made, even by Great Britain, by far the largest of the trustees, to bring this scientific disinterested spirit of inquiry to bear upon the races whose destiny she dominates.[1] The publications of the Aborigines Protection Society, and the report of the Native Races Committee, dealing with South Africa, indicate the vast range of unexplored knowledge, and the feeble fumblings which have hitherto taken the place of ordered investigations.[2] It is natural that this should be so. White pioneers in these countries are seldom qualified to do the work required ; the bias of the trader, the soldier, or the professional traveller, is fatal to sober, disinterested study of human life, while the missionary, who has contributed more than the rest, has seldom been endowed with a requisite amount of the scientific spirit or the scientific training.

Even the knowledge which we do possess is seldom utilized for light and leading in our actual government of native races. There have indeed been signs of an awakening intelligence in certain spots of our Empire ; administrators like Sir George Grey, Lord Ripon, and Sir Marshall Clarke brought sympathy and knowledge to the establishment of careful experiments in self-government. The forms of protectorate exercised over Basutoland and Khama's Country in South Africa, the restoration of the province of Mysore to native government, and the more careful abstention from interference with the internal policy of feudatory States in India, were favourable signs of a more enlightened policy.

In particular, the trend of liberal sentiment regarding

[1] The formation of an African Society, in memory of Miss Mary Kingsley for the study of the races of that continent, was a move in the right direction.

[2] No slight is here intended upon the excellent work of the Society and the Committee here named. They have handled well and accurately their material. It is the work of original research that is so lacking.

government of lower races was undergoing a marked change. The notion that there exists one sound, just, rational system of government, suitable for all sorts and conditions of men, embodied in the elective representative institutions of Great Britain, and that our duty was to impose this system as soon as possible, and with the least possible modifications, upon lower races, without any regard to their past history and their present capabilities and sentiments, was tending to disappear in this country, though the new headstrong Imperialism of America was still exposed to the taunt that "Americans think the United States has a mission to carry 'canned' civilization to the heathen." The recognition that there may be many paths to civilization, that strong racial and environmental differences preclude a hasty grafting of alien institutions, regardless of continuity and selection of existing agencies and forms—these genuinely scientific and humane considerations are beginning to take shape in a demand that native races within our Empire shall have larger liberty of self-development assured to them. and that the imperial Government shall confine its interference to protection against enemies from without, and preservation of the elements of good order within.

The true "imperial" policy is best illustrated in the case of Basutoland, which was rescued in 1884 from the aggressive designs of Cape Colony, stimulated by industrial exploiters.

Here British imperial government was exercised by a Commissioner, with several British magistrates to deal with grave offences against order, and a small body of native police under British officers. For the rest, the old political and economic institutions are preserved—government by chiefs, under a paramount chief, subject to the informal control or influence of public opinion in a national assembly ; ordinary administration, chiefly consisting in allotment of land, and ordinary jurisdiction are left to the chiefs.

" As far back as 1855 Moshesh forbade the ' smelling-out ' of witches, and now the British authorities have suppressed the more noxious or offensive kinds of ceremonies practised by the Kaffirs. Otherwise, they interfere as little as possible with native ways, trusting to time, peace, and the missionaries to secure the gradual civilization of the people." " No Europeans are allowed to hold land, and a licence is needed even for the keeping of a store. Neither are any mines worked. European prospectors are not permitted to come in and search for minerals, for the policy of the authorities has been to keep the country for the natives, and nothing alarms the chiefs so much as the occasional appearance of these speculative gentry, who, if admitted, would soon dispossess them."[1]

These sentences serve to point the path by which most of our Imperialism has diverged from the ideal of a " trust for civilization."

The widest and ultimately the most important of the struggles in South Africa is that between the policy of Basutoland and that of Johannesburg and Rhodesia ; for there, if anywhere, we lay our finger on the difference between a " sane " Imperialism, devoted to the protection, education, and self-development of a " lower-race," and an " insane " Imperialism, which hands over these races to the economic exploitation of white colonists who will use them as " live tools " and their lands as repositories of mining or other profitable treasure.

V

It is impossible to ignore the fact that this " saner " Imperialism has been vitiated in its historic origins in almost every quarter of the globe. Early Imperialism had two

[1] Mr. Bryce, *Impressions of South Africa*, p. 422.

main motives, the lust of " treasure " and the slave trade.
Gold and silver, diamonds, rubies, pearls, and other
jewels, the most condensed forms of portable and durable
wealth by which men in a single hazardous adventure, by
fortune, fraud, or force, might suddenly enrich themselves
—these from the ancient days of Tyre and Carthage have
directed the main current alike of private and national
exploration, and have laid the foundation of white dominion
over the coloured races. From Ophir, Golconda, and the
Orinoco to Ashanti, Kimberley, Klondike, the Transvaal
and Mashonaland it is the same story : to the more precious
metals, tin and copper were early added as motives of nearer
and less hazardous trading ventures, and the machine
economy of recent generations has lifted coal and iron
deposits to the rank of treasures worth capture and exploitation by civilized nations. But gold still holds its own as
the dramatic centre of gravitation for Imperialism.

But along with these motives, and of even wider operation,
has been the desire to obtain supplies of slave or serf
labour. The earliest, the most widely prevalent, and the
most profitable trade in the history of the world has been
the slave trade. Early forms of imperial expansion were
directed less to any permanent occupation and government
of foreign countries than to the capture of large supplies of
slave labour to be transmitted to the conquering country.
The early Imperialism of the Greek States and of Rome was
largely governed by this same motive. Greeks and Romans
did not often effect large permanent settlements among
the barbarians they conquered, but, contenting themselves
with keeping such military and magisterial control as
sufficed to secure order and the payment of tribute, drafted
large numbers of slaves into their countries in order to
utilize their labour. The Greek cities were mostly mari-
time, commercial, and industrial, and the slaves they drew

from Eastern trade or from the Scythian and Thracian "hinterlands" they employed upon their ships and docks, in their mines, and as artisans and labourers in their towns : Rome, the capital of an agricultural State, used her slaves on a "plantation system," ousting by this cheap forced labour the peasantry, who, driven into Rome, were subsisted chiefly upon public charity, defrayed out of the tribute of their foreign conquests.[1]

Now modern Imperialism in its bearing on the "lower races" remains essentially of the same type : it employs other methods, other and humaner motives temper the dominance of economic greed, but analysis exposes the same character at bottom. Wherever white men of "superior races" have found able-bodied savages or lower races in possession of lands containing rich mineral or agricultural resources, they have, whenever strong enough, compelled the lower race to work for their benefit, either organizing their labour on their own land, or inducing them to work for an unequal barter, or else conveying them as slaves or servants to another country where their labour-power could be more profitably utilized. The use of imperial force to compel "lower races" to engage in trade is commonly a first stage of Imperialism ; China is here the classic instance of modern times, exhibiting the sliding scale by which sporadic trade passes through "treaties," treaty ports, customs control, rights of inland trading, mining and railway concession, towards annexation and general exploitation of human and natural resources.

The slave trade or forcible capture and conveyance of natives from their own to a foreign land has in its naked form nearly disappeared from the practice of Western nations (save in the case of Belgium in the Congo), as also

[1] *Cf.* Mr. Gilbert Murray in *Liberalism and the Empire*, pp. 126–129 (Brimley Johnson).

the working of conquered people as slaves in their own country.

The entire economic basis of the industrial exploitation of inferior races has shifted with modern conditions of life and industry. The change is a twofold one : the legal status of slave has given place to that of wage-labourer, and the most profitable use of the hired labour of inferior races is to employ them in developing the resources of their own lands under white control for white men's profit.

" In ancient times the employer would not, if he could, go away from his own country to employ Libyans or Scythians in their native places. If he left home, it was not so easy to come back. He was practically in exile. In the second place, he was not sufficiently master of his slaves in their own country. If they were all of one nation and all at home, they might rebel or break loose. If a strong Government prevented that, it was at any rate much easier for individual slaves to escape—a consideration always of the utmost importance. In modern times, the increasing ease of communication has enabled white men to go abroad to all parts of the earth without suffering much real exile and without losing the prospect of returning home at will. Our Governments, judged by ancient standards, are miraculously strong ; our superior weapons make rebellions almost impossible. Consequently we do not attempt to import blacks, coolies, and Polynesians into Great Britain. The opposition of the working classes at home would be

[1] In the British Protectorate of Zanzibar and Pemba, however, slavery still (1902) exists (notwithstanding the Sultan's decree of emancipation in 1897) and British courts of justice recognize the status. Miss Emily Hutchinson, who was associated with the Friends' Industrial Mission at Pemba, said it was five years since the legal status of slavery was abolished in Zanzibar and Pemba. Every one, including those who were most anxious that the liberation should proceed slowly, was dissatisfied with the present state of affairs. Out of an estimated population of 25,000 slaves in Pemba less than 5,000 had been liberated so far under the decree (Anti-Slavery Society Annual Meeting, April 4, 1902).

furious ; and, even if that obstacle were overcome, the coloured men would die too fast in our climate. The whole economic conditions are in favour of working the coloured man in his own home."[1]

This conclusion, however, requires some considerable qualification in the case of European colonies. Though " imperial " nations do not introduce the subject races into their home labour-markets, they induce an ever-growing stream of labour to flow between different parts of the subject portions of this Empire. The practice of indentured immigration is largely in vogue. The British Colony of Queensland and the French New Caledonia have been fed with labour from Polynesia ; the trade and agriculture of Natal has been largely absorbed by Indian " coolie " labour ; Chinese labour, free or indentured, has found its way into the Straits Settlements, Burma, Borneo, New Guinea, and parts of Australia, America, Oceania, and tropical Africa, a startling illustration of the movement being afforded by the Chinese indentured labour system adopted for the working of the Transvaal mines. Still, it is true that the general modern tendency is to work the coloured man in his own home, or in some neighbouring country to whose climatic and other natural characters he can easily adapt himself.

The chief economic condition which favours this course is not, however, the greater willingness of modern white men to sojourn for a while abroad, but the ever-growing demand for tropical goods, and the abundant overflow of capital from modern industrial States, seeking an investment everywhere in the world where cheap labour can be employed upon rich natural resources.

The ancients carried off the lower races to their own country, because they could use their labour but had little

[1] Murray, *Liberalism and the Empire*, p. 141.

use for their land ; we moderns wish the lower races to exploit their own lands for our benefit. The tastes for tropical agricultural products, such as rice, tea, sugar, coffee, rubber, etc., first aroused by trade, have grown so fast and strong that we require larger and more reliable supplies than trade with ill-disciplined races can afford us ; we must needs organize the industry by Western science and Western capital, and develop new supplies. So likewise with the vast mineral resources of lands belonging to lower races ; Western capital and Western exploiting energy demand the right to prospect and develop them. The real history of Imperialism as distinguished from Colonization clearly illustrates this tendency. Our first organized contact with the lower races was by means of trading companies, to which some powers of settlement and rights of government were accorded by charter as incidental to the main purpose, viz., that of conducting trade with native inhabitants. Such small settlement as took place at first was for trade and not for political expansion or genuine colonization of a new country. This was the case even in America with the London and Plymouth Companies, the Massachusetts Bay Company, and the Hudson's Bay Company, though other colonizing motives soon emerged ; our first entrance into the West Indies was by a trading settlement of the London Company in Barbados ; the foundation of our great Eastern Empire was laid in the trading operations of the East India Company, while the Gold Coast was first touched by the Royal Africa Company in 1692. Holland and France were moved by the same purpose, and the tropical or sub-tropical settlements which later passed from their hands into ours were mostly dominated by commercialism and a government based avowedly on commercial exploitation.[1]

As we approach more recent times, investment of capital

[1] *Cf.* Morris, *The History of Colonisation*, vol. ii, p. 60, etc.

and organization of native labour on the land, the plantation system, play a more prominent part in the policy of new companies, and the British North Borneo Company, the Sierra Leone Company, the Royal Niger Company, the East Africa Company, the British South Africa Company, are no longer chiefly trading bodies, but are devoted more and more to the control and development of agricultural and mining resources by native labour under white management to supply Western markets. In most parts of the world a purely or distinctively commercial motive and conduct have furnished the nucleus out of which Imperialism has grown, the early trading settlement becoming an industrial settlement, with land and mineral concessions growing round it, an industrial settlement involving force, for protection, for securing further concessions, and for checking or punishing infringements of agreement or breaches of order ; other interests, political and religious, enter in more largely, the original commercial settlement assumes a stronger political and military character, the reins of government are commonly taken over by the State from the Company and a vaguely defined protectorate passes gradually into the form of a colony. Sierra Leone, Uganda, and, at no distant date, Rhodesia, will serve for recent instances of this evolution.

VI

The actual history of Western relations with lower races occupying lands on which we have settled throws, then, a curious light upon the theory of a " trust for civilization." When the settlement approaches the condition of genuine colonization, it has commonly implied the extermination of the lower races, either by war or by private slaughter, as in the case of Australian Bushmen,

African Bushmen and Hottentots, Red Indians, and Maoris, or by forcing upon them the habits of a civilization equally destructive to them.[1] This is what is meant by saying that " lower races " in contact with " superior races " naturally tend to disappear. How much of " nature " or " necessity " belongs to the process is seen from the fact that only those " lower races " tend to disappear who are incapable of profitable exploitation by the superior white settlers, either because they are too " savage " for effective industrialism or because the demand for labour does not require their presence.

Whenever superior races settle on lands where lower races can be profitably used for manual labour in agriculture, mining, and domestic work, the latter do not tend to die out, but to form a servile class. This is the case, not only in tropical countries where white men cannot form real colonies, working and rearing families with safety and efficiency, and where hard manual work, if done at all, must be done by " coloured men," but even in countries where white men can settle, as in parts of South Africa and of the southern portion of the United States.

As we entered these countries for trade, so we stay there for industrial exploitation, directing to our own profitable purposes the compulsory labour of the lower races. This is the root fact of Imperialism so far as it relates to the control of inferior races ; when the latter are not killed out they are subjected by force to the ends of their white superiors.

With the abolition of the legal form of slavery the

[1] Mr. Bryce (Romanes Lecture, 1902, p. 32) says : " I was told in Hawaii that the reduction of the native population, from about 300,000 in Captain Cook's time to about 30,000 in 1883, was largely due to the substitution of wooden houses for the old wigwams, whose sides, woven of long grass, had secured natural ventilation, and to the use of clothes, which the natives, accustomed to nothing more than a loin cloth, did not think of changing or drying when drenched with rain."

economic substance has not disappeared. It is no general question of how far the character of slavery adheres in all wage labour that I am pressing, but a statement that Imperialism rests upon and exists for the sake of " forced labour," i.e. labour which natives would not undertake save under direct or indirect personal compulsion issuing from white masters.

There are many methods of " forcing " labour.

Wherever the question of industrial development of tropical or sub-tropical lands for agricultural or mining purposes comes up, the same difficulty confronts the white masters. The Report of the Select Committee of the House of Commons in 1842 on the state of the West Indies, subsequent to the emancipation of slaves, states the problem most succinctly : " The labourers are enabled to live in comfort and to acquire wealth without, for the most part, labouring on the estates of the planters for more than three or four days in a week, and from five to seven hours in a day, so that they have no sufficient stimulus to perform an adequate amount of work." The reason of this inadequate amount of work (how many white men in the West Indies put in a five to seven hours' working-day ?) is that they can get high wages, and this is attributed " to the easy terms upon which the use of land has been obtainable by negroes." In a word, the Committee considered " that the cheapness of land has been the main cause of the difficulties which have been experienced, and that this cheapness is the natural result of the excess of fertile land beyond the wants of the existing population."

The negro would only put in a five to seven hours' day at high pay because he had the option of earning his livelihood on fertile land of his own. The same trouble confronts the white master everywhere where the lower races are in possession of agricultural land sufficient for their low and unprogressive standard of comfort; they either will not work at all for wages, or will not work long enough or for low enough pay.

" The question, in a few words," writes Professor Ireland, " is this—What possible means are there of inducing the inhabitants of the tropics to undertake steady and continuous work if the local conditions are such that from the mere bounty of nature all the ambitions of the people can be gratified without any considerable amount of labour ? "[1]

There are only two genuinely economic forces which will bring such labour more largely into the labour market : The growth of population with increased difficulty in getting a full easy subsistence from the soil is one ; the pressure of new needs and a rising standard of consumption is the other.

These may be regarded as the natural and legitimate inducements to wage labour, and even in most tropical countries they exercise some influence, especially where white settlements have taken up much of the best land. In the lowest races, where the increase of population is kept down by high mortality, aggravated by war and infanticide, and where new wants are slowly evolved, these inducements are feeble ; but in more progressive peoples they have a fair amount of efficacy. Unfortunately, these natural forces are somewhat slow, and cannot be greatly hastened ; white industrialists are in a hurry to develop the country, and to retire with large, quick profits. The case of South Africa is typical. There many of the Bantu races are fairly educable in new needs, and are willing to undertake wage labour for their satisfaction ; many of them, notably the Basutos, are becoming overcrowded on their reserved lands, and are willing to go far for good wages. But the demands of a vast mining industry, growing within

[1] *Tropical Colonization*, p. 155 (The Macmillan Co.).

a few years to gigantic proportions, cannot await the working of these natural stimuli; the mine-owners want an unnatural accession to the labour market. The result is frantic efforts to scour the continents of Africa and Asia, and bring in masses of Zanzibari, Arabs, Indian coolies, or Chinese, or else to substitute for natural economic pressure various veiled modes of political or private compulsion.

The simplest form of this compulsion is that of employing armed force upon individual natives to "compel them to come in," as illustrated by the methods of the South Africa Chartered Company before 1897,[1] which, when the chiefs failed to provide labour, sent out native police to "collect the labour." Save its illegal character, there is nothing to distinguish this from the *corvée* or legalized forced labour imposed on natives in Natal, or the Compulsory Labour Ordinance passed by the Gold Coast Legislature in December 1895, reviving the lapsed custom under which it was "obligatory on persons of the labouring class to give labour for public purposes on being called out by their chiefs or other native superiors," and authorizing the Government to compel native chiefs to furnish as many carriers as were needed for the projected expedition to Kumasi.[2]

Military service, borrowing a semblance of "civilized" usage from the European system of conscription, is utilized, not merely for emergencies, as in the Kumasi expedition,

[1] Sir Richard Martin in his report states his conviction "that the Native Commissioners, in the first instance, endeavoured to obtain labour through the Indunas, but failing that, they procured it by force."

Howard Hensman, defending the administration of the Company in his *History of Rhodesia* (Blackwood & Sons), admits the practice, thus describing it: "In Rhodesia a native who declined to work" (i.e. for wages) "was taken before the Native Commissioners and sent off to some mine or public work close at hand, paid at what, to him, were very high rates, fed and housed, and then at the end of three months he was allowed to return to his kraal, where he was permitted to remain for the rest of the year" (p. 257).

[2] *Cf. Whites and Blacks in South Africa*, by H. R. Fox Bourne, p. 63.

and in our South African campaign, where native labour had everywhere been " pressed," when ordinary economic motives failed, but for regular industrial labour. The classical instance is that of the Congo Free State, where a " militia " levy was made upon the population, nominally for defence, but really for the State and Chartered Company service in the " rubber " and other industries.

In face of unrepealed decrees according " une protection spéciale aux noirs," and prescribing that " l'esclavage, même domestique, ne saurait être reconnu officialement," a system of " voluntary " and " militia " levies has been instituted to be used " in the establishment of plantations and the construction of works of public utility." The accuracy of Mr. Fox Bourne's commentary is attested by numerous witnesses. " The ' force publique ' with its ' agriculteurs soldats ' and others subordinate to it, when not employed on military expeditions, are used as overseers of what are virtually slave-gangs or as collectors of ' tribute ' from the luckless aborigines, whose right to live in their own country, without paying heavily for the privilege, is denied."[1]

So far as " forced labour " is designed merely as a mode of revenue to the State, a system of " taxation in kind," it cannot be condemned as essentially unjust or oppressive, however liable it may be to abuses in practice. All taxation is " forced labour," whether the tax be levied in money, in goods, or in service. When such " forced labour " is confined to the needs of a well-ordered government, and is fairly and considerately administered, it involves no particular oppression. Such " servitude " as it involves is concealed under every form of government.

The case is quite different where governmental regulations and taxation are prostituted to purposes of commercial

[1] *Slavery and its Substitutes in Africa*, p. 11.

profit ; where laws are passed, taxes levied, and the machinery of public administration utilized in order to secure a large, cheap, regular, efficient, and submissive supply of labourers for companies or private persons engaged in, mining, agricultural, or other industries for their personal gain.

Where white settlers find " lower races " in occupation of lands rich in agricultural, mineral, or other resources, they are subject to a double temptation. They want possession of the land and control of a cheap native supply of labour to work it under their control and for their gain. If the " natives " are of too low an order or too untamable to be trained for effective labour they must be expelled or exterminated, as in the case of the " lower nomads " the Bushmen of Australia and South Africa, the Negritos, Bororos, Veddahs, etc., and even the Indians of North America. War, murder, strong drink, syphilis and other civilized diseases are chief instruments of a destruction commonly couched under the euphemism " contact with a superior civilization." The land thus cleared of natives passes into white possession, and white men must work it themselves, or introduce other lower industrial peoples to work it for them, as in the case of slave labour introduced into the United States and West Indies, or indentured labour into Natal, British Guiana, etc.

But where the " lower races " are capable of being set to profitable labour on their own land, as agriculturists, miners, or domestics, self-interest impels the white to work a " forced-labour " system for their private ends. In most tropical or sub-tropical countries the natives can by their own labour and that of their families get a tolerably easy subsistence from the land. If they are to be induced to undertake wage labour for white masters, this must be put a stop to. So we have pressure brought upon government to render it impossible for the natives to live as formerly upon the land. Their land and, when they are a pastoral people, their cattle are objects of attack.

The Torrens Act, by which in 1852 the doctrine of "eminent domain" was applied to South Australia in such wise as to make all the country virtually Crown land, though not ill-meant, has furnished a baneful precedent, not only for encroachment of British settlers, but for the still more flagrant abuses of Belgian adventurers on the Congo. White settlers or explorers, sometimes using legal instruments, sometimes private force or fraud, constantly encroach upon the fertile or mineralized lands of natives, driving them into less fertile lands, crowding them into reserves, checking their nomadic habits, and otherwise making it more difficult for them to obtain a livelihood by the only methods known to them.

A chief object and a common result of this policy is to induce or compel natives to substitute wage labour, altogether or in part, for the ancient tribal life upon the land. Those ignorant of the actual conditions involved often suppose that the alienation of lands or mineral rights, or the contracts for labour, are negotiated in accordance with ordinary methods of free bargain.

The modern history of Africa, however, is rich in instances to the contrary.

The history of competitive knavery and crime, by which Lobengula was inveigled into signing away "rights" which he neither owned nor understood to the Chartered Company, cannot yet be written completely, but its outlines are plain and profitable reading.

A "free contract," implying voluntary action, full knowledge and approximate equality of gain to both parties, is almost unknown in the dealings of superior with inferior races. How political treaties and industrial concessions are actually obtained may be described for us by

Major Thruston,[1] who was sent to negotiate treaties in 1893 in Uganda.

"I have been instructed by Colonel Colvile to make a treaty with Kavalli, by which he should place himself under British protection ; in fact, I had a bundle of printed treaties which I was to make as many people sign as possible. This signing is an amiable farce, which is supposed to impose on foreign Governments, and to be the equivalent of an occupation. The *modus operandi* is somewhat as follows : A ragged, untidy European, who in any civilized country would be in danger of being taken up by the police as a vagrant, lands at a native village ; the people run away, he shouts after them to come back, holding out before them a shilling's worth of beads. Someone, braver than the rest, at last comes up ; he is given a string of beads, and is told that if the chief comes he will get a great many more. Cupidity is, in the end, stronger than fear ; the chief comes and receives his presents ; the so-called interpreter pretends to explain the treaty to the chief. The chief does not understand a word of it, but he looks pleased as he receives another present of beads ; a mark is made on a printed treaty by the chief, and another by the interpreter ; the vagrant, who professes to be the representative of a great Empire, signs his name. The chief takes the paper, but with some hesitation, as he regards the whole performance as a new and therefore dangerous piece of witchcraft. The boat sails away, and the new ally and protégé of England or France immediately throws the treaty into the fire."

This cynical bit of realistic humour expresses with tolerable accuracy the formal process of " imperial expansion " as it operates in the case of lower races. If these are the methods of political agents, it may well be understood that the methods of private " concession-mongers "

[1] *Personal Experiences in Egypt and Unyoro* (Murray).

are not more scrupulous. Indeed, " political protectorate " and " land concession " are inextricably blended in most instances where some adventurer, with a military or other semi-official commission, pushes across the frontier into a savage country, relying upon his Government to endorse any profitable deal he may accomplish.

But since, in the case of England at any rate, political expansion is commonly subordinate to industrial exploitation, a treaty or concession, giving rights over land or minerals, is of little value without control of labour. Enclosure of lands, while it facilitates a supply of native labour by restricting free land for native agriculture or pasture, does not commonly suffice. Various devices are adopted for bringing pressure to bear upon individual labourers to " contract " for wage labour. The simplest, apart from direct compulsion, is to bribe chieftains to use their " influence " with members of their tribe. Such was the system devised by the philanthropic Earl Grey to procure labour for the mines in Rhodesia.[1]

Such bargaining, either with " headmen " or with individual natives, is usually conducted by professional labour touts, who practise every form of craft and falsehood so as to induce ignorant natives to enter a labour contract. In the case of the Transvaal mines this abuse had become so monstrous as to " spoil the labour market," obliging the mine-owners to go ever farther afield for their labour, and eventually compelling them to petition the Government for assistance in putting down the system of private labour touts and substituting authorized respon-

---

[1] " We propose to give to the big chiefs, when they have proved themselves worthy of trust, a salary of £5 a month and a house. . . . The indunas will then be responsible to the Government for the conduct of their people." This, Earl Grey supposes, " is the best way to secure a considerable revenue in the future in the shape of hut tax, and to obtain a fair supply of labour for the mines " (*Times*, November 28, 1896).

sible officials. Alike in the Boer Republics and in Cape Colony, the seizures of land and labour have been chief motives of the border warfare constantly recurring in the history of South Africa. The encroachments of Boers or British colonists upon native territory or reserves, or the seizure of cattle on border land by one party or the other, had led to punitive expeditions, the result of which has been further confiscation of land and capture of prisoners, who, formerly held as slaves, have in more recent times been kept to labour as " apprentices " or indentured labourers.

The case of Bechuanaland in 1897 affords a serviceable illustration. A small local riot got up by a drunken native sub-chief on a trifling grievance, and involving armed resistance on the part of a few hundred Kaffirs, easily put down by a small body of armed volunteers, was exaggerated into a " rebellion," and was made a pretext for driving some 8,000 natives from the lands " inalienably " secured to them by the Bechuanaland Annexation Act of 1895, and for confiscating these lands for British occupation, while the rest of the population, some 30,000, were to be gradually removed from their settlements, and given " equivalent land " in some other district. In the speech introducing the confiscation measure in the Cape Parliament, Sir Gordon Sprigg explained that this was " very valuable land, and probably would be cut up into very small farms, so that there might be a considerable European population established in that part of the country." There was no pretence that most of those who were deprived of their lands or deported were proved to have taken part in the " rebellion." The sequel of this clearing is most significant. What was to become of the people taken from their land ? They were offered a choice between prosecution " on a charge of sedition " and " service in the colony upon such conditions and with such rates of wages as the Government might arrange for a term of five years." The Government, in thus proposing to compound a felony, was well aware of the extreme difficulty of proving " sedition " in a court of justice, and, in point of fact, in two cases which were put on trial the Public Prosecutor declined to bring the case before a jury. The object of the threat of trial was to coerce into the acceptance of " indentured labour," and in fact 584 men, with three times as many women and children were handed over to serve under colonial farmers, wages being fixed at 10s. a month for able-bodied men and 7s. 6d. for women.

Thus did covetous colonials kill two birds with one stone, obtaining the land and the labour of the Bechuana " rebels."[1] It is not necessary to suppose that such incidents are deliberately planned : where empire is asserted over lower races in the form of protectorate, the real government remaining in native hands, offences must from time to time arise, local disturbances which can by rash or brutal treatment be fanned into " rebellion," and form the pretext for confiscation and a forcing of the landless rebels into " labour."

---

[1] The details of this business, recorded in *Blue-book* C. 8,797, relating to native disturbances, are most instructive to the student, of Imperialism.

The inspector of Native Locations in his report of the affair distinctly asserts : " That it was not a general rising of the Mashowing people is certain, because there were not more than 100 natives engaged in the Kobogo fight." Yet the whole of the Mashowing territory was confiscated and all the population treated as rebels.

While only some 450 men were taken with arms, 3,793 men, women, and children were arrested and deported, 1,871 being afterwards " indentured " in the colony. Seven-eighths of the prisoners were women, children, or unarmed men. Even of the men who were taken in arms at the Langeberg Sir A. Milner wrote (January 5, 1898) : " I am inclined to think that in many other cases, if the prisoners had chosen to stand their ground, the same difficulty (as in two cases taken to trial) would have been found in establishing legal evidence of treason. It is probable that, of the men who surrendered at the Langeberg, some had never fought against the Government at all, while many others had done so reluctantly. To bring home treasonable intent to any large number of them would, I conceive, have been a difficult matter " (p. 48).

Among African tribes the most vulnerable point is the cattle, which form their most important, often their only, property. To encroach upon this is a sure way of provoking hostility. The Bechuana riot seems to have arisen from an injudicious handling of precautions needed to deal with the rinderpest. The second Matabele war, with its murders of white settlers and the wholesale slaughter in reprisal, was directly instigated by the seizure of cattle belonging to the tribesmen, on the unproven theory that all cattle belonged to the king and thus came into the possession of the Chartered Company. As a sequel of the first Matabele war large quantities of cattle had been stolen by white settlers to stock the farms which had just been pegged out for them in the land they had taken, and the further threat of a wholesale confiscation of cattle, though not carried into full effect, lay at the root of the subsequent rebellion.[1]

Everywhere these attacks upon the land and cattle of lower races, provoking reprisals, followed by further confiscation and a breaking-up of the old tribal life upon the soil, have as a related secondary object the provision of a supply of cheap labour for the new white masters, to be employed in farming, on mines, or for military service.

---

[1] Here is the account of a Rhodesian writer, defending the British policy :—

" Seeing that Lobengula only allowed his followers to own cattle on sufferance as it were, all the herds in the country might be said to be the property of the late king, and that was the view which the British South Africa Company took. The number of cattle in the country at this time was estimated at not less than a quarter of a million head, and the indunas were ordered at once to drive in the cattle from the districts over which they had control to Buluwayo. Some of the indunas duly complied with this demand, in which they saw nothing more than what was to be expected as the outcome of the war ; but others, and those chiefly who had not taken any part in the fighting, declined to do so, and hid the cattle away out of reach of the Native Commissioners. As the cattle did not come in in such numbers as they ought to have done, the Government ordered the Native Commissioners to collect and send in each month a certain number of cattle. . . . This step proved a highly unpopular one among the natives " (*History of Rhodesia*, by H. Hensman, p. 165).

Such labour commonly preserves a semblance of free contract, engagements "voluntarily" entered into for a fixed period at agreed wages. The amount of real freedom depends partly upon the amount of personal pressure brought to bear by the chief through whom bargains are commonly struck, still more on the amount of option which remains to get a living from the land.

This last is the vital matter in an understanding of "forced labour." In one sense all labour is "forced" or "unfree," where it is not open to the "proletariat" to get a living by cultivation of the soil: this is the normal condition of the vast majority of the people in Great Britain and in some other white man's countries. What is peculiar to the system of "forced labour," as here used, is the adoption by a white ruling race of legal measures designed expressly to compel the individual natives to whom they apply to quit land, which they occupy and by which they can live, in order to work in white service for the private gain of the white man. When lands formerly occupied by natives are confiscated, or otherwise annexed for white owners, the creation of a labour supply out of the dispossessed natives is usually a secondary object. But this "forcing" becomes a system when measures are devised by Government for the express purpose of "compelling" labour.

VII

The simplest method, that of "slavery," is generally abolished by European nations. *Corvée*, the Congo and former Rhodesian methods are seldom openly advocated or defended; but the adoption of various forms of public compulsion in order to drive natives into private service is generally approved by "colonials," and is sanctioned by imperialist statesmen. A chief instrument of this indirect compulsion is taxation. There is nothing essentially un-reasonable in imposing a hut or a poll-tax upon natives to assist in defraying the expenses of government, provided that care is taken in the modes of assessment and collection, and due allowance made for the fluctuating economic circumstances of agricultural populations with narrow markets and small use of money. But these taxes are not infrequently applied so as to dispossess natives of their land, force them to work for wages and even to drive them into insurrections which are followed by wholesale measures of confiscation.

The case of the risings in Sierra Leone during 1898 attests the nature of this impolicy, and the following passage from the report of the Special Commissioner, Sir David Chalmers, deserves attention. His conclusions as to the causes of the insurrection are thus summarized :—

" The hut-tax, together with the measures used for its enforcement, were the moving causes of the insurrection. The tax was obnoxious to the customs and feelings of the people. A peremptory and regularly recurring impost is unknown in their own practices and tradition. The English Government has not as yet conferred any such benefits as to lead to a burden of a strange and portentous species being accepted willingly. There was a widespread belief that it was a means of taking away their rights in their country and in their property."[1] " The amount of the tax is higher than the people, taken together, can pay, and the arrangements by which liability is primarily placed

[1] Miss Mary Kingsley regards this " widespread belief " as justified.
" It has been said that the Sierra Leone hut-tax war is a ' little Indian Mutiny ' ; those who have said it do not seem to have known how true the statement is, for these attacks on property in the form of direct taxation are, to the African, treachery on the part of England, who, from the first, has kept on assuring the African that she does not mean to take his country from him, and then, as soon as she is strong enough, in his eyes, deliberately starts doing so " (*West African Studies*, p. 372 ; Macmillan & Co.).

on the chiefs to make good definite amounts on demand are unworkable." "The mode of enforcing payment provided by the law would probably prove abortive, whether used to meet inability or unwillingness to pay." " Repugnance to the tax was much aggravated by the sudden, uncompromising and harsh methods by which it was endeavoured to be brought into operation not merely by the acts of native policemen, but in the whole scheme adopted by the colonial authorities."

Here Sir. D. Chalmers condenses all the familiar grievances of monetary taxes imposed by strong expensive white Governments upon poor "native" races. White government, if good, is expensive, hence taxation tends to be heavy in amount ; fixed in amount, it must be paid out of very fluctuating industries ; levied in money, it forces self-subsisting families or tribes to find markets for their goods or labours ; collected, as it must be, by native authorities, it breeds extortion, corruption, and cruelty. But Sir D. Chalmers lays his finger on the central vice when he names " a widespread belief that it was a means of taking away their rights in their country and in their property."[1]

Where there exists a large growing demand for native labour this method of compelling natives to pay money taxes is seen to have a new importance. They can only earn money by undertaking labour contracts. Hence a system of direct taxation imposed by hut, poll, or labour-taxes is devised. Everywhere, as we have seen, under free popular government, the tendency is to subordinate direct to indirect taxation. " Imperialism " alone favours

---

[1] Compare the pathetic plaint of the natives in Rhodesia, as voiced by Sir Richard Martin in his official report. " The natives practically said : ' Our country is gone and our cattle ; we have nothing to live for. Our women are deserting us ; the white man does as he likes with them. We are the slaves of the white man ; we are nobody, and have no rights or laws of any kind ' " (Cd. 8547).

direct taxation of the working classes. It does not, however, propose a general system of direct taxation applicable alike to white and blacks. The direct taxes with which we are here concerned are applied exclusively to the "subject" races.

In South Africa their chief avowed aim is, not to provide revenue, but to compel labour. The hut and labour taxation is not strongly developed in Cape Colony or in Natal, because the break-up of old tribal life, and the substitution of individual economic family life favouring wage labour, have hitherto furnished a sufficient supply of labour to countries, mainly agricultural, thinly peopled by white settlers, and only in one district, that of Kimberley, developing a considerable centralized demand for native labour. The hut-tax in these colonies has, therefore, not proved an oppressive burden. Only when the diamond fields found difficulties in obtaining a ready supply of native labour, and wages rose, did Mr. Rhodes, a chief proprietor, use his public position as Cape Premier to procure an Act designed to assist De Beers in obtaining cheap labour. By this statute, the Glen Grey Act, it was enacted that every male native in districts where the Act was adopted, should pay a "labour-tax" of 10s. per annum, unless he could prove that during three months of each year "he has been in service or employment beyond the borders of the district." No secret was made of the fact that this measure was designed, not to provide revenue, but to compel to labour. "If they could make these people work they would reduce the rate of labour in the country," said Mr. Rhodes; and in another speech in Parliament: "It was wrong that there should be a million natives in that country, and yet that they should be paying a sum equal to about £1 a week for their labour, while that labour was absolutely essential for the proper development of the country."

The "labour-tax" has not, however, operated oppressively in Cape Colony; for the diamond industry, being limited in output, has not demanded more native labour than could be easily supplied by ordinary economic inducements. It is in the Transvaal and Rhodesia that taxation of natives ripens into a plan for forcing labour. The mineowners of the Transvaal are agreed as to their right and their need to compel the natives to undergo the dignity of labour, and they regard taxation as one important instrument. The testimony of witnesses before the Industrial Commission in 1897 was unanimous in favouring such compulsion, and Mr. Rudd, of the Consolidated Goldfields, stated the demand very plainly at the annual meeting of his company.[1] "If we could only call upon one-half of the natives to give up three months of the year to work, that would be enough. We should try some cogent form of inducement, or practically compel the native through taxation or in some other way, to contribute his quota to the good of the community, and to a certain extent he should then have to work." The general feeling of the "Outlanders" in the Transvaal has favoured the oppressive hut-tax of £2, imposed by the Republic in 1895, and has only complained of its inadequate enforcement.

Similarly, in Rhodesia, where mines require a larger supply of labour than can be obtained from natives by ordinary economic motives, an increase of the hut-tax and a labour-tax are an integral part of the public policy. Earl Grey, recent administrator and director of the Chartered Company, thus states the case : " Means have to be found to induce the natives to seek, spontaneously (sic !), employment at the mines, and to work willingly for long terms of more or less continuous employment. An incentive to labour must be provided, and it can only be provided by the

[1] November 19, 1899.

imposition of taxation. I look forward to the imposition of a hut-tax of £1 per hut in conformity with the practice which exists in Basutoland, and I also hope that we may, with the permission of the imperial authorities, be able to establish a labour-tax, which those able-bodied natives should be required to pay who are unable to show a certificate of four months' work."

It remains to add that one "imperial authority" of some importance has expressly endorsed this policy of using public finance for private profit-making purposes. In a speech in the House of Commons dealing with the Chartered Company[1] Mr. Chamberlain said : " When you say to a savage people who have hitherto found their chief occupation in war, ' You shall no longer go to war ; tribal war is forbidden,' you have to bring about some means by which they may earn their living in place of it, and you have to induce them to adopt the ordinary means of earning a livelihood by the sweat of their brow. But with a race of this kind I doubt very much whether you can do it merely by preaching. I think that something in the nature of an inducement, stimulus or pressure is absolutely necessary if you are to secure a result which is desirable in the interests of humanity and civilization."

A far more thorough and logical application of the policy of taking natives from their life upon the land in order to perform wage labour is devised by the Transvaal mine-owners. The native labour problem there differs widely from the case of Kimberley, where only some 12,000 natives under strict control are required for the diamond industry. The intention of working out, with the utmost rapidity, the gold of the Rand can only be accomplished by securing a vast and a growing supply of native labour on the spot. In 1899, with great difficulty and at heavy expense, less than 100,000

[1] May 7, 1898.

natives were secured for work upon the mines. If twice or thrice this number are to be procured and at lower prices, this can only be accomplished by using taxation, coercion and persuasion to induce large numbers of Kaffirs to come and settle down with their families upon locations in the mining districts, where the amount of land provided does not enable them to get a living from agriculture, and where they will consequently be dependent on wage labour at the mines, and will breed a permanent supply of young labour on the spot. The wages paid will be determined, not by competition, but by the Chamber of Mines; the houses they will occupy will be the property of the mines, as also the shops where they will be compelled to deal. This has been the policy advocated by the chief mining experts.

Break up the tribal system which gives solidarity and some political and economic strength to native life; set the Kaffir on an individual footing as an economic bargainer, to which he is wholly unaccustomed, take him by taxation or other " stimulus " from his locality, put him down under circumstances where he has no option but to labour at the mines—this is the plan which mine-owners propose and missionaries approve.[1]

[1] This has been the policy of the Glen Grey Act, and the following passage from the official report of a resident magistrate in a district of Cape Colony (Mr. W. T. Brownlie of Butterworth) makes its main economic motive transparent : " I have long held and still hold that the labour question and the land question are indissolubly bound together. In my opinion it is of little use framing enactments to compel unwilling persons to go out to work. It is like the old saw about leading a horse to the water; you can take him there, but you cannot make him drink. In the same way you may impose your labour-tax, but you cannot make your unwilling persons work. Create a healthy thirst in your horse and he will drink fast enough. Similarly create the necessity for the native to work and he will work, and none better.

" Hitherto, under our commercial-tenure system, there has been little absolute necessity for our young natives to leave their homes to work. The land supplies them with food, and a few shillings will buy a blanket, and as soon as the young man marries he is entitled to receive his lot of arable land ; but once this is stopped—and it will be stopped by the survey and individual tenure—a young man before he marries a wife will have to be in a position to support a wife, and

This system of "native locations," fortified by hut and labour-taxes, and by pass laws which interfere with freedom of travel and practically form a class of *ascripti glebœ*, was the method devised before the war by the missionaries for dealing with the labour problem in the Transvaal mines[1]: it is the method still advocated by the South African Native Affairs Commission, reporting in 1905[2]. To limit the access of the growing Kaffir population to the land and to impose taxes with the object of compelling them to wage labour, still remains the sheet-anchor of the South African labour policy. The drafting in of large numbers of Chinese is supplementary to this policy, used partly to afford an increased supply, partly to give mine-owners a better pick of Kaffir labour at a reduced price.

VIII

The introduction of large numbers of Chinese into the Transvaal mines under the Labour Ordinance of 1904, has given great prominence to the indentured labour system which is widely operative in our tropical dominions.

As regards the actual conditions of employment, there is reason to believe that where this system is practised under imperial protection as applied to Indian coolie labour it

to obtain this he must work, and once having married her he must still work to maintain her and himself, and once the necessity of work is created there will be no lack of men ready and willing to work" (*Blue-book on Native Affairs*, C. 31, p. 75).

[1] *Cf.* the Report of the Chamber of Mines for 1898 (quoted *Cd.* 9,345, p. 31), and the Report of the Industrial Commission, Johannesburg, 1897, *passim.*

[2] The gist of the "economic" recommendations of this Commission is that "squatting" of natives upon unoccupied public lands be stopped, that existing native locations for agriculture should be defined and that no more land should be reserved for the use of the growing population of natives; that outside these restricted areas no land should be purchased or leased by natives, that a minimum poll tax of £1 per head should be imposed on all adult male natives except those employed in wage labour or paying rates in towns.

has been free from the worst abuses of " forced labour."
British Guiana, Mauritius, and Trinidad are the West
Indian possessions where the system of importing Indian
coolie labour has been most practised, and where the system
is being tested.

The law[1] governing indentured labour in British Guiana
provided against most of the abuses which beset the
economic relations of white employers towards " lower
races," and appears to be well administered. Here the
Imperial Government in India approves all contracts with
immigrants, and these contracts not only contain a full
statement of time, wages, and other conditions of labour
and of living for the immigrant and his family, but provide
for his return, if necessary at the public expense, at the end
of his time. During the term of his indenture in British
Guiana he is under the protection of authorities appointed
and controlled by the governor alone. An immigration
agent-general, with a staff of agents, who visit all plantations
where indentured labourers are employed, hear privately
all complaints, and bring them, if necessary, into the courts,
retaining counsel and acting in all cases as the principals.
Employers of indentured labour are obliged to keep and
produce full and accurate books of accounts under heavy
penalties, and are forbidden to pay wages below a certain
sum or to overwork their labourers. No punishment of any
kind can be imposed by employers without recourse to the
courts. It is contended by Professor Ireland, who has had
long experience as an overseer, that this system operates
with remarkable success both economically and socially[2]
in British Guiana and in other West Indian islands ; and
in Natal, though " coolies " are regarded with anything

[1] As existing in 1903.
[2] *Tropical Colonization*, chap. v, by Professor Ireland, gives a full and detailed
account of the theory and practice of indentured labour in British Guiana.

but favour by large sections of the population, substantially the same protective legislation is in force, and there is every reason to suppose that indentured labourers are well protected as regards wages and other economic conditions.

But the very encomium passed upon this well-administered system of indenture shows how defective is the grasp of the magnitude and the real nature of the issues involved in the control of tropical labour.

It seems a light and natural thing that large bodies of men, with or without their families, should be driven by economic pressure to quit their native soil in our Indian Empire or in China, and absent themselves for ten years at a time in some unknown and remote colony. Migration to, and colonization of, sparsely peopled lands by inhabitants of thickly peopled lands is a natural and wholly beneficial movement, but the break-up of settled life, implied by long periods of alienation, is fraught with grave injuries to both countries alike. A country which relies for its economic development on continual influxes of foreign labourers who will not settle is impaired in its natural process of industrial and political self-development by this mass of unassimilated sojourners, while the country which they have abandoned suffers a corresponding injury.

Why is it necessary or desirable that large bodies of our Indian fellow-subjects should desert their native land, removing for long periods their industrial services in order to develop another country which is not theirs ? If India is over-populated, permanent colonization is surely the remedy ; if it is not, this practice of " indentured labour " seems to testify to misgovernment and bad husbandry of our Indian resources. To break up considerable areas of Indian society, and remove its able-bodied males for ten years at a time, in order that these men may bring back some " savings " at the end of their term, seems at best a wanton sacrifice of the stability and normal progress of Indian society to a narrow consideration of purely monetary gain. History teaches, in fact, that a peasant people living on soil which they own will not consent thus to alienate themselves for purposes of slight economic gain, unless they are compelled by excessive taxation on the part of Government, or by extortions of money-lenders, which deprive them in large measure of the enjoyment of the fruits of their labour on their land.

However well administered this system of indentured labour may be, it seems vitiated in origin by its artificial character and its interference with normal processes of self-development. It involves a subordination of wider social considerations to purposes of present industrial exploitation. What is true of the system, as applied in the West Indies and elsewhere for agricultural work, is still more true of industrial labour in mining processes. When " civilized " Kaffirs choose to quit their individual farms in the Transkei, or elsewhere, in order to earn extra money by three months' service in the mines, no particular harm may offset their monetary gain ; but when labour agents are employed to break up tribal life and tempt " raw " Kaffirs away from their kraals and the restraints of their habitual life into the utterly strange and artificial life upon the mines, the character of the Kaffir goes to pieces ; he becomes a victim to drink if he can get it, and often succumbs to the vices of the crowded, laborious, unhealthy life to which he has sold himself, while the arbitrary restrictions under which he works and lives, however justified, degrade and damage his personality. According to the evidence of most experienced and competent investigators, he returns home a " damaged " man, and often by his example a damage to his neighbours.[1]

[1] Cf. *Cape Colony Blue-books on Native Affairs*, G. 31, 1899, pp. 5, 9, 72, 75, 91, etc. ; G. 42, 1898, pp. 13, 14, 58, 82.

The least reflection will expose the dangers which must arise from suddenly transferring men from a semi-savage, tribal, agricultural life to a great modern, elaborate, industrial business like that of diamond and gold mining.

What is true of the uncivilized Kaffir is equally true of the more highly developed Chinaman. These men are introduced into the Transvaal as mere economic machines, not as colonists to aid the industrial and social development of a new country. Their presence is regarded as a social danger; they are kept in " compounds," denied the right to acquire property or even to remain in the country as free settlers on the termination of their service. Hordes of able-bodied males, without any women, huddled in close barracks, rigorously guarded during work and at leisure, kept continually at hard routine manual labour, deprived of all the educative influences of self-direction in a free civilized society, however well-fed, however highly paid, these men are inevitably degraded in morals by the conditions of this service, and damage the society to which they return.

Nor is this all. The effect upon the Transvaal is to substitute for a normal gradual and natural development, a hasty artificial abnormal development, to complicate the already grave racial and economic problems of the country by introducing a new factor of dangerous character and dimensions, a supply of cheap labour designed expressly to diminish the demand for white settlers and for black wage-earners. It is difficult to overestimate the gravity of the case in its bearing on the future of South Africa.

The mining industry of the Transvaal is by far the most important industry in the whole country; so far as British interests are concerned, the whole future depends on husbanding and developing these resources so as to keep a large growing number of permanent British colonists in the country. Now the cheapest and most profitable exploitation of the mines involves a minimum employment of white British labour and a short period of over-stimulated industrial activity. Although it is clearly the interest and the intention of the mine-owners, in defiance of the conditions in the ordinance, to displace by skilled Chinese labour most of the white labour formerly required for working the mines, it is possible that a considerable though fluctuating demand for British labour in other industrial and commercial undertakings may be furnished during this artificially shortened life of the richer mines. But upon such an economic foundation no secure fabric of industrial and political civilization can be erected : after a single generation of feverish gold-getting, in which British supremacy is maintained by a constantly changing majority of temporary town residents, the industrial strength of the country must steadily and surely decline, returning not to the more primitive condition of wholesome agriculture from which it temporarily emerged, but to a prolonged miserable struggle of trade and manufactures in a country strewn with the decaying wreckage of disused mines and rotting towns. Hebrew mining speculators, American and Scotch engineers, Chinese miners, German traders will evacuate the country they have sacked, leaving behind them a population of Boers spoiled in large part by their contact with a gambling and luxuriant European civilization, and a host of Kaffirs broken from their customary life of agriculture and hanging around the cities of South Africa—a chronic pest of vagabonds and unemployed.

Such are some of the reactions of the indentured labour system in South Africa. The legitimate and wholesome means of developing a country is by utilizing the labour-power of its inhabitants, inducing them by ordinary economic stimuli to settle where remunerative employment is afforded.

If such a country is under-peopled, emigration is rightly encouraged from more thickly-peopled lands. But such emigration should bring genuine colonists, people intending to become citizens of their adopted country, social as well as economic units. In such fashion, by free flow of populations from less desirable to more desirable regions, the civilization of the world is forwarded, and the social safety and future prosperity of the newly developed countries are best subserved. An indentured labour system, however well administered, sins against the fundamental laws of civilization because it treats the labourers primarily as instruments and not as men. Badly operated, without proper safeguards of impartially administered law,[1] it is a source of grave damage to the political, social and industrial prosperity of the country where it is applied.

It may well be doubted whether there is a net gain to the civilization of the world by increasing the supply of gold and diamonds at such a price.

IX

It may be said : " Whatever the motives of employers may be, it is surely a good thing to take natives, by persuasion or even by force, from a life of idleness and habituate them to labour, which educates their faculties, brings them under civilizing influences, and puts money into their pockets."

Now while the statement that such Kaffirs, West Africans, and other tropical or semi-tropical men, left to themselves, lead an idle life, is commonly a gross exaggeration, due largely to the fact that their work is more irregular and capricious than that of their women, it must be admitted

---

[1] The worst of many evil features in the Chinese Indentured Labour System of the Transvaal is that here alone within the dominions of Great Britain a large body of residents are deprived of the right of appeal to the common law as administered in the Courts of Justice.

that the repression of internecine warfare and the restriction of hunting do set free a large quantity of male energy which it is really desirable should be utilized for industrial purposes. But for whose industrial purposes ? Surely it is far better that the " contact with civilization " should lead these men to new kinds of industry on their own land, and in their own societies, instead of dragging them off to gang-labour on the lands or mining properties of strangers. It can do this in two ways : by acquainting them with new wholesome wants it can apply a legitimate stimulus, and by acquainting them with new industrial methods applicable to work in their own industries it can educate them to self-help. Where native peoples are protected from the aggressive designs of white profit-mongers, this salutary evolution operates. In large districts of Basutoland and in certain reserves of Zululand the substitution of the plough for the primitive hoe or pick has led to the introduction of male labour into the fields ;[1] every encouragement in stock-raising, dairy-farming, or other occupations connected with animals enhances male employment among natives ; the gradual introduction of new manufacturing industries into village life leads to men's taking a larger share in those industries in or near the kraal which were formerly a monopoly of women.

So far as Imperialism seeks to justify itself by sane civilization of lower races, it will endeavour to raise their industrial and moral status on their own lands, preserving as far as possible the continuity of the old tribal life and institutions, protecting them against the force and deceit of prospectors, labour touts, and other persons who seek to take their land and entice away their labour. If under the gradual teaching of industrial arts and the general educational

[1] Cf. *Report of South African Native Races Commission*, p. 52, etc. ; also *The Labour Question in South Africa*, by Miss A. Werner (*The Reformer*, December 1901).

influences of a white protectorate many of the old political, social, and religious institutions decay, that decay will be a natural wholesome process, and will be attended by the growth of new forms, not forced upon them, but growing out of the old forms and conforming to laws of natural growth in order to adapt native life to a changed environment.

But so long as the private, short-sighted, business interests of white farmers or white mine-owners are permitted, either by action taken on their own account or through pressure on a colonial or Imperial Government, to invade the lands of " lower peoples," and transfer to their private profitable purposes the land or labour, the first law of " sane " Imperialism is violated, and the phrases about teaching " the dignity of labour " and raising races of " children " to manhood, whether used by directors of mining companies or by statesmen in the House of Commons, are little better than wanton exhibitions of hypocrisy. They are based on a falsification of the facts, and a perversion of the motives which actually direct the policy.

X

In setting forth the theory which sought to justify Imperialism as the exercise of forcible control over lower races, by regarding this control as a trust for the civilization of the world, we pointed out three conditions essential to the validity of such a trust : first, the control must be directed to the general good, and not to the special good of the " imperialist " nation ; secondly, it must confer some net advantage to the nation so controlled ; lastly, there must exist some organization representative of international interests, which shall sanction the undertaking of a trust by the nation exercising such control.

The third condition, which is fundamental to the validity of the other two, we saw to be unfulfilled, inasmuch as each nation claiming to fulfil the trust of governing lower races assumed this control upon its own authority alone.

The practice of Imperialism, as illustrated in a great variety of cases, exhibits the very defects which correspond with the unsound theory. The exclusive interest of an expanding nation, interpreted by its rulers at some given moment, and not the good of the whole world, is seen to be the dominant motive in each new assumption of control over the tropics and lower peoples ; that national interest itself commonly signifies the direct material self-interest of some small class of traders, mine-owners, farmers, or investors who wish to dispose of the land and labour of the lower peoples for their private gain. Other more disinterested motives woven in may serve to give an attractive colouring to each business in hand, but it is impossible to examine the historic details in any important modern instance without recognizing the supremacy of economic forces. At best it is impossible to claim more than this, that some consideration is taken of justice and humanity in the exercise of the authority assumed, and that incidentally the welfare of the lower race is subserved by the play of economic and political forces not primarily designed to secure that end.

Everywhere, in the white administration of these lower races, considerations of present order are paramount, and industrial exploitation of the land and labour under private management for private immediate gain is the chief operative force in the community, unchecked, or inadequately checked, by imperial or other governmental control. The future progress of the lower race, its gradual education in the arts of industrial and political self-government, in most instances do not at all engage the activity of imperial government, and nowhere are such considerations of the welfare of the governed really paramount.

The stamp of "parasitism" is upon every white settlement among these lower races, that is to say, nowhere are the relations between white and coloured people such as to preserve a wholesome balance of mutual services. The best services which white civilization might be capable of rendering, by examples of normal, healthy, white communities practising the best arts of Western life, are precluded by climatic and other physical conditions in almost every case : the presence of a scattering of white officials, missionaries, traders, mining or plantation overseers, a dominant male caste with little knowledge of or sympathy for the institutions of the people, is ill-calculated to give to these lower races even such gains as Western civilization might be capable of giving.

The condition of the white rulers of these lower races is distinctively parasitic ; they live upon these natives, their chief work being that of organizing native labour for their support. The normal state of such a country is one in which the most fertile lands and the mineral resources are owned by white aliens and worked by natives under their direction, primarily for their gain : they do not identify themselves with the interests of the country or its people, but remain an alien body of sojourners, a " parasite " upon the carcass of its " host," destined to extract wealth from the country and retiring to consume it at home. All the hard manual or other severe routine work is done by natives ; most of the real labour of administration, or even of aggression, is done by native overseers, police and soldiery. This holds of all white government in the tropics or wherever a large lower population is found. Even where whites can live healthily and breed and work, the quantity of actual work, physical or mental, which they do is very small, where a large supply of natives can be made to work for them. Even in the parts of South Africa where whites thrive best, the life they lead, when clearly analyzed, is seen to be parasitic. The white farmer, Dutch or British, does little work, manual or mental, and tends everywhere to become lazy and " unprogressive " ; the trading, professional or official classes of the towns show clear signs of the same laxity and torpor, the brief spasmodic flares of energy evoked by dazzling prospects among small classes of speculators and business men in mushroom cities like Johannesburg serving but to dazzle our eyes and hide the deep essential character of the life.

If this is true of South Africa, much more is it true of countries where climate inhibits white settlement and white energy, the general condition of those countries which represent the expansion of modern Imperialism.

Nowhere under such conditions is the theory of white government as a trust for civilization made valid ; nowhere is there any provision to secure the predominance of the interests, either of the world at large or of the governed people, over those of the encroaching nation, or more commonly a section of that nation. The relations subsisting between the superior and the inferior nations, commonly established by pure force, and resting on that basis, are such as preclude the genuine sympathy essential to the operation of the best civilizing influences, and usually resolve themselves into the maintenance of external good order so as to forward the profitable development of certain natural resources of the land, under " forced " native labour, primarily for the benefit of white traders and investors, and secondarily for the benefit of the world of white Western consumers.

This failure to justify by results the forcible rule over alien peoples is attributable to no special defect of the British or other modern European nations. It is inherent in the nature of such domination. " The government of a people by itself has a meaning and a reality, but such a thing as government of one people by another does not and cannot exist. One people may keep another as a warren or preserve for its own use, a place to make money in, a human cattle-farm, to be worked for the profits of its own inhabitants ; but if the good of the governed is the proper business of a government, it is utterly impossible that a people should directly attend to it."[1]

[1] J. S. Mill *Representative Government*, p. 326.

CHAPTER V

IMPERIALISM IN ASIA

I

THE great test of Western Imperialism is Asia, where vast peoples live, the inheritors of civilizations as complex as our own, more ancient and more firmly rooted by enduring custom in the general life. The races of Africa it has been possible to regard as savages or children, " backward " in their progress along the same general road of civilization in which Anglo-Saxondom represents the vanguard, and requiring the help of more forward races. It is not so easy to make a specious case for Western control over India, China, and other Asiatic peoples upon the same ground. Save in the more recent developments of the physical sciences and their application to industrial arts, it cannot be contended that these peoples are " backward," and though we sometimes describe their civilizations as " arrested " or " unprogressive," that judgment either may imply our ignorance of the pace at which civilizations so much older than our own must continue moving, or it may even afford unconscious testimony to a social progress which has won its goal in securing a well-nigh complete adjustment between human life and its stable environment.

The claim of the West to civilize the East by means of political and military supremacy must rest ultimately upon the assumption that civilizations, however various in their surface growths, are at root one and the same, that they have a common nature and a common soil. Stripped of metaphor, this means that certain moral and intellectual qualities, finding embodiment in general forms of religion, law, customs, and arts of industry, are essential to all local varieties of civilization, irrespective of race, colour, climate, and other conditions ; that Western nations, or some of them, possess these qualities and forms of civilization in a pre-eminent degree, and are able to impart them to Eastern nations by government and its accompanying political, religious, and industrial education. It certainly seems as if " humanity " implies such common factors. The ethics of the Decalogue appears to admit of a wide common application ; certain rights of the individual, certain elements of social justice, embodied in law and custom, appear capable of universal appeal ; certain sorts of knowledge and the arts of applying them appear useful to all sorts and conditions of men. If Western civilization is richer in these essentials, it seems reasonable to suppose that the West can benefit the East by imparting them, and that her government may be justified as a means of doing so.

The British Empire in India may be taken as the most serviceable test. We did not, indeed, go there in the first instance for the good of the Indians, nor have our various extensions of political power been motived primarily by this consideration ; but it is contended that our government of India has in point of fact conferred upon the people the benefits arising from our civilization, and that the conferring of these benefits has of later years played a larger and a larger part in our conscious policy. The experiment has been a long and varied one, and our success in India is commonly adduced as the most convincing argument in favour of the benefits accruing to subject races from Imperialism.

The real questions we have to answer are these : " Are we civilizing India ? " and " In what does that civilization consist ? " To assist in answering there exists a tolerably large body of indisputable facts. We have established a wider and more permanent internal peace than India had ever known from the days of Alexander the Great. We have raised the standard of justice by fair and equal administration of laws ; we have regulated and probably reduced the burden of taxation, checking the corruption and tyranny of native princes and their publicans. For the instruction of the people we have introduced a public system of schools and colleges, as well as a great quasi-public missionary establishment, teaching not only the Christian religion but many industrial arts. Roads, railways, and a network of canals have facilitated communication and transport, and an extensive system of scientific irrigation has improved the productiveness of the soil ; the mining of coal, gold, and other minerals has been greatly developed ; in Bombay and elsewhere cotton mills with modern machinery have been set up, and the organization of other machine industries is helping to find employment for the population of large cities. Tea, coffee, indigo, jute, tobacco, and other important crops have been introduced into Indian agriculture. We are gradually breaking down many of the religious and social superstitions which sin against humanity and retard progress, and even the deeply rooted caste system is modified wherever British influence is felt. There can be no question that much of this work of England in India is well done. No such intelligent, well-educated, and honourable body of men has ever been employed by any State in the working of imperial government as is contained in the Civil Service of India. Nowhere else in our Empire has so much really disinterested and thoughtful energy been applied in the work of government. The same may be said of the line of great statesmen sent out from England to preside over our government in India.

Our work there is the best record British Imperialism can show. What does it tell us about the capacity of the West to confer the benefits of her civilization on the East?

Take first the test of economic prosperity. Are the masses of the people under our rule wealthier than they were before, and are they growing wealthier under that rule? There are some who maintain that British government is draining the economic life-blood of India and dragging her population into lower and more hopeless poverty. They point to the fact that one of the poorest countries in the world is made to bear the cost of a government, which, however honestly administered, is very expensive; that one-third of the money raised by taxation flows out of the country without return; that India is made to support an army admittedly excessive for purposes of self-defence, and even to bear the cost of wars in other parts of the Empire, while nearly the whole of the interest on capital invested in India is spent out of the country. The statistical basis of this argument is too insecure for much reliance to be placed on it: it is probably untrue that the net cost of British government is greater than the burden of native princes which it has largely[1] superseded, though it is certainly true that the extortionate taxation under native rule was expended in the country on productive work or unproductive native services. Whether the increasing drain of wheat and other food-stuffs from India exceeds the gain from improved irrigation, and whether the real income of the " ryot " or other worker is increasing or diminishing, cannot be established, so far as the whole country is concerned, by any accurate measure. But it is generally admitted, even by British officials strongly favourable to our rule, that we have not succeeded in giving any considerable economic

---

[1] About three-eighths of the country is still under native government, with British supervision.

prosperity to India. I quote from a source strongly favourable to our rule :

" The test of a people's prosperity is not the extension of exports, the multiplication of manufactures or other industries, the construction of cities. No. A prosperous country is one in which the great mass of the inhabitants are able to procure, with moderate toil, what is necessary for living *human* lives, lives of frugal and assured comfort. Judged by this criterion, can India be called prosperous ?

" Comfort, of course, is a relative term. . . . In a tropical country, like India, the standard is very low. Little clothing is required there. Simple diet suffices. Artificial wants are very few, and, for the most part are not costly. The Indian Empire is a peasant Empire. Ninety per cent. of the people live upon the land. . . . An unfailing well of water, a plot of land, and a bit of orchard—that will satisfy his heart's desire, if indeed you add the cattle needful to him, ' the ryot's children,' as they are called in many parts. Such is the ryot's ideal. Very few realize it. An acre may stand for the *modus agri*, the necessary plot of ground. A man to an acre, or 640 men to the square mile, is the utmost density of population which India can comfortably support, except near towns or in irrigated districts. But millions of peasants in India are struggling to live on half an acre. Their existence is a constant struggle with starvation, ending too often in defeat. Their difficulty is not to live *human* lives—lives up to the level of their poor standard of comfort— but to live at all and not die. . . . We may truly say that in India, except in the irrigated tracts, famine is chronic— endemic."[1]

A century of British rule, then, conducted with sound ability and goodwill, had not materially assisted to ward off the chronic enemy, starvation, from the mass of the

[1] *India and its Problems*, by W. S. Lilly, pp. 284, 285 (Sands & Co.).

people. Nor can it be maintained that the new industrialism of machinery and factories, which we have introduced, is civilizing India, or even adding much to her material prosperity. In fact, all who value the life and character of the East deplore the visible decadence of the arts of architecture, weaving, metal work and pottery, in which India had been famed from time immemorial. " Architecture, engineering, literary skill are all perishing out, so perishing that Anglo-Indians doubt whether Indians have the capacity to be architects, though they built Benares ; or engineers, though they dug the artificial lakes of Tanjore ; or poets, though the people sit for hours or days listening to the rhapsodists as they recite poems, which move them as Tennyson certainly does not move our common people."[1] The decay or forcible supersession of the native industrial arts is still more deplorable, for these always constitute the poetry of common life, the free play of the imaginative faculty of a nation in the ordinary work of life.

Sir George Birdwood, in his great work on *The Industrial Arts of India*, written more than twenty years ago[2], gives a significant judgment upon the real meaning of a movement which has ever since been advancing at an accelerating pace : " If, owing to the operation of certain economic causes, machinery was to be gradually introduced into India for the manufacture of its great traditional handicrafts, there would ensue an industrial revolution which, if not directed by an intelligent and instructed public opinion and the general prevalence of refined taste, would inevitably throw the traditional arts of the country into the same confusion of principles, and of their practical application to the objects of daily necessity, which has for three generations been the destruction of decorative

[1] *Asia and Europe*, by Meredith Townsend, p. 102 (Constable & Co.).
[2] Now (1938) more than fifty years ago.

art and of middle-class taste in England and North-Western Europe and the United States of America. The social and moral evils of the introduction of machinery into India are likely to be greater." Then follows a detailed account of the free picturesque handicrafts of the ordinary Indian village, and the author proceeds : " But of late these handicraftsmen, for the sake of whose works the whole world has been ceaselessly pouring its bullion into India, and who, for all the marvellous tissue they have wrought, have polluted no rivers, deformed no pleasing prospects, nor poisoned any air ; whose skill and individuality the training of countless generations has developed to the highest perfection—these hereditary handicraftsmen are being everywhere gathered from their democratic village communities in hundreds and thousands into the colossal mills of Bombay, to drudge in gangs for tempting wages, at manufacturing piece goods, in competition with Manchester, in the production of which they are no more intellectually and morally concerned than the grinder of a barrel organ in the tunes turned out from it."

Even from the low standpoint of the world-market this hasty destruction of the native arts for the sake of employing masses of cheap labour in mills is probably bad policy ; for, as the world becomes more fully opened up and distant countries are set in closer communication with one another, a land whose industries had so unique and interesting a character as those of India would probably have found a more profitable market than by attempting to undersell Lancashire and New England in stock goods.

But far more important are the reactions of these changes on the character of the people. The industrial revolution in England and elsewhere has partaken more largely of the nature of a natural growth, proceeding from inner forces, than in India, and has been largely coincident with a liberation of great popular forces finding expression in scientific education and in political democracy: it has been an important phase of the great movement of popular liberty and self-government. In India, and elsewhere in the East, there is no such compensation.

An industrial system, far more strongly set and more closely interwoven in the religious and social system of the country than ever were the crafts and arts in Europe, has been subjected to forces operating from outside, and unchecked in their pace and direction by the will of the people whose life they so vitally affected. Industrial revolution is one thing when it is the natural movement of internal forces, making along the lines of the self-interests of a nation and proceeding *pari passu* with advancing popular self-government; another thing when it is imposed by foreign conquerors looking primarily to present gains for themselves, and neglectful of the deeper interests of the people of the country. The story of the destruction of native weaving industry[1] for the benefit of mills started by the Company will illustrate the selfish, short-sighted economic policy of the late eighteenth and early nineteenth centuries. "Under the pretence of Free Trade, England has compelled the Hindus to receive the products of the steam-looms of Lancashire, Yorkshire, Glasgow, etc., at mere nominal duties; while the hand-wrought manufactures of Bengal and Behar, beautiful in fabric and durable in wear, have had heavy and almost prohibitive duties imposed on their importation to England."[2] The effect of this policy, rigorously maintained during the earlier decades of the nineteenth century, was the irreparable ruin of many of the most valuable and characteristic arts of Indian industry.

[1] *Cf.* the careful summary of official evidence in Mr. Romesh Dutt's *Economic History of British India*, chap. xv. (Kegan Paul).

[2] *Eastern India*, by Montgomery Martin (London, 1838), vol. iii. Introd. (quoted Romesh Dutt, p. 290).

" In India the manufacturing power of the people was stamped out by Protection against her industries, and then Free Trade was forced on her so as to prevent a revival."[1]

When we turn from manufacture to the great industry of agriculture, which even now occupies nine-tenths of the population, the difficulty of alien administration, with whatever good intention, is amply illustrated. Not a few of our greatest Indian statesmen, such as Munro, Elphinstone, and Metcalfe, have recognized in the village community the true embodiment of the spirit of Eastern civilization.

" The village communities," wrote Sir C. Metcalfe,[2] "'are little republics, having nearly everything that they can want within themselves, and almost independent of any foreign relations. They seem to last where nothing else lasts. Dynasty after dynasty tumbles down ; revolution succeeds to revolution ; Hindu, Pathan, Moghul, Mahratta, Sikh, English, are masters in turn ; but the village communities remain the same." " The union of the village communities, each one forming a separate little State in itself, has, I conceive, contributed more than any other cause to the preservation of the people of India through all revolutions and changes which they have suffered, and it is in a high degree conducive to their happiness and to the enjoyment of a great portion of freedom and independence. I wish, therefore, that the village constitutions may never be disturbed, and I dread everything which has a tendency to break them up."

Yet the whole efforts of British administration have been directed to the destruction of this village self-government in industry and politics. The substitution of the individual ryot for the community as the unit of revenue throughout

[1] Romesh Dutt, p. 302.
[2] Letter to the Board of Revenue, April, 1838 (quoted Romesh Dutt, p. 386).

Bombay and Madras struck a fatal blow at the economic life of the village, while the withdrawal of all real judicial and executive powers from the zemindars or headmen, and their concentration in British civil courts and executive officers, virtually completed the destruction of the strongest and most general institution of India—the self-governing village.

Both these important steps were taken in furtherance of the new Western idea of individual responsibility as the only sound economic basis, and centralized government as the most efficacious mode of political machinery. The fact that it should be considered safe and profitable suddenly to subvert the most ancient institutions of India, in order thus to adapt the people to English modes of life, will be taken by sociologists as one of the most amazing lessons of incompetence in the art of civilization afforded by modern history. Indeed the superior prosperity of a large part of Bengal, attributable in part at any rate to the maintenance of a local landlord class, who served as middlemen between the State and the individual cultivators, and mitigated the mechanical rack-rent of the land-tax, is a sufficiently remarkable testimony to the injury inflicted upon other parts of India by sudden ill-advised application of Western economic and political methods.[1]

II

When we turn from industry to the administration of justice and the general work of government in which the ability and character of British officialism finds expression, we are led to further questioning. Is Great Britain able

---

[1] The prosperity of districts under the Bengal settlement, as compared with other parts of British India, must however be imputed largely to the fact that this settlement enables Bengal to evade its full proportion of contribution to the revenue of India, and throws therefore a disproportionate burden upon other parts.

to Anglicize the government of India, is she doing so, and is she thereby implanting Western civilization in India ? How much a few thousand British officials, endowed with the best ability and energy, can achieve in stamping British integrity and efficiency upon the practical government of three hundred million people of alien race and character it is difficult to judge. Numbers are not everything, and it is probable that these diffused units of British authority exercise directly and indirectly a considerable influence upon the larger affairs of government, and that this influence may sometimes permeate far down among native official circles. But it must be kept in mind that those few British officials are rarely born in India, have seldom any perfect understanding of the languages of the people, form a close " caste," never mingling in free social intercourse with those whom they govern, and that the laws and regulations they administer are largely foreign to the traditionary institutions of the Indian peoples. When we remember how large a share of real government is the personal administration of detail, the enforcement of law or regulation upon the individual citizen, and that in the overwhelming majority of cases this work must always be left to native officials, it is evident that the formal virtues of British law and justice must admit much elasticity and much perversion in the actual processes of administration.

" No one can deny that this system of civil and criminal administration is vastly superior to anything which India ever possessed under former rulers. Its defects arise chiefly from causes extraneous to it. The unblemished integrity and unswerving devotion to duty of the officials, whether English or Indian, who occupy the higher posts, no one will call in question. The character of the subordinate officials is not always so entirely above suspicion, and the course of justice is too often perverted by a lamentable characteristic of the Oriental mind. ' Great is the rectitude of the English, greater is the power of a lie ' is a proverbial saying throughout India. Perhaps the least satisfactory of the government departments is the police. A recent writer says, ' It is difficult to imagine how a department can be more corrupt.' This, too, may be an over-statement. But, taken on the whole, the rank and file of the Indian police are probably not of higher integrity and character than those of New York."[1] Now one sentence of this statement deserves special attention. " Its defects arise chiefly from causes extraneous to it." This is surely incorrect. It is an essential part of our system that the details of administration shall be in native hands : no one can contemplate any considerable displacement of lower native officials by English ; the latter could not do the work and would not if they could, nor could the finances, always precarious, possibly admit of so huge an increase of expenditure as would be involved by making the government of India really British in its working. The tendency, in fact, is all the other way, and makes for the more numerous employment of natives in all but the highest grades of the public service. If it is true that corruption and mendacity are deeply rooted in all Eastern systems of government, and that the main moral justification of our rule consists in their correction by British character and administration, it is pretty clear that we cannot be performing this valuable work, and must in the nature of the case be disabled from even understanding where and how far we fall short of doing so. The comment made by Mr. Lilly upon Indian police is chiefly significant because this is the one department of detailed practical government where special scandals are most likely to reveal the failure of our excellent intentions as embodied in criminal codes and judicial procedure.

[1] *India and its Problems*, p. 182.

One would wish to know whether the actual native officer who collects the land-tax or other dues from the individual ryot practises the integrity of his British superior official or reverts to the time-honoured and universal practice of the East.

How much can a handful of foreign officials do in the way of effectual check and supervision of the details of government in a country which teems with populations of various races, languages, creeds, and customs ? Probably not very much, and *ex hypothesi* they, and so we, cannot know their failures.

The one real and indisputable success of our rule in India, as indeed generally through our Empire, is the maintenance of order upon a large scale, the prevention of internecine war, riot, or organized violence. This, of course, is much, but it is not everything; it is not enough in itself to justify us in regarding our imperial rule as a success. Is British justice, so far as it prevails, and British order good for India ? will seem to the average Briton a curious question to ask. But Englishmen who have lived in India, and who, on the whole, favour the maintenance of our authority, sometimes ask it. It must, in the first place, be remembered that some of the formal virtues of our laws and methods which seem to us most excellent may work out quite otherwise in practice. The rigorous justice in the exaction of the land-tax and in the enforcement of the legal claims of userers is a striking instance of misapplied notions of equity. Corrupt as the practice of Eastern tax-gatherers has ever been, tyrannical as has been the power of the userer, public opinion, expediency, and some personal consideration have always qualified their tyranny ; the mechanical rigour of British law is one of the greatest sources of unpopularity of our government in India, and is probably a grave source of actual injury.

There is even some reason to suspect that Indians resent less the illegal and irregular extortion of recognized native autocrats, whose visible authority is familiarly impressed on their imaginations, than the actually lighter exactions of an inhuman, irresistible and immitigable machine, such as the British power presents itself to them.

It is pretty clear that, so far as the consent of the governed in any active sense is a condition of success in government, the British Empire in India has not succeeded. We are deceived by Eastern acquiescence, and our deception may even be attended by grave catastrophe unless we understand the truth. Mr. Townsend, who has brought close thought to bear upon the conditions of our hold of India, writes thus :—

" Personal liberty, religious liberty, equal justice, perfect security—these things the Empire gives ; but then are these so valued as to overcome the inherent and incurable dull distaste felt by the brown men to the white men who give them ? I doubt it greatly."[1]

The reasons he gives for his doubt are weighty. The agricultural populace, whom we have, he holds, materially benefited, is an inert mass : the active classes endowed with initiative, political ambition, patriotism, education, are silently but strongly hostile to our rule. It is natural this should be so. We have spoiled the free career open to these classes under native government ; the very order we have imposed offends their instincts and often thwarts their interests. The caste system, which it is the boast of our more liberal laws and institutions to moderate or disregard, is everywhere consciously antagonistic to us in self-defence, and deeply resents any portion of our educative influences which impairs its hold upon the minds of the people. This force is well illustrated by the almost

[1] *Asia and Europe*, p. 101.

complete failure of our energetic Christian missions to make converts out of any members of the higher castes. The testimony of one of the most devoted of Roman Catholic missionaries after thirty years of missionary labours deserves attention :—

" During the long period I have lived in India in the capacity of a missionary, I have made, with the assistance of a native missionary, in all between two and three hundred converts of both sexes. Of this number two-thirds were Pariahs or beggars, and the rest were composed of Sudras, vagrants and outcasts of several tribes, who, being without resources, turned Christians in order to form connexions, chiefly for the purpose of marriage, or with some other interested views."[1]

This view is borne out in the general treatment of Christian missions in Mr. Barrie's report on the census in 1891. " The greatest development (of Christianity) is found where the Brahmanic caste system is in force in its fullest vigour, in the south and west of the Peninsula, and among the hill tribes of Bengal. In such localities it is naturally attractive to a class of the population whose position is hereditarily and permanently degraded by their own religion."

If British Christianity and British rule were welcomed by large bodies of the ryots and the low-caste and Pariah populations, the opposition of the native " classes " might seem a strong testimony to the beneficence of our rule, as an instrument for the elevation of the poorer working people who always form the great majority. Unfortunately no such result can seriously be pretended. There is no reason to suppose that we hold the allegiance of any large section of the people of India by any other bond than that of fear and respect for our external power. Mr. Townsend

[1] Quoted Lilly, *India and its Problems*, p. 163.

puts the matter in a nutshell when he affirms : " There is no corner in Asia where the life of a white man, if unprotected by force, either actual or potential, is safe for an hour ; nor is there an Asiatic State which, if it were prudent, would not expel him at once and for ever."[1] There are, according to this view, no psychical roots to the civilization we are imposing upon India : it is a superficial structure maintained by force, and not grafted on to the true life of the nation so as to modify and educate the soul of the people. Mr. Townsend is driven with evidently deep reluctance to the conclusion that " the Empire hangs in air, supported by nothing but the minute white garrison and the unproved assumption that the people of India desire it to continue to exist."[2] It was indeed pointed out by Professor Seeley, and is generally admitted, that our Empire in India has only been rendered possible by the wide cleavages of race, language, religion and interests among the Indian populations, first and foremost the division of Mohammedan and Hindu.

But it may be fairly contended that the forcible foundation of our rule and the slowness and reluctance of the natives to appreciate its benefits are no proof that it is not beneficial, or that in process of time we may not infuse the best principles of Western civilization into their life.

Are we doing this ? Is the nature of our occupation such as to enable us to do it ? Apart from the army, which is the aspect of the Empire most in evidence, there is a British population of some 135,000,[3] less than 1 to every 2,000 of the natives, living neither the normal life of their own country nor that of the foreign country which they occupy, in no sense representative units of British civilization, but exotics compelled to live a highly artificial life and unable to rear British families or to create British society

[1] *Asia and Europe*, p. 98.   [2] *Asia and Europe*, p. 89.   [3] At about 1900.

of such a sort as to embody and illustrate the most valuable contents of our civilization.

It is certain that the machinery of government, however excellent, can of itself do little to convey the benefits of civilization to an alien people. The real forces of civilization can only be conveyed by contact of individual with individual. Now the conditions of free, close, personal contact between British and Indians are virtually non-existent. There is no real, familiar, social intercourse on equal terms, still less is there inter-marriage, the only effective mode of amalgamating two civilizations, the only safeguard against race hatred and race domination. " When inter-marriage is out of the question," writes Dr. Goldwin Smith, " social equality cannot exist ; without social equality political equality is impossible, and a republic in the true sense can hardly be."[1]

The vast majority of whites admittedly live their own life, using natives for domestic and industrial service, but never attempting to get any fuller understanding of their lives and character than is required to exact these services from them or to render official services in return. The few who have made some serious attempt to penetrate into the Indian mind admit their failure to grasp with any adequacy even the rudiments of a human nature which differs, in its fundamental valuations and its methods of conduct, so radically from our own as to present for its chief interest a series of baffling psychological puzzles. It is indeed precisely from these students that we come to understand the impossibility of that close, persistent, interactive contact of mind with mind which is the only method by which that " mission of civilization " which we profess is capable of fulfilment. Even those English writers who seem to convey most forcibly what is called

[1] *Commonwealth or Empire* (Macmillan & Co.).

the spirit of the East as it shows forth in the drama of modern life, writers such as Mr. Kipling and Mrs. Steel, hardly do more than present a quaint alluring atmosphere of un-intelligibility ; while study of the great Indian literature and art which may be taken as the best expression of the soul of the people exhibits the hitherto unbridgeable divergence of the British conception of life from the Indian. The complete aloofness of the small white garrison is indeed in no small measure due to an instinctive recognition of this psychical chasm and of their inability to enter into really vital sympathy with these members of an " inferior " race. They are not to blame, but rather the conditions which have brought them there and imposed on them a task essentially impossible, that of implanting genuine white civilization on Asiatic soil. It must clearly be understood that it is not a question of the slowness of a process of adaptation : the really vital process of change is not taking place. We are incapable of implanting our civilization in India by present methods of approach : we are only capable of disturbing their civilization.[1] Even the external life of the vast bulk of the population we hardly touch ; the inner life we do not touch at all. If we are deceived by the magnitude of the area of our political control and the real activity of the machinery of government into supposing that we are converting the Indian peoples

[1] The effects of this disturbance, however, may be of considerable importance. If, as is maintained by some Hindoo politicians of the new school, our influence is sensibly undermining the antagonism between Hindoo and Mohammedan, and is gradually breaking down the rigour of " caste " among Hindoos, it is tolerably manifest that we are sapping the sources of our political rule, by removing the most powerful obstacles to the growth of " nationalism " in India. If the levelling influence of our Western ideas, operating through religious, literary, political and social institutions on the minds of the people, goes beyond a certain distance in breaking down the racial, religious and linguistic barriers which have always divided and subdivided India, the rise of a national self-consciousness upon a basis of common interests and common antagonisms may raise the demand of " India for the Indians " above the margin of vague aspiration into a region of organized political and military endeavour.

to British Christianity, British views of justice, morality, and to the supreme value of regular intense industry, in order to improve the standard of material comfort, the sooner we face the facts the better. For that we are doing none of these things in an appreciable degree is plain to most British officials. Of the nearest approaches to such success they are openly contemptuous, condemning outright the Eurasian and ridiculing the " stucco civilization of the baboo." The idea that we are civilizing India in the sense of assisting them to industrial, political, and moral progress along the lines either of our own or their civilization is a complete delusion, based upon a false estimate of the influence of superficial changes wrought by government and the activity of a minute group of aliens. The delusion is only sustained by the sophistry of Imperialism, which weaves these fallacies to cover its nakedness and the advantages which certain interests suck out of empire.

This judgment is not new, nor does it imply the spirit of a " little Englander." If there is one writer who, more than another, is justly accredited with the stimulation of large ideas of the destiny of England, it is the late Professor Seeley. Yet this is his summary of the value of the " imperial " work which we have undertaken in India :—

" At best we think of it as a good specimen of a bad political system. We are not disposed to be proud of the succession of the Grand Mogul. We doubt whether, with all the merits of our administration, the subjects of it are happy. We may even doubt whether our rule is preparing them for a happier condition, whether it may not be sinking them lower in misery ; and we have our misgivings that perhaps a genuine Asiatic Government, and still more a national Government springing up out of the Hindu population itself, might, in the long run, be more beneficial, because more congenial, though perhaps less civilized, than such a foreign, unsympathetic Government as our own."[1]

III

While India presents the largest and most instructive lesson in distinctively British Imperialism, it is in China that the spirit and methods of Western Imperialism in general are likely to find their most crucial test. The new Imperialism differs from the older, first in substituting for the ambition of a single growing empire the theory and the practice of competing empires, each motived by similar lusts of political aggrandisement and commercial gain ; secondly, in the dominance of financial or investing over mercantile interests.

The methods and motives of the European Powers are not open to serious dispute. The single aim of Chinese policy from time immemorial had been to avoid all dealings with foreigners which might lead to the establishment of inter-governmental relations with them. This did not imply, at any rate until recently, hostility to individual foreigners or a reluctance to admit the goods or the ideas which they sought to introduce. Arabs and other Asiatic races of the West had traded with China from very early times. Roman records point to intercourse with China as early as Marcus Aurelius. Nor were their relations with the outside world confined to trade. Christianity was introduced some fifteen hundred years ago by the Nestorians, who propagated their religious views widely in the Central Kingdom ; Buddhist foreign missionaries were well received, and their teaching found wide acceptance. Indeed few nations have displayed so much power of assimilating foreign religious notions as the Chinese. Roman Catholic

[1] *The Expansion of England*, pp. 273, 274.

missionaries entered China during the Mongol dynasty, and later in the Ming dynasty.[1] Jesuits not only propagated Christianity, but introduced Western science into Pekin, attaining the climax of their influence during the latter part of the seventeenth century. Not until the arrival of the Dominicans introduced an element of religious faction, attended by political intrigue, did Christianity come into disrepute or evoke any sort of persecution. With the introduction of Protestant missions during the nineteenth century, the trouble has grown apace. Though the Chinese as a nation have never displayed religious intolerance, they have naturally mistrusted the motives of Westerns who, calling themselves Christians, quarrelled amongst themselves, and by their tactless zeal often caused local rioting which led to diplomatic or armed interference for their protection. Almost all lay European authorities in China bear out the following judgment of Mr. A. J. Little :—

" The riots and consequent massacres resulting from mission work throughout Indo-China may be justified by the end ; but it is certain our relations with the Chinese would be far more cordial than they are, were we not suspected of an insidious design to wean them from such habits of filial piety and loyalty as they possess, to our advantage."[1]

The main outlines of Chinese policy are quite intelligible. Though not averse from incidental contact with Europeans or with other Asiatics, traders, travellers, or missionaries, they have steadily resisted all attempts to disturb their political and economic system by organized pressure of foreign Powers. Possessing in their enormous area of territory, with its various climatic and other natural conditions, its teeming industrial population, and its

[1] A.D. 1138 to 1644.
[1] *Through the Yang-Tse Gorges*, edition 1888, p. 334.

ancient, well-developed civilization, a full material basis of self-sufficiency, the Chinese, following a sound instinct of self-defence, have striven to confine their external relations to a casual intercourse. The successful practice of this policy for countless centuries has enabled them to escape the militarism of other nations; and though it has subjected them to a few forcible dynastic changes, it has never affected the peaceful customary life of the great mass of little self-sufficing industrial villages of which the nation is composed. The sort of politics of which Western history is mainly composed has meant virtually nothing to the Chinese. It is the organized attempt of Western nations to break through this barrier of passive resistance, and to force themselves, their wares, their political and industial control, on China that gives importance to Imperialism in the Far East. It is not possible here to trace, even in bare outlines, the history of this pressure, how quarrels with traders and missionaries have been utilized to force trade with the interior, to establish treaty ports, to secure special political and commercial rights for British or other European subjects, to fasten a regular system of foreign political relations upon the central government, and at the conclusion of the nineteenth century to drive China into wars, first with Japan, next with a confederacy of European Powers, which threaten to break up the political and industrial isolation of forty centuries, and to plunge China into the great world-competition.

The conduct of European Powers towards China will rank as the clearest revelation of the nature of Imperialism. Until late in the nineteenth century Great Britain, with France as a poor second, had made the pace in pursuit of trade, covering this trading policy with a veneer of missionary work, the real relative importance of the two being put to a crucial test by the opium war. The entrance of Germany and America upon a manufacturing career, and the occidentation of Japan, enhanced the mercantile competition, and the struggle for the Far Eastern markets became a more definite object of national industrial policy. The next stage was the series of forceful moves by which France, Russia, Germany, Great Britain, and Japan have fastened their political and economic fangs into some special portion of the body of China by annexation, sphere of influence, or special treaty rights, their policy at this stage culminating in the ferocious reprisals of the recent[1] war, and the establishment of a permanent menace in the shape of international political and financial conditions extorted from a reluctant and almost impotent central government by threats of further violence.

It is now hardly possible for any one who has carefully followed these events to speak of Europe undertaking " a mission of civilization " in China without his tongue in his cheek.[2] Imperialism in the Far East is stripped nearly bare of all motives and methods save those of distinctively commercial origin. The schemes of territorial acquisition and direct political control which Russia, Germany, and France developed, the " sphere of influence " which has oscillated with " an open door " in our less coherent policy, are all manifestly motived by commerce and finance.

China seems to offer a unique opportunity to the Western business man. A population of some four hundred millions

---

[1] " recent " in 1903.

[2] The *Times* correspondent, in describing the forcible entrance of the allied troops into Pekin, affords this glimpse into Christianity *a la mode* in China. " The raising of the siege was signalized by the slaughter of a large number of Chinese who had been rounded up into a *cul-de-sac* and who were killed to a man, the Chinese Christian converts joining with the French soldiers of the relieving force, who lent them bayonets, and abandoned themselves to the spirit of revenge. Witnesses describe the scene as a sickening sight, but in judging such acts it is necessary to remember the provocation, and these people had been sorely tried " (The *Times*, October 16, 1900).

endowed with an extraordinary capacity of steady labour, with great intelligence and ingenuity, inured to a low standard of material comfort, in occupation of a country rich in unworked minerals and destitute of modern machinery of manufacture or of transport, opens up a dazzling prospect of profitable exploitation.

In our dealings with backward races capable of instruction in Western industrial methods there are three stages. First comes ordinary commerce, the exchange of the normal surplus produce of the two countries. Next, after Great Britain or some other Western Power has acquired territory or invested capital in the foreign country with the aim of developing the resources, she enjoys a period of large export trade in rails, machinery, and other forms of capital, not necessarily balanced by the import trade since it really covers the process of investment. This stage may continue long, when capital and business capacity cannot be obtained within the newly developed country. But a third stage remains, one which in China at any rate may be reached at no distant period, when capital and organizing energy may be developed within the country, either by Europeans planted there or by natives. Thus fully equipped for future internal development in all the necessary productive powers, such a nation may turn upon her civilizer, untrammelled by need of further industrial aid, undersell him in his own market, take away his other foreign markets and secure for herself what further developing work remains to be done in other undeveloped parts of the earth. The shallow platitudes by which the less instructed Free Trader sometimes attempts to shirk this vital issue have already been exposed. It is here enough to repeat that Free Trade can nowise guarantee the maintenance of industry or of an industrial population upon any particular country, and there is no consideration, theoretic or practical, to prevent British capital from transferring itself to China, provided it can find there a cheaper or more efficient supply of labour, or even to prevent Chinese capital with Chinese labour from ousting British produce in neutral markets of the world. What applies to Great Britain applies equally to the other industrial nations which have driven their economic suckers into China. It is at least conceivable that China might so turn the tables upon the Western industrial nations, and, either by adopting their capital and organizers or, as is more probable, by substituting her own, might flood their markets with her cheaper manufactures, and refusing their imports in exchange might take her payment in liens upon their capital, reversing the earlier process of investment until she gradually obtained financial control over her quondam patrons and civilizers. This is no idle speculation. If China in very truth possesses those industrial and business capacities with which she is commonly accredited, and the Western Powers are able to have their will in developing her upon Western lines, it seems extremely likely that this reaction will result.

IV

The inner significance of the joint attack of Western Powers in China lies here. It is the great speculative coup of international capitalism not fully ripened for international co-operation, but still hampered by the necessity under which the groups of capitalists lie, of using national feelings and policies to push their special interests. So long as it is necessary to use diplomatic pressure and armed force in order to secure some special field of investment in railroads, mining rights, or other developments, the peace of Europe is endangered by national intrigues and bickering. Though certain areas may be considered as more or less definitely allocated, Manchuria to Russia, the southern provinces of Tonking, with Hainan to France, Shan-tung to Germany, Formosa and Fokien to Japan, for industrial exploitation and for political control, there are large areas where the industrial and future political control, as spheres of influence, is likely to cause grave discord. Yunnan and Quan-tung on the southern boundary are disputed territory between England and France, the Chinese Government having given to each of these Powers a similar assurance that these provinces should not be alienated to any other Power. Great Britain's claim to the vast indefinite area known as the Yang-Tse basin as her separate sphere of influence for industrial concessions and political dominance is now exposed to the serious avowed encroachments of Germany, while Corea remains an open sore between Russia and Japan. The United States, whose interest in China for investment and for trade is developing faster than that of any European Power, will certainly insist upon an open door, and will soon be in a position to back her claim by strong naval force. The present[1] epoch, therefore, is one of separate national policies and special alliances, in which groups of financiers and capitalists urge their Governments to obtain leases, concessions, or other preferences over particular areas. It is quite possible that the conflicts of national Imperialism thus provoked, skilfully used for self-defence by the Chinese Government, may retard for a long time any effective opening up of China by Western enterprise, and that China may defend herself by setting her enemies to fight among themselves.

But it is idle to suppose that the industrial attack on China can be ultimately evaded. Unless China can be roused quickly from the sleep of countless centuries of peace and can transform herself into a powerful military

[1] The author writes of 1903.

nation, she cannot escape the pressure of the external powers. To suppose that she can do this, because her individual citizens show a capacity for drill and discipline, is to mistake the issue. The whole genius of the Chinese peoples, so far as it is understood, is opposed to militant patriotism and to the strongly centralized government required to give effect to such a policy. The notion of China organizing an army of six millions under some great general, and driving " the foreign devil " out of the country, or even entering herself upon a career of invasion and conquest, ignores the chief psychological and social factors of Chinese life. At any rate this is the least likely of all early issues in the Far East.

Far more reasonable is it to suppose that capitalism, having failed to gain its way by national separatist policies issuing in strife of Western peoples, may learn the art of combination, and that the power of international capitalism, which has been growing apace, may make its great crucial experiment in the exploitation of China. The driving force of the competing Imperialism of Western nations has been traced to the interests of certain small financial and industrial groups within each nation, usurping the power of the nation and employing the public force and money for their private business ends. In the earlier stage of development, where the grouping of these forces is still distinctively national, this policy makes for wars in pursuit of " national " markets for investments and trade. But the modern science of militarism renders wars between " civilized " Powers too costly, and the rapid growth of effective inter-nationalism in the financial and great industrial magnates, who seem destined more and more to control national politics, may in the future render such wars impossible. Militarism may long survive, for that, as has been shown, is serviceable in many ways to the maintenance of a plutocracy. Its expenditure furnishes a profitable support to certain strong vested interests, it is a decorative element in social life, and above all it is necessary to keep down the pressure of the forces of internal reform. Everywhere the power of capital in its more concentrated forms is better organized than the power of labour, and has reached a further stage in its development; while labour has talked of international co-operation, capital has been achieving it. So far, therefore, as the greatest financial and commercial interests are concerned, it seems quite probable that the coming generation may witness so powerful an international union as to render wars between the Western nations almost impossible. Notwithstanding the selfish jealousies and the dog-in-the-manger policies which at present weaken European action in the Far East, the real drama will begin when the forces of international capitalism, claiming to represent the civilization of united Christendom, are brought to bear on the peaceful opening up of China. It is then that the real " yellow peril " will begin. If it is unreasonable to expect that China can develop a national patriotism which will enable her to expel the Western exploiters, she must then be subjected to a process of disintegration, which is more aptly described as " the break-up " of China than by the term " development."

Not until then shall we realize the full risks and folly of the most stupendous revolutionary enterprise history has known. The Western nations may then awaken to the fact that they have permitted certain little cliques of private profit-mongers to engage them in a piece of Imperialism in which every cost and peril of that hazardous policy is multiplied a hundred-fold, and from which there appears no possibility of safe withdrawal. The light-hearted, casual mood in which the nations have been drawn on to the opening up of a country with a population almost as large as that of Europe, nineteen-twentieths of whom are perfectly unknown to us, is the crowning instance of irrational government. In large measure such an enterprise must rank as a plunge in the dark. Few Europeans even profess to know the Chinese, or to know how far the Chinese they do know are representative of the nation as a whole. The only important fact upon which there is universal agreement is that the Chinese are of all the " lower races " most adaptable to purposes of industrial exploitation, yielding the largest surplus product of labour in proportion to their cost of keep. In a word the investors and business managers of the West appear to have struck in China a mine of labour power richer by far than any of the gold and other mineral deposits which have directed imperial enterprise in Africa and elsewhere ; it seems so enormous and so expansible as to open up the possibility od raising whole white populations of the West to the position of " independent gentlemen," living, as do the small white settlements in India or South Africa, upon the manual toil of these laborious inferiors. For a parasitic exploit so gigantic the competing groups of business men who are driving on their respective Governments might even abate their competition and co-operate in the forceful steps required in starting their project. Once encompass China with a network of railroads and steamer services, the size of the labour market to be tapped is so stupendous that it might well absorb in its development all the spare capital and business energy the advanced European countries and the United States can supply for generations. Such an experiment may revolutionize the methods of Imperialism ; the pressure of working-class movements in politics and industry in the West can be met by a flood of China goods, so as to keep down wages and compel industry, or, where the power of the imperialist oligarchy is well set, by menaces of yellow workmen or of yellow mercenary troops, while collaboration in this huge Eastern development may involve an understanding between the groups of business politicians in the Western States close enough and strong enough to secure international peace in Europe and some relaxation of militarism.

This would drive the logic of Imperialism far towards realization; its inherent necessary tendencies towards unchecked oligarchy in politics, and parasitism in industry, would be plainly exhibited in the condition of the "imperialist" nations. The greater part of Western Europe might then assume the appearance and character already exhibited by tracts of country in the South of England, in the Riviera, and in the tourist-ridden or residential parts of Italy and Switzerland, little clusters of wealthy aristocrats drawing dividends and pensions from the Far East, with a somewhat larger group of professional retainers and tradesmen and a large body of personal servants and workers in the transport trade and in the final stages of production of the more perishable goods: all the main arterial industries would have disappeared, the staple foods and manufactures flowing in as tribute from Asia and Africa.[1] It is, of course, idle to suppose that the industrialization of China by Western methods can be achieved without effective political control, and just in proportion as Western Europe became dependent economically upon China would the maintenance of that joint imperial control react upon Western politics, subordinating all movements of domestic reform to the need of maintaining the Empires, and check-

---

[1] Mr. Bryce, in his Romanes Lecture, p. 9, seems to hint at the probability of such a development. "It is hardly too much to say that for economic purposes all mankind is fast becoming one people, in which the hitherto backward nations are taking a place analogous to that which the unskilled workers have held in each one of the civilized nations. Such an event opens a new stage in world history."

mating the forces of democracy by a skilful use of a highly
centralized bureaucracy and army.

How far the advent of Japan into the status of a first
rank political and industrial power will affect the problem
of Imperialism in Asia is a question which presses ever more
vigorously upon the consideration of Western nations.   It
is, however, impossible to deny that the recent manifestation
of Japan as an Eastern nation equipped with all the effective
practical arts of Western civilization is likely to alter profoundly the course of Asiatic history in the near future.

Regarding as the most important issue the economic
development of China upon Western lines, we cannot fail
to see that Japan has great advantages over Western
powers for doing this work and securing the profits which
it will yield.   These advantages are partly derived from
certain energies of mind which the Japanese exhibit, partly
from the geographical and racial factors in the situation.
Summarizing the acknowledged facts, the Japanese, as a
people, seem to have assimilated within two generations
all those mechanical and political sciences of the West
which contribute to the military, commercial and social
strength of a nation, while they can operate these instruments
of civilization quite as accurately and more economically
from the standpoint of the common good than any of the
nations which have been their teachers.   If this is " imitation " it is thoroughly intelligent imitation, for it is admitted
that the Japanese have exercised fine judgment in selecting
the weapons, machines, laws and customs which they have
adopted, and that they work their political, social and
economic institutions easily and efficiently.   The wonderful
success of Japan appears to be in large measure due to two
inner sources of economy.   In the first place they appear
to be able to give out a great quantity of mental energy in
the complex operations of modern life without sustaining

the amount of nervous waste perceptible in Western peoples : they appear to do more easily a larger quantity of cerebral work. Secondly, a more widely diffused, a more intense and a more sustained public spirit appears to produce a better co-operation of individual activities for the common good than is found in any Western people : there is less waste from indolence, corruption and other diseases of officialism, while a high consideration of public service pervades the popular mind. This intense patriotism and self-sacrifice may be only a psychical survival from an old social order which is passing away, but so long as it endures, it supplies a great operative force for further activity.

The proximity of Japan to North China, the associations of race, language, religion, literature, modes of life must give Japan an immense advantage over any European race in the economic development of China. If, as seems likely, the peace following the Russo-Japanese war opens an era of rapid commercial expansion for Japan, and capitalism advances swiftly within her islands, China will be the natural outlet for the investment of her capital and for the employment of her organizing energy in business and in the public services. Whether Japan will be dominated by the same spirit of territorial aggrandisement and political empire as European nations have exhibited depends in large measure upon the part played by the latter in the opening up of China. If the Western powers keep their political and military hands off China, content to encourage private companies to build railways, start mining and manufacturing operations and open up commercial inter- course with the interior, keeping the policy of " an open door," Japan will play this same game, but more successfully because of the better cards she holds, and the prestige of her successful war will stand her in good stead. If, on the other hand, there is closing of doors, ear-marking, and further political absorption of chosen areas by the Western powers, Japan will be driven to enter this sort of competition, and with her better understanding of the conditions of success, and her superior faculty for managing the Chinese, is likely to get the better of her European and American competitors.

Should European nations resent the growing industrial or perhaps political, supremacy of Japan in China and adopt some concerted action to defend their " spheres of influence " or their extorted " concessions," it is not wholly improbable that Japan may organize a great military and naval power in which she will utilize the latent force of China to drive the Western nations out of the China seas.

Such an opportunity for playing a great new part in imperial history may be open to Japan : if so, her temporary alliances with European powers are not likely to divert her from a course which will seem to her people as plain an instance of " manifest destiny " as any of the exploits of imperialism in the annals of England or the United States.

In speculating on the chances of this new chapter of world-history, a great deal depends upon how far Japan maintains her financial independence and is enabled to avoid becoming a catspaw of cosmopolitan capitalism in the great work of developing China. Should the future indus-trialization of Japan and China be conducted in the main out of their own resources of capital and organizing skill, passing quickly through a short period of dependence upon Europe for capital and instruction, the great industrial power of the Far East may quickly launch itself upon the world-market as the biggest and most effective competitor in the great machine industries, taking to itself first the trade of Asia and the Pacific, and then swamping the markets of the West and driving these nations to a still more rigorous Protection with its corollary of diminished production. Lastly, it is conceivable that the powerful industrial and financial classes of the West, in order better to keep the economic and political mastery at home, may combine to reverse the policy which has hitherto been gaining ground in the United States and in our white colonies, and may insist upon the free importation of yellow labour for domestic and industrial service in the West. This is a weapon which they hold in reserve, should they need to use it in order to keep the populace in safe subjection.

Those who regard with complacency the rapid development of China, because of a general conviction that the liberation of these great productive forces must by ordinary processes of commercial intercourse be beneficial to the Western nations, entirely miss the issue. The peaceful, equitable distribution over the industrial world of the increase of world-wealth rising from the development of China implies a successful movement of industrial democracy in the Western nations, yielding not merely increased productivity of their national resources, but a continual rise in standard of consumption of the peoples. Such a condition might, by securing ordinary processes of world-exchange, enrich the nations with a legitimate share of the prosperity of China. But the economic *raison d'être* of Imperialism in the opening up of China is, as we see, quite other than the maintenance of ordinary commerce : it consists in establishing a vast new market for Western investors, the profits of which will represent the gains of an investing class and not the gains of whole peoples. The normal healthy processes of assimilation of increased world-wealth by nations are inhibited by the nature of this Imperialism, whose essence consists in developing markets for investment, not for trade, and in using the superior economies of cheap foreign production to supersede the industries of their own

318

nation, and to maintain the political and economic domination of a class.

V

So far the influence of the " opening " or " break-up " of China upon the Western world has been the subject of inquiry. Let us now ask what this " break-up " means for China. Certain plain features stand out in the structure of Chinese society. China has never been a great Empire, or had any strong national existence in the European sense. The central government has always been very slight, virtually confined to a taxing power exercised through the provincial government, and to a small power of appointment of high officials. Even the provincial government has, in ordinary times, touched the actual life of the mass of the people lightly and at few points. China may be described properly as a huge nest of little free village communes, self-governing, and animated by a genuine spirit of equality. Mr. Colquhoun names the faculty of local self-government as " a main source of national vitality." " Groups of families constitute villages, which are self-governing, and the official who ventures to trench on their immemorial rights to the point of resistance is, according to an official code not confined to China, disavowed by his superiors, and generally finds a change of scene imperative. " The family system, with its extension to village and town groups, is the cheapest form of government extant, for it dispenses with police, while disposing effectually of offenders against the peace or respectability of the community."[1] Similarly the great German explorer Richthofen : " No people in the world are more exempt from official interference."

" The great fact," says Colquhoun, " to be noted as between the Chinese and the Government is the almost

[1] *Transformation in China*, by A. R. Colquhoun, p. 176.

unexampled liberty which the people enjoy, and the infinitesimally small part which Government plays in the scheme of national life."[1]

The family is the political, economic, and moral unit of society, the village commune being either a direct enlargement of a single family or a group of closely related families. Sometimes communal ownership is maintained, but usually a division takes place with each growth of family, and the operative principle in general vogue is an occupying ownership of small proprietors, paying a low land-tax to the State, the sole landlord, in return for a lease in perpetuity. The land-tax is based on profitable use, and unoccupied lands revert to the community. Patrimonial institutions prevent accumulation of large properties. Numerous provisions of law and custom provide against land-grabbing and monopoly. " Nowhere in China would it be possible for a rich man to take possession of a spring and convey its water to his pond by subterranean drains, leaving dry the fields under which it passed. Water is as indispensable to life as air and land. No individual has the right to say ' It is mine, it belongs to me.' This feeling is very strongly rooted in China."[2]

A family council, partly elective, partly hereditary, settles most important issues, punishing crimes, collecting the taxes, and settling divisions of property; recourse to legal processes is rare, the moral authority of the family commonly sufficing to preserve order.

This moral factor is, indeed, the one great vital principle in Chinese life. It not only governs economic relations, and presents a substitute for wider politics, but it figures prominently in the education and the religious or ethical system of the people. " Life seems so little worth living to a man outlawed from family and home that even capital

---

[1] *Transformation in China*, by A. R. Colquhoun, p. 296.   [2] Colquhoun.

sentences are executed by consent " ;[1] and where growth of population drives male members to seek employment in the towns, the closest family associations are retained. The reverence for family history and for the moral obligations it entails constitutes the kernel of national culture and the great stimulus to individual education and ambition in life.

Upon this basis is built one of the most extraordinary civilizations the world has known, differing in certain very vital matters from the civilization of the West.

Two points merit particular attention, because they drive down into the roots of Chinese civilization. The first is the general recognition of that " dignity of labour " which in the West has degenerated into a cant phrase so far as the common forms of work are concerned. Manual labour is not only a necessary means of livelihood, but a genuinely absorbing personal interest for the entire body of the nation ; with simple tools, and scarcely any use of machinery, minute personal skill is applied to agriculture and the manufactures ; most workers have some considerable variety of occupation, and see and enjoy the useful results of their toil. The whole economic system stands on a broad basis of " bread labour," applied in intensive cultivation of the land ; destitute of Western science or Western machinery, the detailed empirical study of agriculture has been carried farther than in any other country, and this " gardening " life is the most prominent factor in the external civilization of the country.

The second point is the wide diffusion of some sort of literary education and a genuine reverence for " things of the mind." The high respect in which a narrow conservative and pedantic literary system is held, the extraordinary importance attached to verbal memory and trivialities of ritual in their culture, have not unnaturally aroused much

[1] Simcox, *Primitive Civilizations*, vol. II.

astonishment and some contempt among educated Westerns. But the general prevalence of schools and libraries, the democratization of the machinery of education, the opening of the highest offices of State to a free competition of the people, conducted on an intellectual test, are indicative of a standard of valuation which entitles China to rank high among the civilizations of the world. In no Western nation do the man of learning and the gardener rank higher in the common regard of the people than the soldier. These valuations, economic and intellectual, lie firmly rooted in the Chinese mind, and have helped through countless generations to mould the social institutions of the people. The civilization, sprung up under these conditions, manifests some serious defects, compared with the best standards of the West. Life and conduct seem unduly cramped by detailed conventions; outside officialism there seems little scope for individual distinction; beyond the range of family, emotional life appears attenuated; the fine arts have never flourished, literature is conventional, morals are closely practical; the rigorous economy of material life seems attended by a less sensitive, nervous organization than that of any Western nation, and individual life seems to run upon a somewhat lower level of consciousness, and to be valued proportionately less.

But it should be recognized that the merits of this civilization are better attested than the defects, for the fruits of Chinese industry, honesty, orderly behaviour, and high regard for learning, are easily discernible by foreigners, while the more serious defects might vanish or be deeply modified by a more intimate understanding of Chinese psychology than any foreigner is likely to possess. The " barbarities " which have commonly won for China an ill-fame in Western lands, the savage punishments inflicted on criminals, the exposure of female infants, the brutal assaults on foreigners, are no normal part of the conduct of the nation, but rather sporadic survivals of brute habits and instincts, not more to be regarded as final tests of the civilization of China than negro-lynching of that of America or wife-kicking of that of England.

If this brief conspectus of the essential features of Chinese civilization is substantially correct, it is evident that " the break-up " brought about by the forces of Western nations will destroy the very foundations of the national order.

Its first fruits have been to impair security of life, peaceful industry and property over large areas of territory, to arouse a disorderly spirit of guerilla, to erect large public debts and so to enhance the burden of central government upon the body of the people, diminishing their communal independence. As the Western economic forces make further way, they must, partly by increased taxation needed for an expensive central government with armies, elaborate civil services and military debts, partly by the temptation of labour agents, draw large numbers of the workers from the position of independent little farmers into that of town wage-earners. This drain of population into industrial cities and mining districts, and the specialization of agriculture for large markets, will break up the communal land system with its fixed hereditary order and will sap the roots of family solidarity, introducing those factors of fluidity, minute subdivision, and concentration of labour which are the distinctive characteristics of Western industry. The economic and social equality which belongs to ordinary Chinese life will disappear before a new system of industrial caste which capitalism will entail. The decay of morals, which is so noticeable in the *declassés* Chinese, will spread with the decay of the family power, and an elaborate judicial and punitory machinery will replace the rule of the self-governing family. This collapse of local status will react upon the habit of commercial integrity attested throughout China by the inviolability of business pledges ; the new credit system of elaborate Western commerce will involve a network of commercial law and an education in that habit of litigiousness which exercises so dangerous a fascination over some other Asiatic peoples. The increase of wealth which this new industrialism would bring would either flow in economic tribute to the West, or would go to the endowment of a new powerful capitalist caste in China itself, who, following the Western lines, would ally themselves with imperialist politics in order to protect their vested interests. Capitalism, centralized government, militarism, protection, and a whole chain of public regulations to preserve the new order against the rising of old conservative traditional forces—such would be the inevitable outcome. The changes of external environment which have come with dangerous rapidity on Europe during the nineteenth century, forced still more rapidly on China by foreign profit-seekers, would produce reactions of incalculable peril upon the national life and character.

It would seem to imply no less than the destruction of the existing civilization of China and the substitution in its place of what ? There has been no serious pretence that European nations can impose or inculcate the essentials of their civilization on China. The psychology of the Chinese is a *terra incognita* : the most experienced European residents are those who are the frankest in declaring their inability to grapple with the mysteries of Chinese character and Chinese morality ; where less discreet writers venture on generalizations, their pages are riddled with the wildest contradictions and inconsistencies. What is, however, pretty clear is this : the Chinaman who detaches himself from the family bond and its moral associations and adopts European manners is distrusted alike by his fellow-countrymen and by his new patrons ; Christianity makes no way among " respectable " Chinese, the educated classes presenting no ground of appeal for any form of supernaturalism ; though Western science may hope in time to make a legitimate impression upon the intellectual life of China, the process will be one of slow absorption from within and cannot be imposed by alien instruction from without.

That the squabbles of European potentates for territorial expansion, the lusts of merchants or financiers, the ludicrously false expectations of missionaries, the catchwords of political parties in European elections, should be driving European nations to destroy the civilization of a quarter of the human race without possessing the ability or even recognizing the need to provide a substitute, ought surely to give pause to those Imperialists who claim to base their policy on reason and the common good.

No thinking man can seriously question the immense importance of free intercourse between the West and the East, or doubt the gain that would accrue to the civilization of the world by a wise communication to the Eastern mind of those arts which peculiarly represent Western civilization, the laborious, successful study of the physical sciences and their application to the arts of industry, the systematic development of certain definite principles and practices of law and government, and the thought and literature which are the conscious flowering of this growth of practical achievement.

That Europe could in this way render an invaluable service to Asia is certain.

" Some strange fiat of arrest, probably due to mental exhaustion, has condemned the brown men and the yellow men to eternal reproduction of old ideas."[1] To revivify the mind of Asia, to set it working again along new lines of rich

[1] *Asia and Europe*, p. 9.

productivity, this might be the boon of Europe. And for this service she too might take a rich reward. The brooding mind of Asia gave to sluggish Europe in past ages the great momenta in religion and philosophy and in the mathematics ; even in its sleep, or what appears to us the sleep of many centuries, it may have had its noble and illuminative dreams. The reason of the West may yet need the insight of the East. A union so profitable in the past may not be barren for the future. It is the right condition of this wholesome intercourse which is of supreme importance to the cause of civilization. Now one thing at least is certain. Force and the pushful hand of material greed inhibit the free interaction of mind and mind essential to this intercourse. The ancient civilizations of India and China, whose duration bears testimony to inherent qualities of worth, have not been directed chiefly to the attainment of progress in the arts of material wealth, though the simpler industries have in parts of China and India attained a high perfection, but rather to the maintenance of certain small types of orderly social life, with a strong hierarchy of social and industrial ranks in India, with a fundamentally democratic character in China.

The energy spared from political and industrial struggles, and in China from military practises, has gone, partly to the cultivation of certain simple qualities of domestic life and personal conduct, partly to the wide diffusion of a certain real life of the soul, animated by profound religious and philosophic speculations and contemplations in India, or by the elaboration of a more practical, utilitarian wisdom in China. These Eastern civilizations alone have stood the test of time ; the qualities which have enabled them to survive ought surely to be matter of deep concern for the mushroom civilizations of the West. It may even be true that the maintenance of these younger and more unstable civilizations depends upon unlocking the treasure-house of the wisdom of the East. Whether this be so or not, the violent breaking down of the characteristic institutions of Asia to satisfy some hasty lust of commerce, or some greed of power, is quite the most fatally blind misreading of the true process of world-civilization that it is possible to conceive. For Europe to rule Asia by force for purposes of gain, and to justify that rule by the pretence that she is civilizing Asia and raising her to a higher level of spiritual life, will be adjudged by history, perhaps, to be the crowning wrong and folly of Imperialism. What Asia has to give, her priceless stores of wisdom garnered from her experience of ages, we refuse to take; the much or little which we could give we spoil by the brutal manner of our giving. This is what Imperialism has done, and is doing, for Asia.

CHAPTER VI

IMPERIAL FEDERATION

I

THE imperial policy of Great Britain after 1870, and more particularly after 1885, was almost entirely absorbed in promoting the subjugation and annexation of tracts of territory where no genuine white settlement of any magnitude was contemplated. This policy, as we have seen, differs essentially from colonization; and from the standpoint of government it implies a progressive diminution of freedom in the British Empire by constantly increasing the proportion of its subjects who are destitute of real power of self-government.

It is important to consider how this new Imperialism reacts, and is likely in the future to react, upon the relations between Great Britain and her self-governing colonies. Will it stimulate these colonies to an assertion of growing independence and final formal severance from the mother country, or will it lead them to form a closer political union with her upon a basis, no longer of Empire, but of a Federation of equal States? This is a vital issue, for it is quite certain that the present[1] relations will not be maintained.

Hitherto the tendency has been towards a steady consistent increase of self-government, and a growing relaxation of Empire in the shape of control exercised by the

[1] 1903.

home Government. In Australasia, North America, and South Africa seventeen self-governing colonies have been established, endowed with reduced types of the British constitution. In the case of Australia and of Canada the growth of self - government has been formally and actually advanced by acts of federation, which have, in fact, especially in Australia, compensated the restriction of the power of the federated States by a more than equivalent increase of governing power vested in the federal Government.

Great Britain has in the main learned well the lesson of the American Revolution ; she has not only permitted but favoured this growing independence of her Australian and American colonies. During the very period when she has been occupied in the conscious policy of extending her Empire over lands which she cannot colonize and must hold by force, she has been loosening her " imperial " hold over her white colonies. While 1873 removed the last bond of economic control which marked the old " plantation " policy, by repealing the Act of 1850 which had forbidden Australian colonies from imposing differential duties as between the colonies and foreign countries, and permitting them in future to tax one another's goods, the Australian Commonwealth Act of 1900 has, by the powers accorded to its Federal Judicature, reduced to the narrowest limits yet attained the constitutional control of the Privy Council, and has by the powers enabling the Federal Government to raise a central armed force for defence obtained a new substantial basis for a possible national independence in the future. Though it is unlikely for some time to come that the federal Government which is contemplated for British South Africa will be accorded powers equivalent to those of the Australian or even the Canadian Federations, the same tendency to increase self-government has in the past steadily prevailed in Cape Colony and Natal, and it is tolerably certain that, if the racial animosities between the two white races are abated, a South African Commonwealth would soon be found in possession of a far larger measure of real self-government than the British colonies which enter it have hitherto possessed.[1]

But while the trend of British colonialism has uniformly been towards increased self-government or practical independence, and has been appreciably strengthened by the process of federating colonial States, it is evident that the imperial statesmen who have favoured most this federation policy have had in view some larger recasting of the political relations with the mother country, which should bind parent and children in closer family bonds, not merely of affection or of trading intercourse, but of political association. Though imperial federation for British purposes is no modern invention, Lord Carnarvon was the first Colonial Secretary to set it before him as a distinct object of attainment, favouring federation in the various groups of colonies as the first step in a process which should federate the Empire. The successful completion in 1873 of the process of federation which formed the Dominion of Canada doubtless stimulated Lord Carnarvon, entering office the next year, to further experiments along similar lines. Unfortunately he laid hands upon South Africa for his forcing process, and suffered a disastrous failure. Twenty years later Mr. Chamberlain resumed the task, and, confronted by the same essential difficulties, the forcible annexation of the two Dutch Republics, and the coercion of Cape Colony, carried his federation policy in South Africa on the road towards completion, while the establishment of the Australian Commonwealth marks another and a safer triumph of the federation principle.

[1] This relates to the situation in 1903.

The process of federation, as bearing on the relations of the federating colonies, is of course a triumph for the centripetal forces ; but, by securing a larger measure of theoretical and practical independence for the federal Governments, it has been centrifugal from the standpoint of the Imperial Government. The work of securing an effective political imperial federation implies, therefore, a reversal of hitherto dominant tendencies.

It is quite evident that a strong and increasing desire for imperial federation was growing among a large number of British politicians. So far as Mr. Chamberlain and some of his friends were concerned, it dates back to the beginning of the struggle over Mr. Gladstone's Home Rule for Ireland policy. Speaking on Mr. Gladstone's Home Rule Bill in 1886, Mr. Chamberlain said : " I should look for the solution in the direction of the principle of federation. My right honourable friend has looked for his model to the relations between this country and her self-governing and practically independent colonies. I think that is of doubtful expediency. The present connexion between our colonies and ourselves is no doubt very strong, owing to the affection which exists between members of the same nation. But it is a sentimental tie, and a sentimental tie only. . . . It appears to me that the advantage of a system of federation is that Ireland might under it really remain an integral part of the Empire. The action of such a scheme is centripetal and not centrifugal, and it is in the direction of federation that the democratic movement has made most advances in the present century."

Now, it is quite true that the democratic movement, both now and in the future, seems closely linked with the formation of federal States, and the federation of the parts of the British Empire appears to suggest, as a next step and logical outcome, the federation of the whole.

Holding, as we must, that any reasonable security for good order and civilization in the world implies the growing application of the federation principle in international politics, it will appear only natural that the earlier steps in such a process should take the form of unions of States most closely related by ties of common blood, language, and institutions, and that a phase of federated Britain or Anglo-Saxondom, Pan-Teutonism, Pan-Slavism, and Pan-Latinism might supervene upon the phase already reached. There is perhaps a suspicion of excessive logic in such an order of events, but a broad general view of history renders it plausible and desirable enough. Christendom thus laid out in a few great federal Empires, each with a retinue of uncivilized dependencies, seems to many the most legitimate development of present tendencies and one which would offer the best hope of permanent peace on an assured basis of inter-Imperialism. Dismissing from our mind the largest aspect of this issue, as too distant for present profitable argument, and confining our attention to British imperial federation, we may easily agree that a voluntary federation of free British States, working peacefully for the common safety and prosperity, is in itself eminently desirable, and might indeed form a step towards a wider federation of civilized States in the future.

The real issue for discussion is the feasibility of such a policy, and, rightly stated, the question runs thus : "What forces of present or prospective self-interest are operative to induce Great Britain and her colonial groups to reverse the centrifugal process which has hitherto been dominant ?" Now, there are many reasons for Great Britain to desire political federation with her self-governing colonies, even upon terms which would give them a voice proportionate to their population in a Parliament or other council charged

with the control of imperial affairs, provided the grace
difficulties involved in the establishment of such a representative, responsible, governing body could be overcome.
The preponderance of British over colonial population
would enable the mother country to enforce her will where
any conflict of interest or judgment arose in which there
was a sharp line of division between Great Britain and the
colonies : the distribution of imperial burdens and the
allocation of imperial assistance would be determined by
Great Britain. If the Crown colonies and other non-self-
governing parts of the Empire were represented in the
imperial council, the actual supremacy of the mother
country would be greater still, for these representatives,
either nominated by the Crown (the course most consonant
with Crown colony government), or elected on a narrow
franchise of a small white oligarchy, would have little in
common with the representatives of self-governing colonies,
and would inevitably be more amenable to pressure from
the home Government. A chief avowed object of imperial
federation is to secure from the colonies a fair share of
men, ships, and money for imperial defence, and for
those expansive exploits which in their initiation almost
always rank as measures of defence. The financial basis
of imperial defence in 1903 is one which, on the face of
it, seems most unfair ; Great Britain is called upon to
support virtually the whole cost of the imperial navy,
and, with India, almost the whole cost of the imperial
army, though both these arms are at the service of any
of our self-governing colonies that is threatened by external
enemies or internal disorders. In 1899, while the population of these colonies was close upon one-third of that of
the United Kingdom, their revenue nearly one-half, and the
value of their sea-borne commerce one-fifth of the entire
commerce of the Empire, the contribution they were

making to the cost of the naval defence of the Empire was less than one-hundredth part.[1] These colonies raised in 1903 no regular or irregular military force available for the general defence of the Empire, though they have supported small contingents of imperial troops quartered upon them by the Imperial Government, and have maintained considerable militia and volunteer forces for home defence. The colonial contingents taking part in the South African war, though forming a considerable volunteer force, fell far short of an imperial levy based upon proportion of population, and their expenses were almost entirely borne by the United Kingdom. From the standpoint of the unity of the British Empire, in which the colonies are presumed to have an interest equivalent to that of the United Kingdom, it seems reasonable that the latter should be called upon to bear their fair share of the burden of imperial defence ; and an imperial federation which was a political reality would certainly imply a provision for such equal contribution. Whatever were the form such federation took, that of an Imperial Parliament, endowed with full responsibility for imperial affairs under the Crown, or of an Imperial Council, on which colonial representatives must sit to consult with and advise the British ministry, who still retained the formal determination of imperial policy, it would certainly imply a compulsory or quasi-compulsory contribution on the part of the colonies proportionate to that of the United Kingdom.

[1] 1899.	Population.	Revenue.	Trade.	Naval Contribution.
United Kingdom	39,000,000	£104,000,000	£766,000,000	£24,734,000
Self-governing Colonies	12,000,000	46,000,000	222,000,000	177,000

Now it is quite evident that the self-governing colonies will not enter such an association, involving them in large new expenses, out of sentimental regard for the British Empire. The genuineness and the warmness of the attachment to the British Empire and to the mother country are indisputable, and though they were not called upon to make any considerable self-sacrifice in the South African campaign, it is quite evident that their sentiments are such as would lead them voluntarily to expend both blood and money where they thought the existence, the safety, or even the honour of the Empire was at stake. But it would be a grave error to suppose that the blaze of enthusiastic loyalty evinced at such a period of emergency can be utilized in order to reverse the general tendency towards independence, and to " rush " the self-governing colonies into a closer formal union with Great Britain, involving a regular continuous sacrifice. If the colonies are induced to enter any such association, they must be convinced that it is essential to their individual security and prosperity. In 1903 they get the protection of the Empire with out paying for it ; as long as they think they can get adequate protection on such terms it is impossible to suppose they would enter an arrangement which required them to pay, and which involved an entire recasting of their system of revenue. The temper of discussions in the Australian and Canadian Parliaments, amid all the enthusiasm of the South African war, makes it quite clear that no colonial ministry could in time of peace persuade the colonists to enter such a federation as is here outlined unless they had been educated to the conviction that their individual colonial welfare was to be subserved. Either Australia and Canada must be convinced that imperial defence of Australia or Canada upon the present[1] basis is becoming more inadequate,

[1] 1903.

and that such defence is essential to them, or else they must be compensated for the additional expense which federation would involve by new commercial relations with the United Kingdom which will give them a more profitable market than they possess already.

Now the refusal of the self-governing colonies hitherto to consider any other contribution to imperial defence than a small voluntary one has been based upon a conviction that the virtual independence they hold under Great Britain is not likely to be threatened by any great Power, and that, even were it threatened, though their commerce might suffer on the sea, they would be competent to prevent or repel invasion by their own internal powers of self-defence. The one exception to this calculation may be said to prove the rule. If Canada were embroiled in war with her great republican neighbour, she is well aware that though the British navy might damage the trade and the coast towns of the United States, she could not prevent Canada from being over-run by American troops, and ultimately from being subjugated.

But, it may at least be urged, the importance of maintaining a British navy adequate to protect their trade will at least be recognized ; the colonies will perceive that in face of the rising wealth and naval preparations of rival Empires, in particular Germany, France, and the United States, the United Kingdom cannot bear the financial strain of the necessary increase of ships without substantial colonial assistance. This is doubtless the line of strongest pressure for imperial federation. How far is it likely to prove effective ? It is certain to educate colonial politicians to a closer consideration of the future of their colony ; it will force them to canvass most carefully the net advantages or disadvantages of the imperial connexion. Such consideration seems at least as likely to lead them towards that definite future severance from Great Britain which, until now, in 1903, none of them has seriously contemplated, as it is to bring them into a federation. This consummation, if it ultimately comes about, will arise from no abatement of natural good feeling and affection towards the United Kingdom, but simply from a conflict of interests.

If the movement towards imperial federation fails, and the recent drift towards independence on the part of the self-governing colonies is replaced by a more conscious movement in the same direction, the cause will be Imperialism. A discreet colonial statesman, when invited to bring his colony closer to Great Britain, and to pay for their common support while leaving to Great Britain the virtual determination of their common destiny, is likely to put the following pertinent questions : Why is Great Britain obliged to increase her expenditure in armaments faster than the growth of trade or income, so that she is forced to call upon us to assist ? Is it because she fears the jealousy and the hostility of other Powers ? Why does she arouse these ill feelings ? To these questions he can hardly fail to find an answer ? " It is the new Imperialism that is wholly responsible for the new perils of the Empire, and for the new costs of armaments." He is then likely to base upon this answer further questions. Do we self-governing colonies benefit by this new Imperialism ? If we decide that we do not, can we stop it by entering a federation in which our voices will be the voices of a small minority ? May it not be a safer policy for us to seek severance from a Power which so visibly antagonizes other Powers, and may involve us in conflict with them on matters in which we have no vital interest and no determinant voice, and either to live an independent political life, incurring only those risks which belong to us, or (in the case

337

of Canada) to seek admission within the powerful republic of the United States ?

However colonial history may answer these questions, it is inevitable that they will be put. Imperialism is evidently the most serious obstacle to " imperial federation," so far as the self-governing colonies are concerned. Were it not for the presence of these unfree British possessions and for the expansive policy which has continually increased them, a federation of free British States throughout the world would seem a reasonable and a most desirable step in the interests of world-civilization. But how can the white democracies of Australasia and North America desire to enter such a hodge-podge of contradictory systems as would be presented by an imperial federation, which might, according to one authority,[1] be compiled in the following fashion : first a union of Great Britain, Ireland, Canada, West Indies, Australia, Tasmania, New Zealand, Newfoundland, Mauritius, South Africa, Malta, to be followed later by the admission of Cyprus, Ceylon, India, Hong-Kong, and Malaysia, with an accompaniment of semi-independent States such as Egypt, Afghanistan, Natal, Bhutan, Jehore, and perhaps the kingdoms of Uganda and of Barotse, each with some sort of representation on an Imperial Council and some voice in the determination of the imperial destiny ?

Is it likely that the great rising Australian Commonwealth or the Dominion of Canada will care to place her peaceful development and her financial resources at the mercy of some Soudanese forward movement or a pushful policy in West Africa ?

An imperial federation comprising all sorts and conditions of British States, colonies, protectorates, veiled protectorates and nondescripts would be too unwieldy, and too prolific of frontier questions and of other hazards,

[1] Sir H. H. Johnston, *Nineteenth Century*, May 1902.

to please our more isolated and self-centred free colonies ; while, if these former were left without formal representation as special protégés of the United Kingdom, their existence and their growth would none the less hang like a mill-stone round the neck of the federal Government, constantly compelling the United Kingdom to strain the allegiance of her confederates by using her technical superiority of voting power in what she held to be their special interest and hers.

The notion that the absence of any real strong identity of interest between the self-governing colonies and the more remote and more hazardous fringes of the Empire can be compensated by some general spirit of loyalty towards and pride in " the Empire " is a delusion which will speedily be dispelled. The detached colonies of Australasia may not unreasonably argue that the very anxiety of British statesmen to draw them into federation is a confession of the weakening of that very protection which constitutes for them the chief value of the present connexion. " The United Kingdom," they may say, " asks us to supply men and ships and money in a binding engagement in order to support her in carrying farther the very imperialist policy which arouses the animosity of rival Powers and which disables her for future reliance on her own resources to sustain the Empire. For our increased contribution to the imperial resources we shall therefore receive in return an increase of peril. Is it not something like asking us, out of pure chivalry, to throw in our lot with a sinking vessel ? " It will doubtless be replied that a firmly federated Empire will prove such a tower of strength as will enable her to defy the increased jealousy of rival Powers. But this tempting proposition will be submitted to cool calculation in our colonies, which will certainly refuse to be " rushed " into a change of policy implying a reversal of the general tendency of half a century. Admitting the obvious political and military gain of co-operative action in the face of an enemy, the colonists will ask whether this gain is not offset by an increased likelihood of having to face enemies, and when they reflect that they are really invited to federate, not merely with the England whom they love and admire, but with an ever-growing medley of savage States, the balance of judgment seems likely to turn against federation, unless other special inducements can be applied.

II

There are two special inducements which might bring the self-governing colonies, or some of them, to favour a closer political union with Great Britain. The first is a revision of the commercial and financial policy of the mother country, so as to secure for the colonies an increased market for their produce in Great Britain and in other parts of the British Empire. In discussion of this issue it is customary to begin by distinguishing the proposal to establish an Imperial Zollverein, or Customs Union, from the proposal for a preferential tariff. But very little reflection suffices to perceive the futility of the former without the latter as an appeal to the self-interest of the colonies. Will these colonies assimilate their financial policy to that of Great Britain, abolishing their protective tariffs and entering a full Free Trade career ? The most sanguine Free Trader suggests no such possibility, nor indeed would such a course afford any real guarantee of increasing the commercial inter-dependence of the Empire. It would simply force the colonies upon processes of direct taxation repugnant to their feelings. Is Free Trade within the

Empire, with a maintenance of the *status quo* as regards foreign countries, really more feasible ? It would simply mean that the colonies gave up the income they obtained from taxing the goods of one another and of Great Britain, each getting in return a remission of tariffs from the other colonies with which its trade is small and no remission from Great Britain, which would continue to receive its goods free as before.

It is now admitted that the colonies will not, and indeed cannot remit or greatly reduce their taxes upon imported goods from Great Britain and from one another. They are prepared to give British goods a preferential treatment upon two conditions : first, that such preference does not involve any net reduction of their income from customs ; secondly, that it does not make British goods to compete more effectively with their own manufactures. A preferential tariff constructed under these conditions implies that any net reductions of the duty upon classes of British imports must be compensated by a general rise of the tariff in regard to other imports, and that where British imports compete with colonial products there can be no reduction of the duty, but only an increased tax in foreign as compared with British goods.

If it does not cost anything to the exchequer of the Dominion and the Commonwealth, or considerably raise prices to colonial consumers, Canada and Australia are willing to oust foreign goods in favour of British, but the tendency will be to do this by raising the duty against foreigners, and not by lowering it against Great Britain. Moreover, the nature of British imports into these countries (i.e. highly manufactured goods) generally involves some amount of competition with home products, so that any actual reduction of duty is inconsistent with protection of home industries. Thus the principles of Canadian protection oblige her to maintain a higher average duty upon British goods than upon American and other foreign goods, many of which are raw materials or semi-manufactured goods which do not compete appreciably with Canadian products. Thus, though the preferences given by Canada to the mother country in 1897 and 1900 have checked the rapid decline in the growth of British as compared with foreign imports into Canada, they have not prevented foreign trade from increasing at a slightly faster pace than British, while the importation (largely of free raw materials) from the United States continues to grow faster than the importation from Great Britain. Moreover, the powerful organized opposition of Canadian manufacturers against favoured British competition is a factor of increasing importance now that Canada is putting more of her own and American capital into manufacturing industry. The tendency will be more and more towards an encouragement of Canadian manufactures by higher duties upon imports, so that a show of British preference can only be maintained by a general raising of duties on imported manufactures. What holds of Canada holds also of Australia. Both nations look forward to a great manufacturing future which will give them that self-sufficing character which is the protectionist ideal; more and more will their desire to favour the mother country conflict with their higher sense of duty towards their own manufactures. The notion that they will abstain from setting up any manufacture which they can successfully establish out of consideration for the English manufacturers who have hitherto supplied these goods is puerile. These being the conditions, such preferences as they give to British imports must be slight and temporary.

To purchase this small boon, Great Britain must give in return preferential treatment involving, first, a reversal of our Free Trade policy; secondly, taxes upon foreign food and raw materials. Grain and flour, cattle and meat, wool, timber, and iron would form the chief commodities which, in the supposed interests of our colonies, would be taxed first. Unless this preference raised prices it could have no effect in enabling colonial producers to displace foreign producers : the tariff, to be operative at all, must remove all profit from some portion of foreign goods previously imported, and, by preventing such goods from entering our markets in the future, reduce the total supply : this reduction of supply acts of necessity in raising the price for the whole market. This well-recognized automatic operation of the law of supply and demand makes it certain that English consumers would pay in enhanced prices a new tax, part of which would be handed over to colonists in payment for their new " loyalty," part would go to the British exchequer, part to defray expenses of collection, and the rest in enhanced rent to British landowners.

Nor is this all, or perhaps the worst. By this very method of binding our colonies closer to us we take the surest way of increasing the resentment of those very nations whose political and military rivalry impels us to abandon Free Trade. The vast and increasing trade we have with France, Germany, Russia, and the United States is the most potent guarantee of peace which we possess. Reduce the volume and the value of our commerce with these nations, by means of the re-establishment of a tariff avowedly erected for the purpose, and we should convert the substantial goodwill of the powerful financial, mercantile, and manufacturing interests in these countries into active and dangerous hostility. It would be far better for us that we had never been a Free Trade country than that we relapsed into a protective system motived by the desire to weaken our commercial bonds with the political and commercial Powers whose rivalry we have most to fear. By the statistics of an earlier chapter[1] it has been shown that not merely is our trade with these foreign nations far greater than the trade with the self-governing colonies, but that it is growing at a faster rate. To offend and antagonize our better customers in order to conciliate our worse is bad economy and much worse politics.

The shrewder politicians in our colonies might surely be expected to look such a gift-horse in the mouth. For the very bribe which is designed to win them for federation is one which enhances for them enormously and quite incalculably the perils of a new connexion by which they throw in their lot irrevocably with that of Great Britain. A monopoly of the imperial market for their exports may be bought too dear, if it removes the strongest pledge for peace which England possesses, at a time when that pledge is needed most. Nor would these colonies share only the new peril of England ; their own discriminative tariffs would breed direct ill-feeling against them on the part of foreigners, and would drag them into the vortex of European politics. Finally, by distorting the more natural process of commercial selection, which, under tariffs equally imposed, has in the past been increasing the proportion of the trade done by these colonies with foreign countries, and reducing the proportion done with Great Britain, we shall be forcing them to substitute a worse for a better trade, a course by which they will be heavy losers in the long run.

III

In face of such facts it will be impossible for Great Britain to offer the self-governing colonies a sufficient commercial

[1] *Cf.* Part I, chap. ii.

inducement to bring them into imperial federation. Is there any other possible inducement or temptation? There is, I think, one, viz., to involve them on their own account in Imperialism, by encouraging and aiding them in a policy of annexation and the government of lower races. Independently of the centralized Imperialism which issues from Great Britian, these colonies have within themselves in greater or less force all the ingredients out of which an Imperialism of their own may be formed. The same conspiracy of powerful speculators, manufacturing interests and ambitious politicians, calling to their support the philanthropy of missions and the lust for adventure which is so powerful in the new world, may plot the subversion of honest, self-developing democracy, in order to establish class rule, and to employ the colonial resources in showy enterprises of expansion for their own political and commercial ends.

Such a spirit and such a purpose was plainly operative in South Africa for many years. That which appears to us as an achievement of British Imperialism, viz., the acquisition of the two Dutch Republics and the great North, is and always has appeared something quite different to a powerful group of business politicians in South Africa. These men at the Cape, in the Transvaal and in Rhodesia, British or Dutch, have fostered a South African Imperialism, not opposed to British Imperialism, willing when necessary to utilize it, but independent of it in ultimate aims and purposes. This was the policy of " colonialism " which Mr. Rhodes espoused so vehemently in his earlier political career, seeking the control of Bechuanaland and the North for Cape Colony and not directly for the Empire. This has been right through the policy of an active section of the Africander Bond, developing on a large scale the original " trek " habit of the Dutch. This was the policy to which Sir Hercules

Robinson gave voice in his famous declaration of 1889 regarding Imperialism: "It is a diminishing quantity, there being now no longer any permanent place in the future of South Africa for direct imperial rule on any large scale." A distinctively colonial or South African expansion was the policy of the politicians, financiers, and adventurers up to the failure of the Jameson Raid; reluctantly they sought the co-operation of British Imperialism to aid them in a definite work for which they were too weak, the seizure of the Transvaal mineral estates; their absorbing aim hereafter will be to relegate British Imperialism to what they conceive to be its proper place, that of an *ultima ratio* to stand in the far background while colonial Imperialism manages the business and takes the profits. A South African federation of self-governing States will demand a political career of its own, and will insist upon its own brand of empire, not that of the British Government, in the control of the lower races in South Africa.

Such a federal State will not only develop an internal policy regarding the native territories different from, perhaps antagonistic to, that of British Imperialism, but its position as the "predominant" State of South Africa will develop an ambition and a destiny of expansion which may bring it into world politics on its own account.

Australasia similarly shows signs of an Imperialism of her own. She has recently taken over New Guinea, and some of her sons are hankering after a "Monroe doctrine" applicable throughout the South Pacific, the opening step of which would consist of the assignation of our Pacific Islands to Australia and New Zealand for administrative purposes. "The same principle," it is suggested, "is applicable to the connexion between Canada and the British West Indies. Economically the latter are important to Canada, as furnishing a tropical market of the kind which the United States possess within their own borders, and also in their newly acquired dependencies. Strategically, also, the islands are becoming important to Canada as a base for the protection of her growing interests, especially in connexion with the Panama Canal, so that here the privilege of administration would enforce the sense of responsibility for naval defence."[1]

If Great Britain is prepared to guarantee to Australasia, Canada and South Africa a special imperial career of their own, placing the entire federal resources of the Empire at the disposal of the colonial federal States, to assist them in fulfilling an ambition or a destiny which is directed and determined by their particular interests and will, such a decentralization of Imperialism might win the colonies to a closer federal union with the mother country. For Great Britain herself it would involve great and obvious dangers, and some considerable sacrifice of central imperial power ; but it might win the favour and support of ambitious colonial politicians and capitalists desirous to run a profitable Imperialism of their own and to divert the democratic forces from domestic agitation into foreign enterprises.

If Australasia can get from Great Britain the services of an adequate naval power to enforce her growing " Monroe doctrine " in the Pacific without paying for it, as British South Africa has obtained the services of our land forces, she will not be likely to enter closer formal bonds which will bind her to any large financial contribution towards the expenses of such a policy. But if Great Britain were willing to organize imperial federation upon a basis which in reality assigned larger independence to Australia and Canada than they have at present, by giving them a call upon the imperial resources for their own private imperial

[1] *Colonial Nationalism*, by Richard Jebb, pp. 306–7.

career in excess of their contribution towards the common purse, business instincts might lead them to consider favourably such a proposal.

How fraught with peril to this country such imperial federation would be it is unnecessary to prove. Centralized Imperialism, in which the Government of Great Britain formally reserves full control over the external policy of each colony, and actually exercises this control, affords some considerable security against the danger of being dragged into quarrels with other great Powers : the decentralized Imperialism, involved in imperial federation, would lose us this security. The nascent local Imperialism of Australasia, Canada and South Africa would be fed by the consciousness that it could not be checked or overruled in its expansive policy as it is now ; and the somewhat blatant energy of self-expression in the Australasian Governments would be likely to entangle us continually with Germany, Japan and the United States in the Pacific, while Canada and Newfoundland would possess a greatly enhanced power to embroil us with France and the United States. If it be urged that after all no serious steps in Australian, Canadian or South African " Imperialism " could be taken without the direct conscious consent of Great Britain, who would, by virtue of population and prestige, remain the predominant partner, the answer is that the very strengthening of the imperial bond would give increased efficacy to all the operative factors in Imperialism. Even as matters stand now there exists in Great Britain a powerful organized business interest which is continually inciting the Imperial Government to a pushful policy on behalf of our colonies : these colonies, the Australasian in particular, are heavily mortgaged in their land and trade to British financial companies ; their mines, banks, and other important commercial assets are largely owned in Great Britain; their enormous public debts[1] are chiefly held in Great Britain. It is quite evident that the classes in this country owning these colonial properties have a stake in colonial politics, different from and in some cases antagonistic to that of the British nation as a whole : it is equally evident that they can exercise an organized pressure upon the British Government in favour of their private interests that will be endowed with enhanced efficacy under the more equal conditions of an imperial federation.

Whether the bribe of a preferential tariff, or of a delegated Imperialism, or both, would suffice to bring the self-governing colonies into a closer formal political federation with Great Britain may, however, well be doubted. Still more doubtful would be their permanent continuance in such a federation. It is at least conceivable that the colonial democracies may be strong and sane enough to resist temptation to colonial Imperialism, when they perceive the dangerous reaction of such a course. Even were they induced to avail themselves of the ample resources of the Empire to forward their local imperial policy, they would, in Australia as in South Africa, be disposed to break away from such a federation when they had got out of it what advantages it could be made to yield, and they felt strong enough for an independent Empire of their own.

It is no cynical insistence upon the dominance of selfish

---

[1] In 1900 the public debts of the Australasian colonial Governments amounted to £194,812,289, for a population of 3,756,894 ; while the New Zealand debt was £46,930,077 for a population of 756,510 *Statesman's Year Book*, 1901).

New South Wales	£65,332,993
Victoria	48,774,885
Queensland	34,338,414
South Australia	26,156,180
West Australia	11,804,178
Tasmania	8,395,639
	£194,812,289

interests which leads us to the conviction that the historic drift towards independence will not be reversed by any sentiments of attachment towards Great Britain. " My hold of the colonies," wrote Burke, " is the close affection which grows from common names, from kindred blood, from similar privileges, and equal protection. These are ties which, though light as air, are as strong as links of iron."[1] But in these ties, save the last only, there is nothing to demand or to ensure political union. The moral bonds of community of language, history and institutions, maintained and strengthened by free social and commercial intercourse, this true union of hearts, have not been weakened by the progress towards political freedom which has been taking place in the past, and will not be weakened if this progress should continue until absolute political independence from Great Britain is achieved.

It is quite certain that the issue must be determined in the long run by what the colonies consider to be their policy of net utility. That utility will be determined primarily by the more permanent geographical and economic conditions. These have tended in the past, so far as they have had free play, towards political independence : they will have a freer play in the future, and it seems, therefore, unlikely that their tendency will be reversed. Though the element of distance between the parts of an Empire is now less important than formerly as a technical difficulty in representation, the following pithy summary of American objections to schemes of imperial federation in the eighteenth century, as recorded by Pownall, still has powerful application :—

" The Americans also thought that legislative union would be unnecessary, inexpedient, and dangerous, because—

" (1) They had already sufficient legislatures of their own.

[1] *Conciliation with America.*

350

" (2) If the colonies were so united to England they would share the burden of British taxes and debt.

" (3) Representatives in England would be too far from their constituents, and the will of the colonies would, therefore, be transferred out of their power, and involved in that of a majority in which the proportion of their representatives would hold no balance."[1]

While then it is conceivable, perhaps possible, that, for a time at any rate, the self-governing colonies might be led into an imperial federation upon terms which should secure their private industrial and political ambitions as colonies, it is far more reasonable to expect that Canada would drift towards federation with her southern neighbour, and Australasia and South Africa towards independent political entities, with a possible future re-establishment of loose political relations in an Anglo-Saxon federation.

It is no aspersion on the genuineness and the strength of the " loyalty " and affection entertained by the colonies towards England to assert that these sentiments cannot weigh appreciably in the determination of the colonial " destiny " against the continuous pressure of political, industrial, and financial forces making towards severance. Though a few politicians, or even a party in these colonies, may coquet with the notion of close federation on an equal basis, the difficulties, when the matter is resolved, as it must be, into financial terms, will be found insuperable. The real trend of colonial forces will operate in the same direction as before, and more persistently, when the nature of the burdens they are invited to undertake is disclosed to them.

The notion that one great result of the South African war has been to generate a large fund of colonial feeling which will materially affect the relations of the colonies

[1] Holland, *Imperium et Libertas*, p. 82.

with Great Britain is an amiable delusion based upon childish psychology. While the rally of sentiment has been genuine, so has been the discovery of the perils of the mother country which have made colonial assistance so welcome and caused it to be prized so highly that imperial statesmen essay to turn the tide of colonial development by means of it.

Reflection, which follows every burst of sentiment, cannot fail to dwell upon the nature of the peril which besets an empire so vast, so heterogeneous, and so dispersed as the British Empire. When the glamour of war has passed away, and history discloses some of the brute facts of this sanguinary business which have been so carefully kept from the peoples of Australia, New Zealand and Canada, their relish for the affair will diminish : they will be more suspicious in the future of issues whose character and magnitude have been so gravely misrepresented to them by the Imperial Government.[1] But the discovery likely to weigh most with the colonial democracies is the unsubstantial assets of the new Imperialism. It is one thing to enter a federation of free self-governing States upon an equal footing, quite another to be invited to contribute to the maintenance and acquisition of an indefinitely large and growing number of dependencies, the property of one of the federating States. The more clearly the colonies recognize the precarious nature of the responsibilities they are asked to undertake, the more reluctant will they show themselves. Unless the democratic spirit of these colonies can be broken and they can be driven to " Imperialism " upon their own account, they will refuse to enter a federation which,

[1] Public feeling in Australia and New Zealand was of a particularly simple manufacture in the autumn of 1899. Mr. Chamberlain communicated the " facts " of the South African war to the Premiers of the colonies and they served them out to the press. This official information was not checked by any really independent news.

whatever be the formal terms of entrance, fastens on them perils so incalculable. The new Imperialism kills a federation of free self-governing States : the colonies may look at it, but they will go their way as before.

The sentimental attractions which the idea may at first present will not be void of practical results. It may lead them to strengthen their preparation for internal defence, and to develop, each of them, a firmer national spirit of their own. The consciousness of this gain in defensive strength will not the more dispose them to closer formal union with Great Britain ; it is far more likely to lead them to treat with her upon the terms of independent allies. The direction in which the more clear-sighted colonial statesmen are moving is and always has been tolerably clear. It is towards a slighter bond of union with Great Britain, not a stronger. The near goal is one clearly marked out for the American colonies by Jefferson as early as 1774, and one which then might have been attained if England had exercised discretion. Jefferson thus describes his plan in the draft of instructions to dele-gates sent by Virginia to Congress : " I took the ground that from the beginning I had thought the only one orthodox or tenable, which was that the relation between Great Britain and those colonies was exactly the same as that of England and Scotland after the accession of James and until after the Union, and the same as the present relation with Hanover, having the same executive chief, but no other necessary political connexion."[1] This same project, that of narrowing down the imperial connexion to the single tie of a common monarchy, was avowed by the " Reformers " who in Upper Canada usually made a majority of the Legislative Assembly during 1830–40, and underlies the conscious or unconscious policy of all our

[1] Quoted *Imperium et Libertas*, p. 70.

self-governing colonies when subject to normal influences. Brief, temporary set-backs to this movement under the stress of some popular outburst of enthusiasm or some well-engineered political design are possible, but unless the real forces of colonial democracy can be permanently crushed they will continue to drive colonial policy towards this goal. Whether they will drive still farther, to full formal severance, will depend upon the completeness with which Great Britain has learnt during the last century and a half the lesson of colonial government which the American Revolution first made manifest. At present, owing to our liberal rendering of the term "responsible self-government," there exists no powerful set of conscious forces making for complete independence in any of our colonies, save in South Africa, where our exceptional policy has given birth to a lasting antagonism of economic interests, which, working at present along the lines of race cleavage, must in the not distant future arouse in the people of a federated South Africa a demand for complete severance from British control as the only alternative to a control which they, British and Dutch, will regard as an intolerable interference with their legitimate rights of self-government.

This forcible interference of the Imperial Government with the natural evolution of a British South Africa, accompanied by a direct attack upon colonial liberties and a substitution of mechanical stimulation for organic growth in the process of a South African federation, will come home later to the other self-governing colonies through its reaction upon British policy. The legacy of this disastrous imperial exploit is enhanced militarism for Great Britain, and the rapacious dominance of armaments over public finance. These considerations almost inevitably goad public policy in Great Britain to make eager overtures to the colonies which will be rightly understood as an invitation to share risks and burdens in large excess of all assured advantages. The endeavours on our part to secure the closer political connexion of the colonies are more likely than any other cause to bring about a final disruption ; for the driving force behind these endeavours will be detected as proceeding from national rather than imperial needs. Australia, New Zealand, Canada have had no voice in determining recent expansion of British rule in Asia and Africa ; such expansion serves no vital interest of theirs ; invited to contribute a full share to the upkeep and furtherance of such Empire, they will persistently refuse, preferring to make full preparation for such self-defence as will enable them to dispense with that protection of the British flag, which brings increasing dangers of entanglement with foreign Powers.

The new Imperialism antagonizes colonial self-government, tends to make imperial federation impracticable, and furnishes a disruptive force in the relations of Great Britain with the self-governing colonies.

CHAPTER VII

THE OUTCOME

I

IF Imperialism may no longer be regarded as a blind inevitable destiny, is it certain that imperial expansion as a deliberately chosen line of public policy can be stopped ?

We have seen that it is motived, not by the interests of the nation as a whole, but by those of certain classes, who impose the policy upon the nation for their own advantage. The amalgam of economic and political forces which exercises this pressure has been submitted to close analysis. But will the detection of this confederacy of vicious forces destroy or any wise abate their operative power ? For this power is a natural outcome of an unsound theory in our foreign policy. Put into plain language, the theory is this, that any British subject choosing, for his own private pleasure or profit, to venture his person or his property in the territory of a foreign State can call upon this nation to protect or avenge him in case he or his property is injured either by the Government or by any inhabitant of this foreign State. Now this is a perilous doctrine. It places the entire military, political, and financial resources of this nation at the beck and call of any missionary society which considers it has a peculiar duty to attack the religious sentiments or observances of some savage people, or of some reckless explorer who chooses just those spots of earth known to be inhabited by hostile peoples ignorant of British power ; the speculative trader or the mining prospector gravitates naturally towards dangerous and unexplored countries, where the gains of a successful venture will be quick and large. All these men, missionaries, travellers, sportsmen, scientists, traders, in no proper sense the accredited representatives of this country, but actuated by private personal motives, are at liberty to call upon the British nation to spend millions of money and thousands of lives to defend them against risks which the nation has not sanctioned. It is only right to add that unscrupulous statesmen have deliberately utilized these insidious methods of encroachment, seizing upon every alleged outrage inflicted on these private adventurers or marauders as a pretext for a punitive expedition which results in the British flag waving over some new tract of territory. Thus the most reckless and irresponsible individual members of our nation are permitted to direct our foreign policy. Now that we have some four hundred million British subjects, any one of whom in theory or in practice may call upon the British arms to extricate him from the results of his private folly, the prospects of a genuine *pax Britannica* are not particularly bright.

But these sporadic risks, grave though they have sometimes proved, are insignificant when compared with the dangers associated with modern methods of international capitalism and finance. It is not long since industry was virtually restricted by political boundaries, the economic intercourse of nations being almost wholly confined to commercial exchanges of goods. The recent habit of investing capital in a foreign country has now grown to such an extent that the well-to-do and politically powerful classes in Great Britain to-day derive a large and ever larger proportion of their incomes from capital invested outside the British Empire. This growing stake of our wealthy classes in countries over which they have no political control is a revolutionary force in modern politics ; it means a constantly growing tendency to use their political power as citizens of this State to interfere with the political condition of those States where they have an industrial stake.

The essentially illicit nature of this use of the public resources of the nation to safeguard and improve private investments should be clearly recognized. If I put my savings in a home investment, I take into consideration all the chances and changes to which the business is liable, including the possibilities of political changes of tariff, taxation, or industrial legislation which may affect its profits. In the case of such investment, I am quite aware that I have no right to call upon the public to protect me from loss or depreciation of my capital due to any of these causes. The political conditions of my country are taken into calculation at the time of my investment. If I invest in consols, I fully recognize that no right of political inter-ference with foreign policy affecting my investment is accorded to me in virtue of my interest as a fund-holder. But, if I invest either in the public funds or in some private industrial venture in a foreign country for the benefit of my private purse, getting specially favourable terms to cover risks arising from the political insecurity of the country or the deficiencies of its Government, I am entitled to call upon my Government to use its political and military force to secure me against those very risks which I have already discounted in the terms of my investment. Can anything be more palpably unfair ?

It may be said that no such claim of the individual investor upon State aid is admitted. But while the theory may not have been openly avowed, recent history shows a growth of consistent practice based upon its tacit acceptance. I need not retrace the clear chain of evidence, consisting chiefly of the admissions of the mining capitalists, by which this claim to use public resources for their private profit has been enforced by the financiers who seduced our Government and people into our latest and most costly exploit. This is but the clearest and most dramatic instance of the operation of the world-wide forces of international finance. These forces are commonly described as capitalistic, but the gravest danger arises not from genuine industrial investments in foreign lands, but from the handling of stocks and shares based upon these investments by financiers. Those who own a genuine stake in the natural sources or the industry of a foreign land have at least some substantial interest in the peace and good government of that land ; but the stock speculator has no such stake : his interest lies in the oscillations of paper values, which require fluctuation and insecurity of political conditions as their instrument.

As these forms of international investment and finance are wider spread and better organized for economic and political purposes, these demands for political and military interference with foreign countries, on the ground of protecting the property of British subjects, will be more frequent and more effective ; the demands of investors will commonly be backed by personal grievances of British outlanders, and we shall be drawn into a series of interferences with foreign Governments, which, if we can conduct them successfully, will lead to annexation of territory as the only security for the lives and property of our subjects.

That this policy marks a straight road to ruin there can be no doubt. But how to stop it ? What principle of safety can we lay down ? Only one—an absolute repudiation of the right of British subjects to call upon their Government to protect their persons or property from injuries or dangers incurred on their private initiative. This principle is just and expedient. If we send an emissary on a public mission into a foreign country, let us support and protect him by our public purse and arms ; if a private person, or a company of private persons, place their lives or property in a foreign land, seeking their own ends, let them clearly understand that they do so at their own risk, and that the State will not act for their protection.

If so complete a reversal of our consistent policy be regarded as a counsel of perfection involving a definite abandonment of domiciliary, trading, and other rights secured by existing treaties or conventions with foreign States, upon the observance of which we are entitled to insist, let us at any rate lay down two plain rules of policy. First, never to sanction any interference on the part of our foreign representatives on general grounds of foreign misgovernment outside the strict limits of our treaty rights, submitting interpretation of such treaty rights to arbitration. Secondly, if in any case armed force is applied to secure the observance of these treaty rights, to confine such force to the attainment of the specific object which justifies its use.

II

Analysis of Imperialism, with its natural supports, militarism, oligarchy, bureaucracy, protection, concentration of capital and violent trade fluctuations, has marked it out as the supreme danger of modern national States. The power of the imperialist forces within the nation to use the national resources for their private gain, by operating the instrument of the State, can only be overthrown by the establishment of a genuine democracy, the direction of public policy by the people for the people through representatives over whom they exercise a real control. Whether this or any other nation is yet competent for such a democracy may well be matter of grave doubt, but until and unless the external policy of a nation is " broad-based upon a people's will " there appears little hope of remedy. The scare of a great recent war may for a brief time check the confidence of these conspirators against the commonwealth, and cause them to hold their hands, but the financial forces freshly generated will demand new outlets, and will utilize the same political alliances and the same social, religious, and philanthropic supports in their pressure for new enterprises. The circumstances of each new imperialist exploit differ from those of all preceding ones : whatever ingenuity is requisite for the perversion of the public intelligence, or the inflammation of the public sentiment, will be forthcoming.

Imperialism is only beginning to realize its full resources, and to develop into a fine art the management of nations : the broad bestowal of a franchise, wielded by a people whose education has reached the stage of an uncritical ability to read printed matter, favours immensely the designs of keen business politicians, who, by controlling the press, the schools, and where necessary the churches, impose Imperialism upon the masses under the attractive guise of sensational patriotism.

The chief economic source of Imperialism has been found in the inequality of industrial opportunities by which a favoured class accumulates superfluous elements of income which, in their search for profitable investments, press ever farther afield : the influence on State policy of these investors and their financial managers secures a national alliance of other vested interests which are threatened by movements of social reform : the adoption of Imperialism thus serves the double purpose of securing private material benefits for favoured classes of investors and traders at the public cost, while sustaining the general cause of conservatism by diverting public energy and interest from domestic agitation to external employment.

The ability of a nation to shake off this dangerous usurpation of its power, and to employ the national resources in the national interest, depends upon the education of a national intelligence and a national will, which shall make democracy a political and economic reality. To term Imperialism a national policy is an impudent falsehood: the interests of the nation are opposed to every act of this expansive policy. Every enlargement of Great Britain in the tropics is a distinct enfeeblement of true British nationalism. Indeed, Imperialism is commended in some quarters for this very reason, that by breaking the narrow bounds of nationalities it facilitates and forwards internationalism. There are even those who favour or condone the forcible suppression of small nationalities by larger ones under the impulse of Imperialism, because they imagine that this is the natural approach to a world-federation and eternal peace. A falser view of political evolution it is difficult to conceive. If there is one condition precedent to effective internationalism or to the establishment of any reliable relations between States, it is the existence of strong, secure, well-developed, and responsible nations. Internationalism can never be subserved by the suppression or forcible absorption of nations; for these practices react disastrously upon the springs of internationalism, on the one hand setting nations on their armed defence and stifling the amicable approaches between them, on the other debilitating the larger nations through excessive corpulence and indigestion. The hope of a coming internationalism enjoins above all else the maintenance and natural growth of independent nationalities, for without such there could be no gradual evolution of internationalism, but only a series of unsuccessful attempts at a chaotic and unstable cosmopolitanism. As individualism is essential to any sane form of national socialism, so nationalism is essential to internationalism : no organic conception of world-politics can be framed on any other supposition.

Just in proportion as the substitution of true national governments for the existing oligarchies or sham democracies becomes possible will the apparent conflicts of national interests disappear, and the fundamental co-operation upon which nineteenth-century Free Trade prematurely relied manifest itself. The present class government means the severance or antagonism of nations, because each ruling class can only keep and use its rule by forcing the antagonisms of foreign policy : intelligent democracies would perceive their identity of interest, and would ensure it by their amicable policy. The genuine forces of internationalism, thus liberated, would first display themselves as economic forces, securing more effective international co-operation for postal, telegraphic, railway, and other transport services, for monetary exchange and for common standards of measurement of various kinds, and for the improved intercommunication of persons, goods, and information. Related and subsidiary to these purposes would come a growth of machinery of courts and congresses, at first informal and private, but gradually taking shape in more definite and more public machinery : the common interests of the arts and sciences would everywhere be weaving an elaborate network of intellectual internationalism, and both economic and intellectual community of needs and interests would contribute to the natural growth of such political solidarity as was required to maintain this real community.

It is thus, and only thus, that the existing false antagonisms of nations, with their wastes and perils and their retardation of the general course of civilization, can be resolved. To substitute for this peaceful discovery and expression of common interests a federal policy proceeding upon directly selfish political and military interests, the idea which animates an Anglo-Saxon alliance or a Pan-Teutonic empire, is deliberately to choose a longer, more difficult, and far more hazardous road to internationalism. The economic bond is far stronger and more reliable as a basis of growing internationalism than the so-called racial bond or a political alliance constructed on some short-sighted computation of a balance of power. It is, of course, quite possible that a Pan-Slav, Pan-Teutonic, Pan-British, or Pan-Latin alliance might, if the federation were kept sufficiently voluntary and elastic, contribute to the wider course of internationalism. But the frankly military purpose commonly assigned for such alliances bodes ill for such assistance. It is far more likely that such alliances would be formed in the interests of the " imperialist " classes of the contracting nations, in order the more effectively to exploit the joint national resources.

We have foreshadowed the possibility of even a larger alliance of Western States, a European federation of great Powers which, so far from forwarding the cause of world-civilization, might introduce the gigantic peril of a Western parasitism, a group of advanced industrial nations, whose upper classes drew vast tribute from Asia and Africa, with which they supported great tame masses of retainers, no longer engaged in the staple industries of agriculture and manufacture, but kept in the performance of personal or minor industrial services under the control of a new financial aristocracy. Let those who would scout such a theory as undeserving of consideration examine the economic and social condition of districts in Southern England to-day which are already reduced to this condition, and reflect upon the vast extension of such a system which might be rendered feasible by the subjection of China to the economic control of similar groups of financiers, investors, and political and business officials, draining the greatest potential reservoir of profit the world has ever known, in order to consume it in Europe. The situation is far too complex, the play of world-forces far too incalculable, to render this or any other single interpretation of the future very probable : but the influences which govern the Imperialism of Western Europe to-day are moving in this direction, and, unless counteracted or diverted, make towards some such consummation.

If the ruling classes of the Western nations could realize their interests in such a combination (and each year sees capitalism more obviously international), and if China were unable to develop powers of forcible resistance, the opportunity of a parasitic Imperialism which should reproduce upon a vaster scale many of the main features of the latter Roman Empire visibly presents itself.

Whether we regard Imperialism upon this larger scale or as confined to the policy of Great Britain, we find much that is closely analogous to the Imperialism of Rome.

The rise of a money-loaning aristocracy in Rome, composed of keen, unscrupulous men from many nations, who filled the high offices of States with their creatures, political " bosses " or military adventurers, who had come to the front as usurers, publicans, or chiefs of police in the provinces, was the most distinctive feature of later imperial Rome. This class was continually recruited from returned officials and colonial millionaires. The large incomes drawn in private official plunder, public tribute, usury and official incomes from the provinces had the following reactions upon Italy. Italians were no longer wanted for working the land or for manufactures, or even for military service. " The later campaigns on the Rhine and the Danube," it is pointed out, " were really slave-hunts on a gigantic scale."[1]

[1] Adams, *Civilization and Decay*, p. 38.

The Italian farmers, at first drawn from rural into military life, soon found themselves permanently ousted from agriculture by the serf labour of the *latifundia*, and they and their families were sucked into the dregs of town life, to be subsisted as a pauper population upon public charity. A mercenary colonial army came more and more to displace the home forces. The parasitic city life, with its lowered vitality and the growing infrequency of marriage, to which Gibbon draws attention,[1] rapidly impaired the physique of the native population of Italy, and Rome subsisted more and more upon immigration of raw vigour from Gaul and Germany. The necessity of maintaining powerful mercenary armies to hold the provinces heightened continually the peril, already manifest in the last years of the Republic, arising from the political ambitions of great proconsuls conspiring with a moneyed interest at Rome against the Commonwealth. As time went on, this moneyed oligarchy became an hereditary aristocracy, and withdrew from military and civil service, relying more and more upon hired foreigners : themselves sapped by luxury and idleness, and tainting by mixed servitude and licence the Roman populace, they so enfeebled the State as to destroy the physical and moral vitality required to hold in check and under government the vast repository of forces in the exploited Empire. The direct cause of Rome's decay and fall is expressed politically by the term " over-centralization," which conveys in brief the real essence of Imperialism as distinguished from national growth on the one hand and colonialism upon the other. Parasitism, practised through taxation and usury, involved a constantly increasing centralization of the instruments of government, and a growing strain upon this government, as the prey became more impoverished by the drain and showed signs of restive-

[1] Chap. xii.

ness. " The evolution of this centralized society was as logical as every other work of nature. When force reached the stage where it expressed itself exclusively through money, the governing class ceased to be chosen because they were valiant or eloquent, artistic, learned or devout, and were selected solely because they had the faculty of acquiring and keeping wealth. As long as the weak retained enough vitality to produce something which could be absorbed, this oligarchy was invariable ; and, for very many years after the native peasantry of Gaul and Italy had perished from the land, new blood, injected from more tenacious races, kept the dying civilization alive. The weakness of the moneyed class lay in this very power, for they not only killed the producer but in the strength of their acquisitiveness they failed to propagate themselves."[1]

This is the largest, plainest instance history presents of the social parasitic process by which a moneyed interest within the State, usurping the reins of government, makes for imperial expansion in order to fasten economic suckers into foreign bodies so as to drain them of their wealth in order to support domestic luxury. The new Imperialism differs in no vital point from this old example. The element of political tribute is now absent or quite subsidiary, and the crudest forms of slavery have disappeared : some elements of more genuine and disinterested government serve to quality and mask the distinctively parasitic nature of the later sort. But nature is not mocked : the laws which, operative throughout nature, doom the parasite to atrophy, decay, and final extinction, are not evaded by nations any more than by individual organisms. The greater complexity of the modern process, the endeavour to escape the parasitic reaction by rendering some real but quite unequal and inadequate services to " the host," may retard but cannot

[1] Adams, *Civilization and Decay*, p. 44.

finally avert the natural consequences of living upon others. The claim that an imperial State forcibly subjugating other peoples and their lands does so for the purpose of rendering services to the conquered equal to those which she exacts is notoriously false : she neither intends equivalent services nor is capable of rendering them, and the pretence that such benefits to the governed form a leading motive or result of Imperialism implies a degree of moral or intellectual obliquity so grave as itself to form a new peril for any nation fostering so false a notion of the nature of its conduct. " Let the motive be in the deed, not in the event," says a Persian proverb.

Imperialism is a depraved choice of national life, imposed by self-seeking interests which appeal to the lusts of quantitative acquisitiveness and of forceful domination surviving in a nation from early centuries of animal struggle for existence. Its adoption as a policy implies a deliberate renunciation of that cultivation of the higher inner qualities which for a nation as for an individual constitutes the ascendency of reason over brute impulse. It is the besetting sin of all successful States, and its penalty is unalterable in the order of nature.

APPENDIX I

	Area (sq. miles).	Population.
DOMINIONS, COLONIES, AND PROTECTORATES—		
Europe	30,709	3,589,000
Asia	2,113,679	364,012,000
Africa	3,093,949	51,583,000
America	4,008,214	13,091,000
Australasia	3,188,405	8,887,000
Total	12,434,956	441,162,000
MANDATED TERRITORIES—		
Asia	9,000	1,036,000
Africa	726,325	6,412,000
Australasia	90,512	768,000
Total	825,837	8,216,000
Grand Total . . .	13,270,793	449,378,000

Compiled from the *Statesman's Year Book* for 1934.

APPENDIX II

	Area in Square Miles.		Population.	
	Mother Country.	Dependencies.	Mother Country.[1]	Dependencies.[2]
Great Britain .	94,633	13,270,793	46,610,000	449,378,000
France . .	212,750	4,617,514	41,880,000	65,179,000
Germany .	181,822	—	65,350,000	—
Netherlands .	13,128	791,907	8,290,000	60,971,000
Austria . .	32,434	—	6,750,000	—
Hungary .	35,909	—	8,841,000	—
Denmark .	16,603	121,395	3,640,000	41,000
Italy . .	119,696	906,213[3]	42,217,000	2,393,000[3]
Portugal .	35,699	807,637	7,090,000	8,426,000
Spain . .	194,216	10,993	24,242,000	1,000,000
Czechoslovakia	54,056	—	15,020,000	—
United States	3,026,200	711,726[4]	126,000,000	15,014,000[4]

[1] Estimates for 31.xii.33.   [2] Estimates for as near the above date as possible.
[3] Excluding Abyssinia.   [4] Including Alaska.

Figures from the *Statesman's Year Book* for 1935, the *Armaments Year Book* for 1935, and the *League of Nations Year Book* for 1934-5.

APPENDIX III

	Total Overseas Trade. (millions of £'s.)	Value per Head of the Population. (£'s.)		Total Overseas Trade. (millions of £'s.)	Value per Head of the Population. (£'s.)
1910 .	1,117		1925 .	2,103	
11 .	1,143		26 .	1,906	
12 .	1,241		27 .	1,939	
13 .	1,306		28 .	1,928	
14 .	1,133		29 .	1,960	
Average	1,188	28·0	Average	1,967	43·3
1915 .	1,238		1930 .	1,619	
16 .	1,460		31 .	1,255	
17 .	1,597		32 .	1,068	
18 .	1,825		33 .	1,044	
19 .	2,436		34 .	1,130	
Average	1,711	42·0	Average	1,223	26·5
1920 .	3,279				
21 .	1,790				
22 .	1,727				
23 .	1,870				
24 .	2,085				
Average	2,150	48·6			

APPENDIX IV

	Imports from		Exports to	
	Foreign Countries.	British Empire.	Foreign Countries.	British Empire.
1913 . . .	75·1	24·9	67·1	32·9
Average 1924–9 .	69·4	30·6	59·1	40·9
1931 . . .	71·2	28·8	58·9	41·1
1933 . . .	63·1	36·9	58·2	41·8

APPENDIX V

	Percentages of Imports into British Empire from United Kingdom.	Percentages of Exports from British Empire into United Kingdom.
1913–4	47·2	40·4
Average 1924–9 . . .	35·6	33·6
1933–4	36·1	39·3

Figures from *Statistical Abstract for the United Kingdom* for 1934, and Sir George Schuster, "Empire Trade Before and After Ottawa," *Economist*, November 3rd, 1934.

APPENDIX VI

BRITISH, IMPERIAL AND FOREIGN TRADE, 1934–35.

	Imports from		Exports to	
	Value (£'s).	Percentage.	Value (£'s).	Percentage.
	£		£	
Foreign Countries . .	460,129,000	62·72	210,412,000	53·15
British India . . .	42,102,000	5·74	36,675,000	9·30
Australasia . . .	90,368,000	12·30	37,681,000	9·50
South Africa[1] . .	16,446,000	2·24	32,509,000	8·20
Canada	50,390,000	6·90	19,726,000	5·00
Other British Dependencies	74,102,000	10·10	58,982,000	14·85
Total . . .	733,537,000	100·00	395,985,000	100·00

[1] Including Rhodesia.

Figures from *Statistical Abstract for the United Kingdom* for 1934.

APPENDIX VII

	Percentage of Imports by Value from United Kingdom.			Percentage of Exports by Value to United Kingdom.		
	1913–4	Average. 1924–9	1933–4	1913–4	Average. 1924–9	1933–4
India	65·4	48·9	41·2	23·5	22·7	31·8
Self Governing Dominions	39·0	36·5	41·9	54·1	46·0	50·2
Other Parts of British Empire[1] .	45·0	23·6	22·8	42·2	20·2	21·4

[1] Including Crown Colonies, Sudan, Southern Rhodesia, and Malaya and Hong Kong (except 1913–4).

Figures from *Statistical Abstract for the United Kingdom* for 1934, and Sir George Schuster, "Empire Trade Before and After Ottawa," *Economist*, November 3rd, 1934.

APPENDIX VIII

Year.	Dominions.	India.	Other British Possessions.
1904 . . .	52,094,444	40,641,277	19,687,997
1905 . . .	52,204,632	42,996,388	19,016,423
1906 . . .	56,923,891	45,181,307	19,904,287
1907 . . .	64,104,666	52,027,221	22,011,879
1908 . . .	56,422,882	49,418,713	20,923,432
1909 . . .	61,585,480	43,581,501	22,071,103
1910 . . .	75,401,799	45,998,500	25,902,643
1911 . . .	80,585,992	52,245,604	26,012,488
1912 . . .	90,183,258	57,626,101	29,283,279
1913 . . .	91,287,754	70,273,145	33,745,909
1914 . . .	79,268,272	62,888,506	29,472,720
1915 . . .	69,923,562	45,603,792	32,892,330
1916 . . .	89,116,567	52,787,920	44,271,384
1917 . . .	64,521,497	59,965,373	48,170,946
1918 . . .	70,879,622	49,180,830	58,301,670
1919 . . .	71,143,432	70,860,991	63,618,037
1920 . . .	180,971,372	181,239,634	139,259,417
1921 . . .	109,843,563	108,868,548	79,904,522
1922 . . .	125,769,446	92,104,778	67,694,500
1923 . . .	133,686,453	86,246,488	80,669,685
1924 . . .	139,356,994	90,577,148	107,530,219
1925 . . .	141,365,824	86,047,757	107,700,581
1926 . . .	140,286,071	81,755,046	94,810,310
1927 . . .	140,350,373	85,044,842	101,254,995
1928 . . .	140,910,867	83,900,440	102,856,595
1929 . . .	143,172,986	78,227,208	103,051,301
1930 . . .	105,145,131	52,944,447	90,255,381
1931 . . .	68,131,620	32,288,579	70,252,593
1932 . . .	64,895,734	34,088,361	66,528,185
1933 . . .	71,686,278	33,402,404	58,428,581
1934 . . .	87,626,611	36,674,581	61,271,842

VALUE OF IMPORTS INTO GREAT BRITAIN (U.K.) IN £'s.

Year.	Dominions.	India.	Other British Possessions.
1904 . . .	70,526,674	42,704,004	12,916,861
1905 . . .	77,158,417	36,039,789	20,212,314
1906 . . .	88,431,030	37,722,235	22,940,401
1907 . . .	94,511,293	43,912,588	25,110,466
1908 . . .	80,177,264	29,588,187	22,977,771
1909 . . .	91,593,058	35,430,771	24,398,063
1910 . . .	103,726,165	42,763,715	32,250,753
1911 . . .	99,517,676	45,423,316	34,585,783
1912 . . .	103,660,165	52,148,731	39,294,383
1913 . . .	113,179,193	48,420,490	41,902,295
1914 . . .	107,622,853	43,348,176	42,301,442
1915 . . .	129,282,519	62,213,614	81,981,097
1916 . . .	143,646,423	72,366,184	91,940,009
1917 . . .	195,276,511	66,836,578	103,014,290
1918 . . .	213,262,757	88,541,217	128,294,040
1919 . . .	313,699,316	108,213,961	172,193,212
1920 . . .	283,339,215	95,721,420	288,075,222
1921 . . .	198,587,225	44,307,742	89,022,436
1922 . . .	188,242,235	47,719,039	85,832,351
1923 . . .	167,332,394	66,950,068	98,316,894
1924 . . .	196,411,435	78,872,953	119,087,035
1925 . . .	227,230,222	80,099,083	129,421,942
1926 . . .	199,924,304	57,638,068	127,808,804
1927 . . .	185,073,001	65,840,065	125,056,495
1928 . . .	189,694,151	64,472,793	116,135,592
1929 . . .	182,271,186	62,844,796	121,903,815
1930 . . .	152,502,896	51,044,435	103,248,648
1931 . . .	127,339,016	36,711,288	81,290,012
1932 . . .	142,099,520	32,308,273	74,376,155
1933 . . .	146,444,670	37,351,929	65,431,482
1934 . . .	153,991,428	42,102,298	76,533,361

This includes Straits Settlements and Dependencies as well as British India.

APPENDIX IX

Number of Outward-Bound British Passengers from the United Kingdom to the Following Countries.

	United States.	Canada and Newfoundland.	Union of South Africa.	Other Parts of the British Empire.	Total.
1912	117,310	186,147	28,216	116,700	448,373
13	129,169	196,278	25,855	99,317	450,619
14	92,808	94,482	21,124	70,409	278,823
15	37,763	19,434	11,699	30,675	99,571
16	28,884	18,953	7,905	17,309	73,051
17	3,981	6,415	2,794	6,508	19,698
18	3,445	3,218	2,374	7,518	16,555
19	32,765	89,102	7,761	39,794	169,422
1920	90,811	134,079	29,019	83,532	337,441
21	67,499	84,145	28,138	76,269	256,051
22	61,826	69,690	21,414	81,371	234,301
23	101,063	121,941	18,938	78,904	320,846
24	39,057	99,717	22,452	85,055	246,281
25	54,898	70,810	21,144	83,921	230,773
26	59,535	83,886	22,958	98,309	264,688
27	58,243	89,571	22,213	87,214	257,241
28	56,508	95,307	22,569	74,144	248,528
29	64,188	107,772	23,870	62,810	258,640
1930	59,390	69,281	21,816	49,426	199,913
31	27,320	38,003	19,491	37,927	122,741
32	23,731	33,911	16,707	37,689	112,038
33	22,189	28,391	19,714	39,966	110,260
34	26,449	30,621	22,878	43,945	123,893

Figures compiled from the *Statistical Abstract for the United Kingdom* for 1934, and Willcox and Ferenczi, *International Migration*, Volume I.

APPENDIX X

	(a) £000's From Public (Governmental and Municipal) Loans to Empire and Foreign Countries.	(b) £000's Income from all British Investments Overseas (excluding undistributed profits).
1929 . . .	64,661	212,365
1930 . . .	64,676	192,175
1931 . . .	65,920	155,513
1932 . . .	62,377	144,118
1933 . . .	61,126	138,274

APPENDIX XI

TOTAL (NOMINAL) BRITISH INVESTMENTS OVERSEAS.

	(a) £000's Imperial Public (Governmental and Municipal) Loans.	(b) £000's Foreign Public (Governmental and Municipal) Loans.	(c) £000's Total (Nominal) Investments Overseas— Public and Private.
1929 .	1,061,000	351,000	3,438,000
1930 .	1,080,000	357,000	3,425,000
1931 .	1,104,000	337,000	3,410,000
1932 .	1,109,000	323,000	3,355,000
1933 .	1,147,000	333,000	3,386,000

From Sir R. Kindersley, " Britain's Overseas Investments," *Economic Journal*, 1931 and 1935.

APPENDIX XII

	Armaments and War.	Colonial Trade : Import and Export Trade with the Empire.
	£000's	£000's
1904	66,055	238,571
05	62,150	247,628
06	59,199	271,103
07	58,256	301,678
08	59,028	259,508
09	63,043	278,660
1910	67,835	326,044
11	70,507	338,371
12	72,432	372,196
13	86,028	398,809
14	361,156	364,902
15	1,001,330	421,897
16	1,414,281	494,128
17	1,767,550	537,785
18	1,977,751	608,460
19	959,192	799,729
1920	386,491	1,072,885
21	178,300	630,536
22	118,000	607,369
23	112,400	633,213
24	116,900	731,921
25	121,500	773,351
26	117,400	704,449
27	118,600	705,004
28	115,700	699,771
29	115,000	693,620
1930	112,700	556,984
31	111,400	420,833

Figures from the *Statistical Abstract for the United Kingdom* for 1914, 1922, and 1934.

APPENDIX XIII

Yearly average or year.	Total.	Crude materials.	Crude foodstuffs.	Manu-factured foodstuffs.	Semi-manu-factures.	Finished manu-factures.
1871–1875	486,128	218,449	75,206	95,282	22,681	74,509
1876–1880	663,650	213,989	158,853	161,915	30,174	98,719
1881–1885	774,607	261,645	162,714	197,457	37,044	115,747
1886–1890	725,685	276,703	108,708	181,521	40,023	118,730
1891–1895	876,326	295,087	150,846	238,580	55,343	136,470
1896–1900	1,136,039	296,664	214,778	272,759	109,500	242,338
1901–1905	1,427,020	432,027	173,972	316,226	161,206	343,589
1906–1910	1,750,980	554,754	155,828	317,374	249,134	473,890
1911	2,013,549	720,611	103,402	282,017	309,152	598,368
1912	2,170,320	731,164	99,899	318,839	348,150	672,268
1913	2,428,506	740,290	181,907	321,204	408,807	776,297
1914	2,329,684	799,838	137,495	293,219	374,224	724,908
1915	2,716,178	591,282	506,993	454,575	355,862	807,466
1916	5,422,642	815,693	421,284	648,039	912,262	2,625,364
1917	6,169,617	832,827	508,762	806,941	1,315,242	2,705,845
1918	6,047,875	972,107	547,436	1,405,820	1,053,270	2,069,242
1919	7,749,816	1,623,085	678,363	1,962,616	922,246	2,563,505
1920	8,080,481	1,882,530	917,991	1,116,605	958,497	3,204,858
1921	4,378,928	983,553	673,334	685,025	410,167	1,626,849
1922	3,765,091	988,456	458,611	587,987	437,730	1,292,307
1923	4,090,715	1,208,468	257,478	583,292	563,718	1,477,759
1924	4,497,649	1,332,746	392,691	573,492	610,668	1,588,052
1925	4,818,722	1,422,058	317,894	573,753	661,683	1,843,334
1926	4,711,721	1,261,325	335,063	503,005	655,547	1,956,781
1927	4,758,864	1,192,776	421,107	463,299	699,727	1,981,955
1928	5,030,099	1,293,257	294,677	465,811	716,352	2,260,002
1929	5,157,083	1,142,352	269,590	484,304	729,013	2,531,823
1930	3,781,172	829,098	178,533	362,650	512,802	1,898,089
1931	2,377,982	566,791	127,072	246,814	317,647	1,119,657
1932	1,576,151	513,659	89,419	152,118	196,727	624,228

APPENDIX XIV

	In millions of £'s
Great Britain . .	114·2
France . . .	90·0
Germany . . .	43·8
Italy . . .	46·4
Russia . . .	242·6
United States . .	145·2

From the *Peace Year Book* for 1935.

APPENDIX XV

GREAT BRITAIN—MILITARY AND OTHER EXPENDITURE, 1904-1931.

	Military.	Munitions.	Military and Munitions.	Cost of Collection.	Education.	Grants to Local Authorities.	National Debt (and Sinking Fund).	Civil Services	Total (excl. P.O.)
1904	66,055,000			3,093,000	15,574,513	12,126,112	31,367,086	7,959,289	136,175,000
1905	62,150,000			3,148,000	16,396,481	12,214,826	32,433,925	8,091,768	134,435,000
1906	59,199,000			3,179,000	16,946,419	12,536,891	35,936,574	5,256,116	133,054,000
1907	58,256,000			3,222,000	17,359,203	11,155,379	38,707,565	5,584,853	134,285,000
1908	59,028,000			3,320,000	17,368,771	9,824,286	34,911,999	9,725,944	134,179,000
1909	63,043,000			3,342,000	17,907,467	9,445,395	26,368,797	19,145,341	139,252,000
1910	67,835,000			3,919,000	18,744,175	9,881,709	29,246,397	22,688,719	152,315,000
1911	70,507,000			3,951,000	18,983,036	9,636,399	31,104,783	23,815,782	157,998,000
1912	72,432,000			4,200,000	19,530,615	9,653,299	34,858,760	24,923,326	165,598,000
1913	86,027,992			4,578,227	19,169,647	9,734,128	24,500,000	38,924,916	182,934,910
1914	361,156,272			4,810,774	20,031,043	9,529,134	22,668,896	114,028,326	532,224,445
1915	754,609,463	246,720,787	1,001,330,250	4,752,177	20,282,996	9,756,851	60,249,311	525,283,334	1,561,405,608
1916	854,840,831	559,439,949	1,414,280,780	5,143,704	20,092,095	9,895,466	127,250,493	692,639,473	2,269,302,011
1917	1,052,449,272	715,101,222	1,767,550,494	5,839,189	24,702,215	9,730,538	189,851,066	948,480,714	2,946,154,216
1918	1,415,523,534	562,227,196	1,977,750,730	6,817,049	25,719,344	9,680,811	269,964,650	813,305,071	3,103,237,655
1919	766,348,663	192,843,559	959,192,222	10,123,896	42,610,904	10,746,142	332,013,708	635,583,836	1,989,790,708
1920	353,568,648	32,922,770	386,491,418	12,740,648	58,318,053	10,785,504	349,598,616	449,409,267	1,267,343,506
1921	178,300,000			12,900,000	53,700,000	9,400,000	328,900,000	413,600,000	996,800,000
1922	118,000,000			10,700,000	47,400,000	10,100,000	321,300,000	264,200,000	771,700,000
1923	112,400,000			10,000,000	46,300,000	13,300,000	344,300,000	224,300,000	750,600,000
1924	116,900,000			10,300,000	46,600,000	13,600,000	353,700,000	206,900,000	748,000,000
1925	121,500,000			10,700,000	47,100,000	14,100,000	354,300,000	226,700,000	774,400,000
1926	117,400,000			10,900,000	48,400,000	14,200,000	374,300,000	219,200,000	784,400,000
1927	118,600,000			11,100,000	48,700,000	15,700,000	374,000,000	214,200,000	782,300,000
1928	115,700,000			11,600,000	47,800,000	16,400,000	369,000,000	202,200,000	762,700,000
1929	115,400,000			11,500,000	48,200,000	31,500,000	359,800,000	205,200,000	771,600,000
1930	112,700,000			12,000,000	53,500,000	45,700,000	360,000,000	241,200,000	825,100,000
1931	111,400,000			11,500,000	56,800,000	46,200,000	354,900,000	245,900,000	826,700,000

Obtained from *British Budgets* (Mallet & George) 1887–1913, 1913–1921, 1921–1931.

INDEX

wild grass

THREE STORIES

OF CHANGE

IN MODERN CHINA

IAN JOHNSON

PANTHEON BOOKS

NEW YORK

Some of the material previously appeared in slightly different
form in the *Wall Street Journal*.

Library of Congress Cataloging-in-Publication Data
Johnson, Ian [date]
  Wild grass : three stories of change in modern China / Ian
Johnson.
        p.   cm.
  Includes bibliographical references.
  ISBN 0-375-42186-6
  1. Political activists—China. 2. Government, Resistance
to—China. 3. Dissenters—China. 4. Civil rights—China.
5. China—Politics and government—1976– I. Title.
JQ1516.J64 2004   323'.04'0951—dc22   2003058082

www.pantheonbooks.com

Book design by Johanna S. Roebas

Printed in the United States of America

First Edition

9 8 7 6 5 4 3 2 1

TO JEAN AND DENIS

Wild grass strikes no deep roots,

has no beautiful flowers and leaves,

yet it imbibes dew,

water and blood and the flesh of the dead,

although all try to rob it of life.

—LU XUN, *Wild Grass*, 1926

Contents

wild grass

Prologue:
One Hundred
Battles a Day

China's rulers have developed a bad case of the nerves. Unemployment is high, corruption permeates daily life and relations with the outside world result in recurring crises. Often these tensions erupt in small protests, sometimes against the government, other times against outsiders. They usually end after a few days, often crushed, sometimes petering out when a few ringleaders are arrested and the protesters' demands partly met. But they are never resolved, surfacing like a corpse that won't stay under.

When the anniversaries of these protests come around a year later, commemorations are held and petitions delivered. Some of these grudge dates are intensely local: a family's memory of its house torn down to make way for a corrupt real estate project, or a village that commemorates a local leader arrested for standing up to abuse. Other commemorations are shared by millions: the killing of students or the banning of a popular religion.

The government, ever watchful for challenges to its rule, tries to keep track of them all. Protests, arrests, detentions: each year the victims try to commemorate these disasters, and each year the government tightens up around these dates. Slowly, the country's mental calendar has become a series of overlapping scabs and sores.

Beijing, the country's political and spiritual capital, where most protests take place, is especially affected because petitioners from around the vast republic ultimately make their way there. Each sensitive date is accompanied by increased police patrols, roundups of dissidents and tapped phones. The signs are not always obvious, but once they are known, they are unmistakable: the triple-teamed soldiers that cordon off diplomatic compounds, late-night police roadblocks, roving patrols on trains heading for Beijing, the sealing off of the cavernous Tiananmen Square, accessible only to those who present their identity cards for inspection.

China's government wasn't always so unsure of itself. Shortly after taking power in 1949, the Communist Party enjoyed some popular success. It united China for the first time in a century, put people to work and redistributed land. Even when the disasters came—and they came fast—the party didn't have to worry too much about unrest. Famines and persecution were regular occurrences during the party's first three decades in power. But China was frozen by totalitarian rule. Even small protests to mark these misdeeds were difficult.

Then, the totalitarian dictatorship of Chairman Mao Zedong collapsed with his death in 1976. Weakened by thirty years of failed policies, the party tried to win back popular support by withdrawing its control over people's personal lives and by allowing capitalist-style economic reforms. Over the past decades this looser form of control has succeeded in raising living standards but hasn't helped the party win deep-rooted legitimacy.

With the government no longer micromanaging their daily lives, people now have time to travel, to reflect and, slowly, to demand more. With prosperity and better education, Chinese people have begun forming independent centers of power out-

side government control—trade unions, religious organizations and clubs. It was the development of this "civil society" that helped bring about the downfall of communism in Eastern Europe late last century. Now, these groups are eroding the power of China's Communist Party.

It would be unfair to say that this cacophony of demands has paralyzed China's leaders. On key economic issues, which they view as vital to their survival, the mandarins can push through reforms. Hence, China's admission into the World Trade Organization, a sign that whatever its name, the People's Republic of China practices little in the way of communist economics. China now has stock markets, labor markets and a more open economic system than some developed countries.

But politics intrudes even in this relatively neutral sphere. This is because economic reforms have progressed to the point that a true market economy is only possible by adopting political reforms—which, put simply, means some sort of an end to the Communist Party's monopoly over power. Only this step can pave the way to a real market economy, which requires a fair judicial system, less corruption and transparent regulations. Despite the government's best efforts to separate the two, economics and politics make the same demands on the government. Political reform now tops every Chinese thinker's agenda. It is widely discussed, even by the party. But in any meaningful sense of the word, it is taboo.

Like other governments under stress, China's has reached for nationalism as a solution. In this it is similar to nineteenth-century Germany—an economic juggernaut run by a backward-looking oligarchy, its masses partly satiated by prosperity and nationalism. This manifests itself in periodic displays of national outrage at perceived slights. Generations of Chinese have been taught

that the world is out to belittle their country, and many believe it to be true. That allows the government to win support by presenting itself as the defender of China's best interests.

But nationalism is a temporary salve. The true source of unrest—the Communist Party's poorly checked powers—continues to breed unrest. Problems continue to rise up, forcing leaders to juggle an increasing number of demands. The effort seems to exhaust the government; unable to lighten its burden through political reform, it resembles a person carrying an ever-heavier weight, its gait slowing to a shuffle, its stoop growing more pronounced.

It is a slow battle of attrition that the government is loath to lose. The police state remains, from the labor camps in China's far west to the toy soldiers in downtown Beijing. The message is clear: we are nervous, possibly even weak, but do not meddle; we can still crush you.

These subterranean tensions are the subject of this book. I do not presume to predict when the crust will crack. Such forecasts are usually wrong, and I believe that China's current political system can probably survive for many more years. But tectonic shifts are grinding away, making change inevitable and giving rise to eruptions felt in China and abroad.

These pressures come mostly from thousands of ordinary Chinese who in small ways demand more from their government than the current system can accommodate. We often expect that history will be made by people like us. Academics think change will come from daring thinkers, journalists look to brave writers, while politicians are eager to meet China's Gorbachev. Such people, except perhaps the Gorbachev figure, all exist in today's China.

But the push for change comes mostly from people we rarely hear of: the small-town lawyer who decides to sue the government, the architect who champions dispossessed homeowners, the woman who tries to expose police brutality. Some are motivated by narrow interests of family or village, others by idealism. All, successful or not, are sowing the seeds of change in China, helping to foment a slow-motion revolution.

Although I have met scores of interesting, brave and forward-thinking people in China, this book focuses on the three most remarkable ones, people representative of the tremors shaking the land. When the current government falls or changes into something more democratic, it will be because of the efforts of this sort of people. Each, wittingly or not, has pushed to change the country's ossified politics. Each represents key problems facing China: the crises in its villages, cities and its soul.

Not surprisingly, the three stories also touch on the country's nascent legal system. For the first three decades of their rule, the communists had little use for laws or the legal system. Disputes were mediated by the party, with little recourse to courts. Economic reforms, however, made laws necessary: people and companies need clear, enforceable rules if they are going to engage in economic relationships. Indeed, the first law promulgated after reforms began was a 1979 law that regulated how foreign and Chinese companies could form joint ventures.

But China's leaders are more ambitious—they want a legal system that can keep order nationwide. This stems from the chaos of the totalitarian era, which made the Communist Party realize that the country needed laws as a bulwark against disorder. So the government has set about "constructing" a legal system. It wrote a constitution in 1982 and since then has promulgated laws at a dizzying rate: General Principles of Civil Law, Contract Law, Intellectual Property Law, Insurance Law, Property Law, a

new Criminal Code and even a Marriage Law. Law schools have been established, with tens of thousands of judges and lawyers trained.

A sense of justice is universal, and Chinese people have enthusiastically tried out their new legal system. On purely economic matters it sometimes works: companies find that contracts can be enforced in the courts, and in some narrow areas the government can even be challenged successfully—for example, for failing to follow a certain procedure in making a decision. But overall, law in China is not neutral. Courts and judges are part of the government, not independent of it. Communist Party committees regularly instruct judges on how to rule. Even the constitution gives a nod to the party's supremacy. So when the party feels challenged by a suit, it uses the courts to its ends. Instead of allowing laws to rule the land, the government uses laws to rule.

Still, living standards continue to rise. Education spreads. Knowledge of rights increases. Try as it might, the party can't put a lid on the demands that people are making for change. The result: China's legal system has become a microcosm of the tensions percolating up, a revolution brewing from below.

This book is an attempt to portray this untenable situation and hint at the sort of more open, fairer country that Chinese people want. Over two millennia ago, the Chinese philosopher Han Feizi wrote a treatise on political philosophy. In it he described the tensions inherent in an autocratic system: "Rulers and ruled wage one hundred battles a day." As these stories show, the battles still rage.

1 THE

PEASANT

CHAMPION

The photo of Ma Wenlin fluttered in my hand, catching the attention of the man sitting across from me on the train.

"He's a lawyer," I said. "I'm looking for him."

The man was silent for a moment and then said, "He looks like a peasant, not a lawyer."

The black-and-white picture showed Mr. Ma staring straight into the camera, his face expressionless except for his faint eyebrows, which arched slightly in a quizzical expression. His hair was short, almost crew-cut, and he had a light stubble above his lips. He wore a plain white dress shirt, buttoned to the neck but with no tie. There was no effort to engage the viewer, no grin, no smile. It was an old-fashioned photo of a man who didn't pose for the camera as modern people do, a man who in the first half of his fifty-nine-year life had been photographed just once or twice.

"He represented peasants," I said. "In a lawsuit against the government."

Like all second-class sleepers, ours had six bunks and no door, allowing people to wander freely down the car, poking their heads in to visit friends and see who else was on board. But we were alone: the only other person in our compartment, a man in a middle bunk, was snoring lightly and the other passengers

bustled back and forth in the corridor, concerned only with finding thermoses of hot water to make tea.

"Those kinds of lawsuits are complicated," the man said ambiguously.

Then he paused and collected his thoughts. He had a shock of gray hair that hadn't receded an inch from his tanned, creased forehead. His suit was Chinese style, the sort worn by the founder of modern China, Sun Yat-sen, and popularized by Mao Zedong, or Chairman Mao, communist China's first leader. Like Mr. Ma, the man wore his shirt buttoned up to the neck, with a fountain pen sticking out of the left breast pocket. It was the outdated uniform of Communist Party cadres from a decade ago, one rarely seen in the country's prosperous areas. But here, in a slow train leaving a remote county seat, it didn't look quite so out of place.

"I'm sure he won't be successful," he continued, looking at me carefully. "This is a poor part of the country."

I nodded but disagreed, casting a glance outside for confirmation. The windows of the train were streaked with rain, and through the blurred glass the denuded hills and earth-colored villages of the Loess Plateau rolled by. Once, this had been fertile forests and steppes, one of the birthplaces of Chinese civilization. Nearby was the grave of the Yellow Emperor, mythic founder of the Chinese people. Down in Xi'an, where we were headed, were the world-famous terra-cotta warriors that had been buried with China's first emperor more than two thousand years ago. He and other rulers had protected this cultural heartland by building fortifications not far from here that later became known as the Great Wall. Seventy years ago the plateau's mountains and gullies had sheltered the Communist Party for a decade, first during China's civil war and later during World War II. It was a region oozing in

history and significance but now was exhausted, poor and relatively obscure.

One commonly hears that these parts of the country are where change is least likely to happen. Instead, one is always encouraged to go to the prosperous coastal metropolises, such as Shanghai or Shenzhen, to look for China's future. But the more I learned about Mr. Ma, the more I understood that this region's backwardness had made it a precursor of change elsewhere in China—the poverty, the intransigence of local officials and the extreme environmental degradation bringing to a boil here problems brewing across the country.

"Well," I said. "This was a poor place when the communists were here, and they ended up running China. Maybe it's not so backward. Maybe it's even avant-garde."

We both laughed, relieved that we could safely turn the conversation to something less risky. We blew on our tea leaves, hurrying their descent to the bottom of the cup.

My cell phone went off. "If you want any information about Ma Wenlin, I suggest you ask me now," a man said quickly. "Because by the time you arrive in Xi'an, I'll be in jail. My phone is bugged."

"I'll call you when I get to Xi'an," I said. "I'm sure there will be no trouble. We'll have dinner tonight."

"I won't be around tonight. I will be in jail."

"No, you won't," I said. "Let's talk later."

We hung up and I switched off my cell phone.

The old cadre sitting opposite poured some water from the thermos into our cups, filling them back up. He eyed me curiously.

"Retired?" I asked.

"Yes, going to visit family in Xi'an."

"Your children?"

"Yes, they've moved to Xi'an and work there. I have grand-children down there."

I liked him, a retired official still dressed for work but on his way to baby-sit. He reminded me of Mr. Ma, who had also been a doting grandfather. It was hard to explain why I had Mr. Ma's picture in my hand, and would probably have seemed incomprehensible to the old man if I had tried. He had been dubbed by locals a *nongmin yingxiong*, or "peasant champion"—a name that conjures up a reckless romantic stirring up revolt among the repressed. It seemed slightly absurd, like something out of a florid South American novel, yet Mr. Ma had scared the government enough to jail him for "disturbing social order." This was a vague, almost meaningless charge, but what I heard about Mr. Ma before my trip only piqued my interest. People said that he had represented tens of thousands of peasants in a lawsuit against the government. Rumors, too, abounded that he'd led protests, traveling from village to village to whip up the peasants against the government. It all seemed a bit hard to believe, so I had come to find out what he had done. I wondered what it meant, at the turn of the millennium, to foment a peasant rebellion, a specter that for thousands of years has haunted China's leaders and has-tened the downfall of more than one dynasty. It was his history— the facts about who he was and what had happened to him—that I was after. I wanted to uncover one man's story from the rumors and half-truths that silt up events in China.

We sipped tea and smiled at each other. The old man closed his eyes, trying to sleep. I stared at Mr. Ma's picture, trying to fig-ure out what I'd learned about him.

My eyes, however, kept wandering to the jagged landscape outside. The yellow alluvial soil that covers the plateau runs up to 300 feet deep and is so prone to erosion that geographers reckon it is the most uneven landscape made of soil in the world,

constantly shifting and breaking. Grotesque outcrops rolled by, formed when huge chunks of loess soil break off the side of a hill vertically, like slabs of lava falling into the sea. Standing on top of such promontories, which centuries of human effort have inevitably turned into a small terraced cornfield or the site of a small temple, you can see dozens of other miniplateaus and fields, some just a few hundred yards away, but separated by cliffs and gullies that can fall hundreds of feet to a dried-up creek below. A newcomer can sometimes feel a sense of panic after scrambling along a few ridges in either direction and finding only precipices.

The cliffs sometimes gave way to the flat, dry riverbeds and smudgy vistas of hills beyond. Underpinning this monochromatic scenery was a supercharged environmental destruction. Each year thousands of tons of topsoil wash down the rivulets and streams into the giant Yellow River. The river, which skirts the plateau in a giant northern loop of several hundred miles, takes its name and silty consistency from the plateau's discharge.

As our diesel locomotive carefully picked its way south, we were embraced by a warm yellow glow, the color of the soil, the water and, on days like this, even the sky. This had been my fifth trip to the Loess Plateau, and I got back about once a year, drawn by the scenery, the stubborn cultural traditions and the tensions bubbling up from below.

I had set off to find Mr. Ma two days earlier, boarding an 8 a.m. flight from Xi'an to Yulin, a small city of 93,000 that boasts the only airport on the Loess Plateau. It was a Monday and the flight was full, a shuttle ferrying small-time officials on coveted trips down south to the provincial capital and back up with booty bought in Xi'an's relatively swank shops.

Yulin has virtually no private enterprise to speak of, so no

one but a bureaucrat or official from a state company could afford the $100 ticket, equivalent to the annual cash income of a Loess Plateau farmer. Unlike the train, there were no retirees on board, no students, no children and almost no women. It was all men, all in two- or three-piece western suits, many lugging consumer goods that were pricier or harder to find up on the plateau. One man had a video disc player in a box bound with twine, another carted a box of apples, a third hauled a wheel rim for a Chinese-made Audi.

An hour later I was in a taxi heading for town. It was only 10 a.m., but in August the sun was already high and we raised a cloud of dust as we raced through the parched streets. After a few minutes we entered Yulin, its roads lined with white-tiled buildings and dusty poplars.

This was a moment I'd rehearsed several times. I knew my driver was going to ask me where to go in Yulin and I knew I'd have to lie to him. What I wanted to do was go to a hotel in town, check in and meet a couple of lawyers who had known Mr. Ma. They had insisted on meeting in a hotel because they were terrified the Public Security Bureau would get wind of our talk if we discussed Mr. Ma's case in public.

Hotels, though, are dangerous places, and I had to stay there for as little time as possible—an overnight stay was out of the question. That's because guests in Chinese hotels are obliged to give their visa number. Mine was a journalist's, with a "J" in front of the number. Each night, hotel guest rolls are handed over to the police and in the morning—depending on the vigor of the local police department—they are checked. The presence of suspicious types, including journalists, is reported to the local government, which then checks if the person has applied to visit its town—or is there illegally. By staying at the hotel for just a few hours, I minimized the chance that the Public Security

Bureau would know of my presence in town; the bureau would have likely completed its morning check for that day, and it seemed unlikely that the hotel manager would call up the authorities and report my presence. After all, the Great Wall is located just a few miles north of the city and tourists were welcome.

But I couldn't tell all this to the taxi driver. Taxis are scarce in small towns like Yulin, and drivers tend to hang around hotels waiting for customers. So, too, do security agents, who lollygag in lobbies watching the people go by. If the driver were to wait for me in front of the hotel, he'd likely get bored and go inside the hotel to chat, possibly with an agent, perhaps telling him about the foreigner he'd just picked up at the airport and taken to a hotel and who intended to go on later today to Yan'an—strange travel plans for a tourist. Another worry was that if the security bureau later checked the hotel rolls and noticed me, they might ask the hotel staff how I'd left town. The doorman or the other taxi drivers waiting at the hotel would probably be friends with my driver. A call to the taxi company would give them the car's license plate and maybe the driver's cell phone. That would allow them to trace me to Yan'an and spoil the rest of the trip.

It sounded paranoid but it had happened to me before, on a trip here eighteen months earlier. I had come to visit a nearby town that had filed a class-action lawsuit against the government. Like Mr. Ma's peasants, the peasants of Peijiawan had been plagued by illegal taxes. Their solution had been to hire a lawyer and charge the government with assessing excessively high taxes.

They did so by taking advantage of China's Administrative Litigation Law of 1990, which allows people to sue the government. The idea is not that you could sue to establish basic rights—for example, one couldn't sue government censors for violating one's right to free speech, which, in theory, is guaranteed in China's constitution. Instead, you were allowed to correct

administrative foul-ups—for example, that an official had erred in denying one a permit or license. It also allowed people to file suits together—like western class-action lawsuits—taking the government to court en masse to correct a wrong.

The case had been much celebrated in China in the late 1990s, trumpeted in a government-run newspaper that covers legal affairs, *Legal Daily*, as an example of how China was developing peaceful, modern ways of solving disputes. But it was also controversial inside the government, with some seeing in it a dangerous precedent.

In 1995 the peasants in Peijiawan had suffered a drought and their crops had failed. The local government, however, wanted to squeeze more money out of the local peasants so had raised taxes. One farmer had told me how his cash income had dropped that year by more than 75 percent to the equivalent of $12, but his taxes had quintupled to $25 from $5. He scraped together $20—which he said the officials took without issuing a receipt—and promised the rest at the end of the month. But a few days later when he was out in the fields, they came by again, broke down his front door and confiscated his television.

Infuriated by this and other acts of bullying, villagers met in secret and elected representatives. The sixty-eight delegates studied central government laws regulating how much tax can be collected and concluded that the local officials had acted illegally. Initially, the leaders asked the government for partial repayment of the $75,000 that they estimated had been taken illegally.

When that was rejected, they sued, collecting signatures from 12,688 farmers, or two-thirds of the residents in the township. Chipping in 25 cents each, they hired lawyers, who filed a very cautious lawsuit. In court the lawyers hadn't brought up the officials' brutal tax-collecting tactics, instead focusing on the amount

collected and the tax regulations. It was an open-and-shut case: in 1999 the farmers got the full $75,000 returned to them.

News of the Peijiawan farmers' victory spread quickly across the Loess Plateau. Farmers in a village one valley over from Peijiawan felt that they, too, had been overtaxed and had hired a well-known local lawyer, Mr. Ma, hoping to duplicate their neighbors' success. So Mr. Ma filed an almost identical lawsuit to the Peijiawan case. But in late 1999, just a few months after the Peijiawan peasants won their suit, he ended up in jail.

When I heard about his case from outraged lawyers in Beijing, I wasn't entirely surprised. When I had left Peijiawan, I had noticed some people standing on top of their houses, glaring at the farmers who had talked to me. Two guides who had accompanied me there started getting nervous and urged me to get out of town. I figured they were exaggerating the risk: after all, the Public Security Bureau couldn't have a post in this tiny village.

But I was wrong. When I returned to Beijing a couple of days later, a message was waiting for me to call the two guides. I did so, and they told me that police had been waiting for them upon their arrival back home in Yulin. They had been let off with a warning, but their story inspired caution: village officials had found a phone in a neighboring village and called to tell the police about our visit, even giving our car's license plate. Meanwhile, police in Yulin had received the hotel register from the night I'd spent at the hotel and noticed my journalist visa. They were quickly able to trace our route, from Yulin to Peijiawan and then on to my next destination. It turned out that I had narrowly escaped being detained in Peijiawan; the police had turned up just an hour after my departure.

That experience and Mr. Ma's fate had made me extracautious. Before leaving Beijing, I obtained a map of Yulin and

found some landmarks near the hotel where I was to meet the lawyers. A hospital was located right across from it, and I had decided to tell my taxi driver to let me out there.

As we drove through town, I told the taxi driver that an old classmate of mine was now living in Yulin and was sick. I wanted to go visit him for a couple of hours before we headed down to Yan'an. Sure, he said, no problem.

I wondered if I wasn't being unreasonable. The driver had told me that he was a former factory worker who'd been laid off and was trying to make ends meet by driving. And even if he were buddies with the security agents, chances are he wouldn't bother to give them a call or even mention me—one should never underestimate human laziness and inertia. It was always a problem in China to figure out the line between excessive caution and carelessness, not only for foreigners like me but for people like Mr. Ma. After all, he'd only done what others had done by representing peasants in a lawsuit. Now he was in jail. What line had he crossed? It seemed like this was the crux of modern China: On a daily level people are quite free to do as they please. But still firmly in place are the old restrictions devised by an authoritarian government. The regime might be dying, but will use these powers when it feels even a little threatened.

We pulled up to the hospital, and I told the driver to go home and pack a bag and a thermos of tea for the trip down south. He thanked me for my consideration and headed home. We agreed to meet back at the hospital in two hours.

After waiting to see him drive out of sight, I walked across to the hotel. Despite my precautions, this was still the trickiest part of the trip. The manager might be very cautious and immediately report my presence to the police, not waiting for the daily visa check. Or a security agent could be killing time in the lobby and go to the Reception out of curiosity, ask to see my registration

form, notice the "J" prefix to my visa number and wonder what a foreign journalist was doing in town.

Entering the hotel, I noticed a couple of men sitting on a red leather couch in the lobby. Dressed in polo shirts and tight polyester slacks, they looked every bit the part of public security officers detailed to check out the local hotels. Men like this seemed to be a fixture in hotels around China: chubby guys, doing nothing, chatting on cell phones and waiting for the karaoke lounge to open. Every time I saw them, I dreamed of a revolution that would sweep them out on the streets where they'd have to earn an honest living.

Well, this town had a tourist draw, I figured, so nothing wrong with me being here. I stopped before a giant plastic relief map of Yulin with the Great Wall marked north of the town. I studied it for a minute and then went to the front desk. A few minutes later I was in my room, waiting for Mr. Ma's colleagues to arrive.

Few other issues are as sensitive as the right to take someone's money. The problem in China started in the mid-1990s, when protests against heavy taxation cropped up repeatedly. The government responded by tinkering with the existing system, hoping to use old-style authoritarian threats to make it work. But it became pretty clear that the government's efforts were inadequate, and taxes remain one of the friction points between rulers and ruled.

When the Chinese Communist Party took control of China in 1949, taxes weren't an issue. The party collectivized agriculture and banned private enterprise. All profits from any enterprise, rural or urban, remained with the state, and these profits were the government's chief source of revenue. It was a classic

communist system, similar to the one in the Soviet Union or Eastern Europe.

As in most communist countries, this system bankrupted itself within a few decades. But while in Eastern Europe communism's economic problems led in the late 1980s to political revolt, China's communist leaders were able to stay in power by reforming the country's economic system early on—in 1978, less than thirty years after taking power. The first and most successful step was abolishing collectivization. Farmers were given control (but not ownership) over plots of land, which they could do with as they pleased as long as they paid taxes, often in grain, to the government.

That led to stunning economic growth—free to profit by their own labor, China's peasants reverted to the hardworking entrepreneurial class they had been before 1949. Other reforms followed, such as lifting the ban on small privately run businesses. Suddenly, small factories sprouted up across China, quickly putting an end to the lack of consumer goods that plagued other communist countries.

Overall, the government benefited from these changes. It recovered some measure of support, which had almost completely dissipated during the first thirty years of disastrous policies. People were so busy getting prosperous that calls for political change were small, albeit insistent. But the changes did have one unforeseen downside: the government had a tough time raising taxes.

The old system of skimming profits from state-owned enterprises was no longer adequate. State enterprises had begun to face competition from new privately run factories and foreign competitors, who had been allowed in the marketplace. In addition, the government needed more money than before. It had ambitious social projects, such as eradicating poverty and enforc-

ing a limit on the number of children allowed per family. It also embarked on a costly modernization of its armed forces, raising salaries for soldiers and buying costly weapons systems from abroad. Since the mid-1990s, for example, annual military budgets have risen by double-digit figures. In addition, corruption continued to siphon off billions of dollars each year, much of it to well-connected party leaders, their friends and offspring.

The peasants' taxes helped, but because they were mainly in the form of grain, they didn't alleviate the fiscal crunch. The grain did allow the government to sell subsidized grain in the cities, helping to buy itself support there, but it was not a substitute for cash.

So Beijing was left with a problem familiar to many governments: how to get more money. Many countries would see this as a political problem—will people accept paying more taxes? If so, raise taxes. If not, cut expenditures or take on debt. But in China the problem was mistakenly seen as simply a technical one. In officials' eyes, the issue wasn't whether people were willing to pay taxes but simply how to collect them. This was reinforced by advice the government got from abroad: the World Bank, for example, supplied the government with plans on how to set up a new tax system, advising it to implement a national income-tax program similar to the ones that exist in other countries. What was rarely discussed is how people would feel about paying more taxes to a corrupt, unaccountable government.

One of the central misconceptions about China is that because it is an authoritarian system it can do anything it wishes. Actually, China lacks the institutions and credibility that allow modern bureaucracies to function effectively. While Beijing can crush a peasant rebellion or student protests, enforcing a fair and reasonable tax system is different. There the question isn't one of sending in soldiers to shoot off guns but of establishing and run-

ning a complicated bureaucratic structure, one that relies on people's trust in the government and a belief that things are fair enough in society so that average citizens feel a sense of duty to pay. Threats can force individuals to pay taxes, but collectively it is belief in the government's legitimacy that allows a tax system to work.

The economic reforms gave the government new legitimacy, but by the turn of the century its biggest successes were a couple of decades old. Gradually, the party's definition of success had become too meager for wider and wider swaths of the population. Having enough food to eat is a wonderful accomplishment, but it's also a bare minimum that a government should offer its population.

Beijing's drive to raise taxes took little of this into account. It launched a massive effort to increase revenues through a simple method: user fees. It was basically the toll-road concept—you use it, you pay for it. It had the advantage of simplicity—money could be collected on the spot from the user—and a semblance of fairness. The disadvantage, of course, is that it falls heaviest on the poorest. A typical tuition fee of $30 per semester for elementary school might be bearable for a prosperous farmer but would be out of reach for a poor farmer. It also was ripe for abuse by local officials, who could slap a fee on everything—and who are held accountable by no one for their decisions.

User fees suddenly began appearing for everything. Farmers could pay a bewildering number of taxes: a vague "village" tax, an agricultural tax, a general education tax, a school repair fee, a market management fee, a head tax, a hygiene fee, an irrigation tax and twenty days of unpaid labor a year for government projects—not to mention special levies, such as the second irrigation fee that caused the furor.

With no checks or balances, farmers suddenly faced huge tax bills. By the mid-1990s, protests had become daily occurrences. The government responded by tinkering with the system. Taxes, it announced in 1991—and has repeated every year or two since then—would be limited to 5 percent of farmers' annual income. That sounds like a great rate—most developed countries tax citizens between 30 and 50 percent—but Chinese farmers have little cash, so 5 percent is still significant. Plus, that rate didn't take into account the user fees—hundreds of local governments simply declared these special taxes exempt from the 5-percent rule.

The central government wasn't blind to the problem and responded with sometimes ingenious solutions. The government, for example, issued a national tax checkbook that farmers were to carry around with them. When a farmer paid a tax, the book would be stamped, and then the farmer could prove that he'd paid his taxes and was exempt from more. But these patchwork solutions were often bypassed by China's tax-starved government. Special fees and surtaxes were still levied and peasants continued to suffer—and protest—despite the regular pronouncement that this time the government was really serious about reducing the peasants' burden.

The rural protests had interesting echoes in Chinese history. Then, as now, uprisings often started against local officials who abused power. When the imperial government supported the officials instead of the victimized peasants, the rebellion often spread and anger became focused against the center. One of the most famous peasant rebels was Chen She, who started the rebellion that led to the downfall of the Qin, which was the first dynasty to unite China. In the summer of 209 B.C., Chen failed to deliver prisoners to a penitentiary on time and faced the death penalty for his tardiness. So he incited a rebellion among peasants

unhappy with local conditions. The rebellion quickly spread and ended up toppling the government and setting up a new dynasty, the Han.

Similar examples can be found throughout Chinese history. Sometimes the peasants' role has been exaggerated or romanticized—for a while it was fashionable to see them as an amorphous arbiter of power in Chinese history, a primordial force that rose up occasionally to topple evil governments. While that is an exaggeration, it is true that some of China's earliest political philosophers saw the populace (which then was almost all rural) as a sort of judge that decided legitimacy. If the government is corrupt, they argued, people had a right to rebel. This has imbued ordinary people with a moral power to choose their rulers. It also helps to explain why the government today treats the countryside with such contradictory policies, at once seeking to raise standards of living but also treating any sign of rebellion with extreme brutality.

Messrs. Zhao and Shao walked gingerly into the whitewashed room, which reflected the morning sun like a floodlit stage. Mr. Zhao strode forward and grasped my hand. He was forty years old but appeared to be in his early thirties, a trim, dapper man who could have been at home in any of China's modern metropolises like Beijing or Shanghai. I couldn't quite place it when I first saw him, but later I realized that he looked a bit like a member of China's Uighur Muslim minority group, with a pencil-thin mustache and a sharp, angular nose. He was dressed in light green trousers, a beige shirt and vented brown leather shoes. Instead of the usual brush cut, his hair was a bit longer and neatly parted down the side. With a gold chain around his neck, he was something of a Loess Plateau dandy.

"Welcome," he said in English. "You are welcome."

"Thanks," I said. Then I switched back to Chinese. "Yulin is a beautiful town."

Mr. Zhao looked at me quizzically, gave a quick shrug and laughed. I liked him already. Most people are intense local patriots, but Mr. Zhao seemed as unimpressed with the dusty little county seat as I was.

"Let me introduce you. This is Lawyer Shao. We are colleagues."

I took one look at Mr. Shao and wished he hadn't come along. Sweaty and bald at age forty-eight, he wore a tight blue polo shirt that hugged his paunch and made him seem the caricature of a lazy official. He looked at me distrustfully, probably thinking that this whole exercise was a dangerous waste of time.

"Ha-ha," Mr. Shao said nervously. "Ha-ha. Ha."

I thought he would keel over from nerves, but instead he plopped himself on one of the beds and wiped his brow with a handkerchief.

Mr. Zhao wasn't ready to sit down yet. With a dramatic flourish he pulled a stack of documents from a plastic shopping bag and dropped them on the bed where I sat.

"You read this and you'll understand everything you need to know about Ma Wenlin. The court transcripts, his self-defense, his appeal, the letter to the governor—it's all here. All except the most recent peasants' petition."

Mr. Shao sat back nervously, as though the documents were a bomb. He kept one eye on them and glanced at me with the other.

"Ha-ha," he said. Then he wiped his brow and cleared his throat. "I have a suggestion: I suggest you leave Yulin immediately," he said, now looking up in my general direction. Still not comfortable about talking to a foreigner, he preferred instead to

address the fan behind my head. Then, turning to Mr. Zhao, he motioned to go.

I jumped up.

"Here," I said, thrusting paper cups filled with green tea at them. "Mr. Zhao. You must be familiar with the Peijiawan case. Why was that different from this case? Just from a legal point of view."

Mr. Zhao wasn't ready to go and accepted a cup of tea, sitting down on the bed next to his colleague, who fidgeted nervously and waved away the tea.

"They're basically the same," Mr. Zhao said, ignoring Mr. Shao. "Both cases are from the same area and involve the same principles. Peijiawan has been handled okay. The government paid the money, and the peasants got what was coming to them. But the government can't accept that such a suit could happen again. If all the peasants in China file class-action lawsuits, then the Communist Party is finished. So Ma Wenlin's case couldn't be allowed to succeed."

Mr. Shao sputtered and his eyes twitched. He looked over at the fan, started to say something and then caught himself. Thinking that he might be the cautious bureaucrat type, I clumsily tried to calm him by imitating what I figured to be the government line.

"Ma was probably also a bit radical," I said helpfully. "Didn't he accompany the peasants to Beijing and help them file an appeal to the central government?"

Mr. Zhao looked at me as if I were a fool, and even Mr. Shao cocked an eyebrow skeptically.

"What you're saying is wrong. That wasn't his problem. No, from the government's point of view his problem was that he linked up the farmers with the legal system. This shouldn't be a

crime, but that's what he did. Isn't that right?" he said, nudging Mr. Shao.

Mr. Shao looked over sternly at Mr. Zhao. Discussing Mr. Ma's crimes seemed to have made him even more wary. He mumbled something about the court documents being secret.

"Nonsense," Mr. Zhao said. "They're not. They're from the courthouse. Anyone can access them."

None of us believed what he'd just said. Criminal court documents in China weren't public, certainly not those regarding as sensitive a case as Mr. Ma's.

Mr. Shao cut in, tapping his watch and looking expectantly at Mr. Zhao. He looked at the fan behind me. Then he finally looked at me and, looking me straight in the eye, spoke: "I have another suggestion: Don't go to Zizhou. The public security is too tight. They've arrested a peasant representative who organized the petition for Ma. It's dangerous. You must not go there." Mr. Shao was speaking fast, as if by spilling out all this information his guilt would be less. He sat back, red in the face.

I sat back, a bit concerned. I had planned to go to Zizhou, the county where Mr. Ma had organized the peasants. It was halfway between Yulin and Yan'an, which is where Mr. Ma lived. I knew that Mr. Shao was ultracautious, but he seemed earnest and I knitted my brow in thought.

Mr. Zhao smiled and lit up a cigarette. Everyone sat thinking for a moment. I looked at him and wondered why Mr. Zhao stayed on the Loess Plateau. Probably, it was simply the fact that Chinese can't easily move from city to city. Without friends or connections it was hard to leave and set up a new life, so he remained here, a small seditious element spreading modern thinking in this backwater.

Outside the window a two-stroke tractor roared by, a small

contraption that looked like a ridable lawn mower. They were ubiquitous in rural China, used to plow fields or haul produce. I was suddenly reminded of the peasants whose fate had so concerned Mr. Ma.

It was time to go. We drained our cups and stood up, shook hands and the two walked out. Mr. Zhao left last, turning to me and saying firmly: "Shao is cautious, but he's right. Don't go to Zizhou. There are police everywhere. I wouldn't even overnight in Yulin if I were you."

I quickly remembered the petition.

"What's that petition you mentioned?" I called out to Mr. Zhao.

"Ask the peasants," he said, turning his head to answer as he walked down the hall.

I ran after him, and he stopped to talk to me as Mr. Shao continued down to the elevator.

"But you said to avoid the countryside," I said.

"They'll find you. It's hard to avoid Ma Wenlin when you get down there."

I stood for a second puzzled, trying to formulate one of the many questions buzzing in my head. But Mr. Zhao had already turned, and was hurrying away after his colleague.

I checked out of the hotel after just ninety minutes, mumbling an excuse to the receptionist, and called the driver on his cell phone. I crossed back over the road to the hospital and waited, eager to be away from the hotel and the men loitering in the lobby. The driver pulled up, I hopped in and we headed south toward Zizhou.

The road was only two lanes, but it was smooth and we started overtaking trucks and tractors as our driver found his

pace. I felt giddy as we gained speed and left urban China's orbit. The valley that spread out south from Yulin zipped past, and I contemplated what had happened. Mr. Zhao's answers had left so much unclear. He said Mr. Ma had linked the peasants to the legal system, but hadn't the other lawyers done the same thing a year earlier? Why weren't they jailed? And the petition was also unusual. How had the peasants organized it, and what did it contain?

The valley around Yulin soon gave way to the Loess Plateau's distinctive hills. The road started to wind around the huge earth and stone outcroppings, their crumbling faces evidence of the unending erosion and decay. Precarious terraces, sometimes marked by slapdash wooden fences, clambered up the hills, which were occasionally dotted with pine and willow trees. Groups of schoolchildren in bright red caps walked past cannibalized trucks and cars, which lay scattered every few miles at the side of the road.

Along the way, cave dwellings would appear halfway up a hill. Many mistake these dwellings for caveman-type accommodations, imagining that the inhabitants are modern versions of Peking Man, living a primitive existence in dark hollows. In fact, as the locals somewhat defensively say, the caves are warm in the winter and cool in the summer. They're practical to build because wood is scarce, but the earth is loose and easy to excavate. Floors are hard-packed or sometimes tiled. The homes usually have one wooden or adobe room that juts out from the hill, giving their homes at least one bright room with natural lighting. Romanticizing this life would be wrong, but a good cave truly is warm and snug, even if sometimes a bit malodorous.

We passed by old cave dwellings, most abandoned for newer ones. The more modern versions were better because they had higher ceilings, 7 or more feet, made possible by better engineer-

ing techniques such as braces and crossbeams. In the older caves one often had to stoop or worry about hitting a beam—often just a tree branch braced against the walls. But the older ones did have exquisite windows, the glass fronted by delicate handmade wood lattice. In the past the lattice wouldn't have had glass behind it; instead, paper would have been glued on. The lattice was to a degree functional, preventing the paper from tearing or blowing in during a storm. Glass made this unnecessary, so the new houses dispensed with the lattices. Probably from a cave-dweller's point of view this was an advantage because the new windows were cheaper and gave more light. Somehow, though, the lack of decoration made the newer homes bleaker, the one bit of frivolity stripped away. Inside the homes, people owned more possessions than in years past—televisions, quilts and fans weren't uncommon, even in this poor region—but from the outside it looked as if the plateau's residents couldn't be bothered to beautify their homes anymore. After centuries of poverty and a progressively deteriorating environment, the region seemed to be hunkering down, concentrating only on material survival.

At noon we reached Zizhou, the county seat just twenty miles north of the center of the rebellion. It was the closest town to the area of unrest, and Mr. Ma had been here numerous times to visit officials on behalf of the farmers. Surrounded by villages that were home to 260,000 farmers, Zizhou's 30,000 residents lived on a small island of urban China. It was typical of hundreds of small cities across China, with almost no structure older than a couple of decades. Buildings were concrete, covered with white tiles. Small shops lined the main road. Government offices hid behind steel gates and high walls. Peasants drove ferociously

through town, their two-stroke tractors barreling past like ancient Industrial Age machines on wheels, belching out smoke and raising clouds of dust in the midday heat.

I stopped at a small noodle restaurant and ducked inside to avoid drawing attention. As I ate lunch, I debated whether to go into the hills where Mr. Ma had been active. Transportation wouldn't be a problem. The roads would be dirt or gravel and steep, and I knew from experience that they could turn to mud, requiring hours of pushing to get a car up them. But the weather was cooperating, and I figured I could probably spend the afternoon in one of the villages and still reach Yan'an by midnight.

The epicenter of Mr. Ma's peasant rebellion was in neighboring Tuo'erxiang Township. A farmer there, Wang Xingwei, had grown rich trading grain and had installed a telephone. His number was among the materials that lawyers had given me earlier in the day, so I decided to give him a call.

I walked out back toward the outhouse, switched on my cell phone and called. It was a bit of a risk to turn the phone on because its signal could be used to track its user. But it would be even riskier to go blindly into the mountains without making a call first. Mr. Wang didn't seem surprised to be talking to a foreign journalist. He said local media had contacted him, but nothing had appeared in the press recently because the case had become too sensitive to report.

"The government has repressed the farmers again and again, but we can only dare to be angry and not say anything," Mr. Wang said in an accent so thick that I had to ask him to repeat every other sentence.

We talked about the local economy, which had suffered from the chronic drought that was affecting swaths of western China. "The natural conditions aren't good. About seventy to eighty

percent of us have to borrow money just to eat. If you want to make ends meet, you have to go out and work as a laborer in the big cities."

What if I came and visited, I asked him. "Sure, come on over," he said quickly. Then he paused and thought better of his offer. "But they'll arrest you. The Public Security Bureau has stationed officers in the village."

He said that the peasants had recently held secret elections and elected several dozen leaders. Like other villages in China, Tuo'erxiang was supposed to have democratic elections—indeed, such grassroots democracy has been the subject of intense study by western academics and funding by western aid agencies. In some model counties these elections do in fact work as a safety valve: although the candidates are screened by the party, outsiders sometimes get in and end up influencing the party's programs. But like most of these elections, the votes in Tuo'erxiang had only resulted in the same clique of party officials winning the posts in the village councils. Mr. Wang had been elected by a real vote, one conducted with secret ballot and multiple candidates. In his view and those of his neighbors, he and the other delegates were their real leaders.

That exercise in grassroots democracy, however, had brought the police in from Zizhou, who arrested or placed under house arrest the village's newly elected leaders. Police, he said, were still in the village, their cars parked in the center of town. It sounded impossible to visit the village—even for Chinese reporters, let alone a foreign reporter. I told him my travel plans, and we agreed that I'd try back in a few hours. I returned to the table, finished my noodles and walked back out onto the street.

I squinted at the town, trying to find something recognizable in the jumble of white-tiled buildings and small shops. This was where I had left my Peijiawan guides eighteen months ago, but

already it had blurred into the other village towns I'd visited. We were now at a crossroads, with a line of stores that sold travel goods: snacks, fruit, alcohol and dried goods, most of them packed in bright red boxes so they could be given as presents. Most of the buyers were farmers who lived elsewhere as laborers and needed to stock up on presents before heading back home into the countless villages that lay in the mountains beyond.

I had a pressing decision to make—to go into these hills or not. I was eager to go because it seemed the best place for me to find out what had happened to Mr. Ma's quest. I had counted on talking to farmers and learning about their problems, what Mr. Ma had done, how they'd been organized and what actions they'd taken. If I didn't go, it seemed impossible to get to the bottom of the rebellion.

But then I ran through the likely outcome of a visit to Tuo'erxiang, the center of the rebellion. The village had just a few hundred residents and I'd be instantly pegged as an outsider. I could hide my appearance, for example by crouching in the back seat of the car and jumping into a peasant's home upon arrival. If the car had dark windows, that could work; I'd done it in other situations and had managed to talk to farmers that way. But this village was so small and controls were so tight that our out-of-town license plates would be instantly recognizable and give me away. The town was probably just a few dozen caves carved into the side of a mountain with everyone in sight of everyone else. If police were already there, I stood no chance.

A bit depressed, I got in the car again, and we continued south, bypassing the rebellion's epicenter. Now I was heading for Yan'an, the communists' headquarters from 1937 to 1947 and Mr. Ma's home for thirty-five years.

When the communists lived here, they relied heavily on peasant support, not just for food but as a way of legitimizing

themselves. By living among peasants here on the Loess Plateau, they showed that they were different from the corrupt Nationalists. The communists had been purified by the soil and unified with the lowest class in China. This played well among some of China's intelligentsia and especially among a group of foreign China-watchers, who saw peasants as strong, earthy figures with ample common sense and a quick smile. Unlike the Nationalists, who took over China shortly after the emperor was overthrown in 1911, the communists would put peasants first.

In fact, Chairman Mao showered money and benefits on China's cities. Rural life might have been celebrated in song and dance, but benefits went to the cities, where health care was free and the capital accumulated through agriculture invested in heavy industry. Peasants had none of that and were seen mainly as food-making machines, best symbolized during the Great Leap Forward when famine-stricken counties were forced to send their last kilos of grain to the cities.

Still, in the official mythology, this part of China was the forge that created the communists. I wondered if living near such a historically important place made peasants more assertive. Being a part of revolutionary history might have raised locals' consciousness, leaving them with the feeling that the revolution was supposed to have been fought for them, not the bureaucrats who ran the country. This was certainly the feeling one got talking to the Peijiawan farmers who had filed the initial, successful lawsuit against high taxes just a year before Mr. Ma's ill-fated suit. I remembered how one farmer had said that Chairman Mao had compared the communists to fish swimming in the sea of peasants.

On the other hand, the peasants' bold actions weren't confined to this one region, with protests occurring across the country. Recently, a national newspaper had published a letter by an

official working in a township in central Hebei Province, a part of the country more prosperous than the area we were now driving through. The letter, "The True Feelings of a Township Party Secretary," was written by Li Changping, a thirty-seven-year-old economist who'd worked in the countryside for seventeen years.

Mr. Li said his district had a population of 65,000, although 25,000 had found conditions so difficult that they'd left to find work in the city. Taxes for a family of five amounted to an astounding $310 a year, virtually wiping out every family's cash income. Despite that, the village governments that collected the taxes were under such pressure to keep channeling money to higher-ups that each village in the township owed on average a staggering $500,000 in back taxes.

The newspaper had been able to print the letter only because of the happy ending tacked on to the bottom. Mr. Li's letter had reached central authorities, who had sent an inspection team to the township. Later, the province convened a meeting and reduced taxes by $6 a person, or $30 for the five-member family. But it wasn't much of a happy ending—the cut amounted to just a 10 percent reduction, which would still leave an average family with a backbreaking $280 a year in taxes. In addition, the inspection team had not only confirmed Mr. Li's analysis but said the situation he described was common across the country. Although this one success story had been written up, most cases were unresolved, or else they, too, would have been trumpeted by the government-controlled media.

We'd been driving now for several hours, and Yan'an was approaching. The plateau's corroded hills came in relentless waves. The sun was now falling, and the hills, which had been tan-colored through the day, now began to soften, turning slightly yellow.

As we bounced down the road, I'd only been able to glance through the court documents that the lawyers had given me back in Yulin. Still, I couldn't help but be amazed at Mr. Ma's audacity. He hadn't just represented the peasants by typing up a dry lawsuit in his office. He'd also canvassed the peasants for support, traveling from village to village trying to find peasants willing to join his lawsuit. He reminded me of U.S. lawyers who filed class-action lawsuits on behalf of victims of industrial pollution. Unlike them, however, he stood to gain little, since legal fees were low.

And even if only part of the files were true, he had led protests and tried to storm the local government offices in Yulin. It seemed bizarre and almost suicidal; the outcome of such actions had to be clear: jail and possibly death. I knew a lot of young people who were sometimes naïve, thinking that the government surely wasn't so brutal as to jail people for expressing their beliefs.

But Mr. Ma didn't fit into the category of young romantic. Born in 1942, Mr. Ma was fifty-five at the time he filed his lawsuit. He had spent almost all his life under communist rule; there had been no overseas education for him, no familiarity with English, no real knowledge of the outside world. In a country where many people retire at sixty, Mr. Ma was an old man born of an old system. I couldn't imagine what could cause such a person to challenge the system, setting in motion a massive lawsuit and, if I believed the court documents, protests and demonstrations across the countryside.

I remembered, too, that Mr. Ma had been shaped by the Cultural Revolution. During that period of totalitarian excess from 1966 to 1976, Mr. Ma had been an enthusiastic member of the Red Guards, Chairman Mao's fanatic followers who roamed the

countryside, destroying temples and humiliating people they didn't like.

Such an experience would affect anyone, leaving them either contemptuous of the law or its fervent supporter. In Mr. Ma's case it had been the latter. Many people who'd survived the Cultural Revolution were intensely self-confident: not necessarily very savvy about the outside world—after all, contact with it was rigorously banned—but many were also unafraid of authority.

A more typical product of his time was Wu Hanjing, whom I met on my first trip to the Loess Plateau, in April 1996. He was the head of Gushui village, which like most villages in the plateau was a series of caves dug up the side of a loess hill. He'd put up me and two friends in the town's official guest cave, which Mr. Wu had set aside for official business and entertaining visitors. The night before, we'd feasted on potato and carrot stew, later playing cards and drinking grain alcohol under a 40-watt bulb. The air in the cave reminded me of a saying—that villagers here bathe but three times in their lives: at birth, at marriage and at death. We had been unlucky enough to catch them in between these auspicious occasions.

After spending a sleepless night in the oxygen-starved cave, I got up early and walked over to our car, an old Czech Skoda that we'd rented in Baotou, Inner Mongolia. When we'd set off, the driver had been terrified that his little car would be splashed by mud. But by the end of the trip, he was just glad that he hadn't broken an axle. I walked over to the car, gray and battered in the morning light, and fished a bottle of water out of the trunk. Above me was a small hill, and I started up it, hoping the water would clear my head.

At the top was a cluster of five temples: four small ones and a big one in the middle. The four smaller temples were fairly routine affairs, one-room, one-story buildings dedicated to popular Taoist gods: the God of the Earth, the Jade Emperor, Lord Guan and the Lady Who Registers Births. But they were just a buildup for the main temple. Two stories, with a slate-gray tiled roof and curving eaves, the building was called the Pavilion in Memory of Heroes. It was a temple to communist China's founding father, Chairman Mao.

Worshiping Mao was a nice twist on his legacy. Although he cultivated the image of a traditional thinker—composing poems and practicing calligraphy—one of his chief hatreds was traditional culture. His goal was to replace China's religions with the cult of the leader—himself. Worshipers were honoring a man who had tried to forbid worship.

A weak early spring light filtered into the temple. Three women prostrated themselves before Mao, a papier-mâché statue about twice his real size, seated with giant hands resting on armrests. The women did three kowtows in quick succession and then got up. Usually, people praying in a Chinese temple will plant three sticks of incense in a burner in front of the god. But the women left after their kowtows. I turned around. Mr. Wu was standing in the doorway watching me watch the women pray. I greeted him and asked about the incense.

"That's superstitious," Mr. Wu explained. He pulled out a cigarette, lit it and stuck it filter side down between Mao's index and middle fingers. "That's how we show respect. He liked to smoke."

Next to Mao were two other oversized statues, one of his premier, Zhou Enlai, and the other of his top general, Zhu De. Cement walls were painted with cartoon scenes of Mao's life. Everything was covered with a light layer of yellow dust.

The second floor of the temple was empty—more shrines were planned, Mr. Wu said, but the village had to raise more money first. We stepped outside and surveyed the valley and the miniplateaus in the distance. Gushui lay below us, a town of 1,200 people who earned on average the equivalent of $100 a year. In the distance were three other villages, all scraping an existence from the worn-out land. The fields were planted with millet and wheat and gradually we could see people moving toward the fields.

Dressed in a Mao suit with a round white cloth cap of a type favored by local farmers, Mr. Wu viewed others suspiciously, preferring to chain-smoke and listen. He'd run the village since the Cultural Revolution, the final and one of the most destructive of Mao's campaigns. He'd got his job in 1952 because his father had died as a "martyr" for the communists in the civil war against the Nationalists. Then he set about doing what every good cadre should do: blindly follow the party's directives. In that era this meant aping absurd government policies. His biggest adventure was a trip to a model village, Dazhai, where he learned how to terrace fields up the sides of steep hills, a costly, backbreaking technique of reclaiming land that requires thousands of hours of labor. Like Dazhai, Mr. Wu's village also had fields that precariously climbed slopes of more than 25 degrees. Those extremely steep terraces, soil conservation experts now reckon, are responsible for about half the plateau's topsoil runoff each year—a prime reason why the environment has worsened so quickly in recent decades.

Mr. Wu had even been to Beijing in 1977 to shake hands with Chairman Mao's ill-starred successor, Hua Guofeng, who lasted just a couple of years before being supplanted by Deng Xiaoping, the leader who implemented economic reforms and ended the Mao cult. But even then, Mr. Wu had kept his job in this

conservative neck of the woods, carefully following the party line as it embraced reforms, all the while not-so-secretly pining away for the good old days. Mr. Wu had one year of schooling and usually expressed himself with grunts. But then I brought up Mao.

"Mao fought on the Loess Plateau for thirteen years. He was one of us for all that time," Mr. Wu said, suddenly eloquent. "Who could forget Mao Zedong? He was first among a thousand emperors."

In 1980, Mr. Wu began building the temple. Or, rather, he began to order his peasants to build it. On his own initiative he forced locals to "volunteer" their free time in the winter to the project and he invested the equivalent of $20,000 of the village's money in the main building. He knew that the peasants were eager to rebuild the other temples, which had been destroyed in the Cultural Revolution. Farmers liked praying to the local God of the Earth, for example, and asking for sons from the Lady Who Registers Births. So he rebuilt those. But he made the centerpiece of the complex the new Mao temple, integrating it into the old religion.

"Who runs these temples?" I asked.

"The temples are controlled by the Taoist Association," Mr. Wu said, referring to the national association headquartered in Beijing.

"Do they have a representative here?"

"That's me. It's one of my duties," he said, suddenly mumbling.

Mr. Wu had a lot of duties. He was party secretary and village chief of Gushui—ostensibly two jobs, the latter of which is supposed to be elected by popular vote.

"What about this new idea from Beijing of holding elections for the village chief. What do you think of it?"

"Oh yes," Mr. Wu said, his voice trailing off again, as though distracted by a memory. "We had elections here."

Like many other elections in rural China, Mr. Wu's had been rigged. He had been the only candidate and the electoral commission, which is charged with vetting candidates, consisted of himself and a few other party members. The talk of modern inventions bothered him and he hurried off to the caves. One had three signs out front nailed from top to bottom on a beam: "Party Office," "Village Council" and "Taoist Association." He unlocked the door and went inside.

Mr. Wu's work had been influential. Farther down the road to the west were the towns of Dingbian and Jingbian. They both had Mao temples built in imitation of Mr. Wu's. We set off to see them, but Mr. Wu didn't come to see us off. He gets a lot of visitors, an aide said, and is very busy.

After arriving in Yan'an at dusk, I checked into a hotel and gave Mr. Ma's wife a call. She invited me over, and I decided to stroll through town to her apartment.

I'd expected that the communists' wartime base would have been pampered, boasting good roads and bleached into an antiseptic cleanliness favored by Chinese urban planners. This usually involves concrete buildings covered in white tile and blue glass, a main street lined with thirsty saplings and a large public square decorated with a few strips of fenced-off grass.

Instead, Yan'an was a chaotic, dirty little city of 300,000. Like the rest of the communists' former strongholds, it had been poor before the revolution and was still plagued by its natural conditions, which left it isolated and surrounded by inhospitable mountains. A few signs of government largesse lay strewn around town. A massive five-story party headquarters domi-

nated the downtown, its streaked concrete walls slowly cracking in the summer heat. During the Cultural Revolution, Yan'an had been a pilgrimage site for youths hoping to imbibe the old revolutionary spirit, and from that era the city had inherited a gargantuan railway station. Now, four of its five platforms lay unused and its giant waiting hall busy only when the train from Xi'an arrived in the morning and departed at noon.

Out on the streets, aggressive beggars accosted passersby, demanding money. Itinerant peddlers hawked cheap shoes and slacks. Streets drained poorly and no one obeyed traffic regulations. Of course, this didn't really matter too much; the town's few streets were permanently jammed with trucks and cars, tractors and horse-drawn wagons. Nothing moved at more than walking pace.

As with most of the Loess Plateau, part of the problem was geography. Unlike Yulin, which was built on a plain, Yan'an is jammed into three valleys. One is along the Yan River, from which the city gets its name. (The suffix *an* means "peace.") The other two valleys follow small streams that feed into the Yan. The confluence of the biggest stream and the Yan is the center of town, basically just a bridge over the river. Rising up from the banks are hills dotted with caves where the communist leaders lived between 1937 and 1947. The hills had been turned into parks, with a Buddhist pagoda atop one hill the city's symbol— an odd choice given the communists' rejection of traditional culture.

Mr. Ma and his wife lived on the campus of the No. 3 Middle School, where Mr. Ma had worked as a teacher and his wife still taught. It was an arrangement not unusual in China. Before economic reforms took hold, most people in China's cities lived in housing provided by their employer, and even now that is still often the case. The housing is often surrounded by walls, mean-

ing visitors have to pass a security guard even for social visits. I was lucky because it was suppertime and the guard wasn't on duty. The gate to the school was open and I walked in.

I had thought Yan'an was a dump, but as I had walked through the gates, the stark beauty of the plateau suddenly overwhelmed me. In front of me was a hill that rose up sharply behind the school yard. Most hills on the plateau are denuded, but this one was dotted with dozens of newly planted willows. As the setting sun caught the hill, the wispy green leaves and yellow soil glowed ethereally, blurring like a watercolor that hung behind the pockmarked school.

The school yard was mostly empty, the students and teachers at home eating dinner. A couple of people out for a walk stared. I went up to the second floor of the building where the teachers lived, and knocked. Mr. Ma's wife greeted me at the door.

Cao Pingfen was a stout woman of fifty-six with short hair parted on one side. She smiled broadly. "Thanks for coming over," she said, ushering me into their living room.

I sat down on a giant black leather sofa and she in a matching easy chair. Ms. Cao pushed a pack of cigarettes across the huge glass coffee table that separated us.

"Have a smoke," Ms. Cao said, her eyes downcast as she made the perfunctory offer.

The pack of Yan'an-brand cigarettes was unopened. She didn't smoke and had bought them to offer the people whom she met on her husband's business—judges, lawyers, journalists and any others she thought worth cultivating with small gifts. I smiled in thanks but didn't pick up the pack.

"Let me get some tea," she said. I had been traveling all day and was exhausted. I thought of the thin green tea leaves slowly sinking in a mug of boiling water, releasing their steady stream of caffeine. I nodded and she got up to boil some water.

I got up and looked around while she busied herself in the kitchen. The apartment was probably twenty years old, a shabby concrete structure with low ceilings and small windows. Mr. Ma and his family had invested a bit of money in fixing up the inside, a sign that, for all the region's problems, living standards had risen. The floor had once been bare concrete but now was covered with big white tiles. The walls had light-colored plywood paneling that ran up from the floor to waist-level. Beige wallpaper covered the rest. The furnishings were black and massive. Up against one wall was a varnished pressboard entertainment center that held an enormous Panda-brand color television. A one-piece desk and chair requisitioned from the school stood up against a wall. The windows were guarded by steel burglar bars—the apartment was on the second floor and crime was a concern. Before sitting back down on the sofa, I studied a giant poster. It showed an enormous flower garden, probably computer-generated but meant to look like the orderly French gardens of Versailles. It was ubiquitous, hanging in countless restaurants and homes around the country.

Ms. Cao returned and quietly put down two paper cups filled with hot water and a few wispy green tea leaves. We were sitting across from each other; I waited for her to finish drinking from her cup. Ms. Cao held the cup gingerly and took a sip. Her face was square and pudgy, with almost no eyelashes and the faintest of eyebrows. She was dressed plainly in a plaid shirt tucked into blue cotton trousers.

I wondered if I should suggest that we go out to get something to eat. Her apartment could be bugged and I was worried about what the lawyers had said. If she was under surveillance, then my arrival might have been noticed. But I knew she was most familiar with her situation and didn't want to create an

unnecessary sense of paranoia. She put down the cup and began to talk.

"Teacher Ma," she said, using his old job title, "was arrested in Beijing on June 7, 1999, and put on trial on November 8 of that year. He was sentenced to five years in jail."

"And you appealed that?" I said.

"Yes, Teacher Ma's lawyer was excellent and he filed a rebuttal to the intermediate court two days later," she said, continuing on with a legal summary of his trial and imprisonment.

I thought it odd that she referred to him so distantly, by a title he hadn't used in years. But as she continued, I could see that she knew his case inside out and had an astounding command of legal vocabulary. She must have spent countless hours reading court documents and even more time recounting Mr. Ma's plight to people who might be of help. Slowly, I realized why she referred to him as "Teacher Ma." She'd dedicated her life to securing his release. The title was a way to keep his imprisonment factual and abstract, as though it were a stranger's fate. I interrupted her.

"How long have you been married?" I said.

"Thirty years."

"How did you meet?"

"We knew each other since childhood. We grew up in the same village up north."

Up north. The county where the peasants lived was north of here—the place I'd stopped for lunch. They came from there?

"In Zizhou County?" I asked.

She nodded.

"Of course. Our families were peasants. We went to elementary school together and junior high. We got married in 1962, when he was still in college. We've known each other all our lives."

Ms. Cao's voice trailed off and she looked down hard. I followed her glance downward and stared at the floor, allowing her to compose herself.

I noticed her shoes. She wore the kind of women's cotton shoes that few wear anymore. They were black, with brown plastic soles and a single black strap that goes over the top of the foot, fastening with a snap. Sometimes the shoes have flower embroidery but hers were plain. I hadn't seen a woman wear such shoes since I had first been in China in the 1980s. They were so old-fashioned they were almost ridiculous. But a different word came to mind, a Chinese word: *laoshi*. It means "honest," "truthful" and "good."

"So you've known him all your life?" I said. I wanted to say something more personal, like "you've loved him all your life," but it wasn't necessary.

"Yes. He's always been very naïve and stubborn. We went back to our hometown for New Year's and the peasants talked to him." Ms. Cao was now speaking in a torrent. "You know, I tried to make some arguments against taking the case, but he's stubborn, so stubborn. . . ."

Before she started crying, her daughter entered the room, carrying a tray of watermelon slices. She was tall, with short hair, thick lips and an angular face. Dressed in a long, tight lime-green dress, she looked eighteen. She put the plate down in front of us and then sat on a wooden chair in the corner by the window, staring intently, almost hostilely, at her mother.

"This is your daughter," I said to Ms. Cao. A boy ran in and picked up some toys that lay scattered around the room and ran over to the daughter. "And this is your son," I said to the daughter, quickly revising my estimate of her age.

The daughter smiled thinly. She looked at me skeptically and I didn't blame her. Maybe I was trouble. At the very least, I was

probably a waste of the family's time. I felt a chill of helplessness in the air and tried to turn the conversation back to a more neutral narrative of facts.

"How did your husband get involved in legal issues?" I asked Ms. Cao.

Ms. Cao picked up her story. She hadn't gone to college, but her husband had attended teacher's college in Xi'an, the provincial capital. He graduated in 1962 when he was twenty and was sent back up to the Loess Plateau. But instead of returning to his village, he went to Yan'an to work in the city's "Foreign Affairs Office." This is a typically communist institution, a committee that coordinates relations with the outside world—defined as anything beyond the narrow confines of the town or even the factory. This meant that officials from other parts of China visiting Yan'an would have their Foreign Affairs Office contact the Yan'an Foreign Affairs Office and arrange lodgings, meals, entertainment and all manner of appointments.

Mr. Ma worked there during the Cultural Revolution, when millions of young Red Guards descended on Yan'an to learn about the communists' legendary wartime base. But in 1978, when China embarked on capitalist-style reforms and Yan'an returned to being a backwater, his office was downsized and he was assigned to teach at a school run by the old Ministry of Post and Telecommunications. He joined the Communist Party in 1985, a normal move for a teacher, especially for someone who owed his education and job to the party.

"He'd always liked to write and did well teaching writing," Ms. Cao said, watching her grandson out of the corner of her eye. "He wrote a few essays on local history for the Yan'an newspaper and this launched his career."

In 1992 the provincial government asked him to write the Yan'an volume in a series of local histories it had commissioned.

That increased his fame, and the local government transferred him to the No. 3 Middle School in 1993 so he could teach Chinese and history instead of the basic-level engineering that he'd taught at the postal ministry's school.

Slowly, Mr. Ma began branching out into law. This might seem odd, but as in imperial China, a mastery of written Chinese is seen as essential for people who want to come into contact with the government. As China started to develop its legal system in the 1980s and 1990s, this is how people saw the law—as a modern form of petitioning that has existed in China for hundreds of years. Who better to work in the legal field than a gifted writer? This is especially true because in China's legal system lawyers rarely make grand speeches as they do in western countries. Juries do not exist, and cases are decided by a panel of judges that—if it hasn't been explicitly ordered to decide a certain way by the local branch of the Communist Party—bases its decision largely on the documents presented. Flowery rhetoric is rare, but a well-crafted letter could be helpful.

"People came by our home all the time, asking Teacher Ma for help writing lawsuits," Ms. Cao said. He bought books on the law and taught himself about it. In 1994 he passed a national test that gave him a Legal Service Work Permit, China's answer to its dearth of fully trained lawyers. Legal workers are allowed to handle civil cases and draw up court documents but not to defend people in criminal cases. Ms. Cao said her husband scaled back his teaching commitments and eventually quit to work as a legal worker for a local law firm, South City Legal Services.

Later, I talked to a representative of that firm who told me that Mr. Ma had been one of its best-known attorneys. Although he didn't have the title of lawyer, he was the firm's star. "People used to ask for him," the lawyer said. "That's uncommon. We usually just assign a lawyer to a case. It's especially uncommon

because he wasn't a lawyer but a legal services worker. But people thought he was the best and wanted him. He had a good track record."

Mr. Ma handled many economic contracts, but he excelled at civil suits, where a descriptive turn of phrase or dash of eloquence could be especially helpful in distinguishing one case from another. He was even allowed to handle the odd criminal case, although as a legal services worker he wasn't technically permitted to do so.

In fact, one of his biggest cases involved murder. It concerned a man whose wife had committed adultery. The two lovers plotted to kill the husband, who learned of the plot and, in a rage, stabbed his wife to death in their kitchen. Mr. Ma was asked to defend the husband and did so. The family was poor and Mr. Ma did it for free. Faced with the death penalty, the man got off with fifteen years in a labor camp after Mr. Ma pleaded extenuating circumstances—jealousy and self-defense.

"Everyone was sure it was execution," the lawyer at South City Legal Services said, making a pistol out of his hand and pointing it to the base of his skull. "But Old Ma pointed out the adultery and that it had been in a fit of rage. It took place during the high point of an anticrime campaign, but he still got the charge reduced to manslaughter. He really had a natural talent."

We took a break from our talk as Ms. Cao and her daughter got the young boy ready for bed. It was dark outside and the weather was changing. Hot and dry since the morning, the air was now damp and heavy. A cicada started to chirp. Others joined in and the buzz swelled into a deafening crescendo, broken only by the roar of two-stroke tractors that drove by every few minutes.

I got up to stretch and walked into an adjacent room. It was

the master bedroom and doubled as Mr. Ma's study. A small desk and bookcase were crowded into a corner. The bookcase had glass doors and I gingerly opened one. As I read the titles, it slowly sunk in that every single book in this bookcase was related to China's legal system. Among others, I saw *People's Republic of China Practical Guide to the Law and Legal Principles, Testing Material on the Law* and the *1998 Legal Yearbook,* filled with statistics on cases, rulings and the number of legal personnel in each city, province and territory. Mr. Ma had one shelf devoted to legal dictionaries, while others were stuffed with primers on the legal system, textbooks with case studies, books on economic law, civil law, criminal law and, most salient, administrative law, which Mr. Ma had used to sue the government on behalf of the peasants.

His desk was stacked with newspapers, the topmost dating from December 1999, by which time Mr. Ma had already been in jail for six months.

"I stopped ordering his newspapers then because I thought he wouldn't need them for a while."

Ms. Cao had walked in. There was a long silence and I fingered the yellowing stack.

"Everything he had was related to the legal system and to rule of law," Ms. Cao said. "All his books. All the newspapers that he read. He was obsessed with rule of law."

I pulled a photo album off the shelf. Inside were grainy black-and-white photos of Mr. Ma's and Ms. Cao's family. Taken in the 1960s, they looked like Mr. Ma in the photo I had of him: stern, formal and lifeless. They also reminded me of photos I'd seen from the nineteenth century, with everyone dour and serious; for many, it was probably the only photo they'd had taken in their lives.

All the men in the photos had white cloth caps on their heads. The caps fitted halfway down to the ears and had flat tops, making the wearers look like health care workers or cooks of some sort. Most men in this dry, barren backwater used to wear these caps, a tradition whose roots had long been forgotten. It was one of the few items of traditional attire that Chinese people still wore, but was found only here in a remote part of the country. It was another reminder that Mr. Ma's people were among the very poorest.

He must have been brilliant to have gotten out. He probably had also benefited from policies, long discarded, that helped find jobs and education for people from "correct" communist class backgrounds—workers, farmers and soldiers—and especially those who grew up in former communist guerilla bases, such as the region around Mr. Ma's hometown. A smart young peasant growing up in the 1950s right after the communists' "liberation" of China could have done worse than to have come from this arid patch of the country.

Few of the pictures were of Mr. Ma or his wife. Some were of his children, but even when they were growing up in the 1970s and the '80s, photography wasn't that widespread, especially in this small city. But his grandchildren—they were represented with dozens and dozens of photos, all in color. Shots of two chubby kids digging into a white-frosted birthday cake, with Mr. Ma peering on tentatively but proudly from the side. Another showing half a dozen adults grouped around a grandchild at a park.

Ms. Cao handed me one to keep. It showed her and Mr. Ma on a sofa with two other grandchildren. Ms. Cao is bouncing the younger on her knee, making him laugh. Next to an eight-year-old, Mr. Ma sits somewhat stiffly in a white dress shirt buttoned

up to the top, a cotton double-breasted blazer buttoned up as well. A glass of beer is next to him and a white birthday cake dominates the foreground. "It's my favorite," she said. "Take it."

I hesitated for a moment and decided to keep it. Then I pointed to one of the old grainy photos. "People like this—peasants—asked him to represent them, didn't they?"

"It was in early 1997 when he went back home to the countryside, up near Zizhou, to visit his mother," she said, sitting on the edge of the bed. "That's when it started."

Mr. Ma's hometown is a small village, Lijiaqu, which is located in Tuo'erxiang Township, which in turn is about seventeen miles from the county seat of Zizhou, the same town where I had stopped for lunch earlier in the day. Every year Chinese try to go back to their old home for Lunar New Year, and 1997 had been no different for Mr. Ma. Along with his wife, he returned to Lijiaqu to be with his mother and some close friends.

The Mas spent the holiday at home, preparing and eating big meals and relaxing—the television was on most of the time and the occasional game of mah-jongg broke out at a neighbor's house. Over the next few days farmers dropped by to visit the local son who'd made good, and they told him about their troubles. Drought had struck and they had difficulty making ends meet. As Mr. Wang had told me on the telephone when I called him from Zizhou at lunch, farmers who refused to pay—or in many cases couldn't pay—were beaten up and thrown in an improvised jail run by county leaders.

They'd all heard about the successful Peijiawan case. Like those farmers just a few miles away, Mr. Ma's relatives and friends had suffered from drought, seen their crops fail and been overtaxed. The farmers told Mr. Ma about their problems and asked him to help them sue the local government, just like the Peijiawan farmers had. I later met a farmer, wearing the same

white cap as Mr. Ma's ancestors, who told me their thinking: "Ma is from this town. He had a license to handle this sort of case. When he came back home, we told him that the township government is corrupt and had set up illegal jails to beat farmers. We begged him for help."

Mr. Ma was touched but refused. "I didn't want him to handle it and neither did he," his wife said. Mr. Ma told the peasants that the case was complicated and he was too busy to take on another big case.

Another reason was that his hometown was controlled by a different district government than the city of Yan'an where Mr. Ma now lived. This is a key distinction in China, where courts often take their instructions from the local government. Mr. Ma lived in Yan'an, and his hometown was controlled by the party office in Yulin. He had no contacts in the Yulin party committee, and if he got in trouble, he'd be on his own. Plus, he knew that China's legal system doesn't have the concept of precedents— courts often make rulings that completely ignore the fact that other courts have ruled differently in similar cases. So even though the Peijiawan farmers had won their case in the same jurisdiction as Yulin, he knew that would be meaningless when his case was tried. The whole enterprise seemed very risky, and after the holiday Mr. Ma went home.

But over the next few months the farmers kept calling Mr. Ma. The family didn't have a phone at the time, but the farmers reached him through a neighbor, who recalls Mr. Ma speaking with people from his hometown on the phone. "You could tell he wanted to help out but that he had some worries," the neighbor said. "He kept telling them how difficult the case would be. He understood the law and understood that their case would provoke a lot of political pressure."

But then, in the summer of 1997, Ms. Cao received a letter

from one of their daughters, who lived in Zizhou. Ms. Cao had to read the letter twice because she couldn't believe it. A rumor was rife in Zizhou that Mr. Ma had turned down the case because he'd been bribed by the Zizhou County government. When Mr. Ma came home that evening, she showed him the letter. He blew up.

"First he blamed our daughter and said she was crazy. Then he made some phone calls and realized it wasn't her fault," Ms. Cao said. "She was telling the truth. People really were saying this."

It was early July 1997, and Yan'an was hot and dry, just like today. Usually, it was a quiet time with little work and days spent outside the apartment block, sitting in the shade with neighbors. Those who could would go somewhere cool: a trip to China's distant coast was possible for the wealthy, but most lazed away the summer at home.

The rumor ate at Mr. Ma. Each morning he got up, bolted down a bowl of rice congee and headed over to his law office. He didn't come home for lunch, burying himself instead in his work in his near-deserted office. Back at home in the evenings, he didn't talk at dinner, stewing silently inside. He didn't speak the whole time.

On the fourth day he came home for lunch. Ms. Cao made a bowl of noodles. Halfway through, he looked at her and said, "I'll take the case." Ms. Cao started to object but checked herself. Her husband wasn't listening. Instead, he was intently polishing off his noodles. Two minutes later he got up and without another word went back to work.

"I think one of the farmers started it," Ms. Cao said to me, "knowing it would get Teacher Ma riled up and that he'd be

forced to take the case to prove he hadn't been bribed. Others say it was just a silly rumor."

Whatever the truth, Mr. Ma was now the farmers' advocate, and he set about winning for them tax relief just as the lawyers for the Peijiawan farmers had a year earlier. To him, just as to the Peijiawan lawyers, he had a straightforward case: local authorities could only tax farmers 5 percent of their income. But he could produce hundreds of witnesses with hard proof showing that they'd been taxed many times this amount. It was a simple administrative lawsuit. As far as he was concerned, it needn't have political implications. After gathering depositions and evidence, he filed the suit on behalf of several thousand farmers in the Yulin Intermediate Court that autumn. The exact number of farmers is hard to ascertain, since farmers continued to join the suit after it was filed. About 5,000 initially signed up, with tens of thousands more following by the end of the year.

Even though Mr. Ma had been reluctant to take on the case, he proceeded with an assumption that people in China have made for centuries: if only the upper levels knew of the true situation, then everything would be fine; it was all a question of lousy local administrators. The case, he figured, would alert regional leaders in Yulin that that farmers were overtaxed. They would order the judges to reduce the taxes and the farmers would win. Case closed.

Up until now I felt I understood Mr. Ma, but this made me wonder. If only top leaders knew? Top leaders benefit mightily from the current corrupt system: their sons and daughters study abroad, work for companies that pay them extravagant salaries for lending their family name and connections. If only they knew about corruption? If anyone was familiar with corruption, it was China's leaders. I had immense respect for what Mr. Ma had tried to do but wondered how he had clung to this idea. It probably explained why China's rulers had stayed in power for so long.

"In the early stage of the case he was naïve," Ms. Cao said. "He didn't know the complexity of society. He thought that the farmers had these difficulties just because the upper-level government didn't know the facts about the real difficulties in the village. He thought he should represent these facts to the upper level. Teacher Ma has always trusted the party and the government, even though he's in jail. He thinks that it's only that people conceal facts."

Over the next two years Mr. Ma was slowly disabused of this view. After preparing his case in the summer of 1997, he went to Yulin and filed. But just six months after it had judged in favor of the peasants in the almost identical Peijiawan case, the court refused to even accept, let alone hear, Mr. Ma's case. He received no written explanation. Later, when he asked around, he heard that the reason was the government had issued a new order instructing the courts to reject such cases.

"If he'd been from Yulin, anyone could have told him that after the Peijiawan case the courts weren't taking any more peasant class-action lawsuits," a lawyer in Yulin said. "That case shocked the district government and it had ordered the courts that no more cases were to be accepted."

Indeed, even the Peijiawan case had attracted a backlash. As I'd learned upon leaving Peijiawan village eighteen months earlier, some people in power weren't happy with the lawsuit. And although Mr. Ma didn't know it at the time he took the case, those responsible for abusing the peasants in Peijiawan hadn't been demoted or fired. Indeed, according to officials in the Yulin government, some had been promoted.

Unsure what to do, Mr. Ma went back to his home and spent a week in September with his mother. The farmers kept coming by to complain. For thirty years he'd been away, returning

only at the holiday season for the annual family reunion, with days spent drinking and feasting. This time around, in autumn, he could see the pitiful harvest that was being wrung out of the cracked fields. The endless droughts were again afflicting the town. And the annual taxes, although not as high as the previous year's, were staggering—on average 100 yuan, or $12, per head.

Many peasants were sure that Mr. Ma had come back to announce his decision to quit. It was a reasonable assumption. After all, the courts had rejected the case and it seemed hopeless. He stayed with his mother, however, and talked to friends. He didn't announce his plans and the peasants held their breath.

Then, two days before he was due to head home to Yan'an, a farmer came by, a man who had been friends with Mr. Ma's father. The man told of how he'd been arrested and beaten the previous year, in the autumn of 1996. His wife had gone to visit the man in the local jail, hoping to give him a blanket. She was refused permission and told to return home. Her husband was a prisoner, she was told, and didn't have a right to a blanket, even though it was below freezing at night and he was being held in a makeshift jail in a pigsty. Angry, she cursed the government official. He struck her. "What's the world coming to when they do this," the peasant told Mr. Ma.

"I remember him sitting in his mother's cave, listening to the story. His face had no expression, but his eyes were wide open, angry like a demon's," the neighbor said. "The government said Ma tried to stir up our sentiment, but it was we farmers who stirred up Ma."

Something changed. Mr. Ma, who had been a legal worker, an amateur lawyer and lover of the law, decided that the law wasn't able to protect the farmers. What was needed, he thought,

was some political pressure from below to break the logjam in Yulin. Lawsuits hadn't worked. He decided to arouse leaders' attention by leading a few small protests.

Naïve, or figuring they had nothing to lose, Mr. Ma and his farmer clients decided that autumn to set up an organization to promote their cause: the Tuo'erxiang County Farmers Anti-corruption and Reducing Tax Burden Volunteer Liaison Small Group. Quite a mouthful, the title was meant to convey the group's apolitical and nonthreatening nature. It was simply "anticorruption" and for "reducing the tax burden"—two officially recognized national priorities. In addition, it was made up of volunteers and its function simply one of liaising—not of "organizing," an action that authorities dread the most. Even the odd term "Small Group" was meant to convey a sense of informality. It is a communistspeak word that means a body that is a step down from a more formal committee or commission and thus not menacing to the government.

Like the Peijiawan farmers, Mr. Ma's farmers elected representatives, who met several times that autumn and collected money. And just like the Peijiawan farmers, who had collected the equivalent of 25 cents from each farmer, the Tuo'erxiang farmers collected roughly the same amount from the 40,000 residents in their township. Authorities later accused the farmers of "United Front tactics"—a reference to a communist strategy of minimizing radical policies and winning support from moderates in society. Authorities consider this dangerous because the Communist Party often preaches United Front tactics—moderation, in other words—as a front for its own radicalism. To a government accustomed to such devious tactics, the peasants' moderation seemed like a cover.

The fateful plunge occurred on November 2, 1997, a Sunday and a market day in the township. A farmer in Mr. Ma's village donated his belching two-stroke tractor. The men draped it with white cloth banners, writing in red and black calligraphy slogans calling for taxes to be reduced. One of the farmers sat up front on the single seat, grasping the long handlebars that control the steering, speed and braking. Attached to the back of the two-wheeled tractor was a small cart draped with the banners and two large speakers that blared out a tape recording of Mr. Ma reading the central government's directives on tax reduction. It was a primitive version of the small trucks with loudspeakers and banners that you see during elections in Taiwan and Japan. The group drove their "propaganda vehicle," as the government later called it, from Mr. Ma's home village of Lijiaqu to the village of Tuo'erxiang, the seat of Tuo'erxiang Township.

At the end of the ten-mile trip, the farmers and Mr. Ma handed out central government documents on taxation. They took the banners off their wagon and hung them up. Hanging limply in the dusty haze, they read: "Reduce Peasants' Burden" and "Taxation According to Law."

Standing underneath the banners, with his propaganda tractor parked nearby, Mr. Ma gave a speech that attracted several hundred onlookers, who crowded the denuded slopes. The market closed down and people roared their approval as Mr. Ma spoke, easily mixing the modern terms of the law with the local dialect.

"All we are asking is that the local government follow the central government's directives," Mr. Ma said. "Our fields have suffered from drought, but officials treat them like they're heavy with corn. They're trying to squeeze oil out of chaff."

About four hours later, the farmers dispersed, heading back to their villages flush with Mr. Ma's ringing rhetoric and clutch-

ing material that explained the government's official tax policies. Unwritten on the flyers but circulating quickly was the story of how Mr. Ma had tried to file a lawsuit but had been rejected. The "liaison small group" believed they had failed because they hadn't garnered the thousands of signatures that the Peijiawan farmers had a year earlier. This rally, they figured, would fire up the farmers and make them willing to sign a petition that would later be circulated.

The next day, the Public Security Bureau contacted Mr. Ma, who was holding a strategy meeting with delegates in a nearby village. Officers asked Mr. Ma to go to Zizhou for questioning. In its charges against Mr. Ma the government says he told the farmers: "We should go together, otherwise I won't go. I won't talk by myself. If we want to talk, we should talk together. If one says something wrong, the other can correct it. They'll take notes. We should take notes as well."

I am not sure why the government put that citation in its charges against Mr. Ma. Perhaps prosecutors thought this showed his devious nature. For example, his advice on taking notes could be construed as giving the peasants clever, lawyerly advice that they wouldn't have thought of themselves—the sort of thing the government must have hated about Mr. Ma. To me it just showed common sense and his desire, even at this stage, not to take too direct a lead in the proceedings. He didn't want to be pegged as the ringleader and wanted to protect the movement against government efforts to split it, perhaps by offering some leaders a bribe to disband.

Agreeing with Mr. Ma's suggestion, about seventy delegates accompanied Mr. Ma the next day to meet with the Public Security Bureau in Zizhou. Some of the farmers saw this meeting with the police as a big victory: at last they'd have a chance to state their case to someone other than the corrupt officials in their

township. Others, probably Mr. Ma himself, realized that this was a dangerous new phase to the confrontation.

The Public Security Bureau occupies one of the best buildings in Zizhou, a five-story white-tiled building off one of the main streets. It is surrounded by a 10-foot wall and has an accordionlike antiterrorist gate that moves from right to left along tracks—the sort of gate designed to stop mobs and suicide bombers driving a truck. I don't think China has ever had such a suicide attack, and it always struck me as incomprehensible why so many government offices in China, from museums and hospitals to schools and welfare offices, had installed this sort of gate. It seemed a mixture of paranoia and fad—the latest way for unaccountable officials to waste people's money.

The seventy farmers followed Mr. Ma through the front gate and into the courtyard. A dozen accompanied him farther inside, where they met the head of the local office over tea at a conference table. Even though some farmers had accompanied him, Mr. Ma was clearly the spokesman. He sat at the center of the table and was the only one capable of speaking the security bureau's language of laws and regulations.

Mr. Ma and his supporters asked for the security bureau's help in righting their wrong, while the bureau insisted they disband and "go through normal channels." Mr. Ma was polite, agreeing that he should have asked for a permit to hold his small rally on market day. But he also said the farmers have a right to protest and appeal—rights enshrined in the constitution, although not taken too seriously by the government.

After an hour the meeting broke up and Mr. Ma returned to the village to spend the night. At first the group had been elated that the government officials had deigned to meet them. But the meeting had been unproductive and the farmers were now angry. Mr. Ma, too, was a changed man. His caution had gone, and he

saw that the government structure in the county—not just the lower-level officials in the village and township—were corrupt and working hand in hand. "Ma asked if we should push forward," one farmer recalled, becoming excited at the memory of the meeting. "And we all said 'Yes, yes, yes.' "

Mr. Ma and the delegates decided they'd have to appeal to the district government in Yulin. This way they'd go over the heads of the county courts and government, in hopes the higher-ranking officials in the district government would order the local courts to accept the case. After all, the Peijiawan case had been tried in Yulin, so judges and their party overseers must be more enlightened there, the farmers figured. They needed to rent trucks to carry the farmers the ninety-miles north to Yulin, so Mr. Ma suggested raising some more money—the equivalent of another 25 cents or so from each farmer should do it, he figured.

On November 4, 1997, the day after the meeting with the Public Security Bureau, Mr. Ma again met with his delegates and planned the trip to Yulin later that month. He was now working closely with two delegates, Ma Quan and Ma Dengde, who despite sharing the same surname weren't directly related to him or each other. The three of them easily raised the money and agreed to expand their publicity campaign to neighboring Nanchuan Township, which also fell under Zizhou County's jurisdiction. Representatives from that township soon pledged support.

On November 19, Mr. Ma and about two hundred farmers traveled to Yulin to submit a written appeal to the district government, asking leaders to reverse their ban on local courts from hearing the farmers' case. A relic of the imperial era, submitting written petitions and appeals has been preserved as a safety valve for those who have lost everything. Many bureaus accept petitions and appeals in China—from district and provincial

offices all the way to the State Council, China's quasi-cabinet that runs the day-to-day operations of government in Beijing. Few petitioners win, but many of China's dispossessed see it as a last hope.

The crowd went to the center of power in Yulin—not the courts or the district government but to the district's Communist Party headquarters. This is the office that holds sway over the courts, appoints government leaders and directly controls the police and security apparatus. For three days the farmers stayed in Yulin, assembling every morning in front of the party head-quarters, holding up banners, many of which had already flown about two weeks earlier during their initial rally in the market town.

According to the government, the rallies were gigantic demonstrations that disrupted the city and government. Mr. Ma, in his defense statement, portrayed the days in Yulin quite differently:

> The truth was that only four or five farmer representa-
> tives and I were broadcasting recordings on the street
> and reading the central government's documents and
> policies. But the prosecutor doesn't care about testi-
> mony or evidence and distorted the facts, even saying I
> was stirring up the masses to confront the government.
> Isn't this a deliberate distortion of facts and claiming
> black is white and white black?

Indeed, the government's charge sheet did seem to be stretching things:

> The appellants created disturbances in the courtyard of
> the prefectural Party committee. They blocked up the

traffic in the lanes to the courtyard of the prefectural Party committee. They grabbed the food from the prefectural Party committee's cooking stove and beat up the cooks and administration people. They stopped the county leaders. They stole local residents' coal and made a "pagoda pyre" of the coal. The normal work order of the prefectural Party committee was disrupted by them until they left on November 22.

It is possible to imagine that the farmers were running out of money, desperate and hungry—so perhaps they asked for a meal. I wondered if the cooks had refused to serve them, or maybe they were just incensed at the food being served to the party cadres while their families went hungry back home.

As for stealing coal blocks, the lawyers I'd talked to in Yulin, even those who thought Mr. Ma probably shouldn't have led the appeal, shook their heads in disbelief. "What would the farmers do with coal blocks?" one lawyer told me, rolling his eyes. "They just had a few trucks so could barely fit all the farmers on the trucks. They weren't about to start carting coal back to the hills."

After two days the peasants and Mr. Ma headed back to the hills. From a hesitant participant, Mr. Ma was now a *nongmin yingxiong*. The term *yingxiong* is often translated as "hero" but I thought that "champion" captured the way that people there viewed him: as someone fighting for their cause. The ambiguities of the Chinese language also allowed for different ways of looking at Mr. Ma. He could be a "peasants' champion" or simply a "peasant champion"—the possessive is often dropped or unclear in Chinese. Probably the former was more accurate because he wasn't, strictly speaking, a peasant anymore. But his roots were in the countryside, and he took on the case because of his rural

pedigree. He was a peasant who'd obtained an education and now returned to the corrupt countryside as its champion.

In December of that same year, Mr. Ma began to spread the word throughout the county. In yet another township, Zhuan-miao, he and peasants held rallies. According to the government documents and interviews with farmers, Mr. Ma was now far beyond his role of passive advocate for farmers' interests. While most of the banners they hung up still had plain, unemotive language such as "Taxation According to Law," new slogans began to appear urging wavering peasants to participate. "What Are You Afraid Of?" hung at one meeting, a elderly farmer recalled.

"We'd been afraid for years, afraid of the government and its police," the farmer said, tugging at the white wisps of a beard growing from his chin. "But Ma's point was that what we wanted was legal. There was nothing to be afraid of."

On January 3, 1998, during what the government called an "illegal" gathering—all meetings must be approved by the government in one way or another—two farmers were detained. Mr. Ma was back with his family in Yan'an but called up the delegates, the government claimed, and "stirred up the people to go to the Public Security Bureau and obtain their release." Mr. Ma said in his written self-defense that he had simply advised the farmers to go to the police and ask for the farmers' release. He didn't participate himself.

Throughout 1998, Mr. Ma devoted more and more of his time to the farmers' suit. Indeed, his family recalls that since taking the case in 1997 he had largely given up other suits, sacrificing his steady income for what at best would result in a meager return. The Peijiawan farmers had won just $75,000 and the legal fees amounted to just 10 percent of this for a team of lawyers, including their expenses. Mr. Ma would have been lucky to cover his expenses and earn a tiny profit.

Far from shielding Mr. Ma from charges of being motivated by greed, his willingness to do basically pro bono work appeared suspicious to the authorities. "They asked me in 1998 what Ma was up to," said a lawyer from the South City Legal Services firm. "If he wasn't making much money on this, which I agreed he wasn't, then they wondered if he wasn't just a troublemaker trying to stir things up."

To make things worse, in the government's eyes, Mr. Ma began spreading his organizational methods to other farmers. In Miaojiaping, a township about ten miles down the road from Tuo'erxiang, peasants set up their own "Anticorruption Liaison Office" that drafted its own plan of action, including propaganda cars, banners and speeches. "Ma planted seeds across the county," a farmer said, scratching his white skullcap. "We were learning about our rights."

The government saw it differently. In assessing blame for crises it creates, the communists like to find "black hands" to blame. In Beijing's myopic world, its inherently corrupt and unstable system of government is never to blame; instead, instigators whip up the innocent masses. This allows the government to avoid confronting the real causes of unrest. This was the way the 1989 Tiananmen massacre was dealt with (a few troublemakers had riled up the students) and how the Falun Gong protests that started in 1999 were explained (a few organizers were to blame). And this was how Zizhou's peasant uprising was seen.

In its charges against him, the procurator laid the blame squarely with Mr. Ma, resorting to subjective, flowery language that reflected the government's anger. "On November 18, 1998, Ma Wenlin even personally attended an illegal gathering in Wancha [village]. He made speeches and his abominable influence radiated to every village and town in the county, seriously affecting the stable unity of Zizhou."

Reading the charges, one gets the feeling the government was searching for something to pin on Mr. Ma. Up until now his actions hadn't been all that radical. Boiled down, they amounted to publicizing government tax policies. Some of the meetings might have been illegal, but it would have been hard to jail Mr. Ma—who after all was a member of the same legal profession as the courts and judges that would try him.

In China, urbanites are afraid of the country's 800 million peasants because of this gut feeling that, once aroused, they can't be controlled. For the most part, this is bunk. Farmers in China are by and large cautious and only do what they figure is in their best interests. But mass action does have its own dynamic, and sometimes things can spin out of control. Maybe this is what happened next. In any case, it was exactly what the government needed to jail the peasant champion.

Ms. Cao and I stopped talking for a moment. We sat facing each other, I on a chair and she on the side of the bed, her face framed by the yellowing white wall behind her. The room was lit by an electric bulb, which hung from the ceiling, its dim rays searching the four bare corners for shadows. It was late and she was tired, the creases on her face made harsher by the crude lighting.

This was the hardest part of the story for her, the event that she'd gone over in her head time and again, trying to re-create a different outcome. She looked at me pleadingly. "I regret that I let him handle this case," she said, carefully putting her hand palms down on her lap as if to straighten out the sequence of events. "But we couldn't prevent him. You know, he found those farmers really pitiful. He tried to be careful. We always urged him to be careful."

On April 8, 1999, the county sent a senior official named

Zhao Liang to Laoshanmao, one of the centers of activism. According to the government, he was sent to check the village's books—in the government's words to "learn about the opinions and come up with an analysis." It sounded as if someone was finally listening to the peasants.

Mr. Zhao arrived late that afternoon and immediately conferred with the local village secretary. They had dinner and then around 10 p.m. went into the local village committee's office to look over the books. After a couple of hours the two men went to sleep in the office, intending to pick up first thing in the morning.

It seemed an odd time to audit the village's finances, and word spread through the village about the odd audit. Seven senior men, all surnamed Ma (but not related to Mr. Ma) walked down to the office, a small one-story building in the center of the village. They conferred outside for about five minutes. They didn't trust Mr. Zhao. He worked in the county seat of Zizhou and oversaw all villages' finances as head of the Village Basic Level Organizational Rectification and Construction Work Team, a powerful body that reported directly to the district's Communist Party. In that capacity he already had copies of the villagers' finances. He must be there to doctor the originals and cover the tracks of the wrongdoers. Their precious evidence was about to disappear.

The seven men decided to act. They threw themselves against the flimsy wooden door, breaking the lock off cleanly. Mr. Zhao and the village party secretary leapt up, the books behind them. The seven men asked for the books. Mr. Zhao refused, saying he still had not finished.

The seven insisted and moved forward. Mr. Zhao swallowed hard and handed the books over. Under the dim bare bulb the nine men huddled over the books. Look at the incomes ascribed to various farmers, they said; such incomes were impossibly high

for poor loess farmers. How could they pay 5 percent on such figures? Mr. Zhao squirmed through the lesson and admitted he had no answers. The farmers' decision: detain Mr. Zhao until he provided satisfaction.

The next morning, April 9, Mr. Ma came to Laoshanmao on one of his now regular semimonthly trips to the countryside. The government says the farmers asked Mr. Ma what to do about Mr. Zhao. Should they release the official? Quoting one of the farmer delegates who oversaw the kidnapping, the government claims that Mr. Ma said, "Don't release Zhao or what we've done for the past two years will be in vain." Mr. Ma supposedly asked for two copies of the village's books and then organized villagers to watch over the official.

This version of events is impossible to corroborate and it was never proved in court. According to Mr. Ma's written self-defense, he never instructed the farmers to keep Mr. Zhao and didn't even know the official was being held. Farmers agreed. "Ma never asked us or advised us about Zhao," one farmer later told me in an interview. "We were just so angry at the idea of him taking away our evidence that we grabbed him."

The government's case is based on the testimony of one of the seven men, Ma Quan, who had worked closely with Mr. Ma over the previous year. He was close to Mr. Ma but also had something to gain by his testimony: the government documents say he had been the chief spokesman for the kidnappers, meaning he faced a stiff sentence unless he cooperated—a decade in a labor camp wouldn't have been unusual. Under many legal systems such potentially biased testimony could have been called into question. But here it formed the sole basis of Mr. Ma's arrest and imprisonment.

Reading through the accounts of events and talking to witnesses, what comes through clearest was the government's anger

that this lawyer had taught peasants all this highfalutin legal talk. For example, in describing Mr. Ma's alleged role in the kidnapping, the court papers said he told the peasants to "speak artfully" with officials, as if this were a crime. In one other case the documents said Mr. Ma told a farmer: "If they want to arrest you, give them your hands and let them. Then send someone to me." This sounds like the soundest advice a lawyer can give a client—don't resort to violence, let your lawyer get you off—yet was used in summation as evidence of Mr. Ma's errors.

"Ma never admitted what he did and never regretted it," the indictment concluded. "Therefore according to the law he should be punished severely." It was the millennia-old slogan used by prosecutors in China: leniency to those who confess, severity to those who do not. Stripped down, this means: we'll break you if you stand up for your innocence.

And indeed, the government did break Mr. Ma.

"This was delivered to us in June, shortly after he was arrested," Ms. Cao said, reaching down under the bed and pulling out a black leather attaché case. It was the sort of shoulder bag that many Chinese men carry—most stuff them in the front basket of their bicycles or carry them under their arm like a football.

She got up and walked back into the living room. I followed and we sat down. She put the bag on the coffee table between us. She opened the bag and pulled out a towel caked in blood.

The alleged kidnapping in April 1999 had ended after fifteen days when the government negotiated the official's release. County officials in Zizhou sent a delegation to the village, and after several days of talks the peasants had agreed to let the official go if their concerns were taken seriously. But they knew that the promises were empty—after all, the officials making the

promises were colleagues of the official whom they suspected of doctoring the books. "They were all in it together," a peasant later told me. "We needed to bypass the county."

Her husband agreed with the peasants, Ms. Cao said.

"He thought that his only hope lay in getting the central government to pay attention," she said, looking down and shaking her head. "He was so naïve."

But it wasn't completely a move of desperation. Mr. Ma's original efforts to file the case—like the successful class-action case in the next valley—had been reported in the national Chinese media. In 1998 the newspaper that is run by the country's Ministry of Justice, *Legal Daily*, published a favorable article. So, too, did *Focus Report*, the country's leading investigative television newsmagazine, run by the central government's television network.

"He thought that with all this favorable publicity and the fact that they'd accepted the other case, all he had to do was make the central government understand and it would support him," Ms. Cao said.

After talking it over with farmers in June 1999, Mr. Ma was ready to set off with five of the elected delegates to Beijing. Their goal was to file a written appeal with the central government asking for intervention. Local authorities were nervous, and before he left for Beijing, the Zizhou County Public Security Bureau made several trips to Mr. Ma's house.

"They were courteous," Ms. Cao said. "But they didn't want Teacher Ma to go. They said that he had done his best for the peasants and that he'd reached the end of his legal appeals. They said we should all be reasonable and drop it," Ms. Cao said.

But Mr. Ma was beyond making the endless compromises that define life in China. He'd backed off cases before and had always been willing to listen to the party's legal affairs committee

when it deemed a case sensitive. This time, however, he felt his countrymen—the families he'd grown up with on the Loess Plateau—were facing an economic catastrophe. This time events would be pushed to their logical conclusion. Mr. Ma listened to the officials and thanked them for the visit. Then he made his travel arrangements for Beijing.

On July 7, Mr. Ma arrived in Beijing with his five companions. The next day they made their way to the State Council's Petitions and Appeals Office. He'd taken farmers to a local-level version of this office in Yulin about eighteen months ago. Now he was at the modern-day equivalent of the emperor's appeal office. Located up an unmarked alley on the south side of Beijing, the office is guarded by plainclothes police, who block people who they think will cause trouble.

Mr. Ma went in and registered. A few minutes later a receptionist came out and asked which of them was Ma Wenlin. Mr. Ma raised his hand, and the receptionist ushered him in for a talk. He was led to a small room where two men sat. They said they were from the Beijing Public Security Bureau. Mr. Ma asked for identification. The two, probably warned by their colleagues in Zizhou that Mr. Ma was a troublemaker, beat him. He lost thirteen teeth and stanched the bleeding with the towel that lay before me on the table.

I picked up the towel. It was caked in blood, but I tried to put myself in the government's position. They'd argue that it could be anyone's blood. Even if it was Mr. Ma's, it could have been from a bad nosebleed.

Then I looked inside the bag. It was filled with legal books, including the *Handbook of Legal Terms* and *Legal Questions*. There was a pair of plastic-framed eyeglasses and a cheap flexband wristwatch. Tucked into a side pocket was a copy of *Legal*

Daily from June 1, 1998, about a year before he was arrested. A long article on page 3 detailed the Tuo'erxiang case and was critical of the court's refusal to accept it. This must have been Mr. Ma's sustenance—an article published by the Justice Ministry's official newspaper arguing that he was right, that the courts should hear his case. The bag belonged to a dedicated lawyer who mistakenly felt he had the system on his side. Not a hell-raiser or criminal.

I sat holding the cloth like a talisman. For Ms. Cao it was a relic, proof of what had befallen her husband. To a government using laws to rule the country, it was easily refutable evidence. Ms. Cao put the articles back in the bag and walked out of the room.

After the beating, Mr. Ma was taken to a hospital, where he was told that said his injuries weren't serious. He was returned to the Public Security Bureau in Beijing, which held him until July 12. Then the Zizhou Public Security Bureau picked him up—odd considering that Mr. Ma lived in another county—and took him to jail in Yulin. It was only four months later, on November 10, 1999, that Ms. Cao was allowed to see him. She picked up his black bag and delivered some clothes. By then Mr. Ma's fate was sealed: five years in a labor camp.

The trial, though, was hardly insignificant. The outcome was never in doubt, but through it Mr. Ma became even more of a rallying point for the legal community—not just here up on the Loess Plateau, but down in the provincial capital of Xi'an, which is one of China's most important cities. It turned Mr. Ma into a local martyr.

The case relied on the flimsiest of evidence: one witness who had overseen the kidnapping of an official. That gave him a

vested interest in fingering Mr. Ma and, indeed, he had received a drastically reduced sentence. In addition, the charges were written in highly unprofessional language. Mr. Ma, for example, was accused of "pretending" to be a lawyer, when in fact he had the legal credentials to handle civil cases, including the peasants' administrative lawsuit.

In addition, the case was marred by procedural irregularities. From the start, Mr. Ma had been vigorously defended by a local lawyer, Feng Xuewen. But Mr. Feng had immediately run up against numerous signals that the trial would be a sham. On October 15, 1999, for example, Mr. Feng went to get a copy of the prosecutor's charges against Mr. Ma and was told he could only copy the first page. The formal list of charges detailing which crimes Mr. Ma had committed were off limits. Only after he protested was he allowed to see the charges.

On October 27, Mr. Feng was told the case would be tried on November 1 and was instructed to hand in his defense statement. Two days later the trial was delayed until November 3 after prosecutors said they wanted to have time to study Mr. Feng's defense plans. On October 31, he handed in his defense statement and the list of witnesses he planned to call. At the top of the list were the peasant delegates who'd hired Mr. Ma.

Police went out and arrested Mr. Feng's six witnesses. Two were released the next day, but four were kept in jail. The next day Mr. Feng asked that his witnesses be allowed to testify in court. The request was denied on grounds that the witnesses didn't want to testify and had also recanted what they'd said in their depositions. Suspicious, Mr. Feng filed another written request to the court, noting that it had the power to require witnesses to testify. Surely, at least those in its custody could testify. Again, a rejection.

The court now delayed the proceedings until November 8. On that day, just before the hearing was due to start, Mr. Feng learned that two of the three judges on the panel deciding the case had participated in drawing up the charges. So intertwined are China's police, prosecutor's office and judicial panels that such events are not uncommon. Mr. Feng asked that at least one of the two be removed from the panel. Another rejection.

The next day, evidence was to be presented to the court. Mr. Feng's six witnesses had now been turned against Mr. Ma, all providing written statements that Mr. Ma was guilty. Mr. Feng stood up and asked that the witnesses give their testimony in court.

"If not," Mr. Feng told the panel of judges, "then one might wonder how the prosecution obtained the testimony."

The allusion to torture wasn't lost on the judges. Infuriated, they ordered him to sit down and not question the evidence. In fact, they said, he had no right to raise questions and must remain silent for the rest of the trial.

Mr. Feng collected his papers and walked out of the courtroom in protest. The trial lasted another day and ended on November 10.

Without a lawyer, Mr. Ma had to represent himself, an irony considering the fact that as a "legal worker" he wasn't allowed to represent clients in criminal cases and had been criticized by the government for overstepping his powers in representing the farmers. As the government presented its case to the judges, Mr. Ma sat in the courtroom in Zizhou and wrote down his thoughts.

What flowed out was an amazing document, a twenty-six-page handwritten self-defense that showed how Mr. Ma had won his reputation. Copies of the document have become coveted among local lawyers. Written on tissue-thin lined paper a bit smaller than regular letter size, the rebuttal cited Chinese law to

show how his legal work had been within the framework of China's existing legal system. It is a robust defense of independent legal work, at times eloquent:

> As is my responsibility as a legal worker, I was just explaining the central government's policies and related laws. The farmers grasped this. The burden on peasants is a key issue that can influence reforms and stability. If it isn't firmly solved then it will harm the national economy and development. But if we could solve the problems, the government would love the people and the people would love the government.

To the end he was unrepentant. As he wrote: "Formerly, when peasants met government cadres who committed illegal activities, they didn't dare confront them. Now those cadres don't dare charge farmers randomly or fine them. They won't dare bully them."

Six days later the verdict was delivered: five years, exactly what the prosecution had requested. His sentence started the day he was arrested and beaten in Beijing. He would be released July 7, 2004.

Mr. Feng immediately wrote an appeal and filed it on November 30, 1999. He also began organizing pressure in the provincial capital of Xi'an. In mid-December he held a meeting of two dozen legal experts, including many prominent law professors. Besides roundly condemning the sentence, the experts called for the case to be reheard and overturned.

Shortly thereafter, Mr. Feng filed his defense statement for the appeal. It is a blunt, eighteen-page document that details Mr.

Feng's travails and Mr. Ma's efforts. Reading it, I couldn't help contrasting its factual analysis with the government's empty rhetorical blasts. In its charges, the government alleged that Ma had committed a dozen crimes, yet it furnishes no proof for any of its charges.

Mr. Feng noted that these crimes—disrupting traffic, disturbing the workings of the government and even of the government's canteen—could be objectively proven if they were true. If the district capital's traffic had been paralyzed, why couldn't the government show one traffic report? If protesters had really overrun the district's Communist Party headquarters—an absurd proposition given the security at such locations—why no police reports of disruptive protests?

He answered his own question in another part of the defense. In it he defended Mr. Ma's goal of representing the peasants in their fight for a more just society. It was an idealistic vision, one that challenged the government on its own terms: China's need for "social order." This is a claim heard endlessly from government officials. Democracy and freedoms, they argue, are well and good, but disorder would be a fatal flaw to China. It would be a throwback to the chaos of the Cultural Revolution and disrupt the steady gains in standards of living and political freedoms.

Mr. Feng didn't deny these arguments. No one, he says, wants to see China slip into disorder. But a death grip is not stability. The inability to change may in the short term look like a virtue, but in the long term it is a weakness, suppressing natural change and leading to violent outbursts.

"During this period [of protests], the social order of Tuo'erxiang was an abnormal social order," Mr. Feng wrote. "It was a social order of increasing burdens that farmers couldn't accept. The farmers rose up, struggling hard to make of Tuo'erxiang a

good, just social order, a social order where reasonable taxes were paid."

On December 28 the appeals court reached its verdict: The lower court's decision was upheld. Mr. Ma faced five years in prison.

Ms. Cao had been confident that the court in Yulin would reopen the case. One good sign was that *Legal Daily,* the newspaper that is run by the Ministry of Justice in Beijing and which had reported favorably on Mr. Ma's efforts in 1998, had written a report in early 2000 criticizing the local courts. The report was an "internal" article written for leaders only, but it was a good sign that word of Mr. Ma's innocence was filtering out.

"I went to Yulin and talked to a medium-level official about the case. I told him that I will keep suing and suing until I die," Ms. Cao said. "That man told me, 'You already have sued and sued and where do you want to sue now? How will you afford it?' "

It was a good question. Even if the court in Yulin were instructed to reopen the case, Ms. Cao would have to hire a senior lawyer—only they can handle suits brought before intermediate courts. One from Beijing would cost the equivalent of $12,500, and even an ordinary lawyer from Xi'an would cost about a tenth of that—completely out of the question for a schoolteacher like herself making $100 a month.

So, like her husband, Ms. Cao decided to learn the law herself. "I ended up using some of Teacher Ma's books," she said, again using his formal title. "I wrote a new defense statement myself last month (July 2000). When some farmers heard that I was going to try to get it reopened, they sent me three written testimonials saying they'd encouraged Ma and that he'd just been their representative. It was courageous. I sent it all to the court in Yulin."

It was indeed courageous. A few days later police went to Tuo'erxiang and arrested the three farmers who had given Ms. Cao the written testimony.

Ms. Cao now sees her husband about once a week. He is held in a labor camp several hours outside town, where he works printing materials for the government. Mr. Ma had been arrested for spreading what was supposed to be the law of the land. Now he was in jail printing government documents.

"He's not mistreated," Ms. Cao said. "But he has a heart condition and there's no medication for him. We've applied for him to be released on medical parole, but people in Zizhou are afraid of him getting out of jail."

I later learned that the Shenmu Prison, where he was being held, put in two requests in 2002 for Mr. Ma to be released early. Prison officials say Mr. Ma is a model prisoner, teaching other inmates reading and mathematics. The request for early release was denied by provincial authorities.

I walked back to the hotel through the honking traffic and heavying air. The crumbling mountains blotted out most of the sky, and threatening clouds covered the rest. The city seemed to revel in the approaching storm, with the late-night streets crowded with people walking, shopping and selling. I bought a bowl of noodles from a street vendor and stared at the dark hills.

The heat that had been building up finally broke the next day. I woke to rain and after talking to a few drivers decided to abandon my plan of driving back to Xi'an. A new highway was under construction, forcing drivers to take a long detour through dirt roads. Those roads had now turned to mud, and the trip to the provincial capital would take eight hours by car.

I decided to take the train later in the day and began to pack my bags. The phone rang.

"Come down to the lobby," someone said in a thick accent. "I want to tell you something about Ma Wenlin."

I went down and looked around the lobby. It was small, with a counter over to the left and a couple of sofas to the right. The receptionist looked at me and, with a frown, cast her gaze at a man who didn't belong here: a farmer with a white skullcap and a faded blue cotton jacket. I walked over and greeted him like an old friend. The sofas were empty, so we sat down and chatted. The receptionist shrugged and returned to her books.

"I heard from friends that you were going to Yan'an, so I came to tell you about us," the farmer said, speaking in quick, low tones.

He'd arrived late the previous night and had stayed with friends, bunking in a dormitory at a construction company. He looked around, eager to go. Then he slid over a big brown envelope. "We're still active," he said. "Look."

I opened the frayed envelope and pulled out a thick document. It was a copy of a typed, twenty-one-page petition signed by 30,166 farmers from Tuo'erxiang and the two neighboring townships where Mr. Ma had campaigned for farmers' rights. Local lawyers had been banned from working on the case, but the petition was clearly a lawyer's handiwork: it repeated in legal language many of the points in Mr. Ma's self-defense. Many farmers were under police surveillance but they, too, had participated, providing nitty-gritty details of police abuse.

So the peasants had found me and I finally had the petition, just as the lawyers had predicted yesterday. I put the packet in my carry bag and we sat there in silence. It wasn't the best place for a conversation.

"Just tell people that we're responsible, not Lawyer Ma," the peasant said. "He was just our lawyer."

I wanted to ask the man his name but hesitated. The lobby was small and we stuck out. We both looked outside.

"The rain is good, finally some rain," he said. "I'm a bit worried about the terracing. Our fields aren't used to this much rain and they might wash out."

He seemed eager to make his trip back home and kept looking outside at the weather, which steadily worsened, the rain now falling in sheets. I stood up and we shook hands, glowing like coconspirators.

A couple of hours later I was on the train back to Xi'an. After getting off the phone with the paranoid journalist and talking to the old cadre, I spent the rest of the ride watching the Loess Plateau recede and reading the court documents. A few hours later I was in Xi'an, a vibrant but filthy city that still boasts its ancient city walls. I tried calling the journalist to arrange dinner as planned but got no answer. I thought nothing of it and instead got in touch with a local lawyer who gave me a copy of a petition sent by the provincial lawyers' association to the provincial governor asking that Mr. Ma's case be heard by the provincial supreme court. Only by bypassing the local courts in the county and district, they felt, would Mr. Ma get a fair shake.

I wondered. Mr. Ma had already tried appealing to higher-level authorities but had been burned as badly by them as by the local officials. He'd gone to Beijing to petition, yet it was Beijing police who'd arrested and beaten him before delivering him into the hands of the local police. The central government's policy was stability above all else. No governor would risk that by tac-

itly appearing to condone the unrest that had consumed one of his counties—and a county of such enormous symbolic importance to the Communist Party.

Still I admired the lawyers. They'd signed their names to the petition. Like all such people in China, they worked either for state-run universities or state-administered law firms—independent schools and law practices don't really exist. As lawyers and teachers, they were expected to toe the government line, not support a rabble-rouser who'd been condemned and jailed by the party. Yet they had done so—more proof, I thought, of the growing courage and independence of Chinese society.

Back in Beijing the next day, I found a fax waiting for me on my desk. It was from a human-rights monitoring agency in Hong Kong, which reported that the journalist who had called me up on the train had been detained a few hours after getting off the phone with me. The journalist hadn't been paranoid. His phone had been bugged. The police had prevented him from speaking to me by detaining him for a few hours. I gave him a call.

"I'm fine now," he said over the crackly line. "It's no big deal. Anytime someone comes here to talk with me about Ma, the police always take me out to the countryside. We had dinner and returned home at one in the morning."

"That was a long dinner," I said.

"Yes," he said. "Great hosts. We even had beer and grain alcohol. At the end of it I realized that the province will never reopen Ma's case. But they are worried. That's a start."

2 DREAM OF A VANISHED CAPITAL

Mr. Luo stepped out from the shadows of the bus stop and walked over to me slowly. He was a good-looking man of fifty-seven, despite dyed hair, a comb-over and bushy eyebrows in need of a trim. I'd met him several times before, and he was always gruff, a bit like a 1930s hard-boiled detective who talked in monosyllables and rarely showed emotions.

He slowly turned his head to the bus shelter and nodded deliberately. His partner, Mr. Feng, stepped out from the shadows, carrying a smart black leather satchel stuffed with documents. He reminded me of a *shutong*, the boy servant to an artist or poet who in ancient China followed behind the great man, carrying his books and works.

Los Angeles detective and classical-era *shutong*, the two walked over to me and we entered our meeting place: a Kentucky Fried Chicken in old Beijing. It was bright and neon-lit, with plastic bucket seats and Formica floors. Mr. Luo motioned for us to go to its upstairs seating area.

"Shouldn't we buy something?" I asked, thinking this would prevent the busboys from throwing us out. "Maybe a tea or coffee?"

Mr. Luo looked at me as if I were the only person in Beijing

who didn't realize that this KFC was his private office. In a concession to his foreign guest he nodded to Mr. Feng and said, "Buy some tea." I started to protest that I'd pay but Mr. Feng looked at me sternly and motioned for me to follow Mr. Luo. No silliness, he seemed to say, just follow the boss's orders.

Mr. Feng went to order tea and we walked upstairs to the restaurant's upper level. Mr. Luo surveyed the scene. It was a weekday at 7 p.m. and most of the tables were taken, including his usual spot in the corner. With a grunt he selected a four-person table in the middle of the room. I cringed at the thought of us on display but figured that if we spoke in low tones, no one would hear us over the noise of other people talking.

After Mr. Luo and I exchanged pleasantries, Mr. Feng arrived with three paper cups of Lipton tea. This was the third time I'd met the two, and as usual we started off with small talk, chatting about the weather, places of interest in China for a foreigner to visit and places that the two of them had visited. It always struck me how different they were. Both had grown up in the old part of Beijing, but they seemed to have little else in common. Although Mr. Luo was the leader and Mr. Feng deferred to him, Mr. Feng kept a superior air about him. At sixty, he was three years older than Mr. Luo, which should have made him the leader of the two. And before retiring he'd helped set policy in the Ministry of Culture. That made him a *ganbu,* a civil servant, and thus a prestigious member of society.

Mr. Luo, by contrast, had worked for the past thirty-eight years in the same agricultural machinery factory as a quality inspector, his hands always a little dirty with the sort of machine grease that never quite scrubs off. But Mr. Luo possessed gravitas. Mr. Feng was sometimes nervous, but Mr. Luo had a strong, commanding presence, the mark of a man who had ordered people around on a hot factory floor for decades.

Both men were dressed smartly, if cheaply—Mr. Luo wearing a green plaid jacket, black pinstriped shirt, leather loafers and dark polyester pants with a crease down the front. Mr. Feng also wore polyester dress pants with a green cotton shirt. I wondered why Chinese men, even those coming straight from a factory, looked smarter than American men, for whom dressing like a slob was some sort of casual proof of their wealth.

Slowly, we got to the topic of their work. Beijing's historic old city was being systematically destroyed at an ever-increasing pace. Tens of thousands of people had lost their homes to government-owned development companies over the past few years, and many residents ended up living on the outskirts of town in poor housing. Quietly, mostly unaware of each other because the local media was barred from reporting their actions, thousands of these former home-owners like Messrs. Feng and Luo had taken the city to court, not so much to protect the historic old city as to demand compensation for their expropriated homes. At first I had been interested only in their lawsuits, seeing a parallel to Mr. Ma's suit in the countryside. Over time I began to see in the effort something different: a more sophisticated effort to mobilize public opinion and a slow recognition by Chinese of their vanishing cultural roots. But now I was just learning about the men's lawsuit, and they were still uncertain about me, fearful that I wasn't really clear about their goals.

Mr. Luo yielded the ritualistic part of the talk—the education of the barbarian—to Mr. Feng. Mr. Feng had a thick, friendly face but seemed slightly ill, his pallid skin made pastier by his jet-black hair, which he dyed. He pulled out a handkerchief and wiped his face in one giant mopping motion. Then I hunched forward dutifully and took notes while he spoke.

"During the 1990s, the city confiscated a hundred thirty-eight billion yuan [roughly $15 billion] in real estate," Mr. Feng

said in a slow, careful way. "More than two hundred thousand people in the old city lost their homes. They got practically nothing in compensation."

"Who got the money?" he said, picking up the tempo. "The government did. How? The local governments cheated the residents."

The district governments, Mr. Feng said, established real estate companies that were given the confiscated land. The real estate companies provided the home-owners little compensation—only a token amount of money and substandard housing in remote suburbs of the city. Then the government real estate companies sold the land to developers, making a huge profit.

"Who benefited? Not the people," Mr. Feng said. "But the local government, which owned the real estate companies."

Mr. Feng was just winding up, but Mr. Luo leaned forward and cut him off, bringing us quickly to the point: "We filed the suit on behalf of twenty-three thousand other home-owners like ourselves. We claimed that the government had forgotten to compensate us. But the administrative hearing officers rejected our case, as did the intermediate courts."

Mr. Feng and Mr. Luo had been brought together by personal tragedy. Both men's homes had been confiscated in 1994, when China was going through an economic bubble and investment poured into real estate projects. Growth rates for the national economy were double-digit and new buildings went up daily. The boom was driven by easy money lent primarily by state banks. Everybody seemed to have the same idea: build concrete and glass high-rises in the center of town. For dozens of cities like Beijing, that meant getting rid of residents and leveling homes. In Beijing, many of the homes dated back six hundred years to the Ming dynasty.

Mr. Luo had lived his whole life in a fourteenth-century

home that his father had bought in 1943. It was just a few blocks away from our KFC and had been torn down in 1996 to build the city's "Financial Street," a real estate development that saw thousands of Ming-era homes razed. As compensation, he was given a substandard apartment in the western outskirts of town, an hour's bike ride from where we now sat.

Mr. Feng had lived near the Forbidden City and was evicted from his home of thirty years to make way for a ritzy shopping mall built by a Hong Kong developer. It was called Oriental Plaza, a giant mirror-and-concrete monolith that didn't have a trace of the Orient in it. The development had caused a furor when it went up because the government not only threw out home-owners like Mr. Feng, but also well-connected commercial interests. A corruption scandal later came to light that caused a vice-mayor of the city to commit suicide.

That didn't save Mr. Feng's 50-square-meter home. It wasn't ancient—it had been put up in the 1950s as housing for government officials—but he was cheated out of a small fortune by the government. His home was sold to the developer for $2,500 a square meter, or $125,000. His only compensation was a small apartment on the tenth floor of a housing silo with dank elevators and cracking cement walls that probably cost a tenth of the $125,000 to build. The local government pocketed the balance, in violation of laws that require fair compensation.

After their individual suits were rejected, they'd independently come to the same conclusion: strength in numbers. Their early suits, they figured, had failed because they had filed alone. Working together, they collected the signatures of 23,000 people and in 1998 filed a class-action lawsuit. It was a heroic effort that was not strictly illegal, but by many measures dangerous. The half-dozen principal leaders of the lawsuit had all been detained several times for questioning. Although the men were released

each time after a few hours, they knew that they were treading on dangerous ground.

Mr. Feng was now surveying the group's finances. Each of the 23,000 participants in the suit had given the equivalent of between $2.50 and $6; the money was used to hire a lawyer. After they lost the initial suits, they used the money to print their materials and try to spread their tale to the local media and government officials, hoping this would pressure the courts to rule in their favor.

"It cost eight yuan [$1] to have a page typeset and then four mao [5 cents] to copy a standard sheet of paper, maybe two mao if you do it in bulk," Mr. Feng said, ticking off their expenses. "Then it cost seven yuan to mail out the packages, seventeen if we had to express-mail it.

"This is what we've produced. What do you think of it?" Mr. Feng said, putting an 8½-by-11-inch book on the table before me. I picked it up and thumbed through it, not bothering to read it very carefully. It seemed to be a collection of their lawsuits. Handy, but I didn't see the point.

"Was this book published?" I said, looking in vain for the *shuhao*, the number given out by the Press and Publication Bureau to every book published legally in China. Then I realized that this wasn't the smartest question. Of course it hadn't been published. It was samizdat, like the Soviet books printed underground to escape censors.

Mr. Feng squinted at me. He was dealing with an idiot. Mr. Feng collected his thoughts, trying to figure out how to simplify the story so that even a slow-witted foreigner would get it. His emotions swirled and then he erupted.

"Corruption—you're familiar with that word, eh? Corruption." If Chinese had an alphabet, he'd have spelled it out, he

said it so slowly. *"Fu bai,"* he said again, drawing out the syllables. *"Foo-buy."* I got it.

"This is *fu bai,*" he said with a slow drawl and a quick sweep of his arm, covering not just the crooked real estate deals but the whole system of government, one that controlled what information was published, which lawsuits were heard and whose homes got demolished.

"If we could get an honest judge, we'd win the case. The constitution is on our side. We have land-use rights and should be compensated according to a fair price. But they don't accept the case."

It slowly dawned on me that he was indeed dealing with an idiot. Mr. Feng had been trying to tell me from the start that my question—"What's new with your case?"—had been stupid. There was nothing new for them to tell me about their case because there couldn't be anything new. With so much money at stake, the courts couldn't accept the lawsuit. But what he was saying was that something else was afoot. The lawsuit might not be going anywhere, but people were organizing. I looked at the book in my hands. The lawsuit might be going nowhere, but something more potent was stirring: public opinion.

"We've given the courts documents this thick," Mr. Feng said, spreading his middle finger as far apart from his thumb as possible. "They've taken away our right to sue. They've denied twenty-thousand people the right to sue."

Mr. Feng stopped for a second to catch his breath, his ashen forehead glistening with sweat.

Mr. Luo now weighed in, speaking with a deep, slightly slurred Beijing accent, a full, manly voice heavy with authority. It reminded me why he was the leader.

"We've filed this suit but to no avail," he said. "The local

media can't report on it. We know many of the journalists. They want to help, but they cannot. What can you do to help us?"

Mr. Feng folded and refolded his handkerchief, but the anger boiling inside him forced him to do something. He busied himself wiping the table clean with an empty sugar sachet, sweeping the loose granules into a neat pile. Then he leapt back into the conversation.

"Who dared to say no when they tore down our house? You say no and it's fifteen days in jail just like that," Mr. Feng said. "Do you call that robbery?

"They beat you" he said, jabbing the table with the sugar sachet. "They arrest you. They jail you. Is that robbery?

"You resist and you're a nail sticking up out of a board," he said, hitting the table with the packet. "They smash you down. Is that robbery?

"You file a suit and they throw it out. You lose. They don't even answer you when you file. Is that robbery?"

He flicked the crumpled paper across the table.

"Not one written answer from the courts. Is that robbery? No, it's not just robbery. It's the Mafia."

He was speaking in short, beautiful sentences, in a cadence I'd never heard from any of China's stodgy leaders, with their wooden clichés and pinched voices. Then I looked around. A couple at the next table had long finished their meal and were staring at their plates. I wondered if they were fascinated by the outburst or repulsed that a foreigner was hearing about their country's problems. I looked back at my two hosts, and Mr. Luo picked up the thread in his steady voice.

"You write it. You write something of value. You seek truth from facts. You report this and you'll have lots of friends, ten thousand friends." Mr. Luo sat back, pleased with himself. A foreigner with 10,000 Chinese friends. That was a generous offer.

Mr. Feng, always eager for the rhetorical trump card, chimed in: "Yes, not just ten thousand friends. We only filed on behalf of twenty-three thousand homes, but two hundred eighty thousand households have lost their homes. They have on average four persons to a household. That's a million friends. You'll have a million friends."

I grinned awkwardly, trying to get their voices down. "That's a lot of friends," I said. "Great, thanks."

I thumbed through the book. I noticed a chop on some of the pages that read, literally, "Ten-Thousand-Person Mass Lawsuit."

"Is this your chop?" I said.

"It's not a chop," Mr. Feng said in an exasperated voice, making sure I understood, once again, that they were on the up and up. "Only the government has the right to issue a chop. A chop is for official use only. This is a stamp, made of rubber. Chops are round and usually made of stone. This is a square rubber stamp. It's just our insignia."

Then I began to flip through the book again, paying more attention. After a minute I looked up at Mr. Feng and shook my head in disbelief at its audacity. He smiled in satisfaction. I seemed to be getting it. The book was 108 pages long, hand-somely printed with a color cover and photos throughout. The front was bright blue with a title in red characters: "A Compilation of Materials Concerning the Demolition of Beijing Residents' Housing Administrative Lawsuit in Accordance with and Under the Protection of the Law."

The compilers wanted the title to be as nonthreatening as possible. The "in Accordance with and Under the Protection of the Law" phrase was a reminder to the reader that what was being done here was legal.

The rest of the cover, however, dispensed with caution. In the upper-right-hand corner was a red box with black characters:

"Demolition of the Capital, No Law—No Heaven." Scattered randomly across the cover were tiny phrases, parenthetical ideas that the authors also thought worth getting on the cover but didn't want interfering with the bigger-type title. They read: "Corruption of Distribution and Leasing of Land"; "Should People's Rights Be Protected and How?"; "Should Power Be Controlled and How?"; "The Trans-Millennium Lawsuit of the Capital"; "The Expropriation of 23,000 People from Prime Real Estate" and "In Broad Daylight Plundering 138 Billion Yuan." Written at the bottom was the name of the publisher: The Demolition of Beijing Residents' Housing Administrative Lawsuit Group. I liked the use of "group." In Chinese it implied something economic, like a group of companies, but was also vague enough not to imply the legal registration needed for a corporation or association.

What was especially striking was the use of color photos. During the Tiananmen student uprising in 1989, copy machines were still tightly controlled by the government. They were seen as a dangerous weapon that people weren't allowed to use without permission. Now copy shops with modern color printers were on every other street block of Beijing, and the result was obvious by looking at this little booklet, with color snapshots on the inside and back covers. One showed Messrs. Feng and Luo and five other representatives of the 23,000 residents standing before the Beijing Municipal Second Intermediate Court, where the lawsuit had been heard. Another showed them presenting the case to an official, while another focused simply on the stack of 23,000 signatures. The inside back cover hinted at what prompted the lawsuit. One snapshot showed a bulldozer leveling an old brick home in September 1996. Another was of an old lady in the rubble of her home, leaning sadly on a tree that used to be in the center of her courtyard. The back cover was even more

revealing: people's belongings strewn through the rubble, a sign that they hadn't left voluntarily. Another showed crowds confronting riot police who were protecting the workers as they went about destroying the homes.

Inside, the book laid out what the compilers said were the two huge scandals to have afflicted Beijing during the 1990s: the corrupt redevelopment of the old town and the corruption of the judiciary. The latter, the authors said, was especially destructive because "this is the largest judicial law incident in the People's Republic of China's history. The corruption of the judiciary legalizes the government's ignoring of the law, which exerts baneful social influence." In other words, if the government ignores the law, others will, too, and society will lose its moral order.

It was incendiary not only because of its contents, but because of the ordinary people who had produced it—people like Mr. Feng and Mr. Luo, not dissidents who'd spent years reading political tracts. As I read through further, I was amazed at the careful research that laid out government corruption on a grand scale.

"These ideas," I said. "The numbers, the analysis of the government's corruption, where did you get them?"

Mr. Luo sat back and smiled. "Fang Ke," he said. "Have you heard of him? He's one of the smartest men in China."

I hadn't but they quickly filled me in. Fang Ke was a young doctoral student at Beijing's elite Tsinghua University who had gathered material throughout the mid-to-late 1990s on Beijing's real estate market. What his meticulous research made clear was the depth of government corruption and its destruction of the old city, which he argued could easily have been avoided with some sensible urban planning.

"We thought the demolition mostly affected us," Mr. Feng

IAN JOHNSON

said. "Fang Ke's studies showed how the problem was bigger. Our heritage is at stake."

As I later noticed when reading through Mr. Feng's and Mr. Luo's book, Fang Ke's ideas had provided the intellectual underpinning for their suit. The precise analysis of the real estate companies' transactions, the sale price of land and the resale to other government-owned entities—all this was the work of painstaking research.

Mr. Luo motioned to get up. Mr. Feng gathered the material and stuffed it into his black briefcase. The audience was over.

We walked downstairs and out into the warm night. Across the street was a twenty-story Bank of China building, a black-glass structure built on the site of several dozen fifteenth-century homes. The street was lined with thick, knotty scholar trees, but they couldn't prevent the bank from overwhelming everything else, ruining what had once been a neighborhood of one- and two-story buildings. The rest of the street was lined with stores selling hardware and stands hawking pirated videos. As far as one could see were restaurants, mostly one-room joints with tiny stools, peeling walls and a bucket of greasy, soapy water out front to wash the dishes.

"I lived just behind there," Mr. Luo said, pointing to one restaurant.

"Poor Luo," Mr. Feng said. "He had a beautiful courtyard home."

"Isn't this an odd place to meet?" I said to Messrs. Feng and Luo, pointing to the Kentucky Fried Chicken where we'd just spent a couple of hours.

"You don't like fried chicken?" asked Mr. Feng.

"No, I mean it's a symbol of westernization and the destruction of the old city. Wasn't it a funny choice?"

Mr. Feng looked at me quizzically.

"KFC didn't tear down a building to build this restaurant," Mr. Feng said. "Plus, it's safe. No one is a regular there and the attendants are all students." He stepped closer to me to make sure I heard him clearly: "Those people who overheard us, we don't know them. We'll never meet them again. It's safe. I like KFC."

We shook hands and they left. I hopped into a taxi. I lived in a new part of the city on the other side of the densely populated old town. The driver was about to take a ring road built on the site of the old city wall that once encircled the old town. But just as we set off, I remembered that a couple of years ago Beijing's urban planners had blasted a six-lane highway through the old city, another in an endless string of egregious wrongs done to the old town. It was called Peace Boulevard. I suggested to the driver that we try that road. The driver was dubious, but I argued and he gave in.

We ended up flying through the old city, speeding over leveled palaces and six-hundred-year-old homes. If we'd taken the ring road, the trip would have taken forty-five minutes, but we pulled up in front of my apartment block in twenty minutes. Even though it was shorter and meant less money, the driver was ecstatic.

"This is when you're happy to pay taxes," the driver said as I got out. "I'd even pay a toll to ride on a road like that."

Up until the 1950s, Beijing was an architectural wonder, an almost perfectly preserved metropolis from the preindustrial era. Many ancient towns and cities exist around the world, but Beijing was enormous: 62.5 square kilometers (25 square miles) large including lakes, parks, palaces and of course the Forbidden City, the emperor's home. Surrounded by some of the greatest fortified walls of antiquity, it was a microcosm of ancient China, a

city that symbolized the political and religious ideals of a system that had existed for twenty-five hundred years.

Beijing was not a historic center of Chinese culture; for centuries it had been a backwater compared to other ancient Chinese capitals, such as Xi'an, Luoyang, Nanjing or Hangzhou. It was primarily the capital of kingdoms of northern nomads, such as the Khitan, the Jürchen and of course the Mongolians, whose dynasty lasted from 1279 to 1368. But in 1403, the Ming dynasty's Yongle emperor usurped the throne and decided to relocate the seat of government from Nanjing to Beijing, where his power base was located. Suddenly, Beijing was home to the emperor, making it the center of the Chinese world.

Becoming the capital meant more than building palaces and other symbols of political power. It meant turning this unremarkable site into holy ground. Unlike many other great cities of antiquity, Beijing was not built near the ocean or a major river. Abutting the Mongolian foothills on the north end of the North China Plain, it was flat and almost featureless.

This made it easy to superimpose China's cosmological system over the new city. Legend has it that Beijing's spiritual underpinnings were drawn up by a geomancer, who handed the Yongle emperor plans for his new capital. The layout of streets and boulevards followed the typical Chinese love of symmetry and clear, square designs. But it was also seen as a spiritual whole, too. Over the city's landmarks was traced the body of Nazha, a young god credited with taming the waters of the Beijing plain. Like an astrological figure drawn over the stars, Nazha's eight-armed body was made the basis of Beijing's layout. His head lies in the south of the city and his feet in the north—south being the most auspicious direction and most Chinese maps pointing south, not north. His head was represented by the Zhengyang Gate, two wells inside that gate were his eyes, the Gate of Heav-

enly Peace (Tiananmen) was his brain, the pathway to the Forbidden City his gullet. His right hand was the Chaoyang Gate, and in that hand rested the East Peak Temple. Each body part, each organ had its counterpart in the city.

Over time, the city became dotted with other links to heaven—temples. In 1911, the year the emperor abdicated, the city had well over one thousand temples—Buddhist, Taoist, Confucian—and a handful of mosques, excluding innumerable tiny shrines that weren't included in official counts. Almost every street had its temple. The guts of the city were its alleys, or *hutong*s. This is a Chinese word that some historians believe stems from an ancient Mongolian word for "well," since water was crucial to such an arid part of the country. Rainfall isn't just sparse: the city abuts the foothills to the Mongolian Plateau, making it susceptible to dry, withering windstorms. Many *hutong* names have the word "well" in it, but others are purely descriptive: "Wei Family Hutong," "Master Wu Liang Hutong," "Vegetable Market Intersection Hutong," "Great Tea Leaf Hutong" and "Green Bamboo Hutong." They are intensely local names, helping to reinforce the identity of those who live in there.

The *hutong*s were also the city's capillaries, carrying traffic the final few hundred meters from the city's major arteries to its final destination. Because few *hutong*s were through streets, most were quiet, almost traffic-free pedestrian zones where people could sit out front of their homes and talk and watch their children play. They were not like European streets, lined with trees and leading to large public spaces. Instead, they were lined with walls—most traditional homes in China are surrounded by walls—and the trees planted inside those walls grew out over the streets, making the city look from the air like a giant park.

Such a cityscape, though, could have its darker side. In the early 1980s, the writer Bei Dao wrote a Kafkaesque short story,

"13 Happiness Street," about a boy whose kite flies over one of these walls. When he climbs the wall to retrieve the kite, he disappears, as does a family member who goes to search for him. The story was claustrophobic and paranoid, but it was easy to see how streets made of walls could breed such feelings.

Encasing the city was the biggest of all walls: the city's fortifications. Up to 62 feet thick at the base and 34 feet thick at the top, the wall dominated Beijing in every respect. Invading nomads faced 50-foot buttresses with crenellated parapets, while local residents knew that they only came and went through the wall's gates with the permission of authorities. Chinese wrote poems about the wall—and the refreshing view when going outside it—while foreigners wrote obsessively about its size, measuring and mapping it in excruciating detail. The city wall gave Beijing its square shape and continues to do so today. Now a series of concentric ring roads enclose the city, each one roughly following the wall's course in wider and wider circumambulations around the old city.

When the imperial system collapsed in 1911, the city slowly rotted. Over the next thirty years, it was ruled by a warlord, a president and a foreign invader. Amazingly, though, Beijing stayed intact. What it couldn't resist, however, was the self-loathing and lack of confidence that had been afflicting China.

For about a hundred years, from the mid-nineteenth to the mid-twentieth century, China was under attack from abroad. Western countries forced it to import opium and agree to a series of humiliating treaties that carved up the country, giving colonies and special legal rights to foreigners. Efforts at gradual reforms were undercut by foreign powers, which continued to carve up China, culminating in Japan's invasion in 1937. As often happens in crises, moderation was supplanted by radicalism. A crisis of confidence swept China, and people began to doubt that

the country's traditional culture had anything of value left. After a four-year civil war, the communists came to power in 1949, advocating an almost complete break with the past.

That applied to urban planning—especially to the country's capital. Like the Yongle emperor, China's new rulers had their own geomantic system, but this one saw progress in the form of oversized squares and boulevards, with smokestacks dotting the horizon. It was a communist vision of urban planning, a particularly radical view of traditional European cities. Reproduced from Ulan Bator to East Berlin, it called for most ancient buildings to be torn down, not in spite of their age but because of it. Temples were closed en masse, with many converted to offices or factories. Today, despite some impressive efforts at restoration, the city of roughly 12 million has just twenty functioning temples.

The most dramatic blow was struck against the city's pride, its walls. China was in the grip of the totalitarian Mao era, but, amazingly, people fought in defense of the city wall. Architects, intellectuals and ordinary people protested, writing petitions and letters to local newspapers. Plans were put forward to reconcile historic preservation with the need to modernize, for example, by preserving the historic core and locating a new government center nearby. But the new government would hear nothing of it. The wall had to go. It took years to destroy the wall, but by the early 1960s it had vanished—almost.

Besides a few gates that were preserved in the center of traffic circles, the wall lived on in street names. It had been punctured by sixteen gates, and from them ran main streets from one end of town to the other, giving the city a gridlike street pattern. Those streets still exist and are still named after the gates that they ran through, with the suffix *nei* (inside) and *wai* (outside) reminding the traveler whether he is outside or inside the old gate. Nowa-

days, for example, one still travels along "Inside the Noble and Refined Gate Street" (Chongwenmennei Dajie), and, when one has passed this gate, which no longer exists, one drives on "Outside the Noble and Refined Gate Street" (Chongwenmenwai Dajie). The street where I met Messrs. Feng and Luo in the KFC was Fuchengmennei, or "Inside the Gate of Abundance." A few steps away would have been the gate, and through it the street still changes to "Outside the Gate of Abundance," as if the gate still stood. It was an interesting way to experience Beijing, traveling along streets that announced gates and walls that no longer existed, a virtual walled city that existed only on street signs.

But except for the loss of the wall in the 1960s, the essence of the old city remained—the hundreds of *hutong*s that weave between the lakes and parks, lined with courtyard homes and the occasional palace. Those probably would have been destroyed next, except that China again slipped into chaos. But instead of fighting foreign invaders, it was now consumed with itself, leaping from one failed version of communism to the next. For much of that time, the city continued to deteriorate, with the courtyard homes that lined the *hutong*s turning into noble slums. But all in all Beijing remained intact, its lost walls a reminder of what could come next.

Lawyer Wu got excited when I pulled Fang Ke's book out of my bag.

"Ah, Fang Ke's book!" he said. "Of course, I know it. I know him well. What a treasure that book is."

Two cell phone calls later and Lawyer Wu had arranged for us to go visit Fang Ke, who was living on the other side of town. We hopped in a car and drove over.

Wu Jianzhong was one of the few lawyers who seemed to

have any chance of successfully suing the city for expropriating residents' property. He was forty years old, quick-witted and eager to try out any new legal technique that came along. At one point he favored U.S.-style civil suits calling for high-priced settlements. When Chinese courts inevitably rejected such cases, he dabbled in real estate law, representing clients hoping to redevelop the city. Now he was on the other side, supporting an administrative lawsuit against government-owned real estate developers. With large glasses, a round face and neatly combed hair, he dreamed of international fame.

He represented an old man named Zhao Jingxin whose house was due to be torn down. Unlike the lawsuit by Messrs. Luo and Feng, whose case hadn't even been accepted by the court, Lawyer Wu had got his case registered by the court and even had had a hearing. After learning of his success, I had decided to meet him and brought with me a copy of Fang Ke's book, which I'd tracked down after hearing about it through Messrs. Luo and Feng.

I wasn't surprised that Lawyer Wu had heard of Fang Ke and his book. After meeting with Luo and Feng, I had begun to look into the destruction of old Beijing. I soon found that everyone had heard of or met Fang Ke and had read his book. In fact, his book was so popular that its press run of 2,500 had rapidly sold out and I'd had to photocopy a friend's copy.

As we headed to see Fang Ke, we sped past buildings that the August smog and heat turned into a concrete blur. Lawyer Wu began to explain the legal steps he had taken on behalf of his client, Mr. Zhao, whom his friends respectfully called Lao Zhao, which could roughly be translated as Old Mr. Zhao.

"The new constitution was written in 1982. That means the constitution was adopted after the [capitalist-style economic] reforms started in 1978," Lawyer Wu said. "But the new consti-

tution isn't less socialist than the old one. Actually, it's more socialist because it says that all urban land is owned by the government. But it does say that use of the land is private, so people do have land-use rights," Mr. Wu said, counting his legal points off on the fingers of his hand.

"Then what about the suit filed by Luo and Feng?" I asked. "Why hasn't their case been heard?"

"Easy," he said. "Their case was too big. They were suing the entire Beijing city government and had, how many, ten or twenty thousand signatures? The courts had a hard time accepting this. It's too broad. It calls into question too much."

"But when they sued individually, they lost, too," I said.

"Yes, but my impression is they weren't specific enough. Basically, they're challenging the government's right to do with the land as it wants. We aren't doing that with Old Mr. Zhao's case. We're attacking their decision on two very narrow and very specific fronts. First, that they didn't adequately compensate him for his land-use rights. His rights are absolutely clear because his father bought the house in 1948 and they have the bill of sale. So we're suing the Property Management Office for inadequate compensation. Second, we're arguing that his home is a protected cultural property and that the local Cultural Affairs Office failed to designate it as such. If it's designated, then it can't be torn down. So you see we have two very specific arguments that allege that the government didn't do its job properly. But we aren't challenging the government's right to expropriate land. The courts wouldn't hear that."

Despite Lawyer Wu's finesse, the suit was still hung up in courts. The initial hearing in a low-level court had gone the government's way, with the judge ruling simply that the government had the right to set compensation as it saw fit and to designate cultural property as it wanted. It could even violate its own

guidelines, the court said, since it set the guidelines. Lawyer Wu had quickly filed an appeal, which hadn't been heard yet.

"Look out the window," Lawyer Wu said. "The destruction is only going to pick up if we win the bid to hold the 2008 Olympics. They're just going to blindly tear down the old city and build new roads and new buildings. Somebody has to put a stop to it. Hundreds of years of culture, being torn down in a decade."

Later on, when Beijing's ultimately successful bid for the games was in full swing, I thought back to that talk. The city had hung banners around town extolling itself. In Chinese and English the banners read: "New Beijing, New Olympics." Then someone in the Olympic bid committee realized how odd that might seem to foreigners. Why a new Olympics? What was wrong with the old one? And why do we want a new Beijing? Wasn't the point of China's bid that it was offering its beautiful old capital as the site for the games? Later the English version of the banners were changed to "New Beijing, Great Olympics." The Olympics might not need renewing, but Beijing apparently did.

"This being the capital, however, perhaps they don't have to pay compensation?" I said.

"That's exactly what the government here argues. But there's a new federal law from January 1, 1999, stating explicitly that all expropriated land must be compensated. There's no exemption for the capital. So now they argue that they've never paid compensation so they don't know how to implement the new law. Imagine how ridiculous that is. The capital government doesn't understand the government's laws so says it should ignore the law. Of course, we didn't say that. We said, fine, then you can't tear down Old Mr. Zhao's house until you figure it out. They say, no, they want to tear down first."

We soon pulled up to the grandly named Movie and Television Mansion, which was actually a rather plain five-story building made of concrete and covered in white tiles. It was the summer break from university and Fang Ke was living in a friend's empty dorm room at a small college nearby. We met in the mansion's cafeteria and sat down in a booth.

Fang Ke looked more like a computer freak than an agent provocateur. He was lanky, with a mop of hair and big glasses. I could imagine him in a suit, but he looked more at home in what he was wearing: an MIT T-shirt, baggy shorts and fat, synthetic rubber sandals that had become an unfortunate global fashion trend. He was vigorous and in shape—twenty-eight years old but gave the appearance of an undergraduate. Talking with him was a joy. He had a winning smile and practical, pragmatic answers to any question. He was someone who'd thought hard about the subject and didn't hold back.

Fang Ke and Lawyer Wu sat down and chatted like old friends. I had figured that Lawyer Wu had become active in the cause of saving old Beijing only because he'd been hired by Old Mr. Zhao to save his house—the latest legal experiment that the curious attorney had undertaken. But as I got to know him better, I saw that although that might have been the case to start with, the case had opened his eyes, turning him into a committed defender of the old town. He and the young doctoral student shared the same friends. They also shared a schoolboy sense of humor.

"I heard you had a hard time getting my book," Fang Ke said, pushing two copies across to me. "Take these and give one to a friend."

Lawyer Wu nodded, smirking at the thought of someone

wild grass

getting Fang Ke's book as a present. "It's not easy reading," he said with a giggle. "Now you've got two."

Fang Ke laughed and continued. "But I'm actually happy that people are interested in this book. It took a while to write and research."

Seven years, in fact, since he'd first started looking into the old city. His teacher at Tsinghua University, Wu Liangyong, had asked him to do a research project on an alley in the old town called Chrysanthemum Hutong (Ju'er Hutong). His interest had slowly grown until he took on the entire old city's redevelopment as his doctoral thesis. He began to look at things a little harder than most people and found some strange contradictions in government policy.

"The first thing I noticed is that all the top leaders live in the traditional *siheyuan* [courtyard] homes. They don't want to live in high-rises, but they try to convince people that the courtyard homes are terrible and old-fashioned. That struck me as odd," he said. "I began to wonder why they were so eager to tear down the old city."

The turning point for old Beijing, Fang Ke said, was in April 1990, when the city announced a new law allowing "dangerous and dilapidated" buildings to be torn down. In October of that year it also promulgated a vague rule to protect twenty-five areas of the old city. When property prices starting rising astronomically a couple of years later, the protected zones were ignored and the city began designating huge swaths of the old town as dangerous and in need of development. They included, for example, Niu Jie, or Ox Street, the center of Muslim life in Beijing. Almost the entire street was leveled, including one of the few ancient mosques in China that was used only by women. The area around the Summer Palace was also meant to be conserved, but developers won exemptions to build high-rises that now mar

the view of the sky from the park. Throughout the 1990s, the city lost more famous buildings than in any of the decades past.

It was a process being repeated across China, with historic sections of cities such as Kunming and Shanghai gutted in favor of slapdash concrete commercial districts. Only in a couple of cities where tourism played a key role, such as Xi'an, could historic preservationists win their arguments.

"They reminded me of Napoleon III of France," Fang Ke said as he sipped a Coke. "He wanted to tear down the old city of Paris and build a new one. He didn't really succeed, but at least he had good architects working for him so that what he built was beautiful. Do you see anything built recently that's beautiful or lasting? It's all ugly."

Lawyer Wu and Fang Ke laughed and then sighed. "Their idea of keeping Chinese characteristics is to put a little pavilion on top of a skyscraper," Lawyer Wu said. "And that's all that's left of Chinese architecture."

"People say it was a death by a thousand cuts in the previous years," Mr. Fang said with a halfhearted grin. "But what has now happened its more like a big blow to the head.

"All I argue is that we should turn the 62.5 square kilometers of the old city into a protected area and then decide what needs to be developed inside it. The urban center of the city has 1,050 square kilometers, so I'm not saying the city should be turned into a museum. Right now the city has a protection plan, but it's only for 5.6 square kilometers, most of which is simply the Forbidden City and Beihai Park.

"Beijing's value is as a whole. Its urban design is unique. Just saving a few streets or buildings doesn't save old Beijing. In 1949 it was complete. The Japanese handed it over peacefully in 1945 and so did the Nationalists in 1949. It was like Jerusalem, a complete medieval city."

I'd heard the comparison before. At first it seemed odd, but the more I thought about it, the more perfect the comparison seemed. Like Jerusalem, Beijing had been a holy city, the center of the Chinese religious world. The two also shared challenges for modern-day urban planners, with the Middle Eastern city showing how an ancient city could be modernized without sacrificing its essence. Proponents of gutting old Beijing liked to argue that its narrow lanes and alleys made it impossible to install telecommunications cables and sewage and water pipes. While conceding difficulties, people like Fang Ke argued that Jerusalem showed that by and large the demands of the modern world could be reconciled with ancient structures. Pipes and electric cables could be laid without destroying everything. The population density had to stay low but there was no need for it to be a medieval slum. On the contrary, living in the old city would become chic, much as it is in scores of western cities.

"None of their arguments make any sense. The city did a survey in 1950 and found that five percent of the buildings were dangerous or dilapidated. Then in 1990 they found that fifty percent were. Of course, nothing had been done to the buildings for forty years, so they became dilapidated. But if they'd give the property rights back to the residents, they'd look after them and fix them up. Instead, the solution is to level everything."

Lawyer Wu had sat silently during his young friend's exposition of his ideas. Occasionally, he gave a theatrical sigh or shook his head sadly.

"There you have it," he said after we had been sitting quietly for a few minutes, absorbing the rush of ideas. "The only thing you haven't mentioned is how much money the officials can make off all this."

Fang Ke looked up cautiously.

"I can't prove individual corruption, but I can show how

much ordinary residents got as compensation and how much the city-owned real estate companies sold the land to the developers. The difference was billions and little of it ended up in the city's treasury. I've calculated it by going through the projects one by one and tallying the numbers. To me there's no doubt that officials were motivated by greed. First, they don't really believe in protection. Second, it's in their financial interest to tear down the city."

We finished our meal and got up. Fang Ke said he had something important to show me, and we agreed to meet in a few days.

At first glance, Fang Ke's book seemed sure to lull even a sharp-eyed censor to sleep. It was published by the China Architecture & Building Press, a publisher hardly associated with radical tracts or investigations of corruption. Its design was smart and modern but nonthreatening. The cover was colored dull turquoise with a sketch map of greater Beijing at the bottom. Above it was the title *Contemporary Redevelopment in the Inner City of Beijing,* with the yawner of a subtitle in lowercase letters "survey, analysis and investigation." Its ultimate protective talisman was stripped in small letters across the top of the cover: "Edited by the Academician Wu Liangyong: Science of Environmental Habitat Series."

The involvement of Mr. Wu, Fang Ke's teacher and adviser, was crucial. Although he sometimes took up popular causes, such as the historic preservation of an old town in a remote province, he was a prudent man. His caution had been rewarded with a post on the Chinese People's Political Consultative Conference, a powerless assembly of prominent academics, artists and non-Chinese ethnic groups, such as Tibetans and Uighurs, whose role was to make it seem like the Communist Party consulted with a

broad range of people. A book published under the auspices of such a man, a censor would reckon, couldn't be that radical.

Despite all this, it was probably only a measure of how many books are published and how cursory censors have become that the book wasn't banned. Its cover might have been cautious, but the book burst with bold ideas and criticisms. One striking point was that it was loaded with pictures. Poorly reproduced black-and-white pictures, perhaps, but photos that couldn't help but grab one's attention. On page 85, for example, was a photo of a deputy in the national parliament who was questioning the government about the tearing down of old Beijing. Below it, in the text, was the statement that the amount of money the deputy believed that developers had misappropriated was in excess of 10 billion yuan, or $1.25 billion—a staggering amount in any country but especially in a developing one where prices are low. To put it in context, during the 1990s, developers had ripped the city off the equivalent of an entire year's worth of economic output, as if every man, woman and child, all 11 million Beijingers, had simply given away everything they produced in one year.

Complementing the pictures were descriptions of the lost buildings, such as the home of China's greatest novelist, Cao Xueqin, who had written the classic novel of manners, *Dream of the Red Chamber*. His home was to be leveled to make way for a wider road. Others were left to rot, such as the homes of two of China's great reformers, Liang Qichao and Kang Youwei. One could imagine that soon they, too, would be leveled as "dilapidated and dangerous" buildings.

The last third of the book was taken up with surveying other Chinese and foreign cities that also had historic centers and discussing how their efforts at preservation could be applied to Beijing. One soon realized that this was something unprecedented and desperately needed, a careful, factual study of how to stop

the destruction of one of the greatest architectural treasures of the world.

As I read along, what gave me the most pleasure were the facts and figures. Usually, books filled with such ballast aren't fun reads. But for years I'd worked in a country where the adjective *chabuduo*—"more or less"—seemed to preface every number, every fact, every figure. One began to realize how one takes for granted straight, factual answers to questions. In China, by contrast, round numbers were so common they were ridiculous. I'd been to innumerable factories or government offices where I'd hear answers like "We have a thousand workers and our output last year was a million yuan." Exactly a million? "Yeah, well, *chabuduo*," followed by the inevitable suspicious glance at me. Why did I want to know that? Nobody knew that number, except the people who needed to.

Here, though, was a book filled with tables and figures, facts culled from documents and endless interviews with developers. Numbers showing the square-meter purchase and sale price of land in different parts of the city—all revealing the fat profits that developers earned by dispossessing people of their homes and tearing down the old city. As a young Ph.D. student, Mr. Fang had had an easier time obtaining the numbers. He wasn't treated with the arm's-length caution given to local journalists or statisticians. Forget about a foreign journalist; few of the developers he surveyed would have given a foreign journalist an interview. What for? They would never list on overseas stock markets and rarely do business with foreign companies. They were engaged in almost inevitably corrupt deals that involved twisting zoning rules, tearing down old buildings and slapping up new "luxury" development. They wanted zero publicity, especially from the outside world.

As a student, however, Mr. Fang could ask questions and use

letters of introduction from teachers to obtain interviews. And as a trained architect, he could work with the raw figures he saw on the construction plans to calculate density and height. Later, he could compare that with the zoning requirements that are not easily obtained by the public but which his connections through classmates and teachers made possible.

For example, he investigated the construction of Financial Street, a real estate development that wiped out 4,000 homes, hundreds from the fourteenth and fifteenth centuries, including the home of Mr. Luo of the Ten-Thousand-Person Mass Lawsuit. He found out, for example, that the buildings exceeded the 70-meter height restrictions by up to 46 meters.

That was a number I'd struggled to get. In 1997, I'd interviewed an official from the government-owned company that was building the street. The two useful facts I got out of the interview were the figure of 4,000 homes being leveled and that 12,000 people had lived there. When I asked about heights or zoning, I got the same blank stare and the platitude that it "was being done in accordance with relevant city regulation. Those were dangerous and dilapidated homes."

Fang Ke's book showed how the city was abusing this argument that much of old Beijing was dangerous. In 1991, he noted, the city claimed that 3.4 million square meters of land was occupied by dangerous housing. During the next eight years, however, it tore down 3.6 million square meters of "dangerous" housing—and still its appetite was insatiable. A new eight-lane boulevard was being built south of the Forbidden City to complement Peace Boulevard to the north. Tens of thousands of residents were being expelled to substandard housing in the suburbs. They, of course, were living in newly discovered "dangerous and dilapidated" housing.

What thrilled many Beijingers about Fang Ke's book was

that he laid out all the lawsuits opposing the redevelopment. He reckoned that between 1995 and 1999, 13,000 residents had filed fourteen class-action lawsuits against the city, in addition to the suit filed by 23,000 that I had heard about from Messrs. Feng and Luo. The suits were listed in a table, and on the facing page was a photo of a man protesting the fact that he'd lost his home to developers.

He also explained the problems that resettled people faced: commutes to work of three or four hours each way in crowded buses; the elderly who had to take buses for hours on end to find a hospital; unhygienic conditions in the new slums and the increase in people living in "temporary housing"—shanties for those who lost their old homes but didn't get new ones. There were 4,900 in 1991; by 1998 the number had increased to 32,000. It was a modest number compared to Beijing's total population of over 10 million, but it showed that despite redevelopment made ostensibly in the name of improving living conditions, they were actually getting worse.

Mr. Fang didn't advocate a political agenda. The logical conclusion, of course, was that a system in which the government is judge and jury, buyer and seller, can't be fair. He never made that argument or drew that conclusion. But his book was still a challenge to the system. He wasn't simply arguing that good rules had been improperly applied or circumvented by a few greedy people. Instead, he was showing that the rules themselves were bad, which he argues are designed to allow the entire old town to be torn down. For example, the city classifies buildings according to their quality from first (best) to fifth (worst) class. According to the regulations, if 70 percent of a district is made up of third-, fourth- and fifth-class buildings, it can be torn down in its entirety. As Mr. Fang points out, these rules mean that almost any

district in the city can be redeveloped. What few monuments are saved will be isolated fragments shorn of the alleys and ordinary courtyard homes that once gave them context.

To some degree what Fang Ke described was universal. Developers around the world try to bypass local governments' urban plans. They ask for exemptions and waivers of zoning rules, always in the name of jobs and progress. In Western countries, historic buildings are under threat, too, but the more common pressure is outward, with agricultural land on the fringes of cities being rezoned for low-density housing that sprawls on endlessly.

In China, urban sprawl is increasing as well—as one can see on the outskirts of any major Chinese city. But suburban life hasn't caught on in China. The wealthiest people, by and large, do not live outside of the city. That's because the high population density makes it impossible to build adequate highways that could make a commute bearable. Rather than commute for hours, the wealthy prefer to live near where they work and shop—as Fang Ke noted early on in his research how senior leaders all like to live in the old town because of its convenience. Thus the pressure to rezone and redevelop is in the center of town, exactly where China's old towns are located. Without any checks or balances to protect the old districts, their fates are sealed.

Another difference from other countries is the intimate relationship between business and government, which is so close that the two are almost synonymous. As Fang Ke bluntly put it early on in his book: "Planning offices cannot say 'no' to the developers. City and district government officials are the senior managers of the developers and the planning offices. When these governments face the problem of choosing between the 'overall interest of the whole city,' represented by the planning offices,

and the 'economic interest of the city,' represented by the developing companies, they often choose the latter one. The planning offices are ultimately always asked to compromise."

Fang Ke's research had got to the core of China's economic and political dilemma: the government's desire to control too much of not only the political field but the economic arena as well. In a country where the government ran large chunks of the economy and was its regulator, corruption and mismanagement were inevitable.

A generation ago, China had a planned economy. In a planned economy, developers didn't exist; instead, the Ministry of Construction simply had "units" that went out and built a building, road or whatever, according to the government's need. Reforms have transformed these "units" into incorporated companies. Although owned by the government, they're charged with making a profit, something that wasn't much of a consideration before. Profits mean that the main shareholder, the state, earns money. If a developer can argue that a project will be profitable, his owners (the state) will make sure that other state offices don't hinder the company's plans.

For example, Fang Ke showed how developers bully the cultural relics bureaus and city planners into giving permission. When the city planners are asked to assess the percentage of dangerous buildings in a district, they only do so after the developers have applied for permits. Since cultural and planning authorities are weak, they're under pressure to come up with as high a percentage of dangerous buildings as possible, making it easy to level the neighborhood, sometimes even with government subsidies. "The so-called examination is just a formality. Once the area is chosen by developers, regardless of its buildings' quality, it can still be listed in the dangerous-building list. The tag 'rebuilding dangerous buildings' just provides an excuse for the

developers to have more preferential policies and to cover their desire for profits."

Another feature spurring destruction is the money pumped into projects by outside investors, mostly from Hong Kong. In the 1980s, only 200 million yuan was invested in rebuilding the old city. From 1990 to 1997, the figure jumped to 17 billion yuan. Hong Kong's richest man, Li Ka-shing, for example, poured billions into the Oriental Plaza, which had cost Mr. Feng his home. In all, outsiders poured in 11.6 billion of the 17 billion total. According to Mr. Fang's figures, the returns on many projects are astronomical as well—on average about 60 percent.

What hurt the most in reading the book was the thoughtlessness of the destruction. It was captured perfectly in an article that a newspaper in a distant city had published on the destruction of a famous bridge in Beijing called Rufuli. Beijing newspapers were strictly forbidden from carrying such news, but the journalists for the *Yangcheng Evening News* in faraway Guangzhou had managed to record the poignant scene as a team of migrant laborers from the countryside wrecked the bridge.

> Under those farmers' hands, the bridge turned to rubbish.
>
> "What should we do about the bricks, tiles and wood?"
>
> "Sell them."
>
> "The bricks can fetch a lot."
>
> "No, they can't. They are too old, nobody wants them. Even fewer will want the wood. The tiles can only be sold for four to five fen [half a penny] each."
>
> "I've worked in Beijing for eight years. I've pulled down many such houses. Two or three months ago, I pulled down a temple near the Directorate of the Impe-

rial Academy. That was a big one. But it doesn't matter. As long as the demolition office gives me money, I can pull down anything, even the Imperial Palace."

A few years earlier I'd come across another book on Chinese architecture. But unlike with Fang Ke's book, I didn't realize the value of Liang Sicheng's *Pictorial History of Chinese Architecture* until it had sat on my bookshelf for a few years. At first I was attracted by Mr. Liang's drawings. He had been a gifted draftsman and the book was punctuated with skillful cutaway sketches of temples, mausoleums and pagodas.

What I hadn't realized is that Mr. Liang had been the first to systematically study Chinese architecture. People knew China had a long history, but most knowledge came from ancient books, which were often based on hearsay and the biased views of one dynasty writing the preceding dynasty's history. Basing history on empirical study was something western civilization had developed as an offshoot of the scientific revolution. Almost no one had applied these new methods to China's architectural heritage.

The idea to do so stemmed indirectly from Mr. Liang's father, the great reformer Liang Qichao, the pending destruction of whose home Fang Ke had noted with distress in his book. The elder Liang had been a loyalist of the imperial system, trying fruitlessly to preserve some of Chinese culture and tradition as the country careened toward revolution.

Mr. Liang's father had been schooled in the millennia-old Confucian system of rote learning. But he soon realized that part of the West's immense advantage over China was its educational system and scientific method. This was how it had developed such sophisticated weapons that allowed a handful of ships and a

few thousand soldiers to seize vast amounts of Chinese territory. It wasn't so much the West's hardware that accounted for such victories, the elder Liang realized, as the software that had developed the material advantage. Most reformers at the time held the opposite view, saying China only needed to buy some up-to-date hardware to catch up to the West. But the elder Mr. Liang was adamant that education was paramount and applied his theories at home. His son was well grounded in China's classic literature, but he was ultimately sent abroad for a modern education.

In 1924 the younger Mr. Liang left for Philadelphia, where he attended the architecture school of the University of Pennsylvania. It was a choice made by his fiancée, Lin Whei-yin, a gifted writer whose marriage to Mr. Liang had been arranged by their parents when they were young. It had been a good match, and they had fallen in love with each other and decided to go abroad together to study. Both were brilliant students and in 1928 returned to China with degrees in hand from the U.S. university.

At the time, no one saw any need to study Chinese architecture. Mr. Liang's father thought it was a waste of time, casually noting that most old buildings were falling down anyway from neglect and the turmoil that had engulfed China since the Opium Wars of the mid-nineteenth century. Instead, he encouraged his son to turn his attention to Chinese painting and encouraged him to write a modern history of Chinese art. Mr. Liang, however, was determined to study China's architectural past and use modern field-research techniques. In traditional China, Confucian scholars worked mostly out of their study, poring over books and writing. No one got dirty by doing fieldwork. He decided to be the first to use the scientific method to catalogue and date the vast trove of buildings that China's thousands of years of history had left scattered across the land.

Mr. Liang made numerous field trips in northern China in

the late 1920s and 1930s. He found examples of architecture dating back one thousand years and identified the different styles, putting them in historical order—all of which were firsts for the history of Chinese architecture. But in 1937, as he was preparing to write a book detailing his work, war broke out with Japan.

The war brought to an end a small renaissance in intellectual and civilian life. Mr. Liang had been part of an educated elite that flourished during the Republic of China, which was founded in 1911 as the last imperial dynasty was being overthrown. (The last emperor abdicated in early 1912.) The new government's capital was Nanjing, a large city near Shanghai, and the dominant political force was the Nationalist Party.

It has been historical orthodoxy for decades to criticize the Nationalists' short time in power on the mainland. They were corrupt and not very successful in resisting Japanese aggression. Some of their leaders frequented Shanghai opium dens and consorted with organized criminals. Famines were common, and most of the country remained hopelessly backward, untouched by modern conveniences like running water and electricity. The communists have been successful in painting them as one of the worst governments China has had, a simplistic view that has taken root in the West.

Yet there were seeds of a modern China sown around that time that look progressive even today—and especially in contrast with the famines, corruption and purges that accompanied communist rule. Large, successful businesses were established and the makings of a modern economy were laid. Organizations independent of government control flourished—as they largely do not today—and academics like Mr. Liang made groundbreaking advances in understanding their own country and the world around them. Literature hit a high point with novelists like Lu

Xun and Shen Congwen (both would have been shoo-ins for the Nobel Prize had it not been so ethnocentrically western back then), while, like Mr. Liang, thousands of young people went abroad to study.

During World War II, the Nationalists fled to Chongqing (better known as Chungking), and it was to this area that Mr. Liang journeyed along with thousands of officials, teachers, writers and patriots of many stripes. A few others joined up with the communists in Yan'an, the dusty mountain town where Mr. Ma the peasant champion later lived, but most went to Chongqing, where they set up universities and research institutes, trying to keep the embers of Chinese intellectual life burning until the war was over.

When World War II ended, Mr. Liang returned to Beijing. When the civil war with the communists started up, Mr. Liang stayed in Beijing. He went abroad—as China's representative to help plan the new United Nations Building in New York—but not as a refugee. While in the United States, he also taught at Yale and traveled to other universities, receiving honors for his work, which had been published in overseas academic journals during the 1930s and '40s. It was a triumphal tour, and his spirits were lifted further by the prospect that China's civil war between the Nationalists and the communists would soon be over.

He ended up returning sooner than he expected. His wife, whose health had been fragile for several years, contracted tuberculosis. He rushed back to be by her side. The Nationalists' fortunes were slipping, and many of Mr. Liang's fellow intellectuals fled with the Nationalists and 2 million of their followers to Taiwan in 1949. Mr. Liang, however, stayed on to be with his wife, also sure that the new government wouldn't be too radical. At first he simply taught at Tsinghua University's new architecture

department. Then, after the communists established control, he was elected to several honorary positions, as well as made vice director of the Beijing City Planning Commission.

Like everything else he did, Mr. Liang threw himself into his job. He drew up a series of principles that he thought should govern the capital's development. It should be a political and cultural center, he said, not an industrial one. The city had never been an industrial center and its old streets and alleys would be inadequate for the demands of modern factories and transport. The Forbidden City should be preserved and surrounding buildings limited in height to a few stories. Most controversially, he called for a new administrative center to be built outside the old city walls—a new center for the city away from the emperor's palaces, which were once the center of the Chinese world.

The communists rejected all these suggestions. The city was industrialized—Chairman Mao was alleged to have said as he stood on the Gate of Heavenly Peace and surveyed the city that he wanted "the sky to be filled with smokestacks." The Forbidden City was only partially preserved, with leaders like Chairman Mao moving into an adjacent palace and much of the rest allowed to fall to pieces, a condition it remains in today. And, most crucially, the administrative center was built in the center of town, forcing the ancient city to bear the weight of a modern bureaucratic state, with old buildings leveled to make way for makeshift ministries and dorms for the huge influx of bureaucrats.

Doggedly—in hindsight one would say foolishly—Mr. Liang stuck to his guns. Every government plan to wipe out the past was met by one of his reasonable and sensible counterproposals. Instead of destroying the walls, for example, Mr. Liang said holes could be punched in them or tunnels built below to allow automobile traffic. The top of the walls, meanwhile, could

be turned into a public park. An apolitical man at heart, Mr. Liang couldn't recognize that the communists brokered no opposition on any question. He was relentlessly attacked, charged with being wasteful and reactionary. His friends were forced to disown him and no one dared stick up for his ideas.

By 1955 his wife had died. During her last months, he lay in a nearby hospital room himself, trying to recuperate from a breakdown caused by overwork, nerves and his own case of tuberculosis. After a partial rehabilitation in the early 1960s, he suffered again during the Cultural Revolution, which Chairman Mao launched in 1966. Red Guards tormented him daily and he was forced to burn his drawings and letters. He was expelled from his apartment and forced to live in a drafty shack. Already suffering from a recurrence of tuberculosis, he was hospitalized and died in 1972 at the age of seventy-one, the last two decades of his life wasted.

Mr. Liang was lucky, however, in his friends. In the 1920s he and his wife befriended John and Wilma Fairbank, two pioneers of Chinese studies. They went on a field trip together and corresponded about Mr. Liang's plans. Mrs. Fairbank later tracked down copies of the photos that he had intended to use in his *Pictorial History of Chinese Architecture*. A maid who had worked for the family also saved some of his writings and notes, providing Mrs. Fairbank with some texts. She published the text in 1984 with the Massachusetts Institute of Technology Press (using a different romanization of Mr. Liang's name, Liang Ssu-ch'eng). In 1994 she came out with a charming biography about Mr. Liang and his wife called *Liang and Lin: Partners in Exploring China's Architectural Past*. It was published by Mr. Liang's alma mater, the University of Pennsylvania.

Mr. Liang's historical work was published in China in 1998 (although of course with no mention of his fate or Mrs. Fair-

bank's role; that would have been seen as unnecessarily dwelling on the party's dark history and an embarrassment that foreigners had saved his work). It was this Chinese version of Mr. Liang's book that I had come across while browsing a bookstore. I had used the book several times when planning outings near Beijing. His description and crystal-clear drawing of the Temple of Solitary Pleasure (or Dulesi) inspired me to visit that temple several times.

One drawing and Mr. Liang's vivid description particularly intrigued me. The drawing was of China's oldest surviving wooden pagoda, built in 1056 in Yingxian, Shanxi Province. Mr. Liang had documented the structure's age, which had an electrifying effect on many Chinese—here, at last, was the scientific method being applied to China's civilization, in this case a discovery that made verifiable previous claims of the pagoda's antiquity. Sure, people knew that this pagoda was old and had existed for centuries. But to be able to prove by use of documents and archives that this structure was nine hundred years old was a milestone. Once, when traveling to Datong in Shanxi Province, I made a special trip to see it. As I drove through the flat, dry Shanxi countryside, the pagoda rose up like a relic from a vanished civilization. I remember thinking how exciting it must have been for a young Chinese researcher to be rediscovering his own people's history. It was like bringing something back to life.

Mr. Liang's work has inspired a new generation of intellectuals to fight to save Beijing. Mr. Liang's brightest student was Wu Liangyong, Fang Ke's adviser. Mr. Liang's son, Liang Congjie, was also active in the movement, although he is mainly known for his work in the environmental field, having founded one of China's few truly nongovernmental organizations, Friends of Nature. And Mr. Liang's idea of moving the ever-expanding

government out of the old city remained the current-day activists' prime demand.

In a widely reprinted article, for example, Fang Ke noted that the construction of Peace Boulevard—the one that had so delighted the taxi driver that evening when I had zoomed home from the evening meeting at the Kentucky Fried Chicken—had once again made Mr. Liang's ideas current. A modern, commercial and industrial city were just not possible in an old city like Beijing, he wrote.

> The suggestion of Mr. Liang was denounced for being "nostalgic, conservative and out of date." It's a tragedy that those who support protection today are given the same label. Today they see the result of placing the administrative center in the old city. One cannot help grasp the far-sightedness of Mr. Liang. It is incomprehensible that even today some people are still unable to grasp this idea.

Old Mr. Zhao, Lawyer Wu's client who was trying to save his courtyard home from demolition, was the descendant of another prominent family that had refused to flee to Taiwan when the Nationalists were defeated. His father, T. C. Chao (whose name could also be Romanized as Zhao Zezhen), had been a president of the World Council of Churches and had obtained an honorary doctorate of divinity from Princeton University in 1947. T. C.'s daughter, Lucy Zhao, a Ph.D. from the University of Chicago who translated Walt Whitman into Chinese, even took the last plane into Beijing in 1948, so determined was she to stand by her family and country. With the city encircled by the communists,

she arrived in a C-46 on Temple of Heaven Road—the airports were already in communist hands.

Old Mr. Zhao and his father shared her optimism, believing that a clean, new government dedicated to social justice was what China needed. Few imagined the horror that would await people like them, with their suspicious foreign degrees and previous allegiance to the republic.

Old Mr. Zhao was eighty-two and had lived in his home for fifty years when I got to know him in the summer of 2000. His father, like Professor Liang in the 1950s and his student, Professor Wu today, had been asked to serve on several powerful "consultative" bodies and was allowed to keep his home. It wasn't the most beautiful courtyard home I'd seen, but part of that had to do with the vicissitudes of the past five decades. During the Cultural Revolution two wings were given to other families and an archway between the two halves of the building were bricked over. The Zhao family, like most Chinese, was reduced to poverty, and upkeep was minimal.

T. C. Chao died in 1979 at age ninety-one, and Old Mr. Zhao continued to live in the home. He'd been a teacher for most of the postwar era after working at a U.S. Army language training center in Honolulu. He still had the ramrod bearing of a soldier, and his square jaw, short silver hair and piercing eyes added to the feeling that he'd live at least as long as his father and remain mentally alert to the end.

He had installed a modern toilet and glass windows and had tiled the floors. He loved the house in his stubborn, blunt fashion. "I lived here for fifty years, why should I give it up?" was one of the first things he said to me when I went to visit him along with a friend and Lawyer Wu.

"You think I couldn't leave? I have family in the U.S. I have other places to go." Then with a snarly growl he added: "But I'm

Chinese and this is our culture. I am not going to leave this place."

I was a bit taken aback by his ferocity. I wondered if this was some sort of stunt or a ploy to get more money from the city. The area was already mostly leveled, and his house was one of the few left standing. On our way to visit him we'd had a bit of difficulty finding the house. It was No. 22 Meishuguan Houjie, a street that ran north from the Fine Arts Center. Not much of the old street remained; it intersected the broad new Peace Boulevard and was slated for redevelopment, a new north-south axis through the old town to complement the broad east-west boulevard.

We had walked north along the street past a few scholar trees that seemed to be bracing themselves for the bulldozers that would soon be coming their way. A newspaper vendor hawked scores of newspapers from a cart, and people jostled each other as they tried to pass along the sidewalk that had been narrowed by previous road enlargements. On our right was a two-meter gray wall with tiles on top. Such walls were found throughout Beijing and used to separate homes from each other. We came to a small red door with no number above it. It was boarded shut. A few yards farther up the road was another door, also with no number. But it had a doorbell and we rang it. Old Mr. Zhao answered and let us in.

Old Mr. Zhao soon got riled up as he began to recount the facts of his case. What angered him most was the arbitrary nature of every decision concerning the home. A low-level director from the Cultural Relics Bureau had been by in March 1998, he said, and declared that the building didn't date from the Ming dynasty (1368 to 1644) and therefore wasn't worth saving.

"Of course, if they'd said it was a cultural relic then they couldn't tear it down, so they said it wasn't one," Old Mr. Zhao said. He had led us into his home and now we were sitting across

from each other on large polished wooden sofas with blue cushions. "But who says a relic is only a relic if it comes from the Ming? There's no rule saying the Ming is the benchmark and everything else can be torn down. It's ridiculous."

Old Mr. Zhao had started his campaign shortly after the official's visit in 1998. He wrote letters and called up his friends in the media. Not much came of it, but the government temporarily backed off its plans. The fiftieth anniversary of the founding of the People's Republic would be celebrated the next year, in 1999, and the government had a "social peace" campaign in force, which called for sensitive or controversial issues to be avoided. Old Mr. Zhao knew a lot of other well-connected people, many of them old-timers with a connection to the old republican era. These people had lived in disgrace for most of the communist era, but now they were seen as useful, besides having some influence through their connections abroad.

In November 1999, a month after the anniversary, the demolition of the neighborhood started. Workers leveled 37,000 square meters of old courtyard homes, including two palaces that had once belonged to princes in the Qing dynasty. Old Mr. Zhao could see that his home would be next, so he and Lawyer Wu filed his first suit, contending that the Cultural Relics Bureau hadn't accurately estimated his home's age. The bureaucrats argued that his house wasn't even on a map of Beijing dating back to the reign of Emperor Qianlong in the mid-eighteenth century and thus wasn't even 250 years old. Old Mr. Zhao, however, pointed out that the name of the street had changed; his home was on the map. The government conceded that point in court but then said it was irrelevant—it still wasn't Ming and still had to go.

"They said in court that it doesn't matter because it was only two hundred fifty years old. That wasn't old enough to be protected. Then they argued that my home is dilapidated and going

to collapse, so it has to be demolished," Old Mr. Zhao said, his watery gray eyes suddenly flashing with anger.

Old Mr. Zhao also argued that the cultural bureau hadn't performed any scientific check of its age. The cultural official had been by twice, each time for five minutes. No wood samples had been taken, nor an analysis of the construction of the bracketed eaves, which can help date a Chinese building. "His only comment was the windows had been renovated and the building had lost its historical character," Old Mr. Zhao said.

The initial hearing was before an administrative judge, where the government's word has especially strong sway. The bureau won, but Old Mr. Zhao and Lawyer Wu immediately appealed. Appeals are heard before a normal civilian court, which are presumed to be less in the government's sway than administrative courts. As we spoke, they were waiting for it to be heard by an intermediate court.

I looked around Old Mr. Zhao's home and could see that the official from the cultural bureau had a point. This wasn't a prince's palace and had been restored in a fairly primitive fashion. The new windows were giant steel-framed structures that looked completely out of place. The floor was an ugly faded linoleum and the interior walls had been covered with some sort of pressboard siding.

But these were matters of taste and money. The structure clearly was ancient and in Beijing's bone-dry climate could probably stand another hundred years even if completely neglected. It didn't look dilapidated at all, and in fact the glazed-tile roof was in top shape, while the structure boasted charming details, such as two stone elephant heads that guarded the eaves of the front door. I couldn't estimate the age, but dozens of architects, city planners and historic preservationists had recently signed a petition calling for the home to be preserved. They rec-

ognized the home for what it was: a typical Beijing courtyard home. If it could be leveled, the entire old city could be gutted.

I also thought about what other countries had done to make their old towns livable. In Europe, medieval structures now boast insulation, double-paned windows, central heating and other modern amenities. Surely preserving the old city didn't mean that the buildings had to preserve preindustrial patterns of living, such as outhouses, woodstoves and the like. On the one hand, the city said the old town was dilapidated and had to make way for modernization; on the other, efforts to modernize the old buildings were used as proof that they no longer were ancient. Like the policies that Fang Ke had outlined in his book, such arguments seemed designed for one purpose: to allow the city to get on with its lucrative redevelopment.

We got up and walked around.

He pointed to his prized possessions, two room dividers—6-by-3-foot panels of carved rosewood that were hinged together. "What I don't get about the government," Old Mr. Zhao said, "is that it says we have this great and glorious history and culture. We have five thousand years and so on. But in the end we only protect a couple of sites like [the cities of] Lijiang and Pingyao and put them on the UNESCO register of cultural sites. And we think that's good enough. What kind of a policy is that?"

Lawyer Wu's two-pronged strategy for saving Old Mr. Zhao's home included a second suit, the one against the city's housing office. Drawing on Fang Ke's studies of Peace Boulevard, he noted that the city's development code allowed commercial redevelopment up to 70 meters back from the broad new road. But Old Mr. Zhao's home was 100 meters back, he argued, and so should be spared the wrecking ball.

Old Mr. Zhao sat back on the sofa and closed his eyes as his advocate picked up the thread. The city, Lawyer Wu said, had

offered Old Mr. Zhao 6,000 yuan (or about $750) per square meter for the 420 square meters of his home. He would get no compensation for his 160-square-meter yard, even though the city-owned real estate office would be able to sell the whole lot to the developers. A few streets over, Lawyer Wu noted, the city is selling newly built old-style courtyard homes for 30,000 yuan a square meter, and buyers had to pay for the yard as well. Using that as a benchmark, the city could pocket well over 3 million yuan, or about $400,000, just by reselling Old Mr. Zhao's yard.

The developer, he said, was the Wangfujing General Commercial Real Estate Development Co., which is owned by the Beijing City East District government. "The buyer of the land is the China Construction Bank, which of course is also owned by the government," Lawyer Wu said. "No one can figure out why they're doing this or why they're allowed to do it. After Peace Boulevard and all the accompanying commercial development opened, occupancy rates fell and the city said no new commercial developments near the boulevard. It's just this blind development. There's no real market functioning here since it's all government money."

Old Mr. Zhao had seemed to be sleeping, but suddenly he bellowed out: "These companies mean nothing. This bank or that construction company—it's all the government. These guys can only make money when they build. They don't care if they rent out the rooms. They only want to sell to builders."

Over the next few weeks I took a closer look at the land deal, and it did indeed seem a bit odd. The bank building that was the ostensible reason for Old Mr. Zhao's move was already under construction. The shell of the six-story building overshadowed the courtyard house and it didn't seem necessary for Old Mr. Zhao to move for the building to be completed.

I couldn't figure out how much the Construction Bank was

paying the city for the land, but I verified Lawyer Wu's statement that one-story homes were selling for 30,000 yuan a square meter. The bank, for a six-story commercial structure, was undoubtedly paying more than that. But even using the 30,000-yuan figure, the city could make $1.6 million by selling Old Mr. Zhao's home to the bank. No wonder they wanted him out.

I called up the city zoning office and found out other odd facts. An official said the new building didn't violate the city's zoning ordinance that commercial buildings were limited to 70 meters from Peace Boulevard. The reason, he said, was that it would be "comprehensive" use, meaning mixed residential and commercial. Later, though, I talked to an acquaintance at the bank who told me it was to be a purely commercial building. Clearly, the "comprehensive" use was a means of skirting the ban on purely commercial buildings in what had been an overwhelmingly residential neighborhood. I also heard from a city planner that the building was only supposed to be 9 meters high, although it was already twice that height.

We had finished walking around Old Mr. Zhao's house and his yard. He'd been through the routine before with journalists. He'd give interviews, we'd write articles, he'd continue to sue and his influential friends would continue to write petitions. One day, he hoped, the city would relent and he'd win. It was like trying to set wet wood on fire.

Overhead, the construction crane swung by and we could hear the migrant laborers yelling to each other. I thought of the newspaper article cited in Fang Ke's book in which some migrant workers boasted that they'd tear down the Forbidden City if the money was right. We tried to take a picture of Old Mr. Zhao and angle the shot so the construction crane would be out of the view. "If you want to know what it looked like before, there have been

some artist friends who took pictures last year," he said. "I'm trying to keep a record of what it was like." We took a shot with the construction crane hovering over Old Mr. Zhao's head like a stick about to fall from the sky.

Fang Ke had said he wanted to show me something in the old city, and we soon set an appointment to meet. We met not too far from Old Mr. Zhao's street, at the north gate of Beihai Park, part of a chain of lakes that runs through the center of town. As earlier, he was wearing sandals, shorts and a T-shirt, this one emblazoned with "MIT Department of Fine Arts." His wife, Zhang Yan, was already in Boston studying at the Massachusetts Institute of Technology and had sent him the shirt and others like it as a gift. We shook hands. "It's on the other side of the road," he said, gesturing with his head toward Peace Boulevard.

The busy road roared with traffic. We could cross it only by taking a pedestrian underpass. As we emerged on the other side, we were beset by men hawking trishaw tours of the *hutong*s around the string of three small lakes that spread out to the northwest of Beihai Park. It was one of the few remaining sections of the old city, one that the city planners had said would be preserved at all costs. I could believe their intentions if for no reason other than that the tiny area had become a tourist draw, one of the few that Beijing had left (the others being the Great Wall, the Forbidden City and the Temple of Heaven).

We brushed off the pesky hawkers and stood in front of a large wooden memorial arch on the south end of the lakes. Soon after we visited, it was torn down, but it used to announce the start of a famous antique market with bright gold characters "Hehua Shichang," or Lotus Market. We turned right and

walked up the east side of the Front Lake (or Qianhai), the first of the three lakes called Shishahai, or Lake of Ten Temples, that are connected to three other lakes to the south.

"I wanted to show you how I got interested in Beijing," Fang Ke said as we strolled along a sidewalk that ran up the lake's east side. "I was a student in the architecture school of Tsinghua University and not interested at all in old Beijing. Like a lot of architects, I wanted to build something of my own and put my name on it, something modern. I was really influenced by western theories of modern architecture and that's what interested me, something big and monumental."

But Fang Ke's teacher had other ideas. Professor Wu was the student of Liang Sicheng and carried on his master's work, at least in a very cautious fashion. He had helped redevelop Chrysanthemum Hutong, an alley on which he was allowed to carry out his and Mr. Liang's theory of "organic renewal"—the idea being that instead of clearing out entire neighborhoods, you saved what could be saved and built similar-sized and similar-looking buildings to replace those that truly were hopeless. He made the comparison to an organism that regenerated parts of itself when they died or were injured. The idea was to preserve as much of the old flavor and ways of life as possible while allowing for the fact that some buildings truly were dilapidated and dangerous.

Professor Wu used the same tactics on his students that he used with authorities. He never ordered his students to take up his cause and recognized the fact that most were going to end up building glass and concrete banks. But he did assign them to work on his projects, hoping that some might see his way.

"I still wasn't interested, even after the Chrysanthemum Hutong project. You have to remember that students live up in the university district. We were young and naïve and cut off from the city. I didn't come from Beijing—my home is in the

south. None of us even wanted to go into the city. We saw it as a dirty old relic of feudal society. We looked down on the residents of the old city. They were poor, members of the underclass, and we didn't have any connection with them.

Then, in the fall of 1995, Professor Wu took Fang Ke on a tour of the old city. The old professor, then seventy-four years old, must have seen some promise in his young doctoral student and decided he was worth winning over. "I was touched by his concern for the city. I have to say I wasn't convinced that the city was worth saving, but I felt obliged to take on the project of studying the old city for my Ph.D. thesis. After all," Fang Ke said in the best tradition of a Confucian scholar, "he was my teacher and I couldn't refuse him."

At the end of his book, Fang Ke described the walk like this:

> I still remember when I started to choose my path of study on November 5, 1995, Mr. Wu, who was seventy-four years old, walked me around old Beijing to investigate and study. At the foot of Prospect Hill, by the Lake of Ten Temples and in front of the Drum and Bell Towers, Mr. Wu was excited and enthusiastic, reflecting on the past in the light of the present. His deep feeling for old Beijing and the people there was from the bottom of his heart and overflowed in his expression, which really moved me greatly. Suddenly, I realized the wide scope of scholarship and the meaning of study. The strong responsibility toward society welled up in my heart. To me, it was a day deeply etched upon my mind. That windy, yet particularly warm, afternoon determined the direction of my thesis and influenced my life over the past few years. What's more, it will influence the track of my journey through life.

We were now walking that same path through the city. After 100 meters, Fang Ke stopped. To our right was a park. The area had been rebuilt recently, and the park was now controlled by some sort of office that barred entrance to the old men who used to go there to play chess.

We looked over the lake. It was around noon, and most people were indoors eating lunch or taking a break from the summer heat. Cicadas, which seem to be everywhere in China in the summer, began to call. In the distance I could glimpse the outline of the Western Mountains, the foothills in a chain of mountains that leads up to the Mongolian Plateau. Yesterday they would have been invisible because the air had been stagnant and the smog had hung heavily over the city. Today, a breeze was blowing, adding a tint of blue to the yellow, washed-out sky and bringing the horizon into a smudgy focus.

I stepped behind one of the willows that lined the lake, allowing a branch to block out the high-rises. From this vantage the city's roofline was still low enough to get a sense of what Beijing had been like for hundreds of years. This is still sometimes referred to as Shishahai, or Lake of Ten Temples, although the temples had long been destroyed. "It's still a pretty lively part of town," Fang Ke said. "People still swim in the lake and go for strolls."

We turned away from the lake and walked up White Rice (Baimi) Street, which used to be lined with rice merchants. The road was only about the width of two automobiles, so car traffic was basically impossible in this part of town. People still drove down the narrow roads, though, and some parked out on the street, making it all but impassable for the flatbed tricycles that delivered goods and picked up refuse.

We stopped at No. 11, a former residence of a provincial

governor in the Qing dynasty, the last dynasty to rule China before the imperial system was overthrown in 1912. The door was open and we walked in. We were in a large yard with a huge plane tree in the middle providing shade and a home for some sparrows.

On the other side of the yard, behind the tree, was a one-story wooden building that would traditionally have been the entrance to some chambers—a reception area, probably—and beyond it to another courtyard with a tree in the middle. The door to that building, however, was closed and signs of construction were everywhere.

Fang Ke's face fell. "An old cadre used to live here. I guess he died and now they've renovated everything," he said. The building had been freshly painted but in a very crude style. Under the eaves wooden beams protruded. Each had the character *shou*, or "Long Life," carved on it and painted in gold leaf for emphasis. But the painting work was shoddy and a bit like a movie set; the closer we got, the worse it looked.

Since we couldn't go in, we walked to the far left side of the courtyard, where there was a passageway to other connected courtyards in the back. Fang Ke stopped for a second and explained our route.

"Western palaces or mansions can have a really intricate number and arrangement of rooms, one here and one there," Fang Ke said. "Chinese courtyard houses are simple. They're like cells that have divided, or replicas of each other."

He took my pen and notebook from my hands and drew a rectangle.

"The courtyard is a rectangle. You enter on the short end and directly ahead on the other end of the courtyard is the main hall. The main hall can be one room, although typically it's made

up of three rooms. In the Forbidden City it's nine, the auspicious number. (Ten is the heavenly number, so nine is the next highest, the highest that mortals can attain.)

"On the left and right of the rectangular courtyard are the long wings, usually rooms for attendants. Big mansions simply copy this pattern over and over. Some courtyards have no buildings and are left open for gardens or lakes, but it's all based on a series of connected rectangles. First, they typically add another rectangle behind the first," he said, adding more and more rectangles to the drawing. "Then more to the left and right. It all depends on the constraints of the land or the ability of the owner to purchase land, but this is the basic pattern."

We had entered a courtyard parallel to the main one. It was typical of how run-down much of Beijing's old housing had become. After the communists took over, they allowed many home-owners to stay in their homes but gradually forced them to share their homes. Where once a family had lived, a dozen now competed for space. The courtyards were turned into small slums filled with shacks and sheds. This yard was filled with about a dozen red brick shanties and endless piles of bric-a-brac. Waist-high piles of dusty bricks attested to someone's plans for further construction. A sheet of corrugated iron stood ready to be tossed on the roof in case a leak should appear. A stack of old flower-pots keeled over against a wall.

Saving it all from appearing too bleak, however, was the human scale—everything was one-story high. Plus, plants were everywhere: potted begonias crowned the heaps of bricks, grass sprouted out of drainage pipes and vines crawled up the crumbling walls. Hovering over it all was a giant chestnut tree planted centuries ago.

It was about two-thirty in the afternoon, and the yard was deserted, with most people at work or on siesta. The summer was

slowly ending, and the heat wasn't as bad as it had been a month earlier when I had traced Mr. Ma's path through the Loess Plateau. For ordinary people, this was still the center of the world, the capital city that one yearned to visit and, if one were incredibly lucky, to work in. At times like this it did indeed seem one of the most desirable cities in the world.

"The silence," Fang Ke said as we stopped to look at a small cactus growing from a pot. "This is the great success of the old urban planning system. The main roads carry traffic, but the *hutong*s are narrow and perfect for children to play or old people to walk. It almost re-creates village life in the big city, yet there's privacy. Everyone lives behind doors. It's very different from western urban life, which is open and everyone has big lawns showing off their wealth. Here people don't want to show what they have. They're worried about making their neighbors jealous but also just want their privacy."

We walked through another courtyard as crowded as the previous one. As we headed back through the series of side wings, we tried fruitlessly to turn right, back to the main axis of the house, which seemed to be cut off from its former wings. We had now walked about 100 meters from the main entrance and geographically were almost back at the lake. The mansion was coming to an end. As we left the second crowded courtyard, we came upon what was traditionally the deepest and best-protected room in the house: the *xiulou*, or bedrooms where unmarried daughters would have lived. Like the rest, the building was one-story high, with curved eaves and a tiled roof. It looked as if it hadn't been renovated in decades, with the paint peeling off the pillars. It was locked and now was probably someone's home.

We walked back to the main courtyard. A group of government officials materialized: a woman in the center, an important-looking man next to her and three flunkies.

"We're just enjoying the beautiful Chinese architecture," I said, eliciting smiles all around. They were here to inspect the refurbished main halls of the house—the crudely renovated part we had been forced to skirt. The doors were now unlocked for the official inspection and we looked inside as the officials discussed construction costs.

Fang Ke gave a start. "Everything here is new. I thought it looked odd, but I mean everything. Look, the pillars aren't wood, but concrete. The floor is concrete. The walls are concrete. . . ." His voice trailed off.

He looked up and saw another abomination: the roof tiles were yellow, the color of the emperor. But this had never been imperial property. The color was arbitrary, a form of cultural vandalism or exoticism—ancient China lite for the country's new ruling class.

The rooms were empty, awaiting their next high-level resident, a lucky cadre who had been chosen to live in this leafy part of town. We didn't dare walk farther in but glanced into the next courtyard. The earthen ground had been covered with sidewalk tiles, giving it an ugly, sterile feel.

"This would be called *ganjing*," I said, and we both laughed at the word, which is literally translated as "clean" but has a fascist connotation to it as well, this sense of sweeping away the old into an antiseptic sameness that is the hallmark of modern Chinese cities and architecture.

Fang Ke couldn't resist putting in a last word.

"You rebuilt it all," he said to the officials, who looked up and nodded. Fang Ke had a lot he wanted to say, but his anger blocked him up and he chewed on his lip to control himself.

"What was wrong with the old structure? The roof is yellow," he said helplessly.

They said nothing. He was clearly irrelevant. We left and continued up Baimi Street.

"It's so disappointing. Every time I come here, the place changes. Even if all this were saved from the wrecking ball, people wouldn't know how to renovate it."

"You really like the *hutong*s," I said. Then, as a joke, added, "Did you fall in love with your wife here?"

"Actually, you could say that. For my master's thesis I expanded on the work I did for Professor Wu. Zhang Yan was an undergraduate, and she also studied urban planning. We spent several days walking the *hutong*s, looking at the architecture. We got to know each other pretty well."

Zhang Yan had always been a bit more focused than Fang Ke and had been determined to study abroad. Immediately after her undergraduate degree she took the entrance exams to U.S. universities. Soon after they were married in 1999, she went to MIT to study.

Our path led us back to the lake. We walked north and came to a construction site that blocked our way. Beijing's lakes, canals and even the moat around the Forbidden City were once linked and part of a living ecosystem—one of the natural wonders in a city that was on the edge of a desert and extremely dry much of the year. Water flowed down from the mountains through streams that have largely dried up and down into the six lakes that run north to south through the capital. The construction work in front of us was the dredging of a canal that ran eastward out of Front Lake and into the Forbidden City's moats.

"Actually, the canal is just for tourists—it won't be reconnected to the moat around the Forbidden City," Fang Ke said as we skirted the construction site by walking along the canal. But maybe this is a start to repairing the damaged waterways."

We couldn't follow the canal anymore because the area was blocked off for the dredging, so we walked along a street parallel to it. We stopped in front of a doorway and looked at the doors. They were made of wood, painted red and with small flower carvings along the edges. The paint was badly worn and the threshold, which on Chinese doorways is raised 6 inches above the ground, was split and cracked from lack of maintenance— nothing had been painted, it seemed, in fifty years.

One of the doors was partly open, and behind it we saw an intricately carved stone screen, meant to ward off evil influences (according to the principles of Chinese geomancy, or *fengshui*) and give residents protection from prying eyes. Fang Ke pushed the door open a bit, and we stepped over the threshold to look at the birds and flowers carved onto the screen. An old lady appeared around the side of the screen.

"Hello, grandma," Fang Ke said, using a polite address for an older woman. "I'm here from Tsinghua University and am studying Beijing's *hutong*s."

The old woman's face immediately lit up and she welcomed us in.

"The Zhang family lives here," she said. "Come in and have a cup of tea."

The courtyard was even more chaotic than that of the house we had just visited. There, shanties had filled the court- yards that we had walked through, but there was an orderliness and abundance of plants—it was, after all, adjacent to the future home of a senior-ranking leader, and those who lived there were probably relatively well-off state employees. This was the home of ordinary people. A broken washbasin hung from a hook. Bricks were piled haphazardly, and a small garlic plant perched atop a precarious stack of tiles.

"We bought the house in 1950, right after Liberation," Mrs.

Zhang said, using the official term for the communist takeover. "Our family had made money trading goods. It was chaos. All the rich people were fleeing to Taiwan and everything was cheap. It was a great deal. We come from Xianghe and thought we'd move into the big city. I don't know if it was such a good idea."

A decade and a half after they moved in, the Cultural Revolution was launched and the family was targeted as capitalists. They were thrown out and forced to live in slums on the edge of town. The government moved in half a dozen families, allowing them to build shanties on what had been the courtyard. After the Cultural Revolution ended in 1976, the family was allowed to move back in but for the past quarter century had been forced to share their home with the people who had taken it away from them. Tensions were high and people ignored each other. It was a common story in the old city.

Mrs. Zhang was seventy-seven, and she pointed with pride to the beautiful doors and the stone screen. She kept insisting we drink a cup of tea, but we wanted to keep moving, so politely declined. "I'm so happy that young people and foreigners are studying our beautiful old Beijing," she said, running a hand over the screen. "We're so proud of this."

It was a response that conventional wisdom said should be rare. One was always reading from commentators that Chinese are apolitical. They don't care about democracy. They're satisfied with their lot. Chinese people even say so themselves. But what most people mean is that they don't want to get mixed up in some insane government political campaign or power struggle in the party—which is what "politics" means to most people. Ask them if they're happy about corruption or other ways that unaccountable officials abuse their power and you suddenly get the opposite answer: they care very much.

So, too, with urban planning. Ask Chinese people if they'd

like to give up their dilapidated old homes for modern apartments in a high-rise and most will say yes. The conclusion is that they don't care about their old homes.

"That was what I thought when I got started on my doctoral work," Fang Ke said as we left Mrs. Zhang and walked down the alleyway. "I thought no one would really want to live here. But people are really friendly once you tell them you're researching or interested in their old homes. You say that and they love you. They're willing to spend time showing you around their courtyards."

"But it is true," I said, "that many say they are happy to leave for a modern home."

"Yes, but their consciousness is so low. If you give them only two choices—live in this slum or move to a high-rise—most will take the high-rise. But people only think in terms of those narrow choices because the government doesn't allow other discussions to take place. We can't publish articles on other alternatives, such as privatizing the houses and allowing people to renovate them according to historic guidelines. If you sit down with people and ask, 'Would you like to stay here if we could install running water and flush toilets?'—they already have electricity, so that's not an issue—then they almost all say they want to stay."

"But what about the excess population here?" I asked. "What about the six families living with Mrs. Zhang. What do you do with them?"

"Where the property rights are clear, then you have to slowly and carefully return houses to people who own them. We need the high-rises on the outskirts of town, that's undeniable. So we will have to move some people out of the old, crowded areas—just like they did in Europe after World War II. But what we don't need to do is to move out everyone, level the old build-

ings and put up shopping malls or luxury housing for a few. That isn't fair and we lose our heritage."

We'd now come out onto Di'anmen Street, having walked parallel to the canal for a few hundred meters. In English it could be translated as the Street of the Gate of Earthly Peace, a counterpoint to the famous Gate of Heavenly Peace on the south side of the Forbidden City. (While the Gate of Heavenly Peace still stands, the Gate of Earthly Peace has been torn down.) The street was narrow and bustling with commerce. Shops sold fresh green tea and small earthenware pots. A row of hardware stores offered knives and Mongolian hotpots. We headed north for a few meters and crossed an old stone bridge over the canal. I looked to the right and could see that Fang Ke had been right—the newly dredged canal passed under us but then just stopped, not continuing on its original path to the Forbidden City's moats. We turned left and walked westward, back along the north side of the canal, returning to the lake.

We passed a shopping center designed to look like some generic old China. It had concrete walls painted to look like whitewashed stone and slate-gray eaves that exuberantly curled up at the ends. It certainly looked nice but was somewhat bizarre. That's because it was a mock version of *Jiangnan* architecture from the Yangtze River valley—but built here in Beijing, about a thousand miles to the north, in a failed effort to fit in with the local architecture.

The walk was depressing me. It seemed like an admission of defeat, a few old crumbling buildings, a shopping center designed by someone who didn't know the characteristics of Beijing architecture and corrupt officials driving all the decisions. I couldn't see the magic of the old city or what had inspired Fang Ke to take up his studies. It all seemed hopeless.

We were now back in the *hutong*s and soon arrived at Silver Ingot Bridge, which straddles the two shores at a narrows where Front Lake meets Rear Lake (Houhai). We'd been walking around for an hour and stopped for a break, leaning against the stone balustrades. This view from the bridge northward to the Western Mountains was one of the famous Eight Scenes of Beijing, which had been captured in painting and poetry over the centuries. Low-rises in the foreground spoiled the view of the mountains, but it was still a lovely spot.

Then a small microtruck tried to cross the humpbacked bridge, but its way was blocked by a trishaw trying to head the other way. A bicyclist coming up behind the truck swerved crazily—like most bicyclists in Beijing, his brakes were shot. He fell off. A taxi came up the other side and started honking. The truck joined in. The bicyclist started shouting.

We looked at each other and laughed.

"Let's walk this way," Fang Ke said. "Professor Wu brought me here five years ago on that walk. We ate some *shaobing* (a toasted sesame roll) at a stall right at this intersection, and we walked up this road. It was here that I fell in love in Beijing."

In 1996 he threw himself full-time into his project. The one-hour commute between the old town and the university district became too much, so Fang Ke rented a room in a house near the Confucian Temple.

"I loved it. I realized people there were cultured and knew the old city's history backwards and forwards. For old people it was really convenient for them to live there because the hospitals and everything they needed were nearby."

And the architecture, which he once shunned as old-fashioned, began to attract him, too. "I was amazed at the variety—Qing and Ming mixing together so well. The family I stayed with wouldn't accept rent. They were so excited I was

studying the old city and wanted to do something to help protect it, so they put me up."

Next to the bridge where we stood was a narrow street. We walked toward it. "Professor Wu told me that when he walked here in 1950 with Professor Liang Congjie this street was a string of beautiful old buildings, one of the best shopping streets in the capital. Now the entire street has been declared dangerous and dilapidated, but no developer wants to build here because the official height restrictions limit buildings to nine meters. So it's just falling down."

The street was called Yandai Xiejie. The latter word simply means "a small, narrow street." The first word, *yandai*, means "smoky belt" because the street resembles a wisp of smoke curling through the old city. Now, instead of leading the visitor past one famous store after the other, it led past ruins and wrecks that were slowly being converted into bars and nightclubs. A five-and-dime store was housed in one, a shabby video rental in another.

But a close look at the buildings showed how beautiful they could be with a bit of work. One was a small, shuttered Taoist temple with faded green eaves and intricate wooden window frames. Another, No. 24, was a building from the late nineteenth century, an effort to blend western and eastern architecture. It was made of stone—a concession to foreign building practices—but its crumbling friezes of flowers and birds attested to its Chinese creator.

"Once everything was collectivized in the 1950s, no one had any interest in keeping up the buildings anymore," Fang Ke said. We had stopped to stare at No. 24 and a couple of people looked at us suspiciously. I could only imagine the thoughts going through their heads: was that foreigner secretly enjoying China's poverty?

We were now back at the Street of the Gate of Earthly Peace and headed north to the Drum Tower. We looked back down the street toward the way we'd come. Directly south at the end of the street was Prospect Hill and beyond it, straight as the crow flies, the emperor's throne.

"We are standing on the axis of Beijing," Fang Ke said. "This is the pole around which the Chinese world turns."

I closed my eyes and pictured where we were in traditional China's cosmology. Traditional western cities are often built around a church, symbolizing the centrality of Christianity to those societies. Palaces of kings are also often found at the center of cities, showing a ruler's power and might. Many modern cities are formed around banking and sporting buildings, highlighting the role of commerce and entertainment.

But the Beijing that existed a few decades ago went far beyond that. It was a complete expression of ancient China's cosmology, with the very buildings, streets, temples and lakes taking on symbolic importance and fitting into a complex system of religious beliefs.

Imposing a cosmic order on earthly space is a key ingredient of Chinese culture. Temples and houses, for example, are laid out in accordance with *fengshui*. When Taoist priests invoke spells, they open up a window into the spiritual world by walking around an altar, temporarily turning the ground into a miniature re-creation of the heavens that they can enter. And in Chinese medicine the human body is a microcosm of the universe, with organs corresponding with the different elements that make up the cosmos.

Beijing, as the epicenter of China's cultural world for six hundred years, became the purest urban expression of this fascination with attaching spiritual principles to earthly objects. Traditionally, Chinese see a bridge between the heavens and

politics—droughts and floods, for example, were expressions that the emperor wasn't fulfilling his duty as the link between heaven and earth. Just as the emperor was the symbolic focal point, the link between heaven and earth, so, too, were his temporal manifestations the center of earthly life. His throne was the city's focus and everything was built around it.

The emperor's throne was located in the Hall of Supreme Harmony, which lay in the center of the Forbidden City, a vast, 178-acre group of 8,700 halls mostly built in the seventeenth century. The popular English name Forbidden City isn't quite accurate and doesn't convey its importance. The proper Chinese name is Purple Forbidden City, with the color purple a reference to a quotation from Confucius in which he said the ruler is like the polestar—the point of reference for the entire country. In Chinese, the polestar is called the "purple pole star" and so the color was added to the Forbidden City's name to show that the emperor was the constant , a reference point to guide the empire.

Likewise, Beijing was fixed on the emperor, not just symbolically or in the sense that all traffic had to stop when the emperor left home, but in a very concrete sense. The main axis or meridian that guided the city's development wasn't a large road or boulevard, but an imaginary north-south line on which Fang Ke and I were now standing. Northward, it ran from the emperor's throne through the center of other halls in the Forbidden City, out through its north gate and over Prospect Hill. The axis then runs north along the Street of the Gate of Earthly Peace to where we stood and continued up to the Drum and Bell Towers, two giant structures whose sounds once regulated the medieval city's life. To the south of the emperor's throne the axis ran out through the Gate of Heavenly Peace and down through two other gates. All the major buildings of the old capital were built either on this axis or just off it on either side.

The axis carried such emotive power that even the communists tried to hitch their pseudoreligion to its power. When they wanted to build the sort of square for mass rallies that every communist capital had, they leveled the houses directly south of the Forbidden City. On it, they built the Monument to the People's Revolutionary Martyrs right on the axis, and when Mao died in 1976, his tomb was built directly on the imaginary line as well. Of course, these structures didn't fit with the traditions. The martyrs' monument is a giant, daggerlike structure that *feng-shui* practitioners say cuts into the energy flow along the axis. The tomb, meanwhile, is a complete abomination—traditional Chinese wouldn't put a dead body on display in the middle of town. Emperors were traditionally buried in the wooded hills outside the capital.

We walked north along the axis to the Drum Tower, a magnificent ten-story structure with a stone base and a wooden top. North of it was a small square and beyond it the similarly shaped Bell Tower. The square in between used to be filled with a warren of small restaurants and market stalls. Stomach indigestion was guaranteed if one ate here, but the chance to eat in the shadow of the two enormous towers was irresistible and several times a year I'd come here to eat spicy tripe, mutton and other Beijing specialties, and then suffer mightily the next day.

Now it was a cobblestoned square with lamps, almost like a European square. A security official lounged on one of the benches set on the square's periphery. His job was to keep people from setting up stalls and hawking things.

"The stalls appeared at the end of the Qing dynasty when the imperial system collapsed," Fang Ke said. "Before then it would have been unimaginable to have disturbed the axis. Even when the stalls were here, you could see a ridge in the center of the square that was right where the axis ran."

It was good that the stalls had been cleared away, but the renovation had been botched. The ridge was supposed to run down the center of the square, but the paving stones had been laid so that the ridge was too far to the right. The square looked lopsided. One couldn't help but conclude that the restorers didn't know the significance of the ridge and had simply repaved the square, not bothering to center it properly.

The buildings along the edge of the square had a Disneyfied look to them. To cover the crumbling stone and rotting wood, the city had put up aluminum siding on the old one-story buildings. The new panels were painted red to look like wooden panels. This was the flip side to destruction: haphazard renovation. As handicraft skills were lost, only a few teams of craftsmen were left to look after an entire city. That meant much of the work was done by people with no idea of how Chinese buildings traditionally looked or were constructed.

Despite all these problems, thinking about the axis—the energy backbone of the city, and in turn, of the imperial system—made me excited that at least this much was left. The buildings around the square had fake façades, but they could be fixed. The fact was that the Drum and Bell Towers still stood, and to the south lay the Forbidden City, its low, sleek buildings testifying to the emperor's broad, vast power. I could see why Fang Ke hadn't given up; the *hutong*s in between these monuments were worth protecting. Together, they formed an ensemble of buildings that hinted at how the Chinese had structured their world for thousands of years.

We walked west from the Bell Tower, weaving through the alleys northeast of the lakes. Walking through a *hutong* was amazingly pleasant, although it can sound tedious if you only imagine a *hutong* as a series of walls. But the *hutong*s' constant turns and twists opened up new vistas every few feet. Trees

stretch out over the street from the courtyards, and the doorways often boast small decorations that intimated the owners' power and rank. Sometimes two *hutong*s converge and a few cars might be parked at this mini-intersection or a couple of children might be practicing badminton.

It was late August and still sultry, but autumn was approaching. Flatbed trishaws carted briquettes of coal from door to door, dumping their loads inside the front door. Residents were already arranging the piles into neat stacks that they make under the eaves of their homes or in corners of the courtyards.

We passed by a small hotel on Small Stone Bridge Lane that had become popular with some savvy travelers. It was a former mansion, with a series of courtyards that led to a small garden with an artificial hill. The threadbare accommodations weren't luxurious, but the location in the old town and the courtyards made it fun. Many people staying there would go for a walk in the morning and have a long, leisurely lunch in the restaurant. Sitting under one of the trees in the front courtyard, sipping a beer, one felt transported into another time. Which era depended on how much one knew about the building.

The mansion had been built in the Qing dynasty and been home to a succession of members of the royal family, but its most famous resident had been Kang Sheng, the head of Chairman Mao's secret police and spy network. Kang had lived there for twenty years, coordinating terror campaigns against the populace and becoming a strong supporter of Mao during the Cultural Revolution. It was a measure of just how terrible Kang was that he was expelled from the Communist Party (posthumously, of course) in 1980. After the Cultural Revolution only the very worst of the worst were expelled from the party; most kept their jobs and positions, part of the party's inability to face its history.

Kang was one of those archetypal secret-police heads. He was often compared to the legendary Soviet henchman Lavrenti Beria, but instead of indulging in sexual perversions, he liked to collect artwork, especially his victims'. During the Cultural Revolution, when people like Professor Liang were forced to burn or somehow dispose of their treasured books, scrolls and old wood furniture, Kang was able to amass a huge collection of goods. As an added twist, he imitated the people he destroyed, retreating to this charming location to practice calligraphy and enjoy his antiques.

One person whom Kang Sheng exploited was Old Mr. Zhao, who lost his furniture and library. Fang Ke told me the story.

"When Kang read a book, he stamped it 'Read by Kang Sheng,' and he catalogued the Ming furniture that he stole," Fang Ke said as we walked past the entrance to the hotel. "After the end of the Cultural Revolution the books were returned to Old Mr. Zhao, but he didn't want to see those stamps in the books anymore so he donated everything to the Shanghai Museum." The pieces are on display there today, with a small label underneath the desk where Old Mr. Zhao's sister translated Walt Whitman. No mention is made of the suffering that brought the pieces to the museum.

That explained the lack of old furniture or books in Old Mr. Zhao's home, save for the wooden screen. I wonder how many times one has to have a heartbreaking loss before one simply gives up on possessions. During the Cultural Revolution, Red Guards took a military medal from Professor Liang's mother-in-law. Her son had been an aviator in World War II and was shot down. The medal, of course, had been issued by the Nationalists, not the communists, since the Nationalists were the official government of China and the only one with an air force. But in the

zealots' eyes it was a contaminated award and they confiscated it. After losing their books, furniture, home, freedom to think and travel, the mother finally lost the last memento of her son. Did she ever think of giving up?

She hadn't, and neither would Old Mr. Zhao. Like Mr. Liang, Old Mr. Zhao's father had probably made a mistake by not fleeing to Taiwan. There, he could have continued his religious work, instead of being forced to kowtow to the communists' erratic policies. But he was an optimist and had stayed on. The house, purchased in 1949 just after the communists took over, was a symbol of that attitude. Professor Liang's mother-in-law had pulled and tugged at the Red Guards, begging them to hand back the medal as they gleefully held it up as "proof" that the family was secretly allied with the Nationalists. Old Mr. Zhao was fighting for his father's home just as stubbornly.

We headed south to the Rear Lake (Houhai), passing a large courtyard home where Fang Ke had held an impromptu book-signing. He had spent quite a bit of time at that particular home while doing his research and brought over a few books to give to the family and neighbors. When the people heard that Fang Ke was back and that his book was out, dozens lined up. He called a friend who quickly brought over a few cartons of books. That night alone they sold more than a hundred.

"People are interested in their homes and their environment," Fang Ke said as we passed the doorway. We decided not to go in but to continue on. "The big issue now is the home of Cao Xueqin [China's famous eighteenth-century novelist] at the Ciqikou intersection. I got a call saying twenty-two families had sued the government over its decision to destroy that neighborhood and Cao's home."

It was midafternoon, but even though the siesta time was

over, the streets remained quiet. The clouds wanted to burst; a month earlier they probably would have. Beijing gets most of its rain in the summer months and the rest of the year is bone-dry. One could feel that dry autumn approaching. Leaves rustled and the cicadas were silent. Everything felt empty, as though we were the only people in the city.

We stopped at No. 47 Nanguanfang Hutong. It was housing provided to employees of the State Council, an administrative arm of the government—more proof that the government had taken the best homes after 1949 and was still occupying them, while telling everyone else that they had to get out of the old city because it was dilapidated. Some children played hide-and-seek, running from courtyard to courtyard. It was a splendid place to play, and the children shrieked with pleasure as they tore around from yard to yard. Big chestnut and scholar trees shaded the ground, and the children hid themselves in the half-ordered stacks of odds and ends—bricks, tiles, tires and whatever else years of hamster economics had taught people to stow away.

We felt like intruders spoiling the kids' fun so walked out again. The walls along the sides of the alley were red instead of the usual gray. Fang Ke began to explain why.

"These are made more simply than gray bricks. Gray ones have water poured on them when they're hot. These red ones, I think, are old, but for some reason the people back then didn't spend as much time on this segment of the wall," he said, peering at the bricks.

Just as he said that, a man was riding by on his bike. He quickly jumped off and corrected Fang Ke.

"No, no, these are new walls. They were just put up a few years ago," he said with a quick, machine-gun delivery.

He was a thin man, wearing just boxer shorts, brown leather

shoes and white socks. He was shirtless in the summer heat but seemed ready to slip into a pair of dress pants and shirt at a moment's notice.

"Why did they make them red instead of gray?" I asked them both.

"Communists like the color red," the man said. "And it's cheap. No one bothers to make the walls in the old ways anymore. Too much trouble."

With that short lecture on urban construction he hopped back on his bike and headed off.

We'd been walking for several hours and were tired. We decided to head over to a project that Fang Ke had worked on in 1998 with some MIT architects. Originally, we wanted to walk over but we weren't sure we'd make it, so we hopped a cab.

The driver took us through several *hutong*s, and then we were suddenly back on Peace Boulevard. Half the shops on it were empty. Under pressure from developers, the city had argued that leveling the old homes and widening the street wasn't just needed to alleviate traffic flows. The old city, they said, needed big new stores along the street, so it built stores in a mock-old style with concrete walls painted red or gray to resemble an old building. The rents, though, were expensive and too large for most of the mom-and-pop businesses that predominate in this part of town. So they remained mostly empty.

We zoomed west and then cut south into a *hutong*. We were back in old Beijing. The traffic slowed as cars and bicycles competed for the limited space.

"See how crowded it is," Fang Ke said as we suddenly stopped moving. "In 1949, between 700,000 and 1 million people lived here. Now it's 1.7 million. I don't think we need to go back to the old population; we've done studies that show we could reduce the overcrowding and restore most of the old homes if we

just moved 100,000 to 200,000 people. That's not that many compared to what's being done now."

We decided to abandon the taxi for the final stretch. We walked south, skirting the White Dagoba Temple (Baitaisi), named after the giant structure shaped like a snake-charmer's bottle. Built in the eleventh century, the dagoba had been frequented by Kublai Khan, who turned it into one of the city's centers of Buddhist worship. The temple was surrounded by six-foot-high walls made of gray bricks that had been gone over with a coat of red paint.

"It didn't look like this originally," he said, running his hand over the flaking paint. They think all old buildings have red paint. But the truth is that the temple walls were originally the same color as the houses'. They should be gray."

To our left as we walked south were rows of old houses. None were as majestic as those we'd seen by the lakes. This had always been a poorer part of town, and it showed in the cramped homes formerly owned by lower-middle-class artisans and shopkeepers.

A few years ago Fang Ke had worked here on a project with some MIT students. The goal was to come up with a feasible plan to renovate the neighborhood, which had been devastated in the 1960s by the destruction of one of Beijing's most famous temples: Huguosi, or the Temple of National Protection. It had been a Buddhist temple but primarily a center of Beijing's largest folk festival on Chinese New Year. The festival had lasted for two weeks, attracting millions of visitors, and had been the focal point of the community for much of the rest of the year. That had made it a target of communist authorities, who pulled it down.

The students had come up with a plan to protect the best-preserved of the homes and build a square in front of the White Dagoba Temple. We walked by the entrance and decided not to

go in. The reliquaries had all been destroyed in the Cultural Revolution, and all that was left was the big white dagoba. We wandered around, and Fang Ke took pictures of the neighborhood for his friends at MIT.

Then we walked up the other side of the temple, now heading north. The narrow road met another small street in a slanting X intersection, forming a small square. Restaurants opened out onto the square, many selling spit-roasted chicken. One man stood in front of the glass-enclosed rotisserie, staring at the birds as they slowly rotated, dripping fat.

Farther up the road we saw a giant, ten-story building, gray and in the style of a Stalinist wedding-cake building.

"It was called a 'communism building' by the locals," Fang Ke said. "It was built in the Great Leap Forward when everyone was supposed to live together. It had one kitchen per floor and one group of toilets."

Each of Beijing's four central districts was supposed to have one, the ultimate in communist city planning. Two were built and one torn down. This was the last one standing, and it was unpopular, with people rejecting the lack of facilities and the shoddy construction.

We walked down the street and then cut over toward the dagoba, which loomed over the low buildings. We passed a former lama residence that had Tibetan prayer wheels on the roof. They contained the scriptures and were proof of the lama's devotion, and wealth. The building looked as if it were going to fall over; I wondered how long it would stand.

Fang Ke seemed to be looking for something. He went off to ask for directions and quickly returned.

"It's down one of these streets," he said as we walked by a couple of two-story warehouses that were built next to the temple. We walked through a wholesale meat market selling freshly

slaughtered beef and ascended a metal fire escape on the back of one building. Perching on a landing, we stared over the temple and neighborhood.

"There he said," like a connoisseur displaying his favorite painting. "It's so low, we can see everything."

From up above, the old city looked like a charming slum. The eaves still sloped upward, and if one had bad eyesight, it looked beautiful, with the giant white dagoba surrounded by gray one-story homes and shops. But the tiles were falling off most roofs, and repairs consisted of throwing sheet metal over the holes and laying bricks along the edges to weigh it down. In other cases people had tossed what looked like bags of rubbish on the sheet metal. Sometimes people had cemented over the holes. I could see what Fang Ke meant by the need for property rights. If the homes were sold, then owners might invest in their upkeep, as they had for centuries.

"The old tiles are so pleasing to look at. They look like fish scales, shimmering in the sunlight. The old capital . . ." he said, his voice trailing off. "It seems lost, vanished."

That term reminded me of a tome by the historian Susan Naquin, who wrote on Beijing's urban life from 1400 to 1900. Beijing had been a capital for the past six hundred years and during that time had come to symbolize many different Chinas. Especially after the Ming dynasty collapsed in the seventeenth century, writers wrote longingly of the "lost" or "vanished" capital, even though of course Beijing was still standing. What they had usually meant was the loss of one dynasty for another, but their works also had a dreamlike quality, a paean to a bygone era.

It was an exercise repeated in the early twentieth century, when many of the writers were foreign and their laments for the loss of "Old Peking" had a colonial ring. Between the two world wars Beijing was filled with romantic westerners who noted how

the new Nationalist government hadn't kept up the temples or monuments. Its decay, they noted, began in the last decades of the old imperial rule, when China's economic and political decline left no money to maintain the temples and palaces that embodied the country's complex religion of ancestor and god worship. Moreover after the emperor abdicated in 1912 many of the temples lost their function. If the emperor was no longer the intermediary between heaven and earth, there was no need for the Temple of Heaven, where he would go to pray for good harvests. The temple stayed (and still exists—it is one of Beijing's best-known tourist sites), but many others fell into decay and were pulled down.

Ms. Naquin was no sentimentalist—indeed her book tries to draw as few implications as possible for the present. But toward the end she allowed herself a few sentences about what had happened to Beijing at the close of the twentieth century. Even though the city lost numerous temples, homes and its great walls in the 1950s and '60s, the destruction during the 1990s, she wrote, was greater than at any other time this century: "My research was not begun as, nor is it now intended to be, an exercise in nostalgia, either for vanished temples or for a lost Peking. . . . Nevertheless, if viewed—just for one moment—against the current destruction of the city, this book reminds even me of a 'record of a dream of a vanished capital.' "

I looked down at the fish scales, their shadows creeping longer as the late-summer sun went down. In the distance the great park of Beihai, where we had met to start our walk, was a giant swath of green. I thought back to Fang Ke's teacher, Professor Wu, and his teacher, Professor Liang. Both had stressed the organic nature of the city, and here it seemed literal. The old city stretched out before us like a broken carapace that the new city was shedding.

•　　•　　•

Huang Yan was deputy head of urban planning at the Beijing Municipal Institute of City Planning and Design and had been walking around an enormous conference room, crossing over from one gargantuan map of Beijing to another, pointing out historic protection zones. Government officials were reluctant to discuss Beijing's urban planning—probably because it had been so contradictory and such an abject failure. But the city had recently announced a new plan to protect the old town and felt obliged to grant an interview.

"In the fifties to the seventies, about a fifth of the old city was torn down for government buildings," she said. "In the eighties not much happened, and then in the nineties we decided to protect the old city. We issued a document in 1992 identifying twenty-five areas that needed special protection," she said, rapping a ruler on one of twenty-five pink squares in the old town.

"The same twenty-five that were announced in 2000?" I asked.

"Well, yes. For whatever reason that plan in 1992 wasn't fully realized. You see, the only people who care about protecting the old city are intellectuals. Residents only care about raising their living standards," she said with a confident smile.

"What about the class-action lawsuits? Many of those people want to protect their buildings," I said.

"That's for the courts to decide," she said firmly.

I felt like I was in a war room, or a movie set of a war room, because nothing real was going on here. Still, I liked Ms. Huang. She was in many ways similar to Fang Ke. She was a bit older, about thirty-five, and had already studied abroad, something Fang Ke was planning to do shortly. Like him, she was part of a group of Chinese who felt part of the outside world. Her

two years at an urban-planning institute in Belgium had influenced her, and she looked distinctly different from most Chinese women. She wore tiny rectangular glasses popular in Europe, a white blouse and a floral-print batik skirt that went down to her ankles. A Chinese person who looked at her would immediately guess that she'd lived abroad.

She had come back to a government job. And like all intellectuals, especially those who have been overseas, her power was limited. The institute wasn't really a key city office. It was a quasi–think tank, where ideas were hatched and sent off to the city's party branch for discussion. Still, she was genuinely concerned about the city but seemed a bit like Fang Ke before his walk with Professor Wu. She didn't live in the old city, and even her institute was located outside of the old town.

"When I visited a *hutong* last year on a bike I realized how hard it was just to ride a bicycle in there," she said. "There are so many cars on them now. The *hutong*s used to be public spaces where children played and old people sat. Now it's too dangerous to do that. The fabric has changed."

"So why not restrict car access," I said. "Like old towns in Europe, you could keep autos on the main thoroughfares and keep them off the *hutong*s."

"The problem, you see, is that the *hutong*s aren't really made for the modern world. It's not just cars, it's other things."

"Like . . ."

"Like gas. The *hutong*s are too narrow for gas pipes. Or sewage. So you see they have to be widened or dealt with in some way."

Maybe Fang Ke had prepped me too well, but I felt I knew her lines better than she did.

"And there's another problem," she said.

"The houses are made of wood?" I said.

"Exactly! You've put your finger right on it."

She'd found an ally.

"Look at European cities. They're made of stone. Not wood. How can you protect wood? You can't. It disintegrates. Old European cities are more modern, even the old parts. They can be wired and there's space for toilets. Beijing is a medieval city. Medieval Paris was destroyed by Napoleon III in the nineteenth century, so when they now modernize old buildings, they only have to modernize structures that are a hundred fifty years old. Ours are five hundred years old."

"So it can't be done," I said.

"Well," she shrugged. "Look at this."

She spread out a big map of the city. It showed the 62.5 square kilometers of the old city, all of which was once inside the city walls and which now was inside the ring road built on the site of the old wall. The old city was shaded in five colors: red, yellow, blue, green and white. Red areas had the strictest protection and included well-known temples and palaces, like the Forbidden City. Yellow was made up of protected streets. Blue was for areas where the "morphology" had to stay the same—street layouts and building heights—but the buildings could be torn down and rebuilt. Green were belts around the protected areas where height restrictions were imposed. In white areas anything was allowed. Most of the map, 62 percent, was white.

Of the remaining 38 percent, about half of it was made up of the Forbidden City and Beihai Park, which formed a giant red and yellow rectangle in the middle of the old town. To the north was another yellow belt of protected areas, which made up much of the area around the Bell and Drum Towers where I'd walked with Fang Ke. These areas were surrounded by a few blue and green belts. A few blotches of yellow or red were dotted on the map, but otherwise it was white.

I looked back on the big map and saw why Old Mr. Zhao's home would be torn down. He lived in a white zone. The plan seemed to be that anything outside these few narrow red and yellow areas would be torn down.

"Look at this," she said, pulling out a large-scale map of one of the yellow belts near the Forbidden City. It was an amazingly beautiful technical work, with almost every courtyard home drawn in and even the ancient trees marked in red. As I studied the map, I noticed that some of the buildings were colored yellow but others weren't.

"On this map, not all the buildings that are in the yellow zone on the big map are yellow on this small-scale map," I said.

"Yes, well even in the yellow zone we can't save all the houses. We'll save about two-thirds. The rest will be torn down."

"So, let me summarize," I said. "Of the 62.5 square kilometers, about 62 percent or two-thirds is open to development. Of the remaining 38 percent, about half is to be protected, so about 19 percent. And of the protected 19 percent, about one-third will be torn down. So the percentage of buildings that will be protected will be about 13 percent of the old town."

"Well, there are the green and blue belts—"

"Which are new buildings with height restrictions."

"Well, we might save a few old buildings in those zones."

After a few pleasantries I left and walked outside. Next door was a bookstore run by the institute and which was devoted to city planning. I asked about Fang Ke's book. It wasn't on sale. Out of stock, perhaps? No, they'd never heard of it.

Old Mr. Zhao finally had his final day in court. It was September 21, 2000, at the Beijing Municipal Second Intermediate Court.

Foreigners were banned, but a Chinese friend went and told me what happened.

The court was located in a tiny room in what seemed to be a regular housing block. At five past nine, the judge and a secretary entered and read the verdict. The reading lasted fifteen minutes, but boiled down it meant this: Old Mr. Zhao had five days to leave his home. If he stayed, the construction company had the right to force him out.

A member of the audience who faced the same problem sighed and said, "This is brutal. We are being robbed."

Lawyer Wu went to talk to the judge. His client, he said, faced a Catch-22: He was appealing a related case but the appeal wouldn't be considered for another month. But according to today's ruling, Old Mr. Zhao's home was going to be torn down in five days. Could the judge extend the five days to thirty so the other appeal could be considered? The judge promised an answer and left.

I went back to Old Mr. Zhao's home a few days later. It was early September and still hot. Dressed in a gray T-shirt and tan cotton trousers, he met me silently at the door and then turned to walk inside. I closed the wooden door behind me, shutting out the busy sounds of the street.

"We're still fighting," he said with a wave of his hand as he shuffled in.

He rattled off a list of prominent Beijing intellectuals who had drawn up a petition in support of him. They included Professor Liang's son, Liang Congjie, and Shu Yi, the son of Lao She, an author who had set many of his short stories and novels in Beijing's *hutong*s. Lao She had been hounded to death during

the Cultural Revolution, jumping off a bridge into one of the lakes I had walked by with Fang Ke. His death gave the son an aura of moral authority.

The men had forwarded Old Mr. Zhao's petition to Li Rui-huan, a senior party member who was the official glad-hander of religious groups, intellectuals, ethnic minorities and so on. He was supposed to be a reformer but was about as powerless as the groups he met.

"So," said Old Mr. Zhao. "We've got some people on our side."

"That's good," I said.

"And don't forget what Mayor Jia Qinglin said: 'Respect the opinion of experts.' "

"When did he say that?" I asked.

"In 1999."

It had come in response to a public rebuke delivered by Fang Ke. He'd attended a meeting of experts called to discuss the construction of Peace Boulevard. Because it had involved the destruction of so many historic structures, another petition had circulated and the mayor had called the meeting to assess the situation. A series of mealy-mouthed officials spoke, and at the very end Fang Ke stood up. His book wasn't out yet, but he had penned a few razor-sharp articles for national publications about the boulevard. He had pointed out then what was obvious now: the boulevard would look horrible and few shopkeepers would be attracted to the fake-looking shops that line it.

After pointing out the lack of market research, the flawed assumptions on traffic flows and so on, he concluded with this rather bold statement—bold, at least, for an academic to say to a powerful leader like Mayor Jia: "Reforming old Beijing by constructing Peace Boulevard only shows that the city lacks a clear understanding of the mistakes it has made before and the severe

problems that are occurring today that are the results of those mistakes."

It wasn't the most stirring rhetoric, but the essence was painfully blunt: you haven't learned from your mistakes. At the end of the meeting Mayor Jia had made a vague summary, thanked everyone and promised to "respect the opinion of experts."

No one thought that Mayor Jia intended to listen to many experts. Instead, he'd listen to his advisers, who'd tell him to "modernize" the city, advice that not coincidentally would also make a lot of officials rich.

"Well," I said to Old Mr. Zhao, "there's some hope still."

We were sitting down again in his living room. His eyes were hard and clear. He was old and knew the fate that likely awaited him.

"And if . . ." I trailed off.

"I'll never agree with this. When they come to tear it down and bring in the Public Security Bureau and the ambulances— they do this, you know, because people often faint when this happens—I'll go. I'm just a simple citizen. I can't fight the law. but I'll never agree with what they do."

I got a call from Fang Ke in late September.

"I'm going," he said. "MIT has agreed to let me take courses and I got a visa yesterday at the U.S. embassy."

"But the semester has already started," I said.

"It doesn't matter. I'm going to audit some courses and improve my English. Then I'll attend next semester and apply for a fellowship somewhere. I'm going really soon. Tomorrow."

It was one of those unexpected calls one sometimes got from Chinese friends. An opportunity would present itself to leave the country, and suddenly they were going, with almost no notice. I

knew he had been planning to go to the United States to study, but I'd thought it would take months. I felt sad. He hadn't saved the old city, I thought, although I knew it was a bit ridiculous to feel that way.

October 26, 2000: Old Mr. Zhao's house was about to be torn down. I got to his house around 9 a.m. The street was partly blocked off and a small crowd had gathered to watch. A few foreign journalists mingled in the crowd, but most of those present seemed to be locals who knew Old Mr. Zhao personally. The local newspapers hadn't been permitted to carry news of his case, so most people didn't know about it.

Old Mr. Zhao had left the night before. A representative from the court had come to tell him that the appeal on his second case wouldn't be heard until after his house was slated to be torn down. The wrecking crew would come the next day, the official told him. Chairman Mao's secret police had stolen his father's library and furniture. Not much was left. He donated his large wooden room dividers to a museum, packed up and that night left his home of fifty years.

Police cleared away onlookers from the front of the house. I breezed past them, pretending to be simply walking down the street on my way somewhere. Old Mr. Zhao's red doors were broken, and I looked in at the little stone wall that is inside every Chinese courtyard house. It is supposed to keep outsiders from looking in and, according to the principles of *fengshui*, evil forces from entering the house. An illegible government proclamation was stuck on it and a dozen peasant workers had climbed onto his roof, just above the stone elephants that were supposed to protect it. The workers ripped up the glazed tiles and then attacked the wooden eaves with crowbars.

As I walked back a second time, a policeman herded me away. He pretended to be friendly and told me that it was "for our safety"—a phrase that in China always means something else. A few other policemen stood nearby. A couple muttered to each other, "What do they want?" and "They should just take off, get out." Two of them strung up police tape that read in Chinese and English "Limit Line."

It was a brilliant, sunny day, a bit cold and hazy but unusually clear. The smog had blown away, and I turned my head upward, soaking in some sun. Nearby was a stall making *jianbing,* a small fried pancake. Another sold newspapers, its rack groaning with a huge array of newspapers that were free to discuss anything, from sex to sports, except for one topic: how people might run their government. A small crowd of people stood and stared, attracted by the police, the foreigners and the peasant workers.

A French artist sat there, sketching the scene in a small notebook. He had just come from the home of Cao Xueqin, the eighteenth-century author whose house was also being leveled. His sketchbook was now open to Old Mr. Zhao's home. The page showed the stone lions and elephants that jutted from the walls. "The doors are superb and the lions really unusual. I've sketched throughout the *hutong*s but haven't seen any like this." A police officer craned over to have a look at what the artist was drawing. He looked bemused and slightly angry.

The street itself was slated to disappear if Beijing won its bid to host the 2008 Olympics. Meishuguan Houjie would be widened and the remaining old buildings leveled. A poster glued to a wall heralded the inevitable change: "Develop Commercial Beijing City—Wangfujing General Commercial Real Estate Development Co." I wasn't sure what the jumble of words meant. Was it an order? A prediction? Next to it was a torn

poster: "Beijing City Exhibition on Fighting and Preventing Economic Crimes."

A Chinese photographer took a few photos. She said she had recorded Old Mr. Zhao's home over the past year. "I have pictures from each of the four seasons," she said. Of course, she knew everyone: Fang Ke, Wang Jun and the older generation of preservationists. She was going to exhibit the photos, she said, and invited me to attend its opening.

A group of schoolchildren was trying to walk north on the street, a path that would have led them by Old Mr. Zhao's home. They were stopped by the police line and spilled out into the street. The street started plugging up. A bus stopped. Cars started honking. The police glared at the foreign journalists. "Go home," one yelled. Once we went home, I guessed the "safety" concerns would evaporate and people would be allowed to walk in front of the home, which was now sinking under the workers' pickaxes and crowbars. It would just become another house being leveled in Beijing, a completely normal sight. My presence wouldn't change anything. I turned around and left.

The day after Old Mr. Zhao's home was torn down, I got an e-mail from Fang Ke. It was an essay called "Eternal No. 22"—which was Old Mr. Zhao's house number on Meishuguan Houjie. It was addressed to a group of friends who had been interested in, and in some cases helped fight to preserve, the old courtyard home. He had written it from Paris.

> It's five o'clock in the morning here in Paris, and I know that over there in Beijing they are tearing down No. 22 Meishuguan Houjie. I can't close my eyes; the whole night through I

keep thinking of a way [for the house] to escape. But I know that it's no use. My friends have told me by cell phone that several cars have already been by to carry away belongings, that the street is filled with several hundred police, 20-odd foreign journalists and that earth-moving equipment is waiting by the side.

I can't close my eyes; I feel that from now on I'll never again be able to sleep. Maybe this is just one courtyard home from the late-Ming or early-Qing but why do they want to tear it down? This is something beautiful that our ancestors bequeathed us, another part of our shrinking capital. It's a crime to tear it down!

For two and a half years I don't know how many times I've knocked at that door. Inside was the owner, over 80, of this courtyard home with at least 360 years of history. It had radiantly yellow chrysanthemums and was so peaceful. I don't know how many times over the past two and a half years I sat on the sofa across from Zhao Jingxin, slowly drinking some scalding jasmine tea, enjoying his Ming-era furniture or listening to his news. I knew clearly that this courtyard home was on [the Emperor] Qianlong's map of Beijing, that one of the emperor's doctors had lived here and that Zhao Jingxin's father, Zhao Zichen, had left a few of his belongings here. The father had been a leader of China's Christians and a hero in the anti-Japanese war and found refuge in the house before he was molested [in the Cultural

Revolution]. Once I saw a big white cat that seemed to possess great intelligence comfortably sunning itself in the corridor.

Every time I closed the door behind me and entered the courtyard, it felt like this was the real Beijing. Outside its walls was noise and confusion, but none of it reached the inside. When I talked to Old Mr. Zhao, I had this illusion that nothing was going to happen, as if the world outside didn't exist. This is what a courtyard house is. In the whole world of architecture only a courtyard house could create such an environment and in all of history only a courtyard house could captivate people so. In all the world no other style has been commended or doted on as much as a courtyard house, with so many authors writing about it. How they would tremble today!

I'm really sad. Sad for the loss of an irreplaceable cultural relic, for the violation of Old Mr. and Mrs. Zhao's civil rights. This has been their private property for 50 years, something sacred that they shouldn't be deprived of or violated. After 1982 when land rights were given to the state, citizens still enjoyed the right to protection of property use—how can it suddenly be taken away?

Old Mr. and Mrs. Zhao are so old and for the last two years have had to live in such fear and had such a hard time to protect their home and this national cultural relic. Their spirits are still exhausted and to have such an unexpected

outcome! How can glass surreptitiously be smashed, walls pulled down and for the courts to write congratulatory letters like the building can "victoriously be torn down"?

I'm really sad. When I return to Beijing and walk to Meishuguan Houjie, I won't be able to knock on the door and a piece of life's beauty won't exist. Close to 400 years of history will be wiped away cleanly in a few hours by earth-moving machines and spades.

Now that Old Mr. Zhao had lost his suit, I wanted to know how Messrs. Luo and Feng had fared. No news, they said over the telephone, but let's meet anyway. It was early 2001, and they wanted to hear the latest about Fang Ke and Old Mr. Zhao. The second floor of the KFC was as brightly lit as ever, but this time we were able to get Mr. Luo's favorite table in the back corner. I slouched low in the plastic bucket seats and tried to make the call as social as possible.

This time we even ordered some food. As I slurped from my paper cup of Lipton, I made my first blunder.

"Old Mr. Zhao lost his case," I said. "Are you worried about your situation? Maybe it's a bit sensitive?"

Mr. Feng stopped eating. He pushed his tray over to the empty side of the table and opened his briefcase. Out of it he pulled a copy of the constitution. The last sentence in Chapter 1, Article 10, was underlined, and he pointed to it: "The state may, in the public interest, requisition land for its use in accordance with the law." The last five words were underlined twice, the strokes so heavy they almost tore through the paper.

"This is my good-luck charm," he said. "You see how tough

our life is. We have no money and the money we raised has run out. We pay our costs ourselves. We're not against the government, but the government is against us. We've both had to meet with the Public Security Bureau so many times that we know their questions before they ask them. But what we do is in accordance with the law. So I don't think it's sensitive."

"How do you answer when the police ask you?" I asked.

"That we're just using the constitution and our right to sue, that we're apolitical and interested in the law."

I bet that's useful, I thought. Then Mr. Feng smiled and trumped me again.

"What I don't tell them is that I have more legitimacy than a member of the National People's Congress."

I jerked forward. "Huh?"

"We didn't appoint ourselves as head of the lawsuit," Mr. Luo said in his deep baritone. "We were elected. January 2000. A secret ballot. Feng and I got ten thousand free and fair ballots for us. How many people vote for a member of the people's congress? Zero."

Our quiet talk was suddenly very loud. A few heads craned around to take a look.

"Let's go outside," I said.

We finished our teas and walked outside. It was a cold winter day and we clapped our hands to stay warm. Mr. Luo crossed the street and we followed him. We walked behind the Bank of China building and into a maze of *hutong*s.

"This is where I grew up," he said.

We walked silently down one alley, into another and then turned quickly into someone's courtyard home. A small coal oven in the corner gave heat. I sat down on a folding chair next to a card table. The room was neat, but everything was worn to the nub. Even the concrete floor seemed ready to sink down into the

earth. The windows were made of wood lattice and glass, but the wood was old and cracked; no one had oiled it for decades and in Beijing's dry climate that meant death. Someone had put in a drop ceiling; I imagined the rafters above it, the elaborate post-and-beam construction waiting for a restorer's hand or the peasant worker's pickax.

The owner of the house was Mr. Luo's previous neighbor. He was a thin man with a two-day growth of beard and a weather-beaten face. The two had grown up together and been fast friends. Mr. Luo's house had been torn down as part of the botched Financial Street development project. The original plan was to extend the street up to the Kentucky Fried Chicken, but the project had run out of money and not even the land where Mr. Luo's house once stood had been built upon. But one day the construction glut would be over and the appetite for more office space return. Mr. Luo's friend knew his house would then fall. Unless, of course, the city had a change of heart.

"We need help," the man said as Messrs. Luo and Feng looked on impassively. "Someone has to change the way the government thinks."

"The lawsuit?" I said, turning to Mr. Feng.

"The last court we could think of has rejected it. We're hoping for help from abroad."

That was usually the sign of a lost cause, and the people who said it knew it. It was like a bankrupt person spending his last dollar on a lottery ticket. But again, I'd misunderstood them.

"What he means," Mr. Luo said loudly, barging into my train of thought, "is that we want you to take this book to Fang Ke. He will help us."

I looked at him in surprise. "What?"

"You are going to go to America, are you not? You will take a copy of our book to him. He will think of something to do."

"Well, I had hoped to see him, but he's just a student at a school. What can he do?" My eyes looked around the room and out into the gray courtyard. An oak tree stood barren in the weak winter light. Would it soon be the lobby of a bank?

"No," Mr. Luo said, shaking his head. "He might not be able to save this courtyard, but he will help people learn about things here. He will come back with new ideas and help us save other streets and other homes."

Fang Ke had joined his wife, Zhang Yan, in Cambridge, Massachusetts. He was due to start soon at a World Bank course down in Washington and had come here for a few months to familiarize himself with the United States and brush up on his shaky English. The course was designed to train young professionals for work in the bank or back in their homelands. It was ideal for him and a chance to put his knowledge of China to practical use, perhaps in the future as someone assigned to fund a bank's urban redevelopment project back in China or another country.

When he came here, he thought of translating his book into English. But as he began to immerse himself in western academia, he set more modest goals for himself. Even though his book was marvelously sourced and footnoted, it was still a polemic tract compared to a western academic study. His book, he was realizing, had been an odd creation. It was supposed to be about architecture, but the outrageous destruction of architecture had led Fang Ke to analyze the cause of this, which he traced to Beijing's corrupt urban planning.

A few months later I got a copy of a paper that Fang Ke presented to a United Nations conference. It had the suitably obtuse title for a western academic paper: "Redevelopment of Historic Neighborhoods of Beijing in a Transitional Economy During

Rapid Urban Development Process." It was also much more detailed in analyzing the economic reasons behind the old city's destruction. Bit by bit, he was reworking his book in a western academic style, making his ideas accessible to people worldwide.

We spent an afternoon walking around Boston, but it wasn't quite the same as in China. Back there he had known the reason for every building's placement, size and shape. Here he was casting an eye at a foreign tradition, figuring out how the lessons learned here could be transferred back home.

"I want to be in China," he said as we rambled through the downtown. "It's not my dream to be here. This is a great place and I'm learning a lot, but it's not my home."

It was a feeling I had never experienced, but I had learned to understand it. It was common throughout China, whose culture and history are so strong that few really break free of its gravity. Like thousands of Chinese students before him, he'd discovered a Chinese grocery store in Boston, bought Chinese ingredients and cooked Chinese food every night. "I think that if you take a person out of their environment, they can't do as much," he said.

Was the same true of his work, I wondered. I couldn't help but draw comparisons between him and his intellectual predecessor, Professor Liang. Both were dedicated to saving the old city and both were supported by remarkable wives who shared their interests. China now was more stable than it was a few decades ago, and I knew that should he return to China, he wouldn't face the persecution that had wasted decades of Professor Liang's life before killing him.

Yet progress wasn't linear. Fang Ke and the home-owners who were suing the government would likely fail in their efforts to save Beijing. Realistically, the government was bent on destroying everything but a few small corners of the old town, turning them into tourist zones where buses could disgorge people for a stroll

through the remaining *hutong*s and pick them up a few blocks later to take them to an authentic "old Beijing" restaurant—or maybe a KFC. Beijing was turning into a vanished capital, vanished at least in the sense that it was too late to preserve enough sections of the city so modern-day people could get a feel for China's old political and cultural order.

Now it was night and Fang Ke had to get home to cook dinner. We took the subway back to Cambridge and said good-bye. As he was leaving, I suddenly realized that I hadn't given him Messrs. Feng and Luo's samizdat book.

I handed it over and he cracked one of his trademark grins.

"They're still at it," he said as we shook hands and left.

3 TURNING THE WHEEL

Chen Zixiu traveled alone. It was late Thursday afternoon, and she avoided her neighbors' watchful eyes, slipping out of the house as it grew dark. It was cold, and she was prepared to sleep outside if necessary, bundled up in heavy padded clothes and corduroy shoes with thick cotton soles. She caught the 8 p.m. bus to Beijing and dozed fitfully, wondering what she'd do when she arrived ten hours later.

Her goal was simple: make her way to the city's gargantuan Tiananmen Square and protest the government's crackdown on Falun Gong, the exercise and spiritual movement that she rigorously followed. It had been over four months since the government had banned Falun Gong as an "evil cult," and during that time many people she knew had been detained for refusing to renounce it. Now the government had sentenced senior leaders of the group to years in prison. Ms. Chen decided that her voice had to be heard, so she joined the piecemeal flow of adherents who were making their way to the capital to protest the crackdown.

It was her first trip to Beijing, but she was sure she could find Tiananmen Square. What she needed was advice on how to avoid being caught ahead of time by police, who she'd heard had plugged the side streets leading there. She hit upon the idea of a

park. She knew that public practice of Falun Gong was illegal, but in her hometown it was still possible to find Falun Gong practitioners in public parks if one got there very early. Her bus arrived in Beijing just after 4 a.m.—early enough, she figured, to find a few adherents. Picking up a shopping bag that she used to carry her personal belongings, Ms. Chen took a slow, creaky bus to Beijing's biggest park, the Temple of Heaven.

She got off the bus on the park's south side and made her way to the entrance. It was now almost 5 a.m. and the park was open. She paid the equivalent of 25 cents to enter—a lot of money for a retiree living on less than $100 a month. She glanced at a map and decided to head toward the Hall of Prayer for Good Harvests, a beautifully proportioned building that looked like an upside-down top. It was a major tourist attraction, and she figured that visiting it was harmless enough.

She started walking toward the hall, its azure roof peeking above the trees. She looked to her left and right, down rows of locust and scholar trees, where she hoped to see people sitting cross-legged in the initial meditation pose, or maybe starting Falun Gong's slow-motion exercises. But after fifteen minutes she had seen nothing but a few joggers and people practicing Chinese shadowboxing. She trudged forward.

It was bitterly cold, and the sun was a gray smudge on the horizon. She clapped her hands. If she could just find a few adherents, she'd be all right. They'd have a place to stay and could tell her the best way to get past the police checks and into Tiananmen Square.

"Where are you going, grandma?"

She slowly turned around. Two policemen were facing her.

"I'm going to see the temple."

"So early in the morning?" one of the officers said dubiously. He looked at her carefully: a short, stocky woman around

sixty years of age, with a square face and roughly cut hair. Her looks, her clothes, her belongings in a shopping bag—all pegged her as a country bumpkin. The officers knew that peasants often came to town to see the sights, but few came alone at 5 a.m.

"Grandma, we have to ask you a question: do you practice Falun Gong?"

Ms. Chen hesitated. Falun Gong was banned, but she wasn't practicing it at that moment. Anyway, Master Li had said that they shouldn't lie; lying was a sin.

"Yes, I do," she said.

"Where are you from, grandma?" one of the policemen said.

"Shandong Province, Weifang City."

"Your ID, please."

She handed it to them. They looked it over for a minute and handed it back.

"Grandma, please follow us. Falun Gong practitioners aren't allowed in the parks."

She started to object, but one of the officers' face hardened. One on each side of her, they escorted her back to the south gate. The two officers accompanied her out of the park and then down a side street. A bus was parked on the right side. An officer opened the door and she climbed up. Inside were half a dozen other people, all from out of town like herself. She had found her fellow practitioners.

Four months earlier, Ms. Chen had been aroused from an almost militant lack of interest in politics. It was July 22, 1999, and a local official from the neighborhood party committee had told her to watch the evening news at seven, saying it would have an important announcement about Falun Gong. Up until then Ms. Chen had avoided the news or reading the newspaper. If the past

few decades of China's twisting and turning politics had taught her anything, it was to avoid politics and keep as low a profile as possible. "Focus on your own life and stay out of politics," she used to tell her children. For most of her life that had worked. But this evening she turned on the news, curious to hear what it would say about her precious Falun Gong.

Ms. Chen used to say that Falun Gong was simply an exercise group, but this didn't do justice to the role it played in her life. Shortly after her employer, an auto-parts maker, had given her early retirement in 1997, Ms. Chen had been walking through a park in the early morning on her way to market. A group of a dozen neighbors were doing Falun Gong's calisthenics and invited her to join. She hesitated but on an impulse decided for the first time in her life to indulge herself.

Her life had spanned some of the most tumultuous decades in Chinese history, from civil war in the 1940s through the famines of the '50s, the insane utopianism of the 1960s and now, since the late '70s, economic reforms that had made people more prosperous but also demanded yet another 180-degree change in how Chinese lived and worked. She had raised two children almost alone after her husband died in an accident when she was twenty-five. Now economic reforms had left her with early retirement and little to show for her life but a minuscule pension and a tiny apartment with concrete floors. At fifty-seven, Ms. Chen was already considered old; there was nothing left for her to do except help out with her grandchildren. She needed a hobby, something to do with her life. She tried Falun Gong that morning in 1997 and never looked back.

Ms. Chen had always been active, but the new exercises made her feel younger, suppler, lither. Instead of burning herself out running one errand after the other, she was finally doing

something for herself. She also liked the fact that the group advocated a strict moral path based on traditional Buddhist concepts of good works and tolerance. Having grown up during an era when religion was virtually illegal, Ms. Chen found the group's guideposts more relevant than the government's ever-changing ideology, which advocated selfless sacrifice but was widely ignored by corrupt officials and cynical citizens. Exercises that made her feel good and a moral compass for her life—the combination was irresistible.

She had a new routine. She'd get up at 5 a.m. and go to the park for ninety minutes of exercise. It was early, but this way younger practitioners would have time to get home and get ready for work. She spent the rest of the day as before: running errands and helping her children and grandchildren. After dinner she read the moralistic texts of Falun Gong founder Li Hongzhi, who preached ethics—summarized by the three principles of truth, benevolence and tolerance—as well as some idiosyncratic notions, such as the existence of extraterrestrial life. Sometimes members would meet in her living room to discuss texts. Other times she'd watch instructional videos of Mr. Li, whom she respectfully referred to as "Master Li." She owned his two main texts and four of his videos. She went to bed between nine and ten.

But as she sat on her sofa in front of the television, the government was saying that all of this was wrong. The announcer intoned that Falun Gong was an "evil cult" and that the government had decided to ban it.

"We must fully understand the serious consequences 'Falun Gong' will have on the physical and mental health of its practitioners. We must fully understand the utmost importance and urgency of dealing with the issues of 'Falun Gong,' " the an-

nouncer said, reading from an editorial that would appear in the next day's edition of *People's Daily*, the Communist Party's mouthpiece.

It didn't make any sense to Ms. Chen, and after the fifteen-minute broadcast she got up and walked to a neighbor's apartment two floors down. Like Ms. Chen, her neighbor had also been a practitioner and had also been at home to watch the broadcast. The seventy-year-old retiree opened the door, her face as distressed as Ms. Chen's. "What does it mean?" Ms. Chen asked. The two sat down and thought for a while. Ms. Chen was deeply depressed.

When Ms. Chen arrived at the park the next morning, most of the group was already there, standing around and discussing the news. Some of her friends said they had suspected that Falun Gong was in trouble because it had been criticized recently in the media for holding a demonstration that spring in Beijing. A couple who had worked in the government before retiring even whispered that some Falun Gong organizers in Beijing had already been detained.

"I can tell you what the newspapers today will say," one of the retired officials said to the group. "They'll repeat last night's announcement word for word. This has become a national issue, a big issue. I'm not coming back here until it blows over."

The group went through its exercises and finished up as usual around 6:30 a.m. Some walked over to a newsstand and picked up the morning papers. The retired official had been right. The papers all had the same article positioned in exactly the same spot on the front page. They all had the same headlines. Ms. Chen studied the article slowly.

> While handling and addressing the "Falun Gong" issue, we must pay attention to ensuring

social stability. Stability is the highest interest
of the country and the people. . . . Without stability, we can accomplish nothing.

For the first time in her life, Ms. Chen began to think hard
about a government policy. She hadn't suffered much during
the Cultural Revolution and during the reform era had concentrated on raising her family. But now she began to wonder about
the government. She'd heard rumblings that the group was in
trouble—that Falun Gong had protested in front of the government's offices in Beijing that spring—but how could they ban
Falun Gong without even consulting with practitioners? How
did they know it was so bad? So she took the first step that many
Chinese take when they disagree with the government: she
decided to ignore it.

Her skepticism was born of self-interest, not idealism, but it
grew strongly inside her. About a week after the ban was
announced, Ms. Chen and her friends were stopped by police,
who were waiting for them at the park. Falun Gong was illegal
and they couldn't practice it publicly anymore, they were told.
The group dispersed and went home. But many of them continued to meet, using Ms. Chen's tiny living room as their meeting
point. They didn't plot to overthrow the government or to
oppose its ban. Instead, they simply practiced their exercises and
read Master Li's texts.

Ms. Chen's group was located in about as typical a place in
China as one can imagine. They lived in Xu Family Hamlet in
Weifang, a small city of 600,000 in eastern China. A dusty maze
of poplar-lined dirt roads and bungalows surrounded by crumbling brown brick walls, the hamlet was a typical village being
swallowed up by its urban neighbor.

Weifang, too, was a fairly ordinary Chinese city, one of the

seemingly endless number of half-million–population cities in China that are all but unknown to the outside world. Indeed, Weifang might be completely obscure were it not for its claim to be the birthplace of the kite and the location of an annual international kite festival. Otherwise the town was an unremarkable collection of newly built white-tiled buildings, home to several state-run factories and a small private sector. Agriculture still played a big role, and Ms. Chen's hamlet sat right between the cornfields of the North China Plain and Weifang's crowded streets.

By August some people from Weifang had gone a step further than Ms. Chen, traveling to Beijing to protest. They joined others from across China and went to Tiananmen Square in the center of the city to perform their calisthenics publicly, hoping to demonstrate that theirs was an inward-looking group with no interest in politics. Facing the Forbidden City, where Chinese emperors had ruled their vast empire for centuries, they sat cross-legged and raised their arms up over their heads—the starting pose for their exercises. Closer to home in Weifang, practitioners had even organized a sit-down strike in front of the local Communist Party headquarters, likewise conducting exercises in defiance of the ban.

The group's demands might have been simple—an end to the prohibition on Falun Gong—but to a government that brooks no opposition, it was a challenge. Plainclothes and uniformed police quickly descended on the small, scattered protests in Beijing and in provincial cities like Weifang. Batons flew. Thousands were arrested, interrogated and most sent back home with a stern warning.

Ms. Chen had stayed out of the protests, quietly practicing at home with her friends. She couldn't imagine participating in such daring protests, although she was secretly proud that her fellow-

practitioners believed in themselves enough to stand up for their rights.

But then, in late autumn, the government ratcheted up the pressure again. First came a Supreme Court decision in early October announcing that existing criminal laws could be used to punish cults. Then came a *People's Daily* article calling Falun Gong a cult. The parliament gave the impending crackdown a legal veneer in late October by passing a "decision" that banned cults. Finally, the Supreme Court ordered lower-level courts not to accept cases filed by Falun Gong adherents.

All this had been preceded by the arrest of all major Falun Gong organizers—people who had served as liaisons between practitioners like Ms. Chen and Master Li, who had emigrated to the United States in 1998. These organizers had distributed Master Li's essays to his followers and did odd jobs like reserve space in the parks for the practitioners. Now the government intended to strike some terror into the Ms. Chens of the world. Like the ban in July that Ms. Chen had seen on television, the government blanketed the country with announcements of the indictments and convictions. Some of the sentences were for up to twelve years in labor camps.

Ms. Chen was stunned. She hadn't known any of the people involved, but the idea that a person would spend a decade or more in a labor camp for practicing Falun Gong angered her. For several months she'd refrained from taking any direct part in the protests, but now she changed her mind, heading off to Beijing to protest, only to be arrested in the Temple of Heaven Park.

Zhang Xueling was at home with her son when the call came from the neighborhood committee. Her mother, Ms. Chen, had been detained in Beijing, the caller on the line said, and Ms.

Zhang was asked to accompany local officials to the capital to bail out her mother. Ms. Zhang immediately agreed to go.

Falun Gong, she thought bitterly. This troublesome organization had been the bane of her family's existence for the past few months. Now, because of it, her mother was in jail and she had to go all the way to Beijing to get her released. It would cost money and none of them had much. Ms. Zhang's husband was a carpenter, and she spent most of her time at home raising her son, working occasionally as a matchmaker.

She sat down to count the money in her purse and collect her thoughts. Falun Gong had started out well enough, Ms. Zhang conceded. Her mother had been, well, cantankerous when she had begun practicing Falun Gong a couple of years earlier. She'd sacrificed much to raise her and her brother and was critical of everyone. It was hard to talk to her without getting into some petty argument.

She remembered how she and her brother had supported her mother's decision to start Falun Gong exercises. Her mother had never been a superstitious or religious person, but the exercises seemed to do her good. And the message of tolerance and doing good works seemed to give her a new outlook.

"She had a bad temper," Ms. Zhang said out loud with a smile. "But then she became a better person."

Still, Ms. Zhang couldn't understand why her mother insisted on continuing with Falun Gong after it had been banned. You could disagree with the government, Ms. Zhang said to herself, but you had to face facts. And the facts were that the government was treating this ban on Falun Gong seriously. Everyone knew that police had searched the homes of people who had led the exercises before the ban. Practicing it was a big risk. She could see that her mother might want to continue practicing alone at home, but inviting friends over seemed to be asking for

trouble. And now going to Beijing to protest! What had possessed her mother to do that? An old lady taking a bus to the capital and getting arrested. Maybe this was an evil cult after all, Ms. Zhang thought to herself.

She walked over to the Chengguan Street Committee offices. The street committee is the lowest level in the mighty Communist Party's system of control, one that starts with a few top men in Beijing and spreads down through its 55 million members to every neighborhood. Ms. Zhang had little contact with her street committee—part Communist Party cell, part social services office and part neighborhood watch. All Ms. Zhang could ever remember the committee doing was organizing occasional "hygiene" campaigns to sweep out the streets. Most of their work involved monitoring women of childbearing age to make sure they had only one child. Ms. Zhang was only thirty-two years old but had a six-year-old son, and so she got only occasional visits from the committee.

She walked in and was introduced to three officials from the Weifang City government's Public Security Bureau. They got into a government car, a Volkswagen Santana, and drove to Beijing. After seven hours, they arrived at the Weifang municipal government's Beijing representative office. It was a lobbying-bureau-cum-dormitory of the sort that scores of Chinese cities and provinces set up in Beijing to house local officials visiting the capital. Ms. Chen was being held there, locked in a dormitory room.

Ms. Zhang paid a $60 fine—a month's wages—and her mother was released. The two broke into tears, but Ms. Zhang couldn't resist a mild rebuke.

"Ma," she said. "How could you do this? Coming to Beijing all the way alone? Please come home and don't do this anymore."

Her mother pursed her lips and didn't answer.

The two were escorted back to Weifang in a police car. The whole way back the officials glared at Ms. Chen, occasionally saying how embarrassing the event had been for them.

Responsibility for Ms. Chen was given to the Chengguan Street Committee. It was the head of the local street committee who had told Ms. Chen to watch the evening news in July—a tip that she was doing something dangerous and ought to take care. They felt they'd warned her, but she'd disobeyed and gotten them all into trouble. Now Ms. Chen was under their control.

The women were told that Ms. Chen couldn't be allowed off without further punishment. The attempted protest had hurt Weifang's standing in the capital. Before she could go home, Ms. Chen would have to serve a two-week prison sentence, a form of administrative detention that authorities can mete out at their will. To make sure that everyone in the neighborhood got the message, Ms. Chen would be held in the neighborhood committee office, which was just a few rooms on the ground floor of an apartment building. One of the rooms was converted into a small jail, and Ms. Chen was to be held there for two weeks. She was also barred from practicing Falun Gong or reading Master Li's books. Ms. Zhang had to pay another $45 for her mother's room and board.

On January 3, Ms. Chen celebrated her fifty-eighth birthday in jail. Despite being under day-and-night observation, she was in good spirits. Ms. Zhang went to see her and began to gain renewed respect for her mother.

"She knew she was right," Ms. Zhang said. "All she wanted was the government not to make a criminal out of her because she knew she wasn't a criminal."

In mid-January, Ms. Chen was released but was still watched carefully by the street committee, which paid her regular visits and confiscated her Falun Gong books and videos.

The new year, however, marked an odd confluence of western and eastern millennialism. On the western calendar, the new year was 2000, which many people in China saw as particularly auspicious. The upcoming Lunar New Year, which fell on February 4, was also seen as especially lucky. It marked the start of the year of the dragon, the mightiest animal in the Chinese zodiac. The year 2000, the year of the dragon; this coincidence seemed to herald the dawning of a new age. A mini–baby boom was in the making as couples wanted their child to be born in this doubly lucky year. Politicians talked of the new age being China's. A sense of a new beginning swept the land.

Even China's avowedly atheist rulers got into the act. They staged a quasi-religious ceremony to mark the new millennium, constructing a "Century Altar" in Beijing that featured a giant needle and a gargantuan incense burner that was lit by President Jiang Zemin at midnight, December 31, 1999.

Galvanized by this millennarian Zeitgeist, hundreds of Falun Gong protesters converged on the capital in late January 2000. Arriving in the weeks ahead of the Lunar New Year holiday, they wanted to protest the ban on their group, hoping that the auspicious date would lend luck to their cause. Despite a massive police presence, scores arrived on the square each day to start their exercise routine. Before they got started, police would swoop down on them, truncheons flying, dragging the bloodied people into waiting vans. The scenes were caught on film by foreign journalists and spread around the world. They made their way through the Internet and word of mouth back to people like Ms. Chen.

For Ms. Chen this was another act of barbarism that she couldn't ignore. Like Falun Gong adherents around China, she didn't feel cowed; she felt outraged. Over a meal during the two-week New Year's celebration, she and her daughter talked.

"The government doesn't understand that we are good people, ordinary people," she said. "We aren't against the government. Falun Gong is good for China."

Ms. Zhang sighed.

"Mom," she said. "Be more realistic. People know that you're still following Master Li. You'll only bring trouble on all of us if you keep this up."

But again Ms. Chen went silent, not wanting to get into an argument with her daughter.

Then, on February 16, as the New Year's holiday was ending, Ms. Chen's doorbell rang. It was the local party district chief, a high-ranking official who was responsible for the political behavior of the 50,000 people in his district. With him were half a dozen local officials, including representatives from the Public Security Bureau and the lady from the neighborhood committee who'd warned her before to quit Falun Gong.

Ms. Chen let the cadres in, ushering the chief and his deputies to the most comfortable place to sit, the couch. The others sat on kitchen chairs. Ms. Chen stood awkwardly and offered them tea. They declined. The chief asked her to sit down, and she found a stool under the kitchen table, dragged it out and sat across from him, like a naughty child facing a school discipline board.

"Chen Zixiu," the chief said, using her full name and dispensing with more familiar forms of address. She stiffened. "We've all heard about the protests in Beijing. Our government is very tolerant of such things. Protests are allowed in the constitution, we all know that.

"Look at how you were treated," the secretary continued. "It was embarrassing to us and cost us a good deal of money, but all that happened after you went to Beijing is that you were

detained and sent home. Nothing more. You made your point and let's leave it at that, okay? The government does not want any more protests. The National People's Congress [China's parliament, which meets once a year] is going to meet soon and we aren't going to disrupt that meeting with protests. My job is to make sure that people understand that."

Ms. Chen sat quietly and dutifully followed each word in the speech, which the chief had already given to several other adherents. She knew this was important: a personal warning from the party chief. The chief continued. Please, he said to Ms. Chen, don't embarrass your hometown. Be a good citizen. No one likes what's happening, but don't make a scene. You know how things are.

The party chief had stopped talking. The lady from the street committee gave her a big smile and added, "We're all one big family. Let's not upset things."

There was silence again. It was Ms. Chen's turn. Now she was supposed to say something reasonable and agree with them. The party chief would smile, everyone would be relieved and they'd go to the next Falun Gong adherent and make a similar speech. It would have lasted ten minutes and no one would know if she practiced Falun Gong at home.

But Falun Gong teaches something that is common among evangelical religions: that it's wrong not to proclaim one's faith—that it's false to practice in private and deny one's belief in public. Despite the past eight months of government propaganda and her experience in Beijing, Ms. Chen was still a believer. Her answer was simple.

"I won't guarantee to anyone that I won't go somewhere. I have the right to go where I please."

There was an awkward silence. The district chief looked

down, his eyes angry. He'd heard this before from these damned Falun Gong fanatics. He left the next part to his aide, who stood up so he could look down on Ms. Chen.

"So far, the government has treated Falun Gong practitioners like wayward children. But discipline can involve harshness. Think about what your attitude means," he said. The officials quickly got up and filed out of her room.

Ms. Chen sat there and pondered her future. A few hours later she left for her second trip to Beijing.

Falun Gong was part of a remarkable religious rebirth that has swept through China since the late 1970s. While outsiders have often focused on the economic reforms that have transformed China from a communist to a largely capitalist country, the collapse of communism as a religion set forth a profound search for meaning, obvious in the arts, such as the novels of Nobel Prize–winning author Gao Xingjian and on a popular level in the rise of dozens of new religions and the rebirth of older, established ones.

Defining what is a religion, especially in China, can be a tricky business. Unlike western religions, which often try to sharply differentiate themselves from each other, Chinese belief systems happily overlap, drawing on ancestor worship, popular beliefs in spirits, the indigenous religion of Taoism and the ideas of worldwide religions like Buddhism. But after it took power in 1949, the Communist Party imposed a Soviet-style religious bureaucracy over this cacophony of beliefs, legalizing only five narrowly defined religions—Buddhism, Catholicism, Islam, Protestantism and Taoism. The myriad folk religions that over the millennia have risen and fallen like waves of faith across the country were either lumped under Taoism or banned as "feudal

superstition." In the most famous case, the government spent years trying to wipe out Yiguandao, or Way of Basic Unity, a syncretic religion that draws heavily from Taoism and also tries to meld in ideas from Islam and Christianity. Thousands of Yiguandao believers were sent to labor camps in the 1950s and forced to confess publicly that the practices were meant to deceive the populace. The group was also charged with treason— complicity with Japanese occupiers during the war—and within a few years was largely destroyed on mainland China.

But about thirty years after taking power, the government all but admitted that Marxism was a useless ideology. It adopted capitalist-style reforms and discouraged leaders from setting up personality cults, such as the one that had centered around the party's totalitarian leader, Chairman Mao Zedong. In effect, it told the Chinese that everything that the totalitarian state had preached—the party leader as god, the primacy of socialism and the goal of communism—was wrong. Predictably, a spiritual crisis ensued. Many turned to the five official religions, which boomed. Temples, mosques and churches were rebuilt, while new monks, nuns, imams and priests were ordained.

But the big religions didn't satisfy everyone's spiritual craving. For years they had been humiliated, their buildings desecrated and their teachings banned. That seemed to break their hold over many in society—who could remain in awe of a god who couldn't protect his own temple from destruction? In addition, the legal places of worship had become unfamiliar. Who knew what went on in a church or a Taoist temple when discussion of them had been taboo for decades and the older generation not allowed to introduce religious practices to the young? Some people also felt that the established religions had discredited themselves by their sometimes toadying association with the authorities. Despite all the humiliations and destruction, their

leaders were men who regularly paid their respects to the Communist Party, pretending—or perhaps genuinely believing—that China had religious freedom.

Into the breach stepped a spiritual, slightly mystical branch of Chinese medicine known as "qigong." The term itself is relatively new, dating back only to the 1950s as a catch-all phrase for various exercises whose origin goes back centuries. These exercises try to regulate "qi," a concept in Chinese medicine that is hard to translate but is the equivalent of a life force or energy. Qi travels through the body along channels that, for example, an acupuncturist taps into and regulates by inserting needles into the skin. Qigong—the second part of the word, "gong," means "discipline" or "exercise"—is a way of adjusting one's flow of qi through controlled breathing, meditation and slow-motion calisthenics.

Before the communist takeover in 1949, these exercises had a strong spiritual component. Both Taoism and Buddhism had their own versions of qigong, and they were accepted parts of the religious healing tradition—a bridge to Chinese medicine. Meditation was crucial to the exercises, with the practitioner not just healing his body but his mind as well. But the communists' rise to power put qigong in conflict with the authorities' suspicion of all things spiritual and their decision that the only accepted religions in society were the five authorized ones. That left no room for traditional qigong. What to do? The answer was to make qigong "scientific."

Science may seem an odd champion for something as spiritual as qigong, but it was important because China's revolution, which began in 1911 with the overthrow of the emperor, has had as its goal "science" and "democracy," both of which were seen as the keys to a strong, powerful country. Although the communists didn't give China democracy, they did elevate science to an

almost cultlike status—much as in the Soviet Union. The party, for example, practices "scientific Marxism"—its policies are therefore not the whims of a gerontocracy but rooted in eternal, provable truths.

Unscientific things, by contrast, are condemned to eternal damnation. In the communist theology, that means they are labeled "superstition" or "feudal superstition." Religion in general is frowned upon, although the five major religions are accepted as temporary necessities. Other forms of religious expression, however, are "superstitious." Shamanism, for example, has had a long history in China, but it and any sort of ecstatic or mystical practice is now taboo because it is not "scientific."

In an effort to avoid the "unscientific" label, qigong's meditative side was downplayed. Instead, it was heralded as a form of physical therapy supervised by doctors. There was less quiet sitting, and qigong's goals were limited to good health. In addition, scientists conducted experiments that purported to show that its regimen of quiet breathing and meditation helped cure chronic problems, such as respiratory or digestive ailments—conclusions not too different from western studies on the benefit of meditation and relaxation in fighting illness.

Research stopped when the Cultural Revolution was launched in 1966 and qigong went into hibernation. Then, as China emerged from totalitarianism, qigong also revived, this time as a national fad. By the early 1990s, qigong was so popular that people talked of a "qigong craze." Qigong was being practiced in parks and outside apartment buildings. It was so widely accepted that China's communist leaders were said to use it to improve their health.

Many people practiced qigong according to traditional precepts, using it as a quiet, meditative form of exercise that could improve one's energy. But it really caught on when it claimed to

promote supernatural powers. Practitioners said they could read words that were hidden—for example, written on paper sealed in an envelope. Other claims included being able to throw needles so fast and so hard that they could penetrate glass, the ability to conduct electricity through one's body or to withstand a blow to the head with a hammer. Military magazines featured reports on qigong, although it's not clear which of these feats the People's Liberation Army figured could help it win a war.

Academics, such as Jian Xu of the University of Iowa, saw in the claims an effort by qigong to win back some of its otherworldly allure. But now, instead of a subtle form of meditation aimed at immortality, qigong had morphed into what he called a "a special, high-powered technology of the self, situated between science and mysticism."

The veneer of scientific respectability—and government control—was given by an organization called the China Qigong Scientific Research Association, which was supposed to register all qigong groups and oversee their "scientific" efforts at improving health through exercise.

That label freed qigong from having to worry about government restrictions on organized religion. Established religions were only allowed to meet in their mosques, temples or churches, and were strictly banned from proselytizing. But qigong was—officially, at least—just an exercise regime. That meant participants could hold meetings in public parks and hand out promotional material to passersby on the street. And, free from the stigma of being a religion, Communist Party members, who are supposed to be atheist, could practice qigong without fear of party censure. Officially, it was simply a branch of medicine that could help cure illness.

◆ ◆ ◆

Millions of Chinese found a deeper meaning in qigong: a rare chance for introspection. One such person was Chen Shouliang, a physicist at Beijing University. In 1984, when he was fifty-three years old, Professor Chen (no relation to Ms. Chen, the Falun Gong practitioner) discovered a cancerous tumor in his neck. Surgery was performed, but Professor Chen was weak and had to give up his promising career as an administrator at the university.

Some years earlier, friends of Professor Chen introduced him to a qigong guru named Zhao Guang, a modest man who lived like a hermit in a tiny, spartan apartment, his only luxury an impressive collection of the Chinese classics. Mr. Zhao had tried to interest Mr. Chen in qigong, but the professor had always been too busy. He had classes to teach and a promising future as a university administrator.

Then, one day in February 1984, they bumped into each other on White Stone Bridge Road. Now the street is a crowded six-lane thoroughfare blanketed with computer shops, but back then it was a narrow, tree-lined road in Beijing's university district. The meeting was an encounter of a mystic, revelatory nature that changed Professor Chen's life and helped solidify qigong's position as an accepted part of Chinese society for the next fifteen years.

Professor Chen was embarrassed when he saw Mr. Zhao. He hadn't taken up Mr. Zhao on his earlier offer and now felt foolish. He badly wanted to learn qigong but didn't want to appear insulting, only interested now that he was ill. But before he could voice his feelings, Mr. Zhao spoke.

"You've got cancer. Now do you have time?"

Professor Chen was surprised. The old master had read his thoughts; he knew that he wanted to learn qigong.

"I do, master. Let me know when it is convenient to come by for a lesson."

"No need," Mr. Zhao said. "I'll teach you here on the street corner, in five minutes."

Mr. Zhao taught him three sentences—mantras, really: Relax your whole body. Breathe calmly and regularly. Keep your thoughts in your belly. The latter was tough. It meant not thinking too much, voiding one's mind. How to do it, Professor Chen asked. Referring to the Buddhist Wheel of Law, which rolls from man to man, place to place, age to age, Mr. Zhao told him: "Think of the Dharma Wheel spinning in your belly. Visualize it turning, overcoming everything else. This will keep your mind off other things."

Mr. Zhao instructed him to do this twenty to thirty minutes twice a day and return a few weeks later for further instruction. Professor Chen did as he was told and went back to Mr. Zhao, who corrected a few errors in his breathing technique. If he kept this up for a hundred days, Mr. Zhao said, Professor Chen would become an adept. One hundred days later he returned to Mr. Zhao, who pronounced him no longer a beginner. He was now an adept, a true practitioner, and over time he started to spread qigong by teaching others.

Professor Chen became more than an enthusiast. As a scientist, he was interested in knowing how qigong worked, so he started conducting studies, hoping to prove that supernatural powers were possible. He surveyed an elementary school class of eight-year-olds, for example, and found that a third could read letters sealed in an envelope. With age, he theorized, we lose our ability to know things intuitively. Qigong, he concluded, helps us regain our youthful innocence. He published his findings in a journal and became a mini-celebrity, often interviewed in the Chinese media. It probably wasn't good science—the study was never accepted for publication at a major international journal

and its results have never been duplicated—but it fit perfectly into the 1980s, a period when China was breaking from its totalitarian past and anything seemed possible, even supernatural powers.

His role was important to qigong's reemergence. Some critics in the Communist Party were beginning to voice their disapproval of qigong, saying it was unscientific and, worse, hinting that it was a pseudo-religion. Professor Chen, with his Beijing University pedigree, helped to deflect these criticisms, lending the imprimatur of scientific respectability to the ersatz religion.

I first met Professor Chen in 1994, a time when the "qigong craze" was at its peak. Over several long summer afternoons on the Beijing University campus, Professor Chen gave me his thoughts on qigong's new popularity. Back then, Falun Gong was just getting started and neither of us was aware of it. Instead, it was qigong's claimed supernatural abilities that interested us.

Professor Chen had the air of an amiable conspiracy theorist, the sort of person who refers to articles in obscure journals and magazines in faraway lands as proof of his idea. He was a small man, with short silver hair and a sharp wit, often making jokes at his own expense. But he also had a naïve earnestness about supernatural powers. Once, for example, he asked me if I'd heard of David Copperfield, whom he greatly admired. The CIA was doing research into supernatural powers, he said, as had the KGB before the Soviet Union fell. He mentioned this as something extremely significant, as though the fall of the Soviet Union was somehow a premeditated blow against qigong research. He reminded me of East Bloc scientists who had been cut off from the outside world for so long and whose thinking was so politicized that they could no longer differentiate between hard fact and intuitive conjecture.

His trump card was a dog-eared copy of his study of elementary school students, which he brought out when I mentioned skepticism about his claims.

"Some people just don't want to believe," he said. "But it's all scientifically proven that qigong can give us superhuman abilities."

Not everyone was convinced. A professor from the Chinese Academy of Sciences wrote a book called *Human Supernatural Abilities and Qigong* that tried to debunk some of the more dubious claims of miracles being ascribed to qigong. Indeed, even Professor Chen conceded that he couldn't explain why qigong gave rise to miraculous powers, only that they existed. His only explanation was: "If we can't explain it, it doesn't mean it's nonsense. It's just that science can't explain it."

It was a rationale that helps explain qigong's popularity. Since the nineteenth century, Chinese people have worried that modernization wouldn't allow them to preserve anything from their ancient culture, which they claim goes back five thousand years. The insistence on science—a western invention—as the answer to all questions seemed to threaten the essence of Chinese culture. Did China have anything of value to offer the modern world? Especially in the 1980s and '90s, with China's brand of communism junked in favor of western market economics, many Chinese thinkers worried that China had become nothing more than an outpost of western civilization. Qigong was something that could be of lasting value, something that could even give people superhuman powers, a feat western science couldn't match. To the skeptic who said that qigong's claims weren't provable scientifically, qigong defenders like Professor Chen turned the tables, saying that the West's vaunted science wasn't developed enough to explain qigong.

That nationalistic streak appealed to China's leaders, who

have been eager to wrap themselves in patriotism and nationalism as a way to legitimize their rule. Some leaders were rumored to practice qigong, and qigong organizations received high-level backing.

But qigong was a double-edged sword. Its existence was an admission that Marxism—a western invention, after all—couldn't satisfy China's spiritual needs. The party began to recognize this threat, which was stated explicitly in a popular novel that pitted a qigong master against a party cadre. The author, Ke Yunlu, wrote in 1994 in *The Great Qigong Masters* that just as qigong requires that science books be rewritten, it also requires that political theories be rewritten. His protagonist displays his fantastic powers to a local Communist Party leader, but the leader is blind to them and organizes a witch hunt against "reactionary" thinking. The message is clear: the party can't be trusted and will only try to destroy qigong.

The novel was prescient, because the party was indeed distrustful of qigong. One reason is that qigong is essentially a private exercise. Formal religions center on temples, churches and mosques, which the government has been able to control by requiring all places of worship to register with the government and be run by officials loyal to the state. Qigong, however, is focused inwardly—outside the government's control. Yet it is often performed publicly in groups. To a government that is used to controlling all aspects of public life, this is perplexing: qigong practitioners are in public and doing something en masse, so by rights they should be formed in an organization and this organization should in some way be run by the government. But what they are doing together is meditating, an inner discipline that the party can't monitor.

The result was an uneasy standoff through the rest of the 1990s. The government kept trying to organize and control

qigong groups, but they kept mutating and expanding, ignoring the government and winning millions of converts.

Falun Gong was the next logical step in qigong's development. While many people continued to practice traditional qigong, using it as a meditation and healing art, more organized groups had been forming since the early 1990s. Led by charismatic leaders, they began distributing texts to adherents. The texts usually contained descriptions of the exercises, but they also contained the moral precepts of the qigong master.

Li Hongzhi formed Falun Gong in 1992 and registered his group the same year with the research association. Master Li's background is unclear, but according to the hagiographic accounts put out by Falun Gong, he was a former government grain clerk, a simple person who achieved enlightenment in an unknown fashion. Like other qigong masters, Master Li wrote down his thoughts, but they were far more sophisticated and complete than earlier efforts at writing texts. While other masters wrote down a few basic moral precepts to go with their exercises, Master Li's two main books, *China Falun Gong* and *Turning the Dharma Wheel*, described a cosmology of heavens and hells, spirits and devils. It was not as complex as the older, better-developed theologies of Buddhism or Taoism, but compared to competing qigong groups, it was a breakthrough: a coherent system of religious thought tailor-made for modern-day Chinese.

While firmly stating that Falun Gong was not a religion, Master Li drew on traditional religions for terminology and symbols. The term "Falun" means Dharma Wheel, or Wheel of Law, the traditional Buddhist symbol of the immutable forces in the world. It was also the same wheel that Professor Chen's guru told him to imagine spinning in his body. It is a well-known sym-

bol of the religion, seen in statues, frescoes or Tibetan prayer wheels—in other words, an established part of Chinese cosmology. Falun Gong's sign is a wheel, a circle made up of a central, counterclockwise-pointing swastika, a traditional Buddhist symbol whose mirror-image was appropriated by the Nazis for their pseudo-religion. The Falun Gong swastika is surrounded by four smaller swastikas and four small yin-yang, or t'ai chi, symbols, a traditional Taoist sign.

At first Falun Gong emphasized its health benefits. Like other qigong groups, Falun Gong claimed that regular practice could maintain good health and even heal serious illnesses. Falun Gong Web sites abroad still carry testimonials of people who were healed by its energy-building exercises. That remains an important claim, with some adherents believing—like Christian Scientists—that medical care is unnecessary.

But over time, the philosophical teachings of Truth, Goodness and Forbearance took on more importance. These three principles require people to live upright lives, to not lie and to follow heterosexual, monogamous lives. Homosexuality is dealt with in only one of Master Li's teachings, but he sharply criticizes it, a stance that critics abroad have used to show Falun Gong's intolerant nature. That isolated reference to homosexuality has now been all but abandoned by the group, which does not feature the speech on its main Web sites. Overall, however, the morality remains traditional, family-oriented—what University of Montreal scholar David Ownby calls "popular fundamentalism," or a return to moral values that many Chinese feel have been lost in the rush to modernization.

Master Li's works also preach exclusivity: either you are with us or you are condemned to hell. To me, this was one of the most unappealing sides to Falun Gong, although I recognized in it the same view found in most major religions. Again, the fundamen-

talist label seemed appropriate. This was a religion trying to overturn the moneylenders' tables in the temple; it wasn't exactly a feel-good religion.

Interestingly—and here Master Li was in tune with his audience—Falun Gong stresses that it is compatible with science. Indeed, like other qigongs, Falun Gong positions itself as a kind of Über-science, something that is modern but even better than modern. His writings refer to extraterrestrial life and the cosmos, but also of the qigong practitioner's ability to surpass these truths. This was probably one of the reasons why Falun Gong appealed so much to Chinese who grew up in mainland China. The group now has branches in most western countries and throughout the Chinese-speaking world, but its adherents remain overwhelmingly Chinese who grew up in communist China, with its environment of stunted major religions and the elevation of science to a pseudoreligion.

In his writings Master Li emphasized that his teachings simply reveal eternal truths that have been known since time immemorial but which have become corrupted over time. He does not claim to be a messiah or god, only a wise teacher who has seen the light. The group also has no formal religious practice typical of organized religion, such as meeting in a special building, lighting incense or candles or worshiping a figure or book.

It was, however, very well organized. Like a modern corporation, its hierarchy was simple but clearly defined. At the top was Master Li, who gave lectures in China and abroad at conferences. His writings were transmitted via book and Internet, with computer-literate members downloading them from official Falun Gong Web sites and printing them out for those without computers. In China before the 1999 ban each of the country's thirty provinces had an "association" and below them were the

thousands of individual exercise groups, each headed by a locally agreed-upon coordinator who arranged the early-morning exercise sessions.

It was this structure that so scared authorities. Falun Gong was banned in 1999 after 10,000 believers protested in front of the government's compound, demanding that the group be recognized as a legitimate organization. Leaders learned that Falun Gong had millions of adherents—one television station referred to 100 million. Although that number was certainly a huge exaggeration, it was clear that the group was as popular as any of the mainstream religions. Shocked, the party banned it and started detaining its leaders and anyone who wouldn't renounce it.

The meeting lasted just five minutes and Brother Li was uncharacteristically nervous. "Here," he said, pulling out a big brown envelope. "Would this be of any use to you?" He looked around and motioned for me to open it.

We were sitting on a park bench in the middle of February, both of us freezing and eager to get going. It was late afternoon and we felt vulnerable, as if the barren birch and scholar trees were watching us. I opened the envelope and pulled out a letter. It was written in pencil on fourteen sheets of tissuelike exercise paper that Chinese students use to write essays. The handwriting was clear and only slightly cursive, the work of an educated woman who had sat down and thought carefully before setting her ideas down in writing.

I skimmed through it, the thin pages snapping in the winter wind. It was a detailed account of a woman's death, with the writer and others apparently present during the woman's interrogation, beating and death.

"May I keep these for a few days?" I asked Brother Li.

He nodded and got up.

"Meet me back here in three days. Make sure you're not being followed," he said in a laconic drawl, barely opening his mouth as he stared into the distance. Then he walked away toward his bicycle.

I'd come to know Li Guoqiang in late 1999 through mutual friends. He was a forty-three-year-old accountant who had worked in a textile mill until losing his job. His transgression was that he had refused to renounce his belief in Falun Gong after it was banned in July 1999. Determined to crush Falun Gong, the government had made belief in it a firing offense. Companies were instructed to purge their ranks of Falun Gong adherents, with state-owned companies ordered to report on employees they suspected had affiliations with the group. He didn't hesitate when asked if he was still a member: he admitted to it and spared his boss the embarrassment of firing him by quitting.

I met him shortly after he lost his job. He was one of the friendliest people I've met, with a ready grin and a slightly shaggy mop of hair that attested to his otherworldly concerns. He had a steady dependability about him that led his friends to give him the nickname of Li Ge, or Brother Li, which could more literally be translated as "Elder Brother Li."

Interested in learning more about Falun Gong, I soon started spending quite a bit of time with Brother Li. Every time we wanted to meet, the drill was the same. I'd go to a pay phone and call him on his beeper. He'd return my call about half an hour later to the pay phone, and we'd make an appointment. It was a time-consuming way to meet, but our home, office and cell phones were bugged, so we had to communicate by public pay phones. The half-hour wait was necessary because he was usually at home when I called and had to go out and find a pay phone. Not unreasonably, he figured that the pay phones near his home

were bugged, too, so he would ride his bike to another neighborhood and call me from there.

These security precautions might seem unusual, but they were instantly grasped by ordinary Chinese, such as Falun Gong adherents. Unlike Mr. Ma's peasants, whose efforts to challenge the government were fundamentally legal, Falun Gong had been declared illegal, and there was no question that the government was out to destroy it. In routine life one rarely came across undercover police or agents, yet only a fool didn't know of their existence and would instinctively not trust one's home phone or cell phones.

Initially, such concerns were minimal. In the months after the group was banned in July 1999, the government contented itself with arresting key organizers and leaders, believing that this would suffice to crush the group. It was a reasonable assumption. Most dissident groups, usually made up of intellectuals who wanted democracy and freedom of speech, were easily broken by detaining a few dozen ringleaders.

Falun Gong, however, wasn't like these groups. It was made up of believers in a religious idea—the concept of salvation and immortality—not a mere political idea. Rational theories could be countered with other rational ideas, such as "I like democracy, but I like labor camps less. Therefore, I'll defer my plans for democracy until conditions are riper and meanwhile stay out of prison." Although millions of casual Falun Gong practitioners came to similar conclusions—"I'll practice quietly at home, I won't demand that the ban on my group be repealed"—tens of thousands were like Brother Li: fervent believers who thought that they had a right, even a duty, to stand up for their beliefs. The government had failed to stem this wave of opposition by arresting the group's formal leaders. Now it was arresting grassroots organizers, making our meetings hard to arrange.

I later got to know Brother Li quite well, but our meetings were at first businesslike. I was a reporter who was covering the crackdown on Falun Gong and the resulting demonstrations. He was a Falun Gong activist who had good contacts with the group's underground structure. We'd discuss ways that I could meet activists who were flooding into Beijing for daily protests against the ban. He'd help arrange meetings but would never be present at them.

When I met Brother Li again three days later, I had photocopied the letters and asked him what he intended to do with the originals.

"Mail them to the government," he said matter-of-factly, as if that was a logical thing to do.

Wouldn't the person in the letter get arrested, and wasn't it a bit naïve—that a complaint letter would cause the government to reform itself?

Brother Li shrugged.

"I'm sending a copy to our fellow practitioners in Hong Kong to keep them on file, but what else should we do with the letters? We have to petition the government to change. Do we have another choice?"

We departed and I had more time to read through the letters. I soon decided I had to meet the people described in them. I'd seen accounts detailing police abuse but rarely with enough detail to track down the person and others familiar with the case. But here were names and addresses, all laid out clearly.

> My name is Jin Hua. I am 22 years of age. I live in Weicheng District of Weifang City. I am a Falun Gong practitioner. A practitioner was beaten to death this February, and most of the other witnesses under illegal arrest at that time were transferred (elsewhere), or

might even be killed, too. In order to prove these things truly happened in the Chengguan Neighborhood Committee training class, including illegal detainment and beating of people, I now set forth what I experienced as a written document, in hopes it can raise the attention of related authorities so that they can punish the evil and the corrupt and stop this from happening again.

I got in touch with relatives and friends of the woman whose death the letter described. Her name was Chen Zixiu, the fifty-eight-year-old grandmother who hadn't heeded the party chief and had returned to Beijing to protest.

Ms. Zhang felt like an unfilial daughter. When her mother had begun to struggle for Falun Gong, she'd been against it, feeling that her old mother was ignorant and backward, wasting her time defending a worthless religion. It's not that she didn't concede that Falun Gong had helped her mother; it had improved her health and temper. But Ms. Zhang was too busy for Falun Gong; she was thirty-two years old, a private entrepreneur and the mother of a rambunctious six-year-old. She had worked in a government-run factory but for the past few years had been a matchmaker, a profession that had been banned by the communists but was now back in favor as a harmless relic of China's past. Plump, with short-cropped hair and a no-nonsense air, she spoke in an equally straightforward manner, only sometimes indulging in imprecisions like "that whaddya-call-it" and "that thingamajig."

Now she regretted having been so harsh to her mother. If she'd been more understanding, she kept telling herself, her mother might be alive. It was a burden that was sometimes crush-

ing, mitigated only by her growing respect for her mother's stubborn insistence on her rights. Slowly, she began to feel that maybe her mother had died for something valuable—a principle.

We met in the seaside city of Qingdao to discuss her mother's death and the letters that Brother Li had let me copy. I later traveled to Ms. Zhang's hometown of Weifang, where she lived a few streets over from her mother's old apartment. I looked at the park where Ms. Chen had first encountered Falun Gong practitioners during her morning walk. I learned how hard Ms. Chen's life had become and how appealing she'd found Falun Gong. I also met the women who had written letters from prison and obtained the letter of another woman who was still in prison. Slowly, I began to reconstruct what had happened to Ms. Chen after the officials had warned her in February 2000 not to go to Beijing.

After delivering their lecture, the officials had gone next to Ms. Zhang, repeating their warning and urging her to control her mother. Ms. Zhang had never been in one room with so many officials. She was petrified and quickly went over to her mother's apartment and pleaded with her to heed the warning.

" 'Stay at home and practice quietly,' I told her. I was having my doubts about the government's ban on Falun Gong, but I could see they meant business."

Ms. Chen didn't listen to her daughter. She left her home that day for the train station, intending to go to Beijing. But she was quickly nabbed by a special squad of informants who roamed the neighborhood looking for Falun Gong participants who dared to leave home. Without knowing it, she had been placed under house arrest; her crime was daring to challenge that by leaving home.

Instead of being sent back home, Ms. Chen was sent back to the Chengguan Street Committee offices. But during the night

she managed to escape—exactly how isn't clear, but the prison there was makeshift and the doors might not have had proper locks. She was arrested the next day, February 17, heading again for the train station, where she hoped to go to Beijing to plead her case before the Petitions and Appeals Office, a last resort for people who feel they've been wronged—the same place where Mr. Ma, the peasant leader, as well as several of the urban activists, had taken their cases.

This time the local officials in Weifang wanted to teach Ms. Chen a lesson, so they sent her to an unofficial prison—a "transformation center"—run by the street committee. Its formal name was the Falun Gong Education Study Class. Unlike the room in the street committee's office, the "Study Class" had been properly outfitted to hold people in custody. It was a square two-story building with a yard in the middle. In the corner of the yard was a squat one-story building with two rooms. People who have been there say it was where people who hadn't learned their lesson were disciplined—by torture.

After her mother was transferred to the detention center, officials called Ms. Zhang and said her mother would be released if she'd pay a $241 fine. Ms. Zhang was fed up with the endless "fines." She'd already paid two exorbitant fines to get her mother out of the jail in Beijing. Now the government wanted more, and not a small amount either. It was the equivalent of four months' wages, a staggering amount to come up with on short notice.

But there was more to it than money. She had to admit that she was tired of her mother's insistence on standing up for her rights. If she'd just give in and renounce Falun Gong, the family's troubles would be over. The fines would stop, and her mother could, after a decent interval, still practice the exercises at home. She didn't see the need for all this.

So she told the officials their fines were illegal and that she'd complain to the local procurator's office if they didn't release her mother.

Ms. Chen spent the night in the jail and heard screams from the squat building. That was the usual practice: newcomers spent a night untouched but were able to hear the cries of those who were resisting. That was often quite effective, with many capitulating without having to be beaten. But Ms. Chen didn't renounce Falun Gong. It was now February 18, and before she was led over to the squat building for interrogation, she was allowed another phone call. She called her daughter and asked her to bring the money. Irritated by the troubles brought on by her mother's uncompromising attitude, Ms. Zhang argued with her mother. Give in and come home, she said. Her mother quietly refused. They hung up.

Ms. Chen's ordeal began that night. A practitioner who was in the next-door room later wrote: "We heard her screaming. Our hearts were tortured and our spirits almost collapsed." Thugs hired by the Chengguan Street Committee used plastic truncheons on her calves, feet and lower back, as well as a cattle prod on her head and neck. They shouted at her repeatedly to give up Falun Gong and curse Master Li, according to her cellmates. Each time, Ms. Chen refused.

The next day, February 19, Ms. Zhang got another call. It was a woman on the line, not her mother. Bring the money, a woman told her. Ms. Zhang hesitated. Her mother came on the line. Her voice, usually so strong and confident, was soft and pained. She pleaded with her daughter to bring the money. The woman came back on the phone: Bring the money.

Ms. Zhang got a sick feeling and rushed over with the money and more warm clothes for her mother. But the building was surrounded by agents who wouldn't let her see her mother. Suspi-

cious that her mother wasn't really in the building, she returned home. An hour later a practitioner came to see Ms. Zhang. Falun Gong adherents—including her mother—were being beaten in the center, the practitioner said.

Ms. Zhang raced back with her brother, carrying fruit as a small bribe for the police. She was refused entrance and her money was refused as well. She noticed an old lady in a room and shouted up to her: "Is my mother being beaten?" The old lady waved her hand to signify "no," although later Ms. Zhang said she might have been trying to wave her away from the prison, fearing she, too, would be arrested. Ms. Zhang and her brother went home to a fitful, sleepless night.

That night Ms. Chen was taken back into the room. After again refusing to renounce Falun Gong, she was beaten and jolted with the stun stick. Her cellmates heard her curse the officials— like many adherents, she told them that the central government would punish them once they were exposed. But, in an answer that dozens of Falun Gong adherents across the country say they heard, the Weifang officials told Ms. Chen that they had been told by the central government that "no measures are too excessive" to wipe out Falun Gong. She would recant or the beatings would continue.

Two hours after she went in, Ms. Chen was pushed back into her cell on the second story of the main building. It was an unheated room with only a sheet of steel for a bed. She fell into a delirium and one of her three cellmates remember her moaning "Mommy, mommy."

The next morning, February 20, she was ordered out to jog in the snow. Two days of torture had left her legs bruised and her short black hair matted with pus and blood, said cellmates and other prisoners who witnessed the incident. "I saw from the window that she crawled out with difficulty," wrote a cellmate in a

letter smuggled out of prison. Ms. Chen collapsed and was dragged back into the cell.

"I used to be a medical major," wrote another. "When I saw her dying, I suggested moving her into another [heated] room." Instead, local government officials gave her *sanqi,* an herbal remedy for light internal bleeding. "But she couldn't swallow and spat it out." Cellmates implored the officials to send Ms. Chen to a hospital, but the officials—who often criticized Falun Gong practitioners for forgoing medical treatment in favor of their exercises—refused. Instead, a doctor was brought in who pronounced her healthy.

But, wrote the cellmate: "She wasn't conscious and didn't talk, and only spat dark-colored sticky liquid. We guessed it was blood. Only the next morning [the 21st] did they confirm that she was dying. Liu [Guangming, an employee of the local Public Security Bureau who the practitioners say did most of the beating] tried her pulse and his face froze." Ms. Chen was dead.

That evening officials went over to Ms. Zhang's house and said her mother was ill. Ms. Zhang and her brother piled into a car and were driven to a hotel, which was surrounded by police. The local party secretary—the man who had visited Ms. Chen and warned her not to go to Beijing to protest—was present. He told the siblings that their mother had died of a heart attack, but he wouldn't allow them to see her body. After hours of arguing, the officials finally said they could see the body, but only the next day, and insisted they spend the night in the heavily guarded hotel. They refused and finally were allowed to go home.

On February 22, Ms. Zhang and her brother were taken to the local hospital, which was also ringed by police. Their mother was laid out on a table in traditional mourning garb: a simple blue cotton tunic over blue cotton trousers. In a bag tossed in the corner of the room, however, Ms. Zhang spotted her mother's torn

and bloodied clothes, the underwear badly soiled. She lifted the new clothes on her mother's body. The calves were black and her back had six-inch-long welts, while her teeth were broken and her ear swollen and blue. Ms. Zhang fainted and her brother, weeping, caught her.

One of the government's most brilliant moves in its persecution of Falun Gong was declaring the group a cult. That put Falun Gong on the defensive, forcing it to prove its innocence, and cloaked the government's crackdown with the legitimacy of the West's anticult movement. The government quickly picked up the vocabulary of the anticult movement, launching Web sites and putting forth overnight experts, who intoned that Master Li was no different from Jim Jones, the head of the Peoples Temple who in 1978 allegedly killed 912 members, or the Church of Scientology, whose members are allegedly brainwashed into giving huge amounts of money.

To prove its point, the government came up with a series of lurid stories about people who had cut open their stomachs looking for the Dharma Wheel that was supposed to spin inside it. Others were presented whose relatives had died after performing Falun Gong exercises instead of taking medicine. The government also tried to cast Master Li as having financially exploited his followers. Snapshots of the group's accounting books were shown on television, purporting to prove that Master Li made huge amounts of money off his books and videos.

The problem was that few of these arguments held up. The government never allowed victims of Falun Gong to be interviewed independently, making it almost impossible to verify their claims. And even if one took all the claims at face value, they made up a very small percentage of Falun Gong's total

number of adherents. In any group of several million it is always possible to find several hundred unbalanced people; the government's examples never proved that the number of unbalanced Falun Gong adherents was higher than one would find in a general sample of the populace.

As for getting rich, I had little doubt that Master Li lived a comfortable life in the United States. His books sold briskly there and his conferences were well attended. In China, Master Li's books had sold even better, but in 1996 the group had gotten into a dispute with the qigong research association and its books had been denied a publishing license. Thus during the most dynamic period of the group's existence in China the books and videos were bootleg, so he hadn't received royalties.

More fundamentally, the group didn't meet many common definitions of a cult: its members marry outside the group, have outside friends, hold normal jobs, do not live isolated from society, do not believe that the world's end is imminent and do not give significant amounts of money to the organization. Most importantly, suicide is not accepted, nor is physical violence.

Broader definitions of cults do exist; in the West the anticult movement's chief theorist is the clinical psychologist Margaret Singer, whose 1995 book *Cults in Our Midst*, claimed that "covert, seductive groups are targeting the elderly, the workplace, the family . . . anyone can be a victim." Ms. Singer gives a three-fold definition of a cult, arguing that it has a self-appointed, charismatic leader with exclusive knowledge, a hierarchical structure that is totalistic or all-encompassing and that its members are forced to give a "total commitment" to the group. This definition, however, is extremely broad and could take in many religious groups, such as Christian or Muslim religious orders.

I knew, however, that as a new spiritual movement Falun Gong had attracted some extremely committed—some might

even say fanatical—members. During the two years that I interviewed Falun Gong members, I had met members who clearly
did see Master Li as a demigod and had centered their life on the
group. Between performing the morning exercises and the evening reading of prayers, not much time was left for other activities besides family and work. And some members' insistence on
not giving in to the government could be seen as unreasonable.
But overall I didn't see an unhealthy rejection of the outside
world, at least no more so than I'd seen among many adherents of
major religions I'd met over the years. I also thought that many
people lost sight of the fact that after Falun Gong had been
banned, believers had been fired from their jobs and forced
underground. If they lived cut off from society, it was the government's doing, not Falun Gong's teachings.

Again, this is not to say that Falun Gong did not have some
troubling beliefs. Its worldview was of unceasing tests that people have to go through to reach a higher plane. Human existence
was thus seen as transitory and in some ways worthless—hardly
a unique concept but one that could lead some adherents to put
their life second to the group's goals. But here I also didn't see
much that was all that different from some established religions,
which have similar concepts.

The final concern about Falun Gong was on one level
irrefutable. Experts on new religions are often concerned that
leaders of these groups are still alive. The argument goes that,
for example, unlike the Jewish prophets, Christ, Mohammed or
Buddha, Master Li was actively preaching. That meant that he
could still issue a dangerous statement in the future. With, say,
Christ, one can argue over interpretations of his statements but
because he is dead (or alive in heaven, depending on one's view-
point), he is not likely to issue a statement for everyone to take
cyanide. With Falun Gong, such a possibility does exist, although

I'd never seen a serious indication that such an order was at all likely. I also wondered if the supposedly safer established religions were that much better; Christ wasn't likely to issue a new statement calling on Christians to commit suicide but arguments over how to interpret his texts had resulted in enough bloodshed to make one skeptical that it was less dangerous than a new religion.

Still, the government's use of the "cult" label was useful. In the West the anticult movement had been losing steam since anxiety over cults peaked in the early-to-mid 1990s. By the turn of the century most anticult activists were confined to adherents of established religions—in other words, people with a vested interest in attacking new groups. In the United States, the most prominent organization, the American Family Foundation, is a Christian-right group, while in Europe the sharpest critics come from the established, state-sponsored churches. In addition, the scientific basis of declaring a group a cult has become suspect. Psychologists are increasingly unconvinced that "brainwashing" can really be performed on people; most people who join cults tend to leave voluntarily after a relatively short time. This is not meant to downplay the damage that small, incestuous religious groups can have on a person or society, but cults are hardly a major challenge facing society.

But China's claim that Falun Gong was a cult gave the western anticult movement a new cause. Many outsiders fixated on the cult label and spent their time debating obscure definitions of Master Li's works, trying to prove that the group was potentially dangerous. One western academic wrote a paper pleading for an understanding of the government's concerns over Falun Gong's teachings, saying it had a legitimate right to fear the group. This even though the government had only interested itself in Falun Gong because of its demonstration in downtown Beijing, not

because of its teachings. And most fundamentally, what was often forgotten in the learned discourse was that the government, not Falun Gong, was killing people.

This point was lost on the United Nations, which to its later embarrassment sponsored one of these anticult conferences in Beijing. In an opening address to the "International Symposium on Cults" in November 2000, the director of the United Nations Development Programme in China, Kerstin Leitner, blamed excessive tolerance for the existence of cults. The U.N. tried to distance itself from its role in the conference. Ms. Leitner's speech was not made public, and its existence was at first denied by the U.N.'s Beijing office—even though China's government-controlled media were happily trumpeting the speech as a sign that the outside world approved of its crackdown.

Later, Ms. Leitner told me over lunch that she had indeed given the opening speech and that the UNDP had sponsored the conference. While she said she opposed the crackdown, she said she'd hoped that, by working from within, the U.N. could help moderate the government's excesses.

On one point, however, Ms. Leitner would not back down. And that was that the government had reason to be concerned about groups like Falun Gong. The reason, she said, was obvious to any student of Chinese history: that the country had long suffered from millennial groups like Falun Gong. The government might be overreacting, she said, but it was understandable. It was an argument heard widely: with a history like China's, the argument went, any government would be wary of religious movements—or peasant rebellions or whatever. It was a popular understanding of Chinese history but one that didn't hold up to scrutiny.

Not to say that religious uprisings haven't dotted Chinese history, or popularly been blamed for a dynasty's downfall.

China's first major dynasty, the Han, fell after the country was partially overrun by religious rebels. That uprising gathered steam during the second half of the second century as China was plagued by droughts and floods. Consumed by an internal succession struggle, the Han rulers reacted slowly to the disasters, fueling the rebellion. A family of healers impressed the population with miracle cures, teaching that poor health is due to sin and confession leads to good health—a striking parallel to Falun Gong, which also preaches that its exercises and moral regime can end illness. In A.D. 184 the group, known as the Yellow Turbans, launched an uprising, defeating armies and capturing cities. It was soon defeated but was followed by a wave of similar rebellions, with names such as Black Mountain and White Wave. They, too, were put down, but the Han court eventually lost control of the army and China broke up into warring factions. The country's unity was only reestablished some three hundred years later.

Likewise, the downfall of China's last dynasty, the Qing, was partially blamed on a series of religious rebellions that started in the late eighteenth century and ran through the middle of the nineteenth. The most deadly uprising was the Taiping, or Heavenly Kingdom of Great Peace, a mixture of folk religion and Christianity. Its founder was convinced that he was the younger brother of Jesus Christ and preached a rigorous moral code, as well as fiery opposition to the Qing. His armies overran much of south and central China, and after ensconcing himself in Nanjing he ruled a huge swath of China for eleven years. The Taipings were finally destroyed by the Qing's foreign-backed armies, but millions died in sieges, countersieges and scorched-earth offensives. The Qing collapsed a few decades later, in 1911.

In traditional historiography, such groups are usually given a disproportionate role in a dynasty's downfall. They are seen as

wild, uncontrollable forces whipped up by demagogues, much like peasants. This, some analysts have argued, is how we should see Falun Gong. Indeed, the existence of groups like the Taipings are seen as explaining or justifying how the communists have dealt with Falun Gong.

This sort of argumentation strikes me as deeply flawed. Most obviously, Falun Gong differs from these other groups in an important way: it does not advocate violence and is at heart an apolitical, inward-oriented discipline, one aimed at cleansing oneself spiritually and improving one's health.

But more fundamentally, the existence of uprisings like the Yellow Turbans, Taipings or even Falun Gong must be seen as a sign of, not the cause of, a dynasty's troubles. Just as the Taipings' rise was due to the Qing's increasing incompetence, corruption and inability to deal with China's contact with the West, so, too, is Falun Gong a reaction to problems in modern Chinese society. A competent regime can deal with floods and droughts; an incompetent one is riven by factions and unable to succor the poor, leading them to find comfort in religious movements and even to rebel. Popular governments have a moral authority that lays claim to its subjects' allegiance—people believe that the rulers should be in power because they are moral and rule well. Corrupt, ossified regimes, regardless of the era, rarely win much loyalty.

Punctually at 8 p.m., Sima Nan strode onto the stage and sat behind a desk. A lamp shone on his face while he talked into a microphone, shock-jock style. "You call yourself Communist Party cadres?" he bellowed. "When you joined the grand party of Marx, Lenin and Mao you swore to atheism, but some of you are cadres by day and proselytizers by night."

His audience of 1,500 sat riveted. They worked for the Wuhan Iron & Steel Works, a venerable communist factory that had more than 10,000 employees. It was August 1999, and the local Communist Party cell was worried that many of them were still Falun Gong adherents even though the government had banned the group a month earlier. Unsure how to cleanse their ranks of Falun Gong, they'd invited Sima Nan, a government-sponsored cult-buster to the grimy metropolis of 7.4 million to give a stern lecture to senior cadres and workers it suspected of still following Falun Gong.

Sima Nan was perfect for the part, a thick, powerfully built former qigong fanatic. Like Professor Chen, he had once believed that qigong could give one supernatural powers. But unlike the amiable academic, who clung to this belief and defended it with questionable science, the forty-four-year-old former journalist had long discovered that most "special powers" granted by qigong were indeed David Copperfield routines that a clever person could learn. Since the early 1990s he'd labored with the conviction of a born-again atheist to expose qigong frauds, developing a performance that had been honed to spellbinding perfection. His message was not always easy for the party to swallow, but at heart he fundamentally supported it and remained a member.

Now he launched into a surprisingly frank criticism of how the Communist Party has failed to fill China's spiritual vacuum. Ever since China's traditional religious world collapsed along with the imperial system in 1911, he said, Chinese have searched for a new spirituality. When the communists took over in 1949, Chairman Mao usurped the role of God.

"But since Chairman Mao's death in 1976," Sima Nan said, leaning across the table to the microphone, "China has been spiritually adrift. We are looking for something to believe in.

Capitalism isn't a religion, so some people are looking for something else."

Especially pitiable, he said, are old party members trying to regain their youth.

"They used to get the best girls," Mr. Sima said as the auditorium roared with laughter and the local party secretary, sitting in the first row, squirmed.

"Now they're just old guys in apartments looking to be strong again."

He then grabbed the microphone and strode across the stage, his powerful arms bulging through his blue banker's suit. Stripping off his jacket, he piled eight bricks on the head of a volunteer from the audience, climbed on a chair and swung a sledgehammer down onto the bricks. Five shattered, but the young man remained standing, somewhat surprised that his head was in one piece.

"Physics," Sima Nan shouted at the audience. "I only smashed five bricks. The bottom three cushioned his head. Magic had nothing to do with it."

Next, he picked up a glass tumbler and another brick. Mimicking a qigong master, he pretended to breathe his qi on the glass to turn it into "iron glass." He then picked up a brick in one hand and the glass in the other and hit the glass against the brick, careful to make sure the thick base of the glass struck the brick first. The brick broke. People whispered in amazement that the glass must truly have been transformed into "iron glass." Looking disgusted at the audience, Sima Nan explained how the thick base of the tumbler is actually stronger than many bricks. To show that thin glass isn't stronger, he smashed the rim of the glass against the brick, shattering the glass into pieces. He topped off the sequence by eating the thin shards, washing them down with water. He later explained that he'd simply practiced carefully

grinding glass with his molars; as long as he drinks water the glass powder goes down fine.

After four hours his assistant dragged him offstage and into a waiting car for a late-night flight home to Beijing. Eager to toe the government line and rid their factories of Falun Gong adherents, many other factory managers had hired Sima Nan, who was now a hot commodity. He'd even won a recent "Hero of Atheism" award.

On the flight back we discussed what a shock Falun Gong was to the government. The iron and steel works was a Communist bastion, built during China's first five-year plan in the 1950s. But local party officials had estimated that hundreds of the plant's Communist cadres were still refusing to give up their belief in Falun Gong, preferring to follow Master Li instead of Chairman Mao.

"Remember how I joked to the steelworkers about the old party cadres who believed in qigong's supernatural powers?" he said. "For years the party flirted with qigong and even embraced it. But they don't really understand it. Sure, the tricks are appealing, but what really attracts people is the spirituality."

The man who really understood Falun Gong lived in the Temple of Universal Succor. No one talked to him and his advice was shunned. He was by now a virtual recluse, a hermit embittered that the world had ignored him. His name was Chen Xingqiao, a lay Buddhist who'd been fascinated and repulsed by Falun Gong for half a dozen years.

It was early evening when I got to the temple, already getting dark as I made my way in. The entrance had been hard to find on the busy commercial street outside, but inside I found a spacious series of courtyards arranged one after another deep

into Beijing's alleys. I walked back from one courtyard to another, past shrines that were empty but for giant wooden statues and the occasional monk reading by candlelight. Most monks were hurrying to supper back in their living quarters, and the incense sticks before the statues were slowly burning down. I stopped and listened to the faint echoes of the city, savoring the quiet.

Despite the tranquil scene of devotion, the temple was primarily a bureaucratic center. It housed the China Buddhist Association, the organization charged with administering the country's 13,000 temples and its 200,000 monks and nuns. Mr. Chen worked for the association's monthly magazine, the *Voice of Dharma*, where he was an editor. Many of the monks I'd just seen worked for the association, and although they were saying their evening prayers, they spent most of their time as little more than employees of the tourist industry, collecting tickets and selling books or souvenirs.

I slowly worked my way back through half a dozen courtyards to Mr. Chen's tiny office. I lost my way and only found him with the help of a friendly cleaning lady. At forty-three, Mr. Chen cut a detached, slightly hostile figure. He was tall and thin, with a carefully combed head of hair and small eyes that carefully watched the world. As he told me his story, I could see that his caution had served him well, allowing him to move up the bureaucratic ladder from a remote province to the association's head office in the capital. But I was also aware from talking to others that Mr. Chen was more complicated than that. He was also a practicing Buddhist, someone who believed in its teachings and studied them carefully. He typified China's religious associations: a legitimate believer who realized he was making compromises but felt he had no choice.

Mr. Chen first came across Falun Gong in 1994, when he still

lived in Harbin, a northern city that lies about a day's drive from the Russian border. I had been in Harbin around the time that Mr. Chen lived there and remember it vividly. Many of China's painful economic reforms—especially the closing of state enterprises, which later led to high unemployment across the country—had begun in Harbin due to its history. The city and the rest of China's northeast had been colonized by Japan, which built heavy industry. Later came the big steel mills and gargantuan machine tool factories built by China's communist economic planners. By now, these factories were out of date and crumbling under the onslaught of free-market competition. This disproportionate concentration of rust-belt industries meant that layoffs started here earlier, giving the city a rotten feel even in the early 1990s. Later a common sight across China, Harbin early on had legions of unemployed camped out on its sidewalks, selling trinkets and leftover products from their bankrupt enterprises. Brazen prostitutes and seedy karaoke lounges were ubiquitous. The appeal of a doctrine promising salvation was obvious.

But something deeper made this region receptive to Falun Gong only two years after Master Li had founded it. In centuries past it was home to non-Chinese tribes like the Manchus—hence the name Manchuria that Japan used and which remained in popular western usage until recently. The Manchus conquered China in the seventeenth century and ran it for nearly three hundred years. During this time they limited the number of ethnic Chinese—the "Han"—allowed to settle in the Manchus' ancestral homeland, hoping to preserve the region's mixed agricultural and hunting economy. The Manchu empire eventually collapsed and the region became overwhelmingly Chinese, but it still retains some of the flavor of a frontier. Unlike China's cultural heartland, where Mr. Ma led his peasant rebellion, this was on the fringes of China's cultural influence. Instead of denuded hills

and tiny temples, here were thick forests and a tradition of shamanism—much closer culturally to Siberia and Mongolia. A religion drawing on this mysticism would find a sympathetic hearing.

A friend took Mr. Chen to hear Master Li speak at the Harbin Ice Hockey Rink, which Falun Gong had rented for the week. It was a revival-style meeting, part of the group's expansion beyond its base in nearby Liaoning Province. "A friend said that Li was a 'great Buddha' and knew I was interested in Buddhism. I thought I might as well go along and listen. It couldn't hurt."

Inside the rink, a stage had been set up, and Master Li addressed the people sitting in the stands. Sometimes adherents would recount their tales, sharing experiences and trying to show how useful Falun Gong had been in ridding believers of illness and pain. During breaks people milled around in the hallways, looking at information posters describing Falun Gong's tenets and how to meditate.

But Mr. Chen didn't like what he heard. Part of Master Li's speech, he said, denigrated Buddhism, which Falun Gong sometimes portrays as a slightly degenerate, worn-out religion that has run its course. Mr. Chen's temple in Beijing, for example, with its mixture of politics and religion, wouldn't meet with approval from many Falun Gong adherents.

As a committed Buddhist, Mr. Chen was slightly insulted.

"I wasn't too impressed. He seemed to be teaching a basic-level qigong and his own personal theory on life. But a lot of people there were really impressed. They're not too familiar with religion and other teachings, and they don't understand much. Many hadn't heard of any religion through the media or at school, so for these people this was really something fantastic. He talked about 'Buddha law' and spent half the time criticizing other qigong masters."

Mr. Chen said that government allegations that Master Li enriched himself through Falun Gong were probably exaggerated, but he said that in the early 1990s, at least, Falun Gong was a profitable business. He estimates that about 4,000 or 5,000 people attended the revival and that each paid 53 yuan to listen to the ten lectures. That's only about 5 yuan, or 60 cents, a lecture, but all told, the Harbin conference still grossed about 200,000 yuan, or about $25,000. After costs, it still probably earned half that— a very tidy sum for the China of that time.

"I went back for the last lecture," Mr. Chen said. "I left thinking it was strange but nothing important. Just a typical northeastern thing. Northeasterners like things big and exaggerated and simple," he said with a laugh, consciously repeating stereotypes of northeastern Chinese. "There were dozens of these qigong guys all around the northeast then, and such boastful teachings were common. I thought he was a crook."

But during the next two years Mr. Chen found it increasingly hard to ignore Falun Gong. Thanks to fervent proselytizing, the group became the most popular of the new religions. Almost every park in Harbin featured a Falun Gong exercise spot. Corner bookstands were lined with the group's books and videotapes. Many Buddhists were even returning their statues and Buddhist sutras, or holy texts, to temples, saying they weren't as powerful as Mr. Li's main work, *Turning the Dharma Wheel.*

At the time, Mr. Chen was only a part-time volunteer at the local chapter of the Buddhist association and earned his living as an administrator at the Harbin Measuring & Cutting Tool Works, a giant state enterprise that then had about 8,000 employees. Falun Gong believers practiced for an hour every morning in the front yard of the plant and met for discussion groups in the evening. They urged Mr. Chen to join them.

He still had a bad impression of the group from the revival

he attended in 1994 but was curious. He picked up a copy of Mr. Li's book and spent several months studying it. His conclusion: Falun Gong was a heretical offshoot of Buddhism that tried to legitimize itself by misappropriating traditional religious terms such as Dharma Wheel.

Basically, Master Li's works call for a reevaluation of Buddhism. The Law of the Buddha, he says, has not been properly conveyed to mankind. Buddhist scholars, for example, quibble over words and categories, paying too much attention to scriptures. Instead, the true "Buddha Law" encompasses the entire universe, and at its core are three principles: Truth, Benevolence and Tolerance. While science has made massive strides forward, it is limited to explaining material existence.

"What can be understood with modern human knowledge is extremely shallow and tiny," Master Li wrote in the introduction to *Turning the Dharma Wheel.* "Only through the Buddha Law can the mysteries of the universe, time-space and the human body be completely unveiled. It is able to truly distinguish what is righteous from evil, good from bad, and eliminate misconceptions while providing what is correct."

People can only improve themselves, Master Li wrote, by cultivating themselves—by meditating and behaving according to the three principles of being truthful, benevolent and tolerant. As people improve, they reach higher and higher levels of cultivation. Eventually, they escape mortal concerns, like illness, and become immortal.

After learning what Falun Gong stood for, Mr. Chen wrote a 20,000-word essay called "Revealing the Original Face of Falun Gong—a New Kind of Folk Religion" and gave it to the local office of the China Buddhist Association.

But Mr. Chen's analysis was too penetrating and his remedy too radical for China's rigid officialdom. The country's religious

bureaucracy recognizes only five religions and limits their growth by banning proselytizing. But Mr. Chen noted that qigong groups like Falun Gong had registered themselves as simple exercise groups and thus labored under no such restrictions.

Mr. Chen's solution: unshackle established religions so they could compete on equal terms. If Falun Gong could hold meetings in sports stadiums and recruit passersby in the park, why not allow Buddhists to do the same? The response from officials, though, was predictable: they ignored his proposals. "They were just interested in keeping everything quiet," Mr. Chen said.

Open discussion of Falun Gong would also expose the central paradox in official policy. Acknowledging Falun Gong as a religion would mean officials would either have to allow a new religion to register, or ban it. Registering a new religion is impossible in China—it hasn't happened in five decades of Communist rule—while banning it would be an admission that the government had allowed a religion to flourish for years in the guise of an exercise group.

Mr. Chen's frustrations came to a head later in 1996, when the Harbin city government convened a meeting called "Socialism and Buddhism." As a senior lay member of the city's Buddhist community, Mr. Chen attended and brought up Falun Gong for discussion.

The issue died after just a few minutes' debate. Representatives from the police said they could act only when a disturbance occurred, while officials from the religion bureau said they are allowed to oversee activities only inside established places of worship, according to people present at the meeting. "It fell through the cracks, so the government simply ignored it and hoped it would go away," said an official at the Harbin Public Security Bureau who attended the 1996 meeting. Adds Mr. Chen:

"It was a new religion, but no one knew what to do about it because new religions are illegal. Therefore it didn't exist."

Mr. Chen decided that if the bureaucracy wouldn't act, he would prod it by publishing his essay, which the local Buddhist association had forwarded to its national headquarters. He appealed for help to its head, Zhao Puchu, a rare figure who managed to remain respected in religious circles while maintaining the trust of party officials.

Mr. Zhao liked the essay and sent it to China's leading party newspaper, *People's Daily*. The paper initially wanted to publish a condensed version in its elite "Internal Reference" edition, which is read by the country's top leaders. But after the newspaper asked Mr. Chen for permission to run such a version, a senior editor killed it. "Several things prevented us from running it," said an editor at the newspaper. "Foremost was that he talked too frankly about religion. We just can't do that."

Mr. Zhao then ordered that the tract be published in early 1997 in *Religious Trends,* an internal publication of the Buddhist association. After a further year of effort, he got the essay printed by a publishing house run by the party's religious affairs office.

These were victories, but small ones. Reflecting government suspicion of religion, *Religious Trends* was allowed to be distributed only to members of the Buddhist association, so its impact was negligible. He also managed to get the manuscript published, but by a tiny publishing house. The book was deemed too sensitive to distribute to bookstores, so interested readers had to contact the publisher in Beijing and pick it up in person.

Mr. Chen said that during the next year, 1998, he was contacted by members of the China Atheist Association, including cult-buster Sima Nan. They also opposed Falun Gong and wanted a copy of his book. He sent one over, but as a Buddhist, Mr. Chen

didn't like what they stood for. "I criticized Falun Gong, but I also talked about the need for religion," Mr. Chen said.

We had been speaking for more than an hour and it had grown pitch black outside and Mr. Chen's office was chilly. His spirits sank as he thought of how the atheists had hijacked the debate over Falun Gong. "Their criticisms are so crude. Their arguments are like objecting to a fake bottle of liquor because it has alcohol in it—not because it's fake and dangerous. So by this logic, all liquor, real or fake, is bad. That's how they treat Falun Gong. They say Li Hongzhi is wrong because he claims to be a god and gods are bad. But what they're doing is criticizing all religions."

Crude or not, it was the atheists who brought down Falun Gong.

Leading the atheists' attack was one of China's most famous scientists, He Zuoxiu. I had heard of Professor He before. He was a semipublic figure, the sort of person who, like Mr. Chen, is more complicated than he first seems. People in Falun Gong portray him as a government pit bull, the stooge who adds a veneer of scientific respectability to the government's attacks on the group, much like Professor Chen had lent credibility to qigong in years past. But Professor He is also a man who speaks his mind and had written letters to the government protesting a planned theater in downtown Beijing. The egg-shaped glass-and-steel theater was President Jiang Zemin's pet project, but that hadn't stopped Professor He from criticizing it as too modern for a building across the street from the Forbidden City.

When I called, he was wary, until I said I didn't want to talk about the theater. He'd received a lot of flak for opposing it, he said, and wanted to let that issue cool down. His work on Falun

Gong, however, had recently been met with government approval, so he quickly invited me over to his spacious but simple concrete-block apartment. Before opening the steel security door he peeked at me through a watch hole. He laughed apologetically. "I've been a target of these Falun Gong types and can't be too sure," he said, tramping into his living room with a motion for me to follow.

He was a rumpled seventy-three-year-old, energetic and quick-witted, if slightly grubby and unkempt. His fingernails were dirty and his unwashed hair stuck straight up. He wore a track suit and plastic sandals. He gave the impression of being either a devil-may-care intellectual or a lunatic.

No sooner had he sat down than he jumped up again and walked to a bookcase, pulling out a plastic envelope, the sort used to store evidence. He unzipped it and carefully pulled out a copy of *Turning the Dharma Wheel.* "I saw it displayed on a roadside stand and was curious what nonsense people were reading," he said, "so I bought it."

As I gingerly opened Exhibit A, Professor He reached over and pulled a receipt out from the back flap. It was dated November 4, 1996. "I thought the book had to do with Buddhism, but I was intrigued because the publisher was the China Broadcast & Television Publishing House. I thought it was strange that a publisher that's supposed to be propagating government information would be spreading Buddhism."

Professor He figured he'd report on the publishing house. After all, such texts are usually only published by obscure companies, such as the one that put out Mr. Chen's treatise on Falun Gong that same year. But then Professor He read the book and became even more fascinated. Here wasn't a simple book on Buddhism but an original religious text, one that outlined a new theology designed to replace major religions. China already had

IAN JOHNSON

five legal religions, which as an atheist he thought was bad enough. Now here was another. Worse, it was brazen enough to publish its tract with a publishing house run by the Ministry of Propaganda.

Then Professor He became involved in a research project at his institute, the Chinese Academy of Sciences' Institute of Theoretical Physics. He put the book on his shelf, intending to come back to it later. Like Mr. Chen, he forgot about it for two years.

By this time, 1998, Falun Gong had exploded in popularity, spreading from Mr. Chen's home in the far north to China's big cities in the south. It had in effect become China's unofficial sixth religion, boasting millions of adherents.

It spread widely on university campuses, even to Professor He's institute. In March 1998, he said, one of his students started to practice Falun Gong compulsively. He refused to eat, lost weight and was sent to the hospital. The next month he was sent to a mental hospital where he stayed for one year. Falun Gong adherents say that such behavior is simply that of a psychologically unbalanced person, but Professor He attributed the young man's behavior to his new passion.

In June 1998, Beijing Television came by his institute to film a report. As usual for China's state-controlled media, it was planned as a puff piece. But Professor He asked if he might air some criticism of his research institute. Coming from Professor He, a respected party member, the criticism couldn't be that controversial, so the producer agreed. "I said we have good things at our institute, but bad things, too. We have people who believe in Falun Gong so much that they've become schizophrenic," he said, recounting his words with a grin.

The day after the show aired on May 11, 1998, Professor He realized he was in for a fight. That morning half a dozen Falun Gong adherents showed up at his house and sat in his living room

for three hours, arguing with him. "I showed them that I'd read their book, and all the parts that I thought were nonsense," he said. "It was a bit unpleasant having all these people coming to your home, but in the end we just agreed that we didn't agree and they left."

Professor He promptly called the television station and found out that a few hundred Falun Gong adherents were outside the station with pickets. Fresh from his experience with the argumentative students, Professor He urged Beijing Television not to buckle. "The idea that they could protest outside a major organization of the party was unimaginable," he said.

But, as Mr. Chen the Buddhist administrator had learned two years earlier, Professor He soon discovered that officials were bent on the path of least resistance. The number of protesters outside Beijing Television quickly grew to 2,000—all peaceful and orderly but shocking to authorities in Beijing, which hadn't seen a significant demonstration since the student protests in Tiananmen Square in 1989. With the ninth anniversary of those demonstrations rapidly approaching—the anniversary always being a sensitive time on China's political calendar—leaders ordered the television station to end the Falun Gong protests at any cost.

The station quickly complied. To show goodwill, it handed out two thousand boxed lunches—one for each protester—and promised to air a sympathetic portrayal of the group. The next day the show ran as promised, the protests dispersed and quiet returned to the Chinese capital.

Professor He was incensed at the weak-kneed television managers. He did more research and got a copy of Mr. Chen's book. Through contacts in the party, he learned that it had regularly yielded to Falun Gong protesters. Over the past few years several media outlets—estimates range as high as fourteen—had

been besieged by Falun Gong adherents angry at reports casting doubt on its claim to foster good health through exercise. In almost every case, the media had backed down, printing or airing apologies to Falun Gong.

Most, Professor He learned, were simply taking their cue from the State Press and Publication Administration, which controls content in China's media. The office had a "three nots" policy on qigong, including Falun Gong: media should not be for it, should not be against it and should not label it good or bad—part of the agency's general policy of avoiding anything controversial.

Newspapers had been following this rule since 1996, when a leading party paper gave in to Falun Gong's first protest. On June 17, 1996, a writer using the pseudonym Xin Ping, wrote in the *Enlightenment Daily* a book review critical of Master Li's work:

> Recently, booksellers in every side street and alley have been selling *Turning the Dharma Wheel,* which is a book propagating feudal superstition and false science. Of all the books I've read, *Turning the Dharma Wheel* is the most wildly arrogant and outrageously boastful.

That incensed Falun Gong adherents, who protested outside the newspaper's office. The newspaper issued a retraction apologizing for the piece. Alarmed at the whiff of controversy, officials in the China Qigong Scientific Research Association expelled Falun Gong, while the State Press and Publication Administration banned Master Li's works, such as *Turning the Dharma Wheel.* [Falun Gong says it voluntarily left the association because Master Li felt it was corrupt.] But the government took no action against Falun Gong for its protest, and the retraction stood. That set a

precedent for the other media outlets, which also issued apologies or retractions whenever they criticized Falun Gong.

To the stability-minded mandarins who run the country, this seemed like sound policy, one that the Beijing Television protests bore out. Opening up a messy debate about Falun Gong would have sparked more protests and allowed people such as Mr. Chen to call for religious freedom. Banning it, on the other hand, seemed pointless because the group was otherwise harmless. Few considered the lesson that Falun Gong was learning: that demonstrations were acceptable and achieved results

Professor He decided to force the party to change its policy—and unlike Mr. Chen, he had more ways to make society take notice of Falun Gong. As a famous academic researcher and government loyalist, he was a member of a top-level consultative committee that advises the Communist Party on policy. Although largely powerless, the committee provided Professor He with some cover to step up his criticism of Falun Gong.

He started by sending a letter to President Jiang Zemin, warning him that a new religion with tens of millions of followers was spreading across China. The letter, which he titled "Reckless Falun Gong," was written by Professor He and five fellow members of the committee. There was no reply.

Refusing to be discouraged, Professor He began writing articles for any publication that would accept his work. Most followed the party's three-nots campaign, but a few regional journals, unaware of the central government's policy, were happy to run articles by the famous scientist. "The bigger papers . . . were afraid they'd have to apologize," Professor He said. "So I had to publish in these small newspapers and magazines."

While Professor He plugged away, Falun Gong enjoyed a banner year in 1998. Though its founder, Master Li, had emigrated to the United States, he returned occasionally to coor-

dinate activities and stayed in close contact with practitioners through a tightly knit organization. Critics such as Professor He continued their pinprick attacks, but the party's do-nothing policies coupled with Falun Gong's assertiveness had marginalized them.

"The government was mostly supportive of us," said Zhang Erping, a Falun Gong spokesman who lives in New York told me in a telephone interview. "Many top leaders seemed to support us."

This impression was understandable but wrong. Most of China's leaders didn't accept or agree with Falun Gong; their crude governing apparatus had simply kept them in the dark, capable only of stifling public debate on the new religion. That was about to change, not because leaders had become wiser, but because Falun Gong was to make a tactical mistake.

As 1998 wound down, Professor He decided to write a short commentary for a small student magazine called *Science and Technology Knowledge for Youth*. The article, "Why Young People Shouldn't Practice Qigong," was one of his typical blasts at all forms of qigong, which he said was more suitable to older, less-active people. Young people, he said, shouldn't sit around meditating; they should be out exercising, running, jumping and in general being as vigorous as he still was. Halfway through the article, Professor He mentioned Falun Gong and then, in a key phrase that angered the group, referred to Master Li in a mildly derisive term as its *toutou*, or "boss."

The response came quickly. The day after the magazine was printed, protesters arrived at its offices on the campus of Tianjin Normal University, located in the port city of Tianjin, about a hundred miles east of Beijing. From April 20 to 23, as many as 6,000 occupied the university, demanding a retraction.

The group's response seemed excessive—after all, the maga-

zine is not widely read and few would have noticed if Falun Gong had let the issue rest. Part of its insistence on apologies and retractions is certainly the self-righteousness found in many religions—the idea that any criticism is an insult against an eternal truth. But there was more to it than that. Falun Gong activists also knew that in communist China small critiques in the media are often a thin wedge. Indeed, the infamous Cultural Revolution began with the critique of a play that might have allegorically criticized Chairman Mao. The group may have been overzealous, but in many ways it understood perfectly how the communists ran society.

This time, however, there would be no retractions. "The publishers called me," Professor He said. "And asked me what was going on. I told them that as a science publication, they had better not print a retraction. They had a duty to the truth." The editors held the line.

With no apology forthcoming, angry Falun Gong members then made their fateful decision to seek help from the very top echelons of the party in Beijing. It was a turn of events that even Professor He couldn't have foreseen. He had hoped his magazine articles would attract leaders' attention; instead, his articles provoked Falun Gong into delivering his message for him.

The protest was like a mirage. It materialized during the morning of April 25, 1999, as Falun Gong adherents converged on the Communist Party's headquarters in central Beijing. Then, after about six hours of quiet sitting outside the compound's perimeter, it slowly vanished as the protesters went home at dark. There were no placards, no shouting, no disturbances. Only about 10,000 people quietly challenging the government to legalize their group.

The leadership compound is called Zhongnanhai, which means Central and South Lakes, in reference to the two lakes around which the group of imperial palaces and modern buildings is grouped. The protesters had gathered to the north, south and west of the compound—the east side abuts the Forbidden City. It was the heart of communist power, just as it had been the heart of imperial China for six centuries.

The quietness only made it odder, even unnerving. Police cars had blocked off the main roads leading to the protest, and central Beijing was turned into a giant pedestrian zone. As I walked by the wall of people, I could only wonder what it was like inside for the government. They could hear nothing, but they knew that under their noses, without any warning from the country's vaunted Public Security Bureau, a group had formed, one whose exceptional organizational power could pull off this well-disciplined demonstration. I heard later that some frantic officials remembered Professor He and called him up, demanding material on Falun Gong. He couriered over a packet, including Mr. Chen's book.

Some of the protesters sat on the ground practicing their exercises, while others stood around, waiting for something to happen. Most were suspicious of outsiders, unwilling to talk or to criticize the government.

"We don't want to say anything," an old man said. "You cannot solve our problem, only the government can do this. Therefore, we want to talk only to the government."

Although Falun Gong would later say that the protest was spontaneous, a fair degree of planning had clearly gone into it. The protesters seemed to have unofficial marshals, who made sure that the protest stayed quiet and that no one said anything. Most seemed to be from Beijing, but from the accents, I and other reporters there knew that some protesters were from Falun

Gong's homeland in northeastern China. Perhaps they had been in Tianjin for the first protest against Professor He's article and made the short trip to Beijing for this protest.

The police presence was light, a reflection of the shock that had engulfed the government. The party maintained, and had largely convinced outside observers, that it had a firm grip on China. Stability ruled in China, unlike those other ex-communist countries that were beset by turmoil. And while China certainly did not have any wars going on and by many measures was stable, here was something that didn't fit: 10,000 people who had somehow been organized without the government's knowledge. In my experience, whenever two or more democratic activists got together they'd be busted. How had 10,000 members of a new religion been organized to travel to Beijing? I wondered if the government's control over society could be as strong as we imagined, or if it wasn't hollowing out.

As I walked on, I saw a policeman ask a group of three elderly women what they were practicing. He shook his head in bewilderment when they said Falun Gong.

Nearby, a young man from the Beijing Post and Telecommunication University said he had come to demonstrate because he'd heard that Falun Gong had been libeled in a student newspaper somewhere. He was clearly referring to the Tianjin article but didn't know the details. It seemed that someone had told him to come down to protest and he'd obeyed.

After walking along the north end of the compound, I wanted to turn left and head south along the side of the compound. The road was blocked, but some marshals tried to keep order.

"Pedestrians, please walk on the right side and do not stand on the road," a middle-aged woman told people entering the street.

I spoke to another old man, who said he was from Hebei Province, which is located next to Beijing.

"Falun Gong is great," he said, dressed in a white shirt, windbreaker and baggy cotton trousers. "If you practice it, you won't get sick. The government could save a lot of money on health care if it allowed Falun Gong. That's why we're here: to make the government understand this."

"Why does the government need to understand this?" I asked.

"It's been criticized in some newspaper. We think it's going to be banned."

"Which paper?"

"I don't know, some youth newspaper. It doesn't matter. We just want to be a legally recognized form of qigong. That's it."

"How long have you been here?"

"Since seven-thirty a.m. I came here after my morning exercises."

Then a young lady came up and stopped him from speaking. "We don't allow interviews," she said. "Sorry."

The old man kept quiet and I moved on.

Many Beijingers stopped and asked questions, but likewise were met with silence.

"What do you want?" a young man said after stopping his bicycle in front of a group.

No one answered.

He shrugged.

"I've never heard of a demonstration where no one says anything," he said and then biked on.

Other locals were less blasé.

"You're just causing trouble," one said to an old man. "Don't rock the boat," another said a bit later. "Look at the disturbance you're causing," a woman said to a third group. "This

is only going to cause trouble for you and all of us. Don't be so selfish."

The comments reminded me of the remarks that family members might make about a troublesome relative: Don't speak about that because it'll only set him off. It was the way a lot of citizens around the world are forced to deal with their governments—as an unpredictable force that is better left alone.

The ordinary citizens' instincts were accurate. The decision to protest in Beijing was a colossal miscalculation by Falun Gong. A crackdown was inevitable and anyone not completely naïve or blinded by belief could see that.

I walked along farther and saw a group of people reading a letter. It was from the Beijing Public Security Bureau and the city's Petitions and Appeals Office. "The government has no intention of banning Falun Gong," the letter read. "Appeals should be made through the usual channels."

That promise turned out to be false, but at the time it seemed reasonable. A group of demonstrators reportedly went inside the leadership compound and met with Premier Zhu Rongji, who also made conciliatory remarks. By nightfall the protesters had dispersed.

But the government soon made its true feelings known. President Jiang Zemin issued an open letter to all senior leaders, calling Falun Gong a threat to the party's authority. In the letter—which was also read aloud in party cell meetings, so everyone got the message—Mr. Jiang chastised the government's security apparatus for allowing the protest to take place.

"We called for 'stability above all,' but our stability has fallen through," Mr. Jiang wrote. "Our leaders must wake up."

Soon, the creaky government bureaucracy that had ignored and unwittingly encouraged Falun Gong for years started to formulate a response to the group. But there was to be no public dis-

cussion on religious freedom, as Mr. Chen wanted, nor the sort of robust, no-gloves debate favored by Professor He.

Instead, the party took the only action it knew. It set up a bureau called Office 610—named for the date, June 10, when it was formed. Its job was to mobilize the country's pliant social organizations. Under orders from the Public Security Bureau, churches, temples, mosques, newspapers, media, courts and police all quickly lined up behind the government's simple plan: to crush Falun Gong, no measures too excessive. Within days a wave of arrests swept China. By the end of 1999, Falun Gong adherents were dying in custody. In February 2000 it was Ms. Chen's turn.

The day after seeing her mother's corpse laid out for cremation in February 2000, Ms. Zhang decided she'd find out who killed her mother. "I felt that something wasn't right, and that they were hiding something," she said. "None of it made any sense."

She hit upon a simple task to start her quest: to obtain her mother's death certificate. Police or hospitals are supposed to issue to family members who request it a person's death certificate, a single piece of paper that confirms that the person is dead and states the cause of death. Ms. Zhang wanted the certificate so she could launch a complaint about how her mother died. Without the certificate, she couldn't request an official investigation—the courts needed proof that her mother had died violently. So she set out to prove that her mother had been killed.

She met with her brother, a twenty-eight-year-old mechanic, and he agreed they should act. But he was not sure what to do. The death certificate seemed like a good idea, but he had no idea how to obtain it. How about asking at the police? he suggested. Ms. Zhang went to her husband and he also agreed that some-

thing should be done, but he also was of little help, other than advising caution: "I didn't think it'd lead to much but, if she had to do it, it's okay," he told me later. "It was a matter of family honor."

What I liked about Ms. Zhang was her bluntness and stubbornness. It was obvious that she had no experience with politics and, at least at first, had little idea how China's political system worked. That was unsurprising because like most Chinese, Ms. Zhang had avoided politics, a messy subject that was only trouble.

In fact, she was once the sort of person who floated easily through reform-era China, taking advantage of the party's cautious economic reforms and relatively relaxed grip on society. She'd worked first as a clerk at a department store, later improving herself by taking accounting classes in her spare time. She married, had a son and went to work as a bookkeeper. Later, after neighbors praised her skill in arranging a few marriages, she worked as a freelance matchmaker—not arranging marriages as traditionally was done, but introducing potential brides and grooms to each other.

Her appearance added to the impression that she was a very ordinary person. She wasn't dressed like many of the Falun Gong bumpkins from the countryside—unlike her mother, for example, she didn't wear old-fashioned padded jackets and cloth shoes. Instead, she wore dark polyester slacks and bright printed blouses, unchic by the standards of China's big cosmopolitan cities but the uniform of a slowly modernizing, slowly prospering hinterland of a billion people. Her hair was cut short, which was practical, but in a concession to fashion was sometimes permed. Her eyes, dark and clear, were remote when she spoke, as though she was trying to visualize what she was saying.

Now she was trying to see justice done for her mother. It was hard to imagine such an abstract idea, but she pursued it with a

matter-of-fact air that I often saw in China's lower classes. There was no hopelessness, only a shoulder-to-the-wheel attitude of people used to struggling and not getting very far. She cried in front of me only once, when describing how she'd refused to pay her mother's fine the day before she was beaten to death. Mostly, though, she was coolly analytical and indefatigable, wanting only to get on with it and obtain that piece of paper.

She turned first to the hospital. They told her that they had just issued a paper ordering the crematorium to burn her mother's body. It wasn't the death certificate, but it confirmed that her mother was dead and stated the cause. She decided to get a copy of that document and went back to the hospital. A receptionist sent her to an official in the records department who handed her a piece of paper on hospital letterhead. It was addressed to the local street committee and read:

> Citizen Chen Zixiu from your district suffered from heart attack and died suddenly at 9:30 a.m. on Feb. 21, 2000, in this hospital after unsuccessful rescue attempts. The corpse has been kept in mortuary for more than 30 hours, and spots have appeared (on the skin). As it has started to rot and the hospital can't maintain it longer, please inform relatives of the dead to transfer the corpse to funeral parlor as soon as possible.
> WEIFANG MUNICIPAL HOSPITAL
> FEBRUARY 22, 2000

Stamped at the bottom was the hospital's seal. Ms. Zhang studied it for a few minutes. This couldn't be true. She spoke to the official: "A heart attack? What about the bruises? The broken teeth? The blood? I want a copy of the death certificate." The official looked at her like she was mad. She asked to see the

corpse again. The official went out, came back five minutes later and said it was impossible. It was in storage and couldn't be brought out without proper authorization. Would she please make arrangements to have the body cremated?

Ms. Zhang left in a daze. It was slowly dawning on her how difficult her battle would be. She went home and conferred with her brother. They'd read about China's legal system, which was in the news all the time, with reports of people suing each other for this or that. It wasn't quite like the lawsuit-happy United States, but China was developing into a litigious society, and the party was trumpeting this in the media as a sign that the country was maturing and that a credible legal system had been created. Ms. Zhang decided to sue the government, demanding that it issue the death certificate.

But unlike the peasant champion or the dispossessed home-owners—who at least could give the appearance that they were simply suing in the name of lower taxes and cultural preservation—Ms. Zhang was challenging the government's stated top priority: crushing Falun Gong. Here one couldn't argue that this was a simple administrative lawsuit; this was as political as it got. She learned this when she called lawyers for help. None would even allow her in the front door for a consultation, let alone file a suit on her behalf. She spent the next three weeks going from one lawyer to another, until finally one told her that they'd been instructed by the government not to handle cases regarding Falun Gong.

On March 17, Ms. Zhang got a letter from the hospital saying her mother's body would be cremated that same day. She called the hospital and said she was launching an inquiry into her mother's death. Don't cremate the body, she said. The official on the phone told her to write a letter. She did but figured the exercise was hopeless and that her mother would be cremated.

Next, she sent letters to the State Council, the highest body of civilian power in China, and to local media, demanding that the state send her a copy of her mother's death certificate. They ignored her. The police, however, didn't; for the next six weeks she was interrogated repeatedly for what she calculates was a total of 107 hours. Finally, in late April, she was sentenced to fifteen days in prison for "distorting facts and disturbing social order."

The detention was a turning point. "I was thrown in with common criminals and could finally see the injustice that my mother had suffered," Ms. Zhang told me after she got out of prison. "I decided to learn everything I could and challenge the authorities using their own language."

Upon her release, she stopped working as a matchmaker to devote herself full-time to pressing her mother's case. She bought handbooks on the law and learned how to make official requests for documents and how to appeal refusals. Her husband remained passively supportive, accepting the family's reduced income but never actively helping her.

She reminded me of Mr. Ma, the peasant lawyer. Like him, she'd taught herself about the law and developed a sophisticated knowledge of appeals and procedures. But Mr. Ma had organized what amounted to a political movement against the government—a band of peasants who traveled hill and valley to spread the word of fair taxes. Others, like Mr. Fang the architect, showed how a person could mobilize thousands by force of intellect, cleverly negotiating his ideas through the barriers and reefs of censors and bureaucrats. Ms. Zhang, though, was more typical. Like most Chinese, she had few allies and little sophistication. She was one person fighting a small battle, the consequences hers to bear.

She was aided in many practical matters by Falun Gong ad-

herents who had withstood the government's onslaught. Brother Li, for example, had given me some of the original documents and had later smuggled them out of China. He and others helped Ms. Zhang find accommodations and locate the petitions and appeals offices. Knowing their location was important because— in another sign of schizophrenia—their location was kept a secret. It was like a test: if you can find us, you can complain to us. "Only they [the Falun Gong adherents] could really understand the frustrations I had and the hurdles I had to face every day," she said to me during a trip to Beijing.

Adherents like Brother Li had managed to survive the government's crackdown by putting together an ad hoc group of volunteers, interchangeable activists who could step in when any were jailed. Before the crackdown, Falun Gong was carefully organized like the government, with a structure that paralleled the government's hierarchy. That was quickly smashed by the Public Security Bureau, which threw thousands in jail. Now it was the Brother Lis of China who were holding the movement together and helping people like Ms. Zhang along the way.

In early July, I set out with Brother Li on a bike ride through the city. Throughout the summer we took several of these trips, avoiding tails and meeting up at a sports stadium in eastern Beijing to tour through the city and chat about life.

We discussed almost anything imaginable, but we always returned to his beliefs. I think he saw in me a possible convert. Like an evangelical Christian, who believes that everyone should be saved and genuinely wants to share the Word with the unbelievers, Brother Li wanted me to understand the good news of Falun Gong. This was a system of beliefs that had made his life meaningful, setting out a strict moral code that stood in contrast

with what he saw as the amorality of daily life in China. It was a complete cosmology, with a creation story, and a promise of salvation and heaven—and of hell to those who did not believe and follow. Of course, he'd want me to know about such a gift, and I accepted his solicitousness as it was meant: as a token of friendship and genuine concern.

Not that I could really get my head around much of the teachings. I had a hard time with the main text, *Turning the Dharma Wheel*, because to me it lacked the beauty of, say, the Buddhist sutras or other religious classics. I could see why the text might be appealing to many mainland Chinese, with its simple language, appeal to science and emphasis on personal health. Perhaps I just lacked this personal history, but in my mind Master Li's writings lacked the genius that had touched some of the writers of the sutras, the Taoist canon, the Bible or the Koran. But I was always eager to talk to Brother Li about how he felt about the texts, and how he interpreted Master Li's message.

One hazy morning we set off on our simple steel-framed bikes toward Tiananmen Square. It was two weeks before the first anniversary of the government's July 22, 1999, ban on the Falun Gong movement, the startling announcement that Ms. Chen had heard on her television. Brother Li knew that scores of out-of-town adherents who had been undeterred by the death of Ms. Chen and others would soon descend on Beijing to appeal against the crackdown. His plan was to help prepare for their arrival. Today was a scouting day, and he intended to provide information on the likely police presence around the square to any adherent who called him for information.

He could expect many calls in the coming weeks. His beeper number was well known among the informal network of protesters, and our two-hour ride was punctuated several times by pager messages from Falun Gong members requesting help. "Everyone

decides for themselves how to be of most use," he said to me as we set off west toward the square. "This is something I can do."

Like our bicycle ride, that year, 2000, was interspersed with the unexpected. The government had an overwhelming advantage over Falun Gong and looked like it would crush the group. But for a year now, small people like Brother Li had resisted, succeeding in staging regular protests in the Chinese capital. They'd be arrested, beaten and some, like Ms. Chen, killed, but their faith kept them coming back. It was at times sickening to watch, like a boxer whose fight should be called before he is permanently injured. But it was also uplifting. A decade earlier a sustained series of protests in the face of a government crackdown would have been inconceivable. Now they were so common that the foreign media soon tired of them and at times only the dutybound foreign wire services sent reporters.

As Tiananmen Square came into sight, Brother Li's beeper went off. It was a message to call a pay phone in Beijing. Brother Li angled his one-speed black bike over to the curb and stopped in front of a bank of pay phones. A wave of cyclists rushed past, and as he dismounted, he noticed that all the phones were occupied.

Experience quelled the temptation to turn on his cell phone. Not only can conversations be monitored, but the phones are dangerous even when they are only switched on. That's because security agents can figure out which transmitter the phone is getting its signal from. In a city like Beijing, where a high density of mobile phones means transmitters are located every few blocks, police could trace Brother Li from one signal tower to the next, triangulating his position and following him through town.

A few weeks earlier one of Brother Li's associates was almost nabbed when he used a mobile phone to set up a meeting. A novice to the group's security measures, he arrived at the ren-

dezvous point to find the area crawling with suspicious-looking people. Although he jumped into a cab and left, the two followers he was supposed to meet were detained. Caution was paramount.

Finally, a public phone came free and Brother Li called. From the receiver came an excited voice—that of a Falun Gong practitioner from northeast China who was in the capital to find someone to help her send an e-mail to the outside world. She told Brother Li that a teenage Falun Gong believer had died trying to escape from police custody by leaping from a train. Like many Falun Gong newcomers to the city, the woman had heard of Brother Li through a friend of a friend. Brother Li had no idea who she was, but after talking to her for a while, he figured she wasn't a police plant. He agreed to meet her later in the day.

"You can usually tell if the people are genuine," he said, hopping on his bike and heading back down the road in the stifling heat. "They make references to things that the police wouldn't know about and have this earnest air about them."

The woman, who had spent the previous night outside in a park, was desperate for accommodation. Practitioners used to stay with Brother Li, but his three-room apartment in Beijing's eastern district was now watched by security agents. Like most people who had continued to practice Falun Gong during the year since the crackdown, the woman had been fired from her job and had little money. She could survive only through the generosity of fellow practitioners.

Helping her was easier because the government's grip over society was continuing to relax. Not too long ago—until the mid-to-late 1990s, depending on the part of the country—state-run factories paid for all manner of social benefits, including insurance, pension and even local schools. Paramount was housing, which was handed out by employers, be they factories or ministries. Truly private companies were few, and even they had to

offer some sort of housing. That meant that neighbors knew each other—they were, after all, colleagues. And the blocks where they lived were guarded by retirees who certainly would know if an outsider was living there.

But as reforms took hold, profits took precedence over control. Companies realized they couldn't be competitive in a market economy if they had to run apartment blocks and provide other social services. So apartments were sold off and began to change hands. Residents couldn't always assume that their neighbors were from their company. They got used to having strangers living next to them. So, too, the watchmen, who no longer could be sure of who was living where.

Brother Li and his colleagues used these changes to their advantage. A fellow Falun Gong adherent who worked for a textile company had an extra apartment, and Brother Li could let the woman stay there without anyone noticing. Over the phone he promised the adherent a place to stay and gave her his friend's beeper number. Another little task accomplished.

As we pedaled across the north end of Tiananmen Square, we didn't attract much attention. Beijing is full of foreigners, and one biking with a Chinese person hadn't been a novelty in years. For his part, Brother Li looked like any of the thousands of other cyclists who at that moment were riding past the cavernous square. Wearing a striped short-sleeve shirt and black polyester pants, he cut a trim figure, his face often breaking out into a broad, easy smile as we chatted. But then his eyes, usually languid and distant, suddenly lit up.

"There and there," he said, making quick mental notes. "The police are all along the entrances to the pedestrian underpasses"— useful information that he would later share with adherents arriving in Beijing.

We met again the next day and cycled past Workers' Stadium

in Beijing, talking about his beliefs. For weeks now he had been agonizing over whether to go to Tiananmen Square himself and protest. He brought up Ms. Chen's death and said he was sure he could resist the torture. After all, he said, it was his duty to let the government know his feelings toward the ban. But he also knew that he was of more use out of jail, where he could continue to coordinate protests.

It was a debate that consumed many Falun Gong adherents. Back in the United States, Master Li had recently started publishing new essays on his Internet site. Computer-literate adherents printed them out and distributed them widely. One, "Toward Consummation," was distributed in August 2000 and was widely reprinted. In it Master Li argues against worldly attachments. In Falun Gong's sometimes turgid jargon, he also urged adherents to protest—to "step forward" and show their belief in the Fa, or immutable law of the universe: "What's unfolding at present was arranged long ago in history. Those disciples who have stepped forward to validate the Fa in the face of the pressure are courageous and admirable."

He wasn't directly ordering people to protest, but the message was clear. It was similar to the Christian idea that one has to "stand up for Jesus." Given the current crackdown, however, I was frightened at the thought of people being encouraged, even if only indirectly, to protest. I kept my thoughts to myself, silently hoping that Brother Li wouldn't go to the square.

His beeper went off again and he pulled over to make a call. It was an adherent from Guangdong Province in the south who had been in Beijing helping people from her region survive in the distant capital, with its incomprehensible dialect and tight security.

A few months earlier the woman had debated going to

Tiananmen Square to protest—an act that always winds up with arrest and detention without charge. At a meeting with Brother Li before heading back, the woman, a thirty-two-year-old unemployed English teacher with a pale face and a tiny voice, decided not to protest. Instead, she said she'd return to Guangdong to tell about the situation in Beijing. "Many followers need to be reminded that others are protesting. This will give them courage."

Now she was calling to say she had made it back safely and to ask for any news. Most of the contact between regions was to exchange basic intelligence—where police are active and who is out of jail and how they can be reached. Members also share stories of police abuse and protests to bolster their spirits. Brother Li told her that demonstrations have been going on daily, even if on some days only a few made it to Tiananmen Square.

We were at a pay phone in a kiosk, and with the vendor listening to our end of the conversation, Brother Li didn't speak too explicitly.

"We've still got a lot of friends visiting town. We're still very active," Brother Li said, referring to the protests. "Let everyone know we're fine in Beijing."

He hung up and we continued to ride. We passed through the capital's bar district, a narrow street lined with pubs called Durty Nellie's and Nashville and, at night, with prostitutes and revelers. In his mind the risks he took were worthwhile because his faith stood in direct contrast to this moral decay. After decades of communist attacks on people's beliefs, morality had been damaged. Brother Li felt he was helping to restore standards.

Not too long ago Mr. Li had given little thought to such spiritual matters, striving for the promotions and business trips abroad that define success in modern China. He had worked as an accountant at a textile mill, got married and had a son. A year ago,

just before the ban was announced, he heard about Falun Gong, and began to practice, at first out of curiosity but then with increasing fervor.

About six months later Brother Li was suddenly forced to decide how much Falun Gong meant to him. Worried about pressure from their government masters, managers at his state-owned mill told him that he should stop practicing. The decision, he said, was easy: he quit his job and since then has occupied his time with odd jobs and with helping the movement survive.

He was living on a monthly $40 stipend from the local welfare office, an amount so small that he liked to say he reminded himself of the famous Chinese aphorism "The great hermit lives in the city"—which means that anyone can be a hermit in a remote mountain cave; resisting the temptations of the material world while among people was a greater feat. Accordingly, he had stripped his life down to the simplest of clothes and only one luxury: a pair of black plastic wraparound sunglasses against the blinding summer sun. Pagers were cheap here, and so were phone calls. He had bought his cell phone, which he rarely used now, when he had a job. With his wife's salary as a clerk in a factory, the Li family just made ends meet.

"We live in a bad world, one that needs good people who believe in doing good deeds," Brother Li said quietly, embarrassed at having to explain his beliefs. "Life is a test to see if you can be a good person."

He was interrupted again by his pager. We coasted to a stop next to a telephone by the side of the road. It was another follower from Guangdong Province who needed a fellow believer picked up at the airport. Brother Li quickly called a Falun Gong member who drove an unregistered cab—one of the thousands of private taxis that had sprung up in recent years. The cabby

agreed to take the passenger without charging; another problem solved.

Arrest was always on Brother Li's mind. To minimize risk he followed a few basic rules. Meetings with adherents lasted just a few minutes. Calls were clipped and ambiguous. Sensitive information was exchanged only in person. Pagers changed as often as he could afford—he had gone through three in the past four months. With adherents regularly arrested, he knew that phone lists, some of which must have his beeper number on them, would fall into police hands. Once police knew his account, they could tell the pager companies to hand over the lists of people who'd left messages for him, a disaster the movement couldn't afford.

We rode around for another hour. Brother Li noted a few pay phones for future use and headed home. The temperature was over 100 degrees, and even Brother Li, usually so cool and calm, started sweating.

He was continuing to agonize over whether he should go to Tiananmen Square to protest. In some ways, a key weapon that Falun Gong practitioners had in their battle against the Public Security Bureau was the randomness of their actions. While protests increased in intensity around certain anniversaries, protesters went to the square almost daily, driven by the dictates of their conscience. Now Brother Li's conscience told him to go to the square. "I feel it is my duty to let the government know it's wrong," he said. "But if I stay out of prison, I might be of more use."

As he weighed his options, the one thing he didn't consider was his timing—but his turned out to be impeccable. Two days later he and his wife went to Tiananmen, sat cross-legged in the Falun Gong meditating position and were quickly thrown in jail. It was early enough in the month so the judges weren't yet hand-

ing down the heavy sentences that some later got for protesting directly on the July 22 anniversary. In fact, as a first-time offender, he was held only fifteen days. But it was long enough for his stay to overlap with the wave of arrests that flooded the prison around the anniversary and the accompanying police brutality. He saw a fellow prisoner beaten unconscious. His wife went on a hunger strike to protest the cramped conditions of ten women to a cell. Suddenly, in late July, he was released.

But as we dismounted to catch our breath, it was still early July, and all he knew was that it was his turn to test his faith. It was late afternoon and the cicadas drowned out everything but Brother Li's voice.

"You know my decision," he said. "I'll call you when I get out."

Unlike Brother Li, Ms. Zhang was also helped by her fame. The United Nations, for example, had cited her mother's case in its triennial review of China's compliance with the U.N. Treaty Against Torture. The U.S. Department of State also drew attention toward it.

That seemed to prevent police from touching Ms. Zhang. After she was briefly detained in April, police left her alone. One friend of hers said she seemed to have a shield around her— while other government opponents were sentenced to long jail terms, she remained free, largely because of the international attention. To some degree I knew that I was like a scientist who changes the thing he is observing simply by observing it. I never told her what to do or gave her any encouragement at all. Indeed, weeks went by without our speaking to each other, and she never called me. But I am sure that my articles in the *Wall Street Journal* allowed her to stay free when others might have been jailed. To

that degree, I abetted her quest; without the coverage, she might have vanished into the prison system.

Ms. Zhang's efforts continued to center on her mother's death certificate. After the police and the crematorium refused her requests for the certificate, she decided to go through more formal channels, filing written requests for the certificate.

After being released from detention in late April, she spent most of May shuttling between offices of the Public Security Bureau in her hometown. Officials at the district office told her that they couldn't release the death certificate and that she should appeal to the higher-level bureau that controls the municipality. That bureau referred her back to the district office, arguing that the lower-level office had to furnish a copy of records before the higher-level office could act. Back at the district office, officials said nonsense: the highers-up didn't need the certificate. Go away.

Frustrated, Ms. Zhang decided in early June to bypass the squabbling officials in Weifang by appealing to officials in the provincial capital, Jinan. Her goal now was to push the provincial procurator's office, which acts like a prosecutor's office in the United States, to file criminal charges against the local Public Security Bureau for failing to release the death certificate.

But the procurator's office, which works closely with security forces, told her to file a civil lawsuit. When she approached lawyers, however, they told her the Ministry of Justice had issued a directive to all lawyers in the country ordering them not to accept cases related to Falun Gong. Stymied again, she headed for Beijing and the central government's Petitions and Appeals Office, where Mr. Ma the peasant champion had been beaten up a year earlier.

I caught up with her in June, a few weeks before my bike ride with Brother Li. Her six-year-old son in tow, she trudged through

the heavy heat toward the Petitions and Appeals Office of the State Council, which is the highest executive body in the central government. Each city, county, province and many ministries have their own petitions office—the Shaanxi farmers, for example, had tried to file a grievance with their local district government's appeals office. But Ms. Zhang was now at the pinnacle of all appeals offices. It was a Mecca for lost causes, the central magnet for the legions of Chinese who felt they'd suffered injustice.

The Petitions Office was located in the south of the city, near a filthy canal. The street had a few scrawny trees that were withering in the dry Beijing air. As we walked down the street, I felt I was back in Shaanxi on the Loess Plateau, the white tile and concrete of Beijing as monochromatic as the barren yellow soil of China's cultural heartland.

As Ms. Zhang hurried from the subway toward the Petitions and Appeals Office, she passed groups of people who, like her, were availing themselves of their right to petition. It was a tradition that went back centuries, and which the party has maintained as a safety valve. We stopped for a moment to look at one bedraggled peasant crouching over a sheaf of papers, moving his pen in the air, trying to remember how to write the word "expropriate." His clan had been trying for fourteen years to recover land that they say had been taken illegally by officials.

The building's entrance is in an alley and is watched carefully by plainclothes police. I drifted back, letting Ms. Zhang walk ahead toward the office. A dozen agents with shifty stares and mobile phones watched her. Security agents at the entrance to the alley stopped her and asked if she was a Falun Gong adherent. Those who answer affirmatively are turned back or even arrested. Ms. Zhang, though, could truthfully say that she didn't practice Falun Gong and that her problem was a simple case of

police abuse. She walked in. I peeled back and waited for her down the street.

Two hours later she came out, shaking her head. "They said it was a criminal case and should be handled by the Public Security Bureau's appeals office," she said, walking back along the garbage-filled canal. "That's my next stop," she said, and disappeared into a subway station.

Ms. Zhang hesitated before going to the Public Security Bureau's appeals office. It wasn't the fear of stepping inside the bureau's offices, a move that would brand her forever as a troublemaker. Instead, it was worry for her son that made her think twice. He had been crying at the sight of uniformed men ever since police had started harassing the family. She didn't want to upset him anymore and wondered whether she was going too far. Perhaps she should just go home. But she knew she had to go through with this. We met later that morning at another subway station and headed to the office.

We were in one of my favorite parts of Beijing—the old city that the urban activists like Mr. Fang were trying to save. The bureau was located in an old courtyard house that used to belong to a prince in the royal family, which was deposed in the 1911 revolution. Like most palaces, it is discreetly located behind a gray-washed wall, the only clue to its noble ancestry being the broad red doors with stone lions out front. I thought back to other former palaces I'd visited, trying to imagine the odd mixture of modern state power and feudal elegance that this office incorporated. I imagined the four wings of a traditional Chinese building set on each side of a small square courtyard. In the middle: a shady plane tree planted several hundred years ago, its

impenetrable foliage rising over the slate roofing tiles and upturned eaves. It was a fitting place for Ms. Zhang to take her appeal, as she followed in the wake of Chinese down the centuries who asked the emperor for help, each sure that if only his majesty knew the truth, the problem would be solved.

It was nearly noon when she arrived and visiting hours were already over for the morning. Another defeat. The adrenaline that had kept her going the past few days ebbed. Her son scampered away, hoping his mother would follow.

Ms. Zhang took a deep breath and decided to visit one more place before giving up. Beijing is dotted with several lesser petitions offices that belong to various minor ministries. Maybe just one of them, she said, could help. Nearby was the petition office of the All-China Women's Federation, a government-run organization that is supposed to look after the interests of China's 650 million women. She grabbed her son by the hand and headed over.

We lost our way in the maze of alleys that make up Beijing's slowly shrinking old city, but finally found the unmarked office. I waited outside, then followed in behind her. The woman behind the reception desk looked up, and Ms. Zhang quickly stated her case. I stood back, holding a map and pretending to have a question about directions. The woman listened carefully to Ms. Zhang, nodded and sighed. Then she pushed her glasses up on the bridge of her nose and spoke carefully: "Rule of law is still rudimentary right now. This case will be hard to solve, but you have to go back to the Public Security Bureau."

The answer was blunt, but was the first civil reply Ms. Zhang had received from the dozens of bureaucrats she had approached. Her courage grew. She gathered up her son and headed out into the heat, vowing to return to the Public Security Bureau in the afternoon.

At 2 p.m. she walked up once again to the unmarked door. Her son had fallen asleep. Ms. Zhang carried him slung over her shoulder and pushed open the red door.

An hour later she emerged, her face beaming. She carefully held a letter sealed by the Public Security Bureau that she suspected contained orders for the local security bureaus to give her the death certificate. She shook her head in amazement. "I don't know," she said, letting her son down gently to the ground as he woke up. "Maybe I can finally get an answer."

Back in Weifang two days later she went straight to the local office of the Public Security Bureau. When an official there opened the letter, she caught a glimpse of the brief order: "Handle this case in writing"—in other words, give a written response. Ms. Zhang was ecstatic. If police had to give a written answer, they couldn't deny her the certificate, she reasoned. A written denial could be appealed, so they'd have to finally give in and hand over the document she'd sought for months.

But then days passed without reply. She returned again and again to the local bureau until finally someone in the office told her that the local police had decided to ignore the order from Beijing—after all, who was going to call them to account?

As the stifling summer slowly came to an end, Ms. Zhang began to realize that she wouldn't get her mother's death certificate. The experience, though, had transformed her. She was still the woman from Weifang who spoke Mandarin Chinese with an accent, lapsing into folksy expressions. She still dressed simply and occasionally permed her hair. Yet she had insights into China that a normal person would never have. Local people, like the peasants in Shaanxi, might know about a local injustice. But like Mr. Ma the peasant champion and Mr. Fang the architect, Ms.

Zhang had been forced to examine her life and her country in ways that most people do not. She did not have a sophisticated political vocabulary, yet I found it easier to talk about China with her than with almost anyone else I'd encountered in China. One didn't have to ignore topics such as repression or pretend that huge segments of one's life were off limits. She knew that. Yet she loved China in ways that I could understand—we both enjoyed green tea, the country's simple northern food, and the dusty beauty of the North China Plain.

The experience also taught her to write essays, something she hadn't done since high school. The constant flow of petitions and appeals that she had to produce focused her mind and forced her to express her frustrations with pen and paper. In September we met for a coffee in Beijing and she handed me an essay she'd written by hand. It was titled "I Am Willing to Trust the Government, But Can the Government Convince Me?"—a description of her travails and the lessons she'd learned.

The process of petitioning, she wrote, "enabled me to meet people being treated unfairly and to listen to the ridiculous things that happened to them. Apart from Falun Gong practitioners, who are taken away by the public security, less than 10 percent of those [other] petitioners expect to have their problems settled. Most petitioners only get a chance to exchange their complaints with each other and end up with empty pockets. Among the dozens of officials who received my petition, nobody talked to me for longer than fifteen minutes and most of them were impatient."

It was a telling comment on the archaic process of petitions and appeals. The petitions system bankrupts already poor people, sometimes leaving them stranded in Beijing, unable to afford the train ticket home. I thought back to peasants I'd seen outside the Petitions and Appeals Office. I'd gone there numerous times

during my seven years in China and met people who'd been in Beijing for years on end, hoping for an audience with the elusive powers that run the country.

As I read on, I realized that Ms. Zhang had become convinced of the need for basic freedoms in a way that the elite of China, most of them corrupted by money or proximity to power, still have not grasped.

"I didn't quite understand Mother's act [of protesting]," she wrote. "On last April 25, I objected to the gathering [of Falun Gong demonstrators]. But after a long march to Beijing this time, I realized that a single person can do nothing to settle any problem. A big crowd of petitioners like in the April 25 affair would cause enough attention. These people petitioned in a peaceful and polite way for the benefit of the group. Seeing the anger and the sadness of other petitioners, I am calm. I'm lucky because I know the reason why we can't make it."

In other words, people have a right to protest, but individual efforts, like her own, are doomed to failure. That is why, she has learned, "we can't make it." It is a sad realization to come to after months of frustration and anger. Similar conclusions had led people like Mr. Ma to organize larger-scale protests and people like Mr. Fang to effect change slowly, by force of his ideas. She has come to realize what all people who want to change China eventually learn: the current system is at a dead end, but its death is not in sight.

After reading Ms. Zhang's essay I tried to call her but could only reach a neighbor of hers in Weifang. The Falun Gong community in the small city is suffocating, the woman said. I asked her what she meant, and she said that more practitioners have died in the months since Ms. Zhang's mother's death. I had been vaguely aware that the suppression was continuing, but with the

protests in Beijing slowing down, I hadn't paid as much attention to the movement. Then she told me that up to another dozen had died in police custody just in this one small city.

I stood at the side of a dark road that ran between a highway and an industrial park. It was cold and dry, but the stars couldn't penetrate the blanket of smog that was choking north China. The industrial park was dark and I could barely see the ground below me. The woman next to me pulled a green army coat up around her neck.

"Be patient," she said. "He's waiting out there somewhere. He saw us get out of the taxi and walk down this road. If we're not being followed, he'll come down and pick us up."

"And if he doesn't come?" I said.

"Then we're being followed and will be arrested," she said, suddenly breaking out of her Falun Gong seriousness and into a schoolgirl's laugh. "We'll go to labor camp together."

"No," I said, playing along with the joke. "You'll go to the labor camp. I'll just be expelled from China."

"Yes," she said, breaking into a fit of giggles and laughs. "You'll be expelled from China, but you'll write me letters in the labor camp."

We suddenly felt depressed and stopped our banter. I'd met this woman a year earlier during the first, almost euphoric wave of protests against the government. We had become e-mail pen pals over the intervening months. At times, she simply talked about her life and interests, but it was like talking to a fundamentalist in any religion—friendship is possible but the lack of shared belief is hard to overcome. I didn't believe in Falun Gong and this was something she couldn't understand. Some months

later, before I left China, she sent me a handwritten letter in English that tried to bridge the gulf:

in many respects you differ greatly from me. but I still tell you: look at "zhuan fa lun [*Turning the Dharma Wheel*]." I know you have one. a good deal of the importance of the book lies in its later influence. you must have a book. I hope you'll always be in touch with me from now on. I want to know if you're fine. write a letter to me. ok?

After a few minutes of waiting I looked up and watched a car crawl along the highway, slow almost to a stop and turn down our road.

"Our friend or the Public Security?" I said.

"Our friend," she said. "Look at the make."

I understood why the car was so slow. It was an old gray Moscow, straight out of the 1950s Soviet Union. It was clearly not the cops, who wouldn't be caught dead in such an old rattle-trap. The design was given to China by the Soviets as a kind of development aid. Although China's auto industry had since moved forward by leaps and bounds, the car was still built and given to army officers as a kind of cheap perk, almost an insulting sign that the army is poor. Cops were different. They were more corrupt than army officers and drove around in confiscated luxury cars or at least in products of foreign-Chinese joint ventures like the Volkswagen Santana.

The car bumped and shook, a dark outline against the glow of the city. Dirt blew across our boots as the first winds of winter blew down from the Mongolian Plateau.

My friend got in the front seat and I got in the back. The

driver wore an appropriately conservative Mao suit, with a collarless woolen jacket buttoned up to the top. Once worn by almost all Chinese, it is now a sign of the wearer's age. The man was a poor Communist Party cadre in his sixties with a brush cut and a clipped, matter-of-fact way of speaking. The suit fit him. So did the car, however he had come by it.

He carefully pushed the gearshift forward, finessing the clutch so the gears wouldn't grind, made a three-point turn and drove back to the highway. In a few minutes the dark suburbs gave way to dimly lit streets. The woman in the front seat reached back and pushed my head down so I wouldn't be visible from the outside. I was back in Weifang, where so many Falun Gong practitioners had been killed.

Weifang hardly seemed like the sort of place that would become the focal point of tragedy. I'd thought that if one were trying to find an Anytown in China, Weifang might be it. It has a famous past as a commercial center and is the hometown of flowing, silk-covered Chinese kites. Today, it is a small industrial center in one of China's wealthiest provinces and boasts a per capita income just above the national average.

Like most Chinese cities, Weifang felt more rural than its population would indicate. Officially, the greater metropolitan area had 8 million residents, but this included a huge swath of densely populated countryside. The urban center had just 620,000 people, and its streets were filled with farmers driving their tractors to markets.

This would be my last trip here and the preparations had been far more elaborate than those for my other trips. Earlier, I'd simply contacted acquaintances on public phones and hopped on a plane. Now the government's campaign against Falun Gong

had gained traction. Like all things the government undertakes, it had started slowly, with a few hundred arrests and a few dozen people sent for long stays in labor camps. But now, nearly eighteen months after it had begun its campaign, the government had mobilized itself fully against the spiritual group. I'd often thought of China's government as akin to a medieval siege engine. It wasn't elegant and was hard to maneuver, but could be deadly when finally set up. Now it was in place and had found its distance. Falun Gong, as an organization in China, was being pulverized, and here in Weifang I could see the rubble.

Although my friend Brother Li was not in jail, many others like him around the country had been imprisoned. In the past the government let him and others like him out of jail after a few weeks. Now if they had any involvement in organizing opposition, they received three years, the theoretical maximum the government could detain someone without charge. In practice, a three-year sentence can be renewed indefinitely. The ability of the group to organize protests was knee-capped. Protests were dwindling in size, while the jails bulged with prisoners. Anecdotal information suggested that criminals were being released to make room for Falun Gong adherents, while *laogai*—reform-through-labor camps—which are not supposed to be used to house people detained without charge, were serving exactly this function.

Falun Gong activists had countered by adopting the most sophisticated underground organizing methods they could think of. For this trip to Weifang, for example, I'd been in e-mail contact with someone who went by the alias of "Mike." He was a graduate of Tsinghua University, China's top technical and scientific university. Midway through 2000 he had contacted me, advising me that in the future all e-mail communication with Falun Gong adherents must be done by encrypted e-mail. I wrote

back saying that I was only in e-mail contact with those living in the United States, so such secrecy didn't seem warranted and might attract government attention. He wrote back and told me that the government could read my e-mail going to the United States even though I used a Hong Kong–based server. In addition, he said obliquely, by using encrypted e-mail I could contact other Falun Gong members—the few, presumably, who were computer-literate and not in jail.

Encrypted e-mail, relatively little used in the West, soon became a standard way of communicating with people in even fairly backward cities like Weifang. After you got the hang of it, encryption was easy to use. It involved downloading free software off the Internet (www.pgp.com) and creating a "key." You used the key to "lock," or encrypt, e-mails that you sent to others, as well as to "unlock" and read encrypted messages sent to you. Only the creator of the key has the password, so only I, for example, could read encrypted e-mails sent to me. It's a bit like having a locker that is closed with a lock that only two people can open—the sender and receiver of the e-mail.

With this software in place, I had sent Mike a note telling him I wanted to go to Weifang and asking for suggestions. Ms. Zhang was now so heavily watched that the police surely had her beeper number and had tapped her phone. That also was true for others I'd previously contacted—all were under heavy police watch. Even meeting people like Ms. Zhang would be tricky because she was often followed. So we arranged for me to contact other people. A few encrypted e-mails later, we'd worked out the details. Several days later I was on my way to Weifang.

According to human rights groups and my own research, by December of 2000 at least 77 Falun Gong adherents had died in police detention. That meant that Ms. Chen hadn't been an anomaly—a significant number of adherents were dying in cus-

tody. Not only that, but a huge number were dying in Ms. Chen's hometown. Weifang, with less than 1 percent of the national population, accounted for 15 percent of those deaths. Clearly, Ms. Zhang's mother hadn't been an isolated case. Something was wrong in China's treatment of prisoners, but something was especially wrong here in Weifang.

As we drove through the empty streets, I asked the driver what he did. It turned out he worked for the city government and had been a devoted Falun Gong adherent for five years. It had caught on early here and across Shandong Province, a densely populated coastal region that has developed rapidly in the past decade. I tried to find out why it was so strong here. The northeast made sense. Chinese culture's hold on it was more tenuous and Master Li came from that province. But Shandong was as Chinese as it got. Confucius was born here and this was a stronghold of China's indigenous religion, Taoism, one of whose holiest mountains lies not far from Weifang.

Some people I'd talked to thought that the group's Shandong organizers were especially gifted; others noted that Master Li paid a successful visit to the province several years ago. I could never really find a satisfactory answer, but what was clear was that by the time of the crackdown, Weifang had one of heaviest concentrations of believers in the province, with an estimated 60,000 adherents, according to an unpublished government report.

After a while the woman told me to get down on the floor of the back seat. She tossed a blanket over me and said not to move. We stopped, turned into a housing compound and drove passed the guardhouse where the doorman kept track of people's comings and goings. No one was on duty this late at night and our biggest threat passed. A few moments later we stopped, I pulled a large, floppy hood up over my blond head and adjusted my scarf so it covered everything but my eyes. Then I put on my gloves,

got out of the car and fixed my eyes on the pavement. I followed the two into an empty apartment building, up two flights of dusty concrete stairs and into our haven. The apartment had five small rooms: a living room, two bedrooms, a kitchen and a toilet. The heating wasn't working, and there was hot water thanks only to a gas burner. The electricity worked, but the apartment was almost barren except for the odd chair, a tatami in one room and a few pieces of calligraphy. The newly whitewashed walls gave the feeling that I was in the workshop of a supercool artist, a minimalist who had hung a few pieces of his work on the walls.

Instead, I was in an abandoned apartment that my companion was using as a safehouse for a few weeks. She'd painted the walls and hung a couple of pieces of calligraphy and pictures that a fellow practitioner had painted for her. One of the pieces of calligraphy was of the three core beliefs of Falun Gong—the characters for Truth, Benevolence and Tolerance. It was done in thick, precise strokes, the work of a self-confident amateur. Another picture showed bamboo bending with the wind, a traditional motif that symbolized the virtuous person's ability to bend but not break. It was an interesting choice of symbols because the group was taking the opposite course of action—it was standing upright and the wind was threatening to break it.

The driver dropped off a roll of bedding for me and a McDonald's bag that had a fish filet in it and a cup of hot chocolate. "We wanted you to have something to eat that you would like," he said with an embarrassed smile. He left to fetch some Falun Gong adherents who wanted to meet me. Over the course of the next days I also went out, mostly at night, and met some contacts I'd made through friends. By the third day I had a fair picture of how the government had operated here and what had gone wrong. Finally, nearly a year after Ms. Chen had been beaten to death, I understood why.

Officials in Beijing had set up the framework that led to the
killings in late 1999. Impatient with the continued flow of protesters from around China into the capital, they decided that
drastic measures were needed. So they reached for a tried-and-
true method of enforcing central edicts, one honed over centuries of imperial rule.

Based on the twenty-two-hundred-year-old *bao jia* method
of controlling society, the system pushes responsibility for following central orders onto neighborhoods, with the local boss
responsible for the actions of everyone in his territory. In ancient
times, that meant the headman of a family or clan was personally
responsible for paying taxes, raising troops and apprehending
criminals.

This method of rule was carried on by the Communist
Party, especially after it launched economic reforms in the late
1970s. In the spirit of the times, it put an economic spin on the
system, signing "contracts" with peasants and factory chiefs, who
had to deliver a certain amount of grain or industrial output but
were given latitude over the methods used. By the late 1980s
provincial governors were also signing similar contracts, being
held personally responsible for maintaining grain output in their
province or holding down births to a certain level. This led to
well-known abuses, such as forced abortions and sterilizations,
because the end, not the means, was all important.

This showed that, instead of creating a modern system to
rule China, the government still relied on an ad hoc patchwork of
edicts, orders and personal connections. It was a classic pattern of
a system under pressure: instead of universal principles and laws,
the system reduces itself to the most fundamental of human relationships: favors. Rule of law was the goal, but here, as with the

peasant champion or the urban activists, laws were secondary to rule by friendship, alliances and obligations.

Now, the problem was Falun Gong. Weifang officials (none of whom were Falun Gong adherents) I talked to, including some in the party's key "organization department," said central authorities told them that they would be held personally responsible if they didn't stem the flow of protesters to Beijing. As in years past, no questions would be asked about how this was achieved—success was all that mattered.

Weifang officials knew the policy meant trouble for them. China has other concentrations of Falun Gong believers, such as in the northeast. But those areas are remote from the capital. Weifang is located just three hundred miles southeast of Beijing, making it easy for protesters to travel to the capital even after the city had taken the initial precaution of sending security agents to train and bus stations to head them off before they left town. The authorities' worries were justified; I remember one forty-eight-year-old practitioner confirming this: "After a while the police were waiting for us at the train station, so we started to bike and walk to Beijing. It takes four days to bike to Beijing, twelve days to walk. I did it both ways."

As the flow of protesters continued into the new year, central authorities didn't have far to look to find a scapegoat. The man held responsible was the province's boss, Wu Guanzheng, Shandong's sixty-two-year-old party secretary. Party Secretary Wu was a member of the Communist Party's twenty-one-member Politburo, making him one of the most powerful men in China. But Party Secretary Wu was in a precarious position. Most Politburo members are central government officials. Only two governors sit on the Politburo: Party Secretary Wu and the party secretary of Guangdong Province, which doesn't have many

protesters. That meant Party Secretary Wu was a focal point of Politburo meetings called to discuss the protests.

One Weifang official put it like this: "The central government told Party Secretary Wu that he was personally responsible. He risked losing his job if he didn't do something. Everyone knew the pressure he was under."

While the official told me his story, I thought back to one of the first letters I'd read from Weifang. A young woman had written the letter to "Uncle Wu." At the time I wondered who that was—some powerful relative who could save her, or perhaps the head of the neighborhood committee? Now I realized it was Party Secretary Wu, the man behind the terror in Shandong.

> Uncle Wu, How do you do!
>
> I'm one of your common people, an originally happy kid, a treasured child of my parents, and a widely known Falun Gong practitioner. Like all other Falun Gong friends, I learned to be a good person through Falun Gong, to have good health and to please my parents.
>
> But, Uncle Wu, I am more and more scared these days. I come across things I never dared to think about.

The letter writer went on to explain about how she had been thrown out of university for practicing Falun Gong and later detained for practicing Falun Gong and for trying to deliver a letter to Party Secretary Wu.

> Why should I be put into jail for practicing Falun Gong and following the doctrine of Truth, Benevolence and Tolerance? Why can't I go to school? I can't get an

answer. Those jailers always made fun of me and beat me with bamboo sticks. They cut my hand, it was very painful and scars still exist now. I lost weight inside and Mum was sick outside for my sake. She couldn't fall asleep at night because of missing me, she kept crying and in this very short period of life she turned very old. Uncle Wu, if your relatives, your kids, were beaten this way, you must feel pain too.

We youth are the hope of the future, but we're scared of society. Uncle Wu, our hope is relying on your effort, please help us!

The letter was dated February 2000 and signed by a practitioner from Weifang. It was followed by a postscript:

Uncle Wu: Before I sent the mail, I heard another piece of news. . . . A practitioner was forced to jump out of the third floor [of the detention center where the practitioner had been held] and was sent to hospital. Another one was forced to commit suicide by hitting himself against a wall. When will this hell on earth end?

Party Secretary Wu almost certainly never saw this letter. Instead, he was busy transferring the pressure he was receiving from the Politburo. First, Weifang city officials say, he ensured that every official in the city knew what was at stake by calling a meeting of police and government officials to a "study session." There, the central government's directive was read out loud. "The government instructed us to limit the number of protesters or be responsible," a government official told me.

Such methods quickly led to abuses. Several Falun Gong adherents imprisoned by local police early this year said their

captors told them that their continued protests threatened to derail officials' careers. "One policeman beat me with a truncheon," said a forty-three-year-old factory worker imprisoned in December 1999. "He said we were responsible for his boss's political problems."

That detainee was beaten after being arrested in Beijing and transferred back to Weifang. City officials said such arrests reflected badly on Party Secretary Wu and the rest of the province because people arrested in Beijing are booked by central security agents and their hometown noted. Statistics were then compiled and provinces with a high number of protesters—like Shandong—criticized. Beating people in Weifang prisons might eventually deter protesters, but this would take time. Authorities wanted results immediately.

So, early in 2000, local officials devised a plan to skirt Beijing's monitoring of their performance. Like many other cities, Weifang maintains a permanent representative bureau in the capital, the place where Ms. Chen had been taken immediately after being arrested in Beijing. I'd been by the bureau several times. It was a two-story building with chrome-plated pillars and looked like a bordello or a karaoke lounge. Located near Rear Lake in the old part of Beijing, the office was surrounded by police cars with Shandong license plates. The office usually had twenty staff members, but by early 2000 the number was doubled, and supplemented by a dozen police officers.

According to an employee in the office and Falun Gong adherents who were arrested, Beijing police had a mutually beneficial agreement with Weifang police. Weifang residents detained in Beijing would simply be handed over directly to the small city's police on duty in the capital. They'd be jailed in the representative office until transportation could be arranged back to Weifang. This suited Beijing police, who were able to shift some

of their work burden. And it helped Weifang's image, because the detainees wouldn't be booked in Beijing prisons and show up on the central government's tally of laggard provinces.

Few detainees say they were beaten in the Beijing representative office. Instead, they were sent directly to one of seven "transformation centers"—like the one where Ms. Chen had ended up. It was at these unofficial prisons that the killings occurred.

I walked by several of these centers in Weifang. One morning I left the apartment early and walked down a street where efforts at building a sidewalk had been abandoned and paving stones lay haphazardly over the cold dusty ground. Trees were bare and a few enterprising shopkeepers stared as I walked past the stores they were unshuttering.

I stopped before a gate that had a vertical white sign out front with printed black letters that read WEICHENG DISTRICT TEXTILE FACTORY STORAGE DEPOT. The entry was barred by a rusty metal gate. I looked in and saw several four-story buildings made of yellow brick that rose seamlessly out of the yellow soil. This was a "transformation center," according to prisoners. It looked empty. I pushed the fence and it wobbled.

A man suddenly hopped out of a small hut inside the gate.

"Whaddya want?" he said, suddenly stopping in his tracks at my foreign face.

"Kites. Kite museum," I said in the worst Chinese possible.

He waved his arm for me to go away. "There are no kites here. This is a government office. Take a taxi to the center of town," he said.

I nodded in agreement, thanked him and walked away.

Along with use of these "centers" came the final ingredient needed for the killings to take place: fear of financial ruin.

Instead of just threatening to ruin local officials' careers,

Party Secretary Wu's colleagues in the provincial government started to fine them as well. The new twist was simple: The provincial government fined mayors and heads of counties for each Falun Gong practitioner from their district who went to Beijing. The mayors and county heads in turn fined the heads of their Political and Legal Commissions, holding them responsible. They in turn fined village chiefs, who in turn fined the police officers—who administered the punishment. The fines varied from district to district, but in one Weifang district the head of the Political and Legal Commission was fined 200 yuan per person protesting in Tiananmen Square, or about $25—a potentially ruinous amount given that his monthly salary is only about $200, according to one of the official's colleagues.

The fines were illegal; no law or regulation has ever been issued in writing that lists them. Officials say the policy was announced orally at government meetings. "There was never to be anything in writing because they didn't want it made public," a member of the city's Political and Legal Commission told me.

Thus a chief feature in torture victims' testimony is that they were constantly being asked for money to compensate for the fines. That's why Ms. Zhang was told to pay a $241 fine in exchange for her mother's release. When she balked, her mother was held another night and beaten to death. I was lucky to have introductions to the officials I talked to. Normally, it would have been impossible to see officials; and all previous efforts at seeking official interviews had been fruitless. But by going through friends, in this case a foreign friend who had relatives living in Weifang, the officials were sure I was trustworthy and wouldn't betray them.

Privately, they told me that they worried that the crackdown had been a terrible mistake. "I wonder why we spend so much time doing this," said the official from the party's organization

department. "We need to undertake economic construction, not beat people."

He and others said that none of the police directly involved in the deaths have been reprimanded. "Reprimanded, for beating a Falun Gong disciple? Don't be ridiculous. You know the motto: 'No measure too excessive,' " an official told me with a sarcastic laugh. In fact, the three officers who oversaw Ms. Chen's interrogation have since been promoted, they say, true to the tradition of giving local authorities a free hand, no questions asked.

The cumulative effect is that at least 11 Falun Gong practitioners died from abuse they suffered in Weifang prisons, according to family members and officials I talked to. An independent human-rights monitoring group in Hong Kong, the Information Centre for Human Rights and Democracy, verified one more death in Weifang. According to the center, the rest of Shandong accounts for another 12 victims, for a total of 24. The next-highest number of deaths is 14 for Heilongjiang Province, the place where Mr. Chen saw Master Li speak at the hockey arena in 1994.

Besides the deaths, which the Information Centre estimated at over 100, the policy seemed to split China in ways that were hard to quantify. Society was polarized and many people turned against the government. A friend of mine liked to argue against this, saying the crackdown showed that Chinese actually didn't care much about each other or the discrepancy in what they saw and what the government said. There was no solidarity with the persecuted, unless they were family members or personal friends. It was like the traffic accidents that one sees in big Chinese cities—crowds only gather to stare; almost no one stops to help. No wonder the government could hold on to power so easily, he said. It doesn't have to divide and conquer its enemies; they are divided of their own accord. I had to agree with him, because I rarely encountered a person who got really angry about the way

the government treated Falun Gong adherents. While some far-thinking people saw the campaign as unjustified and cruel, most simply shrugged and wondered why people bothered to stand up for something they believed in. Concerned with their daily struggles, they couldn't understand why Falun Gong believers insisted on exercising publicly. "Why not just exercise in the living room?" was the most common response I got when I asked about the repression of Falun Gong.

But longer term, society was suffering from the government's one hundred battles a day against Falun Gong and its innumerable other opponents, real and imagined. The sheer number of those jailed—I would conservatively estimate that 30,000 passed through jails during the first two years of the crackdown—meant that many hundreds of thousands more were touched in some way by the campaign.

The woman who met me on the outskirts of Weifang, for example, came from a good family of government officials who all believed in Falun Gong. The last I heard of them the family was split, with the young woman moving from one safe house to another. The parents, meanwhile, had been released from jail and promptly fled to live with relatives in the countryside. If they returned home, the local street committee would come by and demand they denounce Master Li, something they couldn't do.

I wondered at the scores of neighbors who knew that the family's apartment was vacant because of government terror, who knew of their flight to the countryside and the young girl's resistance. The way housing is distributed to government officials, all the people in the apartment building would have been colleagues of the parents. Their children, too, would have gone to university and have been classmates with the young woman. What would these hundreds of people think of the government? How much trust would they have in the ability of the Communist

Party to lead the way forward? And all these hundreds of doubts stem from just one family's suffering. Multiply it by the tens of thousands of Falun Gong adherents who went to labor camps, the peasants who sued and lost, the residents whose homes were demolished.

Eventually, I made it to Weifang's impressive kite museum. I was ready to leave town. My taxi was outside waiting. I walked up to an employee.

"Have you ever practiced Falun Gong?"

His eyes widened and he laughed nervously. "No, why?"

"I was visiting friends here, and one family told me that their grandmother was beaten to death in a transformation center, the one up in Weicheng District, the Chengguan Street Committee. I guess it's pretty dangerous to practice."

He was unpacking boxes of kites, carrying huge stacks of the featherweight boxes into a storage room from a trolley. Then he stopped. It was one of those moments of quiet civic courage that one encountered increasingly in China: "No one can talk about these things," he said. Then without stopping, he added brusquely, "But a lot of people know."

I met Ms. Zhang during my last trip to Weifang but only briefly; the police were outside her house almost all the time, and she had only been able to get away by feigning to go to the market and instead hopping in a cab and traveling across town to meet me. She said she should have been jailed long ago but credited the international publicity and pressure that had accompanied her mother's case with keeping her free.

Slowly, though, that pressure on China was easing. As the international community lost interest, authorities felt they had nothing to lose by detaining Ms. Zhang. In April 2001 she was

picked up by police and taken before an administrative hearing officer. Denied access to a lawyer, she was tried in secret and given three years' "administrative detention," a form of punishment sanctioned by the law. Essentially, the law gives security services the right to jail anyone they want for up to three years—a term that can be extended indefinitely. It was the sort of extra-judicial punishment that, in a more extreme form, had claimed her mother.

Her jailing was brutal on several levels. Her efforts had been aimed at figuring out the law and getting it to work for her. Now she was being told that this was illegal. And she'd essentially given up her efforts at redressing her mother's death. "Now is a time for waiting," she told me during our last meeting in Weifang. "China isn't ready for change."

It was a change from her earlier determination to push change at all costs. She explained it to me during an earlier trip to Beijing, in August, shortly after she'd written her essay. We had gone for a walk along Beijing's main drag, Chang'an Boulevard, a broad Stalinist-style avenue that in the early 1990s had been almost devoid of traffic. Now it was choked with private cars, buses and taxis, which had squeezed the once-generous bike lanes into narrow, crowded corridors along the side of the road. It was hot and we took a seat on a bench. The sidewalks were filled with people, and no one took notice of us as she talked.

"While I was in jail earlier in the year, the only people who were good to me were Falun Gong prisoners," she said slowly, looking down at her feet. The guards had been horrible and the common prisoners were bribed to make her life miserable. When she returned to her cell after an interrogation, the prisoners would also berate her, telling her to give up her struggle for justice. Sometimes they'd take her food away—always, she was sure, at the guards' instruction, and in exchange the prisoners

obtained some small benefit, like bigger rations or early release. She began to doubt human goodness until she started to read the Falun Gong texts that had so captivated her mother.

"I used to be a materialist and believed that everything in life could be gained from hard work," she said. "But Falun Gong makes more sense. At its root are three principles: Truthfulness, Compassion and Tolerance. If we adhere to these, isn't that a deeper meaning to life?"

She said she had started to attend gatherings of practitioners who still meet in secret. They are people of different social status, of different incomes and different backgrounds. But, she says, they treat each other as equals and are nice to each other. "I never knew that a group of people could get along so well," she said, shaking her head and smiling.

Increasingly, she said, she was turning her attention to her son, a reminder of the grandmother who was so fond of him. He was due to start school in September and Ms. Zhang was worried about the government textbooks that he would be reading, with their heavy emphasis on patriotism and nationalism. So she decided to start teaching him the principles of Falun Gong, as a counterweight to the materialism of daily life.

"I teach him that when someone hits him, it's the person who hit him who is wrong," she said as we looked at the people jostling each other on the street and crowding onto the buses. "His grandmother had this belief. I have it now, and so will he."

I asked her if she'd lost faith in the government and in China. She hoisted her duffel bag off the ground and put it between us on the bench. Out of it she pulled a creased, marked-up copy of her essay, opened it to the last page and folded it in half. She pointed to the last line and read it out loud: "China is still trustworthy, we're still waiting."

Notes

A book written in a narrative form is ill suited to footnotes, which break the flow and rhythm of the tales. Readers, though, have a right to know where the information came from. To reconcile these two desires I've included endnotes. Unlike footnotes, these are not numbered and so don't break up the flow of the stories. But they do allow curious readers to learn where I obtained information. For those who see in this exercise nothing but pure pedantry, you are probably right; please feel free to ignore the next few pages.

I have not included notes explaining every fact in the book. Some facts, such as China's population or the location of Weifang, are obvious and don't need sourcing.

Likewise, I have not explained in the notes the source of every quotation. This is a work of journalism, and all quotes are from interviews with the people who said them or from court documents. When accounts differed, I gave precedence to scenes that I witnessed directly or to direct interviews. I tried in all cases to obtain as many sides of the story as possible in order to verify accounts, but was sometimes denied access to participants. In these cases I have relied on the standard journalistic principle of obtaining two witnesses who did not consult with each other before talking to me, and then taking the most conservative version of events. In the case of Chen Zixiu, for example, her words are taken from people who heard her speak them. Many of these quotes first appeared in the *Wall Street Journal*, and the

citations are noted below. I have used people's real names except when this could imperil their safety; these cases have also been noted below.

PROLOGUE

10   "Rulers and ruled wage one hundred battles a day": The Han Feizi quote is often translated as "Superior and inferior wage one hundred battles a day," referring to the ruler as the superior and his ministers or subordinates as his inferiors. Like all philosophical works, however, the quote has been interpreted and translated in many different fashions. Kung-Chuan Hsiao points out this translation and the broader significance of the quote in his book *Rural China: Imperial Control in the Nineteenth Century.*

PART I: THE PEASANT CHAMPION

15   One commonly hears: Here I am referring to the endless magazine and newspaper articles and books touting China's economic future. Almost all focus on big, prosperous coastal cities like Shanghai or Shenzhen.

16   "disturbing social order": The charge "disturbing social order" is one of the most criticized in the Chinese penal code because of its broad scope. It is commonly used to round up undesirables of all shades, from dissidents and labor activists to those who get in the way of China's Olympics redevelopment plan. See reports by Amnesty International, China Labour Bulletin, Human Rights Watch, or Human Rights in China.

18   This was a moment I'd rehearsed several times: This next section on how Chinese hotel rolls are handled is drawn from personal experience, as well as conversations with dozens of journalists and hotel managers who have told me about the regulation of registering at hotels. The rules seem to vary from province to province and even district to district, which

accounts for the differing experiences journalists have faced when traveling without official permission.

19   Their solution had been to hire a lawyer and charge the government: The Peijiawan case is described in detail in Ian Johnson, "Mass Leverage," *Wall Street Journal,* March 26, 1999, A1, or Minxin Pei, "Citizens v. Mandarins: Administrative Litigation in China," *China Quarterly,* December 1997, pp. 832–62.

24   But the changes did have: The most common method of measuring a government's tax revenues is the ratio of revenues to gross domestic product. From 31 percent in 1979, the year reforms begin in earnest, the ratio declined to 10.7 percent in 1995. By contrast, most developed countries have ratios of 30 to 50 percent. Since then the ratio has edged up but remains low.

25   This was reinforced by advice: The China 2020 reports (available online from World Bank publications), for example, discussed the need for a tax system but didn't explore the need for popular support.

26   User fees suddenly began appearing: Limiting users fees was a theme throughout the premiership of Zhu Rongji. See "Farmers Praise China's Anti-Poverty Goals" by William Foreman, Associated Press, March 9, 2003.

28   Messrs. Zhao and Shao walked gingerly: I have changed these men's names to protect their identities from the authorities.

38   Recently, a national newspaper had published a letter: The essay "The True Feelings of a Township Party Secretary" by Li Changping appeared in *Southern Weekend.* I am indebted to David Cowhig, formerly with the U.S. Embassy in Beijing's Environmental, Science and Technology staff for pointing out this essay on the embassy's extremely informative Web site, which he maintained. The translation is also his.

41   A more typical product of his time was Wu Hanjing: I am indebted to George Wehrfritz of *Newsweek* for pointing out to me the existence of the Mao temples.

57 This is a key distinction: See, for example, Lubman, pp 299–19.

59 The exact number of farmers: In China, plaintiffs are allowed to join a suit after it has been filed. Most initial reports spoke of 5,000 coplaintiffs. Human Rights in China estimates 20,000 eventually filed. In 2001, locals spoke of 68,000 having joined the initial suit, but this is impossible to verify.

86 I found a fax waiting: The fax was from the Information Centre for Human Rights and Democracy. See BBC Monitoring Service, August 16, 2000.

PART 2: DREAM OF A VANISHED CAPITAL

105 Today, despite some impressive efforts at restoration: Estimate drawn from author's survey of maps, Chinese guidebooks and interviews. This number will likely increase in the coming years as temples are restored and new ones in the suburbs built. Still, the overall picture of a dramatic decline in religious life is valid.

112 Throughout the 1990s: See, for example, Susan Naquin, especially the epilogue, pp. 706–8.

115 To put it in context: This calculation is based on a 2000 gross domestic product of 217.4 billion yuan. If inflation-adjusted figures are used for the city's output in the 1990s, the rough comparison holds.

157 The pieces are on display: Thanks to Pete Hessler for pointing this out.

163 It was an exercise repeated: See, for example, Arlington or Bodde.

PART 3: TURNING THE WHEEL

187 Anyway, Master Li had said: I use the title "Master Li" because this is how his adherents refer to him.

193 But then, in late autumn: The chronology for measures taken against Falun Gong is reliably reported in Human Rights Watch, *Dangerous Meditation*.

202   Into the breach stepped: For an excellent history of how the term qigong was created in the 1950s, see Miura.

204   Academics, such as Jian Xu: The citation is from Xu Jian, p. 985.

210   Li Hongzhi formed Falun Gong: History according to Falun Gong informants and books. A complete history of the group has yet to be written, but the government uses many of these dates.

211   Master Li's works also preach exclusivity: Falun Gong adherents dispute this interpretation, yet it is a subtext found in many writings.

217–23 Quotes from Ian Johnson, "A Deadly Exercise," *Wall Street Journal,* April 2, 2000, p. A1.

224   Broader definitions of cults: See Singer, pp. 3–9.

226   One Western academic wrote a paper: See Patsy Rahn's "The Falun Gong: Beyond the Headlines," presented at the American Family Foundation's Annual Conference, April 28, 2000.

232–47 Quotes from Ian Johnson, "A Blind Eye," *Wall Street Journal,* December 13, 2000, p. A1.

257–66 Quotes from Ian Johnson, "Brother Li Love," *Wall Street Journal,* August 26, 2000, p. A1.

Selected Bibliography

Arlington, L. C., and William Lewisohn. *In Search of Old Peking.*
Hong Kong: Oxford University Press, 1987 (orig. 1935).

Bei, Dao. "13 Happiness Street." In *Seeds of Fire, Chinese Voices of Conscience.* Edited by Geremie Barme and John Minford. Hong Kong: *Far Eastern Economic Review,* 1986, p. 2.

Bodde, Derk, and M. L. C. Bogan. *Annual Customs and Festivals in Peking.* Taipei: SMC Publishers, 1994 (orig. 1936).

Bredon, Juliet. *Peking.* London: T. Werner Laurie, 1922.

Fairbank, Wilma. *Adventures in Retrieval.* Cambridge: Harvard University Press, 1972.

———. *Liang and Lin: Partners in Exploring China's Architectural Past.* Philadelphia: University of Pennsylvania Press, 1994.

Fang, Ke. *Contemporary Redevelopment in the Inner City of Beijing* (in Chinese). Beijing: Zhongguo Jianzhu Gongye Chubanshe, 2000.

Han, Feizi. *Han Feizi Jijie.* Taipei: Shijie Shuju, 1990.

Hsiao, Kung-Chuan. *Rural China: Imperial Control in the Nineteenth Century.* Seattle: University of Washington Press, 1960.

Human Rights Watch. *Dangerous Meditation: China's Campaign Against Falungong.* New York: Human Rights Watch, 2002.

Liang, Sicheng. *Zhongguo Jianzhu Shi.* Tianjin: Baihua Wenyi Chubanshe, 1998.

Liang, Ssu-ch'eng (Sicheng). *A Pictorial History of Chinese Architec-*

ture. Edited by Wilma Fairbank. Cambridge: MIT Press, 1984.

Lubman, Stanley. *Bird in a Cage: Legal Reform in China After Mao.* Stanford, Calif.: Stanford University Press, 1999.

Miura, Kunio. "The Revival of *Qi*: Qigong in Contemporary China." In Livia Kohn, ed. *Taoist Meditation and Longevity Techniques.* Ann Arbor: University of Michigan Press, 1989, pp. 1–40.

Naquin, Susan. *Peking: Temples and City Life, 1400–1900.* Berkeley: University of California Press, 2000.

Singer, Margaret Thaler. *Cults in Our Midst.* San Francisco: Jossey-Bass, 1995.

Turner, Karen G., James V. Feinerman and R. Kent Guy, eds. *The Limits of the Rule of Law in China.* Seattle: University of Washington Press, 2000.

Watson, Burton, trans. *Han Fei Tzu Basic Writings.* New York: Columbia University Press, 1964.

Wu, Liangyong. *Rehabilitating the Old City of Beijing.* Vancouver, B.C.: University of British Columbia Press, 1999.

Xu, Jian. "Body, Discourse, and the Cultural Politics of Contemporary Chinese Qigong," *Journal of Asian Studies,* vol. 58, no. 4 (1999), pp. 961–99.

Acknowledgments

Readers will have to indulge me for three paragraphs while I thank a host of friends, colleagues and mentors. Although for most people their names will mean little, their sheer number show that behind every book, especially one on such a complicated topic as China, are dozens of people whose moral and intellectual support were crucial.

First, many journalists have nothing but criticism of the Chinese government for hindering their work. That is sometimes justified, but I'd like to thank the more liberal members of the Ministry of Foreign Affairs in Beijing for allowing me to serve as a journalist in China for seven years. If the ministry's rules and regulations were followed to the letter, every one of the roughly four hundred foreign journalists in China should be expelled. I thank the ministry's officials for interpreting the rules liberally, thus allowing me and others to take advantage of China's blooming civil society and penetrate the country in ways that our predecessors couldn't have imagined possible.

Also thanks to: Mr. Harold Givens and Dr. and Mrs. Jean Battle, who over the years have been generous in their moral support and faith; my adviser at the Freie Universität Berlin, Erwin von Mende, whose wide-ranging intellectual interests allowed me to broaden my understanding of China in a very congenial setting; Stephen Feldman of Asian Rare Books, who provided many stimulating and hard-to-find volumes over the years; the former foreign editor of Baltimore's *The Sun,* Jeff Price, who took a chance on sending me to China in

1994; the participants of the chinapol listserv, which was founded by Rick Baum of UCLA and has provided a wealth of stimulating ideas; Brock Silvers of the Taoist Restoration Charity (www.taostore.org) for insightful conversations on Chinese religion; the *Wall Street Journal*'s page-one editing staff for its work on the original Falun Gong series; the *Journal*'s foreign editor, John Bussey, whose unwavering faith in the Falun Gong story was crucial during a very trying period; my former bureau chief at the *Journal*, Marcus Brauchli, who taught me how to write features and helped edit this book; Toronto-based freelance writer Lorne Blumer for his editing work; Jane Kramer of *The New Yorker* for helping to find a beginning to the book; Chris Calhoun at Sterling Lord Literistic for his support and advice; Dan Frank at Pantheon for his superb editing; Leslie Chang, Reginald Chua, Charles Hutzler, Mark Leong and Dali Yang, for conversations and suggestions that helped enormously over the years; and to many Chinese friends and associates who helped out with introductions and, most importantly, unstinting friendship—for obvious reasons most must go unnamed, but I'd like to mention Eldridge Lee and Lijia Macleod for companionship on trips to the Loess Plateau and the rest of China.

Special thanks to: Pete Hessler of *The New Yorker*, for his extraordinary help in editing this book; my wife, Elke; and finally to my parents, to whom this book is dedicated, for never—well, rarely—criticizing their unfilial son even as he spent years abroad.

Index

Peace Boulevard in, *see* Peace
 Boulevard
population density in, 113,
 160–1
pre-1960s, 101–2
protected zones in, 111–12,
 167–8
protests in, 6, 185–6, 190–3,
 195, 197–200, 216, 226,
 243–5, 247–51, 258–9,
 262, 263, 265–6, 274, 282
Public Security Bureau in, 76,
 77, 85, 171, 178, 185–7,
 192, 197, 248, 249, 251,
 258, 261, 263, 268–71,
 285–6
real estate boom in, 92–3
ring roads in, 101, 104
Silver Ingot Bridge in, 150
Street of the Gate of Earthly
 Peace in, 152, 153
temples in, 103, 105, 121–2,
 137, 151, 161–4, 232–3,
 235, 296n
2008 Olympics in, 109
urban planning in, 102–3, 105,
 113, 119–21, 126–7, 165,
 180
walls in, 103–6, 126–7, 159–60,
 161, 164, 167, 172
White Rice (Baimi) Street in,
 140
Yandai Xiejie in, 151
see also Forbidden City; State
 Council; Tiananmen
 Square

Beijing City East District, 135
Beijing City Planning
 Commission, 126–7
Beijing housing lawsuits,
 91–101, 118, 165,
 177–82, 255
 book about, 94, 97–9
 compensation issues and,
 91–2, 95, 114, 135
 legal fees in, 94, 178
 of Luo and Feng, 91–101, 108,
 118, 177–80
 Ma Wenlin's peasant lawsuit
 compared with, 91
 media and, 91, 94, 96
 rejection of, 92, 95
 of Zhao Jingxin, 107–10,
 129–37, 168–9, 177
Beijing Municipal Institute of
 City Planning, 165–8
Beijing Municipal Second
 Intermediate Court, 98,
 168–9
Beijing Television, 242, 243, 245
Bell Tower, 153, 154, 155, 167
Benevolence, 189, 237, 280
Beria, Lavrenti, 157
Black Mountain, 228
Boston, Mass., 181
bribery, 58–9, 221, 291–2
bridges, 121, 150
"Buddha Law," 235, 237
Buddhism, 161, 189, 200, 202,
 203, 232–3, 235–41
 Falun Gong compared with,
 210–11, 237

A Note on the Type

This book was set in Fournier, a typeface named for Pierre Simon Fournier *fils* (1712–1768), a celebrated French type designer. Coming from a family of typefounders, Fournier was an extraordinarily prolific designer of typefaces and of typographic ornaments. He was also the author of the important *Manuel typographique* (1764–1766), in which he attempted to work out a system standardizing type measurement in points, a system that is still in use internationally.

Fournier's type is considered transitional in that it drew its inspiration from the old style, yet was ingeniously innovational, providing for an elegant, legible appearance. In 1925 his type was revived by the Monotype Corporation of London.

Composed by Creative Graphics,
Allentown, Pennsylvania

Printed and Bound by R. R. Donnelley & Sons,
Harrisonburg, Virginia

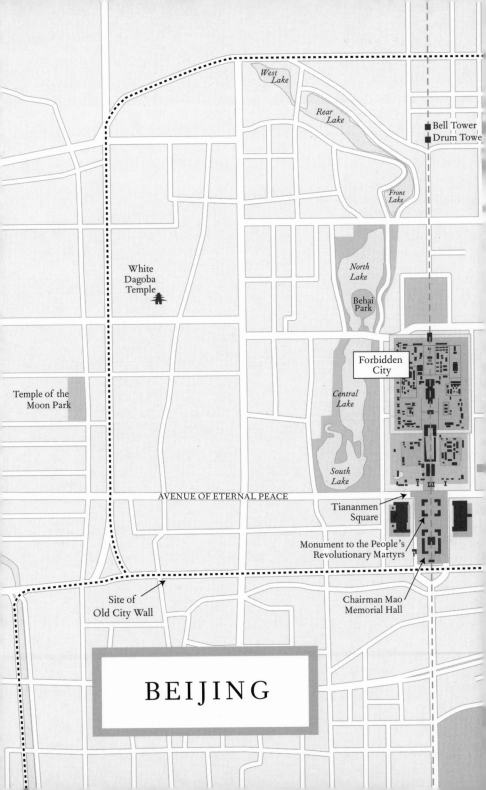

West
Lake

Rear
Lake

■ Bell Tower
■ Drum Towe

Front
Lake

North
Lake

White
Dagoba
Temple

Behai
Park

Forbidden
City

Central
Lake

Temple of the
Moon Park

South
Lake

AVENUE OF ETERNAL PEACE

Tiananmen
Square

Monument to the People's
Revolutionary Martyrs

Site of
Old City Wall

Chairman Mao
Memorial Hall

BEIJING